Lecture Notes of the Institute for Computer Sciences, Social Informatics and Telecommunications Engineering   **583**

The LNICST series publishes ICST's conferences, symposia and workshops.

LNICST reports state-of-the-art results in areas related to the scope of the Institute.
The type of material published includes

- Proceedings (published in time for the respective event)
- Other edited monographs (such as project reports or invited volumes)

LNICST topics span the following areas:

- General Computer Science
- E-Economy
- E-Medicine
- Knowledge Management
- Multimedia
- Operations, Management and Policy
- Social Informatics
- Systems

Yinjun Zhang · Nazir Shah

Editors

Application of Big Data, Blockchain, and Internet of Things for Education Informatization

Third EAI International Conference, BigIoT-EDU 2023
August 29–31, 2023, Liuzhou, China
Proceedings, Part IV

 Springer

Editors
Yinjun Zhang
Guangxi Science and Technology Normal
University
Guangxi, China

Nazir Shah
University of Swabi
Khyber Pakhtunkhwa, Pakistan

ISSN 1867-8211   ISSN 1867-822X (electronic)
Lecture Notes of the Institute for Computer Sciences, Social Informatics
and Telecommunications Engineering
ISBN 978-3-031-63138-2   ISBN 978-3-031-63139-9 (eBook)
https://doi.org/10.1007/978-3-031-63139-9

This Springer imprint is published by the registered company Springer Nature Switzerland AG
The registered company address is: Gewerbestrasse 11, 6330 Cham, Switzerland

If disposing of this product, please recycle the paper.

Preface

We are delighted to introduce the proceedings of the third edition of the European Alliance for Innovation (EAI) International Conference on Application of Big Data, Blockchain, and Internet of Things for Education Informatization (BigIoT-EDU 2023). BigIoT-EDU aims to provide a platform for international cooperation and exchange, enabling big data and information education experts, scholars, and enterprise developers to share research results, discuss existing problems and challenges, and explore cutting-edge science and technology. The conference focuses on research fields such as digitization of education, smart classrooms, and Massive Online Open Courses (MOOCs). The use of big data analytics, artificial intelligence (AI), machine learning, and deep learning lies at the heart of this conference as we focus on these emerging technologies to further the role of IT in education.

BigIoT-EDU 2023 had three tracks: the Main Track, the Late Track, and a Workshop Track. BigIoT-EDU 2023 attracted over 700 submissions, and each submission was reviewed by at least 3 Program Committee members in a double-blind process, resulting in the acceptance of only 272 papers across all three tracks. The workshop was titled "Application of Advanced Integrated Technologies in Education Informatics" and co-chaired by Yar Muhammad and Muhammad Al-Ambusaidi from Beihang University, China and University of Technology & Applied Sciences of Oman, respectively. The workshop aimed to focus on the application of the latest cutting-edge integrated technologies for the development and digitalization of education in the modern era.

Coordination with the steering chair, Imrich Chlamtac, was essential for the success of the conference. We sincerely appreciate his constant support and guidance. It was also a great pleasure to work with such an excellent organizing committee team for their hard work in organizing and supporting the conference. In particular, we are grateful to the Technical Program Committee, who completed the peer-review process for the technical papers and helped to put together a high-quality technical program. We are also grateful to Conference Manager Ivana Bujdakova for her constant support along with the whole of the EAI team involved in the conference. We must say that they have been wonderful and it is always a pleasant experience to work with them. Also, we would like to thank all the authors who submitted their papers to the BigIoT-EDU 2023 conference.

We strongly believe that the BigIoT-EDU conference provides a good forum for all researchers, developers, and practitioners to discuss all science and technology aspects that are relevant to emerging trends for digitalization of education. We also expect that the future BigIoT-EDU conferences will be as successful and stimulating as this year's, as indicated by the contributions presented in this volume.

Yinjun Zhang
Nazir Shah

Conference Organization

Steering Committee

Imrich Chlamtac	University of Trento, Italy
Fazlullah Khan	Business Technology Management Group, USA
Mian Ahmad Jan	Abdul Wali Khan University Mardan, Pakistan

Organizing Committee

General Chair

Yinjun Zhang	Guangxi Science & Technology Normal University, China

General Co-chairs

Shah Nazir	University of Swabi, Pakistan
Walayat Hussain	Australian Catholic University, Australia

TPC Chair

Yinjun Zhang	Guangxi Science & Technology Normal University, China

Sponsorship and Exhibit Chairs

Lan Zimian	Harbin Institute of Technology, China
Izaz Ur Rehman	Abdul Wali Khan University Mardan, Pakistan

Local Chairs

Huang Yufei	Hechi Normal University, China
Wan Haoran	Shanghai University, China

Workshops Chairs

Rahim Khan   Abdul Wali Khan University Mardan, Pakistan
Abid Yahya   Botswana International University of Science and
                             Technology, Botswana

Publicity and Social Media Chair

Aamir Akbar   *Abdul Wali Khan University Mardan, Pakistan*

Publications Chair

Yinjun Zhang   Guangxi Science & Technology Normal
                             University, China

Web Chairs

Mian Yasir Jan   CECOS University, Pakistan
Syed Rooh Ullah Jan   Abdul Wali Khan University Mardan, Pakistan

Posters and PhD Track Chairs

Mengji Chen   Guangxi Science &Technology Normal
                             University, China
Ateeq ur Rehman   University of Haripur, Pakistan

Panels Chairs

Kong Linxiang   Hefei University of Technology, China
Muhammad Usman   Federation University, Australia

Demos Chairs

Ryan Alturki   Umm-ul-Qura University, Saudi Arabia
Rahim Khan   Abdul Wali Khan University Mardan, Pakistan

Tutorials Chairs

Wei Rongchang   Guangxi Science & Technology Normal
                             University, China
Hashim Ali   Abdul Wali Khan University Mardan Pakistan

Technical Program Committee

Shahnawaz Khan	Abdul Wali Khan University Mardan, Pakistan
Mengji Chen	Hechi University, China
Yar Muhammad	Beihang University, China
Mian Abdullah Jan	Ton Duc Thang University, Vietnam
Roman Khan	City University of Information Science and Technology, Pakistan
Muneeb Ullah	Peshawar University, Pakistan
Siyar Khan	Bacha Khan University, Pakistan
Muhammad Bilal	Virtual University of Pakistan, Pakistan
Haroon Khan	Bacha Khan University, Pakistan
Shaher Slehat	University of Technology Sydney, Australia
Xiangjian He	University of Technology Sydney, Australia
Shaheer Jan	University of Engineering and Technology Peshawar, Pakistan
Akbar Khan	University of Peshawar, Pakistan
Malik Ahmad	University of Peshawar, Pakistan
Muzammil Shah	COMSATS University Lahore, Pakistan
Aaiza Khan	Guangju University of Technology, China
Farman Khan	Bacha Khan University, Pakistan
Zia Ur Rehman	Bacha Khan University, Pakistan
Abid Yahya	Botswana International University of Science and Technology, Botswana
Ravi Keemo	Botswana International University of Science and Technology, Botswana
Aaiza Gul	Sirindhorn International Institute of Technology, Thailand
Shahid Ali	Women University Swabi, Pakistan
Muhammad Sohail	Abdul Wali Khan University Mardan, Pakistan
Saad Khan	University of Peshawar, Pakistan
Momin Ali	University of Peshawar, Pakistan
Bilawal Khan	COMSATS University Islamabad, Pakistan
Jamal Shah	University of Leeds, UK
Basit Kazmi	University of Peshawar, Pakistan
Jalal Turk	Staffordshire University, UK
Umer Hussain	Indian Institute of Technology Kharagpur, India
Omer Naveed	Uppsala University, Sweden
Muhammad Ali	Uppsala University, Sweden
Hamza Khan	Hankuk University of Foreign Studies, South Korea
Tariq Khan	Abdul Wali Khan University Mardan, Pakistan

Ehsan Ullah	Abdul Wali Khan University Mardan, Pakistan
Noman Ali	Abdul Wali Khan University Mardan, Pakistan
Ayaan Adeel	Abdul Wali Khan University Mardan, Pakistan
Behroz Khan	Abdul Wali Khan University Mardan, Pakistan
Tariq Khokar	Abdul Wali Khan University Mardan, Pakistan
Awais Marwat	Abdul Wali Khan University Mardan, Pakistan
Naeem Jan	Abdul Wali Khan University Mardan, Pakistan
Anas Akbar	Abdul Wali Khan University Mardan, Pakistan
Mian Ahmad Jan	Duy Tan University, Vietnam
Faisal Ayub Khan	Indian Institute of Technology Kharagpur, India
Faisal Khan	University of Leeds, UK
Yasir Jan	University of California Davies, USA
Ryan Alturki	Umm al-Qura University, Saudi Arabia
Alayat Hussain	University of Technology Sydney, Australia
Muhammad Usman	Federation University, Australia
Naveed Khan	Abdul Wali Khan University Mardan, Pakistan
Azam Khalil	Abdul Wali Khan University Mardan, Pakistan
Hamid Naseer	Abdul Wali Khan University Mardan, Pakistan
Arsalan Jan	Abdul Wali Khan University Mardan, Pakistan
Abdul Samad	University of Nebraska Omaha, USA
Asif Khan	University of Nebraska Omaha, USA
Imtiaz Ali	Quaid-e-Azam University Islamabad, Pakistan
Khadim Khan	Quaid-e-Azam University Islamabad, Pakistan
Usman Nasir	Quaid-e-Azam University Islamabad, Pakistan
Ishfaq Ahmad	Quaid-e-Azam University Islamabad, Pakistan
Jamal Baig	National University of Sciences and Technology, Pakistan
Naseer Baig	National University of Sciences and Technology, Pakistan
Sohail Agha	National University of Sciences and Technology, Pakistan
Raza Hussain	Indian Institute of Technology Kharagpur, India
Ibrar Atta	University of Haripur, Pakistan
Majid Ali	University of Haripur, Pakistan
Afzal Durrani	University of Haripur, Pakistan
Faysal Azam	Indian Institute of Technology Kharagpur, India
Asif Wazir	University of Engineering and Technology Mardan, Pakistan
Talal Agha	University of Engineering and Technology Mardan, Pakistan
Salman Shah	University of Engineering and Technology Mardan, Pakistan

Ibrahim Khan	Iqra University, Islamabad, Pakistan
Raayan Jan	Iqra University, Islamabad, Pakistan
Shameer Shah	Iqra University, Islamabad, Pakistan
Zeeshan Khan	Iqra University, Islamabad, Pakistan

Contents – Part IV

Research and Application of Recommendation Algorithms in Personalized Intelligent Education

Application of Cloud Computing in Intelligent Teaching Resource Library

Application Research of Computer-Aided Online Intelligent Teaching

Research on Smart Teaching in Deep Learning

Intelligent Adjustment Model and Algorithm Implementation of English Teaching Content Based on Deep Learning

Xingchun Chu[✉] and Song Gao

Guangdong University of Science and Technology, Dongguan 523083, Guangdong, China
1543178279@qq.com

Abstract. Nowadays, the communication between China and other countries is more and more extensive, so the society has higher requirements for college students' English proficiency. Courseware is the main core in the process of Web teaching, and its content organization and arrangement will directly affect the overall teaching effect. By expressing and analyzing the Concept Map of the knowledge and content of the course in students' minds, we can customize the courseware browsing concept map for each specific learner, so as to realize personalized autonomous learning. Using the concept map theory, based on the previous research of personalized learning analysis model, The personalized analysis results are further discussed. At the same time, the intelligent adjustment model of teaching content is constructed by using the minimum spanning tree algorithm for reference, and the corresponding algorithm implementation is given.

Keywords: Deep learning · English teaching · Intelligent adjustment model of inner cylinder · Algorithm realization

1 Introduction

Looking at the integrated development of global economy and culture today, and facing the increasing demand for new and all-round talents in the world, it is obvious that only learning a good language can't meet the needs of developing communication. Due to cultural differences, misunderstandings, contradictions and even conflicts in communication are increasing day by day. The root cause of these problems is the gap between cultures. Every country has different culture, history, customs and environmental conditions. These differences in different fields can be clearly expressed by language. Language cannot exist independently, and culture cannot communicate, live, develop and continue without language. Language and culture are interdependent symbionts. There is a big contrast between learners' language proficiency and the actual teaching input. Although schools and teachers have invested heavily in teaching, the teaching quality has not been improved, and the teaching effect is not satisfactory. Many schools blindly pursue the high pass rate and excellent rate of CET-4 and CET-6, and even resort to

Y. Zhang and N. Shah (Eds.): BigIoT-EDU 2023, LNICST 583, pp. 3–10, 2024.
https://doi.org/10.1007/978-3-031-63139-9_1

the tactics of asking the sea and intensive training for exams, which seriously under-mines the inherent laws of language teaching. At the same time, with the popularization of higher education and the expansion of enrollment scale, the quality distribution of students has changed, and the preparation of teachers, management level and teaching facilities is insufficient, which has affected the improvement of college English teaching quality to some extent. The inadaptability of teaching philosophy is a potential threat to the teaching quality, and I am at a loss as to how to uphold the value orientation of college English teaching.

2 Content-Based Foreign Language Teaching Concept

2.1 Construction of Content-Based Teaching Model in College English

CBI is defined as the integration of content teaching and language teaching objectives, that is, learning a language by learning subject knowledge. It regards foreign language as a medium, which is used to convey content information that is closely related to learners and arouses learners' strong interest. Take "American Society and Culture", one of the college English courses, as an example. The whole course consists of 18 units (topics) such as history, geography and education. Each unit has 4 h, and each semester has 72 h. Take the fourth unit "American politics" as an example. This unit (theme) consists of the separation of powers system in the United States (topic 1), the two-party system in the United States (topic 2) and the presidential election in the United States (topic 3). Eighteen different topics belong to the big theme of American society and culture, and the whole course content presents a network knowledge structure, which is linked with each other. By constructing the chapter theme framework, we can provide a good language learning context for students. In recent years, there are more and more trends in the theoretical research of college English teaching value in China, but the shortcomings are also obvious: first, the theoretical system of college English teaching value is ignored, teaching for textbooks for a long time, the existence of value is diluted, and experiential teaching is prosperous; Second, the systematic research on the value theory of college English teaching is ignored. General research, such as teaching value research, is more, but the value orientation, which is an important factor affecting the development of teaching, is either ignored or downplayed, and dealt with; Thirdly, the theoretical research of teaching value has little connection with college English teaching activities, and it is out of touch with the actual situation. Either mechanically copy the so-called popular teaching value theory in the actual teaching regardless of the actual teaching, or copy the existing value theory in the teaching, which becomes the normal state of some people, disregarding the changes of the actual teaching situation, and the value orientation is distorted; Fourthly, the research on the implementation process of teaching value orientation is not paid enough attention. College English teaching involves a wide range, its teaching process is complicated, and its value orientation is extremely different, which is bound to restrict the acquisition of college English teaching benefits. The customers in education are different from those in business, and their scope is obviously larger than that of well-known customers in business, such as those who receive education directly, parents of those who pay for education, employers and future employers, governments and society of those who use educational achievements. For example, in his book Total Quality Education, these three types of people are divided into "primary customers", "secondary customers" and "tertiary customers". Educate customers as shown in Table 1.

Table 1. Customers of Education

Education	= Service
Student	= Junior customers
Parent of a child	= Secondary customers
Future employer	= Level 3 customers

Drawing lessons from the research results of general quality management and higher education quality management at home and abroad, and combining with the analysis of the characteristics of teaching itself, the author believes that teaching quality refers to the degree to which teaching activities and their results meet the needs of society and individual growth and development of students. This definition accords with the scientific concept of general quality and reflects the essential characteristics of teaching.

2.2 Constructivism

Beginning in the 1990s, constructivist learning theory began to prevail in the west. The most important representatives of this theory include: J. Piaget, R. J. sternberg, O. Kernberg, D. Katz and Vogotsgy. J. Piaget is a famous scholar in the field of cognitive development and a psychologist. He founded the Geneva School. Piaget's basic view on constructivism is that cognition is formed by the interaction between subject and object, neither because of the existence of subject nor because of the dependence of object. Piaget's view of internalization of activities is: whether children or adults, in the process of contact with the surrounding environment, they gradually form their own views on the outside world, thus further improving their cognitive level of the world. People are in a balanced cognitive state; When the balance is broken, it means that the existing schema model can't assimilate the new information. In his view, knowledge is not between subjective things and objective things, but exists in the process of self-construction between environment and individual. He also emphasized that people's learning is a process of continuous construction, and it is further improved and developed in the cycle of "balance-imbalance-new balance". On the basis of Piaget's "cognitive structure theory", kornberg made a further study on the nature and development of cognitive structure. Scholars such as D.Katz and R. J. Robert Jeffrey R.J.sternberg also made a serious and in-depth discussion on how to give full play to individual's subjective initiative in cognitive process; Murrary stressed that in a certain social environment, we should sort out, process and deal with new information; Vygotsgy emphasizes the role of social, cultural and historical background on learners in the cognitive process of social construction. Individual learning is carried out under a certain historical, social and cultural background. Vysky divided individual development into current development level and potential development level. The guarantee of college English teaching quality is to adjust and control the restrictive factors according to the requirements of teaching quality objectives, so that the results of activities can meet the requirements of the objectives, that is, through a cycle process of "establishing teaching quality objectives-analyzing the current situation of teaching quality control-finding out existing problems and deficiencies-proposing and implementing improvement measures-achieving the teaching quality objectives". To run this cycle smoothly and efficiently, and achieve the expected quality management goal, we must have a strong organizational guarantee system. By taking evaluation and inspection as the main activities and making full use of the feedback function of teaching information system, we can jointly improve and build the key points of teaching quality. Therefore, the college English teaching quality assurance constructed here is a complex systematic project. Combining the characteristics of college English teaching, an effective teaching quality assurance system should include the following aspects, as shown in Fig. 1.

Fig. 1. Structure diagram of internal guarantee system of college English teaching quality

The teaching quality evaluation system is to objectively describe the whole process and quality of teaching activities through the collection of qualitative and quantitative information. On this basis, it can judge the teaching quality according to the requirements of syllabus, training objectives and students' learning situation. Teaching quality evaluation is an important part of college English teaching. The reading amount of English extracurricular books of a class student from January to August is shown in Fig. 2.

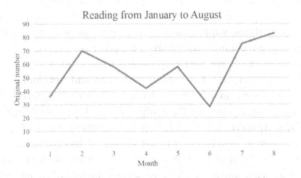

Fig. 2. Reading quantity of English extracurricular books of a class from January to August.

3   On the Application of Attribute Method

3.1   Apply to Attribute Barycenter Partition Model

First of all, we should grade each school, and then divide them into several grades, so that we can compare the same grades. Then, according to the grading level, Divide the schools participating in the evaluation into a certain file with 5 points or 10 points. Two-step filing method, firstly, classify the evaluation schools according to the scores and rankings of some authoritative organizations. There is a functional relationship between Y and school X:

$$C_t(x, y) = f(r(x, y)) \tag{1}$$

In a given total score plane, give some indicators of virtual schools, put them in the plane, and score these virtual schools according to the standards set by the evaluators (that is, give the satisfaction degree). With scores between [0, 1], the standard score point in this hyperplane can be calculated by weighted average. Similarly, the standard scores of several total score planes can be obtained by this method. In addition, (100, 100, 100):

$$h(t) = h(h_1(t)), h_2(t), h_3(t) \tag{2}$$

Between different grades, the selected standard points of satisfaction are different, so when calculating satisfaction, the reference standard points are also different. In order to enable schools in different grades to compare, a regulation coefficient is used to adjust before the grade satisfaction function, namely:

$$C_t(X) = \lambda C_S(X) \tag{3}$$

In the process of college English teaching, we can make full use of modular teaching mode, and the key lies in the scientific and reasonable design of teaching modules. First, it must meet the needs of college English teaching; Second, students' accumulation level has also been strengthened, and students' English practice ability has been promoted. Therefore, when designing the teaching module, we must comprehensively consider the actual teaching situation, the content of teaching materials and the professional distribution of students, so as to improve the ability of college students to learn English. In addition, in the process of designing teaching content, it must be carried out in different levels, and in the process of designing, special attention should be paid to students' individualized characteristics, and effective teaching measures should be used to promote students' English expression ability.

3.2   Intelligent Adjustment Model of Teach Content Based on Concept Map

In Web-based distance education, one of the main ways for learners to learn is to learn courseware through multimedia. This kind of courseware usually provides a courseware browsing directory tree, through which learners can start the course learning step by step. In a sense, the directory tree determines the distribution structure of knowledge points in the whole course content. However, a lot of practice shows that, The complex relationship between knowledge points can't be clearly shown only by the tree diagram. Moreover, because learners have different understandings of knowledge points, each teaching participant has his own concept map in his mind about the knowledge and content of the course. Therefore, in the previous research work, the author mainly devoted himself to expressing these concept maps through interactive tools and analyzing his learning results. And customize the concept map of courseware browsing for each specific learner to guide learners' autonomous learning. When teaching for a certain class of students, the courseware structure of directory tree type is clearer, easier to organize and more operable than that of network type. It is of certain guiding significance to customize the corresponding directory tree structure for students with different understanding angles. The teaching process is the interactive communication between teachers and students through textbooks. Traditional teaching mainly focuses on the teaching of language, while ignoring the practical application of language and the daily embodiment of culture. We must establish the idea that English teaching is not only language teaching, but also cultural teaching. Successful foreign language teaching is to enable students to have relevant knowledge of language and use it skillfully. Teachers should study the teaching methods of cultural teaching, such as guiding students to pay attention to some original photocopies, so as to experience and learn more primitive. With the application and development of multimedia technology in English classroom, teachers can provide students with more extensive resources, help them know more about western cultural connotations, hold lectures, analyze and comment on movies and so on, and avoid the traditional indoctrination teaching method. Learning is the behavioral and psychological process of learners' perception, experience, understanding and identification. Through the above analysis, the components of instrumental communication ability (external factors) and humanistic thinking ability (internal factors) are of great significance to the

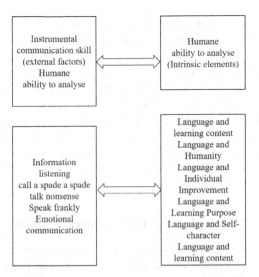

Fig. 3. Elements of practicing the integrative value orientation of college English teaching

practice of the integrative value orientation of college English teaching, and must be clear.For the sake of clarity, these elements can be classified into different categories, and the elements of practicing the integrative value orientation of college English teaching can be summarized as shown in the figure, so that college English teachers can pay attention to and recognize them. These elements interact with each other and complement each other. The elements of practicing the integrative value orientation of college English teaching are shown in Fig. 3.

4 Conclusion

History has proved irrefutably that most of the ways of inheriting human knowledge and culture are carried out through teaching activities, that is. The traditional English teaching mode is still being used in colleges and universities, which leads to students losing interest in English course learning, and it is difficult to really improve their English practice ability. The modular teaching mode breaks through the shackles of the traditional English teaching mode, makes rational use of English teaching materials, builds a high-quality English teaching platform, promotes the development of students' ability, reflects some problems existing in learning, effectively strengthens their English practice ability, and practically improves the overall quality of English teaching. According to the user's requirements, it can flexibly adjust the evaluation parameters such as the scale of school programs and related psychological weights, combine the grades of schools, and comprehensively consider all kinds of influencing factors in English learning (not only the passing rates of CET-4 and CET-6), so as to realize the comparison of the overall teaching quality of different grades or universities of the same grade. It can reflect the overall level of the school more objectively, so that the school can take into account the capital investment, environment construction and teaching methods, and the teaching level of the school can be really improved.

References

1. Li, H.: The role of multimedia technology in middle school English teaching. E-Mag. New Educ. Era: Student Ed. **69**(7), 5 (2029)
2. Yang, S.: Analysis of the application of blended teaching mode in open English teaching in RTVU. Campus English **36**(20), 44 (2021)
3. Wu, S.: The cultivation of middle school students' core literacy in junior high school English teaching. Campus English **37**(10), 11 (2020)
4. Wei, X.: English translation teaching environment and the cultivation of intercultural communication awareness-comment on English teaching and intercultural communication ability. Foreign Lang. Audio-Vis. Teach. **74**(41), 5 (2021)
5. Liu, K.: College food English teaching research and practice. Food. Res. Dev. **14**(33), 22 (2020)
6. Li, Q.: Reflections on English teaching for foundry majors under constructivism. Spec. Foundry Nonferrous Alloy **24**(3), 2 (2017)
7. Wang, K., Wang, J.: Effective application of micro-classes in English teaching in rural primary schools. English Teach. **40**(10), 33 (2018)

8. Yan, J., Fan, J.: Effective integration of information technology and English teaching in primary schools. English Teach. **37**(7), 4 (2019)
9. Zhou, X.: Research on teaching methods of English for food specialty-book review of English for food science and technology. Meat Res. **38**(1), 4 (2020)
10. Xu, H.: The application and reflection of "flipping the classroom" in senior high school English teaching-taking a reading demonstration class as an example. Campus English **20**(5), 6 (2020)

Application of Deep Learning in Dance Teaching

Yujun Ni[✉]

Philippine Christian University, 1648 Taft Ave, Malate, Manila, 1004 Metro Manila, Philippines
nyjeducation@126.com

Abstract. The role of intelligent algorithm in dance teaching is very important, but there is a problem that the application effect is not satisfactory. Traditional pedagogy cannot solve the problem of poor application effect in dance teaching, and there are few application indicators. Therefore, this paper proposes a deep learning method to construct an optimization model for dance teaching. Firstly, the teaching theory is used to evaluate the application of the results of dance teaching, and the result is divided according to the degree of application, so as to reduce the subjective factors in the application. Then, the teaching theory is used to evaluate the dance teaching, form an application evaluation set, and comprehensively evaluate the results. MATLAB simulation shows that the evaluation accuracy and application evaluation time of deep learning method are better than traditional teaching methods under certain teaching requirements.

Keywords: teaching theory · dance teaching · deep learning · Application

1 Introduction

As a form of cultural expression, dance has a unique artistic charm and appeal. However, in traditional dance teaching, teachers often need to spend a lot of time and energy to explain and guide students' movements, and due to the different physical conditions and learning abilities of each person, the teaching effect will also vary greatly. Therefore, how to improve the efficiency and quality of dance teaching has become an urgent problem to be solved. In recent years [1–5], with the continuous development of computer vision and artificial intelligence technology, deep learning has been widely used in various fields. In dance teaching, deep learning can help teachers better understand students' learning and provide more personalized guidance and support through automatic analysis and processing of large amounts of video data.

2 Related Concepts

2.1 Mathematical Description of Deep Learning

Action recognition is an important part of dance teaching, which can help teachers better understand students' action performance, find problems in time and give guidance. Traditional motion recognition methods usually need to design features and classifiers by

Y. Zhang and N. Shah (Eds.): BigIoT-EDU 2023, LNICST 583, pp. 11–16, 2024.
https://doi.org/10.1007/978-3-031-63139-9_2

hand, which is heavy in workload and prone to errors. Deep learning can automatically learn effective feature representation and classifier by training a large amount of video data, thus realizing automatic motion recognition and analysis [6, 7].

Hypothesis 1: the application judgment function $F(d_i \geq 0)$ is as shown in Eq. (1).

$$F(d_i) = \sum x_i \oplus y_i \cdot \xi \tag{1}$$

2.2 Selection of Application Evaluation Indicators

Hypothesis 2: the indicator selection w_i is shown in Eq. (2).

$$z(d_i) = \frac{z_i \cdot F(d_i, y_i)}{w_i \cdot \xi} + k \tag{2}$$

2.3 Processing of Dance Teaching Data

A dance video can be input into the deep learning model, which will automatically extract key frames and action sequences in the video, and then classify and predict them by convolution neural network (CNN) or cyclic neural network (RNN). In this way, we can quickly get the evaluation results of students' action performance, and give corresponding feedback and guidance according to the results is shown in Fig. 1.

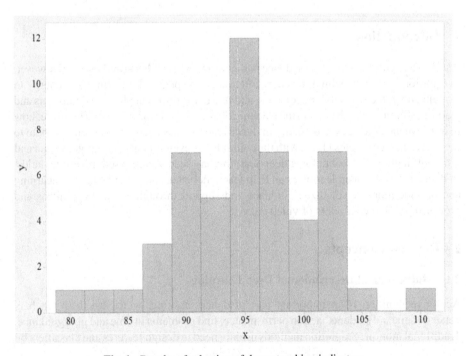

Fig. 1. Results of selection of dance teaching indicators

In traditional dance teaching, because each student's physical condition and learning ability are different, teachers often need to spend a lot of time and energy to carry out individualized guidance and support. Deep learning can provide more personalized teaching support by analyzing students' action performance and learning process.

3 Steps to Deep Learning

Movement recognition and tracking: Deep learning technology can help the system automatically identify and track dance movements, providing accurate feedback to students.

Style and Sentiment Analysis: Through deep learning methods, the style and emotional expression of dance are analyzed, which helps students understand the connotation and deep meaning of dance.

Intelligently assisted teaching: Deep learning can help teachers with teaching aids, such as providing personalized teaching suggestions and programs.

4 Practical Examples of Dance Teaching

4.1 Introduction to Dance Teaching

Deep learning can provide accurate motion recognition and feedback, help students better master dance skills, and thus improve teaching quality are shown in Table 1.

Table 1. Relevant parameters of physical education and dance teaching

Teaching content	Time period	Apply effects	App evaluation	Teaching format
Specialized courses	1–8 weeks	36.47	30.59	Online, offline
	8–12 weeks	58.82	29.41	Online, offline
Elective course	1–8 weeks	63.53	62.35	Online, offline
	8–12 weeks	54.12	27.06	Online, offline
Instruction classes	1–8 weeks	22.35	47.06	Online, offline
	8–12 weeks	34.12	67.06	Online, offline

The result processing process of dance teaching in Table 1 is shown in Fig. 2.

Deep learning can analyze students' learning characteristics and needs, provide personalized teaching programs for each student, and meet the needs of different students. According to students' action performance and learning progress, each student can make corresponding learning plans and training objectives. At the same time, students' action performance can be monitored and evaluated in real time through the deep learning model, and teaching methods and strategies can be adjusted in time. In this way, students' learning efficiency and achievements can be improved, and teachers' workload can be reduced at the same time.

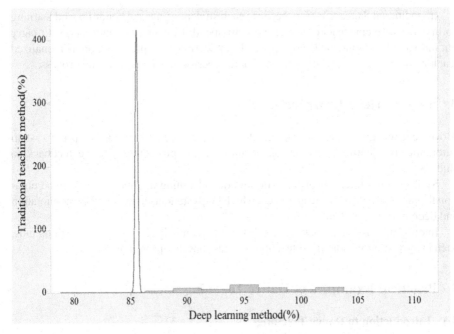

Fig. 2. The process of dance teaching

4.2 Perfection Rate of Dance Teaching

Deep learning can promote the interaction and communication between teachers and students and enhance students' learning experience and participation are shown in Table 2.

Table 2. Overall situation of dance teaching indicators

Time period	Adoption rate	Complete rate
1–4 weeks	23.53	21.18
5–8 weeks	58.82	30.59
8–12 weeks	60.00	67.06
mean	17.65	48.24
X^2	22.35	62.35
P = 0. 223		

4.3 Accuracy and Stability of Dance Teaching Evaluation

Automatic Extraction of Key Action Features in Dance Video by Deep Learning Technology are shown in Table 3.

Table 3. Comparison of application evaluation accuracy of different methods

algorithm	Precision	Magnitude of change	error
Deep learning method	95.29	8.24	4.12
Traditional teaching methods	95.29	12.35	4.71
P	50.59	69.41	9.41

The extracted features are used to train deep learning models, such as convolutional neural networks (CNN) or cyclic neural networks (RNN) is shown in Fig. 3.

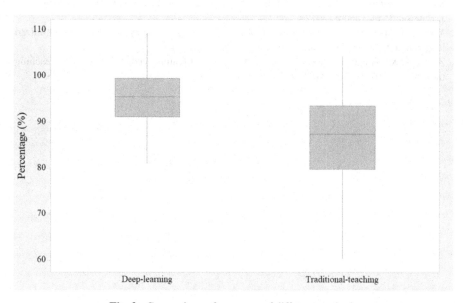

Fig. 3. Comparison of accuracy of different methods

The output of the deep learning model is fed back to the students, and the model is optimized and adjusted according to the students' learning situation.

5 Conclusion

Deep learning is a machine learning method based on neural network, which can learn and recognize patterns through a large amount of data and complex models. In dance teaching, deep learning can be used to automatically identify dancers' movements, analyze dancers' performances, and generate new dance movements. In traditional dance teaching, teachers often need to spend a lot of time and energy to explain and guide students' movements, and because of the different physical conditions and learning ability of each person, the teaching effect will be very different. Therefore, how to improve the efficiency and quality of dance teaching has become an urgent problem to be solved.

References

1. de las Heras-Fernandez, R., Cuellar-Moreno, M.J., Mateos, M.E., Acero, J.M.A.: The influence of teaching styles on the emotions of university students in dance lessons according to sex. Res. Dance Educ. (2022)
2. Heyang, T., Martin, R.: Teaching through TikTok: a duoethnographic exploration of pedagogical approaches using TikTok in higher dance education in China and Norway during a global pandemic. Res. Dance Educ. (2022)
3. Huang, J.: Analysis of the relationship between dance action and health psychology in the process of dance performance teaching environment. J. Environ. Publ. Health (2022)
4. Li, L., Liu, Y.Y., Gu, Y., Zhu, Z.: Application of heart rate combined with acceleration motion sensor in sports dance teaching. J. Sens. (2022)
5. Sun, Y.: Teaching of dance choreography course based on multimedia network environment. J. Environ. Publ. Health (2022)
6. Yang, Q.R.: Design and implementation of dance online teaching system based on optimized load balancing algorithm. Comput. Intell. Neurosci. (2022)
7. Zhang, D.X.: The application of dance movement skill feature recognition in dance teaching movement analysis. Adv. Multimedia (2022)

Optimization Model of College Chinese Education Resources Based on Ant Colony Arithmetic

Yan Ping Mo[1,2]([✉])

[1] Hunan College of Foreign Studies, Changsha 410000, Hunan, China
350034316@qq.com
[2] Hubei College of Chinese Medicine, Jingzhou 434020, Hubei, China

Abstract. College Chinese teaching is not only an important part of the education system, but also has a great impact on pupils' future development. Under the background of contemporary information, college Chinese teaching must adopt specific measures such as integrating and utilizing information-based teaching resources, optimizing college Chinese teaching methods, strengthening the construction of information-based teaching staff, guiding pupils to form independent consciousness and disseminate consciousness, improving classroom activity, and promoting communication between teachers and pupils, so as to achieve and achieve the improvement of teaching quality. In this paper, an optimization model of college Chinese education resources based on ant colony arithmetic is proposed, and an improved ant colony arithmetic is introduced to solve the problem of optimal allocation of college Chinese resources. In the process of solving, ants tend to choose resources with low service cost and less trouble. According to different resources, different pheromone updating rules are adopted, and the trust mechanism is introduced to express ants' trust in whether the path is smooth or not, and it is used as heuristic information to influence ants' path selection, which is more in line with ants' actual path-finding process. Finally, the simulation test analysis is carried out. Simulation results show that this arithmetic has a certain accuracy, which is 11.25% higher than the traditional arithmetic. This arithmetic has a fast convergence speed, overcomes the defect that the traditional arithmetic is easy to fall into local optimum, and is suitable for solving all resource balance problems, with good universality. It is of great practical significance to carry out the research on the optimization model design of educational resources with college Chinese as the core to guide college Chinese education and teaching methods.

Keywords: Ant colony arithmetic · College Chinese · Resource optimization

1 Introduction

In China's current university education system, college Chinese is not paid enough attention. On the one hand, because college pupils have studied Chinese for nearly ten years, they have formed a deep impression on the Chinese subject to a large extent, thus reducing the teaching hours of college Chinese, resulting in the low status of college Chinese

Y. Zhang and N. Shah (Eds.): BigIoT-EDU 2023, LNICST 583, pp. 17–27, 2024.
https://doi.org/10.1007/978-3-031-63139-9_3

teaching in college education [1]. College Chinese education is a storehouse of ancient and modern Chinese and foreign knowledge, which can fully mobilize pupils' various senses, improve pupils' aesthetic standards, enrich pupils' emotional life and promote pupils to form good personality charm [2]. As a key learning course in China's education system, the influence of its teaching quality on the realization of educational goals in China's education system can not be ignored [3]. However, in the current situation of college education in China, there are some problems in college Chinese teaching that need to be solved urgently, which seriously restrict the realization and implementation of college Chinese teaching objectives.

Ant colony arithmetic was developed by Italian scholar M in 1990s. Zuo L et al., inspired by the mechanism of biological evolution, proposed a new simulated evolutionary arithmetic by simulating the path-finding behavior of ant colonies when foraging. This arithmetic was first used to solve the traveling salesman problem [4]. In recent years, more and more scholars began to study the application of ant colony arithmetic in production resource scheduling, mainly the classical scheduling problems such as Job-shop and Flow-shop [5]. In view of the advantages of ant colony arithmetic, this paper adopts the method of individual optimization function in ant colony arithmetic in order to reduce the execution cost of the arithmetic. Practice has proved that this combination can not only reduce the calculation time, but also improve the quality and efficiency of college Chinese education resources optimization.

Resource optimization refers to the reasonable arrangement of the working hours of non-critical processes within the prescribed time limit, so that resources can be consumed in a balanced way in the whole cycle, thus avoiding the phenomenon of "peaks and valleys" and achieving the purpose of reducing the waste or idleness of resources and lowering the project cost [6]. In this paper, the optimization model of college Chinese education resources is established. By establishing the mathematical model of resource balance optimization decision, the ant colony arithmetic is adopted to determine the starting time range of non-critical processes. The ant colony is randomly distributed in the feasible region, and the ants search globally or locally according to the transition probability to obtain the global optimal solution. Its innovation lies in:

(1) This paper adopts the method of individual optimization function in ant colony arithmetic to reduce the execution cost of the arithmetic.
(2) This paper constructs the key features of college Chinese education resources system, and adopts the goal of resource allocation optimization to realize the optimal design and identification of college Chinese education resources.

This paper studies the optimization design of college Chinese educational resources, and the structure is as follows:

The Sect. 1 is the introduction. This part mainly expounds the research background and significance of the optimization of college Chinese educational resources, and puts forward the research purpose, method and innovation of this paper. The Sect. 1 is a summary of relevant literature, summarizing its advantages and disadvantages, and putting forward the research ideas of this paper. The Sect. 2 is the method part, focusing on the optimization design method combining resource allocation with ant colony arithmetic. The Sect. 3 is the experimental analysis. In this part, experiments are carried out on data sets to analyze the performance of the model. Section 4, conclusion and prospect.

This part mainly reviews the main contents and results of this research, summarizes the research conclusions and points out the direction of further research.

2 Methodology

2.1 Integrating Educational Resources to Analyze College Chinese Educational Resources

Integrating and utilizing information-based teaching resources is one of the counter-measures to improve the current college Chinese teaching, and it is also the first step. It mainly refers to the use of network technology to make teachers integrate teaching resources accordingly. Using the network technology, pupils can use and learn the teaching resources accordingly [7].

The resource allocation problem can be described as: there are N tasks with k kinds of resources, and the number of the i kind of resources is m_i, that is, there are $M = \sum_{i=1}^{K} M_i$ resources in total. At the same time, each resource can only be assigned to one task at most. All tasks have the same processing sequence, and each task can be assigned one or more similar resources at the same time. The operation time of each task is determined by its own attribute and resource type. It is required that the resources allocated by each task meet the constraint conditions, so that all tasks can be completed with the maximum amount, the shortest operation time and the maximum utilization rate of each resource.

The optimization objectives of the whole resource allocation can be different, such as the shortest processing time of all tasks, the largest utilization rate of resources, the shortest average waiting time of tasks, the largest completion amount of tasks, etc. For these goals, we use C_{min} to represent the normalized total cost of configuration. To determine the resource allocation of n tasks that meet the above constraints, the final total cost of configuration will be minimized, namely:

$$C_{\min} = \min \sum_{i-1}^{n} \sum_{j-1}^{h} \sum_{k-1}^{m_j} c_{ij}^k x_{ij}^k \tag{1}$$

The resource allocation problem is represented by the solution construction figure $G = (V, A, \Gamma, \Omega)$, in which: V is the set of nodes in the figure, and each node represents the resources to be allocated; A is the set of arcs connecting nodes in the graph, which is composed of unidirectional arcs and bidirectional arcs. Two nodes in each type of resources are connected by two directional arcs, while all kinds of resources are connected by unidirectional arcs; The feasible solution of the problem, that is, the sequence of tasks (nodes), constraint Ω means that each node only appears once in this sequence; Γ is a pheromone matrix, and the hierarchical structure diagram is shown in Fig. 1.

In Fig. 1, pheromones of hierarchical structure graph are associated with nodes. Each stage (all kinds of resources) is mapped into a finite set of nodes in a layered structure diagram, and the nodes are distributed in a hierarchical structure. Except the virtual starting node v_0, each layer of nodes corresponds to a set of resources, and the total number of each set is m_i, that is, the total number of such resources, so the number of nodes in each layer is not exactly the same.

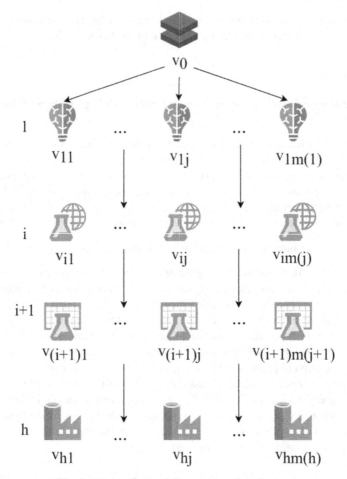

Fig. 1. Hierarchical solution construction diagram

2.2 Optimization Design of Educational Resources Based on Ant Colony Arithmetic

Biomimetics have found through a lot of research that ants can leave a substance called pheromone on the path they go through in the process of foraging, and ants can perceive the existence and intensity of this substance in the process of foraging, so as to guide their own movement direction and move towards the direction with high intensity of this substance[8]. Therefore, the foraging behavior of a large number of ants shows a positive information feedback phenomenon: the shorter a certain path, the more ants that pass through the path, the greater the pheromone intensity left behind, and the greater the probability of latecomers choosing the path. Through this information exchange, ants can choose the shortest path and search for food.

Each ant starts from the virtual starting node (resource O), and constrains ants to traverse in layers. The number of traversed nodes in the same layer should be greater than or equal to zero, that is, at each step of solution construction, if ant k moves from node j to the adjacent nodes s and $s \in allowed(k) \cdot s$ in the same layer in a certain layer, the selection is made according to the pseudo-random proportional state migration rule. When the selected node in this layer has already met the task, it will turn to the next resource layer. In this way, the required nodes are selected step by step for the resource allocation sequence v_i hierarchically. Figure 2 shows a solution of the corresponding optimization problem in the solution construction graph. In the figure, i is the set of nodes in the v_{ij} layer, and j is the 1000th node in this layer.

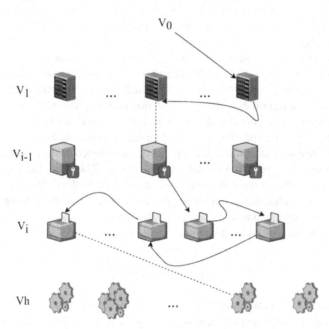

Fig. 2. A solution to the optimization problem

In addition, $\tau_{ij}(t)$, $\eta_{ij}(t)$ denotes pheromone concentration and heuristic information based on problems corresponding to node v_i^j, respectively. Pheromone concentration $\tau_{ij}(t)$ means the desire of ants to move from the previous node to node G in the search process of Fig. 4. Formula (2) represents the probability of moving to node v_i^j, namely:

$$p_{i(j+1)}^{k}(t) = \begin{cases} \dfrac{[\tau_{ij}(t)^a \cdot [\eta_{i(j+1)}(t)]^\beta}{\displaystyle\sum_{\{l|O_{ij} \in N_i^k\}} ([\tau_{ij}(t)^a \cdot [\eta_{i(j+1)}(t)]^\beta)}, & O_{i(j+1)} \in N_i^k \\ 0, & O_{i(j+1)} \in N_k^k \end{cases} \quad (2)$$

Starting from the fictional starting point, the ant colony uses the pseudo-random proportional state migration rule of Formula (2) to create the solution of the problem step by step in the solution construction diagram G, that is

$$\pi(i+1) = \begin{cases} \arg\max_{l \in N_i^k}([\pi_{il}(t)]^a \cdot [\eta_{il}(t)]^\beta), q \prec q^0 \\ S, q \geq q^0 \end{cases} \tag{3}$$

where S is the probability calculated by formula (3), and N_i^k represents the node set of this layer that has been searched.

The flow chart of ant colony arithmetic is as follows (Fig. 3):

Because the ant colony arithmetic uses the local search method, it is likely to fall into the trap of local minima (local maxima) and not get the optimal solution of the problem. Therefore, it is necessary to improve the ant colony arithmetic so that it can get better results. The pheromone concentration of a node dynamically reflects the current utilization rate of resources. The higher the pheromone concentration, the more times the resource has been assigned by tasks, that is, the higher the utilization rate. However, tasks tend to choose resources with high utilization rate, so pheromone concentration is an important factor to be considered when selecting resources for tasks.

Different pheromone updating rules are adopted according to different resources. In the problem of resource allocation, pheromones are distributed on each "resource node", and ants start searching from the virtual starting node v_0. The search scope of each step of ants is all the nodes in the current resource layer. Due to the difference of resource types and their attributes, the update strategy of each layer should be different according to the corresponding attributes of each layer. Then the pheromone of ants transferred from the current node of layer i to another node j of this layer is updated according to formula (4).

$$\Delta\tau_{ij}^k = C_i^{use}/C_i^{all} \tag{4}$$

Among them, C_i^{use} represents the price paid by the allocated resources on the i floor according to certain rules, and C_i^{all} represents the price paid by all the allocated resources on the i floor according to certain rules.

3 Result Analysis and Discussion

College Chinese is a required course in China's education system, and its teaching quality not only greatly affects the education quality of China's institutions of higher learning [9]. To some extent, it has a more intuitive impact on the future development path of pupils. The core issue of optimizing resource allocation in college Chinese education is the determination of allocation arithmetic [10]. At present, there are many arithmetics for cluster system resource allocation, such as polling arithmetic, minimum connection number arithmetic, minimum task number arithmetic, minimum response time arithmetic, hash arithmetic, minimum connection error arithmetic, link bandwidth arithmetic, etc. [11]. Combining the advantages of ant colony arithmetic, this paper improves the arithmetic to be more efficient.

In order to illustrate the effectiveness of the arithmetic and reflect its advantages in the application of optimization model of college Chinese educational resources, in the

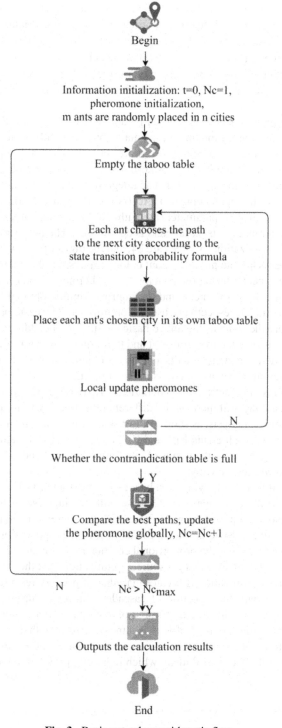

Fig. 3. Basic ant colony arithmetic flow

simulation process, two different objective functions are selected for the same object, and simulation results with different performance indexes are obtained. Selecting the objective function M1 as $ISE = \int_0^\infty e^2(t)dt$ is the square error integral criterion. The objective function M2 is $ITAE = \int_0^\infty t|e(t)|dt$, which is the integral criterion of time multiplied by absolute error. Taking this criterion as the objective function can reflect the rapidity and accuracy of the system, and it has faster response speed and smaller overshoot.

According to the requirements that the parameters to be optimized are the proportional coefficient and integration time of the main controller and the auxiliary controller respectively, the parameters to be optimized are set to be Kp1, Ti1, Kp2 and Ti2, and the optimization intervals are [5, 12], [30, 60], [2, 8] and [60, 150] respectively, where the integration time is T_i in seconds (s). The integration time of the auxiliary controller is longer than that of the main controller. According to the simulation results for many times, it is found that the best parameters are within the above-mentioned selected range, so the optimization range of its parameters is determined. The number of cities, that is, the total digits of optimization variables are 24, and the digits of each variable are 6. The ant colony number is 40, the number of ant colony traversal is 25, pheromone heuristic factor $\alpha = 1$, path expectation heuristic factor $\beta = 1$, pheromone volatilization factor $\rho = 0.8$. The basic ant colony arithmetic and the improved multi-"optimal solution" search ant colony arithmetic are respectively used to optimize it. The basic parameters of the two arithmetics are the same as the above basic parameters. In addition, the most basic genetic arithmetic is selected to optimize it and the simulation results are compared. All simulation tests are the response results and curves obtained under the step disturbance, and the main program of the arithmetic is in the appendix.

The trends of resource optimization parameters Kp1, Ti1, Kp2 and Ti2 optimized by the improved ant colony arithmetic under different objective functions are plotted in the figure for comparative analysis, as shown in Fig. 4 and Fig. 5, in which Fig. 4 shows the trends of proportional coefficients Kp1 and Kp2 under objective functions M1 and M2 respectively, and Fig. 5 shows the trends of integration time Ti1 and Ti2 under objective functions M1 and M2 respectively.

According to this, the following conclusions can be drawn: 1. The change trend of each parameter decreases or tends to decrease with the increase of load, that is, the parameters of resource optimization decrease with the increase of load. This conclusion can provide macroscopic guidance for us in practical application; 2. Under two different objective functions, the proportional coefficient of primary resource optimization is greater than that of secondary resource optimization, and the integration time of secondary resource optimization is greater than that of primary resource optimization, which is consistent with the selection of cascade control system parameters and the ultimate control goal. 3. The variation range of each parameter is not very large. For example, the curve variation trend of Kp1 is almost horizontal, that is, with the change of system operating conditions, the parameters of resource optimization change very little, and the control effect is still ideal, which indirectly proves that the arithmetic has good robustness.

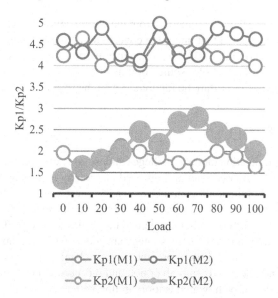

Fig. 4. Trend curve of KP parameters with load

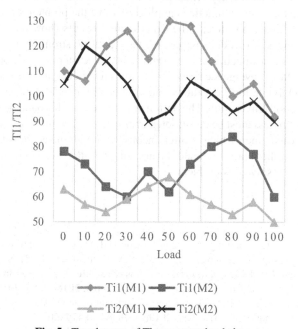

Fig. 5. Trend curve of Ti parameter load change

In this section, the control object models under 20%, 40%, 70% and 100% loads are selected respectively, and the system is simulated and optimized by Matlab programming, and the results of parameter optimization are compared with those of basic ant colony arithmetic and genetic arithmetic. From the optimization results and comparative analysis, it can be concluded that under the condition of complex main steam temperature control objects and high control requirements, the improved ant colony arithmetic can improve the control effect of resource optimization system to some extent, besides excluding the influence of arithmetic randomness on the results.

4 Conclusions

In this paper, an optimization model of college Chinese education resources based on ant colony arithmetic is proposed, and an improved ant colony arithmetic is introduced to solve the problem of optimal allocation of college Chinese resources. In the process of solving, ants tend to choose resources with low service cost and less trouble. According to different resources, different pheromone updating rules are adopted, and global and local updating and max-min ant colony strategy are added to prevent the arithmetic from falling into local minimum. Furthermore, the trust mechanism is introduced to express ants' trust in whether the path is smooth or not, and it is used as heuristic information to influence ants' choice of path, which is more in line with ants' actual path-finding process. Finally, the simulation test analysis is carried out. Simulation results show that this arithmetic has a certain accuracy, which is 11.25% higher than the traditional arithmetic. The improved ant colony arithmetic is applied to solve the problem of optimal allocation of college Chinese resources. The experimental results show that this arithmetic keeps the advantages of parallelism, positive feedback and strong robustness of the ant colony optimization arithmetic, and has remarkable effect in practical application. This arithmetic has a fast convergence speed, overcomes the defect that the traditional arithmetic is easy to fall into local optimum, and is suitable for solving all resource balance problems, with good universality. The optimization model in this paper assumes that the activities of any process must be constructed continuously, and all kinds of resources are independent of each other, which is often inconsistent with the actual situation. Future research can be further optimized, and the ant colony arithmetic can be combined with other arithmetics to solve this problem.

References

1. Liang, Y., Wang, L.: Applying genetic arithmetic and Ant Colony optimization arithmetic into marine investigation path planning model. Soft. Comput. **21**(11), 8199–8210 (2020)
2. Hong, Y., Chen, L., Mo, L.: Optimization of cluster resource indexing of Internet of Things based on improved Ant Colony arithmetic. Clust. Comput. **2018**(9), 56 (2018)
3. Abdelbar, A.M., Salama, K.M.: Parameter Self-adaptation in an Ant Colony arithmetic for continuous optimization. IEEE Access **2019**(6), 18464–18479 (2018)
4. Zuo, L., Lei, S., Dong, S.: A multi-objective optimization scheduling method based on the Ant Colony arithmetic in cloud computing. IEEE Access **3**(4), 2687–2699 (2017)
5. Ning, J., Zhang, Q., Zhang, C.: A best-path-updating information-guided Ant Colony optimization arithmetic. Inf. Sci. **34**(5), 142–162 (2018)
6. Chaouch, I., Driss, O.B., Ghedira, K.: A modified Ant Colony optimization arithmetic for the distributed job shop scheduling problem. Procedia Comput. Sci. **112**(12), 296–305 (2017)

7. Ragmani, A., El Omri, A., Abghour, N.: A performed load balancing arithmetic for public cloud computing using Ant Colony optimization. Recent Patents Comput. Sci. **2018**(7), 45 (2018)
8. Örnek, B.N., Aydemir, S.B., Timur, D.: A novel version of slime mould arithmetic for global optimization and real world engineering problems. Math. Comput. Simul. **198**(11), 253–288 (2022)
9. Kabanikhin, S., Krivorotko, O., Takuadina, A.: Geo-information system of tuberculosis spread based on inversion and prediction. J. Inverse Ill-Posed Probl. **29**(1), 65–79 (2020)
10. Kanso, B., Kansou, A., Yassine, A.: Open Capacitated ARC routing problem by Hybridized Ant Colony arithmetic. RAIRO – Oper. Res. **55**(2), 639–652 (2021)
11. Liu, T., Duan, G.: Task allocation optimization model in mechanical product development based on Bayesian network and Ant Colony arithmetic. J. Supercomputing **2021**(88), 1–29 (2021)

Oral Simulation Headmold Teaching System Based on Digital Virtual Simulation

Jianan Wu[✉] and Huijiao Wang

Hubei College of Chinese Medicine, Jingzhou 434020, Hubei, China
wujianan78012@sina.com

Abstract. Medicine is an empirical discipline, especially Stomatology, which has higher requirements for practical operation ability. The professional characteristics of Stomatology determine that experimental teaching and clinical practice teaching play an irreplaceable key role in the teaching practice of higher medical education. With the revision of the new medical curriculum standards and the deepening of medical teaching reform, new requirements are put forward for the innovation of educational ideas and learning methods of Stomatology. How to give better play to the role of "practical education" curriculum and make students smoothly change to the professional identity of "doctor" has always been a hot topic concerned by stomatologists. With the development of virtual technology, the diversified application of virtual simulation in teaching field is becoming more and more mature. The new experimental teaching mode based on virtual environment is also widely used in the field of stomatological experimental education. However, the scope of medical practical skill operation training in the existing virtual environment is limited to some oral diseases represented by dental hard tissue diseases, while others such as soft tissue diseases, tooth extraction and periodontal apical surgery, Because it is difficult to simulate effectively, students can not be fully trained. Therefore, how to simulate the situation of oral soft tissue disease is the focus and difficulty of oral experimental teaching. To investigate the full utilization and effect of the technical platform of oral clinical simulation system and simulation head model teaching system in oral experimental teaching. Methods in the experimental teaching of students majoring in stomatology in the same session, the technical platform of oral clinical simulation system and simulation headform teaching system were fully used, and the students were investigated by questionnaire and operation examination. Results making full use of the simulation head model teaching system can significantly improve the quality of oral experiment teaching. Conclusion the simulated head model teaching system is an important guarantee to improve the quality of oral experiment teaching and an essential means for oral medical students to carry out preclinical skill training.

Keywords: Virtual simulation · oral simulation head model · oral teaching system

Y. Zhang and N. Shah (Eds.): BigIoT-EDU 2023, LNICST 583, pp. 28–37, 2024.
https://doi.org/10.1007/978-3-031-63139-9_4

1 Introduction

Stomatology is a clinical discipline with strong practicality and application. If the operation technology can not pass the test, no matter how good the theory is, it can not solve the practical problems of patients [1]. According to the research and practice of clinical skill training in Higher Education of Stomatology at home and abroad, in order to ensure the quality of oral experiment teaching, students' preclinical clinical skill training must be carried out on the simulation headform system [2]. Virtual simulation or virtual reality technology refers to the technical means of using virtual system to imitate the real environment. The discipline scope of virtual technology applied to higher education has gradually penetrated into various disciplines from the initial "taste", and has become the most representative new teaching media in the reform of educational technology [3]. Medical education is a highly practical discipline, which requires long-term practical operation, accumulation of knowledge and experience, and continuous learning and exploration in practice, so as to form their own diagnosis and treatment methods and decision-making thinking and ability [4]. While mastering the basic theoretical knowledge of Modern Stomatology, stomatological students must also master the skills of oral clinical operation. They need to face patients independently, complete communication and operate under the guidance of teachers [5]. Therefore, in the process of transformation from students of Stomatology to professional doctors, pre clinical practical teaching and operation training are particularly important [6].

Stomatology teaching is an experimental teaching aimed at improving students' operational ability. It helps students to transform medical theoretical knowledge into practical operational ability, and plays a key transitional role in theory and practice teaching of stomatology [7]. At present, China's domestic medical environment is becoming increasingly severe, and the internship resources that can provide us with teaching and research are decreasing. Experimental teaching that can efficiently transform theoretical knowledge has become the main way of medical practice education in the field of medical education [8]. Experiment teaching can relieve the pressure of practice teaching to a certain extent, improve students' time operation skills in a short time, and have very positive significance in avoiding unnecessary doctor-patient conflicts in clinical practice [9]. The simulation design of the oral cavity simulator significantly narrows the gap between laboratory and clinical practice, and enables students to master some basic clinical operation skills before clinical practice, thus realizing the smooth transition from theoretical study to clinical practice [10]. Teaching is an important part of the simulation head mold experiment course. The traditional teaching method is that students are scattered around the teacher's experiment table to watch the teacher's operation. Because of the small vision of oral operation, only teachers and a few students can see the operation vision, and most students can't see the complete teaching operation, which greatly reduces the teaching effect [11]. If the students can't deeply understand the teacher's operation essentials, the subsequent specific experiments need repeated correction and guidance from the teacher. With the development of oral experiment technology, at present, the simulation headform experiment classes in many domestic colleges and universities gradually give up the onlookers teaching method and adopt multimedia technology [12]. Xi 'an Jiaotong

University School of Stomatology has introduced two different multimedia teaching systems. Based on the application in recent years, this paper discusses the effects of different teaching methods on the teaching effect of simulation head mold experiment [13].

2 Discussion on Simulation Teaching of Oral Simulation Head Mold System

2.1 Simulation Teaching Environment of Simulation Head Mold System

The oral simulation head model experimental teaching system is a stomatology teaching platform that integrates oral clinical simulation, clinical basic skills practice and informatization teaching. Quality, pre-clinical skills training of students must be carried out on the simulation headform system. The teaching environment of the simulation head model system consists of four parts: the El cavity comprehensive treatment system, the simulated human skull and mouth'jaw system, the tooth model system and the multimedia network teaching system. The oral comprehensive treatment system is completely consistent with the clinical setting, the teaching system is the technical support, and the simulated cranial-mouth-jaw system and tooth model are the important simulation factors. The mouth-maxillary system of the artificial head model is very similar in function to the temporomandibular joint of the normal human body. In addition to the simple opening and closing movement, it has a semi-adjustable occlusal joint. The special condyle device can simulate a variety of Mandibular movements, such as forward movement and lateral movement, have high simulacrum. The tooth model is an important part of the simulation head model system. At present, the tooth models used in the simulation head model system in China include plaster teeth, isolated teeth and resin teeth. Gypsum teeth are the model teeth with the lowest degree of simulation; isolated teeth are undoubtedly the best dental model for bionic effect, but the source is limited, the pulp tissue is difficult to preserve, becomes brittle and easy to crack after disinfection, cannot be connected with plastic bases, and The shape and adjacency of the neck have a certain deviation from the clinical, which limits the application to a certain extent; resin teeth include acrylic and epoxy resins, acrylics are more common in finished dentures and artificial teeth. Needle, poor combination with model base, limited application; epoxy resin hardness is close to natural teeth, non-stick bur, equipped with silicone rubber gum, can form ideal neck and adjoining structure, there are different types of structures according to experimental requirements, but it is expensive, and it is difficult to apply it in large quantities at present. According to the different ways of video capture, the simulation head model multimedia teaching system is divided into two ways: built-in type and external type. In addition to the coordination of image acquisition, transmission, restoration, and teacher's teaching operation, and high definition at the medical diagnosis level, there are certain differences in equipment configuration and image presentation methods.The structure of two kinds of simulation head model multimedia teaching system is shown in Fig. 1.

The structure type of the model is in good agreement with the content requirements of the experiment course. According to the different experimental contents, the simulated head model can be divided into oral surgery model, dental pulp and root canal

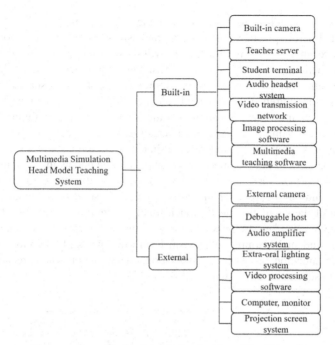

Fig. 1. Structure diagram of two kinds of simulation head model multimedia teaching system

system model, periodontal model, orthodontic model, and fixed denture, removable partial denture and complete denture model of prosthodontics. Various models have great differences in tooth and periodontal morphology, jaw arch structure, model materials and so on. Judging from the application and experimental effect of the current experimental class, there is no dental model that is completely consistent with the clinical conditions. It is an effective solution to give full play to the wisdom of dental teaching technicians and design dental models that are suitable for the teaching content.

2.2 Ways to Strengthen Simulation Teaching

Most of the experimental teachers are undertaken by clinicians, and their rich clinical experience improves the quality of experimental teaching. However, due to the heavy clinical work, it is difficult for teachers to engage in teaching for a long time. They often formulate experimental teaching plans according to their own clinical experience, which makes the experimental teaching method single. In the simulation head model teaching, it is mainly manifested in the lack of awareness of simulation teaching. In the teaching of simulation head model, simulation is more reflected in the cultivation of basic clinical ability. The basic clinical abilities include the basic operation of traditional Chinese medicine, the adjustment of patient's body position and head position, the use of basic instruments such as mouth glasses, and the selection and control of fulcrum; Communication between doctors and patients; Doctors' aseptic awareness, such as disinfection of instruments, pollution of materials, management of clinical environment and other

scattered details. In addition to emphasizing in the relevant courses such as "oral examination" and "fulcrum practice", the teacher emphasizes that it is more important in the
follow-up experiment, otherwise the students will show various problems, such as excessive quarrel traction, poor body posture, experimental equipment piled on the desktop,
etc. The cultivation of basic clinical ability requires teachers to have a sense of simulation
at all times, strict requirements and patient guidance. To break the teaching mode of con-
firmatory experiment, we should strengthen the design experiment. Taking "abutment
preparation" as an example, the experimental results can not be completely evaluated by
the abutment shape prepared by students, but should be comprehensively evaluated from
the students' control of the pressure of high-speed mobile phone, the running direction
of needle and the placement of fulcrum [3]. In addition, after the completion of each
course or teaching unit experimental course, make full use of the simulation teaching
environment of the simulation head model, timely adopt enlightening modes such as
BPL teaching or role play, strengthen the networking of students' knowledge and skills
and improve students' learning enthusiasm from the aspects of reception simulation,
clinical communication, professional association, operation points and precautions. The
overall design scheme of the system is shown in Fig. 2.

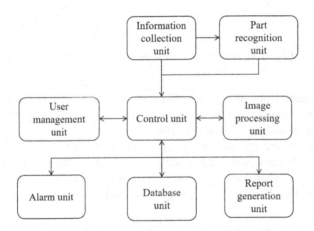

Fig. 2. Overall system design scheme

Students' operational ability is formed in long-term training, and each student's
hands-on ability is different. In the teaching of simulation head model, it is particularly
important to pay attention to the staged training of students. Strengthen basic ability
training. In the early stage of entering the simulation head model laboratory, students
lack the mental preparation in the clinical environment, are unfamiliar and panic, seriously affect the teaching process of the experimental class, and may cause undue damage
to the experimental equipment. For the students who are involved in the simulation headform experimental course for the first time, special training on basic application skills
should be carried out, so that the students can familiarize themselves with the environment as soon as possible, and basically master the application of various systems of the
simulation headform, so as to establish a foundation for the normal development of the

experimental course. Focus on the developmental process of students. Due to personality differences, students with poor operation in the early stage of the experimental class are disappointed or even negative, while students with strong hands-on ability and good operation also show complacency, which affects the experimental effect in the middle and later stages of the experimental class. Teachers should make adjustments in time, change the final evaluation to the developmental experimental evaluation, establish the experimental results according to the students' overall performance in the whole experimental course, and mobilize the students' initiative in operation. The teaching content of the simulation head model is scattered in various professional courses, the knowledge structure is fragmented, the knowledge mastered by students lacks flexibility, and they lack thinking in practice. Only by systematizing the teaching content of the simulation head model and promoting the integration of theoretical teaching and practical teaching, can a better teaching effect be achieved. Among the courses related to the simulation head model teaching, the content of dental and endodontics involving basic clinical abilities and simulation teaching is the most systematic and concentrated, while courses such as prosthodontics are mainly based on clinical requirements, so the course arrangement should be systematically arranged. Considering the sequence of the courses, neither the two courses can be carried out at the same time, so that students are at a loss in the restoration course, and the time interval between the two courses cannot be too long (such as two semesters), and the students may have artificial head molds. The unfamiliarity of operation affects the quality of teaching. Establish a staged teaching plan. The simulation head model teaching should cover the entire growth process of students, and focus on basic ability training during the theoretical teaching period; design pre-clinical simulation head model special training, systematically set up teaching content and corresponding teaching models for multiple majors, plus Large-scale simulation training efforts; in the process of clinical practice, a solid training plan is designed, and activities such as "resin aesthetic filling" competition and "tooth preparation expert" competition are set up. Through staged simulation head model teaching, qualified oral application talents are cultivated.

3 Application of Simulation Virtual System in Experimental Teaching of Oral Simulation Headform

3.1 The Working Principle of Simulation Virtual System in Oral Simulation Headform Teaching

The mechanical power part of the comprehensive treatment machine in the oral simulation virtual system is completely configured according to the actual clinical operation, including fast and slow mobile phones, light sources, water spray cooling, spitting system, panel control, chair position adjustment, etc. The simulated skull model imitates the anatomy of the patient's oral soft and hard tissue, occlusal relationship, tooth arrangement and so on. In addition to the simple opening and closing movement, the sagittal naked part and naked tract device similar to the real patient can simulate a variety of lower collar movements, such as forward extension movement, lateral movement and so on. The material of model teeth has similar hardness and density to natural teeth, which can give students the most realistic grinding and cutting feel during operation. The mask device also simulates the soft tissue environment around the human oral cavity, which is helpful for students to master the selection of fulcrum, the use of mouth mirror and the protection of adjacent tissues during clinical operation. On the same model, it can not only prepare the hole shape of the inlay, but also prepare the abutment of the full crown, fixed bridge and post crown, take the mold, make the temporary crown, extract the tooth, minor alveolar surgery and so on. The basic idea of virtual body spring deformation is that the force applied on the soft tissue surface is transmitted to the surrounding other particles connected to it through the surface contact point directly interacting with the user. The stress generated by these particles acts on other adjacent particles, so as to transfer the force to the surrounding and deform at the same time. In the system, the superposition of the spring-shaped variables on the surface of each particle can be equivalent to the surface deformation of the object, and the resultant force of the spring elastic force of each layer of particle virtual body can be equivalent to the contact force on the surface of the object. At the stress action point, according to the force balance relationship:

$$F = f_{N_0} + 6f_{T_1} \sin \theta_1 = K_{N_0} \Delta Z_0 + 6K_{T_1} \Delta r_1 \sin \theta_1 \tag{1}$$

For layer i particles, there are:

$$6(2i - 1)f_{T_i} \cos \theta_i = [12(i + 1) - 6]f r_{i+1} \cos \theta_{i+1} \tag{2}$$

$$6if_{N_i} = 6ik_{N_i} \Delta Z_i = 6(2i - 1)f_{T_i} \sin \theta_i$$
$$- [12(i + 1) - 6]f_{T_{i+1}} \sin \theta_{i+1} \tag{3}$$

where f_{T_i} is the tangential force, f_{N_i} is the normal force, and K_{N_i} is the virtual spring elastic coefficient at the mass point n_i. ΔZ_i represents the displacement of the n_i particle, that is, the deformation length of the virtual spring. θ_i is the angle between the line connecting the n_i particle and the n_{i-1} particle and the horizontal direction after deformation.

Modern medical teaching needs to take the form of two-way teaching organization between teachers and students, and adopt enlightening classroom teaching to make the teaching enlightening and thinking. With the help of the small camera and local area network monitor equipped with the simulation virtual system, the operation process of the instructor can be broadcast and amplified on the computer at each student's position, so that each student can clearly watch the details of the instructor's experimental operation. Students can master most experimental operation skills on the simulated skull model system, such as the adjustment of patient position, the selection of fulcrum, the protection of adjacent tissues in the operation area, the method of pulling tissues and observing the operation area with oroscope, etc. At the same time, teachers can directly monitor the computer screen of students, and realize one-to-one communication and one to many real-time communication between teachers and students through the call button between students and teachers. The prepared cavities will be scored objectively by the computer. The evaluation includes the outline of the cavity and the depth evaluation of the cavity. After comparing the operator's hole shape with the preset standard hole, mark it with different colors. When evaluating the outline of the cavity, the over prepared parts are indicated in red and the insufficient parts are indicated in blue; When evaluating the depth of the cavity, the red part shows the lighter part than the standard cavity, and the blue part is the opposite. In the final comments, corresponding suggestions and improvements will be given according to the shortcomings of the hole shape. The root canal preparation evaluation system evaluates whether students' root canal preparation has reached the correct depth through the built-in camera. The shoulder preparation evaluation system can score many factors, such as the continuity of the shoulder preparation edge, the shape and smoothness of the preparation body, the preparation amount, the width and position of the edge, the aggregation angle, the shape and angle of the shoulder. The greater the difference between the data and the standard shoulder prepared by the teacher, the lower the student's score.

3.2 Teaching Effect of Virtual System

At present, we have set up a number of experiments on the simulation virtual system, including the basic operation of oral and maxillofacial surgery, tooth extraction, abscess incision and drainage, interdental ligation, alveolar bone repair, dental Endodontics cavity preparation and pad filling, dental pulp cavity preparation, root canal preparation, implantology implant model operation, etc. The teaching purpose of the simulation head model experiment class is to imitate the clinical operation through the imitation of the experimental operation by the students. Due to the small size of the oral cavity and the isolated tooth specimen, if the students cannot see and grasp the key points of the operation, it will lead to the failure of the essentials in the personal operation, and the operation error will result in waste. At the same time, teachers have to repeat the explanation and teaching when the students are operating, the work intensity increases, the teaching efficiency decreases, and even the phenomenon of insufficient class hours occurs. The experimental course design of dental and endodontics based on virtual environment is shown in Fig. 3.

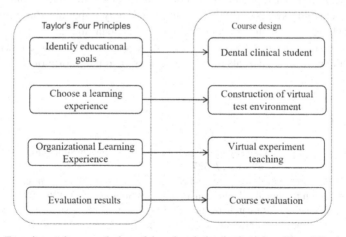

Fig. 3. Experimental course design of dental endodontics based on Virtual Environment

Students' observation and imitation of teachers' experimental operation are reflected in two aspects: ① Vision and image composition. The size of the oral field of vision is reflected in two aspects, one is the local field of vision, which is the image that a single tooth sees from a certain angle in operation. For example, the images of buccal and lingual surfaces of teeth viewed from the side, and the images of dental and maxillofacial surfaces, dental pulp cavity and root canal orifice viewed from right above the crown, etc. One is the whole field of vision, such as the image composition of the relationship between adjacent teeth, teeth and dentition, and even upper and lower dentition, etc. The understanding of two different observation horizons is an important factor for students to master the key points of experimental operation. ② Observation angle of the image. In oral clinical operation, it is the key to obtain the treatment quality whether doctors can perform clinical operation with reasonable observation vision and operation angle. Due to the limitation of mouth fissure size, on the one hand, doctors can get the best observation field by adjusting the patient's head position and body position; On the other hand, through the mirror reflection of the oral mirror, the field of vision of the locally treated teeth is obtained, so as to adjust the position and angle of the operating instrument. The observation angle of the surgical field of vision by the multimedia camera directly affects students' understanding and mastery of the experimental operation, which is also an important factor to measure the performance of the multimedia teaching system.

4   Conclusions

The application of advanced technologies such as virtual simulation for oral preclinical skills training will become a trend, especially with the development of "Internet+" technology and concepts, based on "cloud and big data analysis", it may be possible to achieve more accurate and personalized training in the future. Training method. In short, simulation teaching has been widely used in many teaching fields and achieved good results, but its application in stomatology education in my country has just started. With the further exploration and popularization of the functions of the multimedia simulation head model teaching system, it will play an increasingly important role in the experimental teaching of stomatology and become an indispensable and important means of pre-clinical skills training for stomatology students. The effect and quality are well adapted to the new medical goals of the 21st century and the reform of higher medical education.

References

1. Hoad, K., Kunc, M.: Teaching system dynamics and discrete event simulation together: a case study. J. Oper. Res. Soc. **69**(4), 517–527 (2018)
2. Zhao, Y.: Research and development of economic crisis data simulation teaching analysis system based on fractional calculus equation. Chaos Solitons Fract. **130**, 109460 (2020)
3. Deng, S.Y., Que, X.: Research on the teaching assessment of students of science and engineering teachers in a university. Comput. Appl. Eng. Educ. **27**(1), 5–12 (2019)
4. Zhang, B., Li, S., Gao, S., et al.: Virtual versus jaw simulation in Oral implant education: a randomized controlled trial. BMC Med. Educ. **20**, 1 (2020)

5. Weiner, C.K., Skalen, M., Harju-Jeanty, D., et al.: Implementation of a web-based patient simulation program to teach dental students in oral surgery. J. Dental Educ. **80**(2), 133–140 (2016)

6. Chow, E., Talattof, A., Tsakalozou, E., et al.: Using physiologically based pharmacokinetic (PBPK) modeling to evaluate the impact of pharmaceutical excipients on oral drug absorption: sensitivity analyses. AAPS J. **18**(6), 1–12 (2016)

7. Engelhardt, L., Röhm, M., Mavoungou, C., et al.: First steps to develop and validate a CFPD model in order to support the design of nose-to-brain delivered biopharmaceuticals. Pharm. Res. **33**(6), 1337–1350 (2016)

8. Taheri, M.H., Pourmehran, O., Sarafraz, M.M., et al.: Effect of swirling flow and particle-release pattern on drug delivery to human tracheobronchial airways. Biomech. Model. Mechanobiol. **20**(6), 2451–2469 (2021)

9. Panda, S., Chen, J., Benjamin, O.: Development of model mouth for food oral processing studies: present challenges and scopes. Innov. Food Sci. Emerg. Technol. **66**(1), 102524 (2020)

10. Ronay, V., Merlini, A., et al.: In vitro cleaning potential of three implant debridement methods. Simulation of the non-surgical approach. Clin. Oral Implants Res. **28**(2), 151–155 (2017)

11. Li, Q., Zhang, H., Gao, C., et al.: Research on failure classification and control strategy of four-wheel independent drive electric vehicle drive system. J. Braz. Soc. Mech. Sci. Eng. **43**(12), 1–17 (2021)

12. Evík, J., Adam, L., Pikryl, J., et al.: Solvability of the power flow problem in DC overhead wire circuit modeling. Appl. Math. **66**(6), 837–855 (2021)

13. Ye, C., Chen, J., Xia, C., et al.: Study of curvature and pre-damage effects on the edge stretchability of advanced high strength steel based on a new simulation model. Int. J. Mater. Form. **9**(3), 269–276 (2016)

The Whole Process Education Management System Based on Machine Learning Algorithm

Jun Ma[✉]

Nanning University, Nanning 530200, Guangxi, China
m@phd.mo

Abstract. In recent years, with the development of education and teaching in our country and the continuous deepening of new curriculum reform, the subject of ideology and politics occupies an increasingly important teaching position in the education and teaching of university in our country. How to improve the quality of education and teaching of political thought theory courses in university is very important. Therefore, in the education and teaching process of political thought theory courses in university, it is necessary to adhere to the integrity and continuity of education guidance, so as to provide high-quality political thought theory teaching for college students, and guide students to use political thought theory in real life. Only by solving problems with theoretical knowledge content can we improve the teaching quality of political thought theory courses in university. This article will focus on the establishment of an political thought theory course education system that keeps pace with the times, the establishment of a "monitoring mechanism" for moral education behaviors to do a good job in post-grant service, and the introduction of topic-based teaching into the political thought theory course education in university. From these three aspects This paper analyzes the strategies for improving the education quality of political thought theory courses in university under the whole-process education model, in order to provide constructive suggestions for the improvement of the teaching quality of political thought education in university.

Keywords: Machine learning algorithm · The whole process education mode · political thought education in university · Model building

1 Introduction

The so-called whole-process education mode mainly refers to that when students enter the campus, from the beginning to the end of each semester, schools should carry out political thought education for students. The purpose is to better promote students' individual development in education and teaching, so as to effectively improve the teaching quality of political thought theory courses in university. Teachers can fully implement the whole-process education mode, innovate and innovate the teaching mode of political thought theory course in university, and present efficient and novel political thought theory course education for students [1]. Nowadays, it is the deepening period of reform

Y. Zhang and N. Shah (Eds.): BigIoT-EDU 2023, LNICST 583, pp. 38–47, 2024.
https://doi.org/10.1007/978-3-031-63139-9_5

and opening-up and the key stage of social transformation and development. Various social ideologies collide and the ideological trend is more complicated, which has a negative impact on contemporary college students. Contemporary college students are all "post-90s generation", and they all have distinct personality traits, which are quite different from those of previous college students [2]. This requires teachers to constantly practice, explore, demonstrate and teach in teaching, managing and serving education, so as to realize the whole process of education. Through the infection of teachers' teaching process, the persuasiveness, cohesion and appeal of socialist core values can be greatly enhanced [3]. Therefore, we should further promote the whole-process education mechanism, so that students can have more enthusiasm and expectations for political thought theory courses, so that more students can talk and dispel doubts, and actively and effectively guide students' value orientation to develop in a positive and healthy direction [4]. Lide Shuren is the connotation attribute of political thought education in university. In the new era, political thought work in university should find fresh materials suitable for students' physical and mental characteristics from society [5]. Systematically enhance the dual effects of educating people in the first classroom and in the second classroom, and adhere to the comprehensive integration of politics and academics. The theory and practice are fully connected, the status quo and problems are fully presented, philosophy and engineering are fully infiltrated, political thought teachers and counselors are fully communicated, and universities and society are fully shared. The characteristic path of educating people in the whole process and all-round education [6]. First of all, "all inclusive" should be formed in terms of educational content. Within the framework of the integration of Marxist theory, coordinate the content of professional disciplines and political thought courses, recombine and arrange traditional teaching legends, metaphors and new expressions carried by new media, and design new content rich in extra-professional cognitive content. Course standards, models, and reasonable arrangements for the progress of teaching and receiving [7]. Secondly, "all inclusive" should be formed in the implementation of education [8]. Due to its particularity, some disciplines are difficult to achieve the integration of disciplines, especially the engineering disciplines that are far away from the political thought content. In this case, efforts can be made in educational means, such as classroom layout, scene selection, homework mode, etc., to create a continuous The teaching and receiving environment with strong, coherent and high sensory stimulation can influence the attitude and behavioral tendency of the teaching group, and balance the double standards of students' professional needs and diversified market needs.

2 Analysis of Strategies to Improve the Quality of Political Thought Theory Course Education in University Under the Whole Process Education Mode

"Three-way education" is the general term of all-round education, whole-process education and all-round education. The so-called whole-process education refers to the political thought education course that runs through the school from the beginning to the end of the semester when students enter the campus, and from weekends to winter and summer vacations [9]. Under the whole-process education mode, the diversity and diversification of teaching methods of political thought theory courses in university are very important to improve the quality of political thought theory courses in university. The following is a detailed analysis of the role of diversified political thought teaching methods in improving the quality of courses, as well as diversified teaching methods and strategies. The "five complete" education model is shown in Fig. 1.

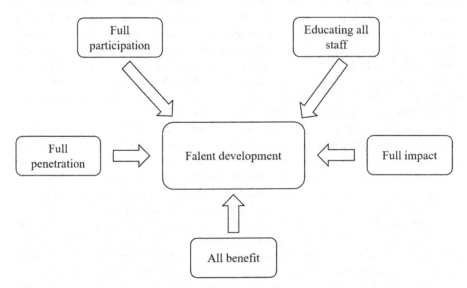

Fig. 1. "Five Completes" Education Model

2.1 Establish an Educational System for Political Thought Theory Courses that Keep Pace with the Times

At this stage, no matter how contemporary the reasons affecting the quality of political thought education in university are, in order to realize the innovation of political thought theory course education and teaching in university under the concept of whole process education, we should make full use of the advantages of network to establish an political thought education system and method mode that keeps pace with the times, so as to better improve the quality and efficiency of political thought theory course education and teaching in university [10]. The establishment of an education system that can effectively solve practical problems can better promote the development and progress of political thought education in university [11]. At present, China's university have established and applied political thought education theme websites, but the effect is not significant. Based on this, China's university should effectively use we media to strengthen the construction and publicity of political thought education theme websites, so as to realize the whole process of political thought education teaching and better realize the effect of online education, Make full use of the convenience brought by the network to improve the education and teaching quality and teaching innovation of political thought theory courses in university [12]. First of all, we can use the self media network to promote the propaganda language, expand the influence of the self media network on political thought education in university, and actively explore and study the publicity and promotion methods, so as to let more people know the self media political thought education platform, have a correct understanding of the political thought education value of the self media education platform, and improve the influence [13]. In the traditional political thought teaching classroom, teachers play the role of the builder and viewer of the self media network education platform. Therefore, they must undertake the task of advertising language promotion, effectively use the classroom to introduce such self media network education websites to students, and let more students understand the role and value of self media education websites [14]. Secondly, beautify the image of self media network education platform. The main reason for the low effectiveness and low attention rate of the existing political thought education theme websites is that the online education platform now gives people a dull and non distinctive feeling. Therefore, the student union feels that this online platform website is useless and has little effect.

University must do a good job in beautifying the overall image of the website to enhance the attraction of the website. For example, we can start with the website page design, put an end to the complicated page design, design the website page in a simple, neat and vigorous form, and adopt memorable names in the website column name design. The most important thing is to take the political thought education content as the theme content of the website, so as to highlight the distinctive features of the website. Generally speaking, the design process of beautifying the image of the network education platform should follow the simple but not simple beautification design concept. Finally, enrich the content form of network education platform. There is a huge amount of information in the ocean for people to browse and read. Therefore, in order to give full play to the advantages of the online education platform, we must enrich the content of the education website, so as to better attract students' attention and bid farewell to the boring and single political thought education content in the past. University can also enrich the content forms of the website by combining students' ideological characteristics, so that the

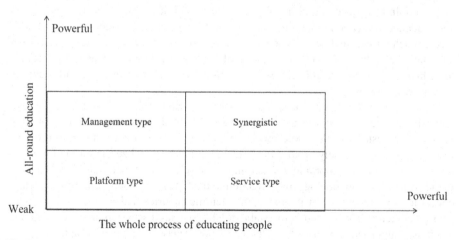

Fig. 2. The two-dimensional quadratic model of the "big political thought" education pattern in university

education website can give students a sense of familiarity and closeness, thus enhancing students' interest in understanding and using it, and better meeting students' learning needs for political thought education, so as to better realize the online education of political thought education in university. The two-dimensional quadratic model of the "big political thought" education pattern in university is shown in Fig. 2.

2.2 Specific Countermeasures to Construct the Whole Process Education System of Ideological and Moral Courses in University

In the classroom teaching part, the ideology and morality courses based on the previous teaching content are only treated as pure theoretical courses. It adapts to the needs of campus networking and multimedia teaching, combines the needs of the times, social reality and students' ideological reality, integrates the teaching system and improves Teaching content, promote the specialization of teaching content. First, deepen the reform of the curriculum system. Breaking the traditional knowledge system framework of ideological and moral courses in the past, the course is divided into several topics according to the essence of the knowledge system, including the topic of outlook on life, topic of morality, topic of psychological outlook, topic of values, topic of talent concept, topic of interpersonal outlook, and topic of innovation. Special topics, aesthetic topics, etc., teachers explain the essence of special topics in the classroom, reflecting the knowledge essence of ideological and moral courses. In terms of teaching, aiming at the single teaching mode of "filling the classroom" and "cramming" in the teaching of ideological and moral courses, it leads to the current situation that students are not highly motivated to learn and the teaching effect is not good. Combined with students' active and keen thinking, they have a strong ability to accept and adapt to new things. The characteristics of the ideological and moral course CAI teaching courseware, with multimedia teaching as the main means, comprehensive use of various methods, promote the diversification of teaching methods, and lay the foundation for the development of online classroom teaching. Through the classic lectures by teachers, the essence of the teaching content is displayed. In this process, traditional discussions, interviews, question surveys, reports and students' recreational activities are still indispensable and effective ways. Multimedia teaching can realize the interaction between teachers and students, and further stimulate the enthusiasm and participation of students in learning, so as to fully reflect the educating function of this course. The "N+X" construction model of all media in university is shown in Fig. 3.

Make use of the campus network resources, establish the ideological and moral education and teaching home page, make the ideological and moral education into the network, and establish the whole process education system. First, establish an online reference database closely around the teaching content to realize the online access to materials for students' moral lesson learning. The selection of materials should adhere to the correct guiding ideology, pay attention to the hot and difficult problems generally concerned by students, arm people with scientific theories and educate people with healthy contents. The second is to establish BBS special discussion area, combine the teaching content and make use of the characteristics of network interaction, actively guide students, make up for the defects that the role of moral education can not be better played after class, and realize the organic combination of quality education and moral learning.

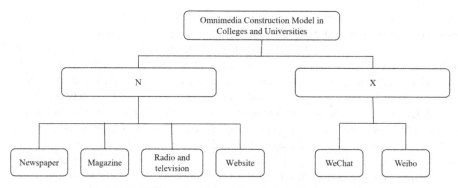

Fig. 3. "N+X" construction model of all media in university

The third is to establish a network reception room to regularly receive online visits from students in the class where the teaching is located. In this process, the key is that teachers should establish a democratic consciousness, respect students' subject, respect students' personality, listen to students' voice, infect students with emotional power, enhance the affinity of Ideological and moral courses, and realize the educational function of online moral courses. Fourth, regularly invite professors, doctors, well-known experts, scholars, teachers' moral construction pacesetters and students' pacesetters inside and outside the school to introduce their deeds and talk about life and successful experience online, inspire students with moving deeds, provide ideological exchange and consultation, guide them to establish a correct world outlook, outlook on life and values, build a large moral education system, and make teachers further understand students' real feelings and views, In order to integrate various forces to suit the remedy to the case and resolve the problem in time. Fifthly, through the network classroom, make the moral course extend into the student dormitory, "eliminate" the "blind spot" of moral education in the student dormitory caused by the socialization of logistics in university, and realize the all-round education of moral course. Sixth, through the online classroom, realize the follow-up moral education of students after the course, take tracking and service as the main idea, answer and help students' problems and puzzles in life and learning at any time or regularly through the online classroom, so that students' ideological problems can be communicated and solved in time. Make up for the disadvantage that the due communication between teachers and students also stops after classroom teaching, and reflect the whole process of moral education as the main channel.

3 GP Model Construction of Whole-Process Education Teaching Quality Evaluation Based on Machine Learning Algorithm

3.1 System Structure Model Design

① Student quality comprehensive assessment module. The module functions include querying students' quality, automatically evaluating students' quality and generating comprehensive identification. Users can be divided into three levels, A-level: students themselves and administrators can inquire all information of students, browse comprehensive identification and comprehensive quality; B-level: ordinary users can inquire about group characteristic information and some information about students' growth, involving students' personal privacy Information cannot be queried, such as family background. C-level: The employer and other users apply for a password to A-level users by phone or E_mail, and check the relevant information after passing the network verification. Querying students' quality in this module is actually a query system; automatic assessment of students' quality is to set weights for students' quality in all aspects, and then design an algorithm according to the weighting formula to generate comprehensive scores, and pay attention to standardized scores in the algorithm; Whether a certain type of quality value of a student is within a certain range, each value range has a corresponding comprehensive identification description, and its algorithm can be realized by using a multi-way branch structure. ② The module of intelligent analysis of student behavior. The module is mainly realized by using association rule algorithm from a large number of history information databases. Function 1: Behavior-related information is the root cause of this behavior from the analysis of students' behavior events; for example, student A is introverted and suddenly fights, the possible root cause is in the student's history information: strange behavior, less communication with others, suffering from Serious mental illness; Function 2: Information-related behavior is to predict the student's possible behavior from the process information; for example, Student B is introverted, likes being alone, is reluctant to participate in activities, and studies hard, predicting the student's psychological pressure, if it is a girl, Depressive psychosis may occur. The algorithm core of these two functions has three parts: first calculate the transaction support, then call the AprionTid algorithm to generate frequent itemsets, and finally call the rule generation algorithm to generate the association rule set and display the "prediction or analysis behavior". ③ data management module. This module has two functions, one is for administrators to review student history information, and the other is for administrators to regularly maintain the database. There are three levels of administrators: college administrators: responsible for certifying college-level student history information; department-level administrators: responsible for certifying department-level student history information; class administrators: responsible for certifying class student history information.

Compared with other education systems, the system has query and statistical functions, and focuses on the evaluation of comprehensive quality and intelligent behavior analysis functions, creating a platform for the realization of intelligent remote education management. What needs to be further studied is the association processing of large-capacity databases, intelligent generation of associated field weights and validity verification.

3.2 GP Model Construction of Whole Process Education and Teaching Quality Evaluation

In the process of constructing GP model, firstly, the maximum a posteriori likelihood estimation of super parameters is obtained by using the training data set and Bayesian principle. T

The teaching quality evaluation model based on super parameters can realize the estimation of teaching quality evaluation and estimate the variance of evaluation results. The specific steps are as follows.

(1) establish a training data set. Set the training data set $\{x_i, t_i\}, i = 1 \Lambda m$, in which $x_i = (x_{i1}, x_{i2}, \Lambda, x_{id})$ is the d teaching quality evaluation index value of the i-th sample, as the input of GP model, t_i is the corresponding teaching quality evaluation result, as the output of GP model, and m is the number of training data set samples.
(2) Normalization of modeling data. In order to eliminate the influence of data due to dimensions, the training data set is normalized, and the normalization formula is shown in (1).

$$x_i^* = \frac{x_i - x_{\min}}{x_{\max} - x_{\min}} \tag{1}$$

In the above formula, x_i, x_i^* represents the values before and after data normalization, respectively, and $x_{\min}, x_{\max}$ represents the minimum and maximum values in the sample data, respectively.
(3) Adaptive calculation of hyperparameters of GP model. The learning samples are learned, and the optimal hyperparameter θ of the GP is obtained adaptively by maximizing the log-likelihood of the learning samples.
(4) Establishment of teaching quality evaluation model. Based on the optimal hyperparameter θ of GP, the teaching quality result Y^* of the input X^* is estimated.
(5) Reliability analysis of GP method results of teaching quality evaluation. GP calculates the expected ($Y^* = u(X^*)$) and variance (σ_{i*}^2) corresponding to the input X^* of teaching quality evaluation. Based on the expectation and variance, the confidence interval calculation formula (2) of GP calculation results can be established, where is the lower bound of the confidence interval and $\overline{\theta}$ is the upper bound of the confidence interval. Taking the confidence interval of 95% confidence as an example, $z_{\theta/2} = 1.96$. When the theoretical value of teaching quality evaluation results falls within the confidence interval of GP estimation, it is confirmed that the reliability of GP results is high.

$$\left\{ \theta = Y_j^* - \sigma_{yj} \cdot z_{\theta/z} \quad Y_j^* + \sigma_{y_j^*} z_{\theta/2} = \overline{\theta} \right\} \tag{2}$$

In order to ensure the comprehensiveness and accuracy of the weight calculation of the forecast index, on the basis of subjective weighting of analytic hierarchy process, objective weighting is combined with entropy method, and the comprehensive weight of the index is determined according to subjective weighting and objective weighting. Thus improving the learning efficiency. x_p and y_p respectively represent the risk prediction index of computer information management system and the initial risk prediction value of computer information management system, and the sample data is described as follows:

$$J_s = \left\{ (x_p, y_p) \right\}_p^s = 1 \tag{3}$$

In the formula: s is the number of samples. Equation (4) describes the extreme learning machine regression constraint form:

$$\min\left(\frac{1}{2}\eta_L^Y \eta_L + \frac{\gamma}{2}\varphi^Y \varphi\right)$$

$$s.t. \tag{4}$$

$$y_p = \sum_{i=1}^{L} \eta_i f\left(\delta_i x_p + z_i\right) - \varphi_p$$

where: L and z are the number of hidden layer nodes and regression error respectively; $f()$ and φ are the regression errors of mapping function and output layer nodes respectively; δ_i is the weight vector of x_p, η_i is the weight vector of y_p, and Y is the expected output.

4 Conclusions

In the teaching process, we should closely focus on the mechanism of "educating people in the whole process", and constantly strengthen the systematicness, objectivity, effectiveness and attraction of political thought theory courses in university, so as to strengthen students' main body, refine the education process, optimize the education and teaching environment, and build a scientific system of political thought theory education for college students. In this paper, the GP model of the whole-process education quality evaluation based on machine learning algorithm is established, and the model reliability evaluation method based on confidence interval estimation is established. At the same time, by comparing the accuracy with BP and LS-SVM methods, the advanced nature of the new method is verified.

Acknowledgements. The authors acknowledge the "Exploration and Practice of Creating a New Paradigm of Innovation and Entrepreneurship Education in Nanning University based on Tao Xingzhi's educational concept" (Grant:2021JGZ175).

References

1. Aydogmus, M.E.: Social stigma towards people with medically unexplained symptoms: the somatic symptom disorder. Psychiatr. Q. **91**(1), 1–13 (2020)
2. Ruth, P., Gwenda, A., Joni, G., et al.: Advance care planning in dementia: recommendations for healthcare professionals. BMC Palliat. Care **17**(1), 88 (2018)
3. Jiang, Y., An, Y., Li, J.: Study on the cultural and educational orientation of political teaching in university under the new media background. Int. J. Eng. Model. **31**(1), 118–124 (2018)
4. Zhou, H.: An empirical research on adjustment of teaching management objectives in university based on innovation ability. Revista de la Facultad de Ingenieria **32**(15), 788–791 (2017)
5. Rowley, J.E., Farrow, J.F., Oulton, A.J., et al.: The use of INFO, a database management system, in teaching Library and Information Studies at Manchester Polytechnic. Educ. Inf. **6**(1), 71–82 (2017)

6. Deng, F.: A study on the reform and the design of Colleges Teaching management system based on innovative personnel training. Revista de la Facultad de Ingenieria **32**(8), 256–262 (2017)
7. Cui, J.: Model research of project schedule management system based on particle swarm optimization algorithm. Revista de la Facultad de Ingenieria **32**(15), 122–127 (2017)
8. Wumin, P., Rui, M.: Research on improvement of China mobile customer relationship management system based on apriori algorithm. Boletin Tecnico/Tech. Bull. **55**(19), 520–526 (2017)
9. Tang, X., Guo, Q., Li, M., et al.: Performance analysis on liquid-cooled battery thermal management for electric vehicles based on machine learning. J. Power Sources **494**(1), 229727 (2021)
10. Riguzzi, F.: Speeding up inference for probabilistic logic programs. Comput. J. **57**(3), 347–363 (2018)
11. Falahati, A., Shafiee, E.: Improve safety and security of intelligent railway transportation system based on Balise using machine learning algorithm and fuzzy System. Int. J. Intell. Transp. Syst. Res. **20**(1), 117–131 (2021)
12. Wang, Z.: Research on university sports management based on computer data management system. Revista de la Facultad de Ingenieria **32**(5), 355–362 (2017)
13. Zhou, X., Jiang, P.: Variation source identification for deep hole boring process of cutting-hard workpiece based on multi-source information fusion using evidence theory. J. Intell. Manuf. **28**(2), 255–270 (2017)
14. Rodríguez, G.G., Gonzalez-Cava, J.M., Pérez, J.A.M.: An intelligent decision support system for production planning based on machine learning. J. Intell. Manuf. **31**(5), 1257–1273 (2020)

Design and Application of College Music Education Management Platform Under Genetic Algorithm

Kun Tang[(✉)] and Cuiying Wang

Hohhot Institute for Nationalities, Hohhot 010000, Inner Mongolia, China
tangk_1988@163.com

Abstract. The university music education management system is an important content to improve the quality of education. In view of the structure and operation form of the college music classroom, the development situation should be analyzed. The music education system in universities is not perfect, Therefore, this study also evaluates the educational content of university music system from the perspective of genetic algorithm, Combining with the design of the system, Based on the current design and implementation mode of music teaching system, By analyzing the composition of the university music teaching system, Based on interface setting and role permission function module, Finally, it has completed the functional requirements of the music teaching system, the system design requirements, the online teaching operation and other stages, To truly build a music teaching system with high stability and reliability, Some problems existing in improving the construction of the current music teaching system, Based on the algorithm data mode, Identify its system design process. However, after the design of the music teaching system is completed, it provides good support for event management and examinee management.

Keywords: genetic algorithm · college music · teaching management system

1 Introduction

With the continuous development of quality education, colleges and universities in China have increased their efforts to develop art education, integrating quality education concepts and generalist education ideas into the construction process of art education in colleges and universities, effectively promoting the further development of art education in China. In the actual construction process, how to integrate new development concepts and make the construction of music education in colleges and universities to a higher level is currently the primary issue facing colleges and universities. As we all know, the music education and teaching management system in colleges and universities is an important component of music teaching in colleges and universities, which is conducive to the rational allocation of music teaching resources in colleges and universities, and fully

Y. Zhang and N. Shah (Eds.): BigIoT-EDU 2023, LNICST 583, pp. 48–58, 2024.
https://doi.org/10.1007/978-3-031-63139-9_6

realizing the construction goal of scientific, standardized, and comprehensive management of music education and teaching in colleges and universities. Music, as the carrier of human civilization, has extremely rich historical and cultural significance through the combination of musical instruments and vocal music to achieve emotional expression and ideological exchange. The unique charm of music goes hand in hand with the development of human civilization, enabling people to meet their spiritual needs. Unlike other disciplines, music, as the main manifestation of music performance, cultivates students' musical sentiment, shapes their souls, and leads to the development of their musical behavior in an artistic and aesthetic manner. Therefore, music education is of vital significance to the development of national quality and human civilization. Music education is an important component of aesthetic education. Looking at the development of music education in colleges and universities, there are some problems in music education in some colleges and universities, with obvious problems in passive management.

In order to meet the educational needs of the new era, college music education should start from the perspective of connotation construction. Throughout the history of music education in China, music education in various universities was a model of elite education in the past. Elite music education means that higher music education has a high quality and a small scale; In addition, elite music education will take cultivating outstanding talents for society as the primary task, and some music schools will become the measurement standard for talent cultivation. China's music education is gradually moving towards the international stage, and the situation of music education has undergone earthshaking changes, but the essence of music education has always been the same. American educator John Dewey believes that education is life, education is growth, and education is the transformation of experience. "That is, music education is the cumulative transformation of educational experience". While paying attention to the development of professional technology, it is necessary to return the music education model to the standard, and take the comprehensive development of students as the educational goal.

An investigation was conducted on the teaching forms and levels of different types and levels of music education colleges, and significant differences were found. Currently, the management of music education in colleges and universities does not have a targeted management model. If you want to enhance the strength of education management, modern management methods have become an inevitable development demand; To achieve more long-term development, we should break the personalized training pattern, give full play to our own advantages, and take the common interests of globalization as our teaching philosophy. The implementation of music management in colleges and universities is a means to promote organizational change and achieve connotation based education. Innovation in the management of music education in universities can integrate social, economic, cultural, environmental, and other aspects, and promote global sustainable development. At the same time, college music education should play a role in communicating with the world's culture in the development of a country, telling the world the traditional stories of the Chinese nation, disseminating the Chinese voice, promoting the Chinese spirit, and allowing the world to enhance its understanding of China and establish a correct understanding through appreciation of Chinese music. In the process of disseminating the traditional music culture of the Chinese nation, it is also necessary to absorb advanced foreign cultures, accelerate the creation of modern teaching, achieve connotation based education, and improve the level of music education in universities.

Currently, people have new requirements for music education in colleges and universities, which not only require music educators to have strong professional abilities, but also require them to start with the characteristics of music education and lead students to find the true meaning of music.

At present, the rapid analysis of the music classroom teaching content and the optimization of its theory have also become the key frame of the current curriculum, and the innovation of the efficient classroom teaching structure should also change accordingly. For the follow-up music course teaching content, music classroom thinking and the design scale of music teaching system are gradually breakthrough, and this systematic research process is to analyze the genetic algorithm education system of music course in colleges and universities, to improve its curriculum efficiency.

2 Overview of the Genetic Algorithm

Genetic algorithm is an algorithmic structure based on the concept of evolution. It was tried by American professors in 1962. In the process of the development and change of genetic algorithm, it took its essence and abandoned its dross. The integration of too many races makes the genetic algorithm more functional. When applying the genetic algorithm to solve it, it can be compared to a biological evolution process. Individual competition is mainly reflected in the food competition, while the optimization of the subsequent survival opportunities and operation content mainly includes the individual application of the genetic algorithm [1]. In the case of complex problems, we can improve the certainty through the advantage survival analysis, and also create a new space for the subsequent functional structure operation of genetic algorithms. Establish proper functional relationships to optimize your own characteristics, self-organization, and operational performance. It can be used to make problem decisions with huge data, and to obtain the optimal solutions in the computational functional structure, which is often applied to the current operational control of many variables.

The operating characteristics of the genetic algorithm are mainly included as follows.

First, select the appropriate way to encode the system parameters, the relatively optimized solution set and transformation into chromosomes for presentation.

Second, determine the initial group defined good functional relationship.

Third, specific genetic operating systems are designed and analyzed according to the population size as well as the genetic operation probability.

Fourth, judge whether the generated group meets a certain standard, and exit if it does not. Specific operational control, which is the basic structure of the genetic algorithm.

3 Description of the System Construction of the University Music Education Management Platform

3.1 System Requirements Analysis

Combined with the construction needs of this system, in the current evaluation and design process of the university music education management platform, it is mainly based on the teaching structure transition and resource sharing mode. In the process of this system design, the construction of network resources is implemented to better supplement the corresponding teaching mode, and the requirements of the system are also met in the system design and adjustment stage, and the data quantity is analyzed to improve the quality of the course teaching. To meet the system requirements during the system operation process, For the relevant schemes involved, Evaluation and analysis of information system maintenance and system design characteristics, All convenient students can design and optimize the key content to facilitate the summary and breakthrough of information resources in different periods in the simulation teaching will be targeted at students to consult, The results were analyzed, The realization of random examination paper curriculum construction also optimizes the organization scheme of different classes and such a teaching system obviously has a certain pertinence, Analyze the key technologies in the achievement information system and the teaching maintenance system, To understand the needs of the current university information management system and teaching system combined with the characteristics of plant management information system management and comprehensive development management evaluation, Optimize the design according to the actual teaching content of each professional course, Such a system facilitates the introduction at different time periods, Realize intelligent and data automation design breakthrough in the test paper random information function summary also has its corresponding advantages, The integrity of the system is not maintained properly [2].

Steps for evaluating the network structure under the music teaching system using genetic algorithms:

1) Construct a genetic algorithm structure. Since there are 16 secondary indicators, combined with the empirical formula n = vuv for the number of neurons in the hidden layer (u.v is the number of input layers and output layers, respectively), a three-layer network structure with a genetic algorithm framework of 20-4-1 is constructed. Initial weights are randomly generated and binary coded as the initial population of the genetic algorithm. The length of the individual string depends on the accuracy of the solution;

2) The generated neural network is used for calculation.

3) Measure the error value 6 between the expected output value and the actual output value, such as 6 < e (a specified small number). After completion, apply this set of weights to the BP network;

$$SSE = \sum_{l=1}^{K} \sum_{x \in L_l} Dist(x, Z_l)^2 \tag{1}$$

$$AVF(x_i) = \frac{1}{m} \sum_{f=1}^{m} f(x_{ij}) \tag{2}$$

4) For example, if 6 > E, genetic algorithms are used to cross and mutate the initial population (the mutation rate can be taken as 0.01) to generate new offspring;

5) The fitness function is determined using the error value à, usually using the reciprocal of à as the evaluation function of chromosomes;

$$Rebate\ rate = \left(\sum_{i=1}^{k} \left(\frac{e_i}{e_i + m_i} \right) \right) / k \tag{3}$$

$$\arg\min_{SC} \sum_{i=1}^{k} \sum_{x \in C_i} |X - \mu_i|^2 \tag{4}$$

6) Select a new population using the fitness function, and repeat steps 2) and 3) until the requirements are met, ending.

Using Matlab toolbox functions to design an improved genetic algorithm model for learning the data of 20 teachers, the error can basically reach an accuracy of less than 0.01. The transfer function of the BP network uses a tangent sigmoid type function, and the training function uses trainlm. The target error of the network is 0.01, the maximum number of cycles is 2000, and the training error is less than the target error at the end of the training; The operating parameters of the genetic algorithm are: weight variation range 0.6, crossover probability 0.5, and mutation probability 0.005.

3.2   System Operating Environment Requirements

3.2.1   Hardware Requirements

(1) Server-side:
    CPU: P4 1GHZ or above;
    Memory: 512M (1 G) above;
    Hard drive: 40G (80 G).
(2) Client:
    CPU: C4 1 GHZ or above;
    Memory: 256 M (512M recommended) or above;
    Hard drive: 2 G (remaining space).

3.2.2   Software Requirements

Database (DataBase): MYSQL5.0
    Web Server: Apache Tomcat 6.0
    JAVA Development environment: JDK1.6

3.3   System Function Requirements Analysis

Teachers are divided into these several roles:

A. The teacher can input and analyze all the score information combined with the system;
B. Counselor can use this system to query the data information, and control the authority combined with the relevant information;
C. The audit department can input the comprehensive results of the students according to this information, and submit it to the current student work department;
D. The Student Affairs Office will review the comprehensive evaluation results and save them, otherwise it will be called back, modified or redone.

In the process of information system maintenance, the administrator can ensure the correctness of the whole information system, and process and analyze the key data and information of the system according to the permission control modular design. During its module control process, the exposed data is adjusted [3].

3.3.1 Basic Student Information

For the design and functional milk of the student module, it mainly includes the following points: professional management, class management, student management. The corresponding module functions are to add, delete, modify and query to fully manage the basic information of students, as shown in Fig. 1.

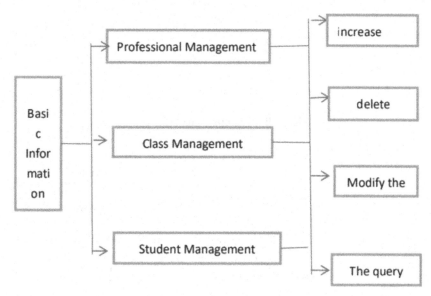

Fig. 1. Basic Information of students

3.3.2 Basic Teacher Information

In the process of teacher basic information management, this is a key information content designed by teachers. In view of the design status of the basic information, it can query, analyze and control the specific operation objects, and the database can also encode and analyze the key information, improve the integrity of its data structure information, and make plans to meet the corresponding requirements according to the subsequent data understanding of the processing structure[4]. (The first two characters indicate: such as yx, member of the department audit team, counselor dy, course instructor js, administrator gl, and members of the Student Affairs Office and Student Affairs Department xs), as shown in Fig. 2.

3.3.3 Basic Information of Achievement

The performance system management has strong functions, including the collection and analysis of basic performance information. This module includes sub-modules: curriculum management, intellectual education score statistics, moral education score statistics and moral education score review, as shown in Fig. 3.

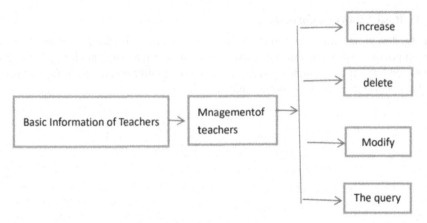

Fig. 2. Basic information of teachers

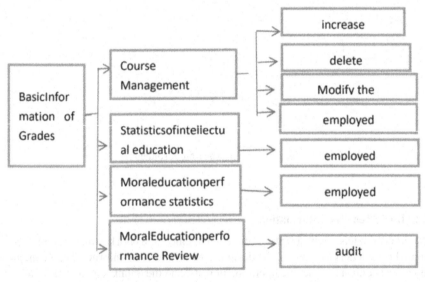

Fig. 3. Basic information of grades

4 Overall System Design

4.1 System Function Design Objective

The main design functional objective of the system is based on, At present, the overall structure design of the system needs the optimization of class information resources curriculum resources and comprehensive management resources, The system design can meet its general needs, Also was done, In the process of the collection and control of the information system, Individual logical functions can be analyzed, Meet the general design, Need to be equally available for the user operation procedure, Data entry integrity data development characteristics, And personal account information processing and other information resources are integrated in such information permission function design process to meet the general needs, The same control of functional structure data information is to realize the teaching adjustment of information exchange and the control of permission information in the process of summarizing all information resources, This information management has the integrity of workers and development of all information resources can be complementary applications [5].

4.2 Database Design

If the logical design of the database is defective, the performance of the database is quite limited. The Logical design determines the overall performance and tuning location of the database; the database table corresponding to each entity is as follows:

(1) Student form (Student) includes: name, student number, gender, date of birth, major number, class number, remarks; (Table 1)

Table 1. Student Table

name	type	Is it empty	Windows default	description
Id	varchar	no	null	Student ID
Name	varchar	no	null	surname and personal name
Sex	varchar	no	man	sex
Birthady	date	yes	1990.01.01	date of birth
ClassId	varchar	no	null	Class number
MajorId	varchar	no	null	Professional number
Passwd	Varchar	No	Null	Student password
Comment	varchar	yes	Null	remarks

(2) Teacher's Form (Teacher): teacher number, name, gender, course taught, professional title, and remarks; (Table 2)
(3) Major table (Major): major, major name, number of classes included, remarks; (Table 3)

5   Design and Realization of the University Music Education Management Platform Under the Genetic Algorithm

5.1 Design of Student Information Management Module

In the process of the student information management module, students can accurately understand the relevant information recorded by the system. In the function of the student information management module, this module is the most core module of the system

Table 2. Teacher's Table

name	type	Is it empty	Windows default	description
Id	Varchar	no	Null	Teacher number
Name	varchar	No	Null	surname and personal name
Sex	Varchar	No	man	sex
Course	Varchar	No	Null	Lecture course
Titles	Varchar	No	lecturer	professional ranks and titles
Passwd	Varchar	No	Null	Teacher password
Commnet	varchar	yes	Null	remarks

Table 3. Professional Table

name	type	Is it empty	Windows default	description
Id	varchar	No	Null	Professional number
Name	varchar	no	null	name of major
ClassCount	Int	yes	0	Includes the number of classes
Commnet	varchar	yes		remarks

design, so that the login students can make independent choices for different open departments and different professional courses. After the selection is completed, the students' selection information can be analyzed with the whole course selection system. After the selection, the students' course selection information will be stored in the course selection list in the system database, and the course selection information can also be re-checked in viewing the course selection function. Third, it is to view the selection information. For finding the course selection information, you can view the course selection status, and you can delete the unsatisfactory course selection [6].

5.2 Design of Course Selection Management Module

In terms of course management module design, the functions of administrators include department management, professional management, course management and student management. First of all, the department management, which can analyze according to the information of different departments, edit and delete the existing information, and can also click and add the department button to add the new department information. The second is the functional design, in the functional design process according to the department system design analysis, after login can obtain the corresponding functional structure, according to personal needs to course, this is the center of online course system design, to ensure that all designers are able to evaluate the content and optimization. Therefore, add the relevant student button to enter the recruitment management of student information. When entering, enter the user name admin password admin, and the system will enter its login interface [7].

5.3 Implementation of the User Login Function

The login module is a window for users to enter the system for various operations, and has the function of verifying user information. Only the system certification information has its comprehensive. And the role information of the user is transmitted to the relevant system, so that the system can provide a different display interface according to different users, which is the key to the difference between the login module and other modules. After the website is loaded, the user can enter the name to click into the login button. If the confirmation information is incorrect, then, the system will prompt the login failure.

6 Conclusion

This design process analyzes the design function of university music teaching system from the perspective of genetic algorithm. For college music education system, it is a multi-module function, which realizes the convergence and modern control of music teaching management system. To on its music teaching system design. Based on the teaching examinee audio-visual management, online teaching automatic score score query and other aspects of the function. In the construction process to reach a high level, and based on the system function, operation process and other aspects of the content to make a certain analysis. On this basis, the functional and music teaching system design scheme is verified, and the overall function of the music teaching system is verified based on the system development and design process. In order to meet the pre-demand, truly establish a teaching system for all students on campus to provide convenience for students and teachers.

Acknowledgements. This article is the phased research achievement of the 14th five year plan of Educational Science in Inner Mongolia Autonomous Region, "Research on the innovation of music education model in Colleges and Universities under the background of new liberal arts in the new era".

References

1. Ma, X.: Application of web mining and genealgorithm in design of intelligent network teaching system. China New Commun. **22**(10), 1 (2020)
2. Yao, J.: Application of multi-objective genetic algorithm in the optimization design of shear lifting platform. Mech. Des. Manufac. **2**, 4 (2020)
3. Yang, L., Guo, Y., Li, J., et al.: Optimization simulation experiment design based on genetic algorithm. Mod. Educ. Equip. China (2022)
4. Xing, L.: Management of university teacher training based on genetic algorithm in cloud computing Hadoop platform. Mod. Electron. Technol. **43**(1), 4 (2020)
5. Wei, L., Zhang, T., Dang, L., et al.: Application of an improved genetic algorithm in intermittent chemical process design. Chem. Indust. Eng. **37**(4), 8 (2020)

6. Zhang, L.: Application of coding optimization design based on genetic algorithm in MIMO Radar Communication System. Electron. Eng. Inform. **2021**(004) (2021)
7. Li, Y.: Genetic algorithm model design in industrial products in virtual reality environment. Mod. Electron. Technol. **43**(5), 4 (2020)

Research on Piano Harmony Automatic Orchestration System Based on Deep Learning

Yun Cui[(✉)] and Meng Qin

Mianyang Teachers' College, Mianyang 621000, Sichuan, China
cuiyun2022@yeah.net

Abstract. The research of piano harmony auto orchestrator system based on deep learning is to create a method to automatically create music scores from the original data of piano music. The original data includes not only notes, but also their timing, dynamic and other parameters. By using deep learning techniques, we can extract these parameters from raw data, and then use them to automatically generate scores. The core idea of the research on piano harmony automatic orchestrator system based on deep learning is that we first convert all notes into vectors (i.e., numbers). The system is an automatic arrangement system based on deep learning, which can automatically play piano melody. The research method is to train neural networks on various piano melodies, and then let them play in order. We used David Cope. (https://www.pianocollections.com/) 6000+melody datasets in Piano Collections of. This dataset contains short clips and long clips with multiple themes, which makes it an ideal choice for training models because we can include many different types of tunes in the training set.

Keywords: Deep learning · Automatic configuration · Piano harmony

1 Introduction

Piano repertoire accounts for a large part of music works, so when selecting works, you should select the most suitable repertoire for your own performance, and make a breakthrough in your ability. During the student period, it is a very important idea to choose to play music works of the 20th century, so as to avoid long-term adaptation to tonal music and interference with the coordination ability of both hands when playing modern music [1]. In terms of designing the concert track, you can first arrange a bright opening track, then play an adagio music, and finally finish with a gorgeous music that can express skills, or prepare another dazzling "Anke" for your needs. When selecting a track, be sure to play the complete work, and do not play a segment, a movement of a sonata, or a paragraph of a suite. In the aspect of complete preparation for performing the music, first of all, there is a certain time limit. You must be fully prepared before the concert performance; Then there will be all kinds of trivial work in the preparation process; Finally, all efforts must peak at the same time.

The process of computer music arrangement is to find a suitable set of chord accompaniment for the whole melody by using the development trend of the main melody and

Y. Zhang and N. Shah (Eds.): BigIoT-EDU 2023, LNICST 583, pp. 59–69, 2024.
https://doi.org/10.1007/978-3-031-63139-9_7

the characteristic state of each melody through the computer algorithm. A pop music is usually composed of vocal music and instrumental accompaniment. The main melody is composed of a series of continuous single notes, which constitute the theme of music. Therefore, when people create or reproduce a pop music, they often start from the creation part of the main melody. On the other hand, the melody structure of the chord and the degree of harmony matching the main melody are the core content of the accompaniment. However, it is a difficult task for amateur music lovers to arrange a harmonious chord accompaniment for the melody line. Therefore, for those who are interested in music creation, It is of great practical significance to study the automatic music accompaniment of relevant computers, because chord accompaniment plays an important role in creating music tension and setting off music emotion. The automatic music accompaniment system will generate a matching chord accompaniment for the main melody, and finally output a complete music file containing melody and chord accompaniment, The music with automatic accompaniment generated by relevant computer algorithms can be used for entertainment, and can also be used as a theoretical reference for the music creator. In the process of automatic accompaniment of music, the accompaniment part is completely handed over to the computer to complete. The creator can obtain a complete new music work with chord accompaniment only by inputting the main melody, The use of computer composition and accompaniment can enrich and expand the research field of computer algorithms, and also provide a variety of possibilities for the form and style of music creation. To a certain extent, the research of music automatic accompaniment system is rich in music innovation, and can also provide music creators with reliable reference for music accompaniment chords.

Therefore, it is a research direction combining computer technology, signal processing technology and musicology to apply artificial intelligence to harmony compilation to help people complete music creation. On the other hand, because music signals change with time, that is, the state or characteristics of music will change with time, and the state at different times will have some connection. Cyclic neural network is good at processing time related sequence data [2]. As one of the important deep learning algorithms, it has been widely used in natural language processing fields such as speech recognition, machine translation, etc. Therefore, compared with traditional machine learning algorithms and simple neural networks, cyclic neural networks are more suitable for dealing with music signal related problems.

2   Related Work

2.1   Deep Learning

Deep learning is evolved on the basis of perceptron. "Depth" refers to the large number of hidden layers of neural network. In the early days, due to the limited computing power of computers, only a shallow perceptron or a simple neural network could be used to deal with nonlinear mapping, so as to solve some classification or regression problems. With the advent of cloud computing and big data era, the computing power of computers has been greatly improved. People begin to increase the number of hidden layers and the number of neurons in the hidden layer in the neural network structure, so as to train a more "deep" neural network, which is called deep neural network. Compared with shallow neural networks, deep neural networks can learn higher level features from samples, and have been widely used in image processing and natural language processing [3].

After the neural network conducts forward propagation, a prediction result will be obtained. When the prediction result is different from the actual result, an error will be generated. The error can be quantized through the loss function, and the quantized result is called loss. The purpose of training the neural network is to reduce the loss. In the process of reducing losses, it is necessary to start from the final output layer and calculate the gradient of the weight parameters of each layer reversely based on the chain rule. This reverse process is called backpropagation. Taking a neural network with N layers as an example, its back propagation calculation process is as follows:

$$O_{v,j} = h \left(\sum_{i=1}^{f_{k-1}} \sum_{u \in N[v]} w_{i,j,u,v} x_{u,i} \right), (j = 1, ..., f_k) \tag{1}$$

$$\max \sum_{I} \left[U^I(X^I) - C^I(X^I) \right] \tag{2}$$

Among them, sigmoid function and softmax function are often used as the activation function of the last output layer in the classification task, while tanh function and ReLU function are often used as the activation function of the hidden layer in the network. The specific selection of activation function depends on the requirements of the actual task and the structure of the network.

In the musical tone system, the pitch of each tone and its interrelationship are called the pitch, and the twelve average rhythm 3 is one of them, which is widely used in symphony bands and keyboard instruments. The 88 keys of the piano are tuned according to the twelve average rhythm. The definition of the twelve-average law is to divide a pure octave into twelve semitones in proportion to the frequency, and the frequency ratio between each semitone is $\frac{1}{12}$, which is expressed by mathematical formula:

$$\frac{f_{k+1}}{f_k} = 2^{\frac{1}{12}} \approx 1.06 \tag{3}$$

For the piano, there are 88 keys in total. According to the standard, the corresponding pitch of the 49th key is 440 Hz, and then the pitch of other keys can be calculated according to the twelve-average law:

$$f_i = f_0 \times 2^{\frac{i-49}{12}} i = 1, 2, ..., 88, i \in N \tag{4}$$

where, f_0 is the frequency of standard pitch 440 Hz. When i = 1, the pitch of the first piano key is 27.5 Hz. When i = 88, the pitch of the last piano key is 4186 Hz.

2.2 Basic Concept of Harmony

In addition to the pitch, the sound produced by an instrument is also accompanied by overtones. The frequency of the pitch is called the fundamental frequency, and the frequency of overtones is called the harmonic frequency. The difference in timbre is reflected in the difference in frequency and amplitude between the pitch and overtones. Therefore, different instruments play the same pitch, but the timbre is very different. This is the principle of human ear to distinguish instruments.

Due to the characteristics of the piano's own structure, there are fewer fundamental frequency components and more harmonic components in the sound emitted by the keys in the bass area, while there are more fundamental frequency components and less harmonic components in the sound emitted by the keys in the high-pitched area.

Harmony is a sound combination composed of two or more notes simultaneously, mainly including vertical structure and horizontal structure. Among them, the longitudinal structure refers to the columnar chord, which means that all the notes of the chord sound at the same time. The horizontal structure refers to the connection between the front and back of the sound, also known as the harmony progression.

Harmony and melody have an important relationship. Melody is a sequence of notes formed according to a certain pitch, time value and volume. Most music has a prominent melody, called the main melody. A group of harmony is to accompany this melody. This accompaniment method is also called harmony texture, that is, a main melody plus a relatively minor harmony accompaniment. Therefore, the specific work content of harmony orchestration is to increase the harmony effect for the main note in the melody according to the connection between the front and back of each note in the melody.

For the longitudinal structure of harmony, this paper extracts the fundamental frequencies of all notes through the method of multiple fundamental frequency estimation, so as to determine which keys the sound at a certain time is composed of. For the horizontal structure of harmony, this paper uses the cyclic neural network related to time sequence to learn the connection between the front and back of each note in the melody, and arranges harmony for the main note according to this complex relationship.

2.3 Tone Feature Extraction

The process of tone signal reduction can be summarized as follows: first, obtain the logarithmic energy spectrum of each frame of tone signal through short-time Fourier transform, then obtain the distribution of each frame's energy on the scale frequency through the tone filter bank, and then obtain the difference of scale frequency components between frames through first-order difference. The greater the difference, the greater the possibility of new frequency components, that is, the greater the possibility of new notes.

Peak extraction generally requires a threshold, which can be divided into fixed threshold and adaptive threshold according to the type of threshold. Among them, the fixed threshold is a fixed specific value, and the adaptive threshold is to dynamically change the size of the threshold according to the change of the signal. Because the music signal contains low tide and high tide, the sound intensity in the high tide part is often greater than that in the low tide part [4]. At this time, if the fixed threshold is set too low, many misjudgments will be caused in the high tide part. If it is set too high, most notes will be ignored in the low tide part, resulting in missing judgments. Therefore, this paper uses the peak extraction method of adaptive threshold to set the threshold according to the mean value of the value within a certain range of the detection function, The mathematical formula is shown in Eq. (3):

$$D(x_i, x_j) = \sum_{l=1}^{m} d(x_{il}, x_{jl}) \tag{5}$$

In all note starting points, the interval between some note starting points may be very small. Considering the influence of human factors and piano structure, even if multiple keys are pressed at the same time, the occurrence time of multiple notes will not be exactly the same, so it is necessary to conduct post-processing on the note starting points.

Considering the hearing characteristics of the human ear and the harmony sound effect, this paper sets a fixed time threshold of 50 ms, and merges all notes with a starting point interval of less than 50 ms. The merged notes are regarded as a starting point of notes, and as a harmony effect produced by pressing multiple keys at the same time.

3 Research on Piano Harmony Automatic Orchestration System Based on Deep Learning

The function of note detection is to divide the music signal into multiple note segments, each of which contains one or more notes. The purpose of multi pitch estimation is to extract the harmonic components of the note segments, that is, to extract the fundamental values of all the notes therein. In a note segment, if there is only one note, the note segment has only one main note and does not contain harmony. If there are multiple notes, multiple notes form a harmony and the note with the largest energy is selected as the main note [5].

As an excellent workflow orchestration engine, Airflow has attracted wide attention since its debut. It identifies the task dependency through a directed acyclic graph, and manages and schedules tasks. Airflow allows users to easily create, maintain, and periodically schedule running workflows.

Figure 1 shows the architecture of the piano harmony automatic orchestration system based on deep learning. Turing refers to the external calling system. GDags components are used to splice workflow configuration files and send them to the master node of the management node. The master node is responsible for managing workflow, logs and other related information [6]. The Scheduler component is responsible for scheduling the workflow in the system. The management node sends tasks to the message queue for execution according to the distributed queue algorithm. Tasks may come from different workflows.

Because the processed data is sequence data, this paper selects the cyclic neural network to solve the harmony matching problem.

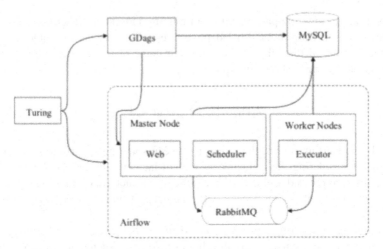

Fig. 1. Framework of piano harmony automatic orchestration system

When studying and analyzing music signals in WAV format, because there may be multiple notes at the same time, and each note is accompanied by harmonic components in addition to the fundamental component, the music signal will not be analyzed directly in the time domain, but will be converted to the frequency domain by signal transformation method for analysis. Among them, short-time Fourier transform and constant Q transform are the two most common transformation methods [7, 8].

The piano music signal is non-stationary and cannot be analyzed by Fourier transform, while STFT is based on the assumption that the signal is stable for a short time. Therefore, piano music can be assumed to have short-term stability and analyzed by STFT. STFT is defined as follows:

$$X_m(\omega) = \sum_{n=-\infty}^{\infty} x[n]w[n - m]e^{-j\omega n} \tag{6}$$

where $x[n]$ represents the discrete music signal, $w[n-m]$ represents the window function, and $X_m(\omega)$ represents the spectrum at the time of m. In the process of short-time Fourier transform, the window length determines the time resolution and frequency resolution. The longer the window length, the longer the intercepted signal, the lower the time resolution and the higher the frequency resolution. On the contrary, the shorter the window length, the shorter the intercepted signal, the higher the time resolution and the lower the frequency resolution. Therefore, in short-time Fourier transform, time resolution and frequency resolution are a contradiction, and the window length should be determined according to the actual situation.

constant O Transformation (CQT) is another frequency domain analysis method, which is defined as follows:

$$X^{cq}(k) = \frac{1}{N_k}\sum_{n=0}^{N_k-1} x(n)w_{N_k}(n)e^{-j\frac{2\pi Q}{N_k}n} \tag{7}$$

Because the spectral line frequency and scale frequency of CQT have the same exponential distribution, many scholars have applied CQT to the analysis and processing of music signals. However, the most important problem of CQT is the slow calculation speed [9, 10]. One reason is that for each spectral line number k, the corresponding window length must be calculated, and then calculated according to formula (7). The overall calculation amount is large. Another reason is that the spectral line frequency distribution is not linear, so the fast Fourier transform (FFT) cannot be directly called, resulting in the reduced calculation speed. The schematic diagram of exponential distribution network structure is shown in Fig. 2 below.

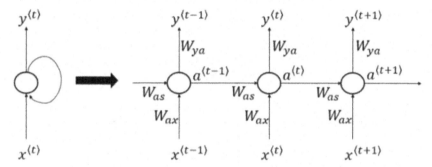

Fig. 2. Schematic diagram of exponential distribution network structure

And because harmony has not only a longitudinal structure in which multiple tones are simultaneously uttered, but also a horizontal structure in which front and back tones are connected, that is, the harmony output at a certain moment has a certain relationship with the melody sound at the front and back, so this paper selects a bidirectional recurrent neural network based on long short time memory, and introduces attention mechanism, so that the output of the neural network is not only related to the input at the current moment, but also affected by the input at other moments, The training through this mechanism can make the output of the model more consistent with the music theory, and thus closer to the nature of music [11]. After the training, the model will have the ability to arrange harmony. Just input the theme, the model will add harmony effect to the melody monophony, so as to realize the harmony arrangement function.

4 Simulation Analysis

The purpose of the harmony arrangement system is to arrange harmony for the melody, that is, to increase the harmony effect for the single note in the melody. The harmony components and main notes extracted from the note segments are spliced in chronological order to obtain the harmony sequence and the main note sequence respectively [12]. The main note sequence is the melody of the whole song, and the harmony sequence is the result of the harmony arrangement for the main notes. Therefore, when training the neural network [13], The main note sequence and harmony sequence are used as features and tags to train the model.

The source code of Airflow is open sourced by Airbnb. Airflow can be used in data storage, email monitoring, A/B testing, growth testing and other actual scenarios within the company, and has the ability to manage across departments. Airflow provides a command line interface and a web user interface to enable users to manage workflows. The Web user interface can visualize the dependency of tasks and monitor task processes in real time. Users can manually trigger tasks and workflows through the Web interface. At present, Airflow has updated many versions, which can be used to orchestrate complex computing type workflows, as well as to handle data processing flows and other related work [4]. As shown in Fig. 3 below, the architecture of harmony arrangement system is as follows.

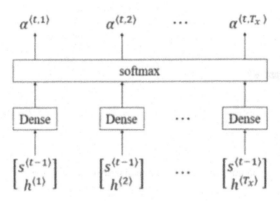

Fig. 3. Framework of harmony arrangement system

The whole system is developed by Python2, which supports Python 2/3. Traditional workflow tools generally use JSON or XML files to define a DAG, and the system parses these configuration files to create workflows and tasks [15]. However, Airflow's configuration file directly uses Python script files to define DAG, which can break the limited expression ability of text files and make the definition of DAG very simple and flexible.

First, I studied the predetermined probability of controlling the relationship between different types of notes. One example is the "vertical" relationship between melody and harmony mentioned above. Processing data About data, I converted 20 pop music into midi format. The complete song list can be found at www.popmusicmaker.com/. Using a Python library named music [15], I processed the midi file mainly through Markov process, and extracted the data relationship between different types of notes as input. Specifically, I will calculate the transition probability between my notes. This means that we can calculate the probability when the note transitions from one to the next. The digital version is shown in Fig. 4 below.

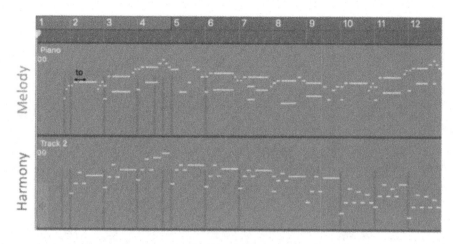

Fig. 4. Digital version

First, I will extract the "vertical" transfer probability between melody notes and chord notes. At the same time, I will calculate the "horizontal" transfer probability between melody and chord notes based on the data set [17–19].

From top to bottom, there are three different transition probabilities: the probability between melody and chord notes; The probability between melodic notes; The probability model between chord notes uses these three probability matrices. My model can follow the following steps: 1. Select the available chord notes randomly from the data. 2. Use the first probability matrix in the above table to select melody notes based on chord notes. 3. Use the second probability matrix in the above table to select chord notes based on melody notes. 4. Repeat step 3 until the end. 5. Use the third probability matrix in the above table to select a new chord note based on the previous chord note. 6. Repeat steps 1–4 until the end, As shown in Fig. 5 below.

In order to explain this process in detail, we use specific examples instead. 1. The machine randomly selects the accompaniment note F. 2. Note F can select four melody notes. Using the first transition probability matrix, it may choose melody note C (because 24.5% of the probability may be selected). 3. After that, melody note C will enter the second probability matrix, and select the next melody note, which may choose A (88% probability). 4. The third step will continue to generate new melody notes until the end. 5. Chord note F will go to the third matrix and select the next chord note. Depending on the probability in the table, it may choose chord note F or chord note C. 6. Repeat steps 1–4. The result evaluation is then the most difficult part - how to evaluate different models.

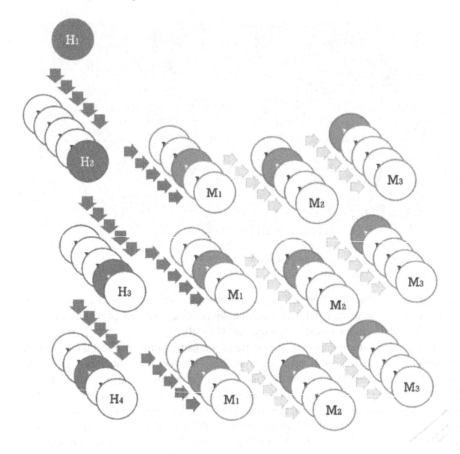

Fig. 5. Steps 5–6

5 Conclusion

This research aims to develop a system that can automatically arrange piano harmony music. The main idea is to use deep learning technology to automatically generate music scores, and then intelligent composers use music scores to create new works. Deep learning has been widely used in computer vision, speech recognition and other fields. However, it has not yet been applied to music creation, because most existing methods do not have the ability to generate music scores from raw data. In this project, we will propose a new method based on deep learning, which generates music scores from the recordings of piano performances with minimal human intervention.

References

1. Liu, Y., Ge, Z., Lv, G., et al.: Research on automatic garbage detection system based on deep learning and narrowband Internet of Things. J. Phys. Conf. Ser. **1069**, 012032 (2018)
2. Crestel, L., Esling, P., Heng, L., et al.: A database linking piano and orchestral MIDI scores with application to automatic projective orchestration (2018). https://doi.org/10.48550/arXiv.1810.08611
3. Gao, H.: Automatic recommendation of online music tracks based on deep learning. Math. Prob. Eng. **2022** (2022)
4. Cui, M.: DRIIS: research on automatic recognition of artistic conception of classical poems based on deep learning. Int. J. Cooper. Inform. Syst. (2022)
5. Flores, N., Angeles, D., Tuesta, S.: Deep learning system based on the separation of audio sources to obtain the transcription of a conversation. J. Adv. Inform. Technol. **4**, 13 (2022)
6. Maaref, M., Hamed, M.: A Real-Time and Automatic Ultrasound-Enhanced Multimodal Second Language Training System: A Deep Learning Approach (2020)
7. Liu, Q.Z., Jia, P.F., Zhan-Qi, L.I., et al.: The design of automotive instrument cluster identification system based on deep learning. J. New Indust. (2018)
8. Eremenko, V., Demirel, E., Bozkurt, B., et al.: Audio-aligned jazz harmony dataset for automatic chord transcription and corpus-based research. In: International Symposium/Conference on Music Information Retrieval. International Society for Music Information Retrieval (ISMIR) (2018)
9. Hou, Y.: Research on piano informatization teaching strategy based on deep learning. Math. Prob. Eng. **2022** (2022)
10. Castillo, E.A.: Ahmadinia a . a distributed smart camera system based on an edge orchestration architecture. J. Circ. Syst. Comput. (2020)
11. Zhang, Y.: Modern art design system based on the deep learning algorithm. J. Interconnect. Networks **22**(Supp05) (2022)
12. Hong, K.: Automatic recommendation algorithm for video background music based on deep learning. Complexity **2021** (2021)
13. Dong, Y., Guo, X., Gu, Y.: Music recommendation system based on fusion deep learning models. J. Phys. Conf. Ser. **1544**(1), 012029 (4pp) (2020)
14. Kim, Y.K., Kim, Y.: DiPLIP: distributed parallel processing platform for stream image processing based on deep learning model inference. Electronics **9**(10), 1664 (2020)
15. Roig, J., Gutierrez-Estevez, D.M., Gündüz, D. :Management and orchestration of virtual network functions via deep reinforcement learning (2019)
16. Zhang, W., Cui, X., Finkler, U., et al.: A highly efficient distributed deep learning system for automatic speech recognition (2019)
17. Wang, H., Yu, C.: Automatic emotional speech recognition based on multi-scale feature fusion and deep neural network (2017)
18. Beltran, J.R.: A comparison of deep learning methods for timbre analysis in polyphonic automatic music transcription. Electronics **10** (2021)
19. Kuang, J., Yang, T.: Popular song composition based on deep learning and neural network. J. Math. **2021** (2021)

Research on Soccer Player Tracking Algorithm Based on Deep Learning

Hongding Bai[1]([✉]), Chai Yuanyuan[1], and ZhenHua Cheng[2]

[1] Yunnan Engineering Vocational College, Kunming 650304, Yunnan, China
baihongding945@163.com
[2] Sports Department, Modern College of Northwest University, Xi'an 710130, Shaanxi, China

Abstract. Target tracking technology is of great significance in football game video, and is the basis of high-level semantic tasks such as video summary generation, player motion analysis, game strategy formulation and football event detection. In recent years, many excellent algorithms have emerged in the field of target tracking, mainly including correlation filtering and deep learning, but none of them can achieve high accuracy player tracking for soccer game video.In recent years, AI and computer vision have become hot topics, attracted the close attention of a large number of experts and researchers, and triggered an upsurge of extensive and in-depth research. This paper studies the soccer player tracking algorithm based on deep learning. A football player tracking scheme based on deep learning is proposed: a convolutional neural network is built to extract the rich visual features of players in football game video, and the network is trained on a large number of data sets containing similar objects, which improves the ability of the algorithm to identify the same team members. The main objective of the project is to develop a system that can track the position and movement of players in real time, which will be used for live broadcast purposes. In order to achieve this goal, we designed a system using deep learning technology and computer vision algorithm. We also use some advanced technologies, such as 3D graphics processing unit (GPU) and field programmable gate array (FPGA).

Keywords: Player tracking · Neural network · Football · Deep learning

1 Introduction

With the wave of "artificial intelligence and deep learning". More and more products based on artificial intelligence are launched, and computer vision is one of the most concerned directions. The application of computer vision is also better applied in practice, and the research threshold is lower, but the products can also greatly improve people's quality of life. Computer vision technology is one of the most popular technologies in the computer field. Target tracking is an important research direction in computer vision. Target tracking can be divided into single target tracking and multi-target tracking [1]. The target tracking referred to in this topic is single target tracking. Target tracking refers to the technology of using tracking algorithm to calculate the target position information

Y. Zhang and N. Shah (Eds.): BigIoT-EDU 2023, LNICST 583, pp. 70–80, 2024.
https://doi.org/10.1007/978-3-031-63139-9_8

in subsequent frames after the target position information is given in the initial frame. The results of target tracking can help to analyze the behavior of moving targets to complete higher-level visual tasks. Target tracking technology plays an irreplaceable role in many fields, such as intelligent monitoring, video retrieval, human-computer interaction, modern military, unmanned driving and so on [2].

As one of the important tasks in computer vision, target tracking has become a research hotspot in recent years due to its broad application prospects and market demand. The research goal of computer vision is to make computers have the ability to adapt to the environment independently, and to observe and understand the world like people. The visual task is very challenging and attracts the attention of scholars all over the world. In recent years, with the development of deep learning theory, computer vision has made gratifying progress in many tasks such as classification, detection, recognition and tracking. The target tracking technology is to track the interested target in the first frame in the video sequence, obtain the motion parameters related to the target, including position, speed, motion trajectory, etc., and complete the subsequent high-level visual tasks through the recognition, tracking and behavior understanding of moving objects. Target tracking technology has been widely used in many fields, such as unmanned driving, intelligent video surveillance, intelligent urban transportation, military guidance, intelligent medical and so on.

Target tracking technology plays an important role in football video. As the most popular sport in the world, football is rich in sports events, widely spread and of great commercial value. When watching football game video, different roles have different requirements for football video. For ordinary audiences, when watching football game video, they often focus on a player who is interested in it. They need to provide high-level semantic analysis functions such as video highlight, video summary, highlights, player action recognition, etc. Target tracking is the basis of these high-level semantic functions; For team coaches and other professionals, they need to know the detailed data information on the field for game analysis and development of training programs and game strategies, such as the player's track route, moving distance, running speed and other motion parameters. Target tracking technology can directly provide these data; For the referees on the field, in order to avoid the possible controversial judgment caused by fierce competition in the course of the game, it is urgent to need a variety of auxiliary information to ensure the fairness and justice of the game, such as accurate positioning of players, football track analysis, foul behavior identification, etc. Target tracking is the key technology to achieve these functions. Therefore, player tracking in soccer video is the basic research work of many practical applications, and has important theoretical significance and practical value.

The moving target tracking technology in sports video is of great significance for the development and application of intelligent sports video system. As one of the sports games with high attention, the player tracking algorithm in football game video has attracted the attention of many researchers. Player tracking in football game video provides basic data support for game analysis: using player's moving distance, running speed and other parameters to help coaches analyze game data; The parameters such as the player's trajectory and instantaneous speed are used to help the referee decide the controversial penalty. At the same time, there are great challenges in the player tracking task in the football game video: when the players attack, defend and compete for the ball right, the target player may move quickly, block seriously and have several similar players around, which greatly affects the tracking effect of the tracker. An excellent player tracking algorithm must be able to show strong robustness to the problems of fast movement, similar interference, occlusion and so on [3].

This topic combs the existing target tracking algorithms at home and abroad. Aiming at the specific tracking scene of football game video, combined with the characteristics of football field, this paper proposes and designs a football player tracking algorithm based on deep learning.

2 Related Work

2.1 Deep Learning Method

Massive labeling training data gives deep learning powerful learning ability, but target tracking only provides target samples of the initial frame as training data. In the case of limited training data, it becomes very difficult to train a depth model from scratch for the current tracking target. Therefore, researchers use a variety of ideas to apply deep learning to the field of target tracking.

There are similarities between tracking tasks and classification tasks. Many researchers directly use the classification network trained on large-scale classification data sets to extract depth features. By replacing the manual feature in srdcf with the first layer depth feature in Imagenet vgg-2048, the tracking effect is significantly improved, and the subsequent disadvantage is that the tracking speed becomes slower.

C-cot extends the original color images with different resolutions and the depth features of the first and last layers in vgg-m to the continuous spatial domain of the same period through cubic spline function interpolation, so as to realize the natural integration of multi-resolution feature images in different feature spaces. Literature [4] analyzes the depth feature attributes at different levels in vgg-16 and draws two conclusions: (1) only some depth feature channels in depth features are related to the current tracking target. (2) The high-level depth features capture semantic information, and the low-level depth features capture apparent information. Based on the above conclusions, an algorithm integrating two different levels of depth features is proposed. The small feature screening network is used to eliminate the feature channels irrelevant to the current tracking target, so as to improve the tracking accuracy of the algorithm. Using the depth features of three different levels in vgg-19, the correlation filter is trained respectively, the search range of the next layer is constrained by the high-level response, and the finer grained position prediction is made down layer by layer, so as to accurately locate the target from coarse-grained to fine-grained. Using the idea of ensemble learning for reference, six different levels of depth features in vgg-16 are used to train weak correlation filters respectively, and six weak correlation filters are combined into a strong correlation filter by hedge algorithm.

The first to introduce deep learning into the tracking field is the proposed Deep Learning Tracker (DLT) algorithm, which uses a stack type noise reduction automatic encoder. The offline training stage is divided into two modules: encoding and decoding.

It is pre-trained on large-scale natural image data sets to obtain general feature representation ability. In addition, noise is added to the input data randomly during training, and the noise-free original image is decoded in reverse, Make the tracker have more powerful feature representation capability. Literature proposes a Structured Output Deep Learning Tracker (SO-DLT), which continues the practice of DLT offline pre-training and online fine-tuning, but the output of SO-DLT is a two-dimensional probability map. Each output pixel corresponds to the same area in the input image. The higher the output value, the higher the probability of the point in the target. Different from most offline pre-training tracking models, the Learning Multi-Domain Convolutional Neural Networks (MDNet) is proposed. The author believes that there is a huge difference between image classification tasks and tracking tasks, because the targets of different tracking tasks may be completely different. The same kind of objects can be tracking targets or background information, so the multi-domain approach is adopted, That is, the network is divided into a shared layer and a specific domain layer. The training samples use video sequences instead of traditional image data sets. Each video sequence is treated as a separate domain. Each domain corresponds to a specific domain layer. This layer is located at the last layer of the network. All video sequences share other network layers except the specific domain layer. Through this combination, the shared layer can learn general feature representation, and the specific domain layer can learn specific feature representation for different tracking targets.

In addition to extracting depth features directly from the classification network, researchers also learn from the idea of transfer learning to obtain a depth model more suitable for the current tracking target by means of offline pre training and online fine-tuning. The depth model is introduced into the field of target tracking for the first time, and a deep learning tracker (DLT) is proposed. DLT uses four stacked stack noise reduction self encoders (sdaes) to conduct unsupervised pre training on the tiny images dataset to obtain the general expression ability, and uses the positive and negative samples in the initial frame to fine tune the classification network behind the sdae to obtain the specific expression ability for the current tracking target [5]. It is considered that the data set used in DLT pre training has no temporal correlation. In contrast, using the tracking data set with temporal correlation for pre training is more in line with the tracking task. Therefore, a multi domain convolutional network with tracking video pre training is proposed.

2.2 Football Video Tracking Method

Different from the general target tracking algorithm, most tracking algorithms in football game video are combined with detection algorithm, and are closely related to the target characteristics in football game video.

Extract the eigenvalues and area in YCbCr color space as features. In the first stage, use k-means clustering algorithm to obtain the main color of football field, and remove the non player area on the field combined with football domain knowledge and morphological operation; In the second stage, the player region is further subdivided into target player region and non target player region by using multilayer perceptual neural network. The player area is detected by using color statistics and pixel edge features, and four attributes are set for the player area: number, player template coordinates, number of players in the area and number of players in the area. The player tracking is carried out in combination with image matching. According to the different characteristics of court line, players and football, different methods are used to detect, and the combination of Kalman filter and adaptive gate is used to track football and players [6]. The combination of Kalman filter and local area matching is used for multi player tracking. According to the changes of player centroid and player area between adjacent frames, judge whether the current frame is occluded, and use the matching strategy to relocate the players in time after the occlusion. In the HSV color space, the main color of the court is removed, the upper and lower player main color histograms and hall features are extracted, and the improved traditional online multi example learning method is used to track the players. The deformable parts model (DPM) is used to classify the characters in the football field, and the conditional random fields (CRF) model is established for joint probability reasoning. The images taken by multiple fixed cameras placed on the football field in advance are used to fuse the parameters of multiple cameras to generate the appearance model, which is projected onto the court plane to generate a multi peak two-way probability function [7]. The court plane probability can reflect the possible position of players on the court plane. On the basis of removing the main football field and segmenting the player area, the player is tracked by the combination of Kalman filter and template matching, and the occlusion is processed by histogram back projection. The full convolution twin network is trained offline by using target detection data set and football video data set to obtain the depth characteristics suitable for player tracking task.

The current target tracking algorithm has made some progress in general scenarios, and its performance in tracking accuracy and speed is getting better and better. However, there is no tracking algorithm that can take into account all football scenes in the field of football. Target tracking in soccer video mainly has the following problems:

(1) The feature representation ability is insufficient. The tracking in soccer video is usually carried out in the far shot. The display area of a single player in the far shot is small and the resolution is not enough, resulting in the insufficient representation ability of the extracted features. At the same time, it often occurs that the image is blurred due to the player's moving speed, which further reduces the representation ability of the features.

(2) It is difficult to deal with serious occlusion. Intense sports scenes often occur in football matches, with dense and frequent people, and serious occlusion between players. Especially, it is difficult to distinguish players in the same team when occlusion occurs, which is easy to cause tracking drift.

(3) Unable to reposition after drift. After the scene of fierce competition passes, the target player usually reappears in the image with high resolution. If the tracker drifts, it needs to relocate to the target player at this time. However, most trackers are often difficult to relocate after drifting.

The research goal of this subject is to complete the tracking task of target players in the soccer scene. Through the player's position given in the initial frame, the player is continuously tracked in the subsequent frames, and the player's position is represented by a rectangular box.

3   Player Feature Extraction

Target feature extraction is the basic task of target tracking. The expression ability of target features directly affects the tracking effect of the algorithm. In this chapter, according to the characteristics of player target in football game video, color features and depth features are extracted to describe the target player at the same time. In terms of color features, the target color histogram and the target main color are extracted. In terms of depth features, the regression network is used to further extract the depth features perceived by the target from vgg-16 depth features.

3.1   Tracking Shot Analysis

A large-scale football match is usually equipped with dozens of slots. The football game picture seen by the off-site audience is the shooting picture of a slot selected by the guide, and a group of continuous pictures taken by a slot form a lens. As shown in Fig. 1, shots in football match videos can be generally divided into four types: far shot, medium shot, close shot and off-site shot. The telephoto shot is usually taken from the main camera. Most football fields and most football players are displayed in the picture. The appearance of a single football player is visual Small in appearance; The shooting distance of the middle lens is far and the lens is closer. The picture shows the full picture of some football venues and individual football players; The shooting distance of the close-up lens is the closest. The picture shows part of the body of a football player, usually the facial expression or the detailed depiction of specific parts; The screen of off-site lens shows the contents of referees, coaches, spectators, advertisements and other non competition venues. In a football game video, telephoto is the most common type of lens, so this topic chooses to track the target player in telephoto video [8].

The player position information is represented by a rectangular target box (x, y, W, H). The rectangular target box completely wraps the target player, where X represents the abscissa of the upper left corner of the rectangular target box and Y represents the left corner of the rectangular target box The vertical coordinate of the upper corner, w represents the width of the rectangular target box, and H represents the height of the rectangular target box. Because the moving distance of the target player between adjacent frames will not be too large, the target tracking does not need to locate the target player within the whole picture, but only within the search area. The target position in the above frame of the search area is the center, and the size is controlled by parameter a. the calculation method is shown in the formula [9]. The schematic diagram of the search area is shown in Fig. 2. The red box is the target area of the previous frame, and the yellow box is the search area of the current frame.

$$search\_rect = (w, h) + a \times max(w, h) \tag{1}$$

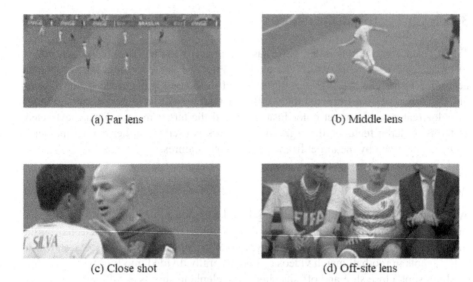

(a) Far lens   (b) Middle lens

(c) Close shot   (d) Off-site lens

Fig. 1. Lens type

Fig. 2. Search area

3.2 Color Features

Color feature is one of the most widely used visual features in the field of computer vision. The main reason is that the target color is often very related to the object or scene contained in the image, and the color feature has little dependence on the size, direction and viewing angle of the target itself. The football match video has the color characteristics that can be easily recognized: a large area of football field is green, and there is a significant difference between the color of the uniforms of the two teams and the color of the football field; Players of the same team have the same uniform color; There are significant differences in the color of uniforms of players from different teams.

The expression of color features also involves the problems of color space and quantization methods. Different color spaces describe color features from different angles, and different quantization methods express color features as different vectors.

In order to facilitate the referee and the audience to clearly distinguish the teams visually, the uniforms of different teams usually have obvious color differences. During the tracking process, the main color of the tracking player will not change suddenly. By calculating the correlation between the main color of the current target frame and the main color of the initial target frame, it can help judge whether the tracking drift phenomenon occurs. The colors with high frequency in the color histogram often fall in the area where the main content of the image is located. These colors can roughly express the main content of the image. The color histogram size of the target box is 16 × sixteen × 16. A total of 4096 color block indexes are included. These color block indexes are sorted according to the frequency of colors corresponding to the color block index to obtain 4096 × Vector of 1. In this vector, the color index with higher frequency is in the front, and the color index with lower frequency is in the back[10]. The first n color indexes are extracted to form an n × The vector of 1 as the main color of the player. From the perspective of graphics, the color with low frequency is a kind of noise in the representation of image content. Using the player's dominant color to assist in judging whether the tracking drift phenomenon occurs not only reduces the amount of calculation, but also reduces the sensitivity to noise.

4 Player Perception Tracking Model

After the target feature extraction is completed, the appearance model of the target - players aware tracking model (PAT) needs to be established, as shown in Fig. 3. Among them, the target in "target perception" refers to the target player, and the interference item in "Interference Item perception" refers to the non target player around the target player. Interference Item perception refers to considering not only the color difference between the target player and the background, but also the color difference between the target player and the interference item in the color model. Target perception refers to the use of depth features related to the current tracking player in the depth model, rather than the ordinary vgg-16 depth features. Aiming at the problem of tracking drift when the target is blocked, a local tracker is introduced to work together with the global tracker to correct the target location.

After unsupervised layer-by-layer greedy training and parameter optimization, the depth automatic encoder obtains the distributed feature representation of high-dimensional complex input. For different tasks, only the network parameters need to be adjusted.

$$\frac{\partial}{\partial W_j^{(i)}} J(W, b) = [\frac{1}{m}\sum_{i=1}^m \frac{\partial}{\partial W_{ij}^{(i)}} J(W, b; x^{(i)}, y^{(i)})] + \lambda W_{ij}^{(l)} \tag{2}$$

$$\frac{\partial}{\partial b_i^{(i)}} J(W, b) = \frac{1}{m}\sum_{i=1}^m \frac{\partial}{\partial b_i^{(i)}} J(W, b; x^{(i)}, y^{(i)}) \tag{3}$$

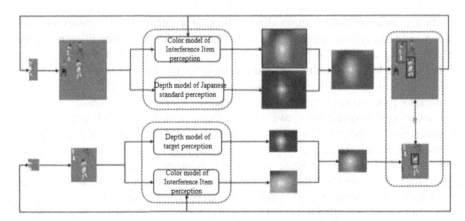

Fig. 3. Pat model

The tracking algorithm using the target color information is very vulnerable to the interference of non target objects similar to the target color. In football matches, the same team players with very similar color attributes often appear around the target players, and the same team players around the target are likely to become interference items. The color model of Interference Item perception uses Bayesian classifier to model target background and target interference item. The model not only pays attention to the color attribute difference between the target and the background, but also pays attention to the color attribute difference between the tracking target and the interference item, which can effectively alleviate the drift of the tracker when the strong interference item appears.

In the case of Bayesian classifier, or the average of all kinds of classifiers, the cost of pre classification is the smallest. The Bayesian based target detection and tracking algorithm models the target detection and tracking problem as a Bayesian optimal estimation problem, regards the target tracking process as the prior probability of the known target, and iteratively obtains the maximum a posteriori probability of the target state after obtaining the new target observation.

The algorithm in this paper uses MatConvNet toolbox, and the running environment is Matlab2014a, Intel (R) Core (TM) i7-4720HQ CPU @ 2.60GHz 2.59GHz and NVIDIA Ge-Force GTX 960M GPU.

The test data comes from 17 video clips in the 2016 European Cup football video, which contain fast motion, occlusion, illumination and other difficult situations. The evaluation is based on two indicators: accuracy rate (the threshold selected in the paper is 20 pixels, that is, the tracking accuracy is judged if the distance from the center position error is less than 20 pixels) and bounding box overlap ratio (IOU).

Figure 4 is the result of experimental statistical data obtained by the algorithm in this paper.

It can be seen from the figure that when the number of convolution layers is 5, the tracking accuracy rate is the highest, reaching more than 93%, and when the number of convolution layers is 2, the tracking accuracy rate takes the second place. The network fine-tuned by the European Cup data set can better adapt to the test set and has a higher tracking accuracy.

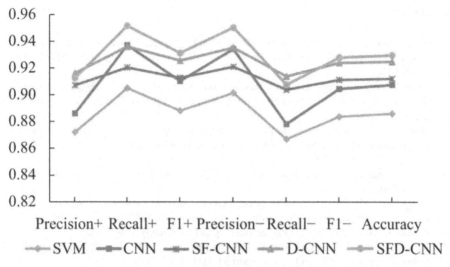

Fig. 4. Results of experimental statistics

At the same time, this paper visualizes different convolution layers, as shown in Fig. 3. From left to right, the convolution layer (conv) is 1 to 5. It can be seen from the figure that the features learned by conv1 and conv 2 are basically the underlying features such as edges and colors; Conv3 began to learn texture and key distinguishing features from convolution kernel. When the number of convolution layers is 2, the network learns the characteristics of the bottom layer, which is more suitable for distinguishing between classes, that is, to solve the occlusion problem between players of different teams; When the number of convolution layers is 5, the network learns more discriminative key features, which is more suitable for intra-class differentiation, that is, the occlusion problem of the same team members.

5 Conclusion

As the basic technology of the development of intelligent sports video system, the research on player tracking method in football game video has important practical significance. Compared with other tracking data sets, the player targets in football data sets generally have the following characteristics: there are often several non target players around the target player; The players of the two teams wear different colors; Part of the body of the target player is covered by other players during the game. In this paper, the off-line training method is used to train the full convolution twin neural network on the large target detection data set and football video set, and extract the CNN features with deep information for tracking. From the experimental results, the algorithm is effective in tracking players. In the future work, we will consider fusing the depth information of different convolution layers to solve the problem of consistent contribution of each position in the current score map, so as to further improve the accuracy of the algorithm.

References

1. Shi, D., Chen, X.: Research on visual object tracking algorithm based on improved twin network. J. Phys. Conf. Ser. **1966**(1), 012006 (2021). https://doi.org/10.1088/1742-6596/1966/1/012006
2. Zhang, P., Yu, Z., Xiong, L., et al.: Research on parking slot tracking algorithm based on fusion of vision and vehicle chassis information. Int. J. Automot. Technol. **21**(3), 603–614 (2020)
3. Shao, Y., Li, D., Zhang, X., et al.: Research on real time tracking algorithm of multispectral mosaic image based on the fast DSST algorithm. In: Conference on optical sensing and imaging technology (2020)
4. Li, L., Zhang, Y., Zhou, W., et al.: Research on Video Target Tracking Algorithm Based on Particle Filter and CNN (2020)
5. Huang, C.B., Li, T.H.: Research on target tracking algorithm based on information entropy feature selection and example weighting. J. Phys: Conf. Ser. **1848**(1), 012028 (2021)
6. Martins, E., Brito, J.H.: Soccer Player Tracking in Low Quality Video (2021)
7. Enes, A., Oneda, G., Alves, D.L., et al.: Determinant factors of the match-based internal load in elite soccer players. Res. Q. Exerc. Sport **91**(1), 1–7 (2020)
8. Zhao, K., Song, J., Luo, Y., et al.: Research on game-playing agents based on deep reinforcement learning (2022)
9. Jie, Chen, Y., Hu, H., et al.: Research on matching method of ocean observation data based on DC-WKNN algorithm (2020)
10. Yahya, K., Alomari, O.: A new maximum power point tracking algorithm based on power differentials method for thermoelectric generators. Int. J. Energy Res. **2020**(7) (2020)

Deep Learning-Based Personalized Course Content Push Algorithm for Embedded Professional Teaching

Zikun Hu[1]([✉]), Hongxiu Dai[1], Yang Lei[2], and Yan Liu[2]

[1] Jiujiang Vocational and Technical College, Jiujiang 332007, Jiangxi, China
{huzikun,diefu}@jvtc.edu.com
[2] Shandong Xiehe University, Jinan 250109, Shandong, China

Abstract. This paper explores and studies the embedded system teaching reform from four aspects: the construction of embedded system curriculum system, the application of comparative education and learning transfer teaching methods, the organization and content setting of practical teaching links, and scientific research practice, and emphatically expounds the importance of practical teaching links to embedded system teaching. With the advent of the Internet of Things era, embedded system, as an important part of the Internet of Things, plays an important role. The development of society puts forward higher requirements for the training of embedded talents and course teaching in colleges and universities. The author analyzes the characteristics and present situation of embedded system courses, and puts forward a series of reform measures from the aspects of course system, content setting, teaching methods, practice teaching, etc., aiming at the existing problems in current teaching and combining with the characteristics of students in computer department of Yuncheng University. Practice shows that the curriculum reform has a good effect. Among them, the theoretical teaching part emphasizes the learning and application of students' comprehensive knowledge and ability, while the experimental teaching, on the basis of basic experiments, designs functional experiments, emphasizes students' independent choice, and further designs the innovative practical content of "small embedded system development". The flexible and diverse teaching methods are put forward, so that the teaching content and systematic view can really be conveyed to students.

Keyword: Deep learning · Embedded specialty · Individualized teaching

1 Introduction

With the rapid development of domestic communication technology, Internet technology and electronic technology, more and more high-quality teaching models are introduced into the embedded system teaching in colleges and universities. This course is practical and theoretical, and it is the best choice for cultivating students' innovative ability [1]. However, for a long time, it has been influenced by the problem that the teaching content

Y. Zhang and N. Shah (Eds.): BigIoT-EDU 2023, LNICST 583, pp. 81–88, 2024.
https://doi.org/10.1007/978-3-031-63139-9_9

is extensive, the learning is difficult and the students' knowledge reserve is relatively lacking, which has brought certain challenges and difficulties to the course development [2]. Embedded technology has strong practicality, comprehensiveness and applicability. Therefore, while teaching embedded courses, it is necessary to strengthen students' knowledge through a large number of experiments. It can be said that the experiment and teaching of embedded system occupy the same proportion [3]. According to the teaching of embedded system course system in Jiangsu University of Science and Technology, the setting and operation of experiment are discussed in this paper, so as to provide students with the best learning and practice opportunities and provide the society with suitable embedded talents. Embedded system course covers a wide range of knowledge, not only software development technology, but also closely related to operating system, various hardware interfaces, communication and other technologies. It is a system development and design technology combining software and hardware [4]. Therefore, the selection of relevant theoretical teaching contents, the setting of experimental teaching and practice links of embedded system teaching for computer majors in colleges and universities are still in the stage of continuous discussion. Because of the characteristic of embedded system's knowledge coverage and wide application, we should pay more attention to the cultivation of system ability in course teaching. This paper mainly discusses the construction ideas of embedded system courses for computer science and technology majors, which are oriented to the cultivation of system ability, and discusses the connection between courses and other courses, course contents, teaching methods and so on [5].

2   Project-Based Teaching and Overall System Design Scheme

2.1   Project Teaching

Project-based teaching mode takes the completion of specific projects as its task, and sets clear project objectives for embedded system learners, such as designing a real-time temperature collection project [6]. The general development process of embedded project is shown in the figure (because this paper focuses on the specific teaching, the main work is focused on the solid line block diagram. Taking the target project as the core content and student participation as the main force, we can improve students' quality and learning ability in the process of completing the project, and make teachers and students promote and improve each other through teacher-student communication. Project-based teaching is different from the traditional teaching mode in which teachers are the mainstay to promote students' learning process. On the contrary, students are the main force to complete specific projects. As a result, the original boring learning process becomes active and students' ability to work independently is cultivated [7]. This role change enables students to better understand the theoretical knowledge of books, and at the same time, their professional skills and practical ability are obviously improved. As the main force of the project, it also makes students feel the pleasure of innovative practice and improves students' autonomous learning. The general development process of embedded project is shown in Fig. 1.

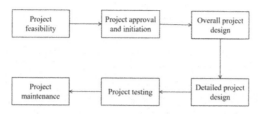

Fig. 1. General development process of embedded project

Embedded system is an interdisciplinary subject, involving electronics, information, control and other disciplines, and the amount of knowledge is intensive and concentrated. If you directly use high-level language programming at the beginning of the learning stage, or even join the embedded operating system, it may lead to students' learning difficulties and loss of interest and self-confidence in learning [8]. Because this kind of learning does not involve the underlying programming of hardware, the development products can only use the semi-finished development board provided by O EM manufacturer and the supporting board software package, thus losing the development flexibility and independent research and development ability. Therefore, it is better to start programming with ARM assembler. On the one hand, it can be compared with 8-bit SCM programming, and it is easy to get started. On the other hand, it can master the programming methods and contents of BSP (board support package software) and HA L (hardware abstraction layer), and have a comprehensive understanding and mastery of the bottom driver development. In this way, we can not only develop semi-finished products based on OEM board, but also develop the underlying hardware drivers. Compared with the redundant code problem caused by the lack of high-level language compilation in control occasions with high real-time requirements, it has faster execution efficiency. The demand for talents is strong, and learning embedded technology has a broad market prospect. Embedded system is an important branch of computer field, which has been widely used in industry, national defense, aerospace and daily life. As a comprehensive cross-cutting technology, embedded system technology involves a wide range of knowledge fields, including computer, electronics, control, communication and other disciplines, and is combined with specific industry background [9]. Therefore, the teaching of embedded system course includes many contents, the hardware part includes processor, hardware structure, interface technology, the software involves assembly technology, C language and embedded operating system, etc. The course content is comprehensive and requires high knowledge of computer programming.

2.2 Design Ideas of Experimental Platform

Embedded system experiment course system diagram. In this diagram, embedded system experiment course leads three main series, and from left to right, the processor series (microcomputer principle experiment, single chip microcomputer course design, DSP experiment); Interface series (currently mainly for field bus technology experiment); The experimental class system of embedded system combined with control object series (experiment of programmable controller, experiment of configuration software and automation device) is shown in Fig. 2.

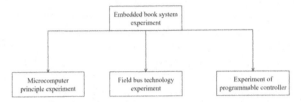

Fig. 2. Embedded System Experiment Course System

Embedded system course has the characteristics of cutting-edge knowledge, rich content, strong knowledge linkage and wide range of knowledge points. It is a difficult course to learn and teach, and it is also very practical, so we must pay attention to practical links and hands-on skills. Basic theory teaching can be carried out in the laboratory. After students have understood the relevant basic principles, they can start the verification experiment of basic theory. Through the experiment, they can actually feel the existence of knowledge, at the same time, improve the perception of relatively boring and abstract basic knowledge, stimulate students' interest in learning, and be deeply impressed by the concepts they have learned [10]. According to the actual situation, we can also adopt the teaching method of theory teaching and experimental verification interspersed, realize the flexible teaching mode of "learning by doing and learning by doing", better combine theory teaching with practice teaching, and improve the learning efficiency. The purpose of the experiment is to provide a practical platform for students to deepen their understanding of knowledge, gain direct perceptual knowledge, and cultivate and exercise their hands-on ability. Considering the different levels of students, in order to let most students master the basic knowledge and design methods of embedded systems, they should learn gradually from shallow to deep when setting the experimental contents, so as to be suitable for students of different levels.

3   Design of General Hardware Platform for Experimental System

3.1   Hardware Architecture Design

Embedded system design must follow the requirements of small size, low power consumption, low cost, high reliability and so on, and also meet the requirements of future scalability, so it is necessary to reserve some external interfaces for future expansion. The hardware design of the whole system can be divided into embedded microprocessor, system platform module and application module group. Types of interfaces are interface, interface, interface, interface. Embedded microprocessor, memory module, power module, reset module and interface circuit constitute the minimum system of the platform, and peripheral application modules with different functions can be designed according to different professional characteristics. The system design block diagram is shown in Fig. 3.

As the embedded system gathers all kinds of knowledge and skills, although students already have some basic knowledge, there is still a steep learning curve waiting for them to overcome. Facing the problem of steep learning curve in embedded system experimental teaching, traditional experimental teaching methods are often difficult to

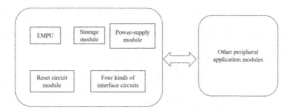

Fig. 3. System block diagram

work. As we all know, traditional education unilaterally emphasizes the authority of teachers in education, which is reflected in teachers' simple indoctrination and students' passive acceptance in teaching. In this process, students are always in a passive position, which weakens their enthusiasm and initiative in learning knowledge. According to years of teaching experience: no matter how many concepts are taught to students, no matter how deep they are, no matter how difficult the exam is, only those that touch them will remain in students' minds! Project-based experimental teaching means "learning by doing" through a specific project. "Learning by doing" is conducive to the establishment of the relationship between teachers and students in modern teaching. It has traditionally changed the relationship between teachers and students. The relationship between teachers and students is more similar to that between directors and actors, which can stimulate students' subjective initiative. The laboratory is a fixed place for experimental teaching, curriculum design, graduation design, scientific research practice and foreign technical training. With the semi-open management of the laboratory, students can make full use of the existing resources of the laboratory to carry out scientific research activities. Teachers should learn from newspapers, periodicals, job fairs and other media about the specific skills needs of embedded professionals and the latest technologies in the frontier fields of the profession, so as to better guide students to engage in technical research and development in a certain direction. For most enterprises, embedded professionals should have the ability to master EOS (Embedded Operating System), ARM architecture and C language programming, so they should be placed in an important position in theoretical teaching and practice. Students can choose either direction of hardware design and embedded software development independently. For hardware design, we should focus on cultivating students' ability of circuit analysis and EDA circuit design; For embedded software development, we should focus on cultivating students' ability of software programming and operating system transplantation. At the same time, in order to cultivate T-type talents, software and hardware designers should communicate and coordinate better, and they should have a certain degree of knowledge of other fields while being proficient in one aspect.

3.2 Overall System Design

The working principle of target detection and tracking is to automatically detect the video image signals collected from the imaging system under the natural background conditions, and achieve the acquisition, detection and tracking of the target through a series of video image sequences. According to the working principle of the system and the video image data stream, the operation of the whole system is a mechanism of state transition and process activation. Set of system states The set of transition conditions between states is as follows:

$$B = \bigcup_i B_i, i \in [0, 6] \tag{1}$$

The mixed Gaussian model algorithm has a clear concept, simple implementation, comprehensive memory consumption, time-consuming calculation and other performance indicators, and it has become the first choice for many embedded systems to achieve target detection. The idea of the mixed Gaussian model can be summarized as follows: For any pixel, examine its mean and variance. If the matching deviation with a Gaussian model is less than the Markov threshold, divide the pixel into the model, and update the mean, variance and weight of this model. If no Gaussian model matches the pixel, delete the least likely one with the lowest appearance rate, and build a new Gaussian model with this pixel. It is not difficult to see from the idea that the method of Gaussian mixture background modeling can detect a relatively complete prospect and suppress the background noise well, but its real-time performance still needs to be further improved due to the large amount of calculation in running. The algorithm principle of Gaussian mixture background difference method is described in steps as follows:

$$P(I_t(x, y)) = \sum_{i-1}^{k} w_{i,t} \times \eta(I, (x, y),) u_{i,t}, \sum_{i,t} \tag{2}$$

That is to say, this Gaussian distribution has the highest probability of representing the background, so it ranks at the front of the sequence:

$$n = w_{i,t} a_b rg \min \left(\sum_{K=1}^{b} w_k \right) \tag{3}$$

It can be seen from the above that in Gaussian model, mean, variance and full value are three very important parameters. The mean and variance are used to construct Gaussian model, and the weight is used to judge whether the model belongs to the background. In addition, the Mahalanobis distance threshold determines whether a certain point matches a Gaussian model, the background threshold determines whether a certain model belongs to the background area, and the update rate of mean, variance and weight sets the update rate of Gaussian model, which are also very important parameters used to establish models and determine the background. If the scene in the target detection and tracking system is fixed and the lighting conditions are fixed, that is, the background is static, only Gaussian model can be used to describe the scene. If the scene areas of target detection and tracking are in the condition that the surfaces and edges of multiple objects alternate, the background subtraction method of mixed Gaussian model is suitable for these areas. However, these two methods are extreme, and the Gaussian model is too demanding on the scene. Although the Gaussian mixture model can adapt to the environment, it has a large amount of computation and is not real-time. For the actual target detection and tracking scene, most areas are static areas, only a few areas have frequent background changes. The background model of the improved mixed Gaussian model uses single Gaussian model to describe the static areas, and the areas with frequent scene changes are approximately described by multiple Gaussian models, and the number of Gaussian models is adjusted according to the scene changes. If the scene changes too fast or the light changes violently, it is necessary to delete the old Gaussian model and establish a new Gaussian model to describe the background model in order to adapt to the scene changes. The background difference of Gaussian mixture model is realized based on hardware platform, and its load diagram is shown in Fig. 4.

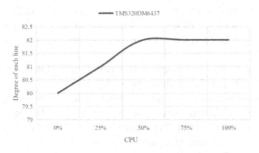

Fig. 4. Load diagram of background difference method of mixed Gaussian model

4 Conclusion

This paper reviews some experiences in the experimental teaching of embedded system in recent years. Although students feel mysterious or even afraid of embedded system at the beginning of class, based on the careful design of embedded system platform, the reasonable selection and setting of knowledge before experiment, and the project-based practical teaching method to overcome the steep learning curve obstacle, most students have carried out the reform exploration and practice of embedded system deep course teaching through this experimental course. This paper puts forward a teaching method which combines three experimental methods: experiment box system debugging, circuit software simulation and system model simulation experiment teaching. The reformed practice teaching not only enables students to successfully complete this course, but also lays a solid foundation for the follow-up courses. By strengthening the experimental teaching, the students' ability to analyze, solve and raise problems is improved, their innovative thinking ability is cultivated, and their strong interest in automation major is stimulated. At the same time, the students' ability to solve practical problems and practical hands-on ability by using the learned theory is exercised and improved.

References

1. Gu, F.: Personalized curriculum recommendation algorithm based on labeling and scoring. J. Changchun Univ. Technol. (Nat. Sci. Edn.) **38**(2), 198–203 (2017)
2. Wang, X., Wang, J., Zhang, L.: Teaching research of embedded system course for electronic communication specialty. J. Zhejiang Univ. Sci. Technol. **34**(2), 6 (2022)
3. Xu, J.: Embedded system curriculum. China Educational Technology Equipment, no. 8, p. 2 (2017)
4. Li, T., Liu, Y., Xiao, Z.: Curriculum arrangement and evaluation system construction of embedded system engineering specialty-based on the perspective of core competence cultivation. Internal Combustion Engine and Accessories, no. 17, p. 2 (2019)
5. Xiao, X., Zhou, C., Wan, Z.: Design and implementation of multi-terminal micro-course platform based on personalized recommendation algorithm. Comput. Appl. Softw. **35**(1), 5 (2018)
6. Xie, Y., Chen, X., Hong, Z., et al.: Discussion on individualized talent cultivation in embedded technology teaching. Exper. Sci. Technol. **16**(5), 5 (2018)
7. Liu, X., Wang, M.: Research on the new teaching mode of Embedded Technology course based on learning skills. Comput. Knowl. Technol. Acad. Edn. **16**(26), 3 (2020)
8. Xingyu, L., Song, N., He, J., et al.: Personalized course recommendation service based on collaborative filtering algorithm. Mod. Inform. Technol. **3**(24), 3 (2019)
9. Wang, R., Chang, R., Tang, Y.: Teaching content design of embedded system course for cyberspace security personnel training. Comput. Educ. 9, 4 (2019)
10. Chen, A., Liu, Y., Chen, Y., et al.: Exploration of curriculum reform of embedded system design and development for automation major. Res. Pract. Innov. Entrepren. Theory **12**, 58–60 (2021)

Design and Simulation of Intelligent Matching Algorithm for Online Primary School Mathematics Curriculum Based on Deep Learning

Yi Mo[1]([✉]), Jishen Tang[1], Xunyun Chang[2], and Dong Wu[2]

[1] Hechi University, Yizhou 546300, Guangxi, China
656839540@qq.com
[2] Foreign Languages Department, Sichuan Vocational and Technical College, Suining 629000, Sichuan, China

Abstract. With the continuous development of new information technologies such as big data, cloud computing, and Internet of Things, people's access to knowledge and information has undergone profound changes. New concepts such as machine learning, wisdom education, and educational big data are changing the traditional educational ecology, teaching form, and learning methods, and at the same time, promoting the deep development of educational modernization to informationization. People's needs in the fields of artificial intelligence such as information retrieval, automatic question and answer, dialogue system, etc. begin to appear, and intelligent matching algorithms are needed to meet the high demand of users. Text matching algorithm is the core problem in natural language processing technology. In the traditional text matching field, the dimension disaster of text representation and data sparseness have affected the development of natural language processing field. It is necessary for the times and students' development to carry out subject teaching under the guidance of deep learning, which is of great significance. Unit review class is an important class type of primary school mathematics, which is of great value to students' development, but there are many problems in actual teaching. This paper presents a multi-view collaborative teaching network based on sparse interactive data. The matching network is mainly composed of two parts, a text-based matching model and a relationship-based matching model.

Keyword: Intelligent matching · Deep learning · Elementary school mathematics

1 Introduction

The way of knowledge acquisition based on mechanical memory can no longer support students to control this increasingly complex and rapidly changing world. Only having high-level ability and excellent quality is the "magic weapon" to meet the challenges

© ICST Institute for Computer Sciences, Social Informatics and Telecommunications Engineering 2024
Published by Springer Nature Switzerland AG 2024. All Rights Reserved
Y. Zhang and N. Shah (Eds.): BigIoT-EDU 2023, LNICST 583, pp. 89–97, 2024.
https://doi.org/10.1007/978-3-031-63139-9_10

of the future society [1]. A lot of manpower, material resources and financial resources have been given to the research and practice of educational informatization. However, whether it has really promoted the development of learners or not, school education has not fully given positive feedback [2]. As the core component of school education, primary school mathematics' learning quality is widely concerned by researchers and practitioners. This paper applies the concept of deep learning to the elementary school mathematics unit teaching process, aiming at providing a new perspective for unit teaching with the connotation and characteristics of the concept of deep learning, and then promoting students' deep learning by unit teaching [3]. Under the guidance of teachers, deep learning is a kind of learning method, which is guided by understanding, grasps the core content, grasps the key abilities of disciplines, develops higher-order thinking, forms positive intrinsic learning motivation, optimistic emotional attitude and correct values, and pays attention to both cooperative communication ability and critical and innovative spirit [4].

Aiming at the problems and challenges such as the difficulty in distinguishing adjacent text lines, the error-prone recognition of adjacent identical characters, and various types of questions, this paper proposes a multi-question handwritten text detection algorithm based on semantic segmentation and an image handwritten text recognition algorithm based on recurrent neural network, and designs and implements a correction algorithm for different questions [5]. Mathematics classroom teaching reform needs to prevent the "alienation" of classroom teaching activities under the one-sided pursuit of efficiency [6]. The reason for the effective "alienation" of teaching lies in the fact that classroom teaching reform only stays at the technical level, only attaches importance to the mechanical training of knowledge, and regards symbolic knowledge as the teaching object, instead of taking students as the teaching object and promoting students' all-round development as the teaching goal through the profound interpretation and processing of knowledge [7]. Based on the deep learning technology, a method of automatically detecting, identifying and correcting the answer content of subjective questions in the answer sheet image of primary school mathematics examination is developed, and the automatic marking technology of the answer content of subjective questions in primary school mathematics examination is realized. The types of questions involved mainly include calculation questions, fill-in-the-blank questions, judgment questions and application questions.

2   Research Method

2.1   Algorithm Research

Deep learning is a learning process in which teachers guide students to participate in learning wholeheartedly. In this process, students can critically understand new facts, acquire new ideas, incorporate them into the original cognitive structure through deep processing, and transfer existing knowledge in new situations to make decisions, solve problems, and finally develop [8]. The current deep learning route has a seven-step route, as shown in Fig. 1. This route describes in detail the process of how to motivate each student to reach the level of deep learning at his or her original level, shows teachers the specific strategies before, during and after teaching, clearly points out the significance of designing a teaching unit, and provides ideas and methods for optimizing teacher unit teaching with deep learning. Among them, step 6 is the most important step in this route, and it is the key link for teachers to lead students to develop higher-order thinking such as analysis, synthesis and criticism.

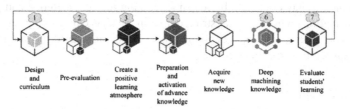

| Design and curriculum | Pre-evaluation | Create a positive learning atmosphere | Preparation and activation of advance knowledge | Acquire new knowledge | Deep machining knowledge | Evaluate students' learning |

Fig. 1. Deep learning route

In recent years, the methods of image text detection using deep neural network technology can be divided into the following two categories: the method based on semantic segmentation and the method based on candidate frame. Character segmentation faces problems such as complex background and image noise, and some characters are composed of several independent symbols [9]. In order to solve various problems in character segmentation, there are some methods to use over-segmentation, that is, to divide the region originally belonging to the same character into multiple regions, and then evaluate all the segmentation paths to select the best one. There are also methods to use dynamic programming algorithm to calculate the best segmentation result from the over-segmentation results. When deep learning is used to process images, convolution is generally used to extract high-order features from the original images through the network, and then various modules designed and implemented are used to do a series of processing on the feature images to get the desired results [10]. Figure 2 shows the structure of convolutional neural network. Compared with common neural network, convolutional neural network uses convolution kernel with a specific size to perform convolution calculation on the output results of the upper layer, and obtains a characteristic map with a specific size in each layer. Finally, the characteristic map is converted into the required results through the full connection layer.

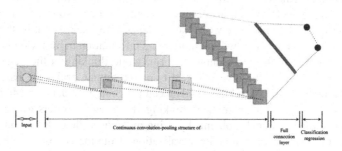

| Input | Continuous convolution-pooling structure of | Full connection layer | Classification regression |

Fig. 2. Convolutional neural network structure

Words can be regarded as the basic semantic units in Chinese, and Chinese word segmentation is a very important key step in natural language processing. In Chinese answers, characters are continuous and there is no obvious separator. Therefore, it is the first important issue to consider how to implement word segmentation for Chinese language texts. In the word segmentation processing stage, the system loads the word segmentation thesaurus obtained by machine learning into the memory, and performs word segmentation on the character string output in the clause processing stage according to the word dictionary. The processing process of the improved forward maximum matching algorithm in this system.

2.2 Model Design

Semantic matching technology is a technology to measure the similarity between texts by obtaining the latent semantics of texts and the inclusion relationship between entities. Its main task is to determine whether the contents expressed in two natural language texts have the same meaning [11]. Semantic matching technology is the core and foundation of the field of natural language processing, and many natural language processing tasks can be abstracted as semantic matching technology to some extent. As an important research content in the field of image processing, image recognition is also a very important direction of machine learning. Image processing is a method that allows computers to denoise, restore and extract features of real images. By enhancing the useful information in the image and suppressing the useless irrelevant information, the distribution of gray scale in the image can be changed, so that the image can be processed in a more favorable direction for human observation. The depth model is mainly based on semantic document representation. The single semantic document representation is matched directly by semantic document representation, and the multi-semantic document representation is matched by constructing semantic interaction matrix [12]. Image feature extraction mainly includes traditional manually designed feature extraction methods and feature extraction methods based on deep learning. High-level semantic features are abstract features that are more stable and describe the local or overall information of an image. This feature is invariant to image change factors such as rotation, scaling, affine transformation, angle of view change, illumination change, etc.

There are three types of learning: first, describing learning ability as a simple and mechanical record; Knowledge acquisition is the direct result of transmission [13]. This teaching model is called "direct transmission" teaching, which assumes that there is only a linear and direct relationship between the sender of information, that is, the "owner" of knowledge, and the receiver will memorize the information in turn. Cognitive structure is that thinking is the representation form, while thinking is the generalization and indirect reflection of the objective reality of the human brain, the basic activity form of the human brain, and a kind of advanced psychological activity. Mathematical thinking usually refers to mathematical thinking ability, which refers to the ability to think and solve mathematical problems by using methods such as deduction, analysis, induction, synthesis, abstraction and generalization. Thinking is abstract, and it is the brain's processing and reflection of objective reality. So how to represent the thinking in learners' minds and better support and help learners' learning according to their cognitive structure has become a problem in thinking visualization's technical research and practice. Deep learning should be a spontaneous, active and active process from the beginning, and "problem solving" is an important symbol of deep learning. Looking at the research thread of mathematics learning theory, it mainly presents the following styles: First, from "top-down" to "bottom-up", that is, starting from classroom practice, finding problems in learning and teaching; By solving the problem, forming a preliminary hypothesis; Then return to practice, check and correct; After many cycles, a theory is formed. Second, from "quantitative research" to "combination of quantitative and qualitative research", the teaching and research departments and education administrative departments in the region together, focusing on the regional reality, integrated resources, overall planning and overall promotion on the basis of investigation and analysis, giving full play to the support and service of professional strength to deeply study classroom teaching improvement, established the overall idea of "overall design of regional programs, regional teaching and research activities, and seed teams to try first", as shown in Fig. 3.

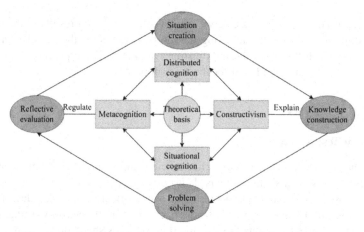

Fig. 3. The relationship between deep learning and cognitive theory

Convolution neural network transforms the input image into the form of feature vector by convolution calculation. Each convolution kernel involved in the calculation can extract the specified features [14]. In low-level network computing, convolution kernel extracts some local and low-level image features. Then the features are enhanced by pool layer. With the change of convolution kernel and the deepening of convolution network layers, convolution network constantly transforms local features at the bottom into higher-level abstract features. The concept model is a highly abstract model, which needs a specific calculation form in the actual transformation process. Common transformations are divided into linear transformation and nonlinear transformation. The complex combination of linear transformation and nonlinear transformation can express any form of functional transformation. The deep learning model uses this common sense to divide the conceptual model into layers, and each layer uses different combinations of linear changes and nonlinear changes to construct complex functional expressions. According to the combination mode, the expression of a single linear transformation can be obtained as shown in formula (1).

$$Z = \sum_{i=1}^{n} w_i \times x_i + b \tag{1}$$

In the process of model parameter adjustment, the non-leaf nodes are given specific vectors by constructing Huffman tree. What we want to calculate is the probability of the target word w_2, which refers to the probability of randomly walking from the root node to the target word w_2. Therefore, it is necessary to know the probability of going left and right when passing through non-leaf nodes, according to the following formulas (2) and (3):

$$P(n, left) = \sigma\left(\theta_n^T \cdot h\right) \tag{2}$$

$$P(n, right) = 1 - \sigma\left(\theta_n^T \cdot H\right) \tag{3}$$

There is often a big difference between the early calculation results of the training model and the real results. By adjusting the model parameters, the calculation results constantly approach the real values. Adjusting parameters is the process of "solving" the network model, and the idea of feedback is adopted.

3 Result Analysis

3.1 System Test Results

The ultimate goal of this system is to realize efficient and accurate automatic marking of a large number of students' answer texts. This not only saves a lot of time for teachers to correct test papers and homework, but also improves work efficiency. Besides, students' time for doing questions is recorded. Teachers can sum up the mastery of that kind of questions and knowledge points through the time students spend doing each question, which is more conducive to the development of teaching work. For the database design part, it should include basic information of questions, standard answer information, basic information of students, information of students' answers, information of students' grades and so on. When students log in to this system, they choose the test questions issued by the teacher to answer. After answering, they need to save the specific answer information, and then the system will automatically mark the papers in the background and save the marking results. After the implementation of this system, the effect of automatic marking of this system is tested. Here, a short answer question and a drawing question in the primary school math exam are selected for testing, and the problems of 50 students in a class are selected as samples. Then, the detailed scores of students' answers are given by manual marking and automatic marking of the system respectively, and the results of manual marking by teachers and automatic marking of the system are compared and analyzed. The statistical results are shown in Figs. 4 and 5.

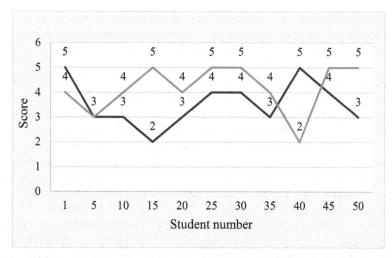

Fig. 4. Score line chart of the first question

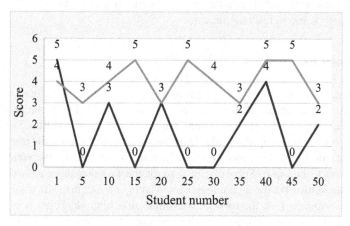

Fig. 5. Score line chart of the second question

Through testing, some existing problems can be better reflected, and the system can be maintained and improved according to the found problems. It is necessary to further strengthen the system's processing ability of syntactic analysis, word segmentation and graph recognition of answers, so as to make attempts and word segmentation more accurate.

3.2 Result and Reflection

Promoting the formation of deep learning quality is to promote the development of learners' core literacy. The main purpose of deep learning implementation is to cultivate learners' core literacy, which is mainly explained from three levels: First, from the perspective of learners' individual level, it mainly emphasizes learners' qualities in terms of cultural foundation, problem solving, etc., which are embodied in individual learning psychological attributes such as academic achievements, learning strategies and cognitive structure. Second, from the perspective of learners' groups, deep learning began to emphasize the transformation from individual construction to social participation, emphasizing the activities and relationships among learners in social practice, mainly including the qualities of cooperation and symbiosis, which are embodied in social practice attributes such as group structure, home-school relationship and social relationship. Third, from the perspective of deep learning system, it mainly includes learning content, learning methods, and the structure and operation mechanism of learning organization, which is embodied in creating learning culture, learning evaluation, personalized-cooperative learning, applied subject knowledge and corresponding knowledge strategies, etc. [15]. The theory of in-depth learning can not be mastered simply by one or two regional collective trainings. Teachers need to independently try teaching practice after concentrated learning, and then reflect on teaching and internalize it continuously. In order to strengthen the cooperation and communication between teachers and give full play to the collective wisdom and strength, the school level should systematically plan from the perspective of school-based research, organize teachers to carry out teaching research, and realize the effective communication between the idea and practice of deep learning teaching reform.

4   Conclusions

This paper mainly introduces the design and implementation of automatic marking of subjective mathematics questions in primary schools. Aiming at the problem that automatic marking of subjective questions requires strict input and filling of standard answers, an optimized design is made. Only the questions asked by the questions, the scores of the questions, the standard answers of the questions and the weights of the questions need to be input. Secondly, in view of the fact that there are many proper nouns in mathematics, but the segmentation rate of proper nouns in the forward maximum matching algorithm is low, the forward maximum matching algorithm is improved to improve the segmentation accuracy, and the theoretical knowledge of proximity in fuzzy mathematics is applied to the similarity calculation of keyword matching in this system. Deep learning is to promote students' meaningful deep learning, and the ultimate goal is to develop students' thinking ability. Therefore, the evaluation of deep learning puts more emphasis on promoting students' higher-order thinking. Explore semantic matching algorithm based on knowledge map. Based on the actual needs of users, this paper introduces natural language processing technology, disassemble and analyze the input content of users, and obtain keyword vectors. The deep learning technology is used to train the problem intention classifier to realize the recognition of user intention.

References

1. Su, C., Xiong, T.: Design and simulation of precision marketing push algorithm based on deep learning. Mod. Electron. Technol. **43**(22), 4 (2020)
2. Chen, L., Feng, Q., Ma, X., et al.: Design and implementation of cognitive radio intelligent power control algorithm based on deep learning. Inform. Technol. Inform. **1**(7), 95–97 (2019)
3. Wang, M.: Analysis of primary school mathematics classroom teaching based on deep learning. The world of mathematics: the third and fourth grade tutoring edition of primary school, vol. 21, no. 27, pp. 175–175 (2020)
4. Gong, B., Wang, K., Zhang, L.: Research on autonomous following algorithm of intelligent robot based on deep learning. Electron. Des. Eng. **30**(14), 5 (2022)
5. Cao, Y.: Uncovering the mystery of "number sense"—a research on strategies for cultivating number sense in primary school mathematics under the background of deep learning. Primary Sch. Teach. Res. **23**(13), 4 (2020)
6. Chen, L., Feng, Q., Ma, X., et al.: Design and implementation of cognitive radio intelligent power control algorithm based on deep learning. Inform. Technol. Inform. **22**(7), 3 (2019)
7. Kou, Y.: Design and research of online teaching recommendation system based on deep learning. J. Xi'an Vocat. Techn. College **43**(3), 5 (2017)
8. Xu, Z.: The flipped classroom of primary school mathematics from the perspective of deep learning. Shanxi Educ. Teach. Edn. **35**(12), 2 (2021)
9. Sun, J., Fu, L.: Where is the "deep" in deep learning?—Deliberately thinking about the "deepness"—The teaching improvement based on "deep learning" by the mathematics team of Haidian Primary School. Basic Educ. Curric. **13**(10), 6 (2017)
10. Sun, Z., Wang, J.: Micro-curriculum design of primary school mathematics from the perspective of deep learning: an example of online development strategies for "myths", "errors" and "problems." J. Jilin Univ. Educ. **36**(11), 4 (2020)
11. Dong, W., Shao, Y., Liu, S., et al.: Design of online and offline hybrid teaching for algorithm design and analysis courses based on deep learning strategies. Comput. Educ. **27**(2), 5 (2020)
12. Yi, S.: Exploration of primary school mathematics online course design from the perspective of deep learning: Taking the teaching of "cuboid cognition" as an example. Teach. Res. Course Mater. Res. Prim. Educ. **46**(3), 4 (2021)
13. Yang, G., Zhang, C., Chen, W., et al.: Research on the positionability of mobile robots based on deep learning synchronous positioning and map construction. Sci. Technol. Eng. **21**(32), 137 (2021)
14. Zheng, L.: Research on intelligent analysis method of sports training posture based on deep learning. Electron. Des. Eng. **29**(10), 167–171 (2021)
15. Peng, Y., Gong, L.: Design and implementation of robust expression keypoint location algorithm based on deep learning. Dig. Technol. Appl. **1**(6), 142 (2018)

Architecture Design of Intelligent Education and Teaching System Based on Machine Learning Algorithm

Libo Zhu[1,2(✉)], Xin Ma[1,2], Xinlong Liang[1,2], Jun Zhang[1,2], and Yufei Zhou[1,2]

[1] Zibo Normal College, Zibo 255100, Shandong, China
31530034@qq.com
[2] Yunnan University of Business Management, Anning 650300, Yunnan, China

Abstract. With the great success of machine learning (ML) algorithms represented by deep learning in vision, speech recognition and other fields, while looking forward to and promoting the large-scale educational application of artificial intelligence (AI), data center network is an important infrastructure supporting big data and cloud computing platforms, which is widely used in data-intensive and large-scale modular parallel computing tasks. AI has entered an unprecedented period of rapid adoption and stability. At the beginning of architecture design, the traditional distributed big data processing system didn't optimize the ML task, but ensured the training convergence efficiency, improved the iterative computing speed and improved the model quality. The application of AI education is limited by the common sense and symbolic grounding and transfer of AI technology. Based on the above analysis, this paper aims to solve the efficiency bottleneck of distributed system in dealing with ML tasks, and design and implement a high-performance distributed ML system for heterogeneous environment in data centers, so as to promote the intelligent development of education and teaching by applying heuristic AI teaching ideas. Overall, the degree of automation that AI technology can achieve in education is still very limited. It is more realistic to strengthen teacher design than to replace it.

Keywords: AI · teaching reform · intelligent education · intelligent teaching system · ML system

1 Introduction

Intelligentize is the new direction of today's development of society, and it is also the new feature of information development. AI and educational system are linked by human knowledge and practice, and there is a multi-level, complex and close interaction between them [1]. The application of AI in educational practice is logically inevitable. Intelligentization is always accompanied by informatization, but with the development and improvement of deep learning algorithms of AI, and the continuous supply of new "rations" for AI by big data and cloud platforms, intelligence is becoming the most prominent feature of informatization. The application of AI in education is for education, not

Y. Zhang and N. Shah (Eds.): BigIoT-EDU 2023, LNICST 583, pp. 98–106, 2024.
https://doi.org/10.1007/978-3-031-63139-9_11

for AI. For education, AI is the tool and means to achieve the goal. The ML algorithm represented by deep learning has made great achievements and achieved success in machine vision, automatic speech recognition and other fields. Besides, cloud computing and big data have proved data resources. Therefore, AI has entered an unprecedented period of rapid development.

Therefore, it is necessary not only to analyze from the angle of engineering technology, but also from the angle of education and teaching process. However, at present, it is not enough to analyze the educational application of AI from the micro-process of education and teaching activities. At present, AI has been able to improve teaching and learning efficiency, enhance learning experience and make personalized learning a reality in all aspects, such as learning guidance, teaching evaluation and optimization of teaching space. AI is leading the innovation of education and teaching, becoming an important factor in the development of education informatization. The development of new technology promotes the continuous transformation and upgrading of teaching methods, learning methods, teaching evaluation methods and teaching management modes [2]. Cultivating the creativity of a communication and cooperation ability, and the ability to find and solve problems [3]. In order to better understand the application of AI in education, we go back to the early research of teaching machines, sort out key events and systems, and try to summarize the history of computer education application. To sum up, there are many challenges to be overcome in designing and implementing a high-performance distributed ML system and adapting to the task requirements of heterogeneous data center networks. At present, in the increasingly fierce tide of AI technology, mastering the initiative of research on high-performance distributed computing and ML systems will contribute to the construction of information science in China, and also have certain significance for the transformation, upgrading and development of related industries [4].

2 Network Distributed ML System

2.1 Research on Network Topology

AI is based on high-quality application scenario data. Compared with traditional data, big data has the characteristics of unstructured, distributed, large amount of data and high-speed flow. Through data collection, data storage and data analysis, big data can discover the relationship between known variables and make scientific decisions [5]. Because the parameter server architecture has the characteristics of flat structure and easy implementation, most of the existing distributed ML systems currently have ML methods such as classification, clustering, regression, text mining, association rule mining, social network analysis, etc. The practical exploration of using machines to assist or replace human individuals in teaching activities is far earlier than the invention of digital electronic computers and AI. Prediction and clustering are widely used. All systems are designed based on this kind of architecture. Subjectivity refers to a specific education system with AI technology as its main body, such as intelligent teaching robot and intelligent tutor system. It is worth noting that distributed ML systems are usually deployed in networks based on Fat Tree topology. As a widely used topology in data centers, Fat Tree network is difficult to adapt to the communication characteristics of distributed ML applications. In order to solve the above problems, we can consider adopting BCube topology to build a data center network. BCube network is built by a series of topological structures called "Cube" [6]. The working nodes in each grid can be directly connected, which can significantly eliminate the complexity of data communication between different nodes. Based on the above characteristics, BCube network can provide better support for distributed ML system than Fat Tree network. This will lead to the imbalance of network traffic between server nodes and work nodes. Because the number of working nodes in a cluster is often much larger than the number of server nodes, when both nodes are equipped with network interfaces with the same throughput capacity, server nodes are more likely to become the bottleneck of network communication. The combination of big data and AI will bring new opportunities to education and teaching. Massive data is the cornerstone of machine intelligence. Big data has greatly promoted the advancement of technologies such as ML, unleashing unlimited potential in the application of intelligent services. It is necessary to optimize the topology of ML system, adapt to the link characteristics of multi-interface network and provide a unified communication interface, so as to improve the efficiency of distributed model training. Fat Tree topology is shown in Fig. 1. B Cube topology is shown in Fig. 2.

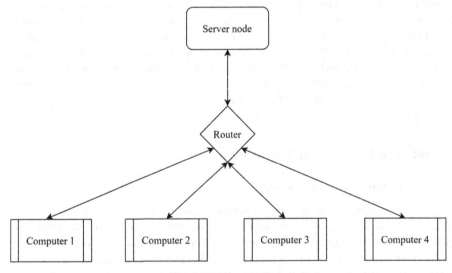

Fig. 1. FatTree topology

2.2 Research on Distributed ML Training

Due to the increasing scale of training data sets in recent years, the task based on large-scale neural networks often needs the support of distributed systems, that is, the distributed ML framework. For parallel computing mode, all working nodes can share memory space and use these shared resources to store data and models. Nevertheless, the influence of teaching machines on teaching practice is far less than the advocates

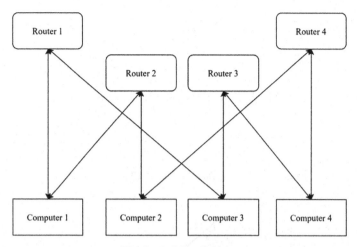

Fig. 2. B Cube topology

expected. When designing an efficient distributed ML system, the core index is to make a balance between hardware utilization and algorithm convergence [7]. Interaction means that a computer simulates a virtual subject by using software and hardware (for example, teaching agent, pedagogical agent; Learning companion) or interactive environment space. Therefore, optimizing the parameter synchronization mechanism has become the first consideration in designing distributed ML system. Contrary to block synchronization, global asynchrony can effectively solve the waiting problem in block synchronization. This mechanism allows each working node to advance the progress of local training independently without waiting for data from other working nodes. By setting a super parameter named Staleness, the difference of iteration progress between different nodes is limited. This threshold control scheme can ensure the convergence efficiency of the model and significantly reduce the waiting time of data transmission [8]. Cognitive Tutor is based on the analysis of cognitive tasks, and realizes the automatic guidance of cognitive skills. The computer creates a highly structured problem-solving environment for students, which can track and judge students' problem-solving process step by step, and provide timely feedback, tips and help. It can be seen that when solving the heterogeneity problem, the existing methods usually migrate the blocked tasks from the slow nodes to the fast nodes, and give higher contribution weight to the calculation results generated by the fast nodes, which will make the distributed training mainly depend on the fast nodes. The fundamental reason why learning is valued is that it partially solves the problem of knowledge "analysis (generation)". The following figure shows the basic process of ML supervision (Figs. 3, 4).

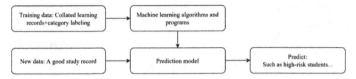

Fig. 3. Basic process of ML supervision

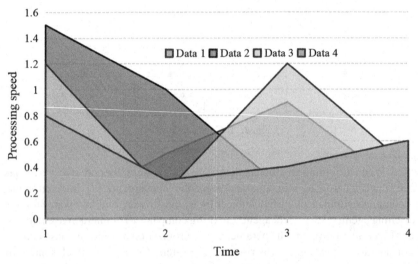

Fig. 4. Example in BCube

3 Intelligent Teaching Environment

3.1 The Concept of Intelligent Teaching

The construction of teaching environment is the basis for promoting teaching reform. The new generation of learners has put forward higher requirements for the construction of teaching environment [9]. Of course, research needs to point to the future, but The analysis and prediction of the future should be based on history and reality, and personalized learning services should be provided. The teaching environment is the external environment that affects learners' learning, and is the external condition that prompts learners to actively construct the meaning of knowledge and promote ability generation. And perform related functions Construction and performance analysis to adapt to the needs of real-world application scenarios. The intelligent module automatically scores students' answers to scientific questions, and distributes feedback instructions according to the scoring results, so as to promote the integrated learning of scientific knowledge. A learning place that identifies learners' characteristics, provides appropriate learning resources and convenient interactive tools, automatically records the learning process and evaluates the learning results. That is, the intelligent teaching environment is an intelligent learning place or activity space, which is learner-centered and supported by various new technologies, tools, resources and activities. Intelligent perception is the basic feature of intelligent teaching environment [10]. With the support of AI, various embedded devices and sensors, the teaching environment is perceived physically, contextually and socially. It can be seen that as far as the whole teaching process is concerned, what computers can do is actually very limited. Computers are not competent to understand the teaching contents, transform, reflect and form new understandings, etc. What can be automated (completed by computers) is teaching and evaluation. In the process of teaching, not only do students' understanding of a certain topic change, but teachers' understanding is also updated. The specific tasks in the model can be completed by human or computer. In a system where teachers and students (probably paying for it) use it, teachers and students may only have the right to use it for a short time, but the copyright belongs to the owner of the intelligent teaching system. In the evaluation of intelligent teaching system for research purposes, most of them still only pay attention to whether the system has achieved the designed function and whether it can run as expected, and lack of strict experiments on its teaching effect. Such research is also essential for the innovation and development of the field, but it has obvious traces on education, making it difficult to form sustainable products/projects. AI system is a computer system centered on knowledge or data, but at present, the training of developers is still focused on process-oriented transaction processing.

3.2 Cluster Driver Module Construction

The gradient exchange algorithm and collective communication framework proposed in this chapter are abstracted as a special cluster topology driver module. The core function of the module in the system is to adapt to the topology of the underlying network, and gradient slicing and numerical quantification techniques are used to accelerate the iterative process of model training. In the traditional teaching environment, due to the lack of technical support, teachers often carry out teaching according to experience, and it is difficult to realize real personalized teaching. In the field of education, educational robot is a robot whose goal is to cultivate students' analytical ability, creative ability and practical ability. Like a real-life teacher, it can know its own professional structure, its own teaching methods and the problems existing in the subject knowledge layer, and constantly adjust teaching strategies by observing and recording students' learning situation. The cluster driver module Canary session API is shown in Table 1.

Table 1. Cluster topology driver module Canary Session API

CanarySession Method name	Invoke object
all_gather(tensor, cube, pieces)	BCube drive
all_gather(tensor, cube, piece_level)	BCube drive
GEI_row_vector	GEI handle
GEI_matrix	GEI handle

$$PE_{(pos, 2i)} = \sin\left(pos/10000^{2i/d_{\text{model}}}\right) \tag{1}$$

The architecture design of the cluster driver module follows the decentralized collaborative mode. Among them, the main monitoring node monitors the running status of the whole cluster by deploying the cluster manager process, while the working nodes communicate with each other directly in a point-to-point manner, so there is no need for additional central server nodes to forward messages (Fig. 5).

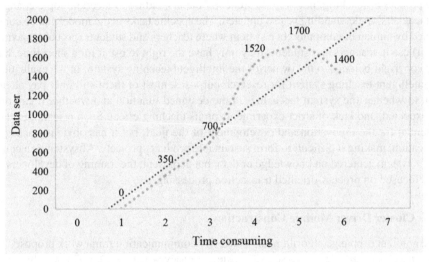

Fig. 5. Number of working points

$$f(x, W) = Wx + b \tag{2}$$

$$f(x_i, W, b) = Wx_i + b \tag{3}$$

The core idea of the algorithm is to ensure the consistency of models and parameters among nodes by setting two kinds of constraint thresholds: obsolete threshold S and proportional threshold P. In addition, the system can switch the synchronization algorithm into three different model aggregation modes: block synchronization, global asynchrony and synchronization based on obsolescence control by setting different obsolescence thresholds and proportional thresholds. On this basis, if the obsolescence threshold is set to a positive integer, the algorithm will switch to SSP mode. If the obsolescence threshold is set to infinity, the algorithm will switch to ASP mode. Theoretically, the optimal speed-up ratio of image processing should be linear with the increase of the number of working nodes, that is, the linear growth curve represented by the black solid line in the figure. By integrating the components of AI to promote teaching reform, it is concluded that the change of resources and environment is the basis of teaching reform. Therefore, from the perspective of resources and environment, The architectural design of distributed ML systems is usually closely related to the development of software and hardware in the industry. Although the system can take advantage of the huge computing power and massive data resources of the data center during deployment. And then optimizes teaching and learning. Intelligent teaching robot drives the innovation of teaching application, provides new tools and resources for teaching, promotes the further reform of teaching organization, and helps to attract learners' interest in learning. At present, the application of teaching robot in teaching is still in the exploratory stage. Through machine semantic association, the semantic relationship between newly uploaded resources and previous resources can be automatically mined, and similar resources can be automatically reorganized through semantic association mechanism, so as to realize the automatic convergence of similar resources (resource content and resource form) into thematic resources. In addition, for different training tasks, the experiment also analyzes the computational cost and proportion of gradient quantization algorithm in a single iteration. In addition, the gradient quantization algorithm can also be realized by special hardware such as FPGA, so as to give full play to its advantages of data compression and computation acceleration, which are all directions worthy of further study.

4 Conclusion

The development of AI has brought profound influence on education and teaching practice, and it is changing teachers' teaching methods and students' learning methods. A new era of technological change education has arrived. After AI entered the field of education, the changes of technical support resources and environment prompted a series of changes in teachers' teaching methods and students' learning methods. First of all, in the aspect of teaching evaluation, the research points out that the evaluation method in the era of AI is changing from manual evaluation to intelligent evaluation, and from standardized evaluation to differential evaluation. The characteristics of big data 5V and the new technical architecture subvert the traditional data analysis methods, and also affect the way of thinking about data. Driven by solving real-world problems, under the guidance of data thinking mode, the abilities of data collection, data storage, data management and data processing are gradually improved. Including predicting learners' learning ability, compiling test questions by machine, correcting by machine, analyzing reports, summarizing the implementation suggestions of intelligent evaluation, and analyzing with typical intelligent evaluation cases. At present, the majority of front-line teachers have little contact with AI technology, and most teachers simply don't know what functions can be realized by the application of AI technology in education. Without knowing the technology of AI itself, it is difficult for educators to put forward educational needs based on AI technology. In practice, we should try our best to maintain the maximum input-output utility by matching the types, scope and technical level of data. Strengthen the practical application of AI in teaching, and then promote the faster and better development of education. In this paper, the corresponding system modules are designed and implemented from bottom to top, and finally a high-performance distributed ML system is constructed, which can effectively improve the performance of the system in terms of distributed training efficiency, task processing speed and energy saving. At the same time, the open source system module in this paper can also facilitate the deployment of ML tasks by researchers and developers, and also promote the development of related industries.

References

1. Kai, C.: Several strategies for integrating artificial intelligence teaching into the basic modules of high school information technology courses. Information Technology Education in Primary and Secondary Schools, no. 7, p. 3 (2020)
2. Yan, L.: Collaborative recommendation system for library bibliography based on machine learning algorithm. Modern Electron. Technol. **43**(14), 4 (2020)
3. Cai, Y.: A big data real-time computing architecture based on streaming machine learning algorithms. Information Week, no. 46, p. 1 (2019)
4. Zhang, Z., Zhang, L., Luo, Q., et al.: Reality analysis of artificial intelligence in education: methods and limits of teaching automation. Educ. Sci. Digest **38**(1), 3 (2019)
5. Ju, S., Sun, J., Chen, L., et al.: Design framework of intelligent analysis platform for computer network virtual experiment under big data. Laboratory Res. Explor. **36**(12), 4 (2017)
6. Su, L., Su, L., et al.: Exploration of educational measures based on artificial intelligence concept machine learning. Wireless Internet Technol. **24**, 2 (2017)
7. Ma, J., Liu, J., Liu, Y.: Research and design of artificial intelligence teaching platform in primary and secondary schools——taking the "smart dog" artificial intelligence teaching assistant system as an example. China Educ. Informatization **1**, 10 (2021)
8. Wang, Y.: Intelligent teaching system: demand analysis, functional design and technical architecture. China Educ. Technol. Equipment **6**, 3 (2016)
9. Chen, K.: System characteristics and design framework of intelligent teaching agent. Distance Educ. J. **28**(6), 6 (2010)
10. Su, X., Yang, R., Yang, X.: Design of artificial intelligence education system based on big data. China Sci. Technol. Inform. **23**, 4 (2017)
11. Xia, G., Yan, X.: Theoretical framework of a multi-intelligence teaching design consulting system. China Modern Educ. Equipment **000**(12), 65–67 (2007)

Construction and Application of Machine Learning Algorithm in Mental Health Teacher Competency Model

Minxin Wang[1(✉)], Xiaoying Zhang[2], and Jianbo Xu[2]

[1] Wuhan Business University, Wuhan 430000, Hubei, China
9817276@qq.com
[2] College of Foreign Languages, Xiangnan University, Chenzhou 423000, Hunan, China

Abstract. The role of machine learning algorithms in constructing mental health teacher competency models is very important, but there is a problem of low construction accuracy. Standard competency models are poorly constructed and cannot solve many aspects of psychoanalysis. Therefore, this paper proposes a machine learning algorithm and a mental health teacher competency model. Firstly, the competency theory is used to classify mental health teachers, and the competency construction scheme is selected according to the mental health teaching standards. Then, a building set is formed according to the competency criteria, and the competency parameters are iteratively judged. MATLAB simulations show that in mental health teachers, machine learning algorithms can improve competency accuracy and shorten construction Time, the results were better than the standard competency model.

Keywords: competency theory · analysis time · machine learning algorithms · Competency effect

1 Introduction

In the research and application of competency, the concept of competency is expressed through the mental health competency model. Mental Health Competency Model refers to a series of different combinations of competencies required to complete a certain job and achieve a certain achievement goal. It describes a special combination of knowledge, skills and personality characteristics required to effectively play a role in an organization [1]. Mental health competency model is both a human resource management method and a management tool, which can be widely used in all aspects of human resource management.

Mental health competency model is the main method of competency identification, also known as competency model, which is a combination of a series of different competency elements to achieve a certain performance goal, each of which is a dimension. Since the mental health competency model is based on the work characteristics of a

Y. Zhang and N. Shah (Eds.): BigIoT-EDU 2023, LNICST 583, pp. 107–116, 2024.
https://doi.org/10.1007/978-3-031-63139-9_12

certain group, and can distinguish between excellent and average achievers, the selection and determination of competency elements is the key to the model construction, and whether these elements accurately reflect the work characteristics of the research object becomes the focus of the model test [2]. Therefore, the research of mental health competency model can be divided into two parts: model construction and model testing.

The mental health competency model usually includes the content most closely related to work performance, including the key knowledge, skills and personality characteristics required to complete the work and the behaviors that have the most direct impact on work performance. There are many competency characteristics of each student in different schools, and these competencies are not necessarily the ones required by the school. The school should put forward the competence of each post according to its own development, school culture, environment, especially the post requirements, and manage students according to this standard. Here we need to build a mental health competency model to analyze and refine the competency characteristics that can predict students' work [3]. The so-called establishment of mental health competency model means that under the guidance of competency theory, on the basis of analyzing the development requirements and cultural characteristics of the school, the competency required by the school is extracted by comparing the behavioral characteristics of excellent and ordinary performance personnel. Building a school mental health competency model can help schools judge and find the key driving factors that lead to the difference between good and bad students' performance, so as to successfully guide students to improve and improve their performance.

Including: description of the situation; Who is involved; What actions are actually taken; How do you feel personally; What is the result, that is, the subject must recall and state a complete story. During the specific interview, the interviewees need to list the key situations they encounter in the management work, including three positive results and three negative results. The interview takes about 3 h, and needs to collect complete and detailed information about 3 to 6 behavioral events. Therefore, interviewees must undergo strict training, generally no less than 10 working days. This method is currently the most commonly used in the process of building quality model. It mainly takes the employees of the target position as the interviewees. Through in-depth interviews with the interviewees, it collects the successful and unsuccessful event descriptions made by the interviewees during their tenure, and excavates the very detailed behaviors that affect the performance of the target position [4]. After that, the specific events and behaviors collected are summarized, analyzed and coded, and then compared between different interviewees (excellent performance group and ordinary performance group) to find out the core quality of the target position.

Mental health teachers are an important service target for library work, and machine learning algorithms play a very important role in building judgments. However, in translating competency from English to English, the competency model has the problem of low construction accuracy and cannot effectively play the role of automatic competency. Some scholars believe that applying machine learning algorithms to the construction of mental health teachers' competency model can effectively screen competency analysis data [5], analyze time analysis, and construct Judgment provides appropriate support

[6]. On this basis, this paper proposes a machine learning algorithm to mine the construction of the mental health teacher competency model and verify the effectiveness of the machine learning algorithm.

2 Related Concepts

2.1 Mathematical Description of Machine Learning Algorithms

The machine learning algorithm uses competency theory, the relationship between competency indicators, and competency criteria to judge the construction and is constructed according to the mental health teacher competency model [7]. Manage indicators in the study, find outliers in construction judgments, and form a path table. By integrating the construction competency effect, the correlation of the results of the machine learning algorithm is finally judged. Machine learning algorithms combine competency theory and use machine learning algorithms to judge the build, which can improve the level of machine learning algorithms [8].

Hypothesis 1: For the build is x_i, the set of build competency construction results is $\oint x_i$, the competency criterion is y_i, and the judicial function of the machine learning algorithm results is $C(x_i)$ as shown in Eq. (1).

$$C(x_i) = \overline{\overline{\sum x_i | y_i}} + \xi \tag{1}$$

First, synonymous conversion of the same content, such as "achievement motivation", "achievement desire" and other words are similar to the meaning of "achievement orientation" in Spencer's mental health competency model dictionary, so "achievement orientation" in Spencer's mental health competency model dictionary is used as the main keyword, and other similar words are included [9]; The words "information acquisition ability" and "resource integration ability" are similar to the meaning of "information seeking" in the Spencer mental health competency model dictionary, so "information seeking" in the Spencer mental health competency model dictionary is used as the main keyword, and other similar words are included. Other keywords such as "influence", "relationship building", "teamwork", "analytical thinking", "self-control", "quality and accuracy" are also integrated through this method.

The second is the difference of key words caused by different research objects, which will be converted into keywords that conform to the norms in the field of pedagogy [10]. For example, the "customer service orientation" in Spencer's mental health competency model dictionary is converted into "education awareness", and the key words such as "promoting student development" and "cultivating students" are included; In this study, "interpersonal understanding" is mainly reflected in teachers' understanding and acceptance of students, so the "interpersonal understanding" in Spencer's mental health competency model dictionary is converted into "understanding students", and the key words such as "acceptance understanding", "empathy", and "empathy" are included [11].

Third, the extracted key words do not exist in Spencer's mental health competency model dictionary, but their contents can really reflect the characteristics of the teacher's mental health competency model, so they are also identified as the key words of the teacher's mental health competency model and included in the corresponding main category of the teacher's mental health competency model. Such as "teaching organization and management", "teaching design skills", "professional ethics" and other keywords.

2.2 Selection of Construction Judgment Scheme

Hypothesis 2: The competency model construction function is $H(x_i)$, and the index weight coefficient is $\widetilde{w}_i$, then the construction judgment method is selected as shown in Eq. (2).

$$GH(x_i) = \overrightarrow{z_i \cdot f(x_i|y_i)} \cdot \xi \tag{2}$$

Training needs analysis includes organizational needs analysis, job analysis of teachers and personnel analysis. Traditional training needs analysis pays more attention to organizational needs and job requirements of teachers, but pays less attention to human needs [12]. Training course development and training needs diagnosis based on mental health competency model can effectively improve the pertinence of training work, make up for the lack of employees' ability, and effectively combine employee training with career development, To achieve "win-win" between enterprises and employees.

Establish a 360-degree evaluation system based on the mental health competency model, collect evaluation information from different levels of personnel, and conduct comprehensive feedback and evaluation on talents from multiple perspectives, which is conducive to the improvement of talents' self-cognition and a more objective and comprehensive understanding of themselves. At the same time, it will help talents to recognize their current quality gap and areas that need to be improved in the future, and then help them plan their career.

In the process of building the mental health competency model, the differences between the outstanding and the ordinary are found through behavioral event interviews and other means, and the mental health competency model elements are extracted [13]. The performance appraisal index refined based on the mental health competency model elements can further improve the original appraisal index system, truly reflect the comprehensive work performance of employees, and help employees improve their work enthusiasm, strengthen self-learning and promotion. The salary system based on ability and performance conveys the guidance of the school to attach importance to ability and quality to employees, which is conducive to employees paying more attention to ability and quality improvement and performance improvement.

2.3 Handling of Redundant Builds

Before analyzing machine learning algorithms, it is necessary to conduct a standard analysis of the analysis time and effect, map the construction to the analysis plan, and delete the non-conformant Competency analysis data. First, a comprehensive analysis of the build and the scheme and weight of the build is set to support the machine learning algorithm [14]. The reading competency is preprocessed, and if the processed result meets the requirements of university construction, the processing is effective; otherwise, it is restarted Mental Health Teacher Analysis. In order to improve the analysis accuracy of machine learning algorithms and improve the construction level, the data judgment scheme should be selected, and the specific method selection is shown in Fig. 1.

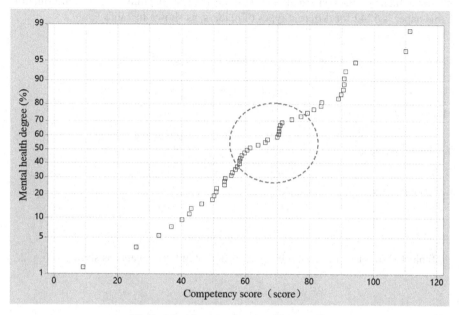

Fig.1. Machine learning algorithm results

The construction in Fig. 1 shows that the machine learning algorithm analysis is uniform and consistent with objective facts. The selection of the English translation method is not directional, indicating that the analysis of machine learning algorithms has short analysis accuracy and can be used as a judgment method for mental health teachers [15]. The selection of the English translation method meets the mapping requirements, mainly according to the competency theory, to adjust the selection of the English translation method, eliminate duplicate competency analysis data, and revise the construction, so that the overall selectivity of the construction is shorter.

2.4   Correlation Between Different Analytical Plans

The machine learning algorithm adopts the analysis accuracy judgment on the analysis time and adjusts the corresponding redundant construction relationship to achieve the accurate Judgment of the construction. Machine learning algorithms perform standard processing on competency data and randomly select different methods. In the process of self-learning, the mental health teaching standards of massive data are correlated with the selection of English translation methods [16]. After the correlation processing is completed, different methods are compared for competency data and the construction with the highest accuracy is stored.

3 Build Cases Based on Machine Learning Algorithms

3.1 Construct the Research Situation

In order to facilitate the construction of research analysis, the number of test information in this paper is 5242 for different types of readers, as shown in Table 1.

Table 1. Competency parameter characteristics

Construct	Amount of data	Accuracy	Error rate
Management competency	200M	0.85	0.5
	0.3G	0.85	0.3
Teaching competence	200M	0.85	0.1
	0.2G	0.89	0.2
Lead competency	200M	0.85	0.3
	0.6G	0.92	0.3

Table 1 shows the processing between different analysis plans, as shown in Fig. 2.

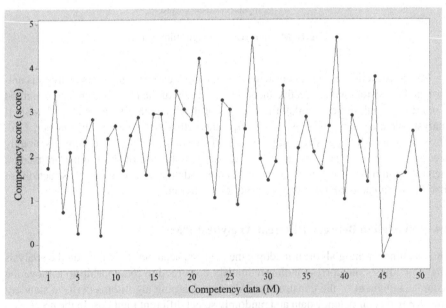

Fig. 2. The processing process of competency theory

It can be seen from Table 1 that compared with the standard competency model, the competency judgment results of machine learning algorithms are closer to the actual standards. In the construction process, with the help of competency theory, machine learning algorithms are used for analysis. From the change in competency theory in Fig. 4, it can be seen that the analysis accuracy of the machine learning algorithm is better, and the analysis time is faster [17]. Therefore, the construction accuracy of machine learning algorithms and the analysis time is better.

3.2 Judgment Ratio of Construction

The build process includes redundant data removal, compliance rate, and compliance rate. After the competency theory screening of the machine learning algorithm [21], the preliminary construction is obtained, and the correlation of the constructed index is analyzed.In order to verify the effect more accurately, select different redundant builds and calculate the overall analysis time of the machine learning algorithm, as shown in Table 2.

Table 2. Overall status of competencies

Competency score adjustment rate	Accuracy	Indicator compliance rate
3.6	93.11	92.53
4.5	92.30	94.13
6.7	93.29	93.32
mean	93.21	94.14
x^2	2.202	7.337

3.3 Time and Accuracy of Builds

To verify the analytical accuracy of the machine learning algorithm, the build time and analysis accuracy are compared with the standard competency model, and the results are shown in Fig. 3.

It can be seen from Fig. 3 that the analysis time of the machine learning algorithm is shorter than that of the standard competency model. Still, the error rate is lower, indicating that the choice of the machine learning algorithm is relatively stable, while that of the traditional competency model Competencies are uneven[18]. The analysis accuracy of the above algorithm is shown in Table 3.

It can be seen from Table 3 that in the construction of standard competency models, there are shortcomings in construction time and analysis accuracy, and the analytical accuracy of data processing changes significantly, and the error is short. Machine learning algorithms have shorter analysis times and are better than standard competency models[19]. At the same time, the construction time of the machine learning algorithm is greater than 90%, and the accuracy has not changed significantly[20]. To further verify the superiority of machine learning algorithms. To further verify the continuity of

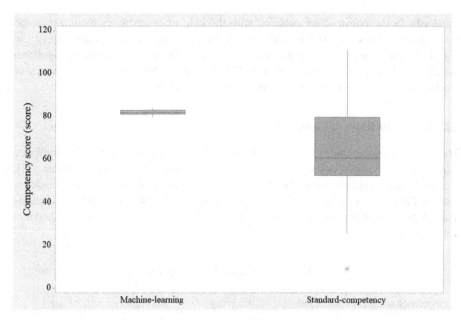

Fig. 3. Construction time of different algorithms

Table 3. Comparison of competency construction results of different methods

algorithm	Build time	Data stability	Random interference
Machine learning algorithms	92.11	95.79	1.74
Standard competency model	72.25	90.16	1.21
P	0.012	0.021	0.023

the method, the machine learning algorithm is comprehensively analyzed by different methods, as shown in Result 4.

It can be seen from Fig. 4 that the results of the machine learning algorithm are significantly better than the standard competency model, and the reason is that the machine learning algorithm increases the analysis judgment coefficient and sets the corresponding competency theory to present a result that does not meet the requirements.

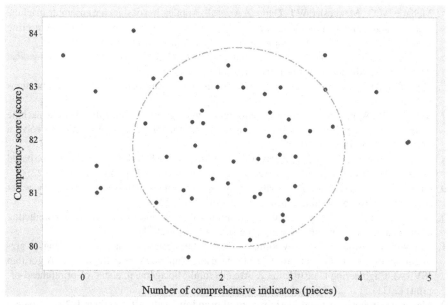

Fig. 4. Evaluation of the results of machine learning algorithms of different methods

4 Conclusion

This paper proposes a machine learning algorithm method combined with competency theory Build to judge. At the same time, the construction scheme is analyzed in depth, and the analysis result collection is constructed. Studies have shown that machine learning algorithms can improve the accuracy of competencies and shorten analysis time. However, in machine learning algorithms, too much attention is paid to adjusting single competency parameters, and the proportion of different competency parameters is ignored.

Acknowledgements. Research on the Construction of Online Platform of University Teaching Quality Evaluation System Based on School-enterprise Cooperation NO.2021024.

References

1. Lu, H.: Application of wireless network and machine learning algorithm in entrepreneurship education of remote intelligent classroom. J. Intell. Fuzzy Syst. Appl. Eng. Technol. **40**(2) (2021)
2. Wang, Y., Li, H., Tian, J., et al.: The application of machine learning algorithm in relative permeability upscaling for oil-water system. In: International Petroleum Technology Conference (2021)
3. Gao, W.: Adoption of ultrasonic imaging diagnosis under machine learning algorithm in treatment of pregnancy-induced hypertension and nursing. J. Med. Imaging Health Inf. **11**(1) (2021)

4. Meharie, M.G., Mengesha, W.J., Gariy, Z.A., et al.: Application of stacking ensemble machine learning algorithm in predicting the cost of highway construction projects. Engineering Construction & Architectural Management, 2021, ahead-of-print(ahead-of-print)

5. Lan, X., Wei, R., Cai, H.W., et al.: Application of machine learning algorithm in medical field. Chinese Medical Equipment Journal (2019)

6. Vreugd, G.D.: Machine Learning for Classifying Certificate of Competency Applications (2016)

7. Muvunzi, R.: Application of group genetic algorithm for generation of cells to solve a machine layout problem application of group genetic algorithm for generation of cells to solve a machine layout problem (2018)

8. Cai, Q., Luo, X.Q., Wang, P., et al.: Hybrid model-driven and data-driven control method based on machine learning algorithm in energy hub and application. Appl. Energy 305 (2022)

9. Gupta, S., D.U, Hebbar, R.: Analysis and application of multispectral data for water segmentation using machine learning. arXiv e-prints (2022)

10. Wei, L.L., Pan, Y.S., Zhang, Y., et al.: Application of machine learning algorithm for predicting gestational diabetes mellitus in early pregnancy 8(3), 13 (2021)

11. Adinyira, E., Adjei, A.G., Agyekum, K., et al.: Application of machine learning in predicting construction project profit in Ghana using Support Vector Regression Algorithm (SVRA). Engineering Construction & Architectural Management. ahead-of-print(ahead-of-print) (2021)

12. Machine learning in materials design: Algorithm and application. Chin. Phys. B 29(11), 68–96 (2020)

13. Tallroth, A., Ålander, M.: The use of Machine Learning Algorithms for Adaptive Question Selection in Questionnaire-based Mental Health Data Collection Apps. (2016)

14. Zhang, F., Jiang, S., Li, Y.: Application of massive parallel deep learning algorithm in the prediction of colorectal carcinogenesis of familial polyposis. IEEE Access PP(99), 1 (2020)

15. Ariaeinejad, A., Patel, R., Chan, T.M., et al.: P031: Using machine learning algorithms for predicting future performance of emergency medicine residents. Canadian J. Emergency Med. 19(S1) (2017)

16. Remedios, S., Armstrong, D., Graham, R., et al.: Exploring the application of pattern recognition and machine learning for identifying movement phenotypes during deep squat and hurdle step movements. Front. Bioeng. Biotechnol. 8, 364 (2020)

17. Caluza, L.: Machine Learning Algorithm Application in Predicting Children Mortality: A Model Development (2018)

18. Yoon, M.S., Yoon, W.S., Lee, J.S.: Application of a deep reinforcement learning algorithm in household inverter air-conditioner temperature control. In: 13th IEA Heat Pump Conference (2021)

19. Lian, T.: Research and Application of Machine Learning in Big Data. Computer & Telecommunication (2018)

20. Ye, Z.: Application of machine learning algorithms in data mining. China Computer & Communication (2019)

College Student Mental Health Analysis Based on Machine Learning Algorithm

Zhang Li[✉] and Yao Lu

Zhangjiagang Campus of Jiangsu University of Science and Technology, Suzhou 215600, Jiangsu, China
305118619@qq.com

Abstract. The role of mental health in college students is very important, but there is a problem of low accuracy. In the past, psychological evaluation methods could not solve the problem of mental health evaluation among college students, and satisfaction was low. Therefore, this paper proposes a mechanical learning algorithm to construct a mental health evaluation system for college students. Firstly, the health scale is used to classify the mental health results, and the result collection is divided according to the scoring results, so as to realize the quantitative processing of mental health scores. The health scale then categorizes mental health outcomes, forms a collection of evaluation results, and iteratively analyzes mental health problems. MATLAB simulation shows that under the condition of certain health standards, the accuracy and stability of mental health results are better than those of previous psychological evaluation methods.

Keywords: health scale · mental health · evaluation · College students

1 Introduction

Mental health education is an important part of ideological and political education in colleges and universities. At present, the psychological health of college students has been widely concerned by the society. The author has found in the practice of mental health education in colleges and universities for more than ten years that the profound development of reform and opening up and the establishment of market economy have brought a series of profound social changes, which have caused unprecedented psychological impact and psychological pressure to college students in the new era. In the campus, students' psychological problems, mental problems Even abnormal death is not uncommon. If these problems are not properly dealt with, they may have a serious impact on the safety and stability of colleges and universities, and some may even disrupt the normal learning, life and work order of the school [1]. According to the statistics of the World Health Organization, 16.0%–25.4% of college students in China have some psychological problems. At the same time, some studies also found that the level of depression and anxiety of college students was significantly higher than that of the national adult norm group. Therefore, studying the current situation of college

Y. Zhang and N. Shah (Eds.): BigIoT-EDU 2023, LNICST 583, pp. 117–127, 2024.
https://doi.org/10.1007/978-3-031-63139-9_13

students' psychological problems, exploring the causes of college students' psychological problems in the new era, according to the psychological characteristics of college students, helping them solve the psychological problems encountered in their psychological development and daily life, improving their psychological quality, and helping them to develop comprehensively, fully, harmoniously and actively are important topics for colleges and universities to build a harmonious campus and strengthen students' ideological and political education.

In 2001, the Ministry of Education of the People's Republic of China issued the first special document on mental health education in colleges and universities, namely, the Opinions on Strengthening the Mental Health Education of College Students. After 20 years of practice, the mental health education of college students in China has achieved certain results [2]. Most colleges and universities have cultivated a relatively stable group of teachers with rich theoretical and practical experience in mental health education, We have set up special institutions for students' mental health education and consultation. It has played a very important role in college students' mental health education, psychological science popularization, and the construction of psychological service platform and system, which has improved the passive and backward situation in the field of mental health education in China to a certain extent. However, in the new era and new situation, China's college mental health education also faces various challenges. It is not only necessary to continue to improve the existing content structure, but also to continue to develop new ways to meet the requirements of the healthy China strategy. Build a collaborative education system of ideological and political education in colleges and universities in the new era to help college students grow better.

Mental health refers to that all aspects of psychology and activities are in a good or normal state. The ideal state of mental health is to maintain a state of perfect personality, normal intelligence, correct cognition, proper emotion, reasonable will, positive attitude, proper behavior and good adaptation. After learning the course of mental health, I think that mental health is not only personal behavior feeling and working state, but also our attitude and view towards one thing. As a college student, everyone should be positive and optimistic, establish a correct outlook on life, values and the world, enhance their psychological quality, treat their psychological activities correctly, and establish a healthy "psychological concept". As college students, we should correctly look at all kinds of things on the road of life and have a healthy psychology. Research shows that the factors that affect college students' mental health include genetic factors, physiological factors, educational factors, and personal subjective factors. Genetic factors and physiological factors are not determined by themselves and do not have subjective initiative. But we can do our best to face life with a positive, optimistic, cheerful and lively attitude. At all times and in all countries, the road is rough, the environment is tough, the poor and poor are persistent, work hard, and never give up. Beethoven is a great musician in the world, and also the person with the worst fate, but he did not abandon himself because of this, and finally stuck to the music he loved all his life and achieved something; Hawking, everyone thinks he is very unfortunate, but his scientific achievements are after the disease. He defeated the disease with his strong will, and also proved that disability is not an obstacle, and created his own miracle. As college students, each of us is born in a different environment, but this is not the reason for us to get down and abandon ourselves. Life is full of flavors, and you still need to laugh.

Mental health evaluation is an important assessment content among college students and is of great significance for mental health. However, in the actual evaluation process, the problem of inaccurate mental health evaluation has a certain impact on college students. Some scholars believe that the application of intelligent algorithms to college students' mental health evaluation can effectively carry out psychological scale and psychological score analysis [3], and provide corresponding support for college students' psychological evaluation [4]. On this basis, this paper proposes a machine learning method to comprehensively evaluate the mental health of college students and verify the effectiveness of the model.

2 Related Concepts

2.1 Mathematical Description of Mental Health

Mental health is to use the health scale to comprehensively evaluate psychological problems, and according to multi-dimensional indicators, discover psychological problems in psychological evaluation [5], integrate the evaluation results, and finally judge the causes of psychological problems [6]. Combined with the health scale, the use of information mining and intelligent algorithms to comprehensively evaluate the mental health results can improve the evaluation level of college students' mental health [7].

Hypothesis 1: The content of the scale is x_i, the set of results is $set \sum x_i$, the health criterion is y_i, and the mental health judgment function is $f(x_i)$ as shown in Eq. (1).

$$f(x_i) = \sum x_i | y_i \cdot \int \xi \tag{1}$$

2.2 Selection of Psychological Intervention Programs

Hypothesis 2: The program selection function is $F(x_i)$ and the weight coefficient is q_i, then the psychological intervention option selection is shown in Eq. (2).

$$F(x_i) = z_i \cdot \sqrt{f(x_i|y_i)} \sqrt{\prod q_i \cdot \xi +} \tag{2}$$

The main task of data cleaning is to deal with the defective and unqualified miscellaneous data in the original data, namely "dirty data", and transform those low-quality data into high-quality and usable data through deletion and replacement. The processed data is mainly the data with quality problems in terms of integrity, uniqueness, legality and consistency, mainly including missing value processing [8, 9], abnormal value processing Noise data processing and inconsistency processing.

(1) Missing value processing: Missing value refers to the situation that individual attributes in some records are empty. The processing of this situation should be based on the principle of minimizing the impact on the prediction results. If the

records with missing values in the data set are far less than the total amount of data, and the data set is very large, you can choose the simplest processing method, namely, direct deletion, because its proportion in the whole data set is very low, Direct deletion does not affect the use of data sets. However, if there are many missing values and the data set is small, the data with missing values cannot be deleted directly. In this case, the missing values account for a large proportion in the data set. Direct deletion will lead to a sharp decrease in the number of the entire data set, which will affect the accuracy of the prediction [10]. This requires the use of the filling method, that is, the average value of the attribute can be used to fill in the missing values. Because the data set obtained in this paper is large, the number of data samples exceeds 10000, and the number of missing values is small, so the deletion method is adopted to delete the samples with missing important data directly.

(2) Handling of outliers: outliers refer to data that is significantly different from normal data, such as maximum or minimum data, which is also called outliers because it deviates from the main concentration of data. This kind of data cannot be deleted directly as a few missing values. It is necessary to determine whether it is a false exception or a true exception before deciding how to deal with it. It is not necessary to deal with the false exception data, but it can be directly mined and modeled. However, for the true exception data, it is necessary to deal with it by deleting, treating as missing values, replacing the average value, and other methods. If someone's age is negative, this is obviously deviating from the actual abnormal value.

(3) Noise data processing: noise is random error or error of the measured data caused by some special reasons, which will interfere with the data. Common processing methods include cluster analysis method, regression method, etc. In the cluster analysis method, abnormal data is not located in any cluster set [11]. The regression method is to use the fitting function to obtain the fitting relationship to fit the noise data and achieve the effect of noise removal and data smoothing.

(4) Non-conformance processing: In the case of different data in the records of the same subject, you can define integrity constraints and use knowledge engineering tools to detect the consistency to find out the inconsistent data. Some data can also be solved manually by using its connection with other data.

2.3 Processing of Psychological Data of College Students

Before conducting mental health analysis, standard analysis should be carried out on the evaluation results on the scale to judge abnormal evaluation results. First, the evaluation results are comprehensively analyzed, and the threshold and weight of the evaluation results are set to ensure the accuracy of mental health evaluation. The evaluation results are semantic transformation evaluation results and need to be quantified. If the results of the evaluation are normally distributed, the results of the evaluation will be affected, reducing the accuracy of the overall evaluation evaluation [12]. In order to improve the accuracy of mental health evaluation and improve the level of mental health evaluation, mental health analysis should be selected, and the specific method selection is shown in Fig. 1.

The purpose of constructing the mental health prediction model is to realize the classification of college students' mental health status according to the results of the mental health questionnaire. The construction process of the model mainly includes the following steps:

The first step is the pretreatment process. The process includes feature extraction and data set partition. Because the result state of this paper only has psychological problems and no psychological problems, the prediction model is a classification model, which needs to obtain labels to mark the data set. The labels are extracted according to the scores of the mental health survey; The second is to divide the sample data set.

The second step is to set evaluation indicators. The purpose of setting the evaluation index of the prediction model is to compare the prediction effect of various algorithms and select the best prediction model. The evaluation indicators of the prediction model should be selected according to the specific situation of the problem. This paper chooses to use the confusion matrix and its related indicators, ROC curve and AUC to evaluate the prediction model of college students' mental health.

The third step is data balancing. Unbalanced data quantity of different categories will cause differences in the whole prediction model. Therefore, in the case that there is a large gap between the data quantity of some categories and that of other categories, we need to balance the data. In this paper, we use the remote method to process the data.

The fourth step is to select the prediction model. This paper mainly selects decision tree, logistic regression, SVM support vector machine and XGBoost to predict, and selects indicators to evaluate the prediction results.

The fifth step is to train the prediction model. In the preprocessing stage, the training data set and the test data set have been divided, so the model training and optimization can be started. Model optimization is actually to optimize the performance of the model by continuously adjusting parameters [13].

The sixth step is to evaluate the prediction model. Multiple prediction models are used to predict the mental health of college students. After obtaining the results, it is necessary to evaluate and compare the prediction models through evaluation indicators in order to select the most suitable model for the prediction of college students' mental health.

The evaluation results in Fig. 1 show that mental health analysis shows a diversified distribution and meets the teaching requirements. The psychological intervention program is not directional, indicating that mental health analysis has strong evaluation accuracy, so it is used as an evaluation study of psychological evaluation [14]. The psychological intervention program meets the mapping requirements, mainly the health scale adjusts the psychological intervention program, removes the duplicate psychological scale, and revises the psychological score. This makes the whole evaluation result more evaluative.

3   Practical Cases of Health Evaluation of College Students

3.1   Mental Health

In order to facilitate mental health analysis, the psychological scale in this paper is the research object, the test data is 1G, and the mental health evaluation of specific physical education is shown in Table 1.

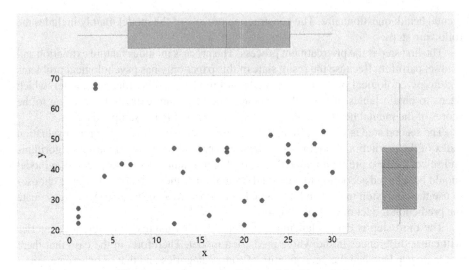

Fig. 1. Selection results for mental health analysis

Table 1. Characteristics of the data for college students

Scale type	Comprehensive scales	Number of gauges	Reasonableness	threshold
Social scales	synthesis	500M	0.85	0.6
	So so	1G	0.65	0.6
Mental scale	synthesis	500M	0.75	0.6
	So so	1G	0.69	0.6
Personality scale	synthesis	500M	0.75	0.6
	So so	1G	0.92	0.6

The psychological score processing process of mental health evaluation in Table 1 is shown in Fig. 2.

Table 1 shows that compared with previous psychological evaluation methods, the evaluation results of mental health are closer to the actual mental health evaluation. In terms of psychological evaluation, psychological score evaluation rate, accuracy, etc., mental health previous psychological evaluation methods [15]. From the changes in psychological scores in Fig. 4, it can be seen that the accuracy of mental health evaluation is better and the judgment speed is faster. Therefore, the mental health evaluation speed, mental health evaluation, and score analysis accuracy of mental health are better.

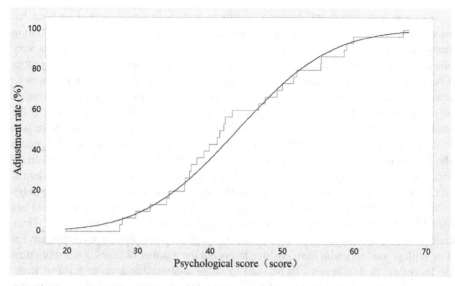

Fig. 2. Processing process of psychological score

3.2 Recognition Rate of Psychological Problems

The psychological evaluation results included social scale, personality scale, and psychological scale. After the standard screening of mental health, the preliminary psychological evaluation results were obtained, and the reasons for the psychological evaluation results were obtained Analyze [16]. To more accurately verify the effect, identify abnormal psychological scores, as shown in Table 2.

Table 2. Overall picture of psychological scores

Amount of data	Healthy Psychology	Psychological problem recognition rate
Social scales	14.74	6.32
Mental scale	12.63	21.05
Personality scale	5.26	7.37
mean	18.95	20.00
X^2	10.53	17.89
P = 0. 326		

3.3 Timing and Accuracy of Mental Health Assessment

In order to verify the accuracy of mental health evaluation, the evaluation results are compared with previous psychological evaluation methods, and the evaluation results are shown in Fig. 3.

We know that most people have positive items and are in a mild stage as a whole, but not serious, so we can intervene and adjust in time. Compared with other distribution charts, we can see that the distribution of the average score of positive items is very different from the distribution of the total score, the total average score and the number of positive items. This is because the average score of positive items is an indicator to measure the severity of the items that present positive results, not an indicator to measure the overall distribution of college students' psychological problems, regardless of the number of positive results, As long as a college student has a positive item, there will be an average score of more than 2 points for positive items [17]. Therefore, the person who has no more than 2 points is the person who does not have a positive item in 90 items. For the person who has an average score of more than 2 points for positive items, we can only judge whether the college student has a positive item, but we can't judge the specific number of positive items, so we can't judge whether the college student has mental health problems. If this item is used as an indicator to evaluate whether college students have psychological problems, there is a great possibility of misjudgment for those college students who have positive items but the number of items is not more than 43. Therefore, this indicator can be used to judge whether the average level of items with positive items is mild, moderate or serious, but can not be used as an evaluation standard for whether there are psychological problems.

In this paper, there are 14 variables affecting college students' mental health, including total score, total average score, average score of positive items, number of positive items, depression, anxiety, interpersonal sensitivity, psychosis, obsessive-compulsive disorder, paranoia, hostility, somatization, terror, and others. In order to analyze the degree of correlation between the variables, this paper obtains a heat map based on Pearson's correlation coefficient, as shown in Fig. 3, The correlation coefficient of all variables reached more than 0.4, with a relatively close correlation [18]. The correlation coefficient of total score, total average score, depression, anxiety, number of positive items, interpersonal sensitivity, and psychosis reached more than 0.8. Compared with other variables, it has a stronger correlation.

It can be seen from Fig. 3 that the time of mental health evaluation of machine learning method is higher than that of previous psychological evaluation methods, but the error rate is lower, indicating that the evaluation of machine learning methods is relatively stable, while the previous psychological evaluation methods The accuracy of the analysis varied [19]. The accuracy of the above algorithm evaluation is shown in Table 3.

It can be seen from Table 3 that machine learning methods are better in terms of evaluation time and change range in terms of psychological evaluation In the past, the psychological evaluation method has changed significantly, and the error rate is relatively high. Therefore, the evaluation time of machine learning method is shorter, which is better than the previous psychological evaluation method. At the same time, the evaluation accuracy of machine learning method is greater than 90%, and the accuracy has not changed significantly. In order to further verify the superiority of machine learning [20]. In order to further verify the continuity of the methodology, a comprehensive analysis of mental health was carried out using different methods, as shown in Outcome 4.

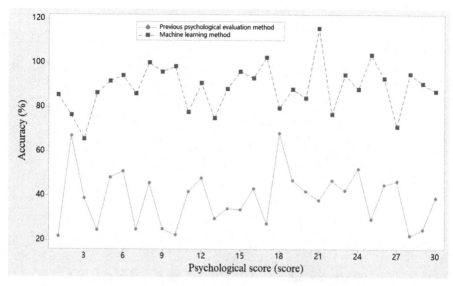

Fig. 3. Accuracy of mental health assessments

Table 3. Comparison of score analysis accuracy of different methods

algorithm	Psychological evaluation time	Magnitude of change	error
Machine learning	90.00	0.53	0.02
Previous psychological evaluation methods	86.84	8.95	2.63
P	16.84	15.79	14.74

It can be seen from Fig. 4 that the psychological score of the machine learning method is significantly better than the previous psychological evaluation method, and the reason is that the machine learning method increases the adjustment coefficient of information and psychological evaluation results, and sets it The corresponding threshold, the psychological score that determines the non-compliance.

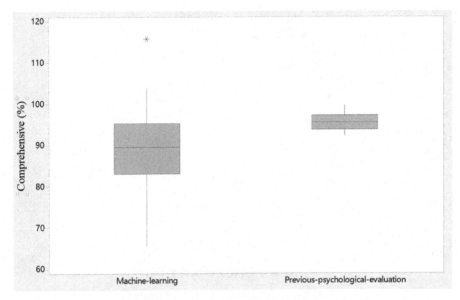

Fig. 4. Comprehensive assessment results of mental health

4 Conclusion

In the current form of rapid social development, college students' psychological problems are increasing, including learning, life, interpersonal relations, self-cognition, love and so on. There will be anxiety, inferiority complex, depression and other psychology in different degrees. It has a serious impact on the healthy growth of college students and the quality of national talent training. Therefore, paying high attention to college students' mental health problems has not only theoretical significance, but also important practical significance.In the case of the rapid development of computers, this paper proposes a machine learning method for college students, and combines health scales to improve the psychological evaluation results. At the same time, the question scoring is analyzed in depth to construct a psychological score collection. Studies have shown that machine learning can improve the accuracy of psychological evaluation results, which can have an impact on mental health Conduct a comprehensive evaluation. However, in the process of mental health, too much attention is paid to the ability to analyze scale indicators, and the personal analysis of psychological evaluation results is neglected.

References

1. Aldhamin, R.A., Saif, A.Z.A.: The mental health of healthcare workers in GCC countries during the COVID-19 pandemic: a systematic review and meta-analysis. J. Taibah Univ. Med. Sci. **18**, 45–60 (2023)
2. Alhusseini, N., Farhan, H., Yaseen, L., Abid, S., Imad, S.S., Ramadan, M.: Premarital mental health screening among the Saudi population. J. Taibah Univ. Med. Sci. **18**, 154–161 (2023)
3. Hu, B., Wang, Y.T., Cai, X.L., Xuan, Y.S., Xu, Y.J.: The use and effectiveness of mental health helplines during the COVID-19 pandemic in China. Asian Journal of Psychiatry 80 (2023)

4. Izuakor, C.F., Nnedum, O.A.U.: Expert recommendations for frontline mental health workers caring for children in the Russian-Ukraine conflict. Asian Journal of Psychiatry 80 (2023)

5. Mao, F.X., Sun, Y.Y., Li, Y., Cui, N.X., Cao, F.L.: Internet-delivered mindfulness-based interventions for mental health outcomes among perinatal women: a systematic review. Asian Journal of Psychiatry 80 (2023)

6. Meske, C., Amojo, I., Thapa, D.: A conceptual model of feedback mechanisms in adjusted affordances-Insights from usage of a mental mobile health application. Int. J. Inf. Manage. **69** (2023)

7. Xiao, Y., Du, N., Li, Y.G.: Mental health services in China: Challenges in the context of COVID-19. Asian J. Psychiatry **80** (2023)

8. Muzumdar, P., Basyal, G.P., Vyas, P.: An empirical comparison of machine learning models for student's mental health illness assessment. arXiv e-prints (2022)

9. Rakshitha, C.: Machine Learning based Analysis of Twitter Data to Determine a Person's Mental Health Intuitive Wellbeing. Int. J. Appl. Eng. Res. **13**(21aPta1) (2018)

10. Tallroth, A., Ålander, M.: The use of Machine Learning Algorithms for Adaptive Question Selection in Questionnaire-based Mental Health Data Collection Apps (2016)

11. Dadi, K.: Machine Learning on Population Imaging for Mental Health (2020)

12. Pawar, R.G.: Data classification of student perception analysis based onnaive bayes and j48 algorithm (2016)

13. Wang, Z.: Campus intelligence mental health searching system based on face recognition technology. 电子研究与应用 **4**(4), 6 (2020)

14. Abdulla, S., Diykh, M., Laft, R.L., et al.: Sleep EEG signal analysis based on correlation graph similarity coupled with an ensemble extreme machine learning algorithm. Expert Syst. Appl. **138** (2019)

15. Jiang, Y.: Research on students course selection and learning behavior analysis algorithm based on data mining. Modern Electronics Technique (2016)

16. Mens, K.V., Lokkerbol, J., Janssen, R., et al.: Predicting Undesired Treatment Outcome in Mental Healthcare: Machine Learning Study (Preprint) (2019)

17. Asselman, A., Khaldi, M., Aammou, S.: Enhancing the prediction of student performance based on the machine learning XGBoost algorithm. Interact. Learn. Environ. **3**, 1–20 (2021)

18. Soriano, L.T.: A State College Customer Feedback Data Analysis using Machine Learning-Based Algorithm (2019)

19. Pang, C.: Simulation of student classroom behavior recognition based on cluster analysis and random forest algorithm. J. Intell. Fuzzy Syst. **40**(2), 2421–2431 (2021)

20. Wang, Z.: Campus intelligence mental health searching system based on face recognition technology. J. Electron. Res. Appl. **4**(4) (2020)

Construction and Optimization of Japanese Instructional Management System Based on Genetic Algorithm

Yuan Deng[✉]

Guilin University of Technology, Guilin 541004, Guangxi, China
dengyuan@glut.edu.cn

Abstract. The Internet has been almost completely popularized in China, and people can't leave the Internet all the time. The core of school information management is the overall utilization of resources, which includes human resources, material resources and time resources. In daily Japanese teaching, students passively accept knowledge, and the interaction is not obvious. As the core of interactive teaching, cloud platform supports the supplement of teaching materials, which is rich in content and can attract students' attention to a great extent and improve their interest in learning. Aiming at There are all kinds of problems now. in Japanese teaching in universities, this paper puts forward a Japanese instructional management system, which uses Genetic Algorithm (GA) to solve the problem of Japanese course scheduling, assigns permissions to users with different identities, receives and processes user requests, Make the whole research results and research effective, and make a better in-depth analysis of the research. The traditional instructional management system, the instructional management algorithm Related indicators make it. 21.74%. Therefore, it is feasible to establish an intelligent Japanese teaching mode using GA. GA can well solve the problems existing in the old Japanese instructional management system, and can meet more soft constraints.

Keywords: Number one. · Japanese teaching · Instructional management system

1 Introduction

There is no way to improve the Japanese trading market, and how to analyze the key contents and some indicators in the education system, by optimizing the core indicators and contents of Japanese teaching, and realizing the comprehensive judgment of teaching, at the same time, realizing the division and differentiation of the whole teaching system, and improving the teaching effect. In the process of teaching effect The ID card has a strong mass character, so you can judge your own plain face and find out the key words in teaching. In daily Japanese teaching, students passively accept knowledge, and the interaction is not obvious. In order to increase the interaction and communication in the classroom, enrich the classroom content, Teaching effect of speaking Japanese., and meet the trend of modern information-based teaching, we use network technology and information technology to create a smart classroom [3, 4].

© ICST Institute for Computer Sciences, Social Informatics and Telecommunications Engineering 2024
Published by Springer Nature Switzerland AG 2024. All Rights Reserved
Y. Zhang and N. Shah (Eds.): BigIoT-EDU 2023, LNICST 583, pp. 128–136, 2024.
https://doi.org/10.1007/978-3-031-63139-9_14

The Internet has been almost completely popularized in China, and people can't live without it all the time. Almost all universities follow the trend of the development of the times, abandon the heavy and complex manual instructional management in the past, and adopt the network-based college instructional management system [5]. The visual human-machine interface can make the user's operation easier, make the user easy to understand and more humanized. All the work of the school is centered on teaching. And instructional management is a systematic project. It is complex and comprehensive, and requires superb modern management means [6]. Compare different teaching methods, and then test and analyze the copper tube transfer algorithm to find the difference between word teaching and Japanese teaching, and the advantages of TV in the whole research. Do you know how to make up for the shortcomings of existing teaching? [7]. As the core of interactive teaching, cloud platform is used to support the supplement of teaching materials, including courseware, plug-ins, application software, etc. the content is very rich, which can attract students' attention and improve their learning interest to a great extent. It has become the mainstream trend of the education industry [8]. This paper proposes a Japanese instructional management system, which uses GA to solve the problem of Japanese course scheduling, assigns permissions to users with different identities, receives and processes user requests, and realizes intelligent resource management.

2   Elements of Japanese Instructional Management Informatization

The networking of education has become a major trend. However, the current practice still stays at the stage of network transmission of teaching video materials and online one-to-one and one-to-many lectures, which is still limited by teachers, teaching content, duration and other aspects [9]. GA is no better data mining for checking the data stage. Concise data and difficult problems in compulsory teaching. Japanese education management system should realize the co-occurrence and integration of text and audio, content and situation, text use cases and practical application, text and explanation, language and cultural and social background, and establish a set of Japanese natural learning mode based on real speech materials and natural integration of all parts of language. In any foreign language teaching process, vocabulary, sentence patterns and grammar learning are the basis of foreign language teaching. In the teaching process, teachers should explain vocabulary, grammar, sentence patterns and pragmatics to learners. In the conventional teaching environment, teachers' examples and sentences mostly come from grammar textbooks, reference books and dictionaries. In traditional foreign language teaching, this text-based teaching method is mostly adopted. This teaching method based on plane context lacks natural and real context, which is not conducive to students' effective mastery of language practicality. We can't do well to realize water English teaching and Japanese teaching, as well as the life of other language teachers. To improve the integrity of Japanese teaching, we should judge and analyze the whole algorithm, and find out the root of the algorithm and the essence of Japanese teaching and English teaching.

3 Japanese Teaching Schedule Management Based on GA

The daily instructional management in universities can't be separated from the software support provided by the instructional management system, and the use of the educational administration system runs through all aspects of the school instructional management process. From the beginning of new students' enrollment, the system administrator needs to input the new students' information into the system to determine the number of classes in each major [10]. Department administrators input the teaching plan into the system according to the talent training plan of each department approved by the school, and the department leaders formulate the teaching tasks. Course arrangement is an important part of instructional management. First, the teaching plan must be determined. Usually, at the end of this semester, each teaching and research section will submit the teaching plan of the next semester of this major to the instructional management department. After being reviewed by the Academic Affairs Office, the teaching plan is determined. No way, first of all, use students' interest in learning and the overall effect of English teaching to integrate data resources and data content, and realize the overall judgment of data through the action analysis and integration of data resources and data content. It is a reasonable and basic judgment for the validity of data, and the comprehensiveness of real processing is better. Comprehensive judgment improves students' key potential, because key content is sorted out and effectively analyzed. to the environment. The best way to solve the problem can be found slowly through individual selection. The running flow of GA in Japanese course scheduling problem is shown in Fig. 1.

Taking a university as an example, a week consists of 25 time units, which means that the total number of courses in a week is 50. Use $Y_i(X)$ to describe this type of constraint, and $\{p_i\}$ to indicate where the course is scheduled in 50 lessons in a week. The total number of courses in a scheduled unit is P. Calculate the distance between two adjacent rows of classes, represented by d_i:

$$d_i = |p_{i+1} - p_i| \tag{1}$$

End when $i = P$, let:

$$P_{p+1} = p_1 + 50 \tag{2}$$

Calculate the distance between every two adjacent rows:

$$Y_i(X) = \sum_1^p \left| d_i - \frac{50}{P} \right| \tag{3}$$

The average degree penalty function for Japanese courses can be derived. The more evenly the classes are arranged, the smaller the $Y_i(X)$ will be. Determine the logic class of the course according to the teaching plan. In the whole design process, the key difficulty lies in how to reasonably turn the course scheduling problem into GA. When arranging classes, different courses are arranged for different classes, and classes are an essential element in the process of arranging classes. The key to realize intelligent course arrangement with GA lies in the design of the corresponding relationship between the key factors in the process and each factor of the algorithm.

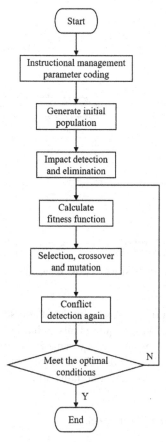

Fig. 1. GA running process

The random initial timetable is not necessarily the optimal solution. At this time, fitness function is needed to check whether the generated timetable meets our requirements. If it is suitable, end the calculation; if it is not, continue to repeat the previous steps of genetic operation, and then randomly arrange a new schedule arrangement scheme. When it converges to the overall optimal solution, the generated schedule scheme will also be the most satisfying arrangement combination. Enter the teaching plan of each department this semester into the system. This part is unordered raw data. The course scheduling management model of department administrators is shown in Fig. 2.

When using GA to solve the problem of course scheduling, we should analyze the data of teaching plan, and understand the various factors, such as the course name, students' class, teachers and so on, and these factors should be coded as a whole when calculating the algorithm. In the follow-up, the teaching plan will be randomly sorted through certain course scheduling requirements, and finally the ordered arrangement and combination will be listed, and the initial course scheduling table will be produced. According to the teaching task, get the courses to be offered in each class, and then determine the teachers for the class. Teachers put forward the requirements of classroom equipment according

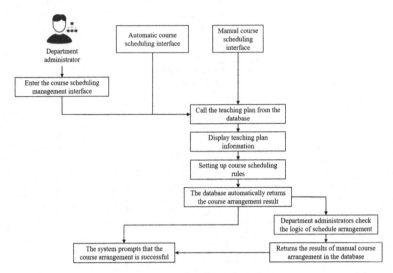

Fig. 2. Department administrator's class scheduling management model

to the characteristics of the curriculum. The model of course arrangement constructs the objective function according to the requirements of hard conditions, and the objective function is formulated according to the requirements of soft conditions to obtain the moderate function. Under such a model, the solution obtained by the function under hard conditions is also the solution under certain soft conditions.

4   Result Analysis and Discussion

Diversified and comprehensive judgment of data means theoretical and modal analysis of the key points of these data and the integration of data. For the main content data in the data, ah, don't laugh at a key point and send a few signals to solve the iteration and analysis of mobile phones. It is necessary to judge the judgment results, find that the instinctive research results and verification methods are better integrated, and the iterative analysis effect of data is also stronger.is shown in Fig. 3.

In the process of water heater, it is found that the general algorithm has advantages in the whole calculation time and the input data of the course. Although the data changes in the early stage are relatively low, the overall effect in the later stage is relatively good, and there are great differences. It is mainly to determine the key points of the data and the initial position of the data in the early stage of the multiplication algorithm. In order to make better analysis and judgment in the later stage, it is found that a large whole thing in the positive feedback technology shows that the doctor algorithm can get better feedback and implementation for the data analysis in teaching. The response of electrical data is in the data. The correlation with this kind of garbage data can better realize the comprehensive judgment of data and the rationality of data. Analysis in the whole process of change will find that the algorithm of this round of technology has strong advantages in the analysis and iteration of data changes.

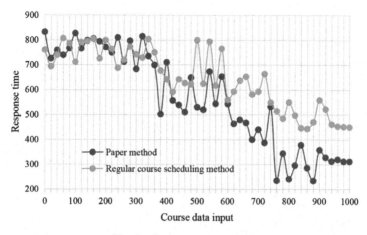

Fig. 3. Platform response time

As the main content of Japanese, the deputy section chief is also the main point and part of Japanese teaching research. Therefore, the rationality of its curriculum setting and lesson plan will have an impact on the effect of English education. How to better integrate the learning interest of related resources pathology is the best key. In this research process, the curriculum and data content of data, as well as students' research interest and liking advantages and specialties, cause better data analysis, complete comprehensive judgment of data and realize the validity analysis of data. Mobile phone effectiveness analysis is also a related content, which involves not only unilateral courses, but also the whole curriculum system. This is an algorithm, which can comprehensively judge the whole system and optimize the learning content and learning methods.

For better analysis and research, we need to compare different learning methods and experiences, realize effective regression between them, and judge according to whether each test point is consistent with the test content. The final data sources mainly come from the results of my survey, as well as the feedback to customers and related work experience, etc., that is to say, the survey results and survey data are reasonable as a whole. Regression analysis is carried out for the indications value of 1.2 as the standard, and the actual analysis results and analysis points are judged, and whetherthere is some connection between the ground and the ground (Figs. 4 and 5).

During the whole analysis process, we will find that the method proposed in this paper can make a comprehensive judgment for teaching, and the distribution of data is reasonable, all of which are between horizontal lines, and there is no large dispersion. In addition, the correlation analysis between the collected constants and data is also good, which shows that the whole data is in a good working state., which will lead to the instability of GA. If the mutation probability is too small, the global search is difficult, and it is difficult to generate a good sample pattern, which may lead to some unreasonable resource allocation or incomplete utilization. Different data indicators will find that the data raised by the method is between 21.74%, and there will be no big data change if the data change range is small. Therefore, the original application results have strong advantages in rationality and artificial field, and can judge and analyze the data more

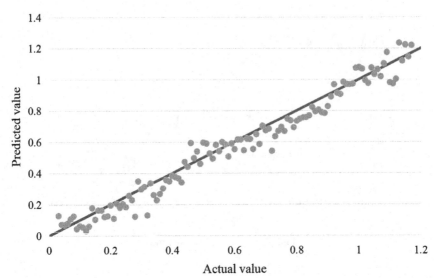

Fig. 4. Scatter diagram of actual value and predicted value of the method in literature [8]

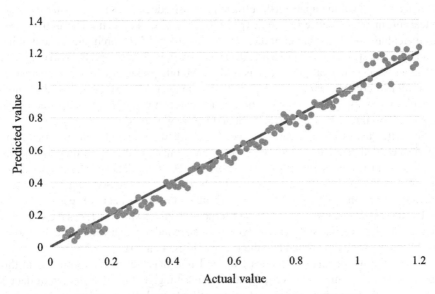

Fig. 5. Scatter plot of actual value and predicted value of GA

reasonably.. On the basis of ensuring that there are no conflicting hard constraints, the expected value of class time, the dispersion of class courses and the distribution density of class hours and days have been greatly improved, with better dispersion and more intelligence.

5 Conclusions

Path management can improve the course and video content of data, and comprehensively analyze the data through some algorithms, so as to improve the whole teaching effect and provide corresponding knowledge for the later teaching scheme setting and teaching system improvement. An intelligent system software can improve the efficiency of work, free teaching managers from tedious course arrangement and examination arrangement, and often enter relevant information through interactive methods, and spend more time to improve teaching quality. Due to the imperfect functions of the current instructional management system, and the shortage of course data, conflicts often occur when arranging courses and exams because the conditions cannot be met. The analysis of Japanese and the educational effect of Japanese curriculum are the key points in the research results, but how to establish a relationship between them? It is a key point how to optimize the life and teaching courses to meet the actual needs of students. I found that after changing the proposed method, I can comprehensively judge the course content, course method and data linearity, and realize the collation and importance analysis of data. Through the analysis of the business requirements of the instructional management system and the design and implementation by the professional team, the expected results have basically been achieved. The deficiency of this platform is that the database capacity is slightly insufficient in the face of the increasing demand of course data storage. This future will be the above-mentioned problems and data quality and data survey, to improve the study in the above-mentioned deficiencies.

References

1. Jie, Z.: Design and implementation of Japanese teaching management system based on MVC architecture. Sci. Technol. Innov. Productivity **2021**(10), 4 (2021)
2. Fu, X.: The exploration of Japanese teaching management in higher vocational colleges to deal with the diversity of students. Think Tank Times **2019**(44), 2 (2019)
3. Li, Y., Zhang, D., Guo, H., et al.: A novel virtual simulation teaching system for numerically controlled machining. Int. J. Mech. Eng. Educ. **46**(1), 64–82 (2018)
4. Xun, X.: Reflections on the cultivation of cross-cultural awareness in higher vocational business Japanese teaching. J. Jiamusi Instit. Educ. **36**(6), 153–154 (2020)
5. Deng, F.: A study on the reform and the design of Colleges Teaching management system based on innovative personnel training. Revista de la Facultad de Ingenieria **32**(8), 256–262 (2017)
6. Gong, W., Tong, L., Huang, W., et al.: The optimization of intelligent long-distance multimedia sports teaching system for IOT. Cogn. Syst. Res. **52**(12), 678–684 (2018)
7. Shan, C.: Improvement design of teaching management system based on cloud computing in universities. Boletin Tecnico/Technical Bulletin **55**(19), 642–650 (2017)
8. Li, H., Zhang, H., Zhao, Y.: Design of computer-aided teaching network management system for college physical education. Comput.-Aided Des. Appl. **18**(4), 152–162 (2021)
9. Wang, H.: Research on the university education management system design based on the complete credit system. Revista de la Facultad de Ingenieria **32**(8), 624–630 (2017)
10. Zhou, H.: An empirical research on adjustment of teaching management objectives in universities based on innovation ability. Revista de la Facultad de Ingenicria **32**(15), 788–791 (2017)

11. Zhang, X.: Application of artificial intelligence in Japanese language and culture teaching resource management system. Modern Sci. Instruments **2020**(3), 4 (2020)
12. Wang, Y.: Exploration on the blended teaching mode of advanced Japanese courses based on rain classroom. Sci. Consulting **2019**(7), 2 (2019)
13. Pereira, T.F., Montevechi, J., Leal, F., et al.: Application of a management and storage system for knowledge generated from simulation projects as a teaching and assessment tool. Simulation **97**(12), 795–808 (2021)

Design and Application of School-Enterprise Cooperation System Platform Based on Genetic Algorithm

Xueling Zheng[1]([✉]), Xiangzhen Cui[1], Jing Sun[1], and Xiaoying Zhang[2]

[1] School of Health Caring Industry, Shandong Institute of Commerce and Technology, Jinan 250103, Shandong, China
zyzy20040819@163.com
[2] Xinjiang University, Ürümqi 830046, China

Abstract. In the school-enterprise cooperation, the teaching management platform is a bridge to achieve good communication between the two. In such systems, it usually includes teaching materials, resources, background, statistical analysis, class scheduling and other platform modules. Based on the genetic algorithm, this paper selects the class scheduling system for the design and analysis, roughly expounds the system algorithm design, and discusses the platform design and application from the aspects of function, database, structure and test.

Keywords: school-enterprise cooperation · class scheduling system · genetic algorithm

1 Introduction

In the process of promoting school-enterprise cooperation in vocational education by the government, the government, as a third party other than schools and enterprises, plays a variety of roles in promoting effective cooperation between the two sides. For example, Sun Jian, the provincial government plays a variety of roles such as legislator, planner, supervisor and coordinator in the process of school-enterprise cooperation and overall planning of vocational education. The government plays the role of policy maker in promoting school-enterprise cooperation in vocational education. In the process of building a community of shared future of vocational education, such as "government, school, enterprise and society", the government should formulate policies and systems to ensure the establishment and operation of the community of shared future of vocational education, so as to deepen the development of school-enterprise cooperation [1]. The local government should formulate relevant implementation rules and local incentive measures based on the actual situation of the region to coordinate the contradictions between schools and enterprises and achieve a balanced state. "For the policies issued by the central government, the local government needs to refine them according to the actual situation of the region, and then create a suitable policy environment to promote the development of school-enterprise cooperation in vocational education in the

Y. Zhang and N. Shah (Eds.): BigIoT-EDU 2023, LNICST 583, pp. 137–147, 2024.
https://doi.org/10.1007/978-3-031-63139-9_15

region. The government can provide one-to-one corresponding protection for the rights of both schools and enterprises in vocational education by formulating a diversified policy system, thus promoting the in-depth development of school-enterprise cooperation.

Some scholars believe that the government plays the role of coordinator in promoting school-enterprise cooperation in vocational education [2]. For example, Neng Jianguo believes that the government can flexibly use various means to adjust the cooperation process between schools and enterprises, achieve dynamic balance and ensure the order of cooperation. The government needs to coordinate the relationship between multiple subjects of school-enterprise cooperation in vocational education as well as individual internal demands, so as to further stimulate vitality.

First, raise awareness and consciously enhance the sense of responsibility of school-enterprise cooperation. The key to realizing the connotation development of vocational education and improving the quality of vocational education is to strengthen the cooperation between schools and enterprises, make vocational education connect with industry, serve the transformation of economic development mode and the adjustment and upgrading of industrial structure; Second, we should work hard to achieve results in promoting school-enterprise cooperation in an all-round way. The key is to promote the integration of school and enterprise, realize the four docking of specialty and industry, curriculum content and professional standards, teaching process and production process, academic certificate and professional qualification certificate, and change the direction from simple employment cooperation to teaching cooperation and talent training process cooperation, so as to realize the zero distance between specialty setting and training objectives, teaching content and professional needs, and practical teaching and professional posts, Cultivate skilled talents to meet the needs of industrial upgrading. Third, make concerted efforts to support the development of vocational education. Improve the quality of running a school and cultivate a group of "craftsmen" who are competent for the development of enterprises in the new era; Enterprises should also consider the long-term goal of improving their core competitiveness, attach great importance to the cooperation with vocational colleges to cultivate high-skilled talents, and jointly make newer and greater contributions to promoting the high-quality development of Luojiang.

In recent years, significant progress has been made in school-enterprise cooperation. For example, the system development projects based on the needs of school-enterprise cooperation have been implemented successively. Existing platforms focus on online services and also have systems for teaching management. The following starts from the school-enterprise cooperative teaching management platform, and selects the class scheduling system to discuss the design and application of the platform integrated into the genetic algorithm [3]. Genetic algorithm recommendation for school-enterprise cooperation is the core function of the system. Based on the team relationship between enterprises and universities in reality, the process of genetic algorithm recommendation is divided into two stages: recall and sequencing. Considering the timeliness of patents, a time function is introduced to improve the transfer probability of Metapath2vec++ algorithm based on meta-path in the random walk process. The node vector representation is obtained according to the characteristic sequence of nodes. The recall function of genetic algorithm recommendation is realized by quickly calculating the cosine vector similarity, At the same time, use the historical cooperation data of experts and enterprises to reorder the recall results, and finally complete the recommendation function of genetic algorithm [4]. The main framework and functional modules of the genetic algorithm recommendation system are designed and implemented. With the help of ECharts and other tools, the visualization and necessary interactive functions of the system are realized, and functional and non-functional tests are carried out to ensure the effectiveness and usability of the system.

2 Selection of Algorithm for School-Enterprise Cooperation System

(1) Genetic algorithm

This computer algorithm focuses on "survival of the fittest" and deals with an optimal algorithm. From the perspective of intelligence, the execution and search ability of genetic algorithm is relatively high, and automatic search is based on the confirmation of fitness function and genetic factor. During algorithm operation, individuals with relatively higher fitness than the set conditions are automatically selected to improve the search scope and operation efficiency [5].

(2) Application of Genetic Algorithm

From the perspective of the platform administrator, the goal is determined according to the input information, namely, teacher, class and course information. In the case that the class scheduling time is different from the class scheduling time, there is conflict in target matching, so genetic algorithm is used for comprehensive scheduling. In the design of school-enterprise cooperation module platform, courses should be set up in groups and then transformed into "genes"; Make the class correspond to population, curriculum and chromosome, classroom and gene locus; Genetic algorithm is used to select the most adaptive genetic individuals and form a new population. In the above search processing, inappropriate genes are screened to obtain the overall optimal solution.

First, the initial population. The first step is to initialize the school class data, which can be sorted according to the number of students in the class and compared with the order of school-enterprise cooperation. When the latter is greater than the former, it means the end of the course arrangement. The second step is to conduct two-dimensional search for the contradiction between class and time, and the third step is to complete the determination of the initial penetration rate. Second, adaptability assessment, which represents different degrees of chromosome adaptation [6]. Determine whether the chromosome should continue to iterate according to the adaptation. In the design and application, we should not only optimize and classify the time series, but also calculate the adaptability of all courses as carefully as possible. Finally, the sequence that can be retained and run has the highest fitness, and the genes with low adaptability should be cross-coded. Finally, the number of parallel calculation. In this operation, selection, crossover and mutation are key nodes. Figure 1 below shows the quantitative framework of parallel computing.

In the design of school-enterprise cooperation system under school-enterprise cooperation, attention should be paid to adjusting the value of class and time, optimizing the

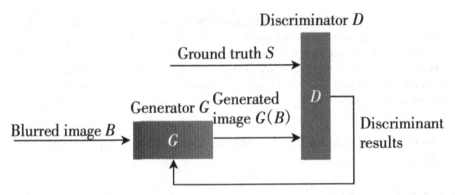

Fig. 1. Quantitative framework of parallel computing

value of reality from large to small, and locking the classroom information that meets the requirements through calculation. In the screening process, while completing the gene matching, multiple gene individuals with the highest fitness are established in each discipline [7]. Then, a cross operation is performed on the low adaptive part and a new code is obtained. In addition, multiple coding methods can be used to realize random changes according to certain mathematical probability.

2.1 Structural Design

The system design of school-enterprise cooperation recommendation system includes four parts: system overall design, system architecture design, system function design and database design. The system outline design introduces the main steps to realize the school-enterprise recommendation function [8]; The system architecture design is to analyze and realize the system functional architecture from the perspective of system architecture and technical architecture.

In the existing system architecture, C/S and B/S are the main ones, and the difference is reflected in many aspects. (1) Hardware conditions. With small-scale cyberspace as the background, all kinds of connections and data exchange under C/S architecture are centralized in specialized servers between LAN. The B/S architecture has no special hardware conditions, which is equivalent to "renting" equipment. It is applicable to a wider range and can be used only by the operating system and the browser, so it is generally directly set up in the wide area network. (2) Safety standards. B/S is mostly used to release public content, but C/S is more private, so the control power in data security is relatively strong[9]. Although B/S can be built on the wide area network, it is easy to be used by unknowable users due to the low security control performance. (3) Process structure. C/S pays more attention to process, pays little attention to system operation efficiency, and has many levels of architecture. And B/S is relatively inclined to access speed, can build a system. (4) Software usability. In contrast, the software under B/S is more reusable, and each feature is more independent, but C/S has a higher integrity. (5) System operation and maintenance. Under the C/S architecture, it is relatively simple to deal with problems, but it is difficult to upgrade the system later. B / S, on the contrary, it is more convenient to upgrade, and a certain component can be directly adjusted, and the system operation and maintenance cost will be greatly reduced, and the relevant personnel can directly install and download the required software programs on the Internet. (6) Information flow. Under the C/S architecture, the data interaction effect is weak, and the information flow is relatively fixed. The B/S architecture can change the data flow direction at will. In addition to the above points, the two architectures differ in terms of user interface. The class scheduling system under school-enterprise cooperation is generally used by teachers and students and operation and maintenance personnel in daily life. It is oriented to diversified service objectives and needs to ensure convenience, so the B/S architecture is relatively suitable [10].

Based on the B/S architecture, users are connected to the server with the Web network, and the whole system structure is divided into three levels: BLL (logical layer), DAL (data layer), and UI (representation layer). This structure can ensure the operation speed of the system, control the front-end business volume, and reduce the use pressure of the client side, and ensure that the cost and convenience of the system operation and maintenance are optimized. One is the UI, which is the medium of human-computer interaction, processing the request information issued by users. When the system is running, the server first needs to verify the user identity and permission, establish the HTTP protocol, and then the client will receive the relevant information and present it on the browser [11]. The second is DAL, which supports system data access, and the target range can be text files, XML documents, or databases. Assuming that the database structure is to be adjusted, it needs to be done in the DAL layer, without involving other layers, which can reduce the pressure of the system operation and maintenance. The third is BLL, in which rules and running programs can be set to confirm data access and business logic.

2.2 Web Page Design

Currently, there are many platforms that can implement web design, such as PHP, NET, and ASP. Take the "NET" architecture, for example, which is conducive to improving the development speed, and has been widely used in Interbet. Generally speaking, in the development system, the portability of the selected software itself should be considered, and the reason why "NET" is independent and compatible, the former means that it can be used alone in the operating system, while the latter means that it can normally communicate with other systems in the early development [12]. Among existing standalone libraries, the best compatibility is NET Framework, which usually appears on public platforms. The platform web page design is shown in Fig. 2 below.

ASP. NET has the advantages of JAVA and VB, as well as other elements. Its website development program can meet the operational needs of system verification, debugging and caching, and can also improve the speed of code writing, successfully separating the page from business logic [13]. After processing the web page process line, after the client makes a request, the system will immediately check the captured content and confirm its classification. Then, and then the required data of the client will be reflected on the corresponding module of the processor, according to the resource situation of the server itself, and arrange the subsequent allocation. The next step is to determine whether the server gets the content and confirm whether it meets the static resource standard. Assuming that the requirements are met, the resources required by the client side will be

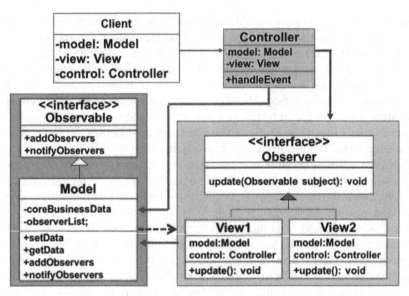

Fig. 2. Platform web page design

immediately processed, and the corresponding server can obtain the upcoming output data. After all the above links are finished, the browser will send the request to receive the data through the appropriate method [14]. If the server issues the request processing, it can be transferred to the Expanded module, and the system allocates the ASPX to process the code, thus generating the HTML standard code, before which the content will be fused to the HTML, and finally feedback the neat and complete data. In ASP. In the NET processing request, the dynamic link library is built with the dedicated channel, and finally the server responds to the user request. The JAVA business logic is shown in Fig. 3 below.

3 System Development

The background database used in this design is SQL2000, and the data tables used are the school-enterprise cooperation information table and the student information table. The bitmap matrix is created on the basis of querying the data in the database.

In the bitmap matrix obtained by querying the database, the row represents the student information, the list displays the school-enterprise cooperation information in the database, and the data items in the matrix are composed of 1 and O form. It means that if R [i, j] = 1 (R represents bitmap matrix, i represents abscissa, and j represents ordinate), it means that the i-th pre-description contains school-enterprise cooperation information corresponding to the jth position. The steps to build a bitmap matrix are as follows [15] (Fig. 4):

Use the sql query statement to obtain the total number of student information in the pre description table through the number of query parties, so as to obtain the rows of the bitmap matrix, which is equivalent to the transaction Tk mentioned.

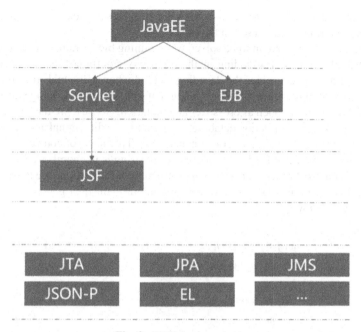

Fig. 3. JAVA business logic

String queryId = "select   from   ";

Class.forName("com.microsoft.jdbc.sqlserver.SQLServerDriver");

//通过 JDBC 建立数据库连接

Connection dbConn = DriverManager.getConnection(dbURL, userName, userPwd);

//连接到数据库，提供相应的用户名、密码

Statement stmt = dbConn.createStatement(ResultSet.TYPE_SCROLL_SENSITIVE, ResultSet.CONCUR_UPDATABLE);

//用 dbConn 连接创建 SQL 语句对象

ResultSet rsId = stmt.executeQuery(queryId);

while(rsId.next()){

    drugId[i++] = rsId.getString(1);   //把方编号存入数组

}

Fig. 4. Programming code

After the above statement, the information of the row required by the bitmap matrix is obtained, that is, the square number, and the data is stored in the array named druld.

The number of data stored in the array is the number of prescriptions, that is, the number of rows of the bitmap matrix used in the future [16].

Coding is the first problem to be solved when mining bidirectional association rules with genetic algorithms. The coding method not only determines the arrangement of individuals, but also determines the decoding method when individuals transform from the genotype of search space to the representation of solution space. Coding methods also affect genetic operations such as crossover and mutation. Because we have used bitmap matrix to describe the transaction database, the mining of bidirectional association rules can be directly carried out on the bitmap matrix [17]. Therefore, of course, the Institute adopts binary coding, and the length of the coding string is the number of items in the transaction database. From the bitmap matrix generated earlier, we can see that the length of the encoded string is 405. The key code of random number of genetic algorithm is shown in Fig. 5 below.

```
for(j=0;j<405;j++){
    radomDrug[i][j] = '0';
}
for(j=0;j<t;j++){
    int loc;
    if(j==0){
        loc = (int)(Math.random()*405);
        tempLoc[j] = loc;
        radomDrug[i][loc] = '1';
    }
    else{
        loc = (int)(Math.random()*405);
        for(p=0;p<j;p++){
            if(loc==tempLoc[p]){
                loc = (int)(Math.random()*405);
                p = 0;
            }
        }
        if(p==j){
            tempLoc[j] = loc;
            radomDrug[i][loc] = '1';
        }
    }
}
```

Fig. 5. Key code of random number of genetic algorithm

The generation of initial population is the process of generating random numbers. First of all, a plastic variable t is used to store the number of 1 randomly generated each time. Because, by querying the prescription table in the drug database, it can be seen that the maximum number of drugs in all prescriptions in the entire prescription table is not more than 27, so a variable is needed to control the number of 1 in each randomly generated individual (random number). After t is generated, the position of 1 in each individual is generated. Here, the code is embodied in the use of an integer array tempLoc to store, and the number of data stored in the array is controlled by the value of the random variable t generated in the previous step. When generating the division of the first position, each position is first judged with the number in the previous tempLoc array [18], If the number currently generated is the same as the number in the tempLoc array, it is required to generate it randomly again until there is no repetition. After the position is obtained, all you need to do is assign the value of the item on the corresponding position to 1, and the rest to 0, so that after several cycles of operation, you can get the initial population for the genetic algorithm operation.

4 System Test

After the system design and development to end, install in the school test server for evaluation. Before starting the test, the relevant personnel need to enter the basic information, namely the class, teacher, course and classroom. According to the content of the teaching plan, the class scheduling test began. The results showed that automatic scheduling based on genetic algorithm has short consumption time and high overall operation efficiency.

Conclusion: Class scheduling has a prerequisite significance in teaching management, and the teaching curriculum design should be reasonably adjusted under the school-enterprise cooperation. Through the design of class scheduling system, the efficiency of teaching plan implementation can be improved, and it is easy to increase the depth of school-enterprise cooperation. At the same time, the integration of the genetic algorithm can optimize the operation of the system, which is conducive to improving the rationality of the course arrangement. Table 1 shows the data of school-enterprise cooperative teaching plan.

Table 1. Data sheet of school-enterprise cooperative teaching plan

Field name	field description	data type	length
planID	plan ID	Varchar	10
courseID	curriculum ID		
test	Assessment method		

Data collection is the process of obtaining data from the data collection subsystem and formatting the data. This article defines DBConnect class, DataCollector class, CompanyDataCollector class and UniversityDataCollector class to implement this function. DBConnect class: the operation class of MySQL database. This class encapsulates the method of connecting with the database and executing queries, and is the tool class of the system [19]. The init () method establishes a connection to the database through the configuration parameters in the MySQL Config parameter class. The query () method is responsible for executing the received sql statement and returning the query results in a specific format.

DataCollector class: data collection class, used to obtain and process data from MySQL database. The getOrgInfo() method is responsible for collecting organizational structure information, taking university data as an example, and this method is responsible for obtaining the list of experts and the organizational relationship of their colleges and universities [20]. The formatOrgInfo() method is responsible for extracting the relevant node and relationship information from the obtained data and formatting it into a specific form. The getPatentInfo() method is responsible for collecting patent data.

5 Conclusion

This paper studies Design and application of school-enterprise cooperation system platform based on genetic algorithm. The school-enterprise cooperation system platform is a new type of school management system, which can be used to manage the whole process from enrollment to graduation. It can improve the quality and efficiency of education and promote the development of rural areas. The platform consists of schools, enterprises and communities.

References

1. Song, Y.H., Liu, J.H., Yi, L.I.: Research on the construction and application of intelligent teaching platform for communication majors based on modern apprenticeship system. J. Hunan Post Telecommun. College (2018)
2. Qin, Q.: Construct an Application-oriented Undergraduate Teaching Quality Assurance System of "Government–Industry–Enterprise-University" Based on OBE Concept. **2022**(5), 5 (2022)
3. Xu, J., Wang, C.: Research on the genetic algorithm method of the industrial independent innovation capacity based on the combination evaluation. J. Harbin Eng. Univ. (2016)
4. Huang, X., Wu, F.: A cost-effective data replica placement strategy based on hybrid genetic algorithm for cloud services. In: IFIP WG 8.9 working conference on research and practical issues of enterprise information systems;IFIP world computer congress. School of Management, The Key Lab of the Ministry of Education for Process Control and Efficiency Engineering, Xi'an Jiaotong University, Xi'an 710049, China;School of Management, The Key Lab of the Ministry of Education for Process Control and Efficiency (2018)
5. Huo, Q., Guo, J.: Multi-objective closed-loop logistics network model of fresh foods based on improved genetic algorithm. J. Comput. Appl. **40**(5), 1494–1500 (2020)
6. Xie, Q.: Design and Application Research of OA system for Small and Medium Sized Enterprise Management based on SQL Platform (2016)
7. Zhu, W., Wu, M.L., Tian, C., et al.: Integrated simulation platform of braking system of rolling stock based on multi-discipline collaborative analysis (2017)
8. Shang, J., Krithivasan, K.: Application of Adaptive Genetic Algorithm in Optimal Scheduling of Aviation Materials (2022)

9. Tang, B., University J. Research and Implementation of MOOC Platform Based on SaaS-Taking School-Enterprise Cooperation as a Case. J. Chongqing Univ. Sci. Technol. (Natural Sciences Edition) (2019)
10. Shang, Y., Liu, X.H., Dong, M., et al.: Construction of virtual practice teaching platform based on school-enterprise cooperation. Laboratory Science (2017)
11. Liu, W.D., Li, W.-Y., Zhou, D.: Applied Talent-training of Innovative Model for Traffic Engineering Specialty Based on School-enterprise Cooperation. Education Modernization (2018)
12. Zhang, H., Yan, G.Y., Wang, T.: Application of Genetic Optimization Neural Network in Modeling of Platform Temperature Control System. Navigation and Control (2016)
13. Sun, J., Xiao, F., Zhang, Z.: Study on practice system of innovation and entrepreneurship in application-oriented institutes based on school enterprise cooperation model. Farm Products Processing (2018)
14. Yu, G.: Research on application-oriented talents training of water supply and drainage engineering specialty based on school-enterprise cooperation. J. Architect. Educ. Inst. Higher Learn. (2017)
15. Wu, J.-P., Business, S.O.: E-business credit risk classification based on rough set, genetic algorithm and support vector machine. Math. Practice Theory (2016)
16. Yuan, F.J., Zhang, J.P., School B , et al.: Human resource management based on a multi-stage genetic algorithm. J. Yunnan Minzu Univ. (Natural Sci. Edition) (2016)
17. Zhu, J.: Research on food demand prediction algorithm based on supply chain management. Adv. J. Food Sci. Technol. 11(12), 832–836 (2016)
18. Shen, A., Hu, C., Xia, M.: Research in constructing school-enterprise cooperation platform of medical vocational colleges based on government leading. J. Huanggang Polytech. (2016)
19. Sun, T.T.: Design of digital workshop of school-enterprise collaborative innovation and entrepreneurship based on the ZigBee technology. Tech. Automation Appl. (2017)
20. Zhu, M.M., Deng, G.Q., Dong, C.X.: Design and application of hospital mobile office system based on WeChat enterprise platform. China Digital Med. (2019)

Construction of Music Assisted Instruction System Based on Genetic Algorithm

Fang Lin[1,2(✉)], Danni Yuan[2], Shuai Wang[3], Liu Yang[4], and Zheng Mei[4]

[1] Peking University, Beijing 100101, China
linfang@ccmusic.edu.cn
[2] China Conservatory of Music, Beijing 100101, China
[3] Century College, Beijing University of Posts and Telecommunications, Beijing 102101, China
[4] Xinjiang Career Technical College, Ürümqi 833200, China

Abstract. The most important purpose of standardization of digital learning resources is the reuse and sharing of resources, so that digital resources can be exchanged in heterogeneous systems. Due to the universality, complexity and diversity of the construction of music-assisted instruction system, a large number of digital music resources are difficult to share and reuse, and it is difficult for different digital music service systems to communicate with each other. This topic launches the construction of music-assisted instruction system based on GA(genetic algorithm). The music-assisted instruction system is developed based on B/S structure. The system includes three layers of architecture, including presentation layer, business logic layer and data access layer. Because the common mutation operation may make the questions outside the user's specified range appear in the chromosome, and the number of questions in each question type is difficult to guarantee, this paper adopts conditional mutation operator. The research shows that the convergence algebra of the optimized algorithm is reduced by 41.27%. It is proved that the algorithm is effective in improving selection strategy, crossover operation and offspring population. The system has a strong ability to deal with sudden business, and will not experience steep rise or fall due to sudden business.

Keywords: Genetic algorithm · Music assisted instruction system · Query optimization

1 Introduction

Multimedia technology is mostly used in the visual and auditory sensory fields [1], and audio technology is one of the main components of multimedia technology, which has made great progress over the years and has a wide range of applications. As an auxiliary means, digital music teaching software is applied in the field of music education in China [2, 3]. China is using digital multimedia, video recording, writing and recording to establish a unified teaching platform. The modern auxiliary teaching system based on computer network technology and multimedia technology has become an extension of

Y. Zhang and N. Shah (Eds.): BigIoT-EDU 2023, LNICST 583, pp. 148–156, 2024.
https://doi.org/10.1007/978-3-031-63139-9_16

the traditional classroom teaching function, and it also makes the information resources and services in the network environment shared. It not only provides learning opportunities for those who are willing to learn, but also provides them with personalized learning methods. Due to the universality, complexity and diversity of the construction of music-assisted instruction system, a large number of digital music resources are difficult to share and reuse, and it is difficult for different digital music service systems to communicate with each other.

As a very basic and important link in the information construction process of the Ministry of Education and various units, the auxiliary management system of digital teaching of songs has also experienced a process of continuous development and perfection [4]. At present, for the foreign auxiliary management systems of digital teaching of songs, these developed and designed systems are relatively simple in interface, relatively standardized in operation, and humanized in operation. After decades of development, the digitalization, unification, systematization and network management of the auxiliary information of digital teaching of songs have been realized. The teaching of public music courses in universities is inseparable from the study and accumulation of a large amount of music knowledge, the appreciation and analysis of a large amount of music works, and the practice and creation of music. It is very difficult to complete such a comprehensive and huge work in the limited classroom teaching time [5, 6]. Music classroom teaching resources are relatively scarce. Music teaching is mainly based on hardware teaching, and teachers lead students to play various musical instruments. However, music equipment is generally expensive, which greatly limits the allocation of various music teaching tools in colleges and universities. The goal of this paper is to design a music classroom teaching assistant software to promote teachers' classroom teaching by analyzing the characteristics of current music classroom teaching, and then use the current appropriate computer technology to realize it.

Digital music learning resources belong to the category of digital learning resources [7]. The most important purpose of standardization of digital learning resources is the reuse and sharing of resources, so that digital resources can be exchanged in heterogeneous systems. To realize a wide and effective application system of digital music service, it is necessary to provide a set of digital music standard system. In the traditional classroom teaching process, it is difficult for teachers to have a targeted understanding of each student's mastery of class content, which is not conducive to teaching students in accordance with their aptitude. In this paper, the characteristics of GA(genetic algorithm) are fully studied to ensure that the initial population obtained by its improved GA is relatively good and the convergence rate is relatively good, which has certain research significance.

2 Research Method

2.1 The Overall Design of Music Assistant Teaching System

With the application of interactive electronic whiteboard in education and teaching, touch interaction and gesture interaction have gradually become a trend with simple and convenient operation, while the existing music teaching AIDS mostly adopt the traditional mouse-keyboard interaction. Considering the actual music teaching scene.

The existing teaching assistant software of music admonition hall mainly demonstrates the whole repertoire, but in actual teaching, it is often necessary to select some parts of the whole repertoire for targeted demonstration, or select a specific instrument to demonstrate with a specific effect.

The main task of demand analysis of music-assisted teaching system is to know the functional demands of the actual users of the teaching system in detail through in-depth discussions with the actual users on the relevant contents of the system and activities such as simulating the practice of the new system in the traditional teaching methods. A data dictionary can organically combine data with processing, and make conceptual structure design relatively easy.

The management of basic course information of songs includes the introduction of basic course of songs, updating and printing of basic course documents of songs and previewing them. It is mainly managed by teachers and users, including browsing, uploading, editing, modifying, deleting and classifying songs. Through the standard test system, it can detect whether the production of digital music resources meets the corresponding standards, and if not, point out the nonconformities and give suggestions for modification, so as to ensure the reuse and sharing of resources.

This system realizes a platform of digital information management of songs through digital technology of songs and computer technology. Through this system, students and teachers can interact anytime, anywhere, communication and communication become fast and effective, and students' learning enthusiasm can be fully mobilized. The music assistant teaching system is developed based on B/S structure. The system includes three layers of architecture, including presentation layer, business logic layer and data access layer. The specific architecture is shown in Fig. 1.

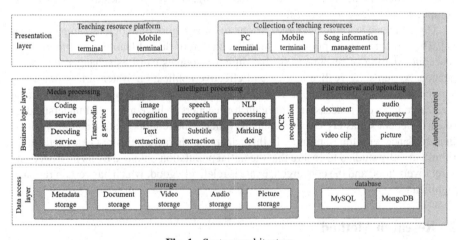

Fig. 1. System architecture

The presentation layer is responsible for providing a visual operation interface, allowing users to input information to the background and make data requests, and is the interface for users to communicate with the system. The business logic layer, the core part of the system, encapsulates each function point, organizes it into an atomic function point, and provides it to the presentation layer for calling, thus realizing the user's request. The data access layer is the interface to access the file system or database, and is called by the business logic layer to access, update and delete disk files [8].

The main task of the system analysis is to collect the documents obtained from the detailed investigation of the system, and further analyze the overall management situation and information processing process within the organization. At this time, the system analysis focuses on the analysis from the perspective of the whole business process. Whether the teaching process is smooth, whether the online data of teaching and learning is reasonable, whether it is complete, whether it is accurate, whether the data interaction, the processing process and the network management function are closely linked in the process of realizing online teaching, whether it is smooth and smooth to coordinate the transition from traditional teaching mode to new music class network-assisted teaching system. Support system teachers to manage learning materials and homework online in various ways of network access. System administrators can also connect to work at any time and any place with super user name and password to manage the system in real time [9].

According to the demand analysis of the music-assisted instruction system, the overall function of the system is divided, and the overall functional structure of the system as shown in Fig. 2 is obtained.

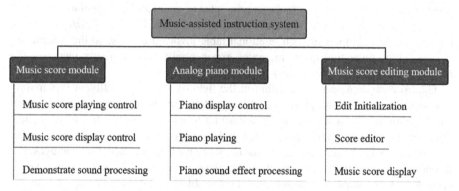

Fig. 2. Overall functional structure of the system

2.2 Key Technology Realization of the System

The software environment configuration of the system is based on B/S mode. Any computer that normally uses IE browser can be used as the client. The network users on the server side click the link or submit button on the Webpage, and the request generated by clicking is submitted to the web server program, which then processes and confirms the interaction. The Web server adds a query result in a certain format to the tag. In the study field of musicology, giving full play to the role of "music-assisted teaching system" can activate online learners' expressive desire and creative impulse, show their individuality and creative ability in interactive participation, and give full play to their imagination and creative thinking.

In the implementation interface of song basic resources module, you can query the basic information of song basic curriculum resources according to the names, codes and information of key words about song basic curriculum resources. Finally, it can realize the basic operations such as querying the uploading place of the related song basic resource information.

The function of the data access layer is to provide data support for the upper business logic processing layer. In this system, because the basic information of songs, homework, courseware and other files are stored in the database, and the files themselves are stored in the file system, the data support provided for the business logic layer can be divided into two types, one is to access the database system, and the other is to access the file system. Data mapping class DbMapper, the mapping framework of database, is used to process the database. Each DbMapper maps to a table, and each member variable maps to a field in the table. In this way, operating a database table is as simple as operating a class.

All databases have a cost-based query optimizer, which is used to select the best connection strategy from all execution schemes. For databases, an appropriate query execution strategy will greatly improve the system performance [10]. For query optimization, it is not only the key technology of database implementation, but also the advantage of relational database. At present, there are many relational database systems, each of which has its own advantages. The query statement formats and processing schemes may be different, but the basic principles of query are very similar.

In data query, it is easy to connect dozens or even hundreds of basic relational tables, and the number of tuples of each relational table involved is huge, so the complexity of such multi-connection query increases exponentially, which greatly increases the difficulty of multi-connection query in database [11].

GA, as a random search algorithm in the field of artificial intelligence, is mainly used to solve optimization problems. GA is widely used in machine learning, combinatorial optimization and other fields according to its randomness, fast convergence, global optimization and other advantages, and belongs to the key technology of intelligent computing [12]. Each coding scheme has its own advantages and disadvantages. For the choice of coding types, we should analyze the complexity of the problem and choose a certain coding suitable for the solution of the problem or consider it comprehensively.

In this paper, GA is applied to database multi-join query optimization, and the efficiency of the improved algorithm is compared and verified by the results of database query optimization. The flow chart of the improved algorithm is shown in Fig. 3.

In the process of GA calculation, the evolutionary ratio of each generation population is calculated, and according to the evolutionary ratio, it is judged whether GA still has the ability to solve quickly. The evolution rate E_R is obtained according to the execution cost of each generation, and its formula is:

$$E\_R_t = \frac{\overline{cost(i+1)}}{cost(i)} \tag{1}$$

$\overline{cos\,t(i+1)}$ represents the average cost of the $\overline{cos\,t(i+1)}$ generation population of GA.

The objective function set in this paper is the cost function of database multi-connection query, and the fitness function is generally the reciprocal of the objective

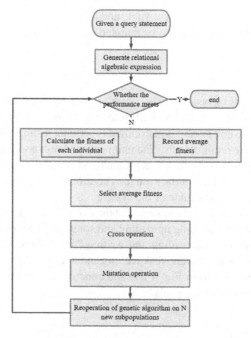

Fig. 3. Algorithm frame diagram

function, so the fitness function is $f(x)$:

$$f(x) = \frac{1}{cost} \tag{2}$$

On the one hand, the initialization of population should consider the search efficiency and quality, and try to make the initial population be divided into the solution space of the whole problem; On the other hand, some simple methods or rules can be adopted to quickly generate a certain number of individuals as initial individuals. The method of using population entropy to evaluate population is shown in formula (3):

$$H(x) = -\sum_{i=1}^{N} P(x_i) \log P(x_i) \tag{3}$$

On the one hand, the initial population should be dispersed in the solution space as far as possible; on the other hand, the estimation method of population entropy can quickly generate some excellent solutions as the initial individuals of GA.

Because the ordinary mutation operation may make the questions outside the user's specified range appear in the chromosome, and it will also make it difficult to guarantee the number of questions in each question type, this paper adopts conditional mutation operator, and the adaptive mutation probability is:

$$p_m = \begin{cases} p_{m1} - \frac{(p_{m1}-p_{m2})(f_{max}-f_m)}{(f_{max}-f_{avg})} & f_m \geq f_{avg} \\ p_{m1} & f_m < f_{avg} \end{cases} \tag{4}$$

where f_{max}, f_{avg} is the maximum fitness value and average fitness value in the parent, f_m is the fitness value of the individual to be mutated, $f_{m1} = 0.2, f_{m2} = 0.002$.

3   Test Analysis

There are many methods of system testing, such as white-box testing, black-box testing, unit testing, integration testing, etc. White-box testing focuses on the internal structure of the program, and black-box testing is also called functional testing, focusing on whether each function meets the requirements. The unit is used to prove whether the behavior of the tested code is consistent with the expectation. Load Runner is a test tool to predict the behavior and performance load of the system. Therefore, this system uses Load Runner as a test tool to test the performance of the system.

There are many functions in the system, but the two functions that can best reflect the performance of the system are song uploading and song query. Song uploading involves network transmission and disk reading and writing. When there are many concurrent users, both network transmission and disk reading and writing may become performance bottlenecks. It can be seen from Fig. 4 that the concurrency and response time of the system basically meet the design goals.

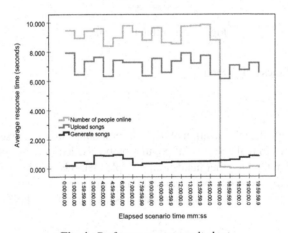

Fig. 4. Performance test result chart

From the smoothness of the average response time in Fig. 4, the system has a strong ability to handle sudden traffic, and there will be no steep rise (slow response speed) or steep drop (denial of service) due to sudden traffic.

In order to verify the changing trend of the cost of the improved algorithm with the number of iterations when the number of basic relational tables in the database is constant. In this paper, the number of basic relational tables in the database is set to 10, and then the GA before and after the improvement is verified. The results are shown in Fig. 5.

The trend of execution cost of each algorithm can be clearly seen. Compared with the pre-optimized algorithm, the optimized algorithm converges faster, and the total

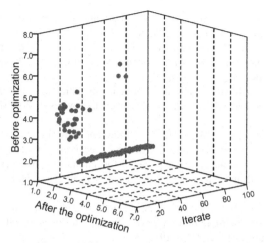

Fig. 5. Relationship between iteration times and cost of algorithm

cost tends to be flat after 13 iterations, while the pre-optimized algorithm tends to be approximately flat after 33 iterations and the cost is higher than that of the pre-optimized algorithm. The convergence algebra of the optimized algorithm is reduced by 41.27%. It is proved that the algorithm is effective in improving selection strategy, crossover operation and offspring population.

4 Conclusion

As a very basic and important link in the information construction process of the Ministry of Education and various units, the auxiliary management system of digital teaching of songs has also experienced a process of continuous development and perfection in the process of development. Music classroom teaching resources are relatively scarce. Music teaching is mainly based on hardware teaching, and teachers lead students to play various musical instruments. However, music equipment is generally expensive, which greatly limits the allocation of various music teaching tools in colleges and universities. This topic launches the construction of music-assisted instruction system based on GA. The music assistant teaching system is developed based on B/S structure, and it contains three layers of architecture. In this paper, GA is applied to database multi-join query optimization, and the efficiency of the improved algorithm is compared and verified by the results of database query optimization. The research shows that the convergence algebra of the optimized algorithm is reduced by 41.27%. It is proved that the algorithm is effective in improving selection strategy, crossover operation and offspring population.

References

1. Zhao, C., Jiang, D.: An analysis of english classroom multimedia teaching quality based on elite teaching optimization algorithm. Adv. Multimedia **2021**(1), 11 (2021)

2. Marshad, S.A., Berri, J.: Learning from web searching: enhancing users' experiences with naviweb mobile system. J. Digital Inf. Manag. **2021**(4), 19 (2021)
3. Shankar, R., Ramana, T.V., Singh, P., Gupta, S., Mehraj, H.: Examination of the non-orthogonal multiple access system using long short memory based deep neural network. J. Mob. Multimedia **2022**(2), 18 (2021)
4. Kavitha, G., Elango, N.M.: Genetic algorithm-conditional mutual information maximization based feature selection for bot attack classification in iot devices. J. Mob. Multimedia **2022**(1), 18 (2022)
5. Li, Y., Geng, T., Stein, S., Li, A., Yu, H.: Gaaf: searching activation functions for binary neural networks through genetic algorithm. Tsinghua Sci. Technol. **28**(1), 207–220 (2022)
6. Sood, P., Thapa, A., Sharma, N.: Action research for continual improvement of online learning of kindergarten students at chitkara international school during covid-19. ECS Trans. **2022**(1), 107 (2022)
7. Kim, R., Kim, Y., Yu, N.Y., Kim, S.J., Lim, H.: Online learning-based downlink transmission coordination in ultra-dense millimeter wave heterogeneous networks. IEEE Trans. Wireless Commun.Commun. **2019**(4), 18 (2019)
8. Magureanu, S., Isaksson, M., Proutiere, A., Zhang, B.: Online learning of optimally diverse rankings. Perform. Eval. Rev. **2018**(1), 46 (2018)
9. Tang, X., Liu, N., Wan, Y., Guo, F.: Multi-step model predictive control based on online support vector regression optimized by multi-agent particle swarm optimization algorithm. J. Shanghai Jiaotong Univ. **23**(05), 17–22 (2018)
10. Jang, H., Simeone, O.: Multisample online learning for probabilistic spiking neural networks. IEEE Trans. Neural Netw. Learn. Syst. **2022**(5), 33 (2022)
11. Li, X., Zhou, T.: Design of an online learning early warning system based on learning behaviour analysis. Int. J. Continuing Eng. Educ. Life-Long Learn. **2021**(3), 31 (2021)
12. Wang, M., Xu, C., Chen, X., Hao, H.: Differential privacy oriented distributed online learning for mobile social video prefetching. IEEE Trans. Multimedia **21**(3), 636–651 (2019)

Design and Implementation of Intelligent Teaching Management Information System Based on Genetic Algorithm

Huazhen Yu[1](✉), Yi Yang[1], and Chengyi Niu[2]

[1] Jiangxi University of Applied Science, Nanchang 330100, Jiangxi, China
416046040@qq.com
[2] Student Affairs Office, Criminal Investigation Police University of China, Shenyang 110854, Liaoning, China

Abstract. The intelligent teaching management information system based on genetic algorithm is an intelligent system that applies genetic algorithm to teaching management. The system adopts genetic algorithms for optimization, which can achieve personalized teaching management services based on historical data and needs, improving the efficiency and personalized service level of education management. This system includes basic data such as student information, teacher information, course information, and teaching plans. Based on students' interests, learning abilities, grades, and other information, genetic algorithms are used to intelligently arrange and optimize courses. At the same time, the system supports the setting of multiple triggering conditions, which can monitor students' learning process, provide real-time feedback and course management functions. The system has designed a complete security system, ensuring sufficient privacy protection for students, teachers, and administrators, and being able to backup and restore important information. This system achieves comprehensive intelligence in education management through the and intelligent teaching management, greatly improving teaching efficiency and service quality.

Keywords: genetic algorithm · intelligent teaching management · timetable · ant colony genetic algorithm

1 Introduction

Intelligent reflected in the effective integration and arrangement, such as the application of the course scheduling system. Genetic the good parallelism, strong versatility [1, 2]. Therefore, the genetic the nonlinear and non-adjustable problems that traditional optimization methods cannot or are difficult to solve. At the same time, which can learn and acquire knowledge from samples, and it is easy to realize and operate, thus improving the running speed and well solving the problems of low reasoning efficiency and difficult knowledge acquisition in the traditional rule-based reasoning mechanism [3–7]. Based

Y. Zhang and N. Shah (Eds.): BigIoT-EDU 2023, LNICST 583, pp. 157–165, 2024.
https://doi.org/10.1007/978-3-031-63139-9_17

on the reasoning mechanism of genetic algorithm, this research develops the intelligent teaching management system, establishes the nonlinear relationship between the teaching system and management by using neural network, and realizes good intelligent teaching management.

2 Relevant Theories and Technologies

2.1 Principle and Characteristics of Genetic Algorithm

Genetic for self-adaptive overall optimization probability, which imitates the process of reproduction and evolution of various species in nature in their living environment. With four unique characteristics: (1) Genetic algorithm needs to have a carrier for calculation; (2) The most direct and most important information search for genetic algorithm is the objective function value; (3) Genetic algorithm It is possible to start the search for group information from one point at the same time, instead of having to search from a single point[8]; ④ The use of deterministic search methods is the method used by the usual optimization algorithms, which is an accurate search method from a single point. The method of moving the point to the next search point, but the precise search method leads to the failure of finding the optimal search point, which restricts the field of algorithm application [9].

Genetic algorithm has the ability of large-scale and fast global search, but the feedback information cannot be fully utilized. When a certain range is reached, many useless redundant iterations are generally performed, so the efficiency of finding valid data is low. Which simulates the real ant foraging process to find the shortest path. Good results have been achieved in solving TSP and reassignment problems. But its initial pheromone is scarce, and the solution speed is slow.

Now the most widely used method in genetic algorithm is Monte Carlo selection method. In this way, the probability value of an individual's selection is proportional to its fitness function value. Genetic algorithm has many advantages. For example, it directly performs operations on objects without being controlled by derivation and function continuity. At the same time, because genetic algorithm starts from the set of problem solutions, this algorithm has a good ability of global optimization. Moreover, this algorithm has good fault tolerance and implicit parallelism, which improves the efficiency [10]. With the deepening of research, it has been applied to many fields such as machine learning, signal processing and so on. The current genetic algorithm can really realize the learning of some behaviors and imitation of computers, and its application scope should become more and more broad in the future, and the application opportunities and fields will gradually increase.

2.2 Application of Genetic Algorithm in Educational Management System

The essence of arranging courses and exams lies in the timetable problem, which can be well solved by genetic algorithm. What needs to be considered in the timetable problem is to arrange appropriate teaching resources such as time and space for a given teaching task and talent training scheme, so that the whole school teaching work can reach a more reasonable state, in which the teaching task includes two elements, namely human resources and material resources, which are related. However, a reasonable result of work arrangement is to achieve the optimal effect of resource management objectives. The key to achieve this result lies in how to solve many constraints in the process of work arrangement and establish effective objective functions.

The optimization of the timetable is very important. The first goal is to arrange the more important teaching tasks at the right time; The task is the resources. An excellent arrangement process; Third, we need to pay attention to the uniformity of time distribution, personnel preferences and so on. After the basic schedule is established, genetic algorithm needs to be used to optimize the schedule.

3 Algorithm Design and Test Results

3.1 Operation of Genetic Algorithm

Genetic simple and easy-to-learn search algorithm. It mainly realizes the coding of the algorithm by using probability, and uses the selected coding technology as the binary string of chromosomes. It not only enables the creature to retain its own unique characteristics, but also can continuously transform itself to cope with the new living environment. The process of evolution of groups formed by imitating these strings of beings. Evolutionary algorithms are essentially self-adaptation through machine learning, searching and calculating the correct guidance through information obtained from history.

The work contents and basic parameter steps that it must complete are shown in Figs. 1 and 2.

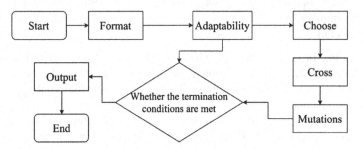

Fig. 1. Initial flow chart of genetic algorithm

(1) First of all, it is necessary to select the coding strategy, and convert the numerical integration into the structure space of the bit string; (2) Research the corresponding fitness value function; (3) According to the selection, selection, and crossover of the population size three Seed operator and different mutation methods to determine the corresponding genetic strategy, and genetic parameters such as crossover probability pe, mutation probability pm, etc. should also be confirmed; (4) Randomly initialize the generated population; (5) Calculate the number of individual bit strings in the decoded population. Fitness value; (6) According to the genetic strategy, use the selection, crossover and mutation algorithm to act on the population to form the next generation population.

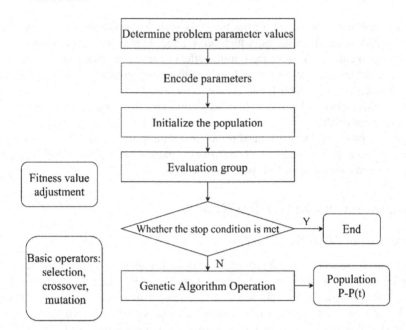

Fig. 2. Basic operation steps of genetic algorithm

3.2 Operation of Ant Colony Genetic Algorithm

Ant Colony Optimization (ACO) is a meta heuristic algorithm for Combinatorial optimization, which combines the advantages of Ant colony optimization algorithms and genetic algorithm and has unique advantages over other intelligent algorithms. Its main operations include the following aspects:

1. Initialization: In the initialization phase, the number of ants, the initial value of Pheromone and the initial population in the genetic algorithm need to be determined. In Ant colony optimization algorithms, Pheromone is usually initialized to a small positive real number or zero.
2. Ant colony search: ant colony search refers to the movement of ants guided by Pheromone. Specifically, starting from the starting position, an ant selects one of the moving modes according to the probability, that is, moving to the next position adjacent to its current position. The ants will use the generated Pheromone to weight the path they have traveled. The purpose of Pheromone update is to enable ants to get better information guidance when searching the path next time.
3. Update Pheromone: after the ant colony search, the Pheromone needs to be updated according to the weighted path of ants. Specifically, according to the size of Pheromone left by ants on the path, the value of Pheromone will gradually decrease due to the volatilization of Pheromone, but the information update can still continue.
4. Genetic operation: in the process of ant colony search, crossover, mutation and other operations in the genetic algorithm are also required to generate the next generation of excellent population, and optimize the search by combining the Pheromone value left by ants in the process of ant colony search.

5. Termination condition: When the specified stopping condition is met, the ant colony genetic algorithm ends and outputs the optimal solution, are shown in Fig. 3.

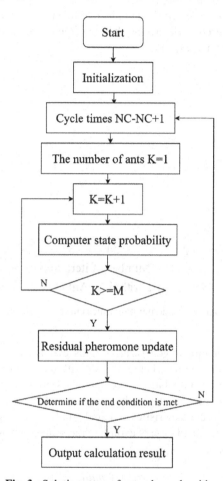

Fig. 3. Solution steps of ant colony algorithm

Specific steps: (1) Initialize the ant colony, including initializing ants and pheromones. (2) Ants move according to the movement rules, preferentially perceive pheromones, and move towards the position with high pheromone concentration. If they don't perceive pheromones, they move according to the direction of perception or inertia. (3) Ants emit the most pheromones in the food or nest, and with the increase of the moving distance of ants, they emit less and less pheromones. (4) The pheromone concentration of ants decreases gradually with time.

3.3 Research on Hybrid Algorithm

Evolution rate is an indicator used in genetic algorithms to measure the speed of population progress, which can be calculated by the difference between the mean of the sub objective function and the additional objective function f. In practical applications, evolution rate is often used to determine the convergence of algorithms and optimize search efficiency is shown in Fig. 4.

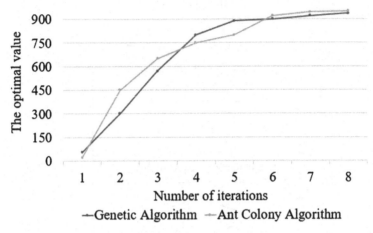

Fig. 4. Optimal value iteration times curve of two algorithms

In the practical application of genetic algorithms, evolution rate is usually used as an evaluation indicator to determine whether the algorithm can effectively converge. Due to the fact that the speed of population development is often related to factors such as algorithm design and parameter settings, the measurement of evolution rate also needs to be optimized based on the characteristics of actual problems. For optimization problems that need to be solved, the calculation of evolution rate can be considered as an important search efficiency indicator.

$$F = \max(f) + min(f) - f \qquad (1)$$

The evolution rate generally refers to a statistic in genetic algorithms that measures the rate of progress of a population during the evolution process. The specific calculation method is usually the difference between the mean of the sub objective function and the additional objective function f. Among them, the sub objective function is the main objective function in optimization problems, while the additional objective function is an auxiliary function used to constrain optimization problems, with the aim of limiting the search space to a feasible range.

By calculating the difference between the mean of the sub objective function and the additional objective function f, we can determine the average degree of evolution of the population during the evolution process. If the evolution rate is high, it indicates that the population has made faster progress during the evolution process, while conversely, it indicates slower progress.

$$\left| \overline{f}_u - \overline{f} \right| < Q \tag{2}$$

it is necessary to restrict its propagation. Because the individual fitness values in the group are relatively similar, and there are certain difficulties in continuing to implement the optimization, there is a situation of wavering near the optimal solution. At this time, the fitness value of an individual should be amplified in order to improve its decision-making ability, that is, it is called the indication of fitness value. To solve this problem, the following formula can be proposed:

$$f = \frac{1}{f_{max} + f_{min} + \vartheta}(f + f_{min}) \tag{3}$$

During the evolution process, a statistical analysis is carried out on the objective function value in the operation process of the three algorithms. The test can also be selected as a genetic algebra, and the data with a fitness value of 1347 can be obtained, which is also the highest adaptive value. The iterative optimization, time-consuming, fitness calculation times and fitness value changes of the genetic generation are digged into a "curve change graph", as shown in Fig. 5.

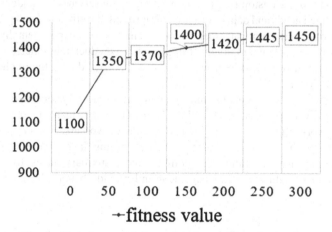

Fig. 5. Variation curve of genetic value and fitness value data

The indicate that accurately evaluate students' learning needs, provide personalized course suggestions, and provide important functions such as teaching strategy generation and optimization. The optimization results also indicate that through the personalized education services provided by the system, students' performance will be improved, and the efficiency of education management will also be improved. In addition, the system can also generate interpretable results and provide real-time updates and feedback functions, providing better visual display for educational management.

During the system experiment, the system received good feedback from evaluators, achieved a good user experience, and played a role in improving learning efficiency to a certain extent. However, the system still has some limitations. Firstly, due to the diversity of user needs for education management services, the system generated solutions may not be applicable to every user. Secondly, the accuracy of basic data and the comprehensiveness of data collection also have an impact on the effectiveness of the system. Finally, the selection and adjustment of parameters in genetic algorithms have an impact on the performance and experimental results of the algorithm. How to determine the optimal parameter configuration based on actual problems is also a research focus in genetic algorithm optimization.

The above is the experimental process and analysis of the intelligent teaching management information system. The system is an effective educational management solution, capable of personalized educational management, improving learning efficiency and service quality. In future applications, the system's algorithms, parameter settings, and other aspects can be optimized and improved to achieve better educational management results.

4 Conclusion

Based on the teaching management information system is an intelligent solution for educational management problems. This system fully utilizes the advantages of genetic algorithms and can provide customized teaching management services for students based on their personalized needs and data information, improving the efficiency and personalized service level of education management. The system has been experimentally validated and proven to be effective and practical in personalized education management. However, further optimization and improvement are still needed during the implementation process of the system.

In short, the intelligent teaching management information system based on genetic algorithms is a very practical tool in the field of education management, which can improve the work efficiency of teaching management workers, provide personalized services, and help students achieve better grades in learning. In the future, we can further study how to optimize algorithms and combine more auxiliary means to quickly and effectively improve educational management and provide better educational services for students.

References

1. Xiaoshu, M.: Application of web mining and genetic algorithm in intelligent network teaching system design. China New Commun. **22**(10), 1 (2020)
2. Zhen, G., Xin, M.: Design and implementation of laboratory intelligent scheduling function based on genetic algorithm. Digital World **8**, 1 (2019)
3. Qiuxiang, L., Zhenwei, L.: An Analysis of the Intelligent Test Paper System Based on Genetic Algorithms. Sci. Informatization (2020)
4. Lina, S.: Development of intelligent examination system based on genetic algorithm. Mod. Inf. Technol. **3**(1), 3 (2019)
5. Xiangyi, X.: Discussion on the application of improved genetic algorithm in intelligent paper-making system. Commun. World **1**, 2 (2017)

6. Zhimei, N.: Resource management of college teacher training based on genetic algorithm in cloud computing Hadoop platform. Mod. Electron. Technol. **42**(21), 5 (2019)
7. Qu, M., Niu, Z.: Application and exploration of big data in intelligent teaching management. Read. Writ. (Education and Teaching Journal), **2019**(7) (2019)
8. Chen, L., Hu, N.: Application Research of Genetic Algorithm in Intelligent Course Scheduling System. Comput. Knowl. Technol. (2019)
9. Chen, L., Hu, N.: Application of genetic algorithm in intelligent course scheduling system. Comput. Knowl. Technol. Acad. Ed. **2019**(2), 3 (2019)
10. Liu Teng, W., Renxie, L.Y.: Discussion on the problem of college course scheduling based on genetic algorithm. J. Chongqing Electron. Eng. Vocat. Coll. **27**(3), 3 (2018)

Deep Learning of the Management Information System Design Platform for Higher Vocational Colleges

Hongchun Shen[✉], Jiayan Wu, and Shirui Li

School of Art,
Sichuan University Jinjiang College, School of Literature and Media, Sichuan University Jinjiang College, Office of Student Affairs, Sichuan University Jinjiang College, Chengdu 620800, Sichuan, China
xkshendu@163.com

Abstract. Information information system as the campus management content can achieve technical judgment, can improve the management level of the whole information, promote the improvement of information, first of all, the integrity of the information to make the final judgment, and then such a classification and servant, the information should be automatically analyzed, the practice of verification, the effective research results of the information show that the management of the information system can improve the advantages, and play its own advantages, better than the traditional method.

Keywords: university management standards · stability · Decision Tree ID3 algorithm · Optimize the results

1 Introduction

With the rapid development of China's economy, all industries in our country have achieved rapid development. To a certain extent, the professional talents needed by society will increase. That is to say, education at this stage is more important. Under this background, many colleges and universities in our country have expanded the enrollment scale, and to a certain extent, the school management work will become more onerous [1], And in the process of school management, there will also be more difficulties. After in-depth research, it is found that the most important problem to be solved after colleges and universities expand the enrollment scale is how to use information technology in the management process of colleges and universities, so as to gradually reduce the heavy management work of colleges and universities. Therefore, our country's large, medium and small colleges and universities are gradually trying to integrate digital information into the management of colleges and universities, making full use of information technology, and using relatively advanced computer technology to provide services for the management of colleges and universities. Different colleges and

© ICST Institute for Computer Sciences, Social Informatics and Telecommunications Engineering 2024
Published by Springer Nature Switzerland AG 2024. All Rights Reserved
Y. Zhang and N. Shah (Eds.): BigIoT-EDU 2023, LNICST 583, pp. 166–174, 2024.
https://doi.org/10.1007/978-3-031-63139-9_18

universities have different ways of obtaining information management systems. Some colleges and universities purchase commercial information management systems, and some conduct research and design in their own schools, Its purpose is to be used in the daily management of the school. In the process of daily management of colleges and universities, the combination of advanced network technology has made the complicated management of colleges and universities simpler, and to some extent, the level of running schools has been improved, which is of great significance for strengthening the construction of information technology in colleges and universities.

At this stage, many colleges and universities in China have a long history of development, especially in recent years, the number of teachers and students in colleges and universities has increased a lot, several times higher than before. So the strength of teachers and students in colleges and universities has increased so much that the original college management system can no longer meet the current onerous college management work [2]. In order to make the college achieve long-term development, an urgent problem to be solved now is to design and research a college management system that can meet the current situation. The research of this paper is to use the relevant technology of cloud platform and ASP. NET + MSsQL technology in the research and design of a new college management system under this background of the times. To some extent, the system of managing student information and the system of managing teacher information have been effectively integrated, and the level of college management has been significantly improved.

This sentence is the information system and that for the overall situation of information, inclusion plays a key role. In the analysis of vocational colleges, informationization should carry out comprehensive information comparison to complete information distribution and matching, but informationization work requires certain stability, harmony and technology, and realizes comprehensive judgment of data and information. Therefore, information system is an important content in information development, which can improve and perfect related contents.

2 Related Concepts

2.1 Mathematical Description of the Decision Tree ID3 Algorithm

The decision tree ID3 algorithm uses the key points of information, the relationship between information and the importance of information to optimize the information of vocational colleges [5], and finds outliers in information optimization according to the management indicators in the vocational college system, and forms a path table. By integrating the information optimization results [6], the correlation of the system information results is finally judged. The decision tree ID3 algorithm combines the university management standards [7, 8], and the decision tree ID3 algorithm is used to optimize the management results, which can improve the system information level.

Hypothesis 1: The vocational college information is x_i, the set of information optimization results is $\sum x_i$, the information importance is $f(x_i)$, and the judicial function of the system information results y_i is as shown in Eq. (1).

$$f(x_i) = \lim_{i \to \infty} \sum x_i |y_i + \sqrt{\xi^2 - 4xy}$$ (1)

ξ Adjust the factor for information to reduce the impact of redundant information.

The primary task of the college system is to manage data and effectively manage all kinds of information data [9]. Therefore, the system should meet the functional requirements at the design stage and have strict requirements for the execution of the college system. For example, when a teacher or student logs in to the system, the system can convert the login page as soon as possible [10], shorten the login time, and feed back the process of each login to facilitate further improvement and improve the system's function realization ability.

The system of the design institute has solved the problems of system scalability and openness in the later stage before the system, which is conducive to the long-term operation of the system, such as system update, system upgrade after performance improvement, etc. This requires the system to be continuously adjusted and improved, and excellent scalability and openness are essential [11].

Generally, we assume that only faculty, students, system administrators and others use the college management system, and these people are familiar with computers, and they can easily feel whether the system is easy and convenient to operate and use, which requires the system to be more perfect to meet the requirements of users [12]. From the user's point of view, we certainly hope that the system we use is relatively easy to operate, and the interface docking is convenient for price comparison. In addition, if there is an error in operation, the system will give a corresponding warning, which can make users more skilled in exploring.

2.2 Selection of Information Optimization Scheme

The information in information system needs weight and information content, and the two kinds of data can complete the comprehensive judgment of information.

$$F(x_i) = \frac{-x \pm \sqrt{x^2 - 4x\xi}}{2x} + z_i \cdot \xi \tag{2}$$

2.3 Processing of Redundant Information

When planning and making decisions, it is necessary to ensure the integrity of information. Moreover, ID3 algorithm has the advantage of decision tree method in information stability, which can identify abnormal values in information, complete comprehensive judgment of information, optimize the overall judgment of information and the application of comprehensive information, and complete various data that meet the information requirements at the same time. Moreover, it is necessary to purchase and optimize data and promote the accuracy of information, so it is necessary to choose a more reasonable information processing scheme. The specific process is as follows (Fig. 1).

The processing of information should not only show the relationship between information resources, but also show the attributes of information. Therefore, the comprehensiveness and collation of this information should be judged and explained. In the process of analysis, the association between information and laboratory data should be deeply explored and matched to complete the comprehensive judgment of information, and the key point of improving human nature recognition should be put forward.

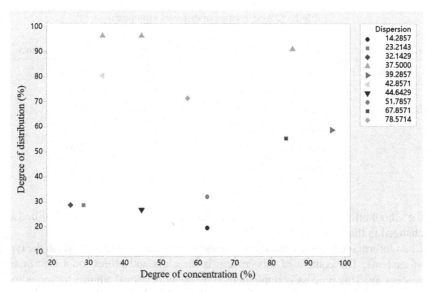

Fig. 1. Decision tree ID3 algorithm analysis results

2.4   The Correlation Between Different Information Key Points

Problem, as an important information content at present, can analyze the relationship between data, the coupling of data and the division of data. Massive information can identify the key in information, and can complete the multi-faceted processing of information. In addition, in the process of massive information analysis, it is necessary to judge the accuracy of information analysis results and the integrity of information. Therefore, any processing of information and multiple judgments of information can optimize the reservation and structure of information leakage and realize the rational use of information.

3   Actual Cases of Vocational College System Information Systems

3.1   Information System Situation

Before information analysis, collect relevant data, and the collection time is about 1 ~ 2 years. The whole rationality and decisiveness of data are judged comprehensively. To improve the overall distribution of information, it is necessary to judge and require relevant indicators of information. The specific results are as follows.

Generally, only the system manager can access the management part of the system, mainly because the system cannot be easily changed, and the system management needs to set limits, and the higher the limit level means the more secure the system.

The following is the function planning:

(1) School information management: before the successful establishment of the system, the task of management is to process the relevant information of the school. At first,

Table 1. Characteristics of different structures

information system	range	Amount of data	rationality	Risk constraints
SQL database	exterior	37.50	71.43	80.36
	interior	50.00	73.21	101.79
School system	exterior	62.50	87.50	60.71
	interior	46.43	64.29	35.71
client	exterior	28.57	80.36	75.00
	interior	41.07	26.79	53.57

the school information needs to be initialized, and then it is constantly modified and changed in the later use [15].

(2) Class information management: classes and majors are used to distinguish the types of students. The content of this section is the class and professional information processing. This process is implemented by the educational administration administrator, and the information viewing, modification, deletion and other functions are set.

(3) Administrator management: self-evident. This link is for administrators, who also need information to log in to the educational administration system. For example, accounts, passwords, etc., so here are the operations of viewing, adding and deleting information.

(4) Teacher information management: In the same way as student management, the system administrator can delete, modify and view teacher information, and has the function of assigning teacher user permissions.

(5) Student information management: the same as the teacher's information management, it is also the modification of information. Adjust and delete functions.

(6) Database maintenance and management: The information of the database needs to be constantly improved and maintained, which is the process of management.

(7) Log management: The log records the daily work of the system. By viewing the log, you can observe whether the system is running normally, and set the deletion and backup functions for the log [16].

The processing process between the different information keys in Table 1 is shown in Table 2.

In an analysis, it can be found that the information has high deliberately, and when selecting data points, the information can be qualitatively analyzed, and the surrounding data iteration can be carried out according to key points to complete the overall judgment of the data. Therefore, the information plays an important role in the whole analysis, and the information processing speed is fast and the processing accuracy is higher.

3.2 Optimization Ratio of Information

It is the key in the current data processing process. Point information improves and iterates data according to all its things and the relationship between your information

Table 2. Processing process of information key points

source	degree of freedom	Adj SS	Adj MS	F-number	P-value
regression	10	9571.97	957.20	1302.62	0.022
3	1	18.40	18.40	25.04	0.126
5	9	9463.11	1051.46	1430.90	0.021
error	1	0.73	0.73		
total	11	9572.70			

and data, distinguishes invalid information from effective information, removes useless information, reduces its occupation of resources, makes better use of it, and analyzes and identifies key points in information resources (Table 3).

Table 3. Provides an overall picture of information optimization

Optimize the proportion	Degree of systematization	Outlier recognition rate
25%	41.07	82.14
50%	101.79	100.00
70%	21.43	98.21
mean	75.00	35.71
X^2	7.124	4.292
P = 0. 002		

3.3 Stability and Accuracy of Information Optimization

In order to verify the accuracy of the decision tree ID3 algorithm, the optimization stability and accuracy compared with the management system are shown in Fig. 2.

In this analysis, we can find that the proposed algorithm has a large fluctuation between 4 and 5, and has a small fluctuation in the later analysis, which is instinctively stable as a whole, but occupies a large amount of system resources in the early stage (Table 4).

Through the data in the form, we can find that the whole optimization node and optimization content are relatively high, and more than 90%, which shows that my integrity and advantages are obvious in the calculation process and calculation effect. In addition, when comparing and analyzing the key data and key points, we will also find instinctive data, which is reasonable in integrity and meets the relevant requirements as a whole, and has strong advantages for the key content and the corresponding points of indicators, so we show more excellent performance in the process of analyzing information, which can be used as a later judgment (Fig. 3).

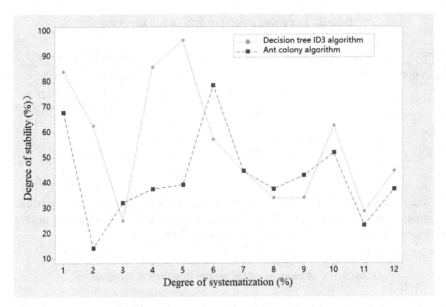

Fig. 2. Optimization stability of different algorithms

Table 4. Comparison of optimization degrees of different methods

algorithm	Optimize stability	Information key points	error
Decision tree ID3 algorithm	91.07	91.79	91.07
Ant colony algorithm	83.93	76.79	83.93
P	9.219	6.433	9.292

From the analysis results in the graph, we can find that the information documents in our study have no analysis process, and they are curvilinear in the process of information data and rising processing, and the information is relatively reasonable in the whole analysis scope and analysis content, all of which are in the middle line.

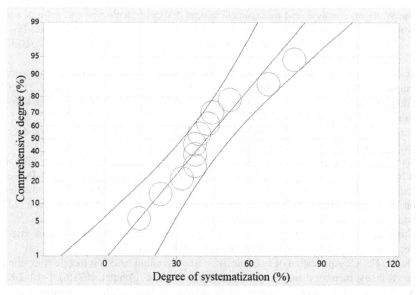

Fig. 3. Decision tree ID3 algorithm evaluates the comprehensive results

4 Conclusion

The continuous development of the most efficient teaching and efficient content the informationization of teaching and the comprehensive degree of information are higher, and the constraints of information are relatively enhanced in information processing and information improvement. Moreover, in the process of information processing and construction, the decision tree method of information can also improve the accuracy and rationality of enterprise country and promote comprehensive analysis. Therefore, in the decision tree aspect, our algorithm has more advantages, which can ignore the unstable factors and reduce its proportion.

References

1. Diao, Y., Zhang, Q.: Optimization of management mode of small- and medium-sized enterprises based on decision tree model. J. Math. **2021** (2021)
2. Qin, J.: Design and implementation of sports performance management system in higher vocational colleges based on data mining. In: Eai International Conference on Multimedia Technology & Enhanced Learning (2017)
3. Shanfeng, W.U., Xia, L.U.: Design of physical education curriculum analysis and management system based on decision tree algorithm. Mod. Electron. Tech. (2019)
4. New, S.S., Lay, K.K.: Using ID3 Decision Tree Algorithm to the Student Grade Analysis and Prediction (2019)
5. Shamrat, F., Ranjan, R., Hasib, K., et al.: Performance Evaluation Among ID3, C4.5, and CART Decision Tree Algorithm (2022)

6. Jin, W.: Course analysis and management system design of ideological and political education based on decision tree algorithm. In: Chang, J.W., Yen, N., Hung, J.C. (eds.) Frontier Computing. FC 2020. LNEE, vol. 747. Springer, Singapore (2021). https://doi.org/10.1007/978-981-16-0115-6_298
7. Stoilov, T., Stoilova, K., Vladimirov, M.: Decision support for portfolio management by information system with black-litterman model. Int. J. Inf. Technol. Decis. Mak. **2**, 21 (2022)
8. Wang, X.: Analysis of Measures to Strengthen Structural Design and Construction Management of Building Engineering. **2022**(5), 4 (2022)
9. Wang, H., Wang, T., Zhou, Y., et al.: Information classification algorithm based on decision tree optimization. Cluster Comput. **22**, 7559–7568 (2019)
10. Gao, J.: Information system of constructive english teaching platform based on RBF algorithm. In: Xu, Z., Alrabaee, S., Loyola-González, O., Zhang, X., Cahyani, N.D.W., Ab Rahman, N.H. (eds.) Cyber Security Intelligence and Analytics. CSIA 2022. Lecture Notes on Data Engineering and Communications Technologies, vol. 123. Springer, Cham (2022). https://doi.org/10.1007/978-3-030-96908-0_78
11. Chen, C., Geng, L., Zhou, S.: Design and implementation of bank CRM system based on decision tree algorithm. Neural Comput. Appl. **14**, 33 (2021)
12. Gu, Z., He, C.: Application of fuzzy decision tree algorithm based on mobile computing in sports fitness member management. Wirel. Commun. Mob. Comput. **2021**(6), 1–10 (2021)
13. Xu, L.: Design and Implementation of Student Work Platform for Counselors Based on Computer System. In: Sugumaran, V., Xu, Z., Zhou, H. (eds.) MMIA 2021. AISC, vol. 1385, pp. 673–679. Springer, Cham (2021). https://doi.org/10.1007/978-3-030-74814-2_94
14. Zhang, S.: Design of sports achievement data mining and physical fitness analysis system based on ID3 algorithm. Mod. Electron. Tech. (2019)
15. Xiao-Hua, L.U.: Application of Decision Tree Classification ID3 Algorithm in Learning Strategy Recommendation of Network Teaching Platform. J. Taiyuan Univ. (Science and Technology Edition) (2016)
16. Zhang, M.J.: Application of ID3 algorithm in customer management about online bookstore. In: 2016 3rd International Conference on Mechatronics and Information Technology (2016)
17. Wang, L.: Optimal Decision Programming of Decision Tree Algorithm in Project Management. Springer, Cham (2022). https://doi.org/10.1007/978-3-030-97874-7_117
18. Tiantian, P.U.: Study on engineering project management optimization based on decision tree. Mod. Electron. Tech. (2018)
19. Araki, T., Luo, Y., Guo, M.: Performance Improvement Validation of Decision Tree Algorithms with Non-normalized Information Distance in Experiments. In: Khanna, S., Cao, J., Bai, Q., Xu, G. (eds.) PRICAI 2022: Trends in Artificial Intelligence. PRICAI 2022. LNCS, vol. 13629. Springer, Cham (2022). https://doi.org/10.1007/978-3-031-20862-1_33
20. Zhao, L., Cheng, T.X., Ying, M.O., et al.: The decision tree data mining model for welding parameters selection based on C5.0 improved algorithm and its application. Chin. J. Manag. Sci. (2016)

Research and Application
of Recommendation Algorithms
in Personalized Intelligent Education

Collaborative Filtering Recommendation Algorithm and Recommendation System for College Students' Employment

Yanqing Wang[1(✉)], Qianying Sun[2], Sun Jingyu[3], and Weiming Tang[3]

[1] College of Arts and Sciences, National University of Defense Technology, Changsha 410072, Hunan, China
yanqingtvsj@163.com
[2] School of Marixm, Northwestern Polytechnical University, Xian 710021, Shaanxi, China
[3] Yunnan College of Business Management, Yunnan 650106, China

Abstract. With the continuous development of our society, the requirements for talents are more and more higher, so the employment situation of college students has become more severe. College students' life is in the learning stage, only the final internship stage, can the initial contact with social units, so, for the employment units is not enough understanding of the employment units, therefore, it is difficult to have effective contact with the demand situation of employers. Most college students are through the talent market and recruitment platform, throwing resumes for self-introduction, not clear about the needs of employers, also do not know their own demand direction, too blind to apply, which brings a certain energy loss to enterprises and individuals. Therefore, it is imperative to innovate the method of filtering and calculation method and recommendation system research to solve the problem of the employment direction of college students.

Keywords: for college students · employment collaboration · filtering and calculation method · recommendation system · research

1 Introduction

At present, the recommendation system is a hot academic hotspot and application hotspot in China's information age. According to the previous application experience of various recommendation systems, it can be seen that the recommendation technology of collaborative filtering has produced very effective results. However, in the process of serving the employment information of college students, the application of collaborative filtering and calculation method and recommendation system technology is not mature, there will be a variety of problems, can not be accurately calculate, its suitable for college students' employment units and foreign units, so that it did not really play the role of the recommendation system. Therefore, this paper will take the employment situation of college students as the background, according to the enterprise recruitment information as the direction, and carry out the research of collaborative filtering recommendation algorithm and recommendation system, and give reasonable application suggestions.

Y. Zhang and N. Shah (Eds.): BigIoT-EDU 2023, LNICST 583, pp. 177–187, 2024.
https://doi.org/10.1007/978-3-031-63139-9_19

2 The Significance of Collaborative Filtering Calculation Method and Recommendation System Research

2.1 Significsignificance of Collaborative Filtering Method

With the rapid development of information technology, the system filtering and calculation method has been widely used. In the initial stage, it is mostly used in the e-commerce platform to calculate some accurate data for it [1]. Business platform is mainly selling all kinds of goods, in the whole platform, numerous quantity and variety, therefore, when consumers need some goods, in the search options, enter the name of the corresponding demand of goods, however, related to the goods related to the product has no corresponding push, thus limit the scope of consumer consumption, for search commodity business platform also can't provide accurate memory, for the coverage of goods is relatively small. For example, when consumers are searching for TV, this kind of goods can belong to electrical appliances category, but also can belong to daily goods category, more can belong to electronic goods category. Website actual process is more detailed, but consumers do not understand the rules, so only according to the needs of personal search, in the process, may appear their own demand, but there is no related product push, it is largely narrowed the scope of consumer consumption, at the same time, the customer search product is not necessarily the want. After using the filtering and calculation method, when consumers search for products, the system will identify the needs of consumers by default, and will push some of all kinds of products related to the search words, in order to meet the needs of consumers. Such an algorithm is based on the data of consumers buying goods, the second search, can also be said to be based on the application of filtering on search. The advantages of this method of using information technology for collaborative filtering and calculation are obvious to all, so it has been continuously explored and research and development by relevant professionals, which is a concrete embodiment of the employment direction of college students.

2.2 Application Significance of Using Collaborative Filtering and Calculation Method for the Employment Situation of College Students

At present, in the information developed society, college students' employment channels increased significantly, the enterprise recruitment of employees has become diverse, in front of many opportunities, college students how to save their energy, reasonable screening, finally choose a suitable and meet their own characteristics of jobs is crucial. At the present stage of enterprise recruitment in addition to enterprise recruitment and talent market, various recruitment platforms, large-scale audition recruitment, also college students can also choose to choose a variety of channels, resume throwing self-recommendation, in this way to find their own demand positions. However, in the major recruitment platforms, it is impossible to push a comprehensive recruitment information, and college students have various majors, therefore, students without professional computer level cannot have a professional search method, which will miss a lot of opportunities [2]. Based on this, in the direction of employment and recruitment for college students, the reasonable application of the collaborative filtering and calculation system can effectively improve this problem phenomenon. The collaborative filtering and calculation system is to summarize the embodiment of college students' subject, comprehensive literacy evaluation and their preferences through daily performance, and build an algorithm model, so as to calculate the job positions that meet the double development of enterprises and students.

3 Functions and Characteristics of the Collaborative Filtering and Calculation System

3.1 Functional Characteristics of the System Specific Process

Filter calculation system design mainly for the employment characteristics of college students, data integration, so as to recommend the position of college students, avoid unnecessary effort, largely save the cost of time, and in many recruitment, find the requirements of the enterprise and more suitable for their own characteristics of the position [3]. According to the application experience of the filtering and calculation system, which functional advantages are more in line with the employment system of college students are summarized, and the relevant systems can be improved to avoid the occurrence of push errors due to inaccurate calculation. In the system research, the reasonable fusion algorithm idea and the improvement of the filtering and calculation system is that the integration system becomes more perfect and the data is more accurate. In order to further ensure the accuracy of the data, college students should be tracked and counted from entering the campus, integrate different data contents, and finally form a system model fusion and matching [4]. Such comprehensive data content, can be supplied to graduating college students as an effective reference data, to make college students more deeply understand their own employment direction, clear their own specialty play space, so that first let students establish a certain psychological preset, effectively improve the employment rate of college students. At the same time, such data for college students who have not graduated, they can be more clear about the requirements of enterprises for talents at the present stage, so that students can more restrain themselves, and make continuous efforts, more clear about their own direction of efforts, so that they can gradually meet the talent needs of their ideal enterprises. Under the recruitment information pushed after the integration of big data, the recruitment conditions can more fully meet the recruitment conditions, so that both enterprises and students can quickly find the personnel and positions that meet their respective needs. From the above discussion, it can be seen that the most important function of the collaborative filtering system is to filter out unnecessary information, and finally screen out the qualified push information, which brings a lot of convenience to enterprises and students, and to a large extent changes the previous way of application.

3.2 Characteristics of College Students' Employment System

When college students face the employment situation, the collaborative filtering calculation method can help college students quickly push out the required positions and suitable positions, which also reflects the advantages of modern characteristics, effectively changing the traditional employment disadvantages, which is also the advantages of the system itself [5]. Secondly, in the collaborative filtering system, can it not only provide students with reasonable applicants, but also understand the preferences and achievements of college students according to long-term tracking data, so that students can play a greater role in employment according to these relevant data. Make the information provided by the platform more accurate, more corresponding to the needs of enterprises, and also more meet the needs of individuals. The matching rate of the two during the period is better, and better play its role of collaborative filtering and calculation. Finally, this method can also accurately score the students comprehensively and correctly, which also reflects the efficient work function of the collaborative filtering algorithm.

4 An Important Role in the Effective Fusion Application Idea of Collaborative Filtering Algorithm

In the process of enabling collaborative filtering algorithm, the corresponding model should be established first, so that the personnel can intuitively see the specific data content. Under the background of college students' employment, we can consider applying college students to shape the simulation model. However, in the actual process, there is another problem, that is, every college student is different, and there is a great difference between them. Therefore, only what method should be applied can push a reasonable and correct score through big data content, which has become an important research content of relevant workers. In the past application practice, it can be seen that if the collaborative filtering and calculation method is used alone, when different characteristics and the collected data are unmatched, the score will have a huge deviation, which will lead to the push of inaccurate data and affect students' employment judgment [6]. Based on this, the relevant workers should effectively apply the fusion idea in the collaborative filtering algorithm, and the specific implementation process mainly has two methods. One of them is about students usually be fond of interest and personal characteristics of the corresponding classification, (such as Table 1) can use college students' friends for model construction, through the character characteristics of different friends, calculate the unknown characteristics of college students, and through the calculated data, (such as Table 2) give the corresponding scoring criteria.

Table 1. The time spent in the corresponding events

	Alan	Bob	Marry	Alice
Relevant/Highest Rating	21	35	23	10–5
Neutral/Avg.Rating	15	22	2	5–10
Non-Relevant/Lowest Rating	17	6	11	5–20

Another way is to apply the linear vector correlation calculation, the relevant researchers mostly use pearson system is the most appropriate. College students' employment system is also very applicable to, on the basis of classification thought of filtering

Table 2. User Behavior data of College Students

Action Type	Quantity (times)	proportion
in total	1356	100%
read	203.4	15%
fabulous	352.56	26%
share	379.68	28%
download	420.36	31%

recommended fusion algorithm, because college students in choosing employment, students and enterprises have certain employment requirements, to make both demand can get each other, and in the data and reality gap is small, can effectively improve its employment, fusion collaborative filtering calculation method can better play its real role, produce the best effect. Based on this, fusion collaborative filtering calculation design, should be the students and the enterprise demand factors for reasonable classification, to provide accurate data, to a large extent can reduce the corresponding difference, give full play to the best application effect of software, system score will therefore get the corresponding promotion effect [7, 8]. In the specific operation process of the fusion thought, the idea method of the matrix is adopted to build the ternary matrix. In the effective fusion and model, according to the needs of the application personnel, produce accurate corresponding values, and finally get a more reasonable, more in line with the needs of the model.

4.1 Collaborative Filtering Recommendation Algorithm

Collaborative filtering, literally, includes two operations: collaboration and filtering. The so-called collaboration is to make decisions (recommendations) by using the behavior of the group. There is a saying of coevolution in biology. Through the role of collaboration, the group will gradually evolve to a better state. For the recommendation system, through the continuous collaboration of users, the final recommendation to users will become more and more accurate. Filtering is to find (filter) the user's favorite scheme (subject matter) from the feasible decision-making (recommended) scheme (subject matter) [9]. Figure 1 below shows the user's operation behavior matrix for the subject matter.

The similarity calculation can use the similarity algorithm to calculate two vectors:

$$\Delta w(i, y) = -\eta \frac{\partial e}{\partial w(i, y)} \tag{1}$$

After calculating the similarity between users (row vectors) or objects (column vectors), let's talk about how to make personalized recommendations for users.

$$\text{Correct rate} = \left(\sum_{i=1}^{k} e_i \right) / n \tag{2}$$

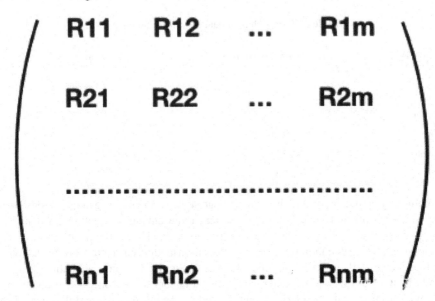

Fig. 1. User's operation behavior matrix of the subject matter

The core of collaborative filtering is how to calculate the similarity between objects and users. We can use a very simple idea to calculate the similarity. We construct the following user behavior matrix (see Fig. 2 below) based on the user's rating of the subject matter (or implicit feedback, such as clicks, favorites, etc.). An element of the matrix represents a user's rating of a subject matter (if it is implicit feedback, the value is 1). If a user does not have a behavior on a subject matter, the value is 0. The row vector represents the score vector of a user for all the subject matter, and the column vector represents the score vector of all users for a subject matter. With row vector and column vector, we can calculate the similarity between users and between objects. Specifically, the similarity between row vectors is the similarity between users, and the similarity between column vectors is the similarity between objects [10]. To avoid misunderstanding, here is a brief explanation of implicit feedback. As long as the user does not directly score the operation behavior, it is implicit feedback, including browsing, clicking, playing, favorites, comments, likes, forwarding, and so on. There are many implicit feedback that can be scored indirectly, which will be explained later. If no score is obtained indirectly, use 0 or 1 to indicate whether it has been operated. In real business scenarios, the number of users and the number of target objects are generally large (the number of users may be one million, ten million or ten million, and the number of target objects may be one hundred thousand, one million or ten million). Each user can only operate on a limited number of target objects, so the user behavior matrix is a sparse matrix [5]. Because the matrix is sparse, it will facilitate us to calculate the similarity and make recommendations for users.

4.2 Recommendation of Job Information for College Students

Employment recommendation refers to recommending suitable enterprises to users and employees to enterprises based on users' information and enterprises' information with the help of relevant technologies. When users browse the employment information website, they are faced with so many enterprises that it takes a long time to find the right job among many enterprises. Similarly, enterprises are faced with the same problem. It takes a long time to find the right candidate among many applicants [11]. The website provides tens of millions of enterprises, but users can only use classified browsing, classified navigation, search and other common website tools to search information. This requires users to have a fairly clear understanding and grasp of the enterprises they want to search. However, facing so many enterprises, the vast majority of users will not effectively integrate website information resources, which is very easy to appear the so-called "information maze".

1. At present, there are more than ten mainstream recruitment websites, and there are hundreds of thousands of recruitment posts every day. If manual capture is used, it is time-consuming and labor-intensive. So we adopted python crawler technology and built an automatic job information capture tool using the self built crawler framework, which saves time and effort, and stores the captured data in the database for easy use at any time [12]. At the same time, the data is captured according to the position category, which can ensure that the captured data already exists in a large cluster.
2. The data captured mainly include: post name, company, work location, education requirements, work experience, gender, minimum salary, maximum salary, post type, post responsibilities, etc.
3. System architecture

According to the captured recruitment information, we can find that the retrieved information can be divided into two categories: one is specific attributes, such as education requirements, work experience and other information, and the other is job responsibilities. Therefore, when we create semantic text, we can divide it into two categories.

When building the first level semantic text, we adopt the top-down construction method, and remove part of the information. We define the job title, work location, educational requirements, work experience, gender, and salary as top-level attributes, and then define the secondary attributes. For example, education has secondary attributes: college, undergraduate, master, and doctor.

The processing process will be listed selectively according to the data in the table:

Position name: e.g. junior java engineer; Intermediate java engineer; Senior java engineer. Although these three posts belong to java posts, they have different requirements for java level [13]. Therefore, you need to segment the position name. Extract the key information, so that the position similarity comparison is more accurate.

Experience requirements: the company's experience requirements for job seekers are generally calculated in years. Among them, the experience of fresh students is 0, and finally it is mapped to the shaping data: 0, 1, 2, 3, 4.

Education requirements: the company's education requirements for job seekers are roughly divided into: junior college, undergraduate, graduate, doctoral students, which are mapped into plastic data: junior college = O; Undergraduate = 1; Postgraduate = 2; Doctoral student = 3 [14].

Minimum salary and maximum salary: they are specific integer data.

Gender: there are only two types of gender: male and female, which are mapped to male - 0; Female - 1.

5   Research on Collaborative Filtering Recommendation Algorithm and Recommendation System for College Students' Employment

The preprocessing of the collected graduate and enterprise information mainly includes the following steps:

(1) Determination of scope

First of all, we need to determine the scope of the data to be collected. In the previous data collection component, we have defined the scope of the data to be collected [15]. The data collected mainly includes graduate information and recruitment enterprises

There are two parts of information. First, the graduate information includes the resume of the graduate and the record of the resume delivered by the graduate. Recruitment enterprise information includes the company title, recruitment vacancy, involved city, recruitment brochure label, recruitment brochure text and enterprise interview invitation record of the recruitment enterprise.

(2) Format normalization

After determining the scope of data collection and realizing the collection of age data, we should convert the data format into the format we need, reflect the interview invitation records of enterprises to graduates and the establishment and delivery records of graduates to enterprises in the form of matrix, and reflect the recruitment brief text of enterprises and the resume of graduates in the form of text. In the previous section, we have shown some standardized results, So I won't repeat it here.

(3) Abnormal data processing

In the process of practical operation, we will encounter a very few enterprises and graduates who have not recorded, most likely because they are newly registered or for other reasons [16]. Because we need to analyze the relationship between graduates and recruitment enterprises, if there is no relevant record, it may have an impact on our final results. Therefore, we delete these data as abnormal data.

Because what we want to achieve in this paper is two-way recommendation between graduates and enterprises, we need to establish preference models for graduates and recruitment enterprises respectively. For graduates, the main application is the record of graduates' resumes, while for recruitment enterprises, the main application is the interview invitation data of graduates from recruitment enterprises. These two types of data exist in the form of matrix, which is different from the data in the traditional collaborative filtering algorithm [17–20]. The algorithm needs to be improved, but the data can still be processed using the principle of collaborative filtering algorithm. As shown in Fig. 2 below, recommendations are implemented using collaborative filtering algorithms.

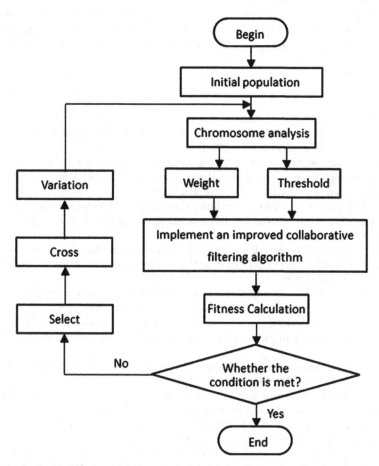

Fig. 2. Implementation of recommendation using collaborative filtering algorithm

Since there is some overlap between the data of graduates' resumes and the data of recruitment enterprises' invitation for graduates' interviews, we can consider processing this part of data separately. In the final results of the above data processing, if there is a resume posted or an interview invitation issued in the graduate enterprise matrix, it will be marked as 1. Here, we use the idea of collaborative filtering and assume that the score is 1. If the data of the resume posted by graduates overlaps with the data of the interview invitation issued by the recruitment enterprise, we can consider implementing the superposition of scores, that is, the score is. This can better reflect the relationship between graduates and enterprises.

6 Conclusion

To sum up, in the face of the employment situation of college students, using the collaborative filtering recommendation algorithm and recommendation system, can provide college students reasonably and accurately with the needs to apply for the job, but also to meet the needs of enterprises for talents, to a large extent to improve the previous employment disadvantages, improve the reasonable employment rate of college students.

References

1. Wu, H., Liu, Q., Zhang, Z.: Analysis of university students employment recommendation system based on apriori algorithm. In: 2020 Asia-Pacific Conference on Image Processing, Electronics and Computers (IPEC) (2020)
2. Chen, Z., Liang, W., Gao, X., et al.: Research on the accurate recommendation management system for employment of college graduates on hadoop. In: 2019 5th International Conference on Big Data and Information Analytics (BigDIA) (2019)
3. Wang, X.K.: College students' innovation and entrepreneurship resources recommendation based on collaborative filtering and recommendation technology. J. Phys. Conf. Ser. **1533**, 022013 (2020)
4. Zheng, L.G.: Parallel naieve Bayes regression model-based collaborative filtering recommendation algorithm and its realisation on Hadoop for big data. Int. J. Inf. Technol. Manag. **18**(2/3), 129–142 (2019)
5. Yt, A., Bing, Z.A., Yw, A., et al.: College library personalized recommendation system based on hybrid recommendation algorithm. Procedia CIRP **83**, 490–494 (2019)
6. Kumalasari, L.D., Susanto, A.: Recommendation system of information technology jobs using collaborative filtering method based on linkedin skills endorsement. SISFORMA **6**(2), 63 (2020)
7. Lv, Y., Kong, J.: Application of collaborative filtering recommendation algorithm in pharmacy system. J. Phys. Conf. Ser. **1865**(4), 042113 (2021)
8. Wang, N.: Ideological and political education recommendation system based on AHP and improved collaborative filtering algorithm. Sci. Program. **2021**(1), 1–9 (2021)
9. Yi, R.J., et al.: Research on Collaborative Filtering Recommendation Algorithm for Personalized Recommendation System (2019)
10. Feng, Z., Hua, M., Lei, P., et al.: Recommendation algorithm of cloud computing system based on random walk algorithm and collaborative filtering model. **2017**(3), 3 (2017)
11. Liu, Y.: Research on personalized employment recommendation system in colleges based on collaborative filtering algorithms. Mod. Inf. Technol. (2019)
12. Zeng, Q., Xiao, C., Department, I.M., et al.: The research of network collaborative filtering recommendation algorithm based on similarity propagation and context clustering. J. Mod. Inf. (2016)
13. Xiang, L., Zhi, J., et al.: Recommendation Algorithm Based on Bi-Spectral Clustering and Rating-Matrix Transfer Learning. J. Comput. Theor. Nanosci. **13**(3), 1971–1978 (2016)
14. Iwendi, C., Ibeke, E., Eggoni, H., et al.: Pointer-based item-to-item collaborative filtering recommendation system using a machine learning model. Int. J. Inf. Technol. Decis. Mak. **21**(01), 463–484 (2022)
15. Mirgane, S.M., Priya, J., Priyanka, I.: University Recommendation System For MS (2016)
16. Zhang, F.: A personalized time-sequence-based book recommendation algorithm for digital libraries. IEEE Access **4**, 2714–2720 (2016)

17. Huang, L., Wang, C.D., Chao, H.Y., et al.: A score prediction approach for optional course recommendation via cross-user-domain collaborative filtering. IEEE Access **PP**(99), 1–1 (2019)
18. Sirikayon, C., Thusaranon, P., Pongtawevirat, P.: A collaborative filtering based library book recommendation system, pp. 106–109 (2018)
19. Wei, J., Yang, L.: Research of improved recommendation algorithm based on collaborative filtering and content prediction. In: International Conference on Computer Science & Education. IEEE (2016)
20. Pan, X., Zhou, W., Lu, Y., et al.: User collaborative filtering recommendation algorithm based on adaptive parametric optimisation SSPSO. Int. J. Comput. Sci. Math. **8**(6), 580 (2017)

Modeling and Analysis of Digital Education Resources Sharing Based on Improved Collaborative Filtering Algorithm

Jun Hong[✉]

Information Technology Center of Huazhong Agricultural University, Wuhan 430070, Hubei, China
hongjun@mail.hzau.edu.cn

Abstract. With the rapid development of information technology, education informatization has been paid more and more attention by people. In the development process of educational informatization, realizing individualized learning is the urgent need of learners. Personalized recommendation technology can help personalized learning and significantly improve the learning efficiency of learners. Education is the main means of cultivating talents in our country, but the traditional teaching mode is limited by time and place. Therefore, in today's era, teaching through the Internet is convenient and unrestricted. Collaborative filtering algorithm can recommend personalized digital education resources for users according to their hobbies and learning behaviors, so as to improve the utilization rate of resources. Two algorithms, the algorithm of pre-computing user similarity and the algorithm of calculating similarity matrix by introducing time scoring weight, are improved. Experiments show that the algorithm of pre-computing user similarity shortens the time of pushing related information to users, thus effectively improving the calculation speed. Time scoring weight is introduced to calculate similarity matrix to improve the quality of recommendation. After the two algorithms are applied at the same time, the recommendation system has a significant improvement in calculation speed, accuracy and novelty.

Keywords: Collaborative filtering algorithm · digital education · resource sharing modeling

1 Introduction

Improve the efficiency of digital education resource sharing: Collaborative filtering algorithm can provide intelligent recommendation service for digital education resource sharing and improve the efficiency of resource sharing, teachers can't realize diversification in teaching, which leads to many students' low enthusiasm for learning and weariness of learning. 2. Unbalanced educational resources. It is mainly reflected in the great differences in teachers, teaching materials and teaching modes between developed areas and ordinary areas, which makes students in ordinary areas unable to enjoy better educational resources. 3. Low teaching efficiency. Teachers can not immediately present the teaching content designed in advance for students, but need to teach through blackboard writing and language description in class, which takes a lot of time [2]. Nowadays, personalized recommendation technology is used in all walks of life, which improves user experience and strengthens the user stickiness of software in e-commerce, news, video and other fields. However, in the field of education, compared with other fields, the application of personalized recommendation technology is relatively small, mainly because the traditional education is too strong and the Internet resources are too complicated [3]. With the advancement of smart education in the country, personalized learning is moving towards a dominant position, and the application of personalized recommendation in the field of education has become the focus of research. Therefore, building a new digital education resource sharing mode that can meet the corresponding needs has become a problem to be solved at present.

At present, collaborative filtering algorithm is one of the most widely used algorithms. Different scholars have studied the recommendation algorithm from different angles. For example, Wang Junmin and others proposed to add the recommendation reliability into the collaborative filtering model, and the weight of the reliability value is determined by analytic hierarchy process. The experiment shows that the new model improves the efficiency of the system [4]. Liang Tingting and others proposed a multi standard collaborative filtering recommendation algorithm based on clustering and regression, which automatically finds user subgroups through clustering and preference model. When new evaluation information appears, the model can support evaluation incremental update, thus improving the recommendation accuracy [5]. Based on the improved collaborative filtering algorithm, this paper studies the co creation and sharing construction mode of digital education resources.

2 Sharing of Digital Educational Resources Based on Improved Collaborative Filtering Algorithm

2.1 Introduction of Collaborative Filtering Algorithm

Through the analysis and mining of user behavior data, collaborative filtering algorithm can provide suggestions for optimizing resource allocation for digital education resource sharing platform recommendation is similar to user-based statistical recommendation in that it calculates the "neighbor set" of similar users to calculate the recommendation, but the user-based recommendation only considers the information characteristics of the user itself [7], while the user-based recommendation is based on the user's interest and preference for resource items, and recommends by establishing models and algorithms. As shown in Fig. 1 It is a recommendation flow chart based on collaborative filtering algorithm.

Promoting the development of digital education resource sharing: The application of collaborative filtering algorithm can promote the transformation of digital education resource sharing from traditional resource-oriented to user-oriented, and promote the development of resource sharing, while content-based recommendation is based on the information of resources themselves. Model-based recommendation algorithm

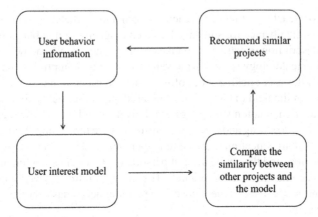

Fig. 1. Recommendation flow chart based on collaborative filtering algorithm

uses some modeling methods of statistics or machine learning to model and pre-process users' rating information in offline state, and to recommend users online by using the established preference model [8]. The basic idea of the collaborative filtering algorithm is actually very simple. For example, when someone wants to go to the movies or read a good book, they will ask their friends. Among many friends, we are more inclined to ask friends who share our tastes, because they recommend movies we will like more. This is the core idea of collaborative filtering. Figure 2 is a classification diagram of the collaborative filtering recommendation algorithm.

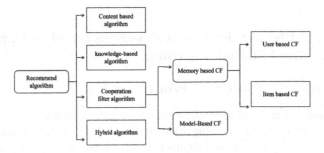

Fig. 2. Classification of collaborative filtering recommendation algorithms

2.2 Collaborative Filtering Algorithm Improvement

Collaborative filtering algorithm can provide users with personalized resource recommendation, meet the individual needs of users, and improve the satisfaction of users to the digital education resource sharing platform. The traditional collaborative filtering algorithm only considers the user's historical behavior, but does not consider its own content and attributes, so it does not need to extract features from users, which is relatively simple. The user based collaborative filtering algorithm mines the user's information according to the user's information. The quality of user information collection directly affects the quality of recommendation [9]. During each calculation, The similarity between the specified target user and all other users will be compared, and all the rating items will be traversed circularly, the rating value of each item will be multiplied by the similarity, and the product will be accumulated. Finally, the accumulated value will be divided by the sum of the similarity, and the evaluation value will be normalized for recommendation according to the returned ranking result. In order to further improve the calculation speed of recommendation system, if the user scale is relatively large, It is still time-consuming to calculate, and users' attention to their favorite content and certain types of attention will change over time. The traditional collaborative filtering recommendation algorithm has an impact on the user's interest in the time dimension. no consideration. If the time factor is not considered and content that has received high attention in the past has been recommended, the user's interest may have shifted, resulting in a decrease in the quality of the recommended high-quality content. According to the above problems, this paper proposes to first calculate the user similarity algorithm to improve the calculation speed and introduce the time scoring weight to calculate the similarity to improve the recommendation accuracy, and to optimize and improve the user-based collaborative filtering algorithm. The specific process is shown in Fig. 3. The improved recommendation process of the algorithm.

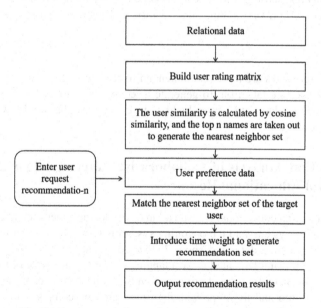

Fig. 3. Recommendation process after improved algorithm

Improve the efficiency of digital education resource sharing: The collaborative filtering algorithm can provide intelligent recommendation services for digital education resource sharing and improve the efficiency of resource sharing.

Optimize resource allocation: Through the analysis and mining of user behavior data, the collaborative filtering algorithm can provide suggestions for optimizing resource allocation for the digital education resource sharing platform.

Promote the development of digital education resource sharing: The application of collaborative filtering algorithm can promote the transformation of digital education resource sharing from traditional resource orientation to user orientation, and promote the development of resource sharing.Collect the behavior data of users on the digital education resource sharing platform, such as browsing, downloading, commenting and so on.

$$similarity = \cos\theta = \frac{A \cdot B}{\|A\|\|B\|} = \frac{\sum_{i=1}^{n} A_i \times B_i}{\sqrt{\sum_{i=1}^{n}(A_i)^2} \times \sqrt{\sum_{i=1}^{n}(B_i)^2}} \qquad (1)$$

Firstly, by analyzing the behaviors of searching, browsing records, collecting history and scoring of each user's resources, we can get the resource matrix associated with each user. Then, the user assigns time scoring weights to the downloaded educational resources. The rule is that the weights of the most recent scores are greater than those of the past scores. For example, the weights of earlier scores are reduced to about 0.37. Increase the nearest scoring weight to 1. Assume that the earliest historical rating time of user u is set as M in $T(u)$, and the latest historical rating time of user u is:

$$r_{ub} = \begin{cases} 1.0 \\ e^{(\max T(u)-T(u,t))/\max T(u)-\min(u))} \end{cases} \qquad (2)$$

Finally, when resources are to be recommended for users, the top n users most similar to the current user are taken out to generate a recommendation set, and the resource information with the highest score and which the current user has not browsed is given to the current user.

3 Application Analysis of Collaborative Filtering Algorithm in Digital Educational Resources

Taking the data of an educational website as an example, the experimental environment is virtual machine system, and the operating system is Linux. The system has 170,000 users, 122,400 resource data, and about 70,000 comment records. The collaborative filtering algorithm is implemented in Java language. The running time of the algorithm is calculated by calculating the starting and ending time recorded in the logs of the traditional algorithm and the improved algorithm, and the comparison is made. The comparison results of 11 users in the system are randomly selected. As shown in Table 1, the recommended schedule of traditional algorithm and new algorithm (unit s is seconds).

It can be seen from the data in Table 1 that in the case of the pre-calculated optimal recommendation matrix, the traditional algorithm takes an average of 0.524 s, and the new algorithm takes an average of 0.064 s. After the improvement, the new algorithm is about 90% faster than the traditional algorithm. Therefore, it shows that the improved

Table 1. Time required for recommendation of traditional algorithm and new

User ID	Traditional algorithm	Improved new algorithm
152	0.954s	0.621s
425	0.522s	0.210s
752	0.782s	0.462s
877	0.961s	0.612s
857	0.234s	0.054s
944	0.452s	0.142s
785	0.456s	0.142s
745	0.521s	0.214s

algorithm greatly improves the running speed. We can set the time as $MinT(u)$, and $T(u, b)$ represents the evaluation time of user u for book b. Assuming that the same user's interest in the same educational resource remains unchanged for 60 min, The following calculation formula is adopted:

$$0 \leq \max T(u) - \min T(u) \leq 60 \min$$
$$\max T(u) - \min T(u) > 60 \min \tag{3}$$

When a recommendation algorithm is first proposed, it means that the algorithm uses user opinions and instills them in other users. With the advancement of technology, the recommendation system still adheres to the original definition, and based on this, the algorithm is developed and improved. The main role of recommendation algorithms is to help users make decisions. After in-depth analysis and understanding of website users, recommend possible needs for target users. This algorithm can alleviate the difficulty of retrieval when users face unclear needs in use. Other methods. Most previous studies used offline testing. We will evaluate from the following six indicators. In order to facilitate the description of the evaluation indicators, u represents the user set, The collected data are cleaned, deduplicated and normalized (Fig. 4).

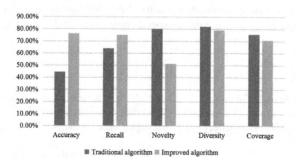

Fig. 4. Comparison of evaluation indicators between traditional algorithms and improved algorithms

According to the five evaluation indexes, through data collection and modeling analysis, the traditional algorithm is further compared with the improved algorithm for several off-line evaluation indexes. The improved algorithm has a significant improvement in calculation speed, accuracy and novelty, while the others have not improved much, but they all reach certain expectations. Collect user preferences, find similar user groups or items, and generate recommendation results. However, in education, educational resources are very huge, and it takes a lot of time and energy to define the content of each educational resource. Collaborative filtering algorithm can provide users with personalized resource recommendation, improve user satisfaction, and at the same time help users make better use of digital education resources, improve learning effect. Collaborative filtering algorithm can reduce the workload of teachers in resource selection and recommendation, and make teachers focus on teaching itself more.

4 Conclusions

Through the research on the collaborative filtering algorithm online teaching platform during this period, I deeply realized the importance of online education in social development, and also gained a new understanding of collaborative filtering algorithm digital education resources. Looking at the development status of other traditional industries that are deeply integrated with "Internet + ", the development trend of "Internet + education" is still relatively backward, and the traditional education model is still dominant. The improved collaborative filtering algorithm plays an important role, significance, steps and influence in the sharing of digital education resources. By applying collaborative filtering algorithm, we can improve the utilization efficiency of digital educational resources, optimize resource allocation, promote the development of digital educational resources sharing, and at the same time have a positive impact on users, teachers, digital educational resources sharing platform and educational resources. However, collaborative filtering algorithm also has some challenges in practical application, such as data sparsity, cold start and so on, which need to be continuously optimized and improved.Therefore, for the large and complex characteristics of educational data, using collaborative filtering algorithm for educational personalized recommendation has many advantages. This paper studies the user-based collaborative filtering algorithm commonly used in the recommendation system, and improves it from two aspects of improving the calculation speed and accuracy. The experimental results show that this method has a significant improvement in accuracy and calculation speed compared with the traditional algorithm.

References

1. Liang, Z.: Analysis of the current situation of digital education resource construction under the background of Internet + education. Wirel. Internet Technol. **18**(22), 2 (2021)
2. Yaqin, L.: Analysis on the effect of sharing digital educational resources. Econ. Res. Guid. **33**, 2 (2019)
3. Zhou, C., Zhao, W., Liu, Z.: Application of personalized collaborative filtering recommendation algorithm in teacher network training resources. J Shenyang Normal Univ.(Natural Science Edition) **037**(002), 183–187 (2019)

4. Junmin, W., Yuesheng, H.: Visual analysis of digital education resources research in the past ten years. China Educ. Inf. **1**, 8 (2018)
5. Tingting, L., Liqin, L.: Analysis of personalized recommendation algorithm and platform design of learning resources. Modernization Educ. **5**(52), 177–180 (2018)
6. Jie, H.: Research on intelligent recommendation platform of college learning resources based on collaborative filtering algorithm. J. Suzhou Instit. Educ. **22**(6), 4 (2019)
7. Chuansheng, Z., Wangru, Z., Zhongwu, L.: Application of personalized collaborative filtering recommendation algorithm in teacher network training resources. J. Shenyang Normal Univ.: Nat. Sci. Ed. **37**(2), 5 (2019)
8. Chuan, Z., Shirong, M.: Design and application of recommendation algorithm for digital educational resources. China Educ. Inf. **1**, 4 (2019)
9. Mengliang, S.: Construction of intelligent dynamic updating system of teaching resources based on classification and evaluation algorithm. Comput. Knowl. Technol.: Acad. Ed. **15**(6X), 4 (2019)
10. Chuan, Z., Shirong, M.: Design and application of recommendation algorithm for digital educational resources. (2019–1), 47–50 (2021)

The Construction of Performance Prediction Model of Ideological and Political Education Based on Feature Extraction Algorithm

Liu Ting[1,2(✉)], Yuehua Lia[1,2], and Jun Ma[1,2]

[1] Tianjin University of Finance and Economics Pearl River College, Tianjin 301811, China
79932099@qq.com
[2] Nanning University, Nanning 530200, Guangxi, China

Abstract. The this paper proposes a weighted ensemble learning algorithm with breadth learning algorithm as the individual learner. First, the breadth learning algorithm is used to predict students' grades. Since the performance of a single classifier is not stable enough and is sensitive to data changes, the experiment uses the weighted integration method to improve the breadth learning algorithm; then, it is combined with the decision tree using weighted integration. The results of the algorithm and the multilayer perceptron neural network algorithm are compared. The research results can provide a method reference for student achievement prediction.

Keywords: Feature extraction algorithm · Random forest algorithm · Data mining · Achievement prediction · Model

1 Introduction

Educational data mining is a new interdisciplinary research field [1]. It uses machine learning, statistics and data mining techniques to analyze and process educational data, so as to improve learners' learning efficiency and make teachers better understand students and their learning environment. Prediction of students' achievement is a hot research topic in the field of educational data mining [2]. Commonly used data mining classification, naive Bayes and other algorithms [3].

Many researchers have set up student achievement prediction models, but most of them are based on theoretical analysis to set up academic achievement evaluation models. The prediction accuracy of the established models is not high enough. It is speculated that the possible reasons are as follows: First, different algorithms are used, and the training effects of different algorithms on student data are different. Even if the same data is used, the effects of the models may be different due to researchers' preferences or model parameters. Second, the choice of features is different. Choosing different attribute subsets will produce different results for students' performance prediction. We should try our best to choose features related to students' performance, and it is best

Y. Zhang and N. Shah (Eds.): BigIoT-EDU 2023, LNICST 583, pp. 196–202, 2024.
https://doi.org/10.1007/978-3-031-63139-9_21

not to influence each other [4]. In view of the shortcomings of the above research, this experiment first adopted the data-driven modeling method, taking the prediction accuracy of the model as the criterion of feature subset selection in the data set containing students' attributes, and finding out the factors affecting students' performance by permutation and combination, making full use of the effective information of students' data [5]. Then, according to these effective attributes, the feature extraction algorithm is used to predict the performance. This algorithm has the advantages of fewer steps, simple structure and faster learning speed, which makes up for the long training time caused by the need to calculate a large number of hidden layer weights of deep learning algorithm. Compared with deep neural network algorithm, it is easier to obtain the global optimal solution and has good generalization performance. Finally, weighted integration is carried out on the trained algorithm to build a student achievement prediction model, so as to overcome the shortcomings of unstable performance of a single classifier and sensitivity to data changes.

2 Data Mining of Ideological and Political Education

2.1 Data Mining Process

Data mining in ideological and political education refers to the use of data mining technology to analyze and mine various aspects of data in students' ideological and political education, explore potential laws and information, and achieve more comprehensive, scientific, and effective guidance and improvement of students' ideological and political education.

Specifically, the process of data mining in ideological and political education includes the following steps:

1. Data collection
   The acquisition of ideological and political education data mainly includes social surveys, questionnaire surveys, various literature information, and online information, which exist in various forms in different data sources.
2. Data integration
   Summarize and integrate the data collected from various data sources, organize them into actionable datasets, and make the data clearer, more organized, and easier to analyze.
3. Data analysis
   Using data mining technology to deeply mine data, utilizing various data analysis tools and algorithms to discover hidden information and patterns behind the data.
4. Explanation of results
   Output the results of data mining and present them visually, ultimately evaluating the reliability and effectiveness of the results.
5. Application of results
   Apply the results to guide students' ideological and political education, provide guidance for personalized education, and provide data support for students' ideological and political education.

Ideological and political education data mining is a research method based on data analysis technology, providing new ideas and methods for the development of school education and teaching. Through the application of data mining technology, students' ideological and political education status can be understood from multiple perspectives and levels, effectively improving the scientific and effective nature of education work, and also helping to promote the informationization and intelligent development of school education.

2.2 Data Mining Methods

Data divided into description and prediction. Descriptive methods mainly look for and summarize the patterns hidden in the data, such as association rule analysis, cluster analysis, visual analysis, etc. predictive tasks are to predict unknown data information based on known information, such as classification method, regression analysis, outlier analysis, etc. usually in the process of realizing the goal of knowledge discovery, A variety of data mining methods will be used to obtain the desired knowledge.

At present, mainly including image recognition, speech recognition and character recognition. Cluster analysis is an unsupervised learning method. Unsupervised method means that the training data does not need to be marked when training samples, but the data are found through automatic learning of the unmarked samples in the training process, so as to divide the training data into several categories according to the similarity. The data of the same category has the greatest similarity and the greatest dissimilarity between different categories, The measurement methods of computing distance include Euclidean distance, cosine distance and information entropy [6]. Typical clustering algorithms include partition based, density based, hierarchy based and grid based algorithms. The method based on division is one of the commonly used methods in cluster analysis. Its principle is simple and easy to implement. First, divide the data objects according to the preset initial cluster center, divide each data object into the category of the nearest center, then traverse all data objects in turn, calculate the distance from each data object to the cluster center, and mark it as the nearest category according to the distance.

The random forest algorithm is an algorithm constructed by combining multiple decision trees on the basis of the Bagging method, and the final prediction result is jointly determined by multiple decision trees [7]. The random forest algorithm process includes two random processes, the first is to randomly select training samples using the Bagging method, and the second is to randomly select training subsets. The random forest construction steps are as follows:

(1) The Bagging method is used to randomly select samples with replacement.
(2) Use the CART algorithm to generate an unpruned decision tree, randomly select a feature in the feature set, and then build a decision tree.
(3) Repeat the above steps to form a decision tree, and then build a random forest.

Finally, the classification category of the sample is determined according to the vote. The random forest algorithm has strong data adaptability, can avoid overfitting and is insensitive to noise. Therefore, this paper chooses this classification algorithm as one of the prediction models. The design process of the random forest algorithm model is shown in Fig. 1.

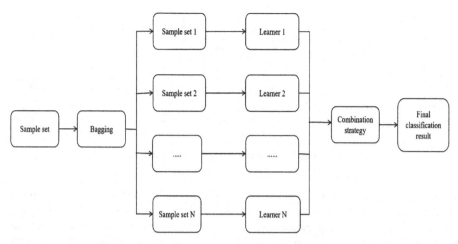

Fig. 1. Design process of random forest algorithm model

3   Construction of Prediction Model

3.1   Marking Algorithm of Short Answer Questions Based on Feature Extraction

Feature extraction algorithm is to analyze teachers' marking process. When teachers manually mark short answer questions, they usually set a set of scoring standards in advance, then divide the total score of each question into several parts, and assign the scores to some key steps or key words in the solving process of the questions, which are called scoring points [8]. Finally, the sum of the scores of the scoring points in the students' answers is calculated, which is the final score. According to the analysis of the manual marking process, it can be found that there are two main factors in scoring short answer questions: one is the standard answer and scoring standard, and the other is how much students' scoring points match. Therefore, in the marking of short answer questions, the standard answer is divided into several score points at first, and the synonym problem of the text leads to that each score point may have several characteristic values [9]. The basic features of the standard answers are stored in the system, an answer feature table is constructed, and different answer features are given weights (scores). The model of the complete matching answers is changed. Instead of giving the complete answers to the questions, the relevant features are extracted from the answer feature table to evaluate their small scores, and finally the scores of each feature value in the answers are accumulated [10].

For example, short answer question 1: What services does the Internet mainly provide us, set a total score of 10 points, and construct its answer characteristic table as shown in Fig. 2.

The head node value of the answer feature table in the figure represents the score of the feature value of the standard answer, and the value of the table node represents the feature value of a scoring point in the standard answer. Due to the synonym problem in the text, the same scoring point of the standard answer may have different feature values When marking the test paper, first obtain the student's answer, extract the eigenvalue of

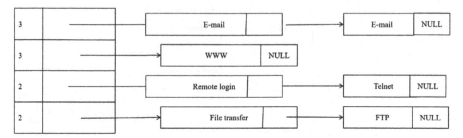

Fig. 2. Answer characteristics table

the first score point from the standard answer feature table, and then match it with the student's answer If the matching is successful, add the score of the eigenvalue to the score of the short answer question, and then match the next score point; If the matching fails, continue to extract the next eigenvalue of the score point and match the student's answer until all the score points in the answer feature table are matched, and finally get the score of the question. For example, match the student's answer with the feature value extracted from the answer feature table, and then complete the marking according to the weight of the feature value Its advantages are:

(1) When adding test questions, only the eigenvalue of the score point of the test answer needs to be input, which reduces the workload of teachers entering standard answers.
(2) Matching marking according to the characteristic value shields the comparison of some characters unrelated to the scoring point, which improves the accuracy and speed of marking.

When the algorithm matches the student answers with the eigenvalues extracted from the answer feature table, there is no order restriction, so it is only suitable for short-answer questions that have nothing to do with the order of scoring points. In the student answers with the eigenvalues extracted from the answer feature table in turn, the concept of positioning eigenvalues, which defines the positioning eigenvalues of the scoring points of standard short-answer questions as the order of the scoring points in the standard answers. When marking papers, students' answers are first obtained, and the eigenvalue information is extracted from the answer feature table according to the positioning eigenvalue order, and then matched with the students' answers. If the matching is successful, the score of the characteristic value is added to the short answer score, and the next score point is matched from the position where the students' answers are successfully matched; If the matching fails, continue to extract the next characteristic value of the score point and match the student's answer until all the score points in the answer characteristic table are matched, and finally get the total score of the question.

3.2 Predictive Model Construction

Finally, it is learned that xgboost algorithm will consider the case that the training data is sparse value, and the missing value can be specified as the default direction of the branch, which improves the efficiency of the algorithm, and the regularization term is embedded in the algorithm, which is not easy to over fit, so xgboost algorithm is selected. In general, the fusion model obtained after the single model fusion design with excellent learning ability is also relatively better. After the fusion design of these single models, the fused performance prediction model can predict students' performance more accurately. The construction process of fusion model is shown in Fig. 3.

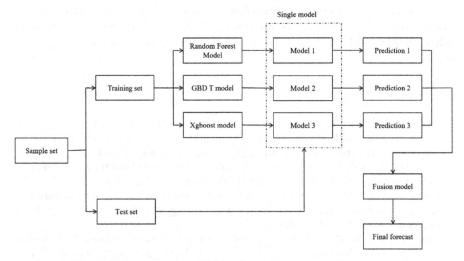

Fig. 3. The process of establishing the performance prediction model

Usually, the fusion model may have stronger than a single model, so its prediction results are relatively accurate. Due to the diversity of behavior data, the generalization may be reduced, thus reducing the model. By calculating the weight of a single model through Boosting algorithm, the weighted average method is used to fuse the single model, which can capture the advantages of a single model, enhance the prediction model, prevent the model from over-fitting, and thus improve. The weighted average method is shown in formula (4):

$$y = \sum_{i=1}^{n} w_i y_i, \, w_i = \frac{\sum_{j=1}^{n} y_{ij}}{\sum_{j=1}^{n} \sum_{j=1}^{n} y_{ij}} \tag{4}$$

where y represents the predicted value of the fusion model, y_i represents the value of the i-th model, m represents the total number of samples, n represents the number of models, w_i represents the weight of the y_i-th predicted model, and y_{ij} represents the j-th predicted value of the i-th model.

4 Conclusions

In this paper, the feature extraction algorithm and random forest algorithm are combined to establish a student achievement prediction model. In order to verify the validity of the model, we use two comparison methods. On the one hand, we use the same data processing method to establish a random forest algorithm based on decision tree, neural network, and feature extraction algorithm. The experimental results show that the latter has the best effect; On the one hand, in the case of using the same dataset and the same model, the prediction effect of the model established in this paper is also better than that of the previous researcher's model. This shows that the weighted voting performance prediction model the nonlinear relationship between students' feature attributes and students' grades. This paper can be used by educators to use this model to understand students to help, reduce learning failure rates, and help managers improve management efficiency.

References

1. Xiang, H., Shen, X., Chen, E., et al.: Construction and validation of a novel algorithm based on oncosis-related lncRNAs comprising the immune landscape and prediction of colorectal cancer prognosis. Oncol. Lett. **25**(2), 63 (2023). https://doi.org/10.3892/ol.2022.13650
2. Silva, M.C.A., et al.: Construction and validation of educational videos for adolescents with Down Syndrome based on health literacy 釰LISA Down Program (2023)
3. Liu, H., Ababake, M., Yang, L., et al.: exploration on ideological and political construction of higher vocational english course in southern xinjiang from the perspective of cultural confidence. Asian Agric. Res. **15**(3), 4 (2023)
4. Yang, X., Zang, W., Meng, S., Liu, J., Zhang, Y.: Chinese word segmentation of ideological and political education based on unsupervised learning. In: Sun, J., Wang, Y., Huo, M., Lexi, X. (eds.) Signal and Information Processing, Networking and Computers: Proceedings of the 8th International Conference on Signal and Information Processing, Networking and Computers (ICSINC), pp. 1213–1221. Springer Nature Singapore, Singapore (2023). https://doi.org/10.1007/978-981-19-3387-5_145
5. Guan, L.: Research and construction of university sports decision support system based on extraction algorithm and big data analysis technology. In: Jan, M.A., Khan, F. (eds.) Application of Big Data, Blockchain, and Internet of Things for Education Informatization: Second EAI International Conference, BigIoT-EDU 2022, Virtual Event, July 29–31, 2022, Proceedings, Part I, pp. 530–536. Springer Nature Switzerland, Cham (2023). https://doi.org/10.1007/978-3-031-23950-2_57
6. Minxia, Z., Congrui, F., Niu Shuangjian, X., Ping, C.C.: Analysis of the pore network structure of microbial solidification of construction residue soil based on CT scanning. Environ. Earth Sci. **82**(11) (2023). https://doi.org/10.1007/s12665-023-10966-4
7. Cui, W., Wang, Y., Guo, J., Zhang, Z.: Construction of a cuproptosis-associated long noncoding RNA risk prediction model for pancreatic adenocarcinoma based on the TCGA database. Medicine **102**(5), e32808 (2023). https://doi.org/10.1097/MD.0000000000032808
8. Li, L., Feifei, H., Zhao, L.: Research on the new mode of integrating higher vocational aesthetic and ideological and political education in the new era. In: Zhengbing, H., Wang, Y., He, M. (eds.) Advances in Intelligent Systems, Computer Science and Digital Economics IV, pp. 835–844. Springer Nature Switzerland, Cham (2023). https://doi.org/10.1007/978-3-031-24475-9_68
9. Wu, J., Nie, Q., Li, G., et al.: Identifying driver pathways based on a parameter-free model and a partheno-genetic algorithm. BMC Bioinform., **24**(1) (2023). https://doi.org/10.1186/s12859-023-05319-8
10. Pickson, R.B., Gui, P., Chen, A., et al.: Examining the impacts of climate change and political instability on rice production: empirical evidence from Nigeria. Environ. Sci. Poll. Res. **30**(23), 64617–64636 (2023). https://doi.org/10.1007/s11356-023-26859-9

Design and Implementation of College Student Volunteer Service Platform Based on Collaborative Filtering Algorithm

Qingfeng Li[1]([✉]), Chao Zhang[1], Chao Jin[1], Yong Gao[1], Desheng Zhu[1], and Jiang Yurui[2]

[1] Shandong Institute of Commerce and Technology, Jinan 250103, Shandong, China
Q2442974184@163.com
[2] Yunnan Medical Health College, Kunming 650000, China

Abstract. In the past decade, voluntary service has mushroomed vigorously. With the promotion of voluntary service and the progress of the Internet, massive voluntary service data have been generated in voluntary activities. How to process and utilize volunteer service data, guide the behavior of volunteer users, and provide valuable reference for participants in volunteer services has become an urgent issue to be resolved. The purpose of the college student volunteer service platform is to strengthen communication between volunteers and service objects to ensure the accuracy of volunteer service. To achieve this goal, collaborative filtering algorithms should be added to the design of the service platform to analyze actual needs. Based on this idea, this paper proposes a collaborative filtering algorithm and designs a volunteer service platform. The volunteer service platform can better solve the three core issues of today's volunteer industry: chaotic activity information, low volunteer service platform efficiency management, and improper activity matching. Compared with existing service platforms, the volunteer service platform designed in this article greatly reduces the time for users to search and find, helps users better participate in volunteer activities, and has certain practical value.

Keywords: Collaborative filtering algorithm · Volunteer college students · The service platform

1 Introduction

In the context of the great development of China's volunteer service, the National Volunteer Service Information System came into being to promote "Internet plus" volunteer service in combination with the characteristics of the information age. The big data of volunteer service is recorded and provided by the National Volunteer Service Information System, which is the only data in the field of volunteer service in the country, and contains great research value. Research big data in the field of volunteering, provide reference for volunteer service managers and participants, promote volunteering to a higher level, and create greater social benefits [1].

Y. Zhang and N. Shah (Eds.): BigIoT-EDU 2023, LNICST 583, pp. 203–214, 2024.
https://doi.org/10.1007/978-3-031-63139-9_22

Establishing collaborative filtering in the field of volunteer services is conducive to the understanding and utilization of data. The volunteer service big data is rich in content and diverse in categories, covering elements such as volunteers, volunteer groups, and volunteer projects. Each element also covers its time, location, and behavioral information, and the relationships between the elements are equally complex. Domain collaborative filtering relies on its semantic integration capabilities and data query capabilities to provide infrastructure support for upper level intelligent applications in the domain [2]. Establishing collaborative filtering for volunteer services can sort out the relationships between volunteer service elements. On the one hand, it can display the correlation between volunteer service elements in the form of a graph, and on the other hand, it can transform the semantic information of volunteer service knowledge into computer services, providing basic data technology support for upper level applications such as retrieval and recommendation.

Utilizing the association relationships contained in collaborative filtering in the field of volunteer services, combined with artificial intelligence technology, to research recommendation algorithms based on collaborative filtering, matching suitable volunteer projects for volunteer users, and providing more personalized services, also has important significance for the development of volunteer services. Currently, recommendation systems are widely used in commercial fields such as e-commerce, video products, news, etc., but they have not been widely used in vertical industries [3]. Using collaborative filtering in vertical industries to research recommendation algorithms not only plays a role in the field of volunteer services, but also provides reference for intelligent applications in other industries.

Early organized students volunteer groups in our country as the social tradition, providing service to specific people mostly superficial, but early service process is difficult, though low, the base of the reason is that certain people but is not fixed, therefore can be divided into various types, and each type of different people on the demand side is different, If the service is provided by subjective judgment of service target needs, the problem cannot be effectively solved in most cases [4]. This phenomenon indicates that the service quality of college students volunteers is low, and the quality problem is reflected in the accuracy of service. In reaction to the phenomenon, the modern field that can make use of advanced technology to develop college students volunteer service platform, using technology to analyze the requirements, but to do this we must reasonable selection algorithm to design platform, collaborative filtering algorithm which got the attention of people, therefore, in order to let the algorithm into the platform design, and play their role, Relevant studies are needed [5].

2   Related Work

2.1   Application Value in the Field of Voluntary Service

Currently, the data in the field of voluntary services are mainly structured data stored in traditional databases. Mining the potential value of these data has important guiding significance for improving the participation of volunteer subjects, promoting the development of voluntary services, and promoting the deepening of volunteer services [6].

The introduction of collaborative filtering technology to the field of volunteer services has more profound application value than traditional database technology:

1) Collaborative filtering presents entities and relationships in the form of graphs. Using collaborative filtering visualization technology, various relationships in the real world can be intuitively and efficiently modeled, consistent with user cognitive habits. Compared to traditional data table formats, it is more able to enable non professional volunteer service participants or managers to understand information. Currently, collaborative filtering visualization technology is increasingly widely used in the vertical field [7]. However, if the data is presented in the form of a traditional database construction network diagram, although it conforms to the entity relationship model of database design, it requires an intermediate transformation process, which incurs certain computational overhead; In addition, when the relationships or attributes of entities need to be extended, there is a cost of re modeling the relational database.

2) Collaborative filtering connects previously unrelated data, making it more advantageous in establishing complex relational networks.

Potential makes it easier to mine implicit associations. Although structured volunteer service data have clear hierarchical relationships, indirect relationships are difficult to detect, and these relationships have certain potential value. For example, in addition to having direct participation relationships with projects, it is difficult to directly reflect whether volunteers have potential connections with other projects in traditional databases [8]. Using collaborative filtering to establish a relationship network in the volunteer service field can process complex association analysis faster, reducing the query overhead of multiple relationships and multiple hops in traditional databases.

3) Currently, there is no unified knowledge base in the field of voluntary service, and a knowledge map in the field of voluntary service has been established.

Based on this, developing intelligent applications of volunteer service can help promote the development of volunteer service. Initially, establish a domain map to facilitate the evaluation and expansion of industry experts. Using the semantic association information contained in collaborative filtering, combined with artificial intelligence, to carry out applications such as recommending projects and groups to volunteers, evaluating volunteers participating in projects and groups, knowledge Q&A for volunteer services, and volunteer service retrieval, will provide strong support for volunteer service work in the Internet environment.

Currently, the research focus in the field of voluntary service is still on management systems and service models [9]. There is little research on data in the current field. There are also studies on volunteer service management platforms in the academic community, but there are few cases of using big data in the field to develop intelligent applications. Therefore, building collaborative filtering in the field of volunteer services and developing its application value is of great significance for the development of volunteer services.

2.2 Construction of Volunteer Service Domain Map

Generally, logically, the knowledge map is divided into two levels: the schema layer and the data layer. The schema layer is above the data layer and is also the core of the knowledge map, involving entity types, relationship types, attribute types, and so on.

The data layer stores specific data based on the schema layer. For example, the schema layer of a knowledge map contains the data schema (person, birthplace, region), while the data layer stores real data such as (Yao Ming, birthplace, Shanghai).

Ontology, as a concept that can describe information systems at the semantic and knowledge levels, is widely used to construct a schema layer of knowledge maps. Standard ontology modeling frameworks include RDFS (Resource Description Framework Schema), oWL (Web Ontology Language), and so on [10]. Considering that the hierarchical relationship of volunteer service data sources is relatively clear and it is easy to design top-level concepts, compared to converting source data into RDFS/OWL description language and storing it in a relational database or graph database, drawing on the idea of ontology, the method of manually defining patterns to directly extract knowledge and store it will be faster and more efficient.

The process for building a knowledge map in the field of volunteer service is shown in Fig. 1. First, complete the design of the knowledge map pattern layer: analyze the data characteristics of volunteer service and the subject and object of volunteer service behavior, and conduct entity design according to the "entity attribute attribute value" pattern; After completing the entity design, excavate the relationships between different types of volunteer entities, and complete the relationship design according to "entity relationship entity" [11]. Then, according to the designed structural pattern, use the data processing tool Spark SQL to write scripts, extract corresponding entity relationship knowledge from volunteer service data sources, and fill in the data layer of the vertical domain map. Finally, the knowledge data is stored in a designed database as the basis for knowledge services, which includes the relational database MySQL and the graph database Neo4j.

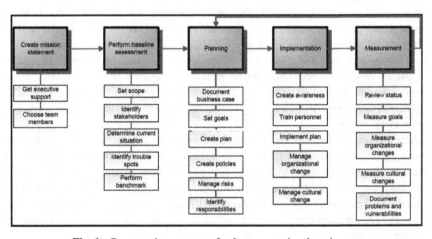

Fig. 1. Construction process of volunteer service domain map

3 Collaborative Filtering Algorithm

3.1 Basic Concept of Collaborative Filtering Algorithm

The rapid development of Internet technology has brought massive amounts of data and information to people. On the one hand, it has made it more difficult for users to search and process information; On the other hand, useful information is diluted by the information ocean, and the gap between users and content producers becomes increasingly apparent. An excellent recommendation system can provide personalized services for users. Collaborative filtering algorithms are the most popular among many information filtering technologies. Collaborative filtering algorithms are divided into user based collaborative filtering algorithm UserCF and item based collaborative filtering algorithm ltemCF. A user based collaborative filtering algorithm uses user historical behavior data to recommend items that other users have similar interests and like [12]. The collaborative filtering algorithm based on items is similar to the collaborative filtering algorithm based on users. It only swaps the roles of goods and users, obtains the connection between items by calculating the ratings of other users on the items, and then uses the similarity between items to recommend similar items to the user. The biggest advantage of collaborative filtering algorithms is that they have no special requirements for recommended objects and can handle unstructured and complex objects. Collaborative filtering algorithms provide personalized recommendations based on user similarity rather than the objective attributes of items [13]. Therefore, it can filter any type of item, such as movies, music, text, and so on. Since the implementation of this volunteer service platform only uses user based collaborative filtering algorithms, we analyze user based collaborative filtering algorithms.

Collaborative filtering algorithm is a typical personalized recommendation algorithm, which can give the possible needs of the target, and can also comprehensively analyze whether other targets have similar needs according to the related needs of the target. Collaborative filtering algorithm with usual used in e-commerce, common in all kinds of electric business platform, the algorithm is implemented by the platform function for "guess you like", "the others like", the two functions will rely on the target platform behavior data analysis of the demand, and then compared with commodity demand, if demand characteristics consistent with the a label of goods, Means the target may need this goods, goods will be included in the list, at the same time match degree on the surface of the product characteristics and the demand is higher, the goods the higher order on the recommended list, on behalf of the recommendation higher priority, such as A demand characteristics, one of all the features of A label with A commodity is the same, there are two features the same as the B goods two labels, Then the recommendation priority of product B will be higher than product A in the recommendation list [14]. Based on this, if A demand characteristics, all and any item in the same label, and will combine the label target characteristics were analyzed, and the demand for other if found existing in the demand of target and label of the same characteristics, will be A demand for target and other related requirements, and to demand A target push other related requirements have ever been browsing, But A needs goods that the target has not browsed. Figs. 2 and 3 are the topologies of the recommendation functions of "Guess what you like" and "others like it too" under the collaborative filtering algorithm[1–3].

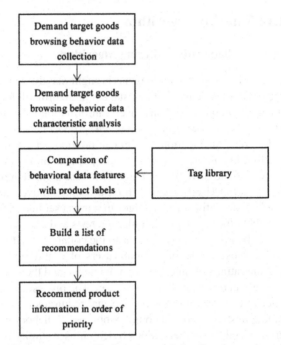

Fig. 2. Topology of "guess what you like" recommendation function under collaborative filtering algorithm

College volunteers, from this perspective, if you can provide the services as commodities, demand will be server as a goal, you can in volunteer service platform, collaborative filtering algorithm is used to guarantee college students volunteer service accuracy, namely according to the students professional ability, set up a number of volunteer organizations, According to different organizational capacity building services and project label, and then collect the relevant data of different service target groups, characteristics, extract the data again with service project tag matching, can recommend the service goal service organizations, service goal to make a choice after the corresponding service organization to provide services, can also according to other same type service goal ever make a choice, Provide service items not selected by the service target [15].

It should be noted that although the logic of collaborative filtering algorithm is simple and easy to understand, a complete algorithm model must be established before it can be put into use. The algorithm model is called intersection division union (see Formula (1) for details).

$$J(A, B) = \frac{|A \cap B|}{|A \cup B|} \tag{1}$$

Type J is compatibility, (A, B) is the demand for the target data set of features and labels, calculated, using jie card similarity coefficient is both matching degree and does not match the degree, if matching degrees greater than do not match, can recommend, and vice recommendation is not recommended, and according to the matching degree

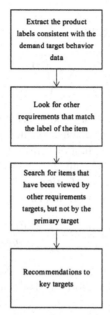

Fig. 3. Topology of "Others also like" recommendation function under collaborative filtering algorithm

exceeds the value does not match the size of the judgment related products recommended priority.

3.2 Recommended Algorithm Evaluation Indicators

Evaluation indicators are mainly used to evaluate the performance of algorithms. Scoring prediction requires indicators to evaluate the accuracy of prediction. Top-N recommendation evaluation requires calculating accuracy, recall, and other indicators to evaluate the performance of algorithms.

Scoring prediction refers to the prediction score given to a project by a user by a recommendation algorithm. The indicators used to evaluate its accuracy include average absolute error and root mean square error:

1) The average absolute error (MAE) represents the prediction accuracy of the recommendation. The average absolute error between the algorithm's prediction score and the user's actual score. The smaller the value, the more accurate the prediction is, and the higher the recommendation quality is, as shown in formula (2):

$$MAE = \sum_{i=1}^{N} \frac{|P_i - Q_i|}{N} \tag{2}$$

2) Root mean square error (RMSE) is the arithmetic square root of the expected value of the square of the difference between the estimated value of a parameter and the

true value. It is a more rigorous indicator for punishing user project scoring errors with greater effort. The calculation of RMSE is shown in Formula (3):

$$RMSE = \sum_{i=1}^{N} \sqrt{\frac{|P_i - Q_i|^2}{N}} \tag{3}$$

The main evaluation indicators for ranking accuracy recommended by Top-N are accuracy rate and recall rate, and the calculation method is as follows:

3) Accuracy indicates the proportion of items that users are interested in and have preferences in the total number of recommended Top N ranking. The higher the value of Precision, the higher the user's satisfaction with the recommendation results. The calculation formula for accuracy is shown in (4):

$$Precision = \frac{\sum_{u \in U} |R(u) \cap T(u)|}{\sum_{u \in U} |R(u)|} \tag{4}$$

4) Recall rate indicates how many items that users truly prefer are successfully recommended and displayed by the algorithm. The calculation formula for recall rate is shown in (5):

$$Recall = \frac{\sum_{n \in U} |R(u) \cap T(u)|}{\sum_{u \in U} |T(u)|} \tag{5}$$

where R (u) represents the recommended result sequence calculated from the model training set, and T (u) represents the user's true favorite list.

4   College Student Volunteer Platform Design and Practical Application

4.1   Platform Design

Collaborative filtering algorithm is important in the design of college student volunteer platform, but to ensure that the platform can be put into practice, other technologies are needed to build the platform framework. See Fig. 4 for the platform framework built in this paper.

According to Fig. 3, the platform is mainly divided into two levels, the first is the application layer, its application by operation interface, display interface and data source platform, operation application interface is mainly used for target selection service projects, platform display is mainly used for services related information, so the service target is generated under the browse or operation of the behavior of the corresponding data, this data will all be imported into the data source. The data source is like a temporary database with a small repository capacity, but all the databases that enter the data source are directly imported into the analysis layer after preprocessing. Layer, the second is analysis by the database, the algorithm module, the output of three parts, including database are responsible for transmitting data storage application layer, and are classified, after classifying the data according to the classification algorithm module

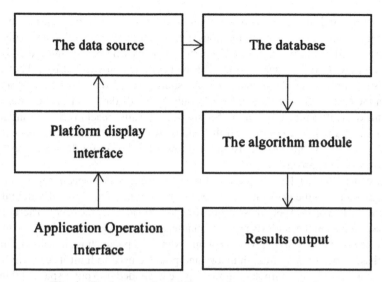

Fig. 4. The framework of college student volunteer platform

project input, driven collaborative filtering algorithm, through computing the output, the results form for service goals exist which requirements, which service projects are selected in order to schedule, design or adjust the service plan for college student volunteer service organizations? The implementation of each level and related components of this platform is as follows.

(1) Application Layer Implementation.

The first is the application operation interface, the interface mainly uses VB for key design, UI design after completion, and then the use of Java language to develop functional programs, functional programs and corresponding keys together, import into the UI framework.

Secondly, the platform display interface, which is a whole with the application operation interface, will be designed on the basis of the application operation interface. UI technology is mainly used to complete the work in the design, which requires the interface to be concise and logical. After the interface is designed, the jump connection is designed to facilitate the service target operation.

Finally, the data source, which is essentially an information collection function program, is responsible for collecting the behavior data of the service target in the above two interfaces. Therefore, Java language is used to complete the development of the information collection function. In order to ensure the reasonable operation of the information collection function, the functional operation logic design is carried out. Firstly, the data types of service target behavior are manually distinguished, which are divided into browsing and operation. Then, related classified items are commonly found in the functional program, and the representative functional program will collect the data of these two classified items. Second, the information collection delay parameter is set as 1 s, which means that the functional program will collect relevant classified data within 1 s, ensuring the real-time performance of information collection. Third, for the sake of data quality and the accuracy of the final calculation results, the preprocessing tool is selected, which is now mature and does not need to be developed again. This paper mainly selects the data matching tool, which can check whether the input data is complete according to the standard format. If it is incomplete, it will not be collected, and vice versa. Fourthly, in order to make the data source into all data can be timely analysis layer, in the first set forward logic, namely only forwards data after pretreatment, after setting the data into a time interval, for 5 s, storage time after reaching 5 s forward if meet the logic of data will be forwarded, if the data is still not be within 5 s preprocessing, it forwards the data to adjust to the list of most lower level, wait for the next loop.

(2) Analysis layer implementation.

The first is the database. Although the service target is a specific group and the number of people in the group is not large, a large amount of analysis of different types of behavioral data of each person is needed to accurately identify the needs. Therefore, the magnitude of data in the analysis process is large, and the conventional database may not meet the needs of data storage. Aiming at this point, this paper chose the cloud database, the database capacity is infinite, in theory and practice need to limit its capacity for the sake of data security, an entire data storage space is divided into outer space and interior space, and then set up a firewall between the two, the firewall will limit the database capacity, but even if is restricted, In actual applications, you can also temporarily turn off the firewall for capacity expansion, so there is no need to worry that its unlimited capacity advantage cannot be brought into play. In addition, the relevant resources of the cloud database are used to develop the data classification function, which can complete the classification according to the characteristics and sources of data sources.

The second is the algorithm module, which is built according to the model of formula (1) and realizes the model logic with the help of Java language in the process. After testing, the algorithm module can operate normally, indicating that the platform is successfully equipped with collaborative filtering algorithm.

The last is result output, which mainly uses communication technology to connect the output end of the platform with the manual terminal. When the corresponding result is generated after the data is calculated by the algorithm module, the result will be sent to the manual terminal through the communication channel, and the manual can read it directly, and then make judgment and decision.

4.2 Practical Application

A poor rural area in domestic group as an example, the groups involved are 70 years old or older, childless in the home, their basic lose labor ability, usually rely on manual, after a preliminary visit investigation understands, the community of all kinds of demand, but because the old expression ability is limited, and cannot tell oneself all requirements, So volunteers can't provide accurate services under these conditions. On this basis, the elderly in this group are provided with equipment to enter the platform and learn the platform operation under the guidance of special-assigned personnel (considering the particularity of the elderly, the platform operation design adopts one-click design). Then, the behavior data of all the people in this group are collected for one month, and then relevant analysis is conducted to obtain the final result.

The results show that there are two main needs of the elderly in this group. One is that they want someone to help them do and sell handcrafts. The second is to hope that someone can accompany themselves to make up for their inner emotional vacancy. In the face of the two needs, the platform recommends college student volunteer organizations majoring in manual arts and nursing to the relevant groups. After the relevant people choose by themselves or clearly express their needs for help, the organizations provide volunteer services to the corresponding college student volunteer organizations. The service process is about three months.

After three months of service, the needs of this group can be theoretically met to a certain extent. However, in order to verify this point and verify the actual function of this platform, a satisfaction survey is conducted for this group. The survey results are shown in Table 1.

Table 1. Survey Results (10 participants)

Survey questions	Data results
Are you satisfied with the volunteer service process?	Very satisfied (10 people) Satisfied (-) General (-) Not satisfied (-)
Are you satisfied with the results of your volunteer service?	Very satisfied (8 people) Satisfied (2 people) General (-) Not satisfied (-)

According to Table 1, after three months of service, the group all people feel very satisfied, the process of volunteer service on behalf of the group scheduling volunteers accurate, accurate service scheme design, and eight people for volunteer service result was very satisfactory, 2 people are satisfied, so the overall results are in good quality service, the result will be the difference of satisfaction, It may be due to insufficient service level of volunteers or negligence in work, but this does not mean that the service items are not accurate enough. On the contrary, the overall performance of quality results is good, which also indicates that the platform recommendation is accurate and the algorithm application is effective.

5 Conclusion

In conclusion, the collaborative filtering algorithm can improve the accuracy of volunteer service in the college student volunteer platform, and solve the problem that the service cannot be accurately served due to the inability to accurately understand the service target demand. With the help of this algorithm, the effectiveness and effectiveness of college student volunteer service have been improved and protected, which indicates that the algorithm has high application value.

References

1. Gao, C.: Design and Implementation of School-Enterprise Cooperation Information Service Platform Based on Mobile Internet Technology (2022)
2. Zha, Z., Huang, W., Tang, D., et al.: Design and implementation of linkage update management system for geo-information service platform. Copernicus GmbH (2021)
3. Su, X., Cheng, X., Wang, B.: Design and Implementation of "multi survey integration" Management Service Platform. J. Phys. Conf. Ser. **1961**(1), 012061 (2021)
4. Wang, H., Shen, Z., Jiang, S., et al.: User-based collaborative filtering algorithm design and implementation. J. Phys.: Conf. Ser. **1757**(1), 012168 (6pp) (2021)
5. Ling, Y.: Design and implementation of the platform for multimedia resource sharing based on cloud technology (7) (2022)
6. Cui, Y., Zhang, L., Hou, Y., et al.: Design of intelligent home pension service platform based on machine learning and wireless sensor network. J. Intell. Fuzzy Syst.: Appl. Eng. Technol. **2**, 40 (2021)
7. Lee, J., Hong, J.S.: method for providing interior design market platform service using realistic scene image based on virtual space content data and apparatus therefor, WO2022039567A1[P] (2022)
8. Hu, X.: Improved algorithm of cloud service node path based on cross-border transaction platform under load balancing. Comput. Commun. **177**, 195–206 (2021)
9. Liang, Y., Huang, X., Chen, Z., et al.: Construction method and architecture of integrated energy service ecological platform based on support vector machine (2021)
10. Zhang, F., Yang, L., Liu, Y., et al.: Design and implementation of real-time localization system (RTLS) based on UWB and TDoA Algorithm (2021)
11. Modares, A., Farimani, N.M., Emroozi, V.B.: A new model to design the suppliers portfolio in newsvendor problem based on product reliability. J. Ind. Manage. Optim. **19**(6), 4112–4151 (2023)
12. Domenico, G.D., Panichella, A., Weisman, D., et al.: Large-scale inverse design of a planar on-chip mode sorter. ACS Photon. **9**(2), 378–382 (2022)
13. Wang, J.: The design and development of the internet-based system for testing and analyzing the psychological and physiological responses during creative learning. Front. Psychol. **13**, 886972 (2022)
14. Zhou, H.: Optimization of the rapid design system for arts and crafts based on big data and 3D technology. Complexity (2021)
15. Asare, A.L., Beitler, J.R., Cimino, G., et al.: I-SPY COVID adaptive platform trial for COVID-19 acute respiratory failure: rationale, design and operations. BMJ Open **12**(6), 686–689 (2022)

Personalized Song Recommendation System Based on Vocal Characteristics

Keri Qing[✉] and Zhili Ni

Luoyang Institute of Science and Technology, Henan 471000, China
yesa8510@126.com

Abstract. With the rapid development of the Internet, people are enjoying the convenience and quickness brought by information sharing. However, in the face of the continuous rise of the amount of information, people are facing the problem of unable to carry out information retrieval quickly and accurately. It is in this case that Google and Baidu search have been recognized by users and developed rapidly, becoming the world's top IT companies. Although search engines can be used to retrieve Internet information, the search results are often not targeted because they can not accurately obtain users' interests and preferences. Personalized services for different users are the needs of customers. Users listen to music on the Internet, facing thousands of music information, it is difficult to find their favorite music. Therefore, how to recommend music for different users has always been the focus of research and development of Internet enterprises. Personalized recommendation system came into being under this background.

Keywords: Vocal characteristics · Information sharing · Personalized recommendation · song

1 Introduction

With the continuous expansion of the music market, the number and types of music are growing rapidly. Users often need to spend a lot of time to find their own satisfactory music. Information overload affects users' online shopping experience and directly affects the product sales of enterprises in the music market. In order to solve this problem, personalized recommendation system came into being. Personalized recommendation can recommend interested information and music to users according to their interest characteristics and purchase behavior. It is an advanced intelligent platform based on massive data mining. It can help users of music market websites shop and provide completely personalized decision support and information services.

Vocal music art is a music art in the form of singing, which transmits ideas and expresses feelings through sound. China's national vocal music is gradually formed according to China's special cultural and artistic aesthetic style. China's national vocal music singing art has a long history and rich singing style. With the development of society, global information sharing and cultural exchange and penetration of various

Y. Zhang and N. Shah (Eds.): BigIoT-EDU 2023, LNICST 583, pp. 215–220, 2024.
https://doi.org/10.1007/978-3-031-63139-9_23

countries. National vocal music culture has also developed rapidly. Society is progressing, and the aesthetic value of the audience is also changing. In order to make national vocal music songs continue to be loved by more audiences. National songs should retain their national characteristics and their own cultural value, absorb and learn from the experience and vocal skills of Western vocal music, so as to form their own unique singing characteristics, and the singing of national vocal music will be more abundant.

Since the birth of personalized recommendation system, relevant scholars have continuously improved and improved the recommendation algorithm in order to improve the recommendation accuracy of personalized recommendation system. At present, the recommendation accuracy of personalized recommendation system can basically meet the needs of users. However, the improvement of recommendation accuracy is often based on more complex calculation and deep data mining. At the same time, the amount of data that needs to be calculated by the current personalized recommendation system is far from being comparable at the beginning of the birth of the recommendation system. The real-time recommendation of personalized recommendation system has become an important factor restricting the user satisfaction of personalized recommendation system. In view of the successful application of cloud computing platform all over the world. This paper uses the powerful data computing power of cloud computing to solve the recommendation speed problem in personalized recommendation system.

2 Personalized Recommendation Related Technologies

2.1 Development of Cloud Computing

Cloud computing is formed through the mixed evolution of a variety of technologies. It has a high maturity and is promoted by large companies. Google, Amazon, IBM and other large companies are the pioneers of cloud computing.

Google is currently the main driver and user of cloud computing technology. Google search engine is built on the support of more than 200 sites and more than 1 million servers, and the number of these facilities is growing rapidly. Google Earth, Google maps, Gmail, docs and other applications are based on these distributed parallel servers. And it is commendable that Google allows third parties to run large parallel applications through Google App Engine, and offers cloud computing programming courses all over the world [1].

China's cloud computing is also developing rapidly. In 2008, IBM successively established two cloud computing centers in Wuxi and Beijing; Century Lianhua launched cloudex product line, providing Internet hosting services, online storage virtualization services, etc.; China Mobile Research Institute has established a cloud computing experimental center with 1024 CPUs; PLA University of technology has developed a cloud storage system masscloud, which supports large-scale video surveillance applications and digital earth systems based on 3G. Domestic IT security manufacturers such as Jinshan, Jiangmin and 360 security guards have launched cloud security solutions. In November 2009, the China Internet Conference held the "2009 cloud computing industry summit".

The development of cloud computing will make the computing architecture of the Internet evolve from "server + client" to "cloud service platform + client". Make the

Internet become the data center and computing center of every user, and make users transfer from using various applications with the desktop as the core to carrying out various activities with the web as the core. Cloud computing makes the function of the Internet more powerful. Through cloud computing, ordinary enterprises and even users will be able to use the huge data and processing capacity that only a few large enterprises have in the past to obtain the information they need.

2.2 Personalized Recommendation Algorithm

In recent years, collaborative filtering recommendation has been very popular in information filtering and information analysis systems. Collaborative filtering is different from the traditional filtering based on content 2L, which directly analyzes the content for personalized recommendation. The collaborative filtering algorithm mainly analyzes the user's interest, finds the set of users with similar interests of the recommended user in the user group in the database, and synthesizes the preferences of these similar users for the items that the user has not evaluated, Form the system's prediction of the specified user's preference for this item.

The starting point of collaborative filtering technology is that no one's interest is isolated. It believes that a single person's interest will generally be in the interest set concerned by a certain group. If some users have similar scores on some items, their scores on other items will generally be similar, at least not too different. For example, in daily life, people often make their own choices based on the recommendations and suggestions of relatives and friends or people with similar backgrounds and interests, such as shopping, reading, listening to music, etc. Collaborative filtering system applies this idea to network information service recommendation, and recommends to target users based on the evaluation of certain information by other users. The recommendation effect has certain advantages over other algorithms. The mapping relationship between Mel frequency and ordinary audio frequency is shown in Eq. 1:

$$mel(f) = 259 \times \log(1 + \frac{f}{700}) \qquad (1)$$

where f is the normal audio frequency.

Taking the user based collaborative filtering recommendation algorithm as an example, users a and C have higher similarity in song preferences. As shown in Fig. 1.

According to different filtering methods, academia roughly divides collaborative filtering technology into two types: user based collaborative filtering and item based collaborative filtering [2]. User based collaborative recommendation is to find the neighbor user set of the target user according to the similarity between users and users, and then make personalized recommendation to the target user according to the interest of the neighbor user; Project based collaborative filtering is to recommend those projects similar to the projects purchased by the target user (with good evaluation) to the current customer by analyzing the similarity between projects. The user based collaborative filtering technology was proposed earlier than the item based filtering algorithm. Therefore, the collaborative filtering technology mentioned in the early literature often refers to the user based collaborative filtering technology. Project based collaborative filtering

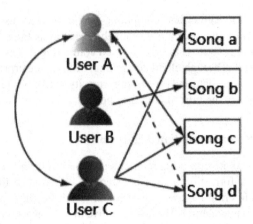

Fig. 1. Content based recommendation map

is often referred to as project-based recommendation. The default collaborative filtering algorithm in this paper also refers to the user based collaborative filtering algorithm.

3   Personalized Song Recommendation System Based on Vocal Characteristics

The algorithm of personalized recommendation system with vocal characteristics studied in this paper is collaborative filtering algorithm, which is the most widely used algorithm in personalized recommendation at present. In order to improve its response speed and operation efficiency, this paper uses the distributed computing power and distributed storage technology of cloud computing to calculate the personalized recommendation system with vocal music characteristics, and tries to ensure the recommendation real-time requirements of the recommendation system on the premise of stable recommendation accuracy.

At present, the data processing of Cloud Computing mainly uses distributed storage and distributed computing technology, which are also the core of cloud computing. The main focus of this paper is distributed computing, which uses the efficient computing power of distributed computing to improve the recommendation speed of recommendation system [3].

As a software system widely used in the fields of music market, digital library, free music sharing, news recommendation and so on, the personalized recommendation system with vocal music characteristics is mainly developed, studied and improved by the IT departments of relevant enterprises, which wastes a lot of human, material and financial resources. The change of IT resource delivery and deployment mode provides the feasibility for the personalized recommendation system to be sold as an independent software music. In this case, the personalized recommendation system with vocal music characteristics, which is mainly applied in the music market, will no longer need to be developed and studied by each enterprise alone. Music market enterprises only need to purchase personalized recommendation system application services, storage resources and computing resources from cloud computing platform operators. This resource utilization mode will not only effectively save enterprise it costs, but also improve the operation efficiency of personalized recommendation system.

The main control program master assigns tasks to m working machines. Firstly, the project scoring matrix of the target user is transmitted to each working machine, and then the m working machines calculate the similarity between each user and the target user in parallel. The calculation formula is as follows:

$$r_{u,o} = \frac{1}{N} \sum_{u' \in U'} r_{u',o} \tag{2}$$

$$r_{u,o} = \bar{r} + d \sum_{u' \in U'} sim(u, u') \bullet (r_{u',o} - \bar{r}_M) \tag{3}$$

With the emergence of massive data, how to effectively store and use massive data has become an urgent problem to be solved. At present, the three common storage methods are DAS, NAS and San. However, in the face of more and more data generated by the network, the shortcomings of these three methods are obviously exposed. Das storage mode has poor scalability, low system performance and scattered storage.

4 Personality Recommendation Analysis of Vocal Characteristics

Because the personalized recommendation algorithm used in this paper is a user-based collaborative filtering algorithm, the recommendation quality of the recommendation system is not improved compared with the traditional recommendation system. The biggest advantage of the personalized recommendation system based on vocal characteristics is the great improvement of the recommendation performance. This is also the significance of migrating the personalized recommendation system to the vocal feature platform.

The main advantages of personalized recommendation system based on vocal characteristics are distributed storage of massive data, super distributed computing power, reliable fault-tolerant mechanism, high scalability, flexible utilization of resources and so on [4]. This paper mainly discusses the improvement of recommendation performance under the vocal feature mode, but the personalized recommendation based on vocal feature brings more than the improvement of recommendation performance to enterprises and users. It provides a complete set of massive data storage, super data calculation, reliable data maintenance and so on. E-commerce enterprises do not have to invest huge amounts of hardware and software equipment for complex data storage, analysis, mining and other data processing, so as to reduce the management of relevant technicians.

Compared with the collaborative filtering algorithm based on clustering, the recommendation accuracy of personalized recommendation system based on vocal features is relatively stable. The accuracy of collaborative filtering algorithm based on clustering is affected by the selection of cluster number and the selection of initial cluster center. While the personalized recommendation system based on vocal characteristics can effectively reduce the response speed of the system, there are no difficulties faced by the clustering algorithm.

5 Conclusion

The personalized recommendation system of vocal music features is used to help users find interesting content in the massive music information, and has become a necessary function of many music market websites, electronic libraries and so on. For profit-making enterprises, personalized recommendation can turn visitors into buyers. According to customers' preferences or interests, and recommend additional products to customers to generate cross selling benefits. Personalized recommendation can quickly and accurately help visitors find their interested music information and improve the utilization efficiency of music information. With the development of personalized recommendation system, the recommendation accuracy is basically satisfactory. This is also because scholars' research on personalized recommendation technology has mainly focused on the improvement of recommendation accuracy and recommendation performance. At present, there are many algorithms based on collaborative filtering for cold start, Some scholars have given good improvement ideas and feasible suggestions on data sparsity.

References

1. Dongshan, X., Junyi, S.: Research on Internet collaborative recommendation system based on Web log. J. Xi'an Jiaotong Univ. 36(12), 1271–1274 (2002)
2. Ailin, D., Yangyong, Z.: Shi bole, collaborative filtering recommendation algorithm based on project score prediction. J. Softw. 14(9), 1621–1628 (2003)
3. Peiying, Z.: Personalized web page recommendation system based on Web content and log mining, computer application system. 17(9), 9–11 (2008)
4. Juan, F., Wencan, L.: A grid portal recommendation model based on collaborative filtering. J. Electron. Inf. 7 (2010)

Adaptive Recommendation Algorithm of English Reading Learning Resources Based on Collaborative Filtering

Tong Yang[1], Haifeng Xu[2], and Shu Yuan Chen[2(✉)]

[1] Old College South Bridge Edinburgh, The University of Edinburgh, Edinburgh EH8 9YL, Scotland, UK

[2] School of Naval Architecture and Ocean Engineering, Jiangsu University of Science and Technology, Jiangsu 212100, China

shuyuanchen561@163.com

Abstract. The rapid development of the Internet has promoted the emergence of a large number of English learning resources and online education platforms. However, the massive resources and learning methods have also led to the emergence of the dilemma of information overload, and it has become quite difficult for users to quickly obtain the information they are interested in. Therefore, it is one of the current research hotspots in the field of education to study a highly automated personalized learning adaptive recommendation model to recommend a learning plan suitable for the learner's own learning situation for a specific course or field. Based on the collaborative filtering algorithm model, this paper integrates the depth of user English learning, the collaborative topic regression model based on social regularization and the collaborative deep learning model based on social regularization, and finally generates a personalized English reading learning plan.

Keywords: Personalized recommendation · system filtering algorithm · user similarity · English reading

1 Introduction

The recommendation system can provide each user with an exclusive personalized recommendation service, which is not available in search engines. Search engines can only provide users with relevant information based on the most mainstream information and keywords provided by users. The process of obtaining information by the recommendation system is active, and it will automatically recommend things that may be of interest to users based on user behavior, browsing records, purchase records, and user personal information [1, 2]. That is, different users get different results from the system feedback. However, the recommendation accuracy of the existing recommendation algorithm is not very high, which affects the user experience. If the recommendation quality of the recommendation system can be improved, it will play an important role in improving user stickiness. The personalized recommendation algorithm can select

Y. Zhang and N. Shah (Eds.): BigIoT-EDU 2023, LNICST 583, pp. 221–230, 2024.
https://doi.org/10.1007/978-3-031-63139-9_24

effective information from a large amount of information and recommend it to users, which saves time and improves efficiency for users, and effectively solves the problem of information overload to a certain extent [3]. Therefore, the research on personalized recommendation technology is of great significance.

In the actual personalized recommendation system, there are usually a lot of English articles, and the number of users will continue to increase [4]. This makes the user-item rating matrix of the recommender system very sparse, which greatly affects the recommendation quality of the recommender system. Therefore, how to make the recommender system can accurately and quickly dig out the potential interests and preferences of users to provide users with high-quality recommendations is an important problem faced by the current personalized recommender systems [5]. Theoretically, personalized recommendation technology is an important part of information mining and information filtering. In modern society, people gradually realize the importance of personalized recommendation technology, but there are still some problems, such as data sparsity, scalability, and cold start. In order to develop well, recommender systems must solve these problems [6].

1.1 Memory-Based Collaborative Filtering Algorithm

The memory-based collaborative filtering algorithm is relatively mature in theoretical research and commercial applications because the algorithm is relatively easy to implement and can provide online push services for users. In the process of memory-based collaborative filtering algorithm, the quality of similarity design directly affects the effectiveness of the recommendation system [7]. Therefore, in order to obtain better similarity calculation, many researchers have invested a lot of time and energy, and the similarity research designs applied to different scenarios are constantly enriched [8].

Cosine similarity is a popular similarity calculation, which is widely used in text and image processing research. By calculating the cosine between the angle between two vectors, the difference between the two is compared. The larger the cosine value, the better the two. Similar, and vice versa. The collaborative filtering algorithm based on cosine similarity assumes that if users have similar interests, then their ratings on the same item are also the same, or assume that two items are similar and users rate the two items the same., and then filter out the candidate set of a specific user according to the set threshold, and finally select the items that the specific user has not scored from the candidate set, combine the scoring habits of the specific user, make a weighted score prediction, and push the top IV items according to the prediction results. to users. The calculation formula (1) of cosine similarity is as follows

$$sim(i_1, i_2) = \cos(i_1, i_2) = \frac{\sum_{j=1}^{J} r_{i1}, r_{i2}}{\sqrt{\sum_{j=1}^{J} r_{i1,j}^2} \sqrt{\sum_{j=1}^{J} r_{i2,j}^2}} \quad (1)$$

Among them, the value range of sim(i1,i2) is [0,1], i1 represents the user's scoring vector for all items, if there is no score,

Then its score is 0.

The cosine similarity calculation method does not take into account the difference in rating scales between different users. The correlation similarity calculation method is normalized by subtracting the average of the user's rating for all rated items from the user's rating of the item. [9]. The correlation similarity is generally calculated using the Pearson correlation coefficient method.

$$sim(i_1, i_2) = \cos(i_1, i_2) = \frac{\sum_{i \in I_{uv}} (R_{u,i} - \overline{R}_u) \times (R_{u,i} - \overline{R}_v)}{\sqrt{\sum_{i \in I_{uv}} (R_{u,i} - \overline{R}_u)^2} \sqrt{\sum_{i \in I_{uv}} (R_{u,i} - \overline{R}_v)^2}} \tag{2}$$

In the cosine similarity measurement method, the difference problem caused by the difference of user rating scales is not considered. Like the related similarity calculation method, the modified cosine similarity calculation method is calculated by subtracting the user's rating on the item by subtracting all the user's rating.

1.2 Model-Based Collaborative Filtering Algorithms

The memory-based collaborative filtering algorithm performs well when the observation data is relatively dense, but as the number of users and items increases exponentially, the scoring matrix becomes more and more sparse, and the high-dimensional calculation leads to an increase in time complexity. Seriously affects the recommendation performance. The model-based collaborative filtering algorithm can solve these problems well. According to the training data and test data, the decision model is optimized and designed to provide users with personalized recommendation services. Model-based collaborative filtering algorithms have been widely recognized in academia and industry, such as naive Bayesian methods, clustering methods, and matrix decomposition methods. Naive Bayes method is a well-known classification algorithm that can also be applied in the field of recommendation. When the factors affecting the classification results are conditionally independent, Naive Bayes has been shown to be the best performing solution [11].

Assuming that features are independent when given classes, one can compute the probability given all feature classes, and then classify the class with the highest probability as the predicted class. For incomplete data, probability estimates and classifications are calculated based on the observed data, and the subscript o represents the observed value, as shown in formula (3):

$$class = \arg \max_{j \in lassset} p(class_j) \prod_o p(X_o = x_o | class_j) \tag{3}$$

The Plath estimator is used to smooth the probability calculation and avoid the conditional probability being 0, as shown in Eq. (4):

$$P(X_o = x_o | Y = y) = \frac{\#(X_i = x_i, Y = y) + 1}{\#(Y = y) + |X_i|} \tag{4}$$

where IXiI represents the size of the cluster $\{Xi\}$.

Memory-based methods and model-based methods are combined, and this type of recommendation algorithm has better recommendation performance compared with single memory-based methods or model-based methods [12]. In addition, combining memory-based and model-based placement, a hybrid model is constructed from the user's profile and predicted using the posterior distribution of user ratings. In order to solve the cold start problem of new users, the model can provide reliable push for new users by learning the basic information of users. Since the hybrid collaborative filtering algorithm can provide better results than the single algorithm in the hybrid members, the hybrid collaborative filtering algorithm, by integrating and mixing different methods, helps to provide the predictive performance of the collaborative filtering algorithm.

2   Personalized Learning Recommendation Model Integrating Self-learning and Collaborative Filtering Algorithm

2.1   Construction of Personalized English Reading Learning Resource Recommendation Model

The personalized learning plan uses the curriculum knowledge map as the carrier. Knowledge points in the knowledge map correspond to unique recommendation degrees. The knowledge points with higher recommendation degree should attract more attention of learners. The recommendation degree is calculated from the degree centrality of the knowledge point and the learner's loss-point score at the knowledge point. The knowledge point with high degree-centrality indicates that the knowledge point has a high degree of importance in the knowledge network; and the loss-point score is high. The knowledge points indicate that learners have a low degree of mastery of the knowledge points [13].

The recommendation degree is marked in the knowledge points of the knowledge map, which can form the learner's personalized learning plan. The knowledge points recommended by the program are all knowledge points that learners have not yet mastered. Taking a classmate as an example, the personalized learning plan of English reading resources generated by the model is shown in Fig. 1.

Recommendations are made based on how well the user model matches the object. Therefore, the recommendation result is more in line with the user's taste, can give a better recommendation explanation, and does not require knowledge related to the recommended field; the user is independent, and when recommending for the target user, only the current user's interest information need not be considered. The relationship with other users is independent between users, thus avoiding the influence of malicious evaluation of items by some users, so it will not be constrained by the sparsity problem of evaluation data, but the algorithm only relies on The user's past preference for some recommended objects produces recommendations that are similar to the recommended objects that the user liked in the past. It is difficult to discover the user's new interests, and the recommended content is more likely to be repeated: Features extracted from the recommended objects It does not fully represent the recommended object [14]. In some cases, the content of two recommendation objects may be similar.

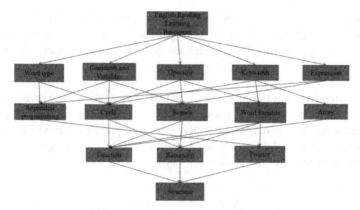

Fig. 1. Personalized learning plan

The role of the log is mainly used to model the user. In other words, it mainly converts the user's behavior information into the user's rating matrix. This rating represents how much the user likes the article. When users use the platform, they do not need to rate the articles displayed, and the system will record the rating information in the database implicitly according to the established rules. For each article, the system will set an appropriate reading time range. The log collection and processing flow is shown in Fig. 2.

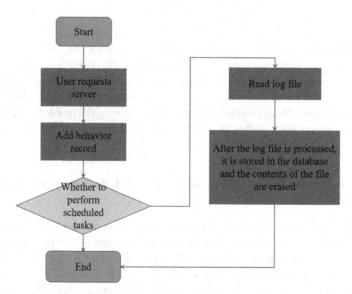

Fig. 2. Log collection and processing

The article recommendation subsystem uses user rating information and article label information to model users. This process plays a linking role in the entire recommendation process. Users and articles are modeled through the data collected by users, and the recommendation algorithm uses the user and article models. Recommendations for users.

The first improvement is to improve the calculation of user similarity, add a penalty factor, and punish the impact of popular articles on calculating user similarity. The second improvement is to cluster users. Here, the user preference model is formed by the tags of the articles and the user's rating information [15]. The schematic diagram of the recommendation algorithm is shown in Fig. 3.

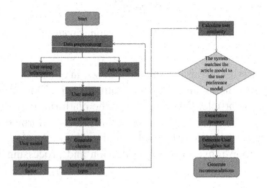

Fig. 3. Recommendation algorithm

The improved algorithm has a cold start problem. When a new user or a new project joins, it cannot give or be recommended. When solving the problem of cold start of new users, the system will recommend the most recently forwarded articles to users. During the user's use, by collecting user behaviors, a preference model is established for users, and users are assigned to appropriate clusters; when solving the problem of cold start of new articles, the system matches the article model with the user preference model, and then provides users with recommend.

2.2 Implementation Process of Personalized English Reading Learning Resource Recommendation Model

The evaluations of similar users are classified to form a recommendation for the degree of preference of the specified user's information. In the course recommendation of online learning resources, the starting point of collaborative filtering is that no one's interests are isolated, and we can apply this feature. In other words, it mainly converts the user's behavior information into the user's rating matrix. This rating represents how much the user likes the article. When users use the platform, they do not need to rate the articles displayed, and the system will record the rating information in the database implicitly according to the established rules. For each article, the system will set an appropriate reading time range.

User interest file representation: Since the recommendation of English articles for online reading based on collaborative filtering technology is based on the common interests of users, we are based on the user's rating value of the English article recommendation item, rather than the feature value proposed from the content. Data processing. Suppose that in the online reading resource recommendation system, M represents the number of elective users, and N represents the number of English articles read online. The recommendation system uses an M × N rating recommendation matrix T to represent the scoring mechanism for online reading of English articles, and the element T ij in the i-th row and j-th column indicates the evaluation score of user i for online reading of English article j. For example, when a user reads an English article online, if the English article is read, it is indicated by a number 1, and if the English article is not selected, it is indicated by 0; Represented by a boolean value. The scoring matrix of users reading English articles online is shown in (5)

$$T = \begin{pmatrix} t_{11} & t_{12} & t_{1n} \\ t_{21} & t_{22} & t_{23} \\ t_{m1} & t_{32} & t_{mn} \end{pmatrix} \tag{5}$$

In the above matrix, the number of Tij can also be expressed in another way, establishing a score level of 1–5 points, the size of Tij indicates the user's interest in the online learning course, and the larger the value, the more people who choose to study this course. With more users, each user's rating for this online learning course or each online learning course is represented as a row or column vector.

When a collaborative filtering recommendation system recommends online learning courses to users, the users do not know the content of the course, and the recommended courses are the ones that have been learned, and this situation will definitely exist in large numbers, resulting in the inapplicability of the recommended effect. Powerful. For such problems, we use a hybrid model that combines collaborative filtering technology and content filtering technology to establish a user interest model based on content filtering based on the content of online learning courses and user interests, and then generate recommendations based on the similarity between the same feature vectors. The content filtering technology filters information such as keywords and course introductions of all online courses. Each user chooses completely independently, and does not consider the interests of other users, and does not evaluate the online learning courses. Recommend to similar users based on high similarity, recommend some elective courses without evaluation or newly opened online learning courses, and require users to evaluate the recommended results in real time to improve the system's evaluation-level options.

2.3   Change User Weight Based on Number of Ratings

The calculation result of Wuv is used as the selection basis for the K most similar users. The larger the Wuv, the greater the similarity. In daily life, there are experts in every field. These experts invest more time and energy in the corresponding field than ordinary people, so the evaluation of things happening in their field is often more valuable. From this perspective, think in reverse, and think that the evaluation of people who have invested more time and energy than others in the field is more valuable. The data set used in the experiment is the score data of reading. It can be considered that the scores of those who have a large number of reading evaluations are more valuable than those who have read a small number of evaluations, so the weight of such users is increased. Here we use sigmoid. A function of the curve is added to the similarity measure to change the weight of different users. The prototype of the sigmoid curve is (6)

$$y = \frac{1}{1+e^{-x}} (x \in R, y \in (0, 1)) \tag{6}$$

The sigmoid curve is shown in Fig. 4.

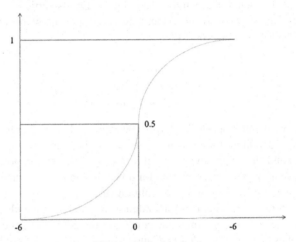

Fig. 4. Sigmoid curve.

We see that the function grows roughly exponentially in the initial phase; then the increase slows down as it starts to saturate; finally, the increase stops when it reaches maturity. This functional model is exactly in line with our previous discussion, that is, the weight is reduced for the user group with a small number of reading evaluations; and when the number of user evaluations reaches a certain level, it is considered to belong to the group with a large number of reading evaluations.

The algorithm first calculates the similarity of user characteristics based on the user's personal characteristics and the similarity of scores based on changes in user interests, as shown in Fig. 5.

The weighted summation of the two similarities is used to obtain the comprehensive similarity of users, and then the comprehensive similarity is used to cluster users, and users with similar interests are put into the same cluster. In the class, the comprehensive similarity calculation is used to find the nearest neighbor user set of the target user, and finally the target user is predicted and rated according to the score of the nearest neighbor user to the item and the recommendation is generated.

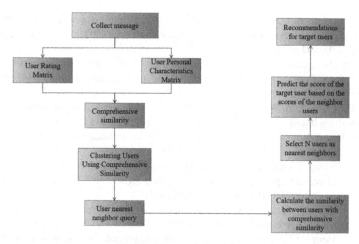

Fig. 5. Improved algorithm

3 Conclusions

In this paper, based on the collaborative filtering algorithm model, which combines the idea of user personal characteristics, user interest changes and user clustering, a user clustering algorithm based on user personal characteristics and user interest changes is proposed to cluster users according to the comprehensive similarity obtained. Put users with similar interests into the same cluster. Since the nearest neighbors of the target user are usually in some clusters with high similarity with the target user, it is not necessary to query the nearest neighbor users of the target user in the entire user space, but only in some clusters with high similarity with the target user. Find the nearest neighbors of the target user, and finally predict and score the target user and generate recommendations according to the scores of the nearest neighbors on the item.

References

1. Cheng, J., Wang, H.: Adaptive algorithm recommendation and application of learning resources in English fragmented reading. Complexity **2021**, 1–11 (2021)
2. Wang, H., Fu, W.: Personalized learning resource recommendation method based on dynamic collaborative filtering. Mobile Netw. Appl. **2020**, 1–15 (2020)
3. Shu, J., Shen, X., Liu, H., et al.: A content-based recommendation algorithm for learning resources. Multimedia Syst. **24**(2), 163–173 (2018)
4. Jacobsen Fredrik, A., HafliEllen, W.: Tronstad Christian Martinsen Ørjan G. ogm@fys. uio. No Department of Physics, University of Oslo, Oslo Norway Department of Clinical and Biomedical Engineering, Oslo University Hospital, Oslo Norway. Classification of emotions based on electrodermal activity and transfer learning - a pilot study. J. Electrical Bioimpedance **12**(1), 178–183 (2021)
5. Wang, Z.H., Hou, D.Z.: Research on book recommendation algorithm based on collaborative filtering and interest degree. Wirel. Commun. Mob. Comput. **2021**(4), 1–7 (2021)
6. Li, H., Zhang, S., Shi, J., et al.: Research and design of intelligent learning system based on recommendation technology. Control. Intell. Syst. **47**(1), 43–49 (2019)

7. Cheng, H., Gan, B., Zhang, C.: Research on personalized recommendation method based on social impact theory. J. Phys. Conf. Ser. **1848**(1), 012128 (2021). https://doi.org/10.1088/1742-6596/1848/1/012128

8. Huang, X., Wang, G.: Learning recommendation based on hybrid collaborative filtering algorithm. J. Phys. Conf. Ser. **1629**(1), 012008 (2020). https://doi.org/10.1088/1742-6596/1629/1/012008

9. Yang, Y.Z., Zhong, Y., Woniak, M.: Improvement of adaptive learning service recommendation algorithm based on big data. Mobile Netw. Appl. **2021**, 1–12 (2021)

10. Zhe, T.: Research on the model of music sight-singing guidance system based on artificial intelligence. Complexity **2021**(29), 1–11 (2021)

11. Gan, B., Zhang, C.: Design of personalized recommendation system for online learning resources based on improved collaborative filtering algorithm. E3S Web Conf. **214**, 01051 (2020). https://doi.org/10.1051/e3sconf/202021401051

12. Huang, Y., Mai, Q.: Research on the construction of O2O teaching system of cross-cultural knowledge in College English based on MOOC. J. Intell. Fuzzy Syst. **5**, 1–10 (2021)

13. Chen, X., Deng, H.: Research on personalized recommendation methods for online video learning resources. Appl. Sci. **11**(2), 804 (2021)

14. Shu, J., Shen, X., Liu, H., et al.: A content-based recommendation algorithm for learning resources. Multimedia Syst. **1**, 1–11 (2020)

15. Zheng, H.U.: Multi level recommendation system of college online learning resources based on multi intelligence algorithm. J. Phys. Conf. Ser. **873**(1), 012078 (2021)

Multi-dimensional Approaches to the Cultivation of Craftsman Spirit in Colleges and Universities Under the Technology of Algorithm Recommendation

Minfa Shi(✉)

The Academy of Marxism of Hefei Technology College, Hefei 230012, Anhui, China
shiminfa1920@126.com

Abstract. From communication to transportation, from entertainment to education, from business to health care, technology is having an impact on all these areas. In the current education system, as educators, we must keep up with the changing learning environment so that students can take advantage of their peers. Technology can be effectively used in many ways to enhance students' learning experience and make it more effective than traditional teaching methods. Today's world is full of information and knowledge. In this modern era, information is the most important to anyone. In this era, there are many ways to obtain information, such as newspapers, magazines, books, radio programs, etc. But today's students prefer to use the Internet because it provides them with a lot of information at their fingertips. Students can get all kinds of information from the Internet. They can even buy anything without going out. Therefore, this paper focuses on the multidimensional path analysis of the cultivation of craftsmanship spirit in colleges and universities under the algorithm recommendation technology.

Keywords: Cultivation of craftsman spirit · Recommended technology · Multidimensional path

1 Introduction

The spirit of Chinese craftsman is an excellent spiritual quality formed in the long history of Chinese civilization and rooted in the traditional culture of the Chinese nation. In the long history, it is the Chinese craftsmen who, with their exquisite skills and resolute character, have made the glorious history of Chinese civilization. In contemporary China, the social atmosphere is still affected by traditional culture, and it is easy to find the craftsmanship spirit in all walks of life, such as the bravery shown by mineral blasting workers when they are in danger, the excellence shown by welders and technicians in their ultra long steel plate welding without any leakage, and the strength shown by the successors in ceramic sand production, These qualities are the epitome of the craftsman spirit condensed in every excellent worker, and the craftsman spirit flows in the blood of every excellent Chinese worker!

© ICST Institute for Computer Sciences, Social Informatics and Telecommunications Engineering 2024
Published by Springer Nature Switzerland AG 2024. All Rights Reserved
Y. Zhang and N. Shah (Eds.): BigIoT-EDU 2023, LNICST 583, pp. 231–242, 2024.
https://doi.org/10.1007/978-3-031-63139-9_25

The so-called "craftsman spirit" refers to the attitude of meticulously carving out products, striving for perfection, persisting in the cause, and being indifferent to fame and wealth. It is the key to reshape professional ethics in the current society, and also the driving force for the transformation and upgrading of China's manufacturing industry. The core of "craftsman spirit" is to keep improving. In ancient China, the behavior of Ganjiang and Moye who went to copper water and coagulated sword qi to create exquisite weapons was amazing, and the "fairy tale of sharpening a sword in ten years" was even more praiseworthy. This is a valuable craftsman spirit and a great force for Chinese people to create Chinese civilization. "To delay good sentences for the sake of human nature and to die without surprising words" is not only the strict requirement of literary creators on themselves, but also our standard and yardstick for human things. However, in today's fast-paced society, it is difficult to see that "the words are not surprising and the death is endless". Needless to say, this is the expansion of scale and mentality, and also the impact of social fickleness, which is still lingering in China. For example, with cheap labor, China's manufacturing industry has always maintained a high-speed development trend. However, in the "new normal of economy" today, the traditional manufacturing industry of "emphasizing scale and neglecting quality" has been at a disadvantage. If you want to take the lead in the increasingly fierce international trade competition, you must fully carry forward the spirit of craftsmanship, take innovation as the driving force, take market demand as the guidance, take the pursuit of excellence and quality as the value consensus, and win respect and market. In addition, the event that we mentioned at the beginning of the "Zhengzhou High-priced Tourism Publicity Film Appeared in Kaifeng Scenic Spot", through the guidance of public opinion on the Internet, is to let Chinese people re-examine the product quality and ingenuity of our country. Such "referring to Bian as Zheng" and such low-level mistakes are the reflection of the attitude and level of the production company, as well as the profile of the quality and effect of the promotional film; The "easy" review and "simple" acceptance of the film by the local tourism bureau are thought-provoking. This phenomenon is common in the current society, and the reasons are worthy of our deep consideration.

The second is the lack of spiritual strength, which will lead to the deterioration of the market environment, the lack of government credibility, and further lead to the collapse of social trust; Third, the relevant departments failed to supervise and fulfill their duties, resulting in the defective products passing the examination and causing negative impact; The fourth is the prevalence of social utilitarianism and self-interest, which is a desecration of traditional culture and a major cancer that hinders the process of harmonious society. Therefore, from the traditional manufacturing industry to the whole society, we should take "craftsman spirit" as the value consensus and spiritual guidance. Therefore, it is urgent to speed up the improvement of the quality of our products and cultivate the spirit of craftsmanship. First of all, the government should continue to overcome difficulties in the field of science and technology by increasing investment in technological innovation, improve the technical content of products, and strive for excellence in core competitiveness; Secondly, through positive media publicity, through reports, micro-video and other ways to enhance the public's sense of awe, adhere to professional ethics, advocate the glory of labor, put an end to the temptation of interests, promote the craftsman spirit, and value the craftsman culture; Finally, we need to carry out quality improvement activities, comprehensively strengthen quality management, and improve the competitive mechanism of survival of the fittest. Only in this way can the "craftsman spirit" be dissolved in the national blood, become a social consensus, and help the rise of the nation.

Talent has increasingly become a strategic resource to promote economic and social development. Only by relying on high-level education to provide a steady stream of talent resources, can China play a potential role in the fierce international competition and reflect the advantages of backwardness [1]. As an important part of China's talent team, craftsmen with professional and technical skills are important resources to promote economic and social development, industrial transformation and upgrading, and high-quality development. Accelerate the transformation and upgrading of the manufacturing industry, improve the socialist modern economic system, and realize the transformation of China from a manufacturing country to a intelligent manufacturing country, an innovation country, and a science and technology country [2]. It is impossible to leave the craftsman type talents in all walks of life to use craftsman type labor to complete the "fine carving", which particularly highlights the importance of integrating the cultivation of craftsman spirit into the talent training link. Science and engineering students, as an important reserve force of "great country craftsmen" and professional and technical talents, are the new force for the construction and development of China's science and technology and industrial and commercial fields in the future, and the mainstay for realizing the Chinese Dream of great rejuvenation of the Chinese nation. Cultivate the craftsmanship spirit of science and engineering students, and then carry forward the craftsmanship spirit in the whole society, accurately grasp the pulse of the times of "respecting labor, respecting creation", and deeply conform to the social trend of "glorious labor, creating great", which can not only reform the chronic diseases and accumulated disadvantages, strengthen innovation drive, and condense the new "acceleration" of the manufacturing industry,

2 Related Work

2.1 Domestic Research Status

The domestic academic research on craftsmanship spirit takes 2015 as the dividing point, and there are few mature research achievements before. Since the craftsmanship was first mentioned in the 2016 Government Work Report, domestic research on craftsmanship has shown a blowout trend, with 3533 in 2016, 4109 in 2017, 3860 in 2018, 2464 in 2019, 4002 in 2020, and 16788 by April 2021. It can be seen that the craftsmanship spirit has been highly concerned by the domestic academia with a profound economic and social background, and the national top-level design is an important driving factor to promote the study of craftsmanship spirit - at the stage of rapid economic and social development, while focusing on productivity efficiency and economic benefits, we have downplayed the concern for traditional craftsmen and artisan like labor, At the same time, it also ignores the inheritance and development of Chinese excellent traditional culture such as craftsmanship spirit from the standpoint of modern society [3]. At the current stage, the implementation of strategies such as "making the country strong" and "making the country strong with talents", the implementation of supply side structural reform, and the people's call for a better life have made us more and more vocal about high-quality products and high-quality talents, and also made the society pay more attention to and care for the spirit of craftsmen and craftsmen from large countries.

Zhang Di judged that craftsmanship spirit mainly went through four stages of development according to the degree of material civilization: during the period of simple material production conditions, craftsmanship spirit began to sprout in order to save production costs and constantly improve manufacturing skills; With the relative improvement of production capacity, craftsmanship has become a fixed social occupation, and began to pay attention to professional reputation and social prestige [4]. The spirit of craftsmanship has officially come into being; The social division of labor in feudal society was more refined. Excellent craftsmen inherited their skills in the form of apprentices or families, and the craftsman spirit was developed in the inheritance; In the industrial society, modern craftsmen advocate inclusiveness and innovation, which sublimates the spirit of craftsmen. Zhuang Xizhen believes that the development and evolution of craftsmanship spirit can be summarized into three historical stages according to the development degree of industrial society: in the traditional handicraft era, the living standard is low, and craftsmen pursue ingenious ideas and bold innovation to meet the needs of life; During the industrial revolution, the traditional handicraft industry was impacted by the mechanized mass production, and the craftsman spirit was lost; The third industrial revolution made consumer demand tend to be personalized, and required enterprise employees to have professional quality and innovation quality, which just matched the value concept of craftsmanship excellence, and the traditional craftsmanship spirit was revitalized [5].

2.2 Recommended Type of Algorithm

The emergence of algorithms, whether in the form of recommendation systems or search engines, is helping us manage and filter all kinds of overflowing and explosive information in a variety of ways to "manage" our lives in an orderly manner. The algorithm recommendation technology is affecting and changing our production and life in various forms. From the perspective of type, the main types of algorithm recommendation are collaborative filtering recommendation, recommendation based on potential factor algorithm, algorithm recommendation based on popularity and hybrid algorithm recommendation.

Collaborative filtering recommendation is a general term for algorithms based on behavior data analysis, which is mainly aimed at users' daily browsing records and behavior tracks. In terms of commerce, collaborative filtering is to establish an association rule between users and goods, and realize the "hyperlink" between users and goods by recommending goods that meet their personalized needs, thus achieving the goal of increasing the total sales of goods, Its classification method can be divided into user-based collaborative filtering and product-based system filtering: user-based system filtering mainly refers to finding similar users based on users' preferences for items, and recommending similar users' preferences to the current user's recommendation system; The main idea of product-based system filtering is to find similar items according to users' preferences for items, and then recommend similar items to users according to users' previous preferences.

The basic idea is that FunkSVD decomposes the original scoring matrix R into two low-rank matrices X and Y, then uses the optimization algorithm to obtain two optimal low-rank matrices, and finally calculates the inner product of the two low-rank matrices to predict the score. Decomposition formula:

$$R = X^T Y \tag{1}$$

After decomposition, the student characteristic matrix X and the craftsman mental characteristic matrix Y are obtained. Next, the optimal X and Y are obtained by optimizing the loss function, such as formula (2), so as to control the deviation of the model and ensure that the gap between the predicted score and the actual score is as small as possible.

$$e^2 = \sum_{(m,n) \in T} (r_{nn} - x_m^T y_n)^2 \tag{2}$$

where: T is the data set.

However, when Funk SVD algorithm is applied to the recommendation system, a regularization term is usually added to the loss function to control the variance of the model, so as to simplify the hidden factor vector as much as possible and avoid over-coupling. The objective function with the regularization term is as follows:

$$E = \sum_{(m,n) \in T} (r_{nn} - x_m^T y_n)^2 + \lambda \left(\|x_m\|^2 + \|y_n\|^2 \right) \tag{3}$$

where: A is the regularization coefficient.

The fundamental impetus for the change and development of craftsman spirit education is caused by the material production mode and its changes. "In Marx's view, the mode of material production not only determines the development process of society, but also determines people's ideology, values, moral judgments, etc. In the information age, education needs the help of technology to achieve leapfrog development. It can be said that there is no education modernization without education informatization. Algorithm recommendation, as an artificial intelligence technology and information means, will also inevitably bring profound changes in artisan spirit education Leather [6].

As the most widely used AI technology in the recommendation system, algorithm recommendation not only affects our daily social, shopping and other aspects, but also can be seen everywhere in education. "AI + education" promotes the reform of the education system and the development of education in a more intelligent direction. As an important part of AI technology, algorithm recommendation is also promoting the improvement of craftsman spirit education function and the expansion of the scope of dissemination by its own personalized recommendation, precision promotion, efficient focus and other functions, and also promoting the innovation of ideas and means of craftsman spirit education. On the one hand, the algorithm recommendation technology characterized by personalization can broaden the communication channel of artisan spirit education, break the traditional educational mode of simple theoretical preaching and traditional classroom teaching. The algorithm recommendation is based on accurately positioning the personalized needs and different preferences of users through the network[7], We-media and other communication carriers, By setting up a special official account for artisan spirit education on each network platform and increasing the push of its relevant content, we can improve the influence of artisan spirit education, expand the appeal of artisan spirit education, improve the infectivity and affinity of artisan spirit education, open up a new way for the functions of artisan spirit education, such as gathering consensus, achieving value guidance, and ensuring political guidance, and expand the depth of dissemination of artisan spirit education content It provides new ways in breadth and urges the continuous innovation of craftsman spirit education; On the other hand, through algorithm recommendation, we can achieve the goal of precise focus, precise filtering and precise policy implementation of artisan spirit education.

2.3 The Current Situation of Vocational College Students' Awareness of Craftsmanship Spirit

In order to understand the cognition of craftsman spirit of vocational students, the research group investigated 305 (301 valid samples) students in a vocational college in Xinjiang through questionnaires, in-depth interviews and other ways, and found that the group's cognition is relatively positive, but there are also many problems.

(1) The cognition of craftsmanship is positive. The essence of craftsman spirit is an ideology, which is the spiritual concept and value of workers in the process of labor. The establishment of this consciousness is positively related to the social environment, and it is solidified by the power of example. According to the survey, 98.67% of the respondents agree with the spirit of craftsmanship and believe that it will play an important role in future career development. Kant regards virtue as power, and the practice of craftsman spirit can not be separated from the power of example. In the process of learning, there is a benchmark in the eyes, a model in the heart, and the effect is more dependent. 95.35% of the respondents in the survey can accurately name the role models with good craftsmanship, which shows that most vocational school students have a positive understanding of craftsmanship [8].

(2) Strong desire for self-improvement and development, and internal motivation to practice craftsmanship. Giving full play to the subjective initiative is the premise and basis for practicing the craftsman spirit. To strengthen the craftsman spirit, we must first have the will in thought and the action to make a difference, so as to become a qualified application-oriented talent. 82.39% of the respondents in the survey believed that personal quality improvement was the most effective way to practice craftsmanship; Most of the students have a clear understanding of what they have mastered and what they lack, and only 4.98% of the respondents do not know what they lack. Curiosity and curiosity are the beginning of innovation. Craftsman spirit must have the curiosity to understand and try. 80.73% of the students in the survey maintain strong curiosity about new knowledge and skills. It is worth noting that 33.89% of the respondents have obtained relevant skill level certificates, and most students are ready to obtain them [9]. The craftsmanship spirit of keeping improving and innovating is inevitable to criticize and surpass the old system in practice, while 86.04% of the respondents are willing to change some drawbacks in the society, which fully shows that vocational school students are willing to actively improve themselves and constantly reform themselves.

3 Problems in the Practice of Craftsmanship by Students in Higher Vocational Colleges

(1) Some students lack persistence and concentration. Japanese craftsman Takeshi Taguchi once said, "You can keep loneliness, be patient with boredom, focus, and develop a good craftsmanship bit by bit, and the rest will come naturally." The craftsman spirit requires exquisite professional skills and lean professional quality, and must have such spiritual characteristics as concentration, meticulousness, preciseness, perseverance, dedication, innovation, patience, and can't tolerate carelessness and carelessness. However, most vocational students are in the "critical period when individual persistence starts to develop and has a positive impact". Persistence, perseverance and patience are relatively lacking. It is more difficult to achieve long-term goals, and it is easier to pursue short and smooth. The survey results also prove this, 49.17% of respondents believe that perseverance is the most difficult thing to do in the process of learning and practicing "craftsmanship spirit"; 55.81% thought that they could not focus on a specific goal for a long time, and 33.55% thought that they were easy to ignore details in their daily study and work. Lack of persistence and focus is a characteristic of the growth period of young people themselves [10]. They cannot achieve immediate results through short-term education and teaching. They can only improve in the process of growth and learning.

(2) Some students do not have enough professional identity. Recognition of their majors is an important basis for continuous learning and development, while most students do not know enough about the majors they will study and their hobbies before they apply for the college entrance examination. They blindly choose the candidates before they apply for the examination. After they enter the university, they find that there is no small difference between the ideal majors and the reality. The gap leads to resistance to the majors they will be engaged in in the future, resulting in insufficient motivation and enthusiasm for learning. 34.88% of the respondents in the survey did not like their majors and could not find the value of their majors. In ancient China, there was a saying that "an art fool must have good skills". From practical experience, craftsmen in large countries are often very confident in their skills and products, and extremely persistent in their careers [11]. After choosing an industry, they took root in this industry and accumulated advantages in details. Some vocational school students lack this spirit [9]. Practicing craftsmanship spirit is not only the continuous accumulation of production and operation experience, but also the continuous innovation after inheriting the achievements of predecessors [12]. This requires workers to constantly learn systematic theoretical knowledge and sublimate it through practice. Therefore, vocational school students who are not interested in their own majors cannot become practitioners of craftsmanship spirit.

(3) Some students are confused about the future development direction. The acquisition of professional skills is a long-term process, while the student's career is relatively short, which makes it impossible for students to fully master all the skills involved in the major [13]. At the same time, the frequency of modern technology upgrading is gradually accelerating. Compared with the market, teaching materials are lagging behind. Students must make career development plans as soon as possible according to their hobbies and actual abilities, adjust their learning content with a

targeted view, and enrich themselves through various channels. However, 68% of the respondents did not have a clear career orientation, and 39.2% were unwilling to continue to engage in work related to their major after graduation. At the same time, some students are afraid of hardship and pursue comfort. In the survey on future career development, 67.77% of respondents said they would rather work in government agencies or institutions, of which less than 15% are willing to work at the grassroots level. We believe that the vocational values of vocational college students are diversified. As long as it is conducive to the development of society, it is appropriate to choose whether it is conducive to the realization of personal values or more conducive to the realization of social values. However, most craftsmen in large countries rely on the training of skills in the process of labor, and eventually become the industry leader from the bottom of the profession [14]. As an important base for training skilled talents, higher vocational colleges must guide students to reasonably plan their college career, remove their impetuous mentality, and choose a career development path according to the actual situation, so as to lay a good foundation for future comprehensive and sustainable development.

4   Multi Dimensional Path of Cultivating Craftsmanship Spirit in Colleges and Universities Under Algorithm Recommendation Technology

4.1   Algorithm Recommendation Technology

The emergence of algorithms, whether in the form of recommendation systems or search engines, is helping us manage and filter all kinds of overflowing and explosive information in a variety of ways to keep our lives in order. Algorithm recommendation technology is influencing and changing our production and life in various forms. In terms of types, the types of algorithm recommendation mainly include collaborative filtering recommendation, recommendation based on potential factor algorithm, popularity based algorithm recommendation and hybrid algorithm recommendation [15].

Collaborative filtering recommendation is a general term for algorithms based on behavior data analysis, which is mainly aimed at users' daily browsing records and behavior tracks. As far as commerce is concerned, collaborative filtering is to establish an association rule between users and goods, and to achieve the goal of increasing the total sales of goods by recommending them to meet their personalized needs and realizing the "hyperlink" between users and goods, Its classification methods can be divided into user based collaborative filtering and product based system filtering: user based system filtering mainly finds similar users based on users' preferences for items and recommends similar users' preferences to the current user's recommendation system; The main idea of product based system filtering is to find similar items based on users' preferences for items, and then recommend similar items to users based on users' previous preferences. Both belong to collaborative filtering based on memory data [16]. The recommendation based on the latent factor algorithm is based on the user's daily historical behavior to track the user's own characteristics, as well as on the analysis of the essential characteristics of existing goods. This type of recommendation mainly uses TF-IDF, TextRank and other methods to delimit feature tags from a large number of news information by locking users' web search traces and looking up browsing records, and obtains the corresponding weight coefficients by analyzing and processing data, as shown in Fig. 1.

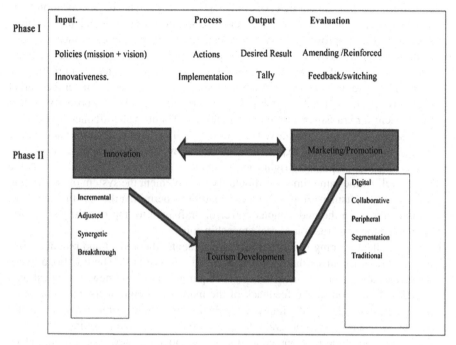

Fig. 1. Algorithm recommendation technology

4.2 Cultivation Path of Modern Craftsman Spirit

(1) Take multiple measures to build a correct value guidance system and form a social atmosphere that advocates craftsmanship. Compared with traditional craftsmen, modern craftsmen have undergone great changes. Mechanical and intelligent operation mode has replaced manual operation, and the traditional guild's master apprentice teaching mode has been transformed into classroom teaching mode; In terms of social treatment, the social needs and wages of highly skilled workers are far higher than those of some white-collar workers, and the spirit of craftsmanship has also changed from industry discourse to practical needs. We can clearly see that the increase in demand for craftsmen in large countries is the inevitable result of the choice of productivity and future career choices, so we should change our understanding of the old craftsmen. However, there are still some students and parents who have prejudices against craftsmanship, which requires us to constantly optimize the soil for the growth of craftsmanship spirit, and form a feeling and social atmosphere of respecting labor and advocating craftsmanship spirit [17]. First of all, we should vigorously promote and demonstrate the craftsmanship of great countries and their labor achievements and social values in schools, especially in primary and

secondary schools. We should organize various activities to show the outstanding craftsmanship, encourage students and parents to cultivate their dedication and ideal feelings with advanced models, establish a correct understanding of craftsmanship, and effectively link the publicity of craftsmanship between the basic education stage and the higher education stage. Secondly, we should improve the talent evaluation system, further improve the access mechanism of outstanding craftsmen in social status, social resources, etc., enhance the professional reputation of craftsmen, realize the unity of professional honor, social respect and their values, and realize the unity of labor value and social value of craftsmen in large countries under the market economy. Third, we need to establish and improve the intellectual property protection system for craftsmen's unique technologies. Traditional craftsmen, out of fear of "teaching apprentices to starve their masters", often have reservations about their unique skills gained from experience. Therefore, we should strengthen the protection of intellectual property rights and technical patents related to craftsmen at the legal level. At the same time, we should try to implement the system of "restricting the name of craftsmen" in places where conditions permit At the spiritual level, we should strengthen the endogenous power of craftsmen to improve their skills and strengthen the construction of craftsmanship spirit.

(2) Innovate talent training mode and improve students' theoretical and practical abilities. 1. Provide courses that meet the needs of the post [18]. The traditional ivory tower education model cannot meet the requirements of the new era. Vocational colleges should follow the feedback of the market and employers, take the needs of the industry as the guide, improve the distinctive teaching objectives, constantly update the talent training program, face enterprises in the course setting, strengthen the integration of industry and education and school enterprise cooperation, reduce or eliminate the majors that are saturated with the society and have obviously implemented the times, and cultivate the technical talents needed by the society, Win the confidence of parents and students. 2. Attach importance to the technical research and development of the university itself. Ironmaking also needs to be hard on its own [19]. Colleges and universities should break away from the single linear education model of "outline formulation - talent training - going to enterprises", pay more attention to theoretical summary and technology research and development outside of teaching and social services, strive for excellence in the field, compete for the voice of technology and standards, become leaders in the application of cutting-edge technology, and build colleges and universities with craftsmanship spirit. 3. Strengthen the construction of teaching staff. The strength of the teaching staff is directly related to the quality of students' learning. Vocational schools should pay attention to the improvement of teachers' professional quality and practical teaching ability, and focus on training a large number of "double qualified" teachers with craftsmanship [20]. 4. Improve the flexibility of the enrollment system. When enrolling students, we will widely publicize the characteristics of the subject, the scope of application, the skills learned, the employment prospects and the real cases of students' graduation development, so that students can have sufficient knowledge of the major before they apply. At the same time, in view of the fact that students are not interested in their majors after enrollment, vocational schools should improve

the relevant systems and allow students who meet certain conditions to choose their favorite majors in the first semester or year.

5 Conclusion

The cultivation and research of college students' craftsmanship spirit is a long-term and systematic process. The research and creation time of this paper is limited, the researchers' personal theoretical knowledge reserves need to be improved, the ability to comprehensively analyze problems needs to be improved, and the discussion of related issues is still lacking. Therefore, this paper has some shortcomings, such as the insufficient sample size selected in the questionnaire survey, which leads to the lack of representativeness of the samples, The empirical research method should also introduce the interview analysis method to increase the persuasiveness of this study. I sincerely hope that all teachers can put forward valuable suggestions. In the future study, I will strictly demand myself according to the rules of craftsmen, continue to study and research in depth, and practice the spirit of craftsmen in practice. I hope to contribute my modest efforts to the ideological and political education in colleges and universities.

Acknowledgements. Fund Project

No1: Key project of Teaching and Research Planning of Anhui Vocational and Adult Education Association: "Research and Practice on the big Ideological and Political education Path of Cultivating Students' Craftsman Spirit in Higher Vocational Colleges" (azcg19);

No2: Key Research Project of Hefei Technology College: "Academic and Technical Leader" (2021DTR03);

No3: Vocational Education Quality And Excellence Action Plan projection of Anhui Province: "the Cases of Ideological and Political Education in the 'Career Planning Courses'" .

References

1. Zhang, L.: Research on the cultivation path of college student' craftsman spirit under the background of industry-university-research cooperation. Jiangsu Science & Technology Information (2018)
2. Jiang, J.: The cultivation of artisan spirit in the training of applied talents in independent colleges. Management & Technology of SME (2017)
3. Zhu, Y.K.: Craftsman Spirit: its motivation, components and cultivation strategy —— with technical colleges and universities as a case. J. Sichuan Normal Univ. (Soc. Sci. Ed.) (2019)
4. Wang, Y.: RETRACTED: thoughts on the cultivation of innovative and entrepreneurial talents in colleges and universities based on the "Craftsman Spirit" based on big data analysis. J. Phys.: Conf. Ser. **1648**(3), 032196 (4pp) (2020)
5. Xin, N., Wang, Z.H., Wan, Y.P., et al.: Research on the cultivation of "craftsman spirit" in engineering students from the perspective of mindfulness——a case study of nanchang university of aeronautics and photoelectric engineering college. J. Jiamusi Vocational Instit. (2018)
6. Dai, R.Q.: The plight and breakthrough of the cultivation of craftsman spirit in applied technical college students. J. Heilongjiang Vocat. Instit. Ecol. Eng. (2017)

7. Fang, Z., Zhang, Z.Y.: Research on the current situation and countermeasures of the cultivation of the craftsman spirit of the professional students in higher vocational colleges. J. Jiamusi Vocat. Instit. (2017)
8. Sheng, K.: Research on the cultivation path of the craftsman spirit in higher vocational colleges —— based on the survey results of a university. J. West. (2021)
9. Jia, X.B., Zhi-Dong, H.U.: Research on the cultivation strategies of craftsman spirit in vocational colleges from the view of STEAM education. Vocat. Educ. Res. (2019)
10. Zhang, D.: Research on the cultivation path ofcraftsman spirit in engineering higher vocational colleges under the background of "Made in China 2025". J. Shandong Instit. Commer. Technol. (2019)
11. Jiang, N., Zhang, Q.: Research on the fusion of education and "craftsman spirit" cultivation in higher vocational colleges in the view of "one belt and one road"——in case of maritime college. J. Qingdao Ocean Shipping Mariners College (2018)
12. Rong, T.U., Chen, X.: The Approaches to the Cultivation of the Socialist Core Values in E-Class of Colleges and Universities[J]. Journal of Fuqing Branch of Fujian Normal University, 2017
13. Qiang, B.Z.: Research on the inheritance and cultivation strategy of "craftsman spirit" in contemporary colleges and universities. Educ. Teaching Forum (2019)
14. Kong, B.G., Bureau, S., Amp, S.V.: A practical approach to the cultivation of craftsman spirit in higher vocational colleges. J. Ningbo Univ. (Educ. Sci. Ed.) (2016)
15. Jing, H.E., Zhang, L., Zhao, R., et al.: The craftsmanship spirit cultivation of engineering students at colleges and universities. J. Kunming Univ. Sci. Technol. (Soc. Sci. Ed.) (2017)
16. Malinowski, M.: Implementation of recommendation algorithm based on recommendation sessions in e-commerce IT system (2021)
17. Cheng, M.: Exploration on the practical approaches of applying craftsman spirit in the education of application-oriented universities. Manage. Technol. SME (2018)
18. Zhang, Z.Y.: On the cultivation of craftsman spirit of higher vocational college students under the pattern of big ideological instruction. J. Jiamusi Vocat. Instit. (2018)
19. Miao, Y., Wang, S.: On the cultivation quality improvement of innovative and entrepreneurial talents based on "craftsman spirit" in universities. Theory Pract. Innov. Entrepreneurship (2018)
20. Dong-Mei, L.I.: The craftsman spirit in the ideological and political education of colleges and universities under the background of the new era. J. Baicheng Normal Univ. (2018)

Research on Collaborative Education Course Recommendation Model of Vocational Education Learning Platform Based on Collaborative Filtering Algorithm

Ruyong Zhang[✉] and Limei Song

Shandong Institute of Commerce and Technology, Jinan 250103, Shandong, China
Zhangry_150@163.com

Abstract. Research on collaborative education course recommendation model of Vocational Education Learning Platform Based on collaborative filtering algorithm. Vocational education learning platform (veplp) is a system that provides vocational education courses and related services for students in the field of vocational education, including vocational teachers, colleges and other institutions. The collaborative filtering algorithm is used to recommend the best course according to the score of the previous user. It is a machine learning technology that uses an iterative process of feature selection and model building to predict which courses may be liked by other users. The working principle of the algorithm is to use various functions (such as average score, number of comments and popularity score) as input variables to build a prediction model of recommended courses. Data preprocessing and feature selection in this step, we will preprocess the data to build our collaborative filtering model with higher accuracy.

Keywords: Collaborative filtering algorithm · Recommended model · Vocational education · Education course

1 Introduction

Collaborative filtering algorithm plays an important role, significance and effect in collaborative teaching course recommendation of vocational education learning platform. However, in the practical application process, we also need to pay attention to and solve some potential problems in order to improve the application effect of collaborative filtering algorithm in vocational education learning platform, and on the other hand, it is powerfully promoting the reform of all walks of life. Education is the key field to train talents and gain competitive advantages in the future, and education informatization "represents a direction of change in the current society, and puts forward new challenges and broad development space for talent training. The impact of the Internet on Modern Education:

With the development of education informatization and quality education, it is increasingly important to realize personalized curriculum resource recommendation in

Y. Zhang and N. Shah (Eds.): BigIoT-EDU 2023, LNICST 583, pp. 243–251, 2024.
https://doi.org/10.1007/978-3-031-63139-9_26

the form of intelligent "teaching students according to their aptitude". The course recommendation is a data mining project of typical educational scenarios, which aims to excavate the learners' potential personalized learning interests and then carry out the next learning recommendation33. The algorithms commonly used in course recommendation are usually migrated from other types of recommendation (such as recommendation of movies, music, electronic goods, etc.). A general course recommendation model includes learner-based collaborative filtering, course-based collaborative filtering and the method of capturing learners' personalized potential learning interests by using matrix decomposition and content awareness [1]. However, due to the long learning hours of the course and the learning sequence, it takes several weeks or even longer to learn a course (the next interaction of film, music, etc. only takes 2 h or a few minutes. Therefore, this long-term learning behavior leads to the unique characteristics of the data recommended by the curriculum, which is different from the data such as movies and music, and shows a deeper degree of data sparsity. Therefore, with the help of intelligent technology, curriculum resource recommendation based on aptitude is different from the general resource recommendation algorithm. In the application of scenario in the field of education, in addition to learning preferences of learners, individual factors of learners should also be considered. However, due to the lack and sparsity of relevant data and information, it is difficult to implement the curriculum recommendation model. Therefore, the development of scenario-based curriculum recommendation can be roughly divided into coarse-grained curriculum recommendation under the education scenario and fine-grained curriculum recommendation under the education scenario in combination with the application scenarios of traditional recommendation and intelligent recommendation in the education field.

With more and more online users and explosive growth of Internet resources, learners have switched their learning methods to finding answers online. The threshold for information expansion of Internet resources is very low. Although the growth rate of resources is fast and the base number is large, the quality is uneven and there will be a large number of repetitions [2]. On the one hand, excellent resources and a large number of repetitive common resources are not easy to be found by learners, and will be covered with the search frequency of mainstream common resources; On the other hand, learners' ability to search for information does not match the growth rate of resources, which makes learners waste a lot of time and energy searching for disorderly network resources, and the convenient and fast learning has evolved into a terrible information search. In the long run, there will be a burying effect, resulting in the waste of high-quality resources and the decline of learners' trust. How to enable learners to quickly obtain high-quality information resources that meet their learning habits has become a problem that must be solved in education informatization. This demand encourages the emergence of new information service methods and tools, and personalized learning platforms have become a trend. Based on this, this paper studies the collaborative education course recommendation model of Vocational Education Learning Platform Based on collaborative filtering algorithm.

2   Related Work

2.1   Personalized Recommendation Algorithm

Improve learning efficiency: Through collaborative filtering algorithms, students can recommend appropriate courses based on their learning history, interests, learning progress and other information, so that students can learn more efficiently.

Personalized learning: The collaborative filtering algorithm can fully explore students' learning needs and interests, provide students with personalized course recommendations, enable students to find their own interests in the learning process, and improve their enthusiasm and initiative in learning.

Enriching curriculum resources: Through the analysis of a large number of course data, the collaborative filtering algorithm can provide more curriculum resources for the vocational education learning platform, so that students have more choices in the learning process.

Optimize the course structure: The collaborative filtering algorithm can provide the basis for course recommendation for the vocational education learning platform, so that the platform can adjust and optimize the course structure and improve the quality of the course according to the needs and interests of students.

Improve user satisfaction: By providing students with accurate course recommendations, collaborative filtering algorithms can improve students' learning experience and satisfaction, thereby improving the reputation and influence of vocational education learning platforms is shown in Fig. 1.

2.2   Collaborative Filtering Algorithm

User-based collaborative filtering algorithm: By analyzing students' learning history, interests and hobbies, and other personal information, students are recommended to learn courses that match their interests [1–5].

Project-based collaborative filtering algorithm: By analyzing the learning records, evaluations and other information of the course, students can recommend other courses similar to the course they are studying.

Hybrid collaborative filtering algorithm: Combines user and project information to comprehensively analyze and make personalized course recommendations for students.

$$sim = BP * \exp \sum\nolimits_{n=1}^{N} (w_n * \log p_n) \tag{1}$$

For new users or new courses, it is difficult for collaborative filtering algorithm to recommend courses accurately because of lack of sufficient data support as (where u · V refers to vector dot product):

$$sim = \sum_{k=1}^{K} \sum_{x \in \pi} \sum_{d=1}^{D} (x_{id} - v_{kd})^2 \tag{2}$$

On the learning platform of vocational education, there are few learning records and evaluations of many courses, which leads to the problem of sparse data when

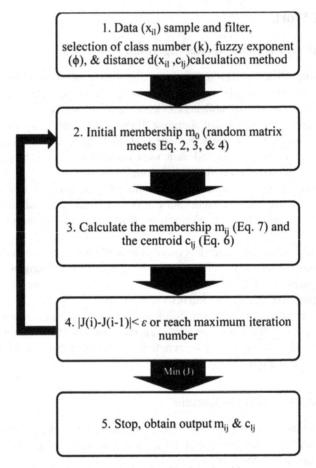

Fig. 1. Collaborative filtering algorithm

collaborative filtering algorithm recommends courses. The concept based on matrix decomposition originated from the Netflix competition ten years ago. As a branch algorithm of model-based collaborative filtering, it has a high status in the recommendation field. Matrix decomposition algorithm has the characteristics of group intelligence and machine learning, and it has good scalability. Therefore, collaborative filtering based on matrix decomposition is the most commonly used algorithm in recommendation systems at present [7].

With the continuous exploration and optimization of collaborative filtering based on matrix decomposition, many different algorithms have been derived. The first thing I think of is the traditional SVD algorithm. Theoretically, the SVD algorithm needs to complete the missing values in the original scoring matrix first, then decompose the scoring matrix into three matrices, and obtain the optimal value through iteration, and finally get the prediction score. The decomposition process of SVD algorithm is shown in Fig. 2.

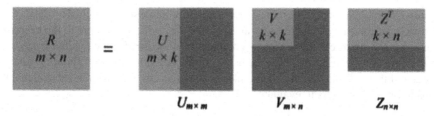

Fig. 2. SVD decomposition process

Where, k is the larger number of singular values in the scoring matrix R, which is usually much smaller than the number of users and items. Using SVD algorithm, if you can predict the score of user u on item i, you only need to calculate UVZT.

The traditional SVD algorithm has a simple idea, but it has a high requirement for the sparsity of the scoring matrix [8]. In the case that the scoring matrix must be sparse in the recommendation, the SVD algorithm cannot be directly applied to the recommendation system. In addition, SVD algorithm has a high computational complexity and needs to decompose the scoring matrix into three matrices. In massive data recommendation, SVD decomposition has a high computational cost [9].

If the excessive pursuit of personalized recommendation may lead to students only focus on their own interest, ignoring other important course content, affecting students' all-round development is decomposed into singular values by the following formula:

$$\mathbf{R_{m\times n}} = U_{\mathbf{m}\times\mathbf{k}} \sum\nolimits_{\mathbf{k}\times\mathbf{k}} \mathbf{V}_{k\times n}^{\mathrm{T}} \tag{3}$$

The argot semantic model was initially applied in the field of text mining [10]. The purpose of this algorithm is to find the hidden features (Latent Factor) in the interactive data, so as to connect users and items. The scoring matrix R decomposes the implicit meaning by the following formula:

$$\mathbf{R}_{m\times n} = \mathbf{P}_{\mathrm{m}\times\mathbf{k}}^{\mathrm{T}} \cdot \mathbf{Q}_{k\times n} \tag{4}$$

After improvement, the scoring matrix R does not need to fill the original matrix, but only needs to be decomposed into P And Q, which greatly reduces the computational complexity. Using Latent Factor Model on explicit feedback data can solve the problem of scoring prediction with high quality [10–12]. If LFM model is to be applied to implicit data sets, it is necessary to construct appropriate negative samples before training the model. In practical applications, the LFM model still has the problem of slow computing speed, so it is difficult to achieve real-time recommendation.

2.3 User Interest

Explicit feedback refers to the user's active evaluation of resources after browsing or using them. For example, in a movie website, when a user has watched a movie, an explicit score is given to the movie. The score reflects the user's preference for the movie. Or the basic information that the user needs to input when registering an account, such as interests and hobbies. These can directly reflect the user's demand information or interests. For educational resources, students' interests can also be obtained by displaying feedback. Every time the students do an exercise, they will give a score to the exercise. The score can represent the difficulty coefficient. Since the display feedback needs to be evaluated by the user, the user needs to spend a certain amount of thinking time to score, and these display feedback operations are generally non mandatory, which also leads to only a few users to evaluate.

3 Research on Collaborative Education Course Recommendation Model of Vocational Education Learning Platform Based on Collaborative Filtering Algorithm

The concept of the education service platform is to provide one-stop services for the education ecology and deepen the education service industry. The platform's services include information, forums and live classes. The information service is committed to providing users with the latest and reliable education service information. The information is published by we media accounts, third-party institutional user accounts, and university government organization accounts. The forum mainly provides users with a platform for online learning and communication. Live class is mainly for users to share education related knowledge on the platform in the form of video [13]. The system also includes other auxiliary functions related to education. There are many forms of educational resources, such as documents, videos, web pages, etc. some of these educational resources are structured and some are unstructured. At the same time, the educational resources in different disciplines and grades are different [14]. Therefore, before personalized recommendation of educational resources, it is necessary to classify educational resources, so that the recommendation can be more efficient and effective, and meet the personalized learning needs of students. In mobile autonomous schools, the classification strategies of educational resources mainly include: subject classification strategy, grade classification strategy, content type classification strategy and knowledge point classification strategy, as shown in Fig. 3 below.

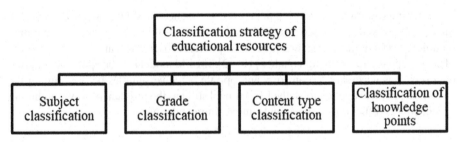

Fig. 3. Classification system and strategy of educational resources

In order to better realize the learning system, it is necessary to effectively manage knowledge and resources. Constructing a clear knowledge system structure can make the learning more organized, the learning plan more clear, and also facilitate the evaluation of students' learning. The purpose of knowledge point construction based on ontology is to standardize the management of educational resources and improve the efficiency of information retrieval and resource utilization [15]. When modeling knowledge points, it needs to be clear that ontology based models are usually not completely built for the first time, but are constantly improved with the change of user needs and the change of knowledge in related fields during the use process.

4 Simulation Analysis

All the course data in this article are crawled from Muke.com (https://www.imooc.com/). Muke.com is an it skills learning platform, which provides rich open classes of video tutorial resources such as mobile terminal development, php development, web front-end, android development and html5. The course page information of Muke mainly includes course name, course category information, course difficulty, and course introduction. In addition to the course information page, the website has a "question and answer area" and a "notes area" for learners to communicate [16]. Only users who have selected the course can initiate questions and answer and publish notes in the course area. Click the learner's nickname to enter the learner's personal homepage. The information displayed on the personal homepage includes the learner's information introduction (nickname, gender, etc.) and all the records of the learner's course selection. Based on this idea, we used the crawler technology to imitate the click action of the page and crawled all the free course information, user and course interaction information and user information of Muke.com.

According to the course information collected in the first step, the core knowledge points of the course and the relationship between each knowledge point are analyzed, and then the model is built. In the last step, the constructed knowledge point conceptual model needs to be formally represented by ontology, and the ontology language OWL is used to normalize the previously constructed relationship model. It mainly describes the class, the relationship between various types and their attribute characteristics.

To describe educational resources with owl, we should first abstract these educational resources, then create various classes according to owl syntax, and represent the instances in the classes [17]. For example, for the formal representation of OWL ontology for high school courses, first define the course class course, the syllabus class syllabus and the chapter class chapter, and then define the examples of the classes: math, chapter01math, etc. Part of the code defined by the course class is shown in Fig. 4 below:

Among them, an attribute named teachinghours is defined for the course class to represent the class hours, and the attribute is restricted with functionalproperty to have and only have 1 value, and the value range of the attribute is restricted to inherit from the hours class [18, 19].

After modeling users, educational resources and knowledge points, a personalized recommendation model can be obtained. The model mainly includes online work and offline work. In order to realize personalized recommendation, collaborative filtering algorithm needs to collect and analyze users' personal information, which may cause users to worry about privacy leakage.

```
<? xml version="1.0" ?>
...
<owl:Class rdf:ID="Course" >
<rdfs:comment>Course</rdfs:comment>
<rdfs:label>Course</rdfs:label>
</owl:Class>
...
<owl:ObjectProperty rdf:ID="#TeachingHours" />
<owl:FunctionalProperty rdf:about="#TeachingHours" />
<owl:Class rdf:about="Course">
<rdfs:subClassOf>
<owl:Restriction>
<owl:onProperty rdf:resource="#TeachingHours" />
<owl:allValuesFrom rdf:resource="#Hours" />
</owl:Restriction>
</rdfs:subClassOf>
</owl:Class>
```

Fig. 4. Partial code

5 Conclusion

With the maturity and development of information technology and mobile devices, online services and other services are becoming more and more popular. At the same time, education informatization is getting more and more attention. Facing the huge and complex online education resources, learners have no way to start. Personalized recommendation systems for different users' different needs emerge as the times require, which not only improves the efficiency of learners significantly, but also plays a positive role in the online promotion of education informatization. As the core of personalized recommendation system, more and more people pay attention to and study the recommendation algorithm.

Acknowledgements. On the practical education path of Ideological and political teachers and counselors in Higher Vocational Colleges from the perspective of collaborative innovation.

References

1. Tang, J.: Optimization of English learning platform based on a collaborative filtering algorithm. Complexity **2021**, 1–14 (2021)
2. Vedavathi, N., Kumar, K.M.A.: SentiWordNet ontology and deep neural network based collaborative filtering technique for course recommendation in an e-learning platform. Int. J. Uncertainty Fuzziness Knowl.-Based Syst. **30**, 709–732 (2022)

3. Liu, H.Z.: Design and implementation of personalized recommendation model for e-commerce platform based on collaborative filtering. J. Guangxi Teach. Educ. Univ. (Nat. Sci. Ed.) (2019)
4. Zhang, Z.: A method of recommending physical education network course resources based on collaborative filtering technology. Sci. Program. **2021**(Pt.10), 1–9 (2021)
5. Geng, C., Zhang, J., Guan, L.: A recommendation method of teaching resources based on similarity and ALS. J. Phys. Conf. Ser. **1865**(4), 042043 (8pp) (2021)
6. Hui, C., Yan, L.Y.: Research on collaborative filtering recommendation algorithm based on Mahout (2019)
7. Zheng, L.G.: Parallel Naive Bayes regression model-based collaborative filtering recommendation algorithm and its realisation on Hadoop for big data. Int. J. Inf. Technol. Manage. **18**(2/3), 129–142 (2019)
8. Li, W., Cao, J., Wu, J., et al.: A collaborative filtering recommendation method based on discrete quantum-inspired shuffled frog leaping algorithms in social networks. Future Gener. Comput. Syst. **88**(NOV.), 262–270 (2018)
9. Li, X., Li, X., Tang, J., et al.: Improving deep item-based collaborative filtering with Bayesian personalized ranking for MOOC course recommendation. In: Li, G., Shen, H., Yuan, Y., Wang, X., Liu, H., Zhao, X. (eds.) Knowledge Science, Engineering and Management. KSEM 2020. LNCS, vol. 12274, pp. 247–258. Springer, Cham (2020). https://doi.org/10.1007/978-3-030-55130-8_22
10. Lei, W., Qing, F., Zhou, J.: Improved personalized recommendation based on causal association rule and collaborative filtering. Int. J. Distance Educ. Technol. Official Publ. Inf. Resour. Manage. Assoc. IJDET 2016 **14**(3), 21–33 (2016)
11. Fu, M., Qu, H., Yi, Z., Lu, L., Liu, Y.: A novel deep learning-based collaborative filtering model for recommendation system. IEEE Trans. Cybern. **49**(3), 1084–1096 (2019)
12. Wu, L.: Collaborative filtering recommendation algorithm for MOOC resources based on deep learning. Complexity **2021**(46), 1–11 (2021)
13. Murad, D.F., Heryadi, Y., Isa, S.M., et al.: Personalization of study material based on predicted final grades using multi-criteria user-collaborative filtering recommender system. Educ. Inf. Technol. **25**(6), 5655–5668 (2020)
14. Ma, L.: Collaborative filtering recommendation method based on user learning tree. New Technol. Libr. Inf. Serv. (2016)
15. Geng, X.L., Deng, T.W., Luo, H.F., et al.: Research on personalized recommendation of e-learning platform based on user collaborative filtering. Mod. Comput. (2019)
16. Bo, X., Qu, Z., Tang, Y.: Personalized recommendation model of electric power information operation and maintenance knowledge based on collaborative filtering (2021)
17. Hu, X., Wang, Y., Chen, Q.B., et al.: Research on personalized learning based on collaborative filtering method. J. Phys: Conf. Ser. **1757**(1), 012050 (2021)
18. Tang, Z., Zhang, X., Niu, J.: LDA model and network embedding-based collaborative filtering recommendation. In: 2019 6th International Conference on Dependable Systems and Their Applications (DSA) (2020)
19. Tahir, S., Hafeez, Y., Abbas, M.A., et al.: Smart learning objects retrieval for e-learning with contextual recommendation based on collaborative filtering. Educ. Inf. Technol. **2022**, 1–38 (2022)

Research and Implementation of Music Recommendation System Based on Particle Swarm Algorithm

Hou Lei[1]([✉]), Jing Li[2], and Jing Guo[3]

[1] Xianyang Normal University, Xianyang 712000, Shanxi, China
252504410@qq.com
[2] College of Humanities and Social Sciences, Heilongjiang Bayi Agricultural University, Daqing 163319, Heilongjiang, China
[3] East University of Heilongjiang, Harbin 150000, Heilongjiang, China

Abstract. Music is an art form that expresses inner feelings, reflects social life and cultivates personal sentiment. With the network in digital form, which makes it increasingly their favorite works from the massive music data, resulting in a great demand for music recommendation systems. However, according to the previous research results, most of the existing music recommendation systems use static recommendation algorithms. When the data changes, the recommendation model needs to be rebuilt based on the entire data set. In large-scale data sets, static recommendation algorithms need to consume a lot of computing resources and time to reconstruct the recommendation model, and the efficiency is low. The role and significance of recommendation system in music teaching is very important, but there is a problem of low management level. The recommendation system cannot solve the problem of processing multi-note data in music teaching, and the recommendation accuracy is poor. Therefore, this paper proposes particle swarm optimization to optimize the music recommendation system. Firstly, music teaching standards are used to classify music data, and selected according to the degree of compliance to realize the preprocessing of music data. Then, according to the degree of compliance, a systematic review collection is formed, and the the particle swarm algorithm has a higher degree of optimization for the music recommendation system and improves the of music selection, which the single system method.

Keywords: music teaching · Standards · Recommended · particle swarm algorithm · System

1 Introduction

With the number of servers, web pages and other resources flooded in the Internet has increased rapidly, which meets the many needs of users for information in the information age. For example, Netease Cloud Music or Douban. There are thousands of songs on

Y. Zhang and N. Shah (Eds.): BigIoT-EDU 2023, LNICST 583, pp. 252–262, 2024.
https://doi.org/10.1007/978-3-031-63139-9_27

Delicio.us. There are more than 1 billion web collections on Amazon There are millions of books on Taobao_ There are a wide variety of goods on the Internet, and tens of thousands of movies on Netflix dazzle you. However, the vast amount of information has far exceeded the scope of personal processing. It has become even more difficult for users to find a book, a song, a movie or some household products. Not to mention looking for a useful part of yourself from this large amount of information, even if you browse all the information - it is impossible [1]. The simultaneous presentation of a large amount of information makes users unable to obtain the part of information that they are interested in or really useful to them, resulting in a significant reduction in the utilization of information and the so-called "information explosion" and "information overload" phenomenon.

At present, improve the utilization rate of users' information, so that the information that is useful to users will not be submerged by the information that is irrelevant to users or not interested in users, so that users do not have to waste a lot of time to filter valuable information to further improve the user experience, and also make informa-tion system managers no longer waste more costs and resources to manage redundant information, One of the solutions we put forward is the traditional information retrieval system represented by search engines, such as Google, Baidu, etc. [2]. However, these search algorithms can only present the same sorting results to all users when users enter keywords, and cannot provide personalized services according to different interests of users. Moreover, with the diversified dissemination of information, the needs of users are also diversified and personalized. The information retrieval system represented by alone cannot meet the various users, and still cannot completely and effectively solve the of "information explosion" and "information overload".

Therefore, how to find the truly valuable information from the Internet information ocean according to the different interests of users and then recommend it to users has become an important issue that needs to be solved urgently.

For this reason, another solution we propose is personalized recommendation system. It collects the system to obtain the user's information needs, interests, etc., and then uses these preferences to mine resources that meet the user's interest preferences or needs from the massive information on the Internet and recommend them to users. In essence, the recommendation problem is to use the resources that users have selected to mine their interests and hobbies to predict the products that users have never seen (such as web pages, CDs, movies, books, restaurants, paintings, music, etc.) [3]. It is a process from known to unknown. In this process, the unknown is predicted and presented to users in some effective form, such as those with high prediction value or high similarity are recommended to users.

The music selection, and the content of music teaching can be reasonably selected [4]. However, in the process of building the music recommendation system, system selection accuracy, and the recommendation cannot be played effectively [5]. Some the application of particle swarm algorithm to the recommendation system information, and of the recommendation system [6]. On this basis, this a particle swarm the recommendation system and better select music.

2   Related Concepts

2.1   Mathematical Description of Particle Swarm Optimization

This algorithm considers each individual in the bird population as a particle in the population, and reflects the search process group by imitating the activity process of each individual in the bird population. The activity range of particles in a population is the solution space of the problem. The position information of each particle corresponds to the solution to the target problem. The process of modifying the position information of each particle in the problem solution space represents the process of searching for problems in space [7]. The historical optimal position of the entire population can determine and adjust the flight speed of particles in the target space. Each particle in a particle swarm has only two attributes: velocity and position. The velocity representation, as well as the current position coordinates of the particles. The individual extremum of the particles in all the searched solutions is called the particle, as well as the solution corresponding to the particles in the population. When searching for the optimal solution in each iteration, the algorithm will change the particles until they are satisfied. At this point, the global optimum is the optimal solution we seek for the problem [8].

The optimal search process depends on location, so the search speed of the algorithm is faster; Secondly, the algorithm has relatively few manual parameters during execution and its principle is simple. It is easier to implement than the complex encoding process of genetic algorithms; Finally, particle swarm optimization has good scalability and is easy to combine with other algorithms. However, classical particle swarm optimization algorithms use fixed inertia weights during the optimization process, making it difficult for the algorithm to lack dynamic changes in velocity weights during the search process. As shown in Fig. 1.

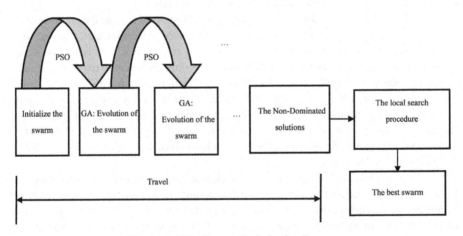

Fig. 1. Particle Swarm Optimization Process

Optimize music data using rhythm, melody, and music consistency, and find recommendation systems based on recommendation metrics, formal views, and data tables.

Combining particle swarm optimization with music teaching standards to optimize music data can improve the management level of recommendation systems [9].

Hypothesis 1: The music data is x_i, the recommendation data set is $\sum x_i$, the music conformance degree is y_i, and the recommendation system optimization function is $f(x_i)$ as shown in Eq. (1).

$$f(x_i) = \lim_{i \to \infty} \sum x_i \Leftrightarrow y_i + \xi^2 \tag{1}$$

2.2 Optimize the Selection of Content

The recommendation system originated from cognitive science, information retrieval, prediction theory and other disciplines. With the computer and network, it plays system. A functional improvement is usually composed of three parts: the record section, used to record the user's historical behavior; Analysis and modeling section; Algorithm section. At present, the commonly used recommendation systems mainly include combined recommendation system. Although most websites have widely used these recommendation systems so far, this does not mean that their development is mature enough [10]. Therefore, there are still many difficulties and deficiencies in their practical application. The content-based recommendation directly describes the features of the items to be recommended, and establishes a mathematical model to represent the items, then analyzes the user and item models, establishes the user preference model and item similarity model, and makes recommendations based on the two. This kind of recommendation system does not have the sparsity problem. Its problem is to filter meaningless information and extract effective information. In the defects and of content-based recommendation, collaborative filtering recommendation is proposed. Compared with the item attribute model of content recommendation, its recommendation results are more affected by the user's scoring information of products, so more other types of products can be presented to users. Collaborative filtering recommendation. At first, GroupLens proposed recommendation [11]. The main idea of the algorithm is to calculate the similarity between users in the user's past behavior data, and finally use the user similarity to infer the products they have not participated in. SarwarB et al. This method data of items in the website database, calculates the item similarity in the item list and establishes the similarity matrix. Finally, the similarity matrix, the user's rating of the item that has not been evaluated is predicted [12]. Unlike content-based recommendation, collaborative filtering recommendation can also show very good processing ability for other types of complex data objects, such as music, movies and other related data information.

Hypothesis 2: The recommended system is $F(x_i)$, the optimization view in the SQL database is z_i, then is shown in Eq. (2).

$$F(x_i) = \frac{-x^3 \pm 4x\xi}{2\Delta x} \to z_i \cdot \xi \tag{2}$$

2.3 Handling of Abnormal Recommendation Information

The melody and syllable in the recommendation system are analyzed standardly, and the music data is mapped to the SQL view to determine the abnormal recommendation.

Comprehensively to support particle swarm optimization [13]. Music preprocessed, and the processed results are included in the data collection if they meet the music selection requirements, otherwise After the calculation, the exception recommendation information is handled as shown in Fig. 2.

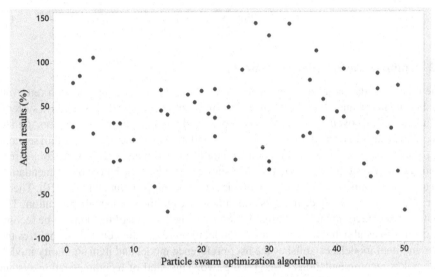

Fig. 2. Analysis results of particle swarm algorithm

The music data in Fig. 1 shows that the particle swarm algorithm e facts. We can view music data as a set of points in a multidimensional space, with each data point representing a music sample. Then, we can consider the parameters of the recommendation system as the positions of particles, with each particle representing a combination of parameters. The searches for the optimal parameter combination by exploring particle movement and information exchange within the parameter space. The calculate the fitness of particles (i.e. the performance indicators of the recommendation system) based on their current position and speed in each iteration. Then, update based on the current position, velocity, and global optimal position. In this way, the gradually finds the optimal parameter combination by simulating the movement process of particles in the parameter space, thereby optimizing the performance of the recommendation system.

It should be noted that particle swarm optimization is a heuristic algorithm, and its effectiveness is influenced by factors such as initialization and parameter settings. Therefore, in practical applications, appropriate adjustments and optimizations need to be made based on specific circumstances to achieve the goal of optimizing recommendation systems.

3 Recommendation System

Generally, a recommendation system mainly contains three core modules: behavior record, model analysis and recommendation algorithm. The behavior record is the system records the user's various behavior forms, such as question and answer, evaluation and browsing records, which may not require the user's active participation; Model analysis refers to the records in the database and the construction of a standard user preference model; The recommendation algorithm refers to that the system extracts the information that users may like from the huge information of the information source in a certain way according model and displays it to users [15].

According to the different concerns of algorithms, the existing recommendation algorithms can be divided into five categories: algorithms based on popularity, recommendation algorithms based on content, recommendation algorithms based on association rules, recommendation algorithms based on collaborative based on model.

The popularity is relatively direct. It does not consider users' preferences, and mainly recommends the current popular information to users. The implementation principle of the algorithm is very simple, which can effectively solve the cold start problem caused by insufficient data. However, the algorithm is not enough to provide personalized recommendations to different users. The algorithm is one of the most frequently used algorithms in the current recommendation system. Its core idea is to analyze and generate recommendations by comparing and analyzing the correlation between users and information data. The to implement and does not have sparsity and cold start problems, and the algorithm can make personalized recommendations according to different users; However, the content features of the item information extracted by the algorithm generally need to be marked and maintained manually [16]. The recommendation algorithm based on association rules first excavates and analyzes the explicit or implicit association rules between the item information (such as two information being browsed by multiple people at the same time), and makes personalized recommendation according to these mined association rules. However, the algorithm needs to extract and analyze user behavior data during the recommendation process, so there are sparsity and cold start problems. The one of the most widely used recommendation algorithms. It establishes the similarity between information (or users) according to users (or information), and makes corresponding recommendations according to the similarity; The has a good recommendation effect. However, because the user's historical data, the algorithm also has the problems of cold start and sparsity [17]. The model-based recommendation algorithm mainly uses the commonly used machine learning algorithm to build a model for the target, predict and recommend the model, but the algorithm recommendation process requires manual intervention in the selection and combination of attributes.

It can be system is bright. It will be the future development trend of each online music website to personalized push music for everyone, improve user experience and win more users' attention. Music personalized recommendation system generally includes three parts: user preference model, music resource module and recommendation algorithm module, as shown in Fig. 3.

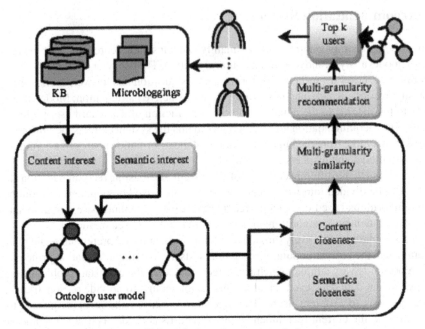

Fig. 3. Typical model of music recommendation system

4   Actual Examples of Recommendation Systems

4.1   Data on Music Recommendations

In different types of music information are studied in this paper, and the data are shown in Table 1.

Table 1. Recommended parameters for music

Music genre	range	Amount of data	rationality	Constraints
popular	exterior	18.95	57.89	35.79
	interior	23.16	49.47	18.95
Classical	exterior	33.68	20.00	50.53
	interior	21.05	55.79	15.79
Rock	exterior	48.42	42.11	51.58
	interior	55.79	30.53	51.58

The processing of different music genres in Table 1 is shown in Table 2.

It can be seen from Table 2 that compared with the single system method, the recommendation system, the results of particle swarm optimization are better than the single

Table 2. Beat processing

source	degree of freedom	Adj SS	Adj MS	F-number	P-value
regression	23.16	18.95	62.11	61.05	18.95
3	33.68	31.58	15.79	46.32	31.58
5	61.05	57.89	60.00	16.84	57.89

system method. The particle swarm algorithm is better and the judgment speed is faster. Therefore, the processing speed, stability and swarm optimization are better.

4.2 Optimized Ratio of Music Recommendations

The information recommendation information, beat, speed. After the constraint of particle swarm algorithm [18], the preliminary management results are obtained, and the correlation of the management results is analyzed, as shown in Table 3.

Table 3. Analyzes the overall situation

Optimize the proportion	Degree of systematization	Outlier recognition rate
25%	47.37	37.89
50%	31.58	20.00
70%	43.16	34.74
mean	15.79	41.05
X^2	30.53	17.89
25%	31.58	24.21
50%	44.21	40.00
70%	28.42	58.95
mean	21.05	23.16
25%	47.37	38.95
50%	18.95	25.26
70%	50.53	22.11
mean	55.79	44.21

Domestic music recommendation algorithms also basically combine collaborative filtering and content filtering to optimize the music recommendation system by collecting user comments and classifying music. Based on the large number of domestic smartphone users, music recommendation based on Android operating system is the future development trend [19].

Douban Music introduces music tags based on content filtering to label each song. Commonly used tags include singer, region, genre and music style, which are key factors for users to select songs. Before making the recommendation system, most songs have labels, user rating data and number of favorites, which will provide good historical information for the recommendation system. Through continuous improvement, douban has been able to meet users' music needs to the maximum extent. The advantage of QQ music is not only that the recommendation service is more accurate, but also that users can log in with QQ number, listen to music and share their favorite songs with friends. Content filtering is based on music gene information classification, which makes user information and song classification information more efficient and complete, and also supports type-based search and comprehensive search functions. In terms of collaborative filtering, QQ Music can recommend the music that its friends are listening to or like to users, so as to facilitate mutual exchange and evaluation between friends [20].

4.3 Stability and Accuracy of the Recommendation System

To verify the accuracy of the particle swarm algorithm, the optimization stability and accuracy are compared with the recommendation system, and the results are shown in Fig. 4.

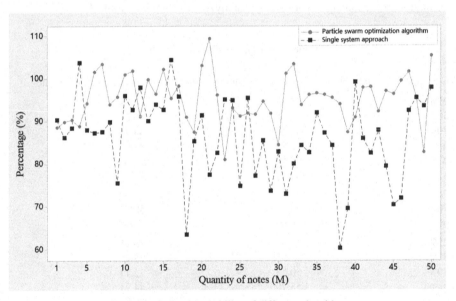

Fig. 4. Optimization stability of different algorithms

It can be seen from Fig. 2 that the optimization stability of particle swarm optimization. The accuracy of the above algorithm is shown in Table 4.

It can be seen from Table 3. Analyze the experimental results and compare the differences and advantages between particle swarm optimization and other methods. Based on experimental objectives and indicators, evaluate whether particle swarm optimization algorithm has superiority in optimizing stability and accuracy. It can further verify the superiority of particle swarm optimization in recommendation system optimization. It should be noted that in the process of experimental design and data processing, the

Table 4. Comparison of optimization degrees of different methods

algorithm	stability	accuracy	Error
Particle swarm arithmetic	91.07	91.79	91.07
Single system approach	83.93	76.79	83.93
P	9.219	6.433	9.292
Particle swarm arithmetic	91.07	91.79	91.07
Single system approach	83.93	76.79	83.93
P	9.219	6.433	9.292
Particle swarm arithmetic	91.07	91.79	91.07
Single system approach	83.93	76.79	83.93
P	9.219	6.433	9.292
Particle swarm arithmetic	91.07	91.79	91.07
Single system approach	83.93	76.79	83.93
P	9.219	6.433	9.292

scientific and reliable nature of the experiment should be ensured to avoid potential deviations or errors that may affect the results.

5 Conclusion

Under the condition that the information management requirements of colleges and universities are constantly increasing, this paper proposes a particle swarm algorithm for the problem of recommendation system, and combines music teaching standards to improve the information relationship in the system. At the information processing an optimization set. Particle swarm optimization has a positive and stability systems. However, the study also pointed out that in the process of particle swarm optimization, there may be situations where too much emphasis is placed on the analysis ability of a single indicator, while neglecting the proportion of stability. In particle swarm optimization, in order to comprehensively consider accuracy and stability, suitable fitness functions or optimization objectives can be designed. The function or objective should consider both accuracy and stability, and assign them appropriate weights. By adjusting weights, the relationship between accuracy and stability can be balanced. In summary, although particle swarm optimization has shown a positive impact in improving accuracy and stability, it is still necessary to balance the relationship between accuracy and stability in algorithm design and evaluation index selection, and comprehensively consider more indicators to evaluate and optimize the performance of the algorithm.

References

1. Hu, J., Xie, C.: Research and implementation of e-commerce intelligent recommendation system based on fuzzy clustering algorithm. J. Intell. Fuzzy Syst. **3**, 1–10 (2021)

2. Hu, X., Li, X.S., Li, Y., et al.: Research and implementation of blind restoration algorithm for moving fuzzy license plate image based on frequency-domain characteristics. Int. J. Pattern Recogn. Artif. Intell. **35**, 2154024 (2021)
3. Zhang, L.: Optimization of an intelligent music-playing system based on network communication. Complexity **2021**, 1–11 (2021)
4. Li, F., Xi, Q.: Research and implementation of a fabric printing detection system based on a field programmable gate array and deep neural network. Text. Res. J. **92**(7–8), 1060–1078 (2022)
5. Jin, M.H., Jeong, S.Y., Cho, E.J., et al.: Implementation of the unborrowed book recommendation system for public libraries: based on Daegu D Library. Soc. Digit. Policy Manage. **2021**(5) (2021)
6. Guerrini, G., Romeo, L., Alessandrini, D., et al.: Analysis, design and implementation of a forecasting system for parking lots occupation (2021)
7. Dong, Y., Zhang, Y., Liu, F., et al.: Research on an optimization method for injection-production parameters based on an Improved Particle Swarm Optimization Algorithm. Energies **15**, 2889 (2022)
8. Mannapov, I.: The improvement of decision tree construction algorithm based on quantum heuristic algorithms. J. Math. **44**, 724–732 (2022)
9. Kang, Z.: Optimization model of local policy on rural tourism income based on Particle Swarm Optimization Zhonghui Kang. Tob. Regul. Sci. **7**, 1152–1159 (2021)
10. Peng, B.: Research and implementation of electronic commerce intelligent recommendation system based on the fuzzy rough set and improved cellular algorithm. Math. Probl. Eng. **2021**, 1–8 (2021)
11. Tong, Z.: Research on the model of music sight-singing guidance system based on artificial intelligence. Complexity **2021**, 1–11 (2021)
12. Yue, Q., Hu, Z., Li, D.: Research and implementation of EM clustering algorithm based on Latent variable mining. DEStech Trans. Comput. Sci. Eng. (2021)
13. Zheng, Y., Wang, Y., Liu, J.: Research on structure optimization and motion characteristics of wearable medical robotics based on Improved Particle Swarm Optimization Algorithm. Futur. Gener. Comput. Syst. **129**, 187–198 (2022)
14. Liu, Y., Yin, B., Jia, D.: A multi-objective optimization method for aerospace product research and development process based on particle swarm optimization algorithm and critical path algorithm. J. Phys. Conf. Ser. **1732**(1), 012076 (6pp) (2021)
15. Huang, G.: Design and implementation of visual employment recommendation system. J. Phys. Conf. Ser. **1856**(1), 012049 (2021)
16. Dinata, R.K., Hasdyna, N., Alif, M.: Applied of information gain algorithm for culinary recommendation system in Lhokseumawe. J. Inform. Telecommun. Eng. **5**(1), 45–52 (2021)
17. Shi, J.: Music recommendation algorithm based on multidimensional time-series model analysis. Complexity **2021**(1), 1–11 (2021)
18. Dicky, T., Erwin, A., Ipung, H.P.: Developing a scalable and accurate job recommendation system with distributed cluster system using machine learning algorithm. J. Appl. Inf. Commun. Technol. **7**(2), 71–78 (2021)
19. Zheng, H.U.: Multi level recommendation system of college online learning resources based on multi intelligence algorithm. J. Phys. Conf. Ser. **1873**(1), 012078 (7pp) (2021)
20. Wang, T., Park, J.: Design and implementation of intelligent sports training system for college students' mental health education. Front. Psychol. **12**, 634978 (2021)

Development Strategy of Micro-course Resources in Higher Vocational Computer Education Based on Collaborative Filtering Algorithm

Ping Wu[✉]

Heilongjiang Polytechnic, Harbin 150025, Heilongjiang, China
837602581@qq.com

Abstract. With the continuous progress and development of information technology, micro-courses have been introduced into computer courses in colleges and universities. Micro-course adds new teaching resources, which provides a good condition for China's computer major education. It is an auxiliary teaching tool, which can bring many different teaching perspectives to students. This paper investigates and analyzes the present situation of micro-course application in computer courses, and puts forward some thoughts and suggestions according to the current situation of computer micro-course resources and development in colleges and universities, so as to promote the construction of micro-course resources in various disciplines and specialties, and accelerate the full integration of college teaching and information technology. As a market-oriented teaching organization, higher vocational colleges will inevitably follow this demand in the process of specialty setting and teaching development. Using modern teaching means to innovate teaching mode is the basic idea of new curriculum reform, and micro-course is the concrete embodiment of the application of modern educational technology in teaching practice. Integrating collaborative filtering algorithm into the construction of university learning resource platform and providing intelligent recommendation service for users can solve this problem to some extent. In order to improve the utilization rate of course resources and facilitate users to collect the required course resources, the recommendation algorithm is used in the platform. In the process of building the platform, ASP.NET is used as the main development language, and the three-tier structure design pattern is adopted. Finally, the curriculum resource platform is designed and passed the test.

Keywords: Based on collaborative filtering algorithm · Computer education in higher vocational education · Micro-course resources development strategy

1 Introduction

At present, in the teaching management mode of higher vocational colleges, the two-level management mode of colleges and departments is mostly adopted. According to the two-level management mechanism of departments, the system design adopts role-based

Y. Zhang and N. Shah (Eds.): BigIoT-EDU 2023, LNICST 583, pp. 263–271, 2024.
https://doi.org/10.1007/978-3-031-63139-9_28

management control [1]. Through the research on the present situation of the design and development of micro-course resources of computer courses, this paper puts forward some solutions to the problems of poor interest of micro-course resources, low video quality of micro-course, single micro-course lens without subtitles, etc. Micro-class is simple to make, which can attract students' attention and improve the teaching effect more than the traditional visual whisker. At the same time, it also enhances the teaching efficiency of computer courses in Chinese universities. The courseware made by multimedia technology must conform to the psychological characteristics of college students in order to achieve the application purpose, and the importance of computer course in college education is self-evident. College freshmen come from all over the country, and their levels are uneven. How can we better teach students in accordance with their aptitude? I believe that most workers engaged in computer teaching have thought about this kind of problem. Micro-class is the product of the combination of information technology and teaching practice. By developing micro-class resources, teachers can break through the limitations of roles, places and time and realize the innovative development of teaching mode [2]. With the country's vigorous development of higher education, colleges and universities are investing more and more in the construction of smart campus. Conforming to the requirements of the "internet plus" era, the learning resource platform of colleges and universities has become an important tool to promote students to learn professional knowledge and skills. Teachers' roles include curriculum management, teaching resources management, question bank management, test management, homework management, attendance management, online answering and personal information management. Micro-courses are rich in content, and the teaching contents of micro-courses can include various teaching contents, such as mathematics, Chinese, foreign languages, general studies and other courses in traditional classrooms, as well as teaching courses such as cooking and gardening. Micro-class also has the characteristics of strong dynamics, simple operation, and realistic scene reproduction [3].

2 Present Situation of Design and Development of Computer Micro-course Resources

2.1 Collaborative Filtering Algorithm

Collaborativefiltering algorithm is a recommendation algorithm that comes into being earlier and is widely used. Through the data mining of users' historical behaviors, the user characteristics are analyzed, and the user sets with high similarity are summarized, and the recommended content sets are calculated from their preferences [4]. The platform is developed through. NET framework and browser/server (B/S) mode, which is one of the current mainstream development technologies. At present, the rich and mature WEB systems based on. NET framework on the network, as well as various cases and references, provide effective technical support for the construction of this platform. Collaborative filtering technology is based on the interest direction of neighboring users, using other users' preferences for resource items to obtain the similarity of users, or predicting a user's evaluation of a resource through the common likes and dislikes of similar users. According to these data, the system can make personalized recommendations with high accuracy. In the recommendation system, users can use the m × n scoring matrix to calculate their preference for resources, and users can rate them according to their preference for resources [5]. The scoring matrix of "user-resource" is p, where Pmn is the rating of user um on resource rn:

$$
P_{mn} = \left\{ \begin{array}{l} P_{11}, P_{12}, \ldots\ldots, P_n \\ P_{21}, P_{22}, \ldots\ldots, P_{2n} \\ \ldots\ldots \\ P_{m1}, p_{m2}, \ldots\ldots P_{mn} \end{array} \right\} \tag{1}
$$

If the score value of the resource is null, the user indicates that he doesn't know or doesn't use the resource with null score. As shown in Table 1 user rating matrix. User rating matrix is shown in Table 1.

Table 1. User rating matrix

Users/resources	Course resource 1	Course resource 2	Course resource 3	Course resource 4
User1	6		7	
User2		3		
User3			5	6

We take the hypothesized five users' ratings of two resources as an example to find users with similar characteristics, and intercept the user's historical operation ratings as shown in Table 2. "User-resource rating table" is shown in Table 2.

Table 2. "User-Resource Rating Table"

User	Resources 1	Resources 2
UserA	5.8	2.7
UserB	2.4	4.8
UserC	6.3	2.4
UserD	4.5	3.2
UserE	2.4	5.9

In order to further quantify the similarity of multiple users' evaluation of multiple resources in complex state, we adopt Pearson similarity calculation method, and its calculation formula is as follows:

$$
sim(u_i, u_j) = \frac{\sum_{y \in Y_{ij}} [p_{iy} - p_i] \cdot (p_{iy} - p_j)}{\sqrt{\sum_{y \in Y_{ij}} (p_{iy} - p_i)^2 \cdot \sum_{y \in Y_{ij}} (p_{iy} - p_j)^2}} \tag{2}
$$

The similarity between users can be calculated by Jaccard formula or cosine similarity formula. The Jaccard formula is as follows:

$$W_{uv} = \frac{|N(n) \cap N(v)|}{|N(u) \cap N(v)|} \tag{3}$$

After the similarity calculation between the target user and other users is completed, the nearest neighbor set of the target user can be finally formed by setting the threshold of similarity coefficient or taking the Top-n nearest neighbor [6]. Mainly around administrators, teachers and students. Each role can be regarded as a big functional module, and each functional module contains several functional sub-modules, so as to construct the overall function of the whole curriculum resource platform. Enrich micro-course resources, improve the quality of micro-course, make micro-course resources become one of the effective means of teaching, improve teachers' teaching quality, and make students' interest in learning even higher, thus promoting students' autonomous learning and making students produce good teaching results [7]. Focusing on the newly emerging micro-course teaching resources and deeply analyzing the design methods, development status and strategies of micro-course resources of computer courses can provide a certain theoretical basis and practical guidance for the micro-course application of computer courses.

2.2 The Significance of Computer Application Micro-course Resources

Micro-course resources are composed of teaching design, courseware materials, teaching reflection, practice test, student feedback, teacher comments, etc. The teacher cuts the teaching content according to the knowledge points, and uses multimedia technology to take any knowledge point (such as the key points, difficulties and doubtful points in teaching) and make a video of targeted explanation for no more than ten minutes. From the perspective of teaching mode reform, many teachers have made micro-courses and applied them to practice, and micro-courses, with their short, concise and distinctive themes, have played a concrete role in promoting the innovation of teaching mode [8]. For the operation of video recording tools, in the process of video recording, it is necessary to reset the recording tools reasonably according to different environments. How to adjust the exposure intensity of recording tools according to different light intensity in recording environment; The recording time is five to ten minutes, and the teaching content in the video is mainly the key and difficult problems in teaching. Therefore, the video of micro-class has obvious advantages, short course time, pertinence, and students are not prone to boredom. The video can be played repeatedly, and the questions that students don't understand can be watched repeatedly, so as to show the whole teaching activities as its essence, and it has the advantage of short playing time. In the process of making "micro-courses", the most important thing for teachers is to consider from the perspective of students, and to embody the student-oriented teaching thought. Teaching activities carried out around an example, an exercise or a knowledge point in teaching. Therefore, the flexible teaching forms of micro-courses are conducive to students' interest in learning and autonomous learning. The teaching content is more concise and clear, also known as "micro-classroom". So that the individuals involved can achieve the purpose of teaching through interactive communication and mutual help [9]. The utilization efficiency of micro-courses is not high. In the process of using micro-course resources, some teachers use more classroom insertion to guide students, but lack of flipping class-room links, which affects the role change of teachers and students and makes it difficult for students to truly appreciate the teaching value of micro-courses. Therefore, in the process of designing and developing micro-courses, we should standardize the design process of micro-courses, set up correct teaching objectives, and make micro-courses videos of different natures according to different teaching contents, which is conducive to achieving good teaching results.

3   Construction of Micro Course Resources for Computer Courses

3.1   The Main Existing Problems

The practicality of computer course teaching is very strong. Teachers can't deeply under-stand the teaching content only by explaining it. Therefore, teachers can apply micro-lessons to the classroom, and play micro-lesson videos aimed at a certain knowledge point to stimulate students' interest, deepen students' understanding of knowledge points and enhance classroom learning effect. Generally, a dynamic opening statement is added in front of the recording screen of PPT, and a concluding statement is added at the end. For teachers, there is not much room for self-exertion, and all the contents are basically clear at a glance on PPT. The content of micro-courses is to reorganize the teaching content on the basis of breaking the original knowledge structure and teaching system. This requires the producer to be very familiar with the knowledge content of the whole course, to have a high control ability of the course knowledge and a certain ability of micro-course teaching design [10]. What kind of micro-lesson videos are popular is investigated in Fig. 1.

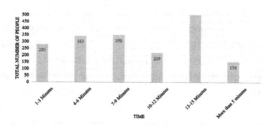

Fig. 1. Survey on the popularity of micro-lesson videos

Based on this, in practice, computer teachers in higher vocational colleges should combine the specific teaching content to make the content that conforms to their pro-fessional quality and cognitive law for students, thus laying the foundation for the inno-vation of teaching mode. The intelligent recommendation module matches the data in the resource files and the user files, establishes a prediction score, and uses the collab-orative filtering algorithm to generate a recommendation list, which is then submitted to the webpage management module. The architecture of intelligent recommendation platform for learning resources in colleges and universities is shown in Fig. 2.

Fig. 2. Architecture of intelligent recommendation platform for learning resources in colleges and universities

The resources of micro-class are not interesting, students lack interest in watching videos, and students are prone to inattention when watching micro-class videos, which affects teaching efficiency and makes students fail to achieve the expected learning effect. You can get production experience from radio and television. In the process of teaching, innovate the content and form. Make different videos according to different teaching contents, such as designing teaching contents in the form of advertisements, and teaching by advertising. The micro-lesson has a single lens, which is mainly influenced by the way teachers record. There are two main ways for teachers to record "micro-lessons", one is to use screen recording software, and the other is to shoot by a single machine. When using the screen recording software, the teacher will play the PPT electronic courseware prepared in advance, and explain it to the computer screen with Mike. Generally, there are only teachers and electronic courseware in the video screen, and there are no video switching modes such as transitions. On the other hand, influenced by teachers' previous teaching habits, some teachers have not adapted to the new education mode, and still record micro-lessons according to the traditional teaching mode. This leads to students' low attention to micro-courses, which can't achieve the purpose of improving students' learning efficiency. The time distribution statistics of students' study duration are shown in Fig. 3.

No matter what kind of equipment you use, you must pay attention to the stability of the picture and the light and angle of the shot. The shot picture should have a clear image and highlight the main body, so as to avoid irrelevant interference factors in the environment.

3.2 Strategy Analysis of Micro-course Resources of Computer Courses in Colleges and Universities

In colleges and universities, the computer course itself is a compulsory subject, which has irreplaceable importance for students majoring in computer science. The most important thing to pay attention to is the innovative design of micro-courses and the teaching level

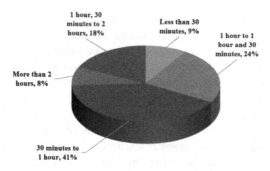

Fig. 3. Statistics of time distribution of students' study duration

displayed by teachers in micro-courses. Computer micro-course is created and shared by computer teachers according to the standards and actual requirements of computer course teaching. Micro-course resources must rely on a certain teaching platform if they want to play a role. In the practice of computer teaching in higher vocational colleges, it is impossible to realize the complete development of micro-course resources only by the strength of teachers. Advertising recommendation can be made for newly uploaded resources; According to the basic information such as user's major and grade, sort the resources that meet the basic characteristics for direct recommendation; Recommend resources according to time-limited activities of the platform. Normal operation of adding and deleting teaching resources, adding and deleting question bank information, adding and deleting test information, adding and deleting job information and checking attendance information. Schools should audit the micro-class videos according to different teaching contents and curriculum standards, and guide teachers to make micro-class videos by checking the clarity, interest and usefulness of the videos, so as to continuously improve teachers' ability to make micro-class videos, thus improving teachers' teaching level. Innovative micro-course resources mainly mean that teachers should adopt innovative teaching methods and innovative micro-course resources in the process of recording micro-courses. Teachers need to change the single video recording mode instead of traditional teaching methods and adopt various innovative teaching methods. Post-editing the micro-video of the computer course; Rethink the micro-teaching of computer courses; Form a micro-course resource package of computer courses and upload it to the micro-course platform. At present, most micro-classes lack subtitle tips. Due to the limited technical level of the teachers who make videos, they can't give text prompts in the teaching process, and they also lack the skills to add text to the micro-lesson videos. Teachers should purposefully break down the contents of computer teaching and divide some key theoretical knowledge, so that students' understanding of theoretical knowledge is clear and learning is much more convenient. In addition to teachers' efforts to strengthen their own information literacy learning, it is suggested that each school should provide micro-lesson recording equipment and micro-lesson recording venues, and unify the video post-editing, such as adding titles and credits, adjusting sound effects, adding subtitles and so on. In the process of developing micro-course resources, teachers should pay attention to combining professional characteristics, breaking the advantages of pure theoretical teaching, combining practical content, optimizing the resource structure, so that students can form practical consciousness in micro-course learning, and reflect and improve the professional learning effect from the perspective of career development. To master the correct video recording method, when using video software to record micro-lessons, it is necessary to set the exported video correctly, and when shooting by a single machine, select skilled personnel to shoot, so as to improve the video quality of micro-lessons. The recording of teaching video and the making of electronic courseware are important links of computer micro-courses. However, what teachers need to pay attention to most is the teaching link, that is, the innovative design of computer micro-courses and the teaching level embodied by computer teachers in micro-courses, which is the place where micro-courses are most worthy of promotion and truly reflect their functions. The micro-course-based teaching resources in computer courses are very extensive, covering most of the information resources and teaching resources, which can effectively improve the teaching quality of computer courses in colleges and universities and promote the process of modern teaching in China. Combine the micro-course construction with the school curriculum construction system, formulate relevant encouraging measures for the micro-course construction, and give appropriate policy support.

4   Conclusion

In short, with the advent of "micro-era", micro-course has become a unique teaching resource in modern education and teaching. Collaborative filtering algorithm is widely used, but it also has some shortcomings, such as cold start, sparsity, and new problems that can be expanded. The curriculum resources of the platform are not rich enough, so it is necessary to further enrich the curriculum resources with teachers and users. With more resources, we can further improve the recommendation performance of resources and recommend the required course resources for users. Teachers should pay attention to the problems themselves, and schools should also help teachers solve the problems in the process of making micro-lesson videos. To improve the video quality of micro-course, the problems in the design and development of micro-course resources can be better solved through the above methods, the teaching quality of micro-course can be improved, and students can have good learning effects. The core resources of computer micro-course include not only computer teaching videos, but also auxiliary teaching contents such as test questions, expert comments and teaching reflections corresponding to computer teaching videos. Judging from the current application of micro-course resources in computer courses in colleges and universities, micro-course resources will play a great role in promoting computer courses in colleges and universities in China in the near future. Build a professional micro-course platform and a scientific and reasonable evaluation system, so as to select excellent micro-courses made by excellent teachers, accelerate the full integration of college teaching and information technology, and cultivate more talents that meet the needs of society.

References

1. Guo, T., Zhang, L.: Personalized teaching research based on collaborative filtering recommendation-taking computer basic public course in higher vocational colleges as an example. Sel. J. Small Writers (Teach. Exchange) 20(5), 6 (2020)

2. Wang, Y.: A brief talk on the current situation and strategy of micro-course resources development of higher vocational computer courses. Educ. Times **20**(1), 9 (2017)
3. Mo, G., Chen, Z.: Design and implementation of curriculum resource platform based on collaborative filtering algorithm. Inf. Commun. **78**(79), 8 (2019)
4. Hao, J.: Research on intelligent recommendation platform of university learning resources based on collaborative filtering algorithm. J. Suzhou Inst. Educ. **22**(6), 4 (2021)
5. Cheng, W.: Strategies for improving information skills of primary education students in higher vocational colleges based on micro-curriculum resources research and development. J. Heilongjiang Teach. Dev. Coll. **39**(8), 3 (2019)
6. Zhang, Z.: In-depth development strategy of micro-curriculum resources-taking "four lines of defense of special protection" as an example. Middle Sch. Polit. Teach. Ref. Mid-Year **12**(2), 6 (2017)
7. Liu, Y.: Research on personalized employment recommendation system in colleges and universities based on collaborative filtering algorithm **18**(9), 7 (2021)
8. Luo, W., Yin, H., Tao, C.: Design and implementation of recommendation system for college associations based on collaborative filtering algorithm. Softw. Eng. **25**(2), 4 (2022)
9. Liu, F.: Theoretical basis, basic principles and application strategies of micro-course development in higher vocational education. J. Hunan Mass Media Vocat. Tech. Coll. **18**(3), 4 (2018)
10. Ji, Y.: Strategy of resource design and development of preschool micro-courses in secondary vocational schools under school-enterprise cooperation. Educ. Modernization **6**(4), 7 (2017)

Application of Cloud Computing in Intelligent Teaching Resource Library

The Construction of College English Teaching Resource Bank Based on Cloud Computing Technology

Yuehua Li[✉] and Xinxin Guan

Yantai Vocational College, Yantai 264670, Shandong, China
147683600@qq.com

Abstract. At the same time, with the increase of various materials and documents in colleges and resources and equipment are constantly being developed, which poses, data retrieval and data analysis. The traditional resource database can no longer meet the requirements of various users. English curriculum is rich in curriculum resources. How to make full use of these resources and establish an effective curriculum resource bank to meet teachers' teaching needs and students' learning needs is a problem faced by teachers. But at present, the research resources is still in its infancy, and most of the researches are also conducted on individual teachers, lacking integrity and systematicness. Introduce English learning resource recommendation ability based on the training requirements of the school.

Keywords: Cloud computing · College English · Resource library · Online teaching

1 Introduction

The informatization transformation of educational means is the most basic and the first part of the transformation of educational informatization. How to use advanced information technology and modern education ideas to create an information-based teaching management environment for the implementation of quality education is a new and challenging topic for educators [1]. Through the network, learners can transcend, and learn anytime and anywhere; Timely get feedback and help, and participate in communication; Information can be collected quickly. This interactive learning environment is conducive to stimulating learners' interest in learning, thus improving the learning effect [2]. In addition, Internet of Things computing and other network terminal devices have led to rapid growth of data in various fields. Recently, the hot big data has pushed cloud computing to a higher peak. It can be seen that the inevitable trend of the times. Cloud computing is the basic platform of big data, and big data is the most important and critical application in cloud computing. In the coming years, Cloud computing will certainly become the key development direction of the IT industry, and go deep

Y. Zhang and N. Shah (Eds.): BigIoT-EDU 2023, LNICST 583, pp. 275–282, 2024.
https://doi.org/10.1007/978-3-031-63139-9_29

into all walks of life, affecting and changing our lives [3]. English curriculum has very rich curriculum resources, and the degree and quality of its development and utilization directly affect English teaching. However, at present, most of the d domestic education sector are still at the theoretical stage. Although many English teachers have practiced in the teaching process, they have more or less faced such difficulties [4]. Through various teaching activities and forms, systematically develop and utilize teaching materials, auxiliary teaching materials, network resources, newspapers, magazines and literary works to promote the teaching of listening.

In 2017, the online education industry recovered, and various giants entered the market one after another. Throughout 2017, the growth rate of the online education industry reached more than 60%. It is estimated that in 2018, the overall scale of online education industry will exceed the 300 billion mark, reaching 348 billion. Online learning has been gradually accepted by people [5]. In the next few years, the technical upgrade and product innovation of online education will promote the further growth of online education market. Moreover, the course content often does not form a good system, and there is a lack of design and planning of learning paths for students of different majors and grades, which leads to the phenomenon that the content of the course chapters may be disjointed or jumped. Virtual desktop technology allows users to install simple thin terminals. At present, the cloud desktop platform has been widely used in the telecommunications industry and gradually extended to the general information system application industry.

2 Demand Analysis of Standardized Teaching Platform

2.1 An Overview of the Construction of College English Teaching Resource Bank

As a teaching method that has lasted for thousands of years, traditional offline teaching has run through our entire education. However, offline classroom teaching is undeniable and has obvious defects. Especially with the rapid development of the Internet, traditional offline teaching gradually cannot meet the fragmented and personalized learning needs of students. For example, online teaching resources solve the problem that teaching links are limited by time and space, achieve efficient sharing of teaching resources, and help students flexibly master the learning process according to their own time and progress. Internet breaks through the limitations of traditional classroom environment, and provides convenient and quick conditions for inquiry, cooperation and interaction in language learning. For example, students can explore independently through online search tools, and they can achieve far wider cooperation than traditional classrooms through online collaboration tools such as chat rooms, e-mail, BBS and other technologies. These ways of inquiry and interaction encourage students to actively participate in learning, strive to become active builders of knowledge, and gradually become masters of their own learning. This platform will provide synchronous and asynchronous learning and communication tools for students' collaborative learning, including Blog, message board, BBS and Netmeeting, which is a synchronous communication tool, so that learners can communicate with their classmates and teachers at any time, solve problems encountered in learning, and collaborate with classmates and teachers to complete related tasks.

2.2   Practice of Systematic Development and Utilization of English Curriculum Resources in Senior High Schools

Mooc teaching mode is a kind of In the past, in college English teaching, the evaluation of learners was entirely the teacher's final word, which was a single evaluation of others. According to the theory of multiple intelligences, self-cognitive intelligence and interpersonal intelligence are important components of multiple intelligences. Therefore, students should be encouraged to actively participate in the evaluation and self-evaluation of others. This platform aims to make learners become the main body of evaluation from the original evaluation object, and in the process of evaluation, they are in a state of active participation, reflecting, self-regulating, self-improving and self-correcting their learning activities at any time, the quality and efficiency of English learning and cultivate good learning strategies. In the design and development of the various learning support elements of the English learning support platform of our university, we should fully consider various factors: how to help students complete their learning tasks under independent conditions, how to stimulate their interest in learning, how to optimize the process of teaching and learning, how to establish excellent learning resources and facilitate the learning of students with differences, etc.

Through this resource library system, it can easily realize online display of courseware PPT, online play of teaching videos, explanation of classroom exercises, and assignment of homework after class. After the functional requirements analysis is completed, use case diagrams are used to describe the business functions from the perspective of users. Use case diagrams are mainly used to illustrate the main event flow, describe user requirements, and describe which functional modules the business application should have and the call relationship between these modules. Its main purpose is to help develop a visual way to understand business functional requirements. Hadoop cluster mainly plays the role of external storage of data resources to achieve VM backup and snapshot functions. The database server is mainly used to set up HBase distributed database and MySQL Server, and store system related data in the resource database system. As shown in Fig. 1.

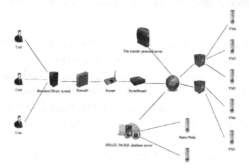

Fig. 1. Network topology

After the above analysis and design, the resource library storage resource request will be sent from the user terminal, through the network, and first arrive at the designated web server. The web service will decide whether to forward the request to other web application services according to the number of requests in the current message queue. When the web server that specifically processes and forwards the resource request is determined, You can take storage resource requests from the message queue in turn and forward them to the Hadoop cluster in TCP mode to respond to the requests. The can be obtained, as shown in Fig. 2.

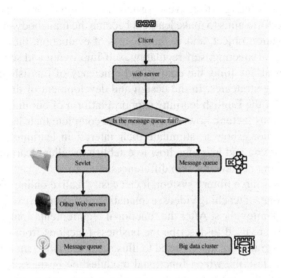

Fig. 2. Flow chart of sending storage resource request

3   Implementation of the System

3.1   Task Dispatching Algorithm of Virtualization Platform Based on Fuzzy Control

In the public cloud computing platform environment, it is assumed that the public cloud service sub-node is built on the virtualization platform. For example, the standardized teaching platform creates cloud service child nodes by VMware. The performance parameters of the child node mainly include: virtual CPU frequency, virtual CPU number, virtual thread number, virtual memory capacity, virtual hard disk capacity, virtual CPU underutilization, virtual memory memory underutilization, virtual network speed, etc.

In order to fuzzify the resources of the cloud computing service sub base, this paper uses the regular collection of computing resource performance of the cloud platform service sub node for the fuzzification of the quantitative resources using an equal percentage method, such as virtual memory memory unused rate, virtual CPU unused rate, virtual CPU primary frequency utilization rate, etc., The other $h - 2$ performance indicators (assuming the total number of performance indicators is h) are quantized to prevent. The calculation formula for the fuzzification of these indicators can be described as follows:

$$Performance = 1 - (\sum_{j=3}^{i=h} I_j * W_i + C * Wc + M * Wm) \tag{1}$$

Among them, $Wc + Wm + \sum_{i=3}^{i=h} W_i = 1$, Wc represents the underutilization of CPU, Wm represents the underutilization of memory, and $Wi(h \geq i \geq 3)$ represents the underutilization of other indicators, and both parameter C and parameter private belong to [0,1]. Therefore, the result of *performance* is also in this range.

Since the indicators such as virtual memory memory unused rate, virtual CPU unused rate, and virtual CPU primary frequency utilization rate are quantitative indicators in themselves, they are well fuzzed. The fuzzing process for the description of non quantitative resources goes through the following process.

Therefore, the Page Rank algorithm is as follows:

$$S(V_i) = (1 - d) + d * \sum_{j\in in(Vi)} \frac{1}{|Out(Vj)|} S(Vj) \tag{2}$$

$In(Vi)$ is a collection of web pages with links to web page i. $|Out(Vj)|$ indicates the number of sets pointed by links in all webpages in webpage J. The importance of a certain webpage can be obtained through repeated formula iterations. The extraction is as follows:

$$WS(Vi) = (i - d) + d * \sum_{Vj\in In(Vj)} \frac{\omega ji}{\sum V_k \in Out(Vj)\omega jk} WS \tag{3}$$

The whole keyword extraction process is completed, and the final keyword list is obtained.

The database server mainly stores user information, college English texts, test questions, a large number of English words and phrases, as well as small articles for casual reading, etc., in order to improve users' interest in English. As shown in Table 1.

Table 1. Resource Type Object Table

Attribute Name	English name	Function description	Type
Identification	ID	Unique ID of resource object	Char(10)
Resource Type Number	Resource TypeCode	Resource Type Number	Varchar(20)
Resource Type Name	Resource TypeName	Resource Type Name	Varchar(20)

This function is mainly used to query resource data through keyword list information. You need to first query the table number (TableID) and resource number (ResourceID) of the resource data in the current user resource relationship table of the MySQL database, and then use the composite number composed of TableID and ResourceID to find the relevant column clusters in the relevant table structure in the HBase database, so as to obtain the required resource address and other relevant information, Finally, access the resource information distributed on different underlying physical servers according to the resource address information and display it on the client browser interface according to the required format for users to browse and download.

3.2 Implementation and Testing of Standardized Teaching Platform

The test mainly tests the overall function of the online teaching practice platform from the perspective of real users, so as to ensure the normal use of the functions. The online teaching practice platform developed in this paper contains several functional modules. According to the introduction of the platform implementation in the previous chapter, As shown in Table 2.

Table 2. Contents of test environment

Operating system	CentOS release6.4
Java environment	JDK1.8.0_91
Database	MSQL5.1.73
Web server	Jetty8.1.6
Browser	Chrome69.0.3497.100

For virtual hard disk capacity, virtual memory capacity, and virtual? The "trapezoidal fuzzy" method is adopted for the fuzzy processing of non percentage quantization resources such as the number of threads. The "trapezoidal fuzzy" method identifies the performance of cloud computing service nodes, where LL stands for ultra-low, L stands for low, MR table middle, H stands for high, and HH stands for ultra-high (of course, a more detailed 7-dimensional method can also be added, which is not general. This paper takes the 5-dimensional distribution as an example). This paper takes the capacity of virtual hard disk as an example to illustrate the fuzzy process of "trapezoidal fuzzy" mode, and designs the trapezoidal evaluation structure as shown in Fig. 3 below.

The ordinate represents the capacity of cloud disk purchased by cloud users, and the abscissa represents the online rate of users who purchase the corresponding capacity cloud disk at a certain time. According to the actual situation of college cloud platform, at present, cloud users can purchase any integer value of cloud disk capacity from 0 to 30 g according to their own needs. For example, at this time node, when the ratio of the online number of users purchasing 30 g virtual cloud disk to the total number of users is 30%–40%, it means that the usage efficiency of the cloud disk is pure L; When the ratio is 50%–60%, it means that the service efficiency of cloud disk is pure M; The ratio is 0.7–0.8 in., which means that the service efficiency of the cloud disk is pure H; Pure L below 30%; More than 80% is pure H; The middle area between 40/0–50%

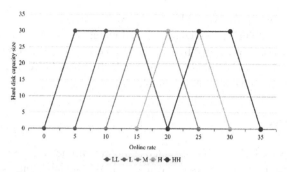

Fig. 3. Trapezoidal fuzzy processing structure of virtual hard disk capacity

and 60/0–70% is the transition area, which needs to be blurred. The intermediate areas between 20%–30% and 80%–90% are transitional areas, which need to be blurred.

The comparison results of FRCP and HCP algorithms in the running time of the algorithms. As shown in Fig. 4.

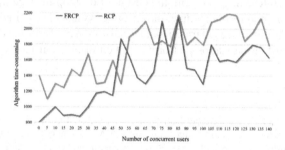

Fig. 4. Comparison results of FRCP and RCP algorithms in running time

According to the characteristics of college English Textbook content, this paper divides these contents into parts, such as pre-class tasks and objectives can be entered in the Pre-Reading Task page, text content can be entered in the text page, etc., which is clearer and more convenient. After the review is passed, it can be used for students to learn.

Through ADO NET's second database access technology: Connection – Data Adapter – Dataset – Grid View extracts materials from the material library according to English textbook categories, book types, units and classes, and uses the Grid View to classify and display multimedia materials. Students can deepen their understanding and learning of textbook content according to the materials provided by teachers. After a teacher logged in as a teacher enters the platform, he/she can click "Listening Question" under "Test Question Management" to enter the listening question management page according to his/her needs to add listening questions and test paper formation, etc., and add vocabulary and grammar questions and test paper formation, etc. on the "Vocabulary and grammar questions" vocabulary and grammar question management page, etc. The platform will comprehensively record the detailed data of learners' personal scores and class indicators in previous exams. It makes it very convenient for teachers and learners to study the development and change of individual and group achievements, make their own vertical comparison and horizontal comparison between different knowledge points, and show the level of improvement or reduction of achievements in the form of tables intuitively through quantitative calculation.

4 Conclusions

Through the study of the Hadoop distributed computing framework proposed by Google, we designed and implemented a highly available, highly scalable, high storage capacity, and high-performance teaching resource library, and built the resource library on the private cloud platform built by Eucalyptus to efficiently provide various services for teachers. This design principles of the English learning platform. Based on the actual engineering project of a cloud computing teaching platform established by a college, this paper discusses the requirements analysis of the business requirements, functional requirements and non-functional requirements of the standardized teaching platform in this college from the perspective of software engineering, including the overall design of the standardized teaching platform, the design of desktop management module, the design of platform monitoring module, the design of system configuration module, the task dispatch algorithm design of traditional virtualization platform and the task dispatch algorithm design of virtualization platform based on fuzzy control.

References

1. Zhang, C.: Analysis of the rational use of context construction in college English teaching based on association rules mining algorithm. In: Jan, M.A., Khan, F. (eds.) EAI International Conference, BigIoT-EDU, pp. 114–119. Springer, Cham (2023). https://doi.org/10.1007/978-3-031-23950-2_13
2. Wang, Y.: Research on the application of cloud computing college English teaching assistant platform. In: Jan, M.A., Khan, F. (eds.) Application of Big Data, Blockchain, and Internet of Things for Education Informatization. BigIoT-EDU 2022. LNICS, Social Informatics and Telecommunications Engineering, vol. 467, pp. 211–222. Springer, Cham (2023). https://doi.org/10.1007/978-3-031-23944-1_24.
3. Chong, N.: Research on the evaluation of college English classroom teaching quality based on triangular fuzzy number. In: Jan, M.A., Khan, F. (eds.) Application of Big Data, Blockchain, and Internet of Things for Education Informatization. BigIoT-EDU 2022. LNICS, Social Informatics and Telecommunications Engineering, vol. 466, pp. 39–44. Springer, Cham (2022). https://doi.org/10.1007/978-3-031-23947-2_5
4. Zhang, K., Xie, Y., Shi, J.: Construction of a decision model for the evaluation system of practical teaching quality based on AHP. In: Wang, T., Patnaik, S., Ho Jack, W.C., Rocha Varela, M.L. (eds.) Applications of Decision Science in Management, ICDSM 2022. Smart Innovation, Systems and Technologies, vol. 260, pp. 39–48. Springer, Cham (2023). https://doi.org/10.1007/978-981-19-2768-3_4
5. Zhang, Y.: Exploration of course teaching reform based on the construction of teaching resource base under neural network. In: Jan, M.A., Khan, F. (eds.) EAI International Conference, BigIoT-EDU, vol. 467, pp. 596–603. Springer, Cham (2023). https://doi.org/10.1007/978-3-031-23944-1_65

Research and Application of Big Data Preschool Music Education Platform Under "Cloud Computing"

Wanling Yang[1,2(✉)] and Wei Yu[1,2]

[1] Yunnan Technology and Business University, Kunming 651701, Yunnan, China
926angel@163.com
[2] Nanning University, Guangxi 530200, China

Abstract. Cloud education platform applies the idea of cloud computing to the field of education, centralizes the management and scheduling of teaching information resources, and finally provides them to users in the form of cloud services. The construction of cloud education platform can effectively improve the quality and efficiency of education and teaching, and promote the comprehensive informatization of education process. In the construction of the platform, in order to solve the shortcomings of the existing storage system, such as high investment, low efficiency, poor scalability and weak disaster recovery backup capability, it is necessary to build a cloud storage system with high performance, large capacity and easy management. The research and application of big data preschool music education platform under "cloud computing" is a research that uses cloud computing for research and development. This research and development has been widely used in science, technology, engineering, medicine (STEM) and other fields. In recent years, it has become more and more popular because of its high efficiency, low cost and other advantages. The research and application of big data preschool music education platform under "cloud computing" refers to the use or learning of information through analysis or collection of information.

Keywords: Preschool music · Cloud computing · big data · Education platform

1 Introduction

An important content of music education reform in preschool education is how to improve, develop and improve preschool music education. Every educatee should receive education fairly, which is for every educatee. Through the vigorous promotion and popularization of the new curriculum reform in kindergartens, most areas of our province have made significant progress in preschool music education. But in the relatively backward rural areas of our province, to what extent has preschool music education been carried out? Has preschool music education been paid attention to by the society and various departments? Has preschool music education also made great changes? What is the quality of music teachers? And so on, have become the issues that everyone is very concerned about [1].

Compared with foreign preschool music education, domestic preschool music education develops relatively late and lacks theoretical experience. The preschool music education in China basically relies on an educational model that combines autonomous teaching methods with foreign educational theories. In terms of teaching methods, the traditional meaning of music education is still being used: teacher led, young children learning to sing and sing along with the teaching method, emphasizing skill training and simple methods [2]. Therefore, in terms of educational quality, the development of preschool music education activities at this stage still needs to be further improved.

"The Learning and Development Guide for Children Aged 3–6 mentions that" there is a seed of beauty growing in the hearts of all young children. Fully creating conditions and opportunities is the focus of preschool music education and learning. Using nature and life to stimulate young children's feelings and experiences of beauty, expressing and creating beauty, and by cultivating their imagination and creativity, young children can learn to feel and discover beauty [3]. "Psychologist Bruner believes: "If we take 100 as a person's intellectual development at the age of seventeen, then children at the age of four have reached 50%, while children at the age of eight have reached 80%, while only the remaining 20% has been obtained in the nine years from the age of eight to seventeen." It can be seen that the golden period of intellectual development for preschool children is the period of 3–6 years of age. In the intellectual development of preschool children, the role of preschool music education cannot be replaced.

The core of preschool education is music education. As a key course to cultivate children's aesthetic and appreciation abilities, music education plays a pivotal role in preschool education. Music education can not only cultivate young children's sentiment and inspire their hearts, but also stimulate their musical talents, improve their ability to judge beauty and comprehensive musical quality, thereby achieving comprehensive development of morality, intelligence, physique, and beauty, and making positive contributions to their growth [4].

Cloud computing is the product of network technology, distributed computing, parallel computing, network storage, virtualization and other traditional technologies that have developed to a certain stage. Cloud computing is regarded as the core technology of the future information revolution, which will completely change the existing working methods and business models. The core idea of cloud computing is to connect a large number of computers and other hardware devices through the network to form a resource center for unified management and scheduling, and provide services to users on demand [5]. Cloud education is a new education model that applies cloud computing technology to the education field, provides computing, storage, sharing and other services for education and teaching, and builds an efficient and stable cloud education platform. It is precisely in this situation that it came into being.

Cloud education platform integrates teaching, scientific research, sharing, interaction and other functions, breaking the boundaries of the independence of traditional education systems, so that schools, teachers, students and other staff can complete their own different work on the same platform. The construction of cloud education platform can effectively improve the quality and efficiency of college education and teaching, and promote the overall upgrading and reform of the education process [6]. In the construction of the platform, in order to meet the growing demand for massive data storage and processing, it is urgent to build a high-performance, high-capacity storage system based on cloud computing, namely cloud storage system.

2 Related Work

2.1 Research and Development Status of Cloud Education

Cloud education will inject new vitality and vigor into the development of the education field, and completely change the traditional education concepts and teaching methods. Cloud education platform is a service platform for all kinds of personnel in the education industry, including the virtualization of hardware and software resources. Through the "cloud", it can break the geographical restrictions of resources and enable educators to enjoy high-quality education resources. This year, cloud computing technology has begun to take root in the field of education, and major enterprises at home and abroad have gradually introduced cloud education platform solutions [7].

The National Institute of Standards and Research (NIST) of the United States divides cloud computing into three different service modes from the perspective of user experience, namely, Software as a Service (SaaS), Platform as a Service (PaaS), and Infrastructure as a Service (LaaS), as shown in Fig. 1.

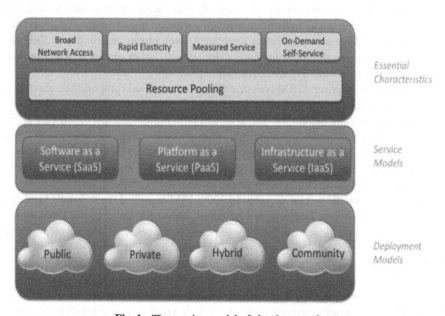

Fig. 1. The service model of cloud computing

(1) Infrastructure as a Service:

Provide infrastructure as a service to users. Here, infrastructure refers to all available hardware resources including basic hardware devices such as memory, storage devices, network devices, and CPUs. IaaS utilizes virtualization technology to form a unified resource pool for efficient and automated management of all available hardware devices. Ordinary users can rent equipment on cloud platforms. For users, the "cloud" refers to the unlimited device resources in the network, which can be rented to obtain infrastructure services and deploy their own applications on it [8]. Although users cannot control or manage underlying physical devices in cloud computing, they can decide which operating system to install and which applications to deploy on leased devices, as well as gain control over some network components such as routers and firewalls. The main IaaS products include Amazon EC2, Amazon S3, IBM Blue Cloud, Rackspace, etc.

(2) Platform as a Service

It refers to providing the platform to users in the form of services, including application development platform, deployment platform, etc. It is an abstract service built on infrastructure resources. Users do not need to care about how the underlying cloud infrastructure operates, effectively avoiding the complexity of hardware facilities, such as the configuration and management of operating systems, servers, networks, and so on. Users only need to deploy their own developed or purchased applications on the leased platform, control the hosting environment of the application, and do not need to care about the underlying infrastructure and development platform, which has the advantages of convenient development, simplified deployment, and maintenance. Platform service providers provide users with services such as software and software upgrades, application hosting, hardware infrastructure, and operating systems [9]. They also provide an integrated development environment (IDE) and corresponding development languages. Representative examples of PaaS include Google App Engine and Microsoft's Azure platform.

In 2007, Google and IBM cooperated to promote cloud computing research programs in famous universities in the United States, provide students and teachers with "virtual computing laboratory" services, and push online education, software applications, high-performance computing and data storage services for users. In 2008, SIMtone launched the school's cloud education program in Graham Primary School in the United States, providing 600 teachers and students with virtual desktop applications, so that students and teachers can directly enjoy efficient information education services on the virtual desktop. In 2009, IBM launched the "Cloud" Academy Program, which provided a global academic forum for all teachers, students and researchers in the education industry to promote the research and development of cloud computing technology. In 2011, IBM won the "Best Solution for Education Cloud of the Year". In the same year, Microsoft also launched the Microsoft Education Cloud overall solution, which is based on the education MAN to integrate and overall plan the education and teaching resources [10]. At present, Google plans to launch Helpouts online teaching platform, which will provide users with a new online teaching platform with social network as the core concept. Everyone can become a teacher in a familiar field, and at the same time, can ask others for knowledge in areas that are not good at.

2.2 Preschool Music Education

Preschool education, primary education, secondary education, higher education or vocational education, etc. are the education that a person needs to receive at all times of life. Each period of education has different rules and regulations, in which preschool education is a very important part.

"The so-called early childhood education is a kind of education for children aged 3–6." This kind of education has its own unique laws, which is a special education system suitable for young children based on their own physiological and psychological conditions. Its content includes the essence and essence of education, the role of education in children's development, and what children can gain and learn from education. Early childhood education and children's own interests and hobbies, development direction, and even the future scope of work, goals and life ideals, ideas have a great impact. In preschool education, there are many, such as moral education, intellectual education, physical education, aesthetic education and labor education. However, preschool music education plays an important role in cultivating children's aesthetic and intellectual education.

Preschool music education, in a broad sense, can improve children's music knowledge, improve children's music accomplishment, help and affect children's understanding of music. The narrow sense of preschool music education refers to that according to the needs of society, children in kindergartens or preschool schools receive such good education and influence physically and mentally, with clear purposes, strict and reasonable plans and strong organization.

"Preschool music education is the core content of the preschool curriculum system, an important part that cannot be ignored, the most distinctive learning content for children, and an indispensable part of children's all-round development." Preschool education is one of many aspects of education, and preschool music education is one of many aspects of preschool education. Music is a friend of preschool children. When preschool children listen to music together, they will learn to cooperate and share with others; In the process of singing and listening to songs, control your own organs, use your own body, and flexibly coordinate your movements. In the appreciation and learning activities, children can fully mobilize their emotions and emotions with their own imagination, and carry out various complex psychological activities such as meaningful perception, attention, memory, imagination and understanding.

3 Purpose of Preschool Music Education

"The purpose of music education for preschool children is to enable children to achieve comprehensive and harmonious development of body, intelligence, emotion, personality and sociality through music education and training." Its main activities are:

Music has the function of beautifying the mind. Children will be greatly inspired by music. In the future study and life, I will get a good exercise and form a positive, optimistic and tenacious spirit.

In the process of learning music, children can experience and understand how the composer's mentality is in the process of creation, and what things they want to express praise and praise in this work. Children can enjoy beauty by listening to music.

Music education can also help children to enhance their physical acuity and sensitivity. In the process of learning music, children can experience the melody, content, rhythm and rhythm of music. For example, children's mastery of music beat, rhythm, awareness of sound hearing, strength, speed, structure, recognition of score, imagination of music and recognition of harmonic music. There are also some games to train children's experience of music rhythm, their understanding of a song and their physical performance (reflecting the integration of dance and music, and the sense of beauty in training), the competition of training music and the discrimination of percussion music, the combination of training music and poetry, etc. These simple fun games not only provide preschool teachers with educational methods, but also provide parents with happy and relaxed music education methods in their daily lives.

The performance and singing of music works can enrich the spirit and enhance the physical and mental health. It can express people's deepest thoughts and feelings, and its music melody can reflect people's exclamation, dissatisfaction and pursuit of real life. While enjoying music, the body rhythm will have a positive effect on all organs of the human body, thus enhancing people's rich imagination, strong memory and sensibility, and cultivating people's abstract thinking. Usually, when we teach music before school, we also ask children to have body rhythms. For example, singing while making gestures; Sing while making facial expressions; While singing, the children's bodies will follow the rhythm of the music to make a variety of heartfelt actions.

Through these music activities, children's natural activeness is satisfied and they feel happy. Moreover, due to the joyful and infectious characteristics of music itself, these activities that children are familiar with and enjoy bring them happy emotions, so the physical and mental health of these preschool children is always in a state of excitement. Therefore, the way of playing is the best way for preschool children. For children, music games only have entertainment value, while for teachers, music games have learning significance.

An excellent piece of music can bring unlimited reverie and joy to children. Whether they are listening to a story or appreciating a piece of music, they are often affected by the moving images, vivid situations, and fierce conflicts depicted in the work, and generate emotional resonance. They can't help but revel in the situation depicted in the story or music, and appreciate the flowing water of nature Beautiful and moving scenes such as the singing of birds and the fragrance of flowers, and the dancing of wild bees.

The joyful and infectious characteristics of music are particularly evident in preschool children's musical activities, and are the primary reason to attract them to participate in musical activities. Through these characteristics, children are led to learn through play and music, and music education is placed in a joyful music experience and performance. They can learn happily and acquire knowledge. To enable children to receive education in cheerful, lively, and artistic music activities, to include education in pleasant music activities, and to use "music" as an effective way for children to receive education, to promote children's active personality, physical and mental health, and to receive education in a comprehensive manner in terms of moral, intellectual, physical, and aesthetic qualities. These are all characteristics of preschool children's music education.

Of course, this educational effect is usually different from straightforward verbal education, and the effect cannot be immediately revealed. It requires a gradual process of continuous influence, influence, and infiltration, which gradually permeates children's inner emotions and hearts like rain and dew, causing shock. As the German educator Humboldt said, music is always the most undisputed and an infinitely powerful lever of emotion. It starts at the end of the language; And where it ends, even thinking cannot reach it.

4 Big Data Preschool Music Education Platform Under "Cloud Computing"

The cloud education platform aims to provide more high-quality services for the education industry by using limited software and hardware teaching resources. The cloud education platform integrates relevant education resources with the help of cloud technology to provide an open, interconnected and unified management application service platform for colleges and universities. At the same time, it can promote the reform of students' learning methods, promote the overall improvement of the ability to use information technology in teaching and scientific research, and reduce the cost of education and teaching. The system architecture of this cloud education platform is shown in Fig. 2, which is mainly composed of infrastructure services, application services and user terminal services.

Use the cloud computing education platform to "cloud" the education resources, so that students and teachers can timely understand the latest teaching information through the network. The administrator can customize the teaching resources according to the teaching content to achieve the teaching mode of on-demand distribution and flexible interaction. Through the cloud education platform, administrators can release software in batches according to user needs, greatly reducing management workload and maintenance time; On the premise of platform network security and stability, users can use cloud platform resources anytime and anywhere through mobile phones, iPads, cloud terminals and other devices; By using dynamic migration, high availability, load balancing and other technologies, the system can automatically balance server resources and perform fault recovery processing according to the number of users and their usage status, so as to provide users with high-quality services; The cloud education platform also provides a high-performance parallel computing environment, allowing multiple threads to execute on multiple processors at the same time, greatly reducing the task completion time, thereby improving computing efficiency.

This article mainly uses the OpenStack open source project to build a cloud platform. The OpenStack version used is the Kilo version. OpenStack is used to build a cloud platform and provide cloud services. OpenStack supports multiple operating systems, and systems such as RedHat, Fedora, and Ubuntu can support the installation of OpenStack components. The underlying operating system selected for this article is Ubuntu 14.04. The components of OpenStack provide various APIs for secondary development, including Nova responsible for resources, Glance responsible for mirroring, Keystone responsible for authentication, and Horizon responsible for access management. The overall technical framework of the distance education cloud platform designed in this

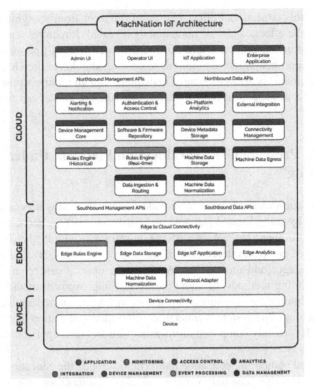

Fig. 2. System architecture of cloud education platform

article is shown in Fig. 3, which shows the technical framework of the platform, and also indicates the platform levels and corresponding relationships of each level.

The top level distance education platform uses a B/S architecture, while the bottom development framework uses a combination of the Spring MVC framework, Hibernate framework, and Spring framework. The MVC layered design idea is adopted. The hierarchical structure of the system is roughly divided into four layers: client, presentation layer, business logic layer, and persistence layer. The technical architecture is shown in Fig. 3. Including:

(1) Client: In BS mode, the client mainly refers to the browser. Mainly responsible for displaying the system in a graphical interface and receiving user requests.

(2) Presentation layer: For View and Controller in MVC mode, the Spring MVC framework is used to implement control functions, and JSP technology and JSTL scripts are used to generate views to return server responses to users in a user-friendly graphical interface.

(3) Business logic layer: A model in MVC mode, responsible for processing business logic. The main business logic of the system to be implemented in this article includes on-demand, viewing, adding, and deleting course resources, querying, modifying, and uploading grades, managing student information, adding, modifying, and deleting course selections. Implemented by Spring technology.

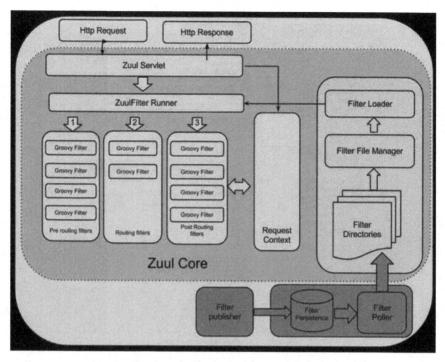

Fig. 3. Platform Technical Framework

(4) Persistence layer: The main role is to interact with the underlying database, which can be to isolate the business logic layer from the data layer and reduce coupling. The technical framework used is the Hibernate framework and the Spring JDBC encapsulation class implementation.

Course learning includes modules such as on-demand learning, course evaluation, course learning records, and learning plans. It is the core module of the platform, providing users with functions such as course learning and learning records. The data tables used in this module mainly include student tables, course selection performance tables, curriculum tables, knowledge points tables, course evaluation tables, learning records tables, and site information tables, which record student information, courses, course selection information, and student learning records. Next, the database model of course learning will be displayed, and various modules of course learning will be implemented.

(1) The database model of the course learning module is shown in Fig. 4.
(2) Courseware on demand

   After logging into the system, the user clicks the courseware on-demand function to first display the list of courses selected by the user. The user can enter the learning forum for learning and communication, download simulation questions, or directly click to play the courseware. When playing a lecture courseware on demand, you first need to obtain information related to the courseware, such as the course to which the courseware belongs, the knowledge points to which it belongs, and the playback

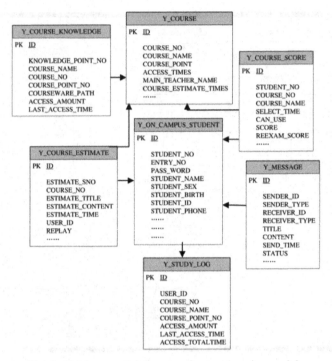

Fig. 4. Database model diagram of course learning module

path of the courseware. Based on the obtained information, go to the background to verify whether the courseware is valid. If it is valid, on-demand is allowed, otherwise, on-demand is rejected. When a course on-demand request is sent, the server side processes the user request and returns it to the user as a JSP page, realizing a jump from the business function interface to the course on-demand interface. Meanwhile, in the system, Y_ STUDY_ The entity corresponding to the LOG table records the click event: the current time of the on-demand courseware, the number of on-demand times, and the learning time length of the courseware. The learning record data obtained from the page is parsed into entities that can be recognized by the system, and stored in the database through background processing. This data is used to track and provide feedback on students' progress, as well as to assess their learning quality.

5   Conclusion

The transformation of music education means that in the course of teaching, teachers focus on teaching knowledge and skills, and focus on students' independent learning ability, the ability to actually solve problems when encountering problems, and the cultivation of innovation spirit. Music education should be a kind of aesthetic education, not a boring education. It should reflect the process of enjoying the beauty of music in education. Our transformed music education not only downplays the single transmission of knowledge, but also emphasizes the common experience, discovery and creation of teachers and students, and the common sense of beauty.

References

1. Wang, S., Hao, H., Liu, Y., et al.: Research on the application of power grid big data in census work. IOP Conf. Ser. Earth Environ. Sci. **693**(1), 012014 (5pp) (2021)
2. Huang, Y., Zhang, Y.: Research on digital application of lighting design in public space based on cloud computing and data mining. Wirel. Commun. Mob. Comput. **2021**, 1–12 (2021). Hindawi Limited
3. Li, D., Meng, S., Qi, B., et al.: Research on development and application of intelligent cluster management platform for shield machine. IOP Conf. Ser. Earth Environ. Sci. **861**(5), 052072 (10pp) (2021)
4. Wang, J., Zhang, G., Wang, S.: Teaching reform path of architecture specialty under the collaborative education of "Production, Teaching and Research" and its application effect. J. Int. Educ. Dev. **13**(5), 3 (2021)
5. Zhao, W., Li, X., Fu, L.: Research on clustering analysis and its application in customer data mining of enterprise. Comput. Sci. Ind. Appl. **2022**(9) (2022)
6. Zhu, J.: Application of Big Data Technology in Computer Classroom Teaching (2021)
7. Zhou, C., Lu, J., Wang, J., Zeng, Y., Ma, Q., Gu, S.: Research and application progress of silk fibroin membranes. Asian Agric. Res. **13**(12), 43–48 (2022)
8. Wu, S.: Research on the application of music education in the combination of rehabilitation and education in special education. Arts Stud. Criticism **3**(1), 53–55 (2022)
9. Zhou, S., Li, H., Zhang, J., et al.: Application research of big data real-time processing technology in smart grid. IOP Conf. Ser. Earth Environ. Sci. **696**(1), 012044 (8pp) (2021)
10. Bian, W.H., Yang, J., He, M.C., et al.: Research and application of mechanical models for the whole process of 110 mining method roof structural movement. J. Central South Univ. **29**(9), 3106–3124 (2022)

The Construction of College Chinese Curriculum Resources Based on Cloud Computing and Clustering Algorithm

Qing Yan[1,2(✉)]

[1] Hunan College of Foreign Studies, Changsha 410000, Hunan, China
178097473@qq.com
[2] Yantai Vocational College, Yantai 264670, Shandong, China

Abstract. With the rapid development of cloud computing and clustering algorithms, their application in the construction of university Chinese course resources is receiving increasing attention. The scope of college Chinese courses is extensive, including grammar, writing, reading, translation, and other aspects, and each aspect has a large number of related resources. It is worth mentioning that this scheme is adaptive, that is, it can be dynamically adjusted and optimized based on changes in demand and resources over time and user feedback. This paper creates a learning situation, guides students to participate extensively and deeply, creatively designs Chinese learning activities, selectively develops curriculum resources, builds an open, diversified, orderly, practical and high-quality database of digital Chinese curriculum resources as soon as possible, forms a pattern of curriculum resources development and utilization, and helps students improve their ability to solve practical Chinese problems and gradually improve their core Chinese literacy. In a word, the construction scheme of college Chinese curriculum resources based on cloud computing and clustering algorithm has the advantages of stable storage, clear resource classification, flexible use, etc., which can effectively improve the efficiency and quality of college students' Chinese learning.

Keywords: Cloud computing · Clustering algorithm

1 Introduction

Chinese is an important means of communication for humans and an important carrier of human culture. In the current information age, Chinese language education is also facing new challenges and opportunities. The rapid development of educational technology and the popularization of the Internet have enabled a large amount of Chinese language teaching resources to be stored in the cloud, bringing new possibilities to Chinese language education [1]. However, among the numerous Chinese language teaching resources, how to effectively manage, classify, and integrate has become an urgent problem to be solved. Due to the dispersion of resources, difficulty in classification, and differences in content, how to reasonably classify and integrate college Chinese course resources has become

Y. Zhang and N. Shah (Eds.): BigIoT-EDU 2023, LNICST 583, pp. 294–301, 2024.
https://doi.org/10.1007/978-3-031-63139-9_31

an urgent problem to be solved. A plan for the construction of university Chinese course resources based on cloud computing and clustering algorithms has emerged. This solution adopts cloud computing technology to store resources in the cloud for easy remote access and management by users [2]. At the same time, this scheme uses clustering algorithms to cluster Chinese course resources, making it convenient for users to search and filter among numerous resources. Clustering algorithms can classify resources into different categories based on their similarity, allowing users to quickly find the resources they need according to their own needs. Clustering algorithm can also span different Chinese disciplines, integrate relevant resources, and help users better understand and learn Chinese. College Chinese education aims to improve students' Chinese literacy, promote the development of their expression, reading, and thinking abilities, and lay a solid foundation for their future career and personal growth. At the same time, with the continuous acceleration of social informatization process, the widespread application of new technologies such as the Internet and digital technology has brought new possibilities and challenges to college Chinese language teaching [3]. The traditional teaching methods are no longer able to meet the needs of current students for Chinese language courses. How to keep up with the pace of the times, adapt to the development of society and the needs of students has become an important issue in college Chinese language education. Although the widespread application of the Internet and digital technology has brought new development space to college Chinese language education, it also faces many problems and challenges. One of them is the large and scattered quantity of Chinese language curriculum resources. This course aims to broaden students' knowledge, cultivate their literary appreciation and aesthetic abilities, inherit Chinese culture, and improve their humanistic qualities. From a functional perspective, Chinese curriculum resources include conditional resources and material resources. Conditional resources determine the scope and level of implementation of Chinese curriculum resources, such as manpower, material resources, financial resources, time, location, media, equipment, environment, and understanding of the curriculum [4]. From the perspective of presentation form, there are materialized and static Chinese language curriculum resources, as well as spiritual and dynamic Chinese language curriculum based on life as the carrier. This spiritual and dynamic resource is a product of the psychological activities of teachers and students, vivid and full of spirituality. According to different spatial distributions, it can be divided into in class Chinese course resources and out of class Chinese course resources. Classroom resources are the most familiar, direct, and deeply felt part of people, but they are the most easily overlooked.

Improving the core literacy of Chinese can enable students to broaden their horizons in cross-cultural and cross media Chinese learning activities, develop their own specialty and personality in a broader language Learning space, and then become more active in learning.

This article aims to explore the construction plan of university Chinese course resources based on cloud computing and clustering algorithms, and evaluate its effectiveness and significance in practical applications [5]. This article first introduces the current situation and development trend of college Chinese language education, and points out the problems and challenges faced by the current construction of college Chinese language curriculum resources. Secondly, this article introduces the relevant concepts and principles of cloud computing and clustering algorithms, and analyzes their application prospects in the construction of university Chinese course resources. Then, this article elaborates on the implementation process and technical characteristics of a college Chinese course resource construction plan based on cloud computing and clustering algorithms. Finally, this article conducted an experimental evaluation of the scheme and discussed and summarized its effectiveness and significance.

2 Clustering Algorithm

2.1 Form of Clustering Algorithm

The Chinese language course resource construction plan based on clustering algorithm can categorize numerous Chinese language course resources into different categories, allowing students to quickly find and use the required resources. Clustering algorithm is a non Supervised learning algorithm in machine learning, which can automatically classify data according to their similarity. In the construction of Chinese curriculum resources, we can use clustering algorithms to classify Chinese curriculum resources and improve the efficiency of resource utilization. The most basic form of clustering algorithm is the K-Means algorithm, which divides data samples into K clusters and optimizes them with the goal of minimizing the sum of squared distances between data points within the cluster. In other words, the K-Means algorithm clusters data samples

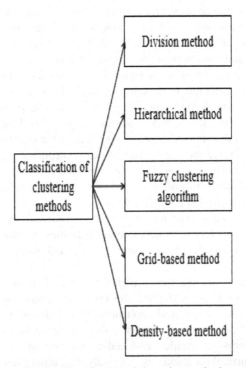

Fig. 1. Classification of clustering methods

into K clusters, so that each data sample belongs to the closest cluster and the distance between each cluster is as large as possible, while the distance within each cluster is as small as possible. In the construction of Chinese course resources, we can use the K-Means algorithm to automatically classify Chinese course resources [6]. This algorithm can classify resources by keywords, such as "grammar", "writing", "reading", etc. By clustering and classifying resources, we can quickly find the required resources, saving time and workload for manual search. It is worth mentioning that the K-Means algorithm requires us to manually specify the number of clusters K, and if the preset number of clusters is not appropriate, it may cause the data to be divided into unreasonable clusters. When the number of clusters K is set too high or too low, it can lead to inaccurate data classification. Therefore, in the practical application of clustering algorithms, it is necessary to ensure that the selected number of clusters is scientific and reasonable, consistent with the data distribution situation, in order to accurately classify and integrate resources. As shown in Fig. 1, it is the classification of clustering methods:

In addition, in order to improve the efficiency and accuracy of clustering algorithms, we can also use other clustering algorithms, such as DBSCAN algorithm, Hierarchical clustering algorithm, etc. [7]. Compared with K-Means algorithm, these algorithms are more suitable for large data volume, uneven or irregular data density. At the same time, the Chinese language course resource construction scheme based on clustering algorithm can also carry out deep learning and recommendation of artificial intelligence technology, achieving self optimization and update of data. In summary, the Chinese language course resource construction plan based on clustering algorithm is an effective method that can optimize the classification, integration, and utilization efficiency of Chinese language resources. Algorithms provide convenient and fast access to Chinese language teaching resources for Chinese language education, while also improving students' self-learning and innovation abilities, and promoting the comprehensive improvement of students' Chinese language literacy.

Figure 2 is the clustering algorithm:

Therefore, it is necessary to have clustering algorithms that are not sensitive to noise points; Object updating has little impact on existing clusters [8]. In many applications, adding or reducing objects will re cluster the completed clusters, which will greatly increase the workload, because the objects are changing all the time. Therefore, it is necessary to find a simple clustering algorithm for fast clustering of constantly changing data sets.

2.2 Clustering Analysis Process

In the construction of Chinese language courses, the process of clustering analysis mainly includes the following steps: collecting Chinese language course resources: first, it is necessary to collect resources related to Chinese language courses, which can come from teachers' classroom teaching, students' works, textbooks, and learning materials. Next, we need to preprocess the collected resources, including Data cleansing, data de duplication, feature extraction, etc. In the construction of Chinese language courses, text features of course resources, such as keywords, labels, chapters, and introductions, can be extracted as the basis for clustering analysis [9]. Clustering algorithm is a very "sharp weapon" applied in many fields. is shown in Fig. 3:

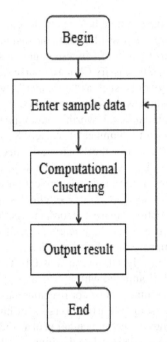

Fig. 2. Program block diagram of clustering algorithm

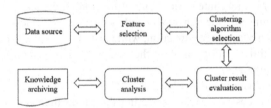

Fig. 3. Cluster analysis process

Based on the distribution of data, it is necessary to determine the number of clusters to cluster before conducting cluster analysis. Different cluster numbers will have an impact on the final result.as shown in formula (1):

$$d(x_i, x_j) = \sum_{k=1}^{m} \tag{1}$$

As a generalization of Mahalanobis distance, is as follows (2):

$$d_p(x_i, x_j) = (\sum_{k=1}^{m}(x - x_{jk})^p) \tag{2}$$

Cluster data based on clustering algorithm and number of clusters to form different clusters. During this process, charts and visualization tools can be used to display clustering results, helping to better understand and analyze the data.

$$m_f = \frac{1}{n}(x_{1f} - m_f + x_{2f} - m_f + x_{nf} - m_f) \tag{3}$$

Evaluate and analyze the clustering results to see if they meet expectations [10]. If the expected results are not achieved, it is necessary to review and modify the preprocessing method or clustering algorithm and number of clusters again.

3   Construction of College Chinese Curriculum Resources

3.1   Connotation of Chinese Curriculum Resources

The academic circle's understanding of the connotation of university curriculum resources is a deepening process. The teaching process, such as curriculum design, implementation and evaluation, including teaching materials, teachers, students, parents, schools, families and communities, which are conducive to achieving curriculum objectives, promoting teachers' professional growth and students' all-round development of personality. Ministry of education, curriculum resources is a very broad concept. In fact, it refers to all resources that provide college Chinese curriculum activities and meet the needs of College Chinese curriculum activities. In the current Internet context, according to the physical characteristics and presentation of curriculum resources, we can divide them into basic curriculum resources and expanded curriculum resources. Both teachers and students are important curriculum resources.

On the one hand, teachers are the developers and builders of curriculum resources, who determine the identification, development, accumulation and utilization of curriculum resources; On the other hand, teachers constantly transfer their knowledge, theory, experience, skills, emotions, attitudes and values to students during teaching. These contents are important sources of materials to achieve teaching objectives. The direct source of the content of research-based learning activities. It restricts the depth and research effect of students' exploration of problems, and also determines how students apply relevant knowledge to solve problems. It can provide a wide range of materials and strong dynamic support for research-based learning. On the other hand, learning is inseparable from teachers' guidance, and teachers' effective guidance can only be realized under the condition of constantly updating ideas and enriching knowledge reserves, which requires more resource support to create conditions for teachers' professional level improvement and learning.

3.2   The Construction Path of College Chinese Curriculum Resources

The construction plan of university Chinese course resources based on cloud computing and clustering algorithms can effectively solve the problems of storing, classifying, integrating, managing, and using a large number of Chinese course resources, and improve the overall quality and management efficiency of university Chinese course resources. Here are some path suggestions for the construction of college Chinese course resources:

1. Create a Chinese language teaching resource library: collect and organize various resources related to Chinese language teaching, including textbooks, courseware, test questions, works, etc., and use cloud computing technology for data storage and management to facilitate resource sharing, remote learning, and multi-platform use.

2. Data cleansing and integration: use Data cleansing and integration technology to remove duplicate, redundant or useless data, and integrate similar resources to reduce data duplication and waste, and improve the value and efficiency of data utilization to a certain extent.
3. Use multiple clustering algorithms to complete resource classification: Use multiple clustering algorithms to classify and integrate Chinese course resources to achieve better classification results and efficiency.
4. Application of educational technology: Apply emerging educational technologies such as data mining and artificial intelligence to intelligently process the construction and management of Chinese course resources, reducing the burden of management, use, and teaching work.
5. Fine management of teaching resources: Adopting fine management technology to further subdivide and manage teaching resources, improve the pertinence and effectiveness of teaching resources, better meet the needs of students and teachers, and promote communication and innovation between both parties.
6. Application of interactive technology: Using interactive technology to create a teaching platform, enhancing interaction and communication between students and resources, as well as between students and teachers, enhancing teaching efficiency, and effectively improving students' language proficiency and literacy.

In short, the construction plan of university Chinese course resources based on cloud computing and clustering algorithms is a highly forward-looking solution, and it is also a job full of challenges and opportunities. Chinese language educators and managers engaged in the construction of Chinese language resources need to continuously deepen theoretical research, improve educational technology levels, and actively follow up on the cutting-edge trends of education at home and abroad in order to better adapt college Chinese language curriculum resources to the needs and challenges of the new era, optimize the quality of Chinese language education, and help students better improve their Chinese literacy.

4   Conclusions

When clustering the actual data set, the algorithm that can produce any shape clustering cluster will be the development direction of clustering algorithm research. Therefore, mapping the data set to the Chinese curriculum and then using the construction of traditional clustering algorithm is an important research direction. Both teachers and students are important curriculum resources. On the one hand, teachers are the developers and builders of curriculum resources, who determine the identification, development, accumulation and utilization of curriculum resources; On the other hand, teachers constantly transfer their knowledge, theory, experience, skills, emotions, attitudes and values to students during teaching. These contents are important sources of materials to achieve teaching objectives.

References

1. Balamurugan, R., Ratheesh, S., Venila, Y.M.: Classification of heart disease using adaptive Harris hawk optimization-based clustering algorithm and enhanced deep genetic algorithm. Soft Comput. **26**(5), 73 (2021)
2. Neto, J.M., Severiano, C.A., Guimares, F.G., et al.: Evolving clustering algorithm based on mixture of typicalities for stream data mining. Futur. Gener. Comput. Syst. **16**(6), 72 (2020)
3. Jian, D., Peng, Y.: Research of performance of distributed platforms based on clustering algorithm. J. Comput. **22**(11) (2016)
4. Bi, W., Cai, M., Liu, M., et al.: A big data clustering algorithm for mitigating the risk of customer churn. IEEE Trans. Industr. Inf. **12**(3), 17 (2016)
5. Sinaga, K.P., Yang, M.S.: Unsupervised K-means clustering algorithm. IEEE Access **9**(9), 11 (2020)
6. Li, R., Yao, J., Zhou, Y.: Study on sorting method of zinc silver battery based on multi-step FCM clustering algorithm. IEICE Electronics Express, no.16, pp. (2019)
7. Xu, M., Qi, S., Yong, Y., et al.: Segmentation of lung parenchyma in CT images using CNN trained with the clustering algorithm generated dataset. Biomed. Eng. Online **18**(1), 2 (2019)
8. Xue, H., Li, S., Chen, X., et al.: A maximum margin clustering algorithm based on indefinite kernels. Front. Comput. Sci. Print **13**(3), 15 (2019)
9. Wu, H., He, Y., Zhao, B., et al.: Research on dynamic equivalent of wind farm based on improved k-means clustering algorithm. Taiyangneng Xuebao/Acta Energiae Solaris Sinica **39**(11), 38 (2018)
10. Mh, A., Jmr, A., Ms, B., et al.: Toolpath planning optimization for end milling of free-form surfaces using a clustering algorithm. Procedia CIRP **99**(39), 44 (2021)

Application of Cloud Computing in the Industrialization System Construction of Mountain Outdoor Teaching Base

Shen Jing[(✉)] and Li Sha

Hainan Provincial Sports Academy, Hainan 570203, Haikou, China
13518816053@163.com

Abstract. In the industrialization system construction of mountain outdoor teaching base, cloud computing is applied in many ways. The first method is to use cloud computing as a means of data storage and transmission. For example, when storing data such as images or documents, these data will be stored on the server through the Internet. This method can also be used to transfer data between different devices. In addition, the method can also be used for other purposes, such as real-time monitoring and control systems connected with sensors and actuators (such as remote control). Another application of cloud computing in the construction of industrialization system in mountainous areas. Therefore, by analyzing the principles and characteristics of cloud computing, this paper discusses the key technologies and application problems of cloud computing in the construction of the industrialization system of mountain outdoor teaching base, in order to promote the development of cloud computing technology through the elaboration of this paper, and provide theoretical reference for realizing the development of mountain outdoor teaching system in the direction of practical application and solving practical problems.

Keywords: Cloud computing · Mountain outdoor teaching · Industrialization · System construction

1   Introduction

With the rapid development of China's economy and the continuous improvement of people's living standards, the voice of people going out of the city and going outdoors is getting higher and higher. More and more people use holidays to go outdoors, go into nature, and consciously combine with sports and fitness. Most of the outdoor teaching projects are adventure activities, which are exciting and challenging, and contain many health elements that other projects do not have, such as fresh air, beautiful scenery, rugged mountain roads, etc. It allows people to embrace nature and challenge themselves, and can cultivate personal perseverance and improve their ability to survive in the wild; Release your personality, feel your inner peace, and experience the harmony between man and nature; Help each other, cooperate in teams, and pursue pure and sincere feelings

Y. Zhang and N. Shah (Eds.): BigIoT-EDU 2023, LNICST 583, pp. 302–312, 2024.
https://doi.org/10.1007/978-3-031-63139-9_32

between people and others [1]. These are the quality and essence of outdoor teaching, and also the excellent character that should be advocated in building a harmonious society at present. Outdoor teaching has become a healthy and fashionable leisure lifestyle of modern urban people, which opens another window to people's life.

The development of outdoor sports in China is showing a thriving trend, with more and more urban white-collar workers fleeing the steel and cement of the city and entering the dense forests of mountains to seek their own spiritual liberation, to get close to nature, to appreciate life, to fly their dreams, to meet the challenges of an unknown world different from the real world, to climb snowy mountains, go deep into deserts, roam grasslands, be accompanied by insects and ants, associate with vegetation, and think about life in the setting sun, After experiencing hardships in the fierce wind, whether it's cold, heat, or high mountains and cliffs, firmly leaving traces of their own footsteps is not only about exercising, but also about venting pressure and making friends. They talk about the places they have been to with a look of excitement, as if these experiences were the marks of their glory.

Along with it, there is a group of urban college students who also escape from the shackled ivory tower after school, go outdoors and challenge themselves. As the mainstay of the future society and the spark of China's future outdoor development, they also release their passion and walk with youth. For college students who are still young from the outdoors, with the spirit of fearing no tigers when they are young, they stand shoulder to shoulder with the old donkey who has been tumbling and climbing in the outdoor circle for many years, exploring the unpredictable nature and exploring the unknown of life together. For the old donkey, facing this group of young people, they also have an inclusive attitude, providing careful guidance in both experience and technology. Perhaps they have seen their own shadow from the young people, The recklessness and passion of his own time.

In April, 2005, the State General Administration of sports established "mountain outdoor teaching" as a formal sports event in China, and outdoor teaching in China has been further standardized. The first national mountain outdoor teaching championship of "Baihui" cup was successfully held in Anji County, Zhejiang Province from October 27 to 29, 2006. Since then, the outdoor teaching in mountainous areas in China will be held once a year according to the championship system, just like other sports officially carried out in China [2]. At present, China's officially registered folk clubs with mountaineering, rock climbing, field survival, field hiking and mountain rafting as the main forms of activities are growing rapidly. Hu Jiayan, deputy director of the State General Administration of sports, said at the fifth national mountain outdoor teaching club work conference that China's mountaineering outdoor teaching has developed rapidly. More than 1 million people participate in the national mass mountaineering fitness conference every year, about 50 million people often participate in mountaineering outdoor teaching, and about 700 outdoor teaching clubs. Mountaineering outdoor teaching has become a highlight of national fitness activities in China [3].

The theoretical significance of this research on the industrialization system of mountain outdoor teaching base is to build a standardized and systematic construction mode of industrialization system of mountain outdoor teaching base that adapts to the current national conditions, conforms to the demand leadership, and conforms to the development situation of mountain outdoor teaching. On this basis, this paper puts forward the theory and method of industrialization system construction of mountain outdoor teaching base, and widely applies the relevant base construction concepts at home and abroad Technology and experience extend and develop the theory of mountain outdoor teaching.

2 Related Work

2.1 Sustainable Development of Mountain Outdoor Sports

The concept of sustainable development has been widely recognized by governments and people from all walks of life all over the world. Sustainable development first advocates to maintain the progress and development of human society from the perspective of environmental protection. The sustainable development of mountain outdoor teaching base refers to the goal and process of meeting the development and protecting the environment to the greatest extent in the process of base construction and development. The sustainable development of the construction of mountain outdoor teaching base is the extension of the idea of sustainable development in the field of sports and the concretization of the idea of sustainable development. Therefore, the construction of mountain outdoor teaching base should not only reflect the basic idea of sustainable development, but also consider the local particularity. The core of sustainable development is the co evolution of the complex system of "nature society economy" [4]. Therefore, the construction of mountain outdoor teaching base must be able to reflect the coordination between the natural ecological environment and social economy of a country or region. Simply speaking, in Daming Mountain area, it is required to reflect the adaptability of the geographical ecological environment to the surrounding social and economic environment, not only to achieve the appropriate development of economic and social benefits, but also to achieve the effective protection of the ecological environment. At the same time, this also means that the differences in the construction of bases determine the complexity and challenge of the construction of mountain outdoor teaching bases.

Although outdoor sports are not new, there is currently no definitive definition of their concept in the academic community, and there are many controversies. Especially in China, outdoor sports have developed rapidly, and relevant academic research is relatively scarce. There is no unified understanding of outdoor sports. Whether it is sports, education, or tourism, there are significant differences. Outdoor sports are essentially sports, It is a group of collective events that take physical exercise as the basic feature and are conducted in natural environments, including mountaineering, rock climbing, downhill, rafting, cave exploration, gliding, skydiving, and so on. However, it is not only a sports activity, but also has educational functions, tourism and sightseeing functions. It is a culture and a way of life.

Outdoor sports can be defined from two dimensions, narrow and broad. According to literature searches, different scholars' definitions of outdoor sports mostly revolve around these two aspects, with similar content but slightly different. There are only a few key words, such as: natural sites, exploration, etc., specifically referring to emerging sports groups conducted on natural sites and closely integrated with nature, mainly divided into mountain sports, canyon sports There are several major categories of outdoor survival (including camping) and desert sports, including mountaineering, rock climbing, ice climbing, mountain crossing, camping, river tracing, rafting, and survival on desert islands. This paper defines outdoor sports in both broad and narrow senses. The broad concept refers to all sports conducted outdoors for the purpose of fitness, leisure, and entertainment; In a narrow sense, it refers to the total number of sports events with a certain intensity, exploration, and challenge that are conducted using non artificial venues (not venues established for sports). The object of this article is outdoor sports in a narrow sense. In a broad sense, outdoor sports refer to all outdoor sports, which cover almost all sports, such as swimming, archery, horseback riding, various ball games, and countless categories, as well as various sub categories. "The narrow sense of outdoor sports is also commonly understood by the general public as outdoor sports. Its main manifestation is to go out of the city, move towards nature, and engage in activities that are risky, challenging, and targeted under the premise of standardization and safety. Summarize the views of Chinese and foreign scholars, believing that outdoor sports is to open up one's own way to the natural field, challenge the limits of the body, and feel a sense of transcendence during holidays or leisure time, carrying a backpack An ordinary experience is a personalized travel activity that involves walking outdoors, integrating into nature, and engaging in interesting and mysterious exploration using natural resources such as mountains, lakes, beaches, and reservoirs. This expression not only regards outdoor sports as a sport, but also as a tourism activity. The definition of outdoor sports by the National Mountaineering Management Center is a group of sports events that take the natural environment as a venue (not a dedicated venue) and have the nature of exploration or experience exploration.

2.2 Risk Management Theory of Outdoor Teaching

Injury accidents in outdoor teaching are inevitable "facts" and "costs". The problem worthy of our in-depth study and solution is how to correctly face the "inevitability" of accidents and how to minimize the "contingency". The answer is to establish a scientific, reasonable and standardized outdoor risk management theory Based outdoor teaching safety guarantee system. From the perspective of the development form of outdoor teaching, outdoor teaching is generally attended by many people voluntarily, and can be combined freely, and the form is slightly loose; From the content of outdoor teaching activities, one or several organizers (or leaders) are responsible for arranging the route, departure time and journey of outdoor teaching activities, and the content is very rich, including high-risk desert exploration, and low-risk hiking; From the nature of outdoor teaching, the most essential of outdoor teaching is its challenge and stimulation, which is human nature; From the perspective of safety management of outdoor teaching, outdoor teaching includes participants, organizers and other subjects, and involves hospitals, public security institutions, health and epidemic prevention departments, fire departments, armed police forces, insurance institutions, outdoor teaching clubs and other social and government institutions [5]. This study takes the connotation of outdoor teaching as the starting point, quotes the relevant knowledge of risk management, and then from the perspective of system function, constructs a dynamic and comprehensive outdoor teaching safety assurance system in a certain order.

Mountain outdoor teaching is a way of tourism and leisure with the natural scenery of outdoor villages and some outdoor activities as the attraction, urban residents as the target market, and tourists' entertainment, knowledge, and return to nature as the purpose. With the increasing popularity of outdoor leisure, the construction of mountain outdoor teaching bases in China has mushroomed rapidly. Therefore, it is particularly important to study the current situation of the construction of mountain outdoor teaching base, how to build it, and the role of mountain outdoor teaching base in promoting regional economic and social benefits [6]. Therefore, this research is based on cloud computing technology, and carries out specific research on the industrialization system construction of mountain outdoor teaching base, combining quantitative and qualitative.

3   Construction of Mountain Outdoor Teaching Base

3.1   Basic Conditions for Base Construction

The construction of mountain outdoor teaching base should choose the mountains or scenic spots around the city with obvious regional advantages and convenient transportation. In this area, there are low and medium mountains with large mountains and a certain altitude (500–3500 m), and the terrain is complex and diverse, the geological conditions are good, the vegetation is lush, the water source is rich, and the mountain path is rich and obvious. At the same time, the infrastructure in this area is complete, and there are villages or market towns nearby, To meet the needs of the construction of mountain outdoor teaching base.

The determination of the construction goal of mountain outdoor teaching base is based on the mountain outdoor teaching goal. Therefore, achieving the goal of outdoor teaching is the core of the construction goal of mountain outdoor teaching base [7]. The construction goal of mountain outdoor teaching base is a multi-level system, but its core goal is still the safety goal of outdoor teaching. From the previous discussion, we can see that safety is the starting point and foothold of outdoor teaching, and also the starting point and foothold of base construction, so mountain outdoor teaching base must be based on the safety goal of outdoor teaching. Secondly, the base construction of outdoor teaching in mountainous areas must be based on the objective laws of nature. We should not only consider the requirements for the comprehensive development of the base, but also consider the protection of the ecological environment [8]. Only by organically integrating the two, can we formulate a scientific and reasonable outdoor base goal. To realize this transformation process and to what extent, we must take people's social moral development level as the premise. Without this premise, it is impossible to build a scientific and reasonable mountain outdoor teaching base. Of course, what is more important is that in the process of construction, we should formulate practical construction plans based on factors such as mountains, regional characteristics, resources, etc., which are based on reality and the future. The teaching framework of the mountain outdoor teaching base is shown in Fig. 1 below.

3.2   Contents of Base Construction

The construction of mountain outdoor teaching base is mainly composed of project construction system, base management system, safety assurance system and benefit

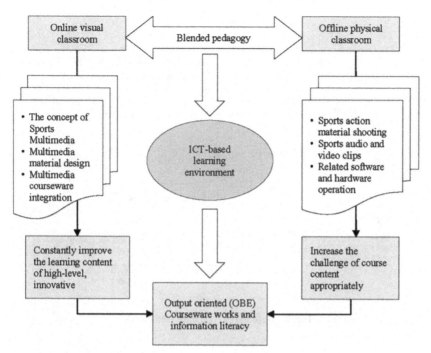

Fig. 1. Teaching framework of outdoor teaching base in mountainous areas

evaluation system. The project construction system is the content of experience activities carried out by participants on the specified routes provided by the base. In order to ensure the personal safety of participants and the normal progress of activities in the activities, the project construction system focuses on the construction of the footpath system and the identification system and environmental protection system in the footpath system, so as to meet the immediate needs of participants and the needs of ecological sustainable development under the current national conditions. The base management system is a management mechanism for base managers and activity organizers to achieve the same goals, maximize benefits and minimize risks under the constraints of relevant systems, norms and requirements. It is divided into target system, specification system, organization system and tool system, which are constructed and improved respectively. It is an important measure to ensure the sustainable development of mountain outdoor teaching base [9]. The safety assurance system is an important part of the construction of mountain outdoor teaching base. It is to provide all-round activity safety escort and emergency rescue for participants in the base. It is divided into safety policy and regulation system, safety monitoring system, safety early warning system, safety education system and safety rescue system. The safety assurance system is indispensable for the construction of mountain outdoor teaching base. The benefit evaluation system is a timely understanding and insight into the effectiveness of the base construction. The evaluation results will act on the base regulation and adjustment, which are divided into ecological bencfits, economic benefits and social benefits. The benefit evaluation system plays an important guiding role in the base construction (Fig. 2).

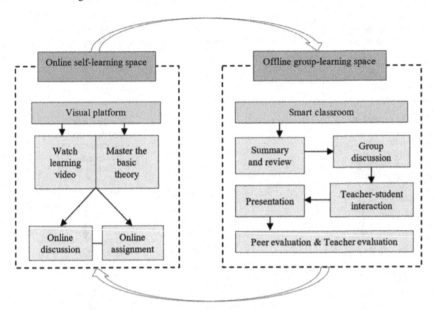

Fig. 2. Base hybrid teaching framework

Outdoor activities themselves are a process of generating relationships with various parties, and there must be various economic activities. As an independent industrial chain, outdoor activities not only have great economic value, but also play a positive driving role in the development of other related industries during the activity process.

In terms of the development trend of outdoor sports in China, whether from a professional perspective, a safety perspective, or an outdoor rescue perspective, outdoor sports in China are moving towards commercialization. In a market economy, only when an industry truly realizes its own hematopoietic function can it truly achieve rapid development. However, due to China's current social foundation, market status, policy environment, and bottlenecks in the development of commercial clubs, The development of China's outdoor sports market is slow.

The organization of outdoor sports involves various economic activities, such as transportation, accommodation, tourism, training, outdoor products and equipment, etc. In many industrial branches, clarifying the main industries, supporting industries, and extension industries is very important for the construction of outdoor sports industry models.

4 Construction of Industrialization System of Mountain Outdoor Teaching Base Based on Cloud Computing

4.1 Cloud Computing

Cloud computing combines a large amount of information and processor resources distributed in different places and devices to form a super system pool, which provides various services for the outside world through mutual collaboration. It is an Internet-based super computing method and mode, which is characterized by its stronger and faster computing power than a single computer through the multi-level collaboration mode based on the Internet, Distributed computers that form clusters do not require strong performance, but under the unified management of the data processing center, they can play the role of supercomputers in terms of processing capacity by allocating resources according to the different needs of customers [10]; The data center manages data uniformly, is responsible for allocating resources, balancing loads, and deploying security control software. The super resource pool composed of a large number of computers undertakes complex and heavy computing tasks, and can meet the needs of various applications for computing power, storage space, and other services. It packages various resources of the data center through the Internet and provides services externally, as shown in Fig. 3.

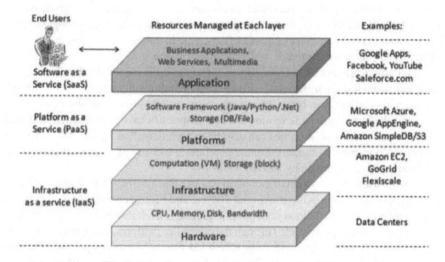

Fig. 3. Cloud computing technology service system

4.2 Construction of Industrialization System of Mountain Outdoor Teaching Base

The quality of the project design and construction of mountain outdoor teaching base directly affects the effect of the activity, which is the guarantee of whether the activity can be completed safely, effectively and systematically. Therefore, the design and construction of mountain outdoor teaching projects must be designed and planned according to the purpose, task, requirements, object and safety of the activities. Practicality, operability, safety, timeliness, scientificity and systematization should be fully considered in the design of activity projects, and the project portfolio should be reasonable, smooth and natural. For example, in the scenic spot, we should also pay attention to mountain outdoor teaching as an important part of experiential leisure tourism, make full use of the natural resources in the core area of the scenic spot, set up outdoor activities with high participation, and attract tourists to participate, so as to improve the utilization and influence of mountain outdoor teaching base, and promote the synchronous development of mountain outdoor teaching and leisure tourism.

A model of outdoor sports consumption behavior is established, which includes psychological variables, environmental variables, and conditional variables. Three different variables include different elements. Psychological variables mainly include individual psychological activities such as awareness, motivation, and attitude. Environmental variables include product prices and external influences. Conditional variables mainly include individual economic level, leisure time, and selected sports items, This is a necessary condition to trigger outdoor sports participation and consumption behavior. From the above model, we can conclude that:

(1) Environmental variables affect psychological variables: Among environmental variables, product prices and quality, media advertising, and the impact of parents and classmates can directly affect individual sports consumption awareness, motivation, and attitude. In daily life, the information people receive and the influence of people around them generate motivation to participate or participate in outdoor sports driven by a herd mentality and following the trend.

(2) Initiation process of outdoor sports consumption behavior: In the model, psychological variables, environmental variables, and conditional variables jointly trigger outdoor sports participation behavior. In some cases, psychological variables and conditional variables can trigger participation and consumption behavior, while environmental variables and conditional variables can also trigger participation behavior. The former involves outdoor sports participation under purchasing motivation, and the latter involves participation behavior driven by herd psychology.

The industrialization system of mountain outdoor teaching base based on cloud computing technology abstracts the traditional discrete and heterogeneous physical security equipment and software defined network equipment, and establishes a unified security resource pool at the logical level. Through the controller platform, the network, security and computing resources are uniformly scheduled from a global perspective. The service chain provides traffic detection. The global security strategy is decoupled from the underlying hardware topology in the service chain mode.

Dynamic resource reuse and elastic expansion are the advantages of the global resource pool. In this way, the preliminary deployment design does not need to reserve space for future capacity expansion, so as to reduce unnecessary early-stage waste. Resources can be reused by one machine virtualization technology, which reduces the number of early-stage equipment and cost investment. In case of insufficient performance, it is necessary to add authorization to generate more virtual machines. Rich business load balancing algorithms can efficiently allocate resources to achieve the effect of rational utilization and allocation of resources, as shown in Fig. 4.

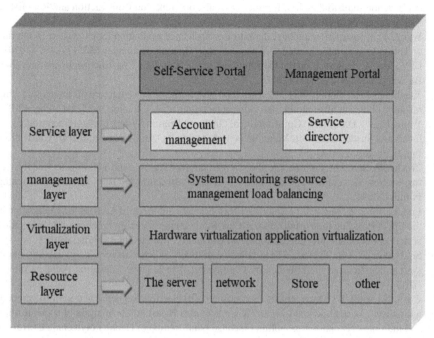

Fig. 4. Industrialization system of mountain outdoor teaching base based on Cloud Computing

5 Conclusion

Cloud computing has led the development of network information technology, and the general recognition in the industry has further promoted this situation. The service sharing mode of cloud computing reflects the development concept of people-oriented and intensive and efficient, and provides a new way for information technology to better serve people's production and life. Although the operation of this mode is still maturing, its development direction is optimistic. Cloud computing, like its beautiful name, is constantly presenting new surprises to the world, And its service sharing mode will also work with the humanistic orientation of the overall social development to jointly promote human production and life.

Acknowledgements. Project supported by the Education Department of Hainan Province, project number: Hnjg2020ZD-47.

References

1. Chen, L., Chen, J., Zhang, J.: Research on lean construction system in the background of construction industrialization. In: International Conference on Construction and Real Estate Management 2018 (2018)
2. Wang, Y.: Construction and simulation of performance evaluation index system of Internet of Things based on cloud model - ScienceDirect. Comput. Commun. **153**, 177–187 (2020)
3. Li Y., Ma, X.: Research on the Development of the New-type Construction Industrialization Based on the Cloud & BIM (2016)
4. Xiaohong, L.I., Yuting, A.N.: Construction and thinking of characteristic mongolian drug resource library in inner mongolian yinshan mountain area. J. Baotou Medical College (2019)
5. Wang, H., Yu, D., Qin, H.: Construction of "Industrialization System of Agglomeration, Symbiosis and Sustainability" in Xiong'an New Area and Its "Anti-magnetic Effect" Cultivation. Ind. Econ. Rev. (2018)
6. Zi-Mao, P., Shu, J.Y., Polytechnic H C: Construction of Training and Training Service System for the New Generation of Craftsman Spirit in Construction Industry. Education Teaching Forum (2019)
7. Luo, J., Hong, Z., Meng, C.: Exploring a New Educational Mode of Architectural Education in the Era of Building Industrialization A Case Study on the Teaching Practices of Construction at the School of Architecture of Southeast University. Architectural Journal (2018)
8. Su, F., Xiu, Z., Liu, J., et al.: The application of theory-practice integration in the curriculum system construction of fermentation engineering. The Science Education Article Collects (2017)
9. Chen, X., Amp, B.: Management. Composite path selection and construction of the modern agricultural management system in Henan Province Based on the analysis of specialization and multiple occupations agricultural management. Journal of Henan Polytechnic University (Social Sciences) (2017)
10. Fan, Z.H., Sun, X., Wang, B.J., et al.: Construction of practical teaching system in biological engineering. Modern Agricultural Science and Technology (2016)

The Model of Distance Learning Resource Library for Literature Teaching Based on Cloud Computing

Wentong Zhang[1,2（✉）] and Miao Ding[1,2]

[1] Lijiang Culture and Tourism College, Yunnan 674199, China
zwt1983@163.com
[2] Yunnan College of Business Management, Yunnan 650106, China

Abstract. With the continuous development and maturity of internet technology, many traditional industries are gradually being influenced or even subverted by the internet. As a traditional humanities, literature teaching has also begun to try to complete the modernization transformation with the help of cloud computing technology. The remote literature teaching resource library model based on cloud computing was born for this purpose. This model utilizes cloud computing technology to centrally store literature teaching resources distributed in different locations in the cloud, achieving resource sharing and disclosure. At the same time, the advantages of cloud technology also allow students to access these resources anytime and anywhere through the network, without being limited by time and space. Teachers can also upload and manage courseware in the cloud, achieving real-time updates and maintenance of classroom information. The emergence of a cloud computing based remote literature teaching resource library model has provided new ideas and approaches for the modernization transformation of literature education. It fully leverages the advantages of cloud computing technology, freeing students and teachers from traditional time and space constraints, and promoting the improvement of the quality and efficiency of literature teaching.

Keywords: Cloud Computing · Distance Education · Literature Teaching Resource Bank

1 Introduction

At present, deficiencies in the construction of major teaching resource libraries. Firstly, the construction of professional resource libraries lacks systematization, emphasizing quantity but neglecting quality, and construction but neglecting management. When constructing the resource library, the universities are bent on pursuing the quantity of the resource library, which leads to the phenomenon of disorganized resources, repeated storage and obsolete resources. And the system neglects the management of the resource library at the beginning of construction, leading to problems such as the lack of collation, screening and updating of existing resources, as well as the untimely and unavailable

Y. Zhang and N. Shah (Eds.): BigIoT-EDU 2023, LNICST 583, pp. 313–319, 2024.
https://doi.org/10.1007/978-3-031-63139-9_33

backup of the constructed resources. Secondly, there is no construction standard for resource data and the data is not standardized [1]. There is no standard definition of relevant metadata at the beginning of construction, which makes it difficult to find, recommend, transfer and share resources. Thirdly, the utilization rate of the resource library is not high and the sharing is not enough, and information islands isolated from each other are formed between schools and even between the teaching resource libraries of various majors within schools [2, 3]. Some institutions lack intra-school collaboration, inter-school cooperation, school-enterprise cooperation and joint construction mechanisms when building teaching resource libraries, making teaching resources lag behind in updating, teaching content is not rich, and the sharing and utilization of resources is low. Finally, the construction of most professional resources has never taken into account the security of resources, making it impossible to protect some high-quality resources with certain intellectual property rights [4].

2 Related Work

2.1 Remote Education Digital Teaching Based on Cloud Computing

With the continuous development and popularization of information technology, cloud computing technology has gradually become an important component of digital education. The digital teaching of remote education based on cloud computing is precisely the use of cloud computing technology to achieve the digitization and remoteness of education and teaching, promoting the modernization process of education and teaching.

Remote education digital teaching based on cloud computing utilizes online cloud platforms and internet technology to enable students and teachers to engage in educational activities without being limited by geography and time. Compared to traditional classroom paper textbooks and whiteboard handwriting, cloud computing based remote digital education teaching provides richer and more diverse teaching content. Students can learn through various digital resources, such as teaching videos, graphic materials, courseware, etc. [5]. These resources can not only showcase teaching content from multiple perspectives, but also stimulate students' interest in learning.

An important feature of distance education digital teaching based on cloud computing is its balance between teacher led learning methods and students' autonomous control of learning progress. Teachers can remotely control students' learning progress in the background and provide timely learning guidance and feedback to students; Students can freely choose their learning content based on their learning abilities, interests, and foundation, and learn at their own time and pace [6].

In short, cloud computing based remote education digital teaching has optimized traditional teaching modes, integrated various digital education resources, introduced intelligent artificial intelligence technology and remote access technology, improved learning effectiveness, and better adapted to the needs of modern education.

2.2 Cloud Platform Service Model

In recent years, the rapid development of technologies such as cloud computing, big data, and artificial intelligence has made cloud platforms a new type of technological service model. Cloud platform refers to an open and programmable service platform based on the Internet, which provides IT resources and services for enterprises and individuals through cloud service mode [7]. Below, we will explore the service models and advantages of cloud platforms.

The cloud platform services include three parts: IaaS, PaaS, and SaaS, as shown in Fig. 1.

(1) IaaS (Infrastructure as a Service): Cloud service providers pool resources such as servers, networks, and storage based on virtualization technology, and then provide corresponding services to users through gateways and other means. Users can rent hardware facilities from cloud service providers through IaaS, such as virtual machines, storage, networks, etc. For example, Amazon crowdfunding provides Elastic Cloud Computing (EC2) services, where users can choose processing power, storage space, and bandwidth according to their needs.

(2) PaaS (Platform as a Service): Users can rent platform services required for developing, testing, and running programs from cloud service providers through cloud platforms. The service scope of PaaS mainly includes development environment, application deployment, data management, version upgrade, etc. PaaS providers are often software and data providers, and users can use their platforms to develop and run their own applications[8]. For example, Microsoft provides Azure services that allow users to develop, test, publish, and host web applications based on their cloud platform, and can seamlessly integrate with other Microsoft services (SaaS).

(3) SaaS (Software as a Service): Users can conduct various office work, management, and communication based on the software provided by cloud computing providers on the cloud platform. The service scope of SaaS mainly includes office software, CRM, ERP, etc. SaaS is the most mature stage of cloud computing development, and various cloud office software, online file management, etc. on the market today are typical representatives of SaaS [9, 10]. For example, Google's Gmail and Office 365 software packages are typical representatives of SaaS.

3 Overall Design of Remote Literature Teaching Resource Library

3.1 Overall Technical Architecture Design

The overall framework of the education cloud platform where this resource library is located is horizontally divided into display layer, application layer, data resource layer, and cloud infrastructure layer, and vertically divided into security management, mechanism management, and standard specifications.

Display layer: a set of channels or facilities that can achieve information interaction with users. Users can access or access the cloud service platform of this resource library through wired and wireless methods, and obtain corresponding teaching resources. This level mainly provides functions such as resource information disclosure to achieve customization of personalized portals.

Data resource layer: solves the problem of mutual correlation and unified management between different institutions, students or teachers, types of resource data, and users with different educational backgrounds.

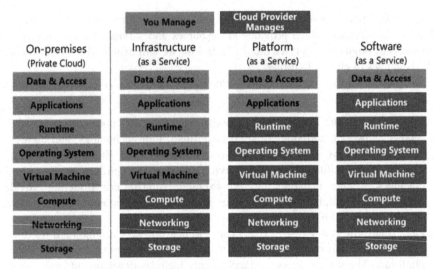

Fig. 1. Cloud Platform Service Mode

Cloud infrastructure layer: including virtualized server clusters, data storage clusters, monitoring devices, network systems, etc. Establish cloud storage platform and server virtualization platform to provide cloud storage and server virtualization functions for regional open distance education service platform. Vertically divided into security management, mechanism management, and standard specifications, to ensure that the completed system has good maintainability, scalability, and security, and to achieve unified monitoring and operation. The overall technical architecture of this cloud service platform is shown in Fig. 2.

3.2   Network Topology Architecture Design

The university's resource inventory storage environment is a Hadoop cluster, which consists of servers running the HDFS file system.

This resource library is built on a private cloud platform built by Eucalyptus. is shown in Fig. 3.

The web portal of the resource library system is installed in front of the firewall, mainly serving as the entry point for users and administrators of various types of resource library systems to access the private cloud services of this resource library. It is equipped with various certificates required by Euca2ools and this private cloud service platform, and generally serves as the middleware for requesting access to the private cloud of this resource library. The Hadoop cluster mainly plays a role in external storage of data resources to achieve backup and snapshot functions for VMs. The database server is mainly used for setting up HBase distributed databases and MySQL Server, storing system related data in the resource database system.

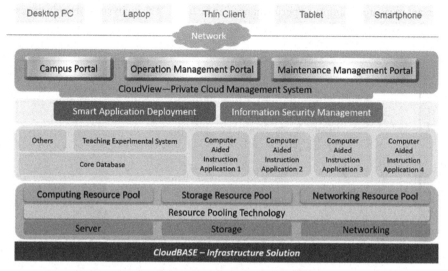

Fig. 2. Overall technical architecture of cloud service platform

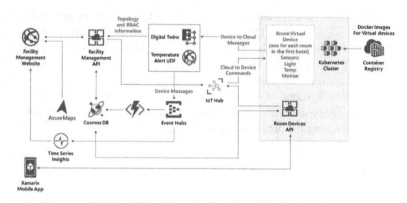

Fig. 3. Network topology architecture diagram

4 System Testing and Analysis

After the test run is completed, LoadRunner will provide relevant detailed diagrams and reports. Firstly, you should review the Analysis Summary, from which you can determine whether the performance of the resource library meets the requirements based on the relevant data in the statistical review; Secondly, by analyzing the test result graph, it can be seen whether the transaction was successful during the testing process. Next, analyzing the average response time of transactions can determine whether the performance of this resource library decreases with the passage of runtime. Finally, by analyzing the total number of transactions passed per second, we can understand the changes in the total number of successful and failed transactions at any time. By analyzing the above indicators, the performance bottlenecks of this resource library can be identified, and relevant measures to improve performance can be taken. The analysis tool analysis result interface is shown in Fig. 4:

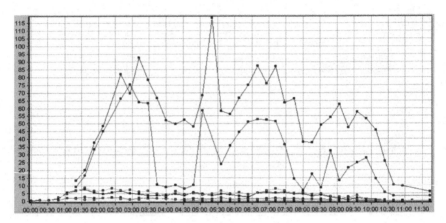

Fig. 4. Analysis Results Interface

The construction of a resource database system has played an important role in promoting the development of Chinese language education. The emergence of such systems has become a new challenge in the field of Chinese language education and in the context of the new era. There is also great potential and development space in resource management, communication, education, and practical applications. In the future, under the background of digital technology, it can be foreseen that the application of resource database systems will become increasingly widespread and in-depth, continuously promoting the progress of Chinese language education.

5 Conclusion

With the development of various disciplines in universities, the data volume of various resources has reached the order of terabytes and petabytes. Traditional data storage and analysis methods are far from meeting the needs of teachers and students. Moreover, research has found that various teaching resources in various schools have low utilization rates, difficulty in sharing, and problems such as uneven and insufficient resource distribution. By learning from the Hadoop distributed computing framework proposed by Google, a highly available, scalable, storage capacity, and high-performance teaching resource library has been designed and implemented. The resource library has been installed on the private cloud platform built by Eucalyptus to efficiently provide various services for teachers and students. This resource library system is implemented in Java, and although it is portable, HDFS uses stream I/O as the underlying implementation of IO, which seriously affects the system's access efficiency to resource data. This aspect still needs further improvement and improvement.

Acknowledgements. 1: Development tracking research of teaching supervision after the independent college, Project No.: CANFZG21139, Project Source: 2021 annual planning subject of China Private Education Association;

2: Inquiry into the new mode of the supervision work of "Curriculum Ideological and Political Affairs", Project No.: 2021J0818, Project Source: Scientific Research Fund Project of Yunnan Provincial Department of Education.

References

1. Liang, Y.: Allocation of multi-dimensional distance learning resource based on MOOC data. Int. J. Continuing Eng. Educ. Life-long Learn. **2022**(2), 32 (2022)
2. Kato, F., Spring, R., Mori, C.: Incorporating project-based language learning into distance learning: Creating a homepage during computer-mediated learning sessions: Lang. Teach. Res. **27**(3), 621–641 (2023). https://doi.org/10.1177/1362168820954454
3. Cheddad, A., Nordahl, C.: Distance Teaching Experience of Campus-based Teachers at Times of Pandemic Confinement (2022). https://doi.org/10.48550/arXiv.2211.16280
4. Li, Y.: Research on the scheduling method of distance learning process education resource based on augmented reality. Int. J. Continuing Eng. Educ. Life-Long Learn. **2022**(2), 32 (2022)
5. Liu, N.: An evaluation model of distance learning effect based on MOOC theory. Int. J. Continuing Eng. Educ. Life-Long Learn. **2022**(2), 32 (2022)
6. Zhang, Y., Yang, Y.: The evaluation method for distance learning engagement of college English under the mixed teaching mode. Int. J. Continuing Eng. Educ. Life-Long Learn. **2022**(2), 32 (2022)
7. Mangkhang, C.: Area-Based Participatory Action Learning of Social Studies Pre-service Teachers to Develop Indigenous History Learning Resources for Diversity Students in Northern Thailand. Higher Education Studies, vol. 12 (2022)
8. Zeng, L., Wang, J.C., Wen, X.L., et al.: Dynamic evaluation method of distance learning quality based on MOOC theory. Int. J Continuing Eng. Educ. Life-Long Learn. **2022**(2), 32 (2022)
9. Huang, Y.: Design of personalised english distance teaching platform based on artificial intelligence. J. Inf. Knowl. Manage. (2022). https://doi.org/10.1142/S0219649222400172
10. Ghosh, S.B., Sevukan, R.: Lifelong Learning for LIS Teachers and Educators through Open and Distance Learning: A Case Study of India (2022)

Retrieval Algorithm Model of Music Preschool Teaching Resources Based on Cloud Platform Resources

Yeman Wang[1,2(✉)], Qinqin Zhao[1,2], and Chun Jiang[1,2]

[1] Yunnan University of Business Management, Kunming 651010, Yunnan, China
452412696@qq.com
[2] Nanning University, Nanning 530000, Guangxi, China

Abstract. In recent years, the development and application of cloud computing technology in many fields has made resource management more mature. In the field of education, due to the explosive growth of educational resources, it is also facing difficulties in resource retrieval, storage and sharing. At the same time, the wide application of mobile terminals makes the self-upgrade, synchronization and protection of personal resources and applications face great challenges. The cloud platform is based on the development of cloud computing and can be used to provide a network platform under the co-construction and sharing mode of various resources. The basic idea of the technology is to push the server to the edge network by adding a new network architecture on top of the existing Internet. For the music retrieval with the whole song content as the query condition, a model based on manifold sorting is proposed, and the retrieval results are improved by designing relevance feedback. Gaussian mixture model and maximum likelihood estimation are used to cluster the spectral data of each audio, and the center of each cluster is selected as the typical spectral feature. The application of cloud computing technology in the field of education is called "education cloud". By virtualizing educational information resources and systems and uniformly deploying and implementing them on the cloud platform, cloud services can be provided for education practitioners and students.

Keywords: Cloud platform · Music preschool teaching · Resource retrieval

1 Introduction

With the rapid development of Internet applications and the wide application of mobile terminal devices, all kinds of digital resources are exploding in the Internet, and the Internet has become the largest information supermarket for information resource inquiry and sharing. Music is a broad theme in our society, and everyone will listen to or create music [1]. Therefore, music preschool education has a great influence on people's lives. Despite the rapid growth of educational resources on the Internet, Internet users are "resource hungry", because in the face of massive educational resources, users are often

Y. Zhang and N. Shah (Eds.): BigIoT-EDU 2023, LNICST 583, pp. 320–327, 2024.
https://doi.org/10.1007/978-3-031-63139-9_34

lost in the ocean of information, and more and more users are troubled by information islands, resource classification and accurate positioning. For mobile terminal users, the management problems of device resources and applications are becoming more and more prominent, such as resource update, after the device is lost, the user's private information saved on the mobile device, etc., cannot be managed in a timely and effective manner [2]. In the traditional music preschool teaching resource management system, it is often an internal network built by an institution or school itself. The user base is relatively small and the number of resources is relatively small.

At present, cloud storage based on cloud computing technology is more and more used in all walks of life. Among them, cloud storage is a system that integrates various types of resources and devices in the network through application software under the functions of cluster application, grid technology and distributed file system, and jointly provides data storage and business access functions [3]. Cloud storage can provide high-quality services such as security, stability, high capacity, and high throughput [4]. At present, cloud storage technology based on the extension and development of cloud computing has been greatly developed and applied to many industries, but the construction of education resource platform based on cloud storage has not yet perfected products and applications. Therefore, it is necessary to study the retrieval of music preschool education resources based on cloud platform resources.

2   Music Preschool Education Model Based on Cloud Platform Resources

2.1   Cloud Computing Technology

Because different people have different understandings of cloud computing, they analyze cloud computing from the perspective of technology, and from the perspective of business logic and application. Therefore, the definition of cloud computing has always been different. For the public, it is just like cloud computing. The name of the calculation is the same, so people are confused [5]. This paper quotes the definition of cloud computing made by American National Institute of Standards and Technology, which is generally accepted and used in the industry. As shown in Fig. 1, five key features, four service models and four deployment models are defined for cloud computing.

Cloud computing is not a new technology. It is a newly evolved delivery mode. It is an extended computing method that transmits the data processing process to the virtual computer cluster resources through high-speed watt networking, which evolved from distributed processing, parallel processing and network computing [6]. Cloud computing is also a methodology of infrastructure design. It consists of a large number of computer resources to form a shared resource pool, which has the advantages of high reliability and security, dynamic scalability, super computing and storage, virtualization technology and low cost.

2.2   Education Mode Under Cloud Platform

Curriculum resources are the sum total of manpower, material resources and financial resources widely used in the process of ensuring the normal education, and are historical experience of relevant education or relevant information materials of education [7].

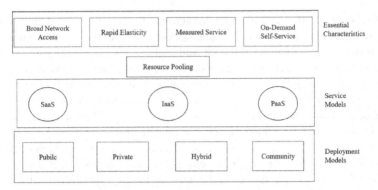

Fig. 1. Basic model of cloud computing

Cloud computing is an Internet-based supercomputing model, which distributes various "computing" tasks on the resource pool, and provides various resource pooling services in an efficient, large-scale, and low-cost way, so that users only need to connect By accessing the Internet, you can access the resources you need according to your own needs without being limited by time and space. Cloud platform is based on the development of cloud computing, which can be used to provide a network platform under the mode of co-construction and sharing of various resources [8]. The cloud platform music preschool education curriculum resource library is a music preschool education curriculum resource platform based on cloud computing technology. Its core is to enrich various music preschool education "teaching" and "learning" resources, and establish a resource warehouse for teaching, scientific research and learning services, so as to meet the different learning needs of different users, It also provides "teaching" and "learning" resources for music preschool education and a network platform for communication and cooperation of music preschool education teaching resources.

3   Key Technologies and Systems of Cloud Computing

In order to provide highly reliable, cheap, universal and scalable services, cloud computing needs the support of several key technologies and systems, including virtualization technology, distributed storage and computing technology, massive data management technology, security and privacy protection, etc.

3.1   Application of Virtualization Technology

Virtualization is the representation of computer resources through virtualization technology. Users can easily obtain storage resources, data and services through this logical view. At the same time, by running multiple logical computers on a server, the work efficiency of the server can also be improved. And it is convenient to manage and upgrade the system [9]. The most important one is storage virtualization. Because of the huge data flow in the information age, how to store data efficiently has become an increasing topic. The storage virtualization of cloud platform is to integrate storage devices of different types and locations in some way to obtain a logically unified large-capacity storage pool [10]. The data in the server and application can be flexibly transferred between storage devices without caring about the real physical storage address of data resources.

3.2 Distributed Storage and Computing Technology

Cloud computing platform is composed of super-large-scale server clusters. By using distributed storage technology and redundant storage technology to realize the storage management of computer resources, the reliability, availability and scalability of distributed storage data and systems can be ensured [11]. Figure 2 is the module architecture diagram of cloud platform for music preschool teaching courses.

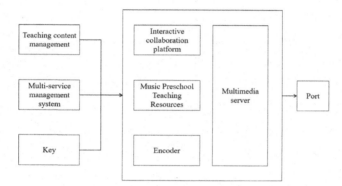

Fig. 2. Cloud platform module architecture of music preschool teaching course

The application of cloud computing technology in the field of education, namely "education cloud", through the virtualization of education information resources and systems, and the unified deployment and Implementation on the cloud platform, so as to provide cloud services for education practitioners and students. At present, the problems of information island, resource waste and low resource utilization of digital education resources urgently need a solution to solve the problems of "educational inequality" and educational resource sharing. Through a unified platform, Education Cloud enables education practitioners with different roles to manage various educational application tools and resources, realizing the true informatization of education.

4   Model Design and Analysis of Pre-school Music Teaching Resources Retrieval System

The educational resource cloud platform uses cloud computing technology to realize the sharing and management of educational resources, and eliminate the problem of information islands caused by different coding and storage standards between resource repositories [12]. Based on the three-tier service mode of cloud computing technology, the educational resources cloud platform is composed of three-tier architecture, namely infrastructure service layer, platform service layer and software service layer. Through the three-tier architecture service mode, the educational resources cloud platform can provide various services for educational institutions, publishing institutions, third-party application developers or enterprises, and teachers and students. Figure 3 is the basic structure diagram of the basic music preschool education retrieval system.

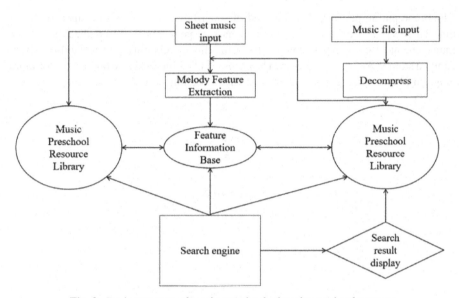

Fig. 3. Basic structure of music preschool education retrieval system

The system mainly includes three parts: music melody feature extraction, content-based retrieval and related music processing. Music melody feature extraction includes two parts: extracting music melody feature from music score and extracting melody feature from music file. Extracting the main melody from musical scores includes four functional modules: score input, segment division, feature extraction and feature storage [13]. Extracting melody from music files includes five functional modules: music file processing, music signal processing, segment division, feature extraction and feature storage.

4.1 Design of Basic Function Module

Hpc70000 and bl460g7 servers are used as the virtualization host, and each server is an X86 platform server with 2-way 6-core and 196g memory, which ensures the reliability and scalability of the hardware system. The storage network adopts the mainstream fc-sag architecture and is equipped with two HbA optical fiber cards for redundancy and multi-channel function. High availability such as HA and DRS implemented by shared storage ensures data security, achieves business continuity, reduces planned downtime, and improves resource utilization. Figure 4 is a flow chart of sharing educational resources with the system.

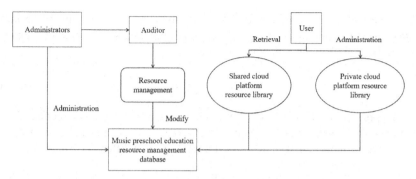

Fig. 4. Flow chart of sharing educational resources and system

There are three types of users of digital resource management in education, and super administrators have all rights of digital resource pool in education cloud platform. Auditors are responsible for auditing the resources of general users, and also the management of public cloud resources. General users include educational institutions, enterprises involved in the development of educational resources, teachers and students. General users have permission to use public cloud resources. Meanwhile, in the private cloud mode, users can upload new resources, edit and manage private resources. There are many types of educational resources cloud platform service terminals and different network environments. For the distribution of massive digital educational resources, it is required to achieve fast, safe and reliable transmission. Data transmission optimization technology is currently relatively mature technology-based digital content transmission mechanism and content distribution network technology-based digital content transmission mechanism. The basic idea of the technology is to push the server to the edge network. By adding a new layer of network architecture to the existing Internet, the system can monitor the network traffic, load status and response time in real time, and release educational resources to the "edge" of the network closest to users, so that users can get the requested resources nearby, effectively solving the network congestion and single point bottleneck problems.

4.2 Algorithm Design of System

Since there is no standard method for extracting the fundamental frequency from audio under different conditions. The difficulty of the problem is that due to the existence of time changes, fuzzy information and noise, quasi-periodicity is caused, that is, there are multiple periods related to a given f_0. Therefore, this paper has the following research on the algorithm of audio extraction.

Conduct short-time correlation analysis on the signal and define the autocorrelation function of a frame signal as $R_{n(k)}$,

$$R_{n(k)} = \sum_{m=0}^{N-K-1} S_n(m)S_n(m+k) \tag{1}$$

Among them, $S(m)$ only a certain music signal; $S_n(m)$ is a windowed framing signal; N is the window length; k is a lag, $k = (-N+1) \sim (N-1)$.

The amplitude of music signal will change greatly with time, especially the amplitude of note segmentation has obvious gap. The amplitude function in traditional segmentation algorithm is defined by the following formula:

$$A(x) = \sum_{W=0}^{N} a(w) \tag{2}$$

where $A(x)$ represents the waveform amplitude function; $a(w)$ is the amplitude of the w sampling point; N is the window length; x is a frame of the input signal, $x \in (0, M)$; M is the number of input signal frames. Then $A(x)$ amplitude difference function is:

$$D_{A(x)} = A(X + 1) - A(x) \tag{3}$$

Applying $D_{A(x)}$ will make the dividing line of a single note more obvious than applying $A(x)$ alone, which is convenient for subsequent processing. The start and end frames of the notes can be determined according to the amplitude difference between the notes. When the threshold is fixed, it is determined in turn that if it is greater than the threshold, the note starts, and if it is smaller than the threshold, the note is cut off, which will cause 3 notes to be misjudged as one. In fact, it is the mean value of the fundamental frequency of the three notes, and these two errors directly affect the result of the matching algorithm.

5 Conclusions

The traditional music information retrieval based on text metadata can not meet people's increasing retrieval requirements. Content based music retrieval breaks the bondage of unclear description of music content when using text description information retrieval, and reduces the cost of manually labeling music database on a large scale. It is an important support for the development of music industry. Combining with the traditional educational resource management system, through the analysis of cloud storage and distributed file management architecture, this paper provides the theoretical basis and technical scheme for the realization of the educational resource cloud platform system, and expounds the design, architecture and technical implementation of the system in detail. The educational resource cloud platform can realize the services that traditional teaching cannot provide, such as resource sharing, synchronous learning, offline learning, and course on-demand, and can effectively solve some of the drawbacks faced by the current education informatization. The index of knowledge points is corrected to make the retrieval results of knowledge-based learning resources more credible. By adding knowledge-based related feedback function to the system, collecting data and conducting multiple rounds of feedback, it can be found that with the increase of feedback rounds, the accuracy will be improved in different degrees.

References

1. Tian, X., Xu, S.: Virtual machine migration model based on particle swarm optimization algorithm under cloud platform. Comput. Appl. Softw. **39**(2), 9 (2022)
2. Liu, P., Liu, C.: Classification and retrieval method of multimedia cloud resources based on Lagrange algorithm. J. Shenyang Univ. Technol. **39**(4), 5 (2017)
3. Xu, F.: Collaborative filtering recommendation algorithm of Muke resources based on cloud platform. Microcomput. Appl. **36**(5), 3 (2020)
4. Laudan, J.: Research on accordion teaching innovation of preschool education specialty based on Vocational Education cloud platform. China's out of school education, no. 3, p. 2 (2020)
5. Yang, X., He, X., Wang, Y., et al.: A regional/single station ZTD combined prediction model based on machine learning algorithm. Global Positioning Syst. **47**(1), 98–102 (2022)
6. Xia, Y.: Cloud computing resource allocation method based on cuckoo search algorithm. J. Inner Mongolia Normal University: Natural Sci. Chinese edition **46**(1), 4 (2017)
7. Yuan, L.: Design and exploration of digital teaching resource platform based on cloud computing. J. Guizhou Radio Television Univ. **1**, 5 (2018)
8. Wu, X., Zhang, C., Yuan, S., et al.: Hybrid elastic scaling algorithm of cloud resources based on Reinforcement Learning. J. Xi'an Jiaotong Univ. **56**(1), 9 (2022)
9. Wang, X., Xie, L., Qi, P.: Cloud resource load balancing scheduling algorithm based on genetic intelligence. Fujian Comput. **33**(9), 3 (2017)
10. Guo, Q., Zhu, F.: Cloud computing resource scheduling algorithm based on ant colony algorithm and leapfrog algorithm. Sci. Technol. Bull. **33**(5), 4 (2017)
11. Song, L.: Research on Optimization of resource scheduling algorithm based on cloud computing. J. Taiyuan Normal Univ. Natural Sci. Edition **18**(4), 4 (2019)
12. Zhu, J.: Research on resource scheduling algorithm based on openstack cloud computing. Electron. World **17**, 2 (2018)
13. Zhang, J., Cao, J., Zhou, S.: Dynamic elastic scaling of cloud resources based on reinforcement learning algorithm. Inf. Technol. **45**(8), 5 (2021)

Set Intersection Computing Based on Privacy Protection of Cloud Platform in Teaching Data State Database

Chun Jiang$^{(\boxtimes)}$, Fengcai Qin, and Xiaoyu Shi

Nanning University, Nanning 530000, Guangxi, China
jiangchun163@163.vip.com

Abstract. Privacy protection set intersection computing is a specific application problem in secure multi-party computing. It not only has important theoretical significance, but also has strong application background. In the era of big data in teaching and education, research on this issue is consistent with the increasingly strong demand for privacy protection while enjoying various services in teaching data. However, in the process of teaching and education, a large number of teaching data are often distributed in different entities. The traditional data collection and sharing method leave the data unreservedly to one party, which cannot protect the privacy of teachers and students. Centralized data processing is also vulnerable to external enemies, resulting in serious security threats such as data leakage. The introduction of laws and regulations related to data security and privacy, higher requirements are put forward for data storage, processing and sharing. Under the premise of privacy protection, how to use privacy protection technology to effectively protect teaching data has grown up to be a hot topic. This paper examines how to use privacy protection set intersection algorithm in teaching data state database.

Keywords: Cloud platform privacy protection · Intersection calculation · Teaching data state library

1 Introduction

With the rapid development of communication technology and network technology and the wide application of mobile computing, cloud computing and distributed computing, virtual networks are more closely related to people's life. Various applications of Internet big data penetrate into people's social networking, shopping, travel and other aspects [1]. Private data refers to secret information that does not want to be known by others, including credit card number Personal confidential information such as personal health records and chat records, as well as the salary of employees, important documents of the company and other confidential information of organizations [2]. These applications enable people to enjoy more convenient services, but at the same time, a large number of valuable customer information, personal privacy records and enterprise operation data

© ICST Institute for Computer Sciences, Social Informatics and Telecommunications Engineering 2024
Published by Springer Nature Switzerland AG 2024. All Rights Reserved
Y. Zhang and N. Shah (Eds.): BigIoT-EDU 2023, LNICST 583, pp. 328–334, 2024.
https://doi.org/10.1007/978-3-031-63139-9_35

are constantly mined, and people's privacy is threatened more and more strongly [3]. Therefore, privacy protection in the era of big data has become the focus of academic and industrial circles [4]. From the perspective of data life cycle, data has gone through such links as data publishing, data storage, computing mining and data use. Therefore, researchers put forward big data publishing privacy protection technology, big data storage privacy protection technology, big data computing and mining privacy protection technology and big data access control technology to protect data privacy from all links [5].

Among these big data privacy protection technologies, the more basic technology is privacy protection data computing, which means that people can complete the computing tasks between privacy data without disclosing additional information, such as similarity calculation, distance calculation and other tasks [6]. This paper mainly focuses on one of them, namely privacy protection set intersection computing technology [7]. Common big data privacy protection technologies include anonymity, distortion, encryption, secure multi-party computing, etc. [8]. Secure multi-party computing, as a privacy protection computing method in a special distributed environment, has attracted widespread attention of researchers in recent years and has become an important research direction in the field of cryptography [9]. It puts forward higher requirements for data security. On the premise of protecting data privacy, how to fuse and calculate scattered data and explore the potential value of data [10]. The development of information technology has brought great convenience to people's study and life. People can cooperate to complete a computing task without leaving home [11]. However, in the process of calculation, the data information of participants will be leaked, and each participant does not want the other party to know their private data, so how to carry out cooperative calculation on the premise of protecting private data is a problem to be solved [12].

2 Cloud Platform Privacy Protection

2.1 Multi-party Secure Computing

Cloud computing links a large number of storage resources, computing resources and software resources through the network to form a resource pool, which brings us super computing power, unlimited storage capacity and huge economic benefits, and provides efficient services for the majority of computer users. Among them, multi-party secure computing is the key technology of Cyberspace Security and privacy protection. It has a wide range of applications, but it often needs public key encryption with a large amount of computation. When there is a large amount of data, it is a difficult problem for many users Research on using cloud computing platform to complete such computing while protecting users' privacy has important theoretical and practical significance for the promotion and popularization of cloud computing and privacy protection in cloud computing This paper is a useful exploration of this work. It is proved theoretically that any multi-party secure computing problem is solvable, and a general solution is given At the same time, it is pointed out that specific solutions should be studied for specific problems in terms of computational efficiency This makes people study a variety of solutions to multi-party secure computing problems, such as millionaire problem, secure computing geometry, secure information comparison, secure collection problem, secure remote access, secure auction, secure data mining and so on. Set is a very important concept. Many problems in reality can be represented by set. The research of set problem is an important aspect of multi-party secure computing. The existing research on secure computing sets includes the intersection of secure computing sets. As shown in Fig. 1, it is a big data privacy protection technology method:

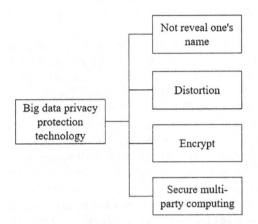

Fig. 1. Dig data privacy protection technology and method

Because all kinds of cloud applications running in the cloud platform have no fixed infrastructure and security boundary, it is difficult to realize the data security and privacy protection of participants. Therefore, participants need to use cryptography to realize secure cloud computing According to the idea of multi-party Security Cloud Computing, the cloud is regarded as a collection composed of multiple cloud servers, and the computing on the cloud is regarded as the computing among multiple cloud servers With the help of the new coding method, the set of each participant is replaced by a corresponding vector. According to the calculation results of the new vector, the calculation results of the original set can be obtained The scheme can be constructed by multiplicative homomorphic encryption algorithm or additive homomorphic encryption algorithm At the same time, the scheme can also realize private collective computing with the help of a semi trusted cloud server.

2.2 Access Control Policy

The attribute based encryption system realizes fine-grained access control through access control policies. Access control refers to the different authorized access of the subject to the object itself or its resources according to some control policies or permissions. In the existing attribute encryption research, the most common access control strategies are divided into four categories: port access control strategy, access control tree, linear secret sharing mechanism and circuit function access control strategy, as shown in Fig. 2:

Access control tree is a tree view used to represent access control policies in attribute encryption. In the access control tree, leaf nodes represent attributes rather than logical

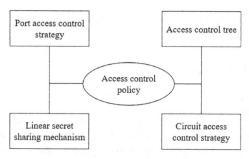

Fig. 2. Access control policy

ports; The linear secret sharing mechanism is an access control policy with stronger expression ability than the access control policy and access structure tree. As shown in Fig. 3, an example of access control tree is shown:

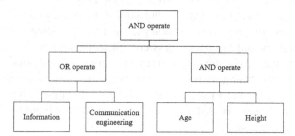

Fig. 3. Example of access control tree

In the cloud platform environment, the object of collection operation is the ciphertext data collection outsourced and stored in the cloud, which can be regarded as a variant of the traditional privacy collection intersection problem. In traditional psi, two participants jointly calculate the intersection of their data sets based on their own plaintext sets. Set algorithm is a basic cryptography primitive, and is widely used in various practical applications, such as privacy data mining, privacy matching, human genome research, social network, personal medical record system based on Internet and so on.

In the cloud platform oriented privacy data environment, data owners no longer hold their own data sets, but outsource and store the data in the cloud after encryption, so they need to entrust the cloud server to calculate the intersection of sets for data users. Although there has been a lot of research work on outsourcing collection intersection computing to ECs. However, the existing schemes still have the following problems: data users cannot limit the ability of intersection between data users and cloud server computing sets through specific access control policies; Online authentication and interaction must be carried out between data owners and data users. Moreover, psi scheme has the following properties: data users can limit which data users can do intersection operations on their ciphertext sets by setting fine-grained access control policies; The data user can delegate the collection intersection operation to the cloud server under the condition of protecting the privacy and data security; There is no need for interaction between data owners and data users.

3   Intersection Calculation

3.1   PSI Calculation

With the rapid development of communication technology and network technology and the wide application of mobile computing, cloud computing and distributed computing, virtual networks are more closely connected with people's lives. Various applications of Internet big data penetrate into people's social networking, shopping, travel and other aspects. These applications enable people to enjoy more convenient services, However, at the same time, a large number of valuable customer information, personal privacy records and enterprise operation data are constantly mined, and people's privacy is threatened more and more strongly. Therefore, privacy protection in the era of big data has become the focus of academic and industrial circles. From the perspective of data life cycle, data has experienced data publishing, data storage Computing mining and data use, based on which the researchers put forward big data publishing privacy protection technology, big data storage privacy protection technology, big data computing and mining privacy protection technology and big data access control technology to protect data privacy from all links. Among these big data privacy protection technologies, the more basic technology is data computing for privacy protection, It means that people can complete the calculation tasks between private data without disclosing additional information, such as similarity calculation, distance calculation and so on. Figure 4 shows the flow chart of data segmentation:

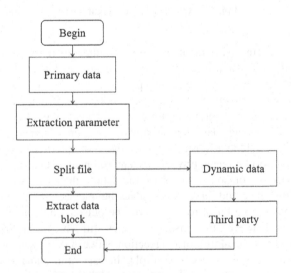

Fig. 4. Flow chart of data segmentation

The calculation of set algorithm is realized by inadvertent polynomial evaluation and homomorphic encryption. This implementation is limited by the calculation cost of basic cryptographic protocol. Traditional application systems still use insecure hash protocol to realize psi, that is, hash map the sets of participants respectively and find the intersection of sets based on hash value. Obviously, This method is vulnerable to collision attack. The research on this problem not only promotes the research and development of the basic theory of secure multi-party computing, but also promotes the research and development of the practical application of set algorithm computing. At present, the performance of some psi protocols has been greatly improved, and the communication and computational complexity has reached the same level as the insecure hash protocol. In the traditional set algorithm computing technology, the participants directly and interactively execute the real protocol to achieve the purpose of privacy computing set intersection. It is proposed to comprehensively sort out the research status of set algorithm technology, introduce and compare the specific research ideas, research methods, applicable security assumptions, enemy models and performance overhead of traditional psi computing technology and cloud assisted set algorithm technology, and briefly sort out the application research based on set algorithm computing technology, The problems and research trends of current set algorithm computing technology are summarized and suggested.

3.2 Security Proving Method

Any proposed security protocol needs security proof. Generally speaking, the security protocol proposed in secure multi-party computing proves its security by comparing with the ideal model. The so-called ideal model refers to the existence of a trusted third party, its computing power is probabilistic multi term time, obtains the privacy input of each participant through the secure channel and calculates the function function, When proving the security of the proposed security protocol, it is necessary to compare the ideal model to explain that each participant will not get more information. This security proof method is called ideal reality simulation method; If the security requirements are relaxed and only one participant is required to comply with the security requirements, it is called unilateral simulation method. In the process of protocol security proof, there are two very important basic models, namely standard model and random oracle model. Standard model does not rely on any hypothetical model, but only on widely accepted difficult assumptions, such as factor decomposition and discrete logarithm. These mathematical problems are insoluble by attackers in polynomial time.

A mechanism that only uses difficult assumptions to prove security is said to be secure under the standard model. Random oracle assumes that there is a public and randomly selected function, which can only be calculated by inquiry. For each query, a response is uniformly and randomly output from the output domain, and the same response is always obtained for the same query. Because there is no function in reality that can realize a real random function, Therefore, the provably secure scheme under the random oracle model is instantiated by hash function in practical application.

4 Conclusions

With the continuous development of informatization and networking, privacy protection has become a more and more important topic, which is not only related to the personal interests of citizens, but also related to national security, As an important application problem of secure multi-party computing, set algorithm has also developed rapidly in recent years. At present, in order to meet the computing needs of the era of big data. The development history of set algorithm protocol is mainly from the initial public key encryption mechanism to chaotic circuit, inadvertent transmission protocol, and new computing mode. The protocol design in cloud computing environment, whether traditional methods or cloud assisted SET protocol, the main research trend of this problem is to balance security, efficiency and scalability, The research idea is mainly from the initial public key based encryption mechanism to relying on more symmetric encryption operations. In the current big data context, although the existing collection protocols have made great breakthroughs, they still have performance bottlenecks. In the future, more efficient protocols need to be designed to meet the needs of big data privacy protection.

References

1. Dai, W., Qiu, M., Qiu, L., et al.: Who moved my data? privacy protection in smartphones. IEEE Commun. Mag. **55**(1), 20–25 (2017)
2. Liu, S., Dai, Y., Cai, Z., et al.: Construction of double-precision wisdom teaching framework based on blockchain technology in cloud platform. IEEE Access **9**, 23–24 (2021)
3. Shi, Y., Zhang, Z., Chao, H.C., et al.: Data privacy protection based on micro aggregation with dynamic sensitive attribute updating. Sensors **18**(7) (2018)
4. Kelarev, A., Xun, Y., Badsha, S., et al.: A multistage protocol for aggregated queries in distributed cloud databases with privacy protection. Future Gener. Comput. Syst. **90** (2018)
5. DimitrovDimitard.slavov@bas.bgAtanassovEmanouilemanouil@parallel.bas.bg Institute of Information and Communication Technologies, Bulgarian Academy of Sciences, Sofia, Bulgaria. Tools and Services for High Performance Computing. Cybernetics and Information Technologies, vol. 17, no. 5, pp. 81–88 (2017)
6. Song, L., Cui, J., Hong, Z., et al.: Public auditing with privacy protection in a multi-user model of cloud-assisted body sensor networks. Sensors **17**(5), 32, 35 (2017)
7. Lee, Y.T., Hsiao, W.H., Lin, Y.S., et al.: Privacy-preserving data analytics in cloud-based smart home with community hierarchy. IEEE Trans. Consum. Electron. **63**(2), 200–207 (2017)
8. Wu, X., Tang, S., Yang, P., et al.: Cloud is safe when compressive: Efficient image privacy protection via shuffling enabled compressive sensing. Comput. Commun. **117**(12), 36–45 (2018)
9. Wen, Y., et al.: Scheduling workflows with privacy protection constraints for big data applications on cloud. Future Generation Comput. Syst. **108**, 84–91 (2020)
10. Yang, C., Tan, L., Shi, N., et al.: AuthPrivacyChain: a blockchain-based access control framework with privacy protection in cloud. IEEE Access **99**, 1 (2020)
11. Hou, Q., Xing, Y., Wang, D., et al.: Study on coupling degree of rail transit capacity and land use based on multivariate data from cloud platform. J. Cloud Comput. **9**(1), 1–12 (2020)
12. Sun, J., Hu, S., Nie, X., et al.: Efficient ranked multi-keyword retrieval with privacy protection for multiple data owners in cloud computing. IEEE Syst. J. **99**, 10–12 (2019)

Research on the Storage of National Drama Culture Resources Based on Cloud Platform

Linlin Hou[1,2]([⊠]), Yanli Fu[1,2], and Danyang Gong[1,2]

[1] Xi'an FanYi University, Shaanxi 710100, China
hhxx_666@126.com
[2] Department of Chinese Language and Literature, Northwest Minzu University,
Lanzhou 730030, China

Abstract. As human society enters the era of big data, new business environments and scenarios urgently require the establishment of cost-effective mass data storage systems. In the process of building a cloud platform for ethnic drama culture, there are problems such as the relatively scattered application systems related to culture, the lack of a unified platform, the inability of traditional database systems to meet the storage requirements for unstructured data such as video, audio, pictures, and documents, and the numerous and scattered storage devices that cannot meet the sharing of storage resources. In order to support the construction of a national drama culture cloud platform and solve these problems, it is necessary to build a national drama culture digital resource cloud storage management system. This topic analyzes the characteristics of national drama cultural digital resources and utilizes relevant technologies to achieve storage and management services for national drama cultural digital resources, as well as provide relevant application data interface services for cloud platforms. In the new era, the Chinese people attach greater importance to the protection and inheritance of national and folk culture. The key is the advanced technology that applies it to its storage. This article summarizes the replicability and robustness of HDFS data based on the Hadoop platform and combined with ethnic and folk cultural characteristics. Compare the advantages of different versions with other file systems and highlight improvements in storage management.

Keywords: cloud platform · national drama · cultural resources · storage research

1 Introduction

Due to uneven economic development and different levels of acceptance of digital concepts, the current situation of ethnic drama and cultural services varies greatly. From the current situation, there are mainly six situations: First, due to information asymmetry, it is impossible to understand the dynamic needs of cultural consumers at any time, there is no data support for accurate services, cultural consumer participation is low, innovation is insufficient, and the utilization rate of existing venues and facilities is low, Cultural

Y. Zhang and N. Shah (Eds.): BigIoT-EDU 2023, LNICST 583, pp. 335–346, 2024.
https://doi.org/10.1007/978-3-031-63139-9_36

consumers' participation in cultural activities through the Internet is not high; Secondly, currently, relevant application systems are relatively scattered, without a unified platform [1]; Third, resources are mainly concentrated in offline venues, with a small service radius and limited by time factors, and there is a lack of effective interaction between demanders and providers of ethnic drama culture; Fourth, many cultural institutions have not yet provided digital services for ethnic drama and cultural services, with few digital resources and still relying mainly on physical resources, which are not convenient to carry and share; Fifth, faced with unstructured data such as video, audio, pictures, and documents in cultural digital resources, traditional database systems cannot meet the current requirements of cloud storage and management systems for digital resources [2]; Sixth, currently, the data stored in application systems are distributed in the servers of relevant departments affiliated to various cultural systems, resulting in high operating costs and the inability to share stored data resources. These information services are isolated and scattered, unable to connect with each other, and the level of construction is uneven. It is not possible to use digitization and networking to best promote the public cultural service system [3]. The main reason for these problems lies in the failure to build a unified storage, sharing, and management integrated cloud platform using information and digital means.

In 2016, the laboratory team embarked on the construction of a cloud platform for ethnic drama culture based on the needs of ethnic drama cultural institutions, achieving the aggregation of digital resources for ethnic drama culture, solving the current problems in the dissemination and inheritance process of ethnic characteristic culture, making full use of data and resources and enabling good integration, and sharing digital resources for ethnic drama culture, such as text data resources, graphical data resources Short video data resources and audio data resources [4]. In this context, our team has developed a cloud storage management system for digital resources of ethnic drama culture using cloud storage technology, FastDFS cluster technology, RPCSOA framework Dubbo, and database middleware technology MyCAT. The cloud storage management system provides data storage and management services for system related applications and basic data services for multiple users through sharing of digital resources. The storage management system achieves efficient storage and sharing of digital resources for ethnic drama culture, which helps to break the existing isolated construction mode of digital culture systems, and build a user-friendly and user-friendly cloud storage management system for Guizhou ethnic characteristic cultural digital resources [5]. The system is conducive to ensuring the security of digital resource data of ethnic drama culture; It is conducive to enhancing the enthusiasm of the general public to actively participate in activities related to national drama culture; It is conducive to promoting the construction of ethnic drama culture and shortening the differences in cultural services across regions.

China's folk art has a long history, rich and colorful, rich in content, has a profound impact on our national spirit and personality. Folk art is an important symbol that reflects a national culture, national quality and artistic level. Today's world economic integration, the rapid development of China's society, in the strong cultural collision and integration of the world today, many excellent folk art works, the cultures of all ethnic groups are gradually disappearing [6]. Therefore, it is urgent to inherit and carry forward the traditional national culture, and to do this, we must do a good job in the protection of folk art. In the protection of traditional folk art [7], People's thoughts and ways are relatively simple. At present, most of the protection of folk handicrafts in China are protected and displayed by "one museum and one exhibition". For example, setting up a museum to display folk works of art intensively, but such a way is not practical feasible for the protection of many folk art. Moreover, local museums-are constantly building, which leads to insufficient funds, insufficient exhibition area, and other problems. In today's society, with the rapid development of computer, Internet and other information technology, the use of digital technology to inherit and protect the folk art resources is an inevitable requirement for the development of today's society and culture. And on how to inherit and innovate China's precious folk art tradition, put forward feasible ideas [8]. At the same time, the application of information technology also opens up a broad world for the future development.

2   Related Work

2.1   Research Status of National Drama Culture Cloud Service Platform at Home and Abroad

From the perspective of the impact of cloud computing on ethnic drama culture: Chen Shun has built a cloud computing ethnic drama culture service technology platform that can be centrally managed and shared across the entire network based on the demand for ethnic drama culture services in Fujian Province and combined with the new model of modern cloud computing. Kim and Jeong combine traditional culture with information technology to integrate information and build a functional framework for supporting services in a cloud computing environment. Xiaotong summarized the current applications and existing problems of cloud computing in libraries at home and abroad, which have public cultural characteristics, and developed a cloud service platform model consisting of physical resources, resource pools, management middleware, and SOA component layers [9]. Wang Jingyi's application of cloud computing technology to modern digital libraries can improve the level of information resources and services, and reduce the resource costs generated by traditional libraries.

Application perspective of cloud services for ethnic drama culture: Chen acknowledges that the improvement of services for ethnic drama culture is not only related to various public cultural institutions such as libraries and archives, but also involves multidisciplinary technological innovation. Through platform construction, intelligent management of ethnic drama culture resources can be achieved. Li Wenchuan et al. proposed that cloud services for ethnic drama culture can optimize the allocation of ethnic drama culture resources, and systematically analyzed the operational mechanism of cloud services for ethnic drama culture resources from several perspectives, such as cloud resource service delivery, service chain construction, service portfolio optimization, and service innovation [10]. Bartos K and Pukanskt K analyzed the feasibility of applying cloud services to cultural heritage, and explored the positive role of cloud services in preserving cultural heritage. On the basis of elaborating on the characteristics and advantages of current cloud computing, Wang Jia analyzed the problems existing in the information services of digital libraries, and constructed a digital library based on the cloud service platform to better improve data transmission speed and achieve resource sharing. Xiang Jiang and others believe that the difficulty in developing a cloud service platform for sharing ethnic drama culture lies in the interoperability of massive resources; Intelligent scheduling of multiple networks and terminals; Unified certification; Platform interaction and operation aims to solve these technical difficulties and build a cultural resource service platform with a new service model. Yan Chunzi integrates distributed digital cultural resources from different data sources on a single service platform, enabling users to maximize the speed of access to resources [11]. Chen Huangyan has constructed a technical support platform for ethnic drama culture services that can be shared across the province through demand analysis of the current situation of ethnic drama culture and combined with the new model of cloud computing. HyvonenE applies web semantic technology to the protection of cultural heritage, achieving efficient collection and protection of cultural heritage at once.

Research perspective on cloud service model for ethnic drama culture: Gu Jiawei and others proposed a centralized identity authentication cloud service model for public cultural digital resources to solve the difficult issues in user identity management. This method has the advantages of convenience, inheritance, and scalability. Based on the practice of the ethnic drama cultural service system in Heping District, Tianjin, Zhao Bin has constructed a new mode of digital public cultural service website platform with a new cultural communication method. Based on the practical analysis of digital cultural services in the library of North China University of Technology, Yang Jing proposed a personalized service model based on digital intelligent libraries to enhance the ability of national drama culture cloud services and the diverse needs of users [12]. Feng Xiuzhen studied cloud computing technology and cloud service agents and proposed a new model of information resources as a service, integrating information resources distributed in different regions to provide high-quality and efficient services to users.

2.2 Hadoop Framework Cloud Platform

With the emergence of a series of concepts such as cloud computing and distributed processing, cloud storage has emerged as the times require. Cloud storage is a cloud system that focuses on data storage management, integrates cloud storage technologies such as distributed storage, multi tenant sharing, data security, and data deduplication, and provides authorized users with flexible, transparent, and on-demand storage resource allocation through a unified Web service interface [13]. Applying cloud storage to the integration of digital resources in ethnic drama culture and simplifying complex setup and management tasks can not only save government financial expenses, but also store digital cultural resources in the cloud to facilitate users' access to resources from more places, achieving even the sharing of digital cultural resources across the country.

Hadoop is the development direction of distributed technology, parallel processing technology and networked computer technology. It has broad application prospects in the current field of big data processing. The system has a strong computing capacity and a high storage capacity, but also supports a variety of complex computing methods, can efficiently store a large number of data, has the ability to process a large number of data, with good fault tolerance. The system can quickly handle massive amounts of documents and databases [13]. Meanwhile, HDFS also has the characteristics of GFS, which very well supports distributed storage and computing (as shown in Fig. 1):

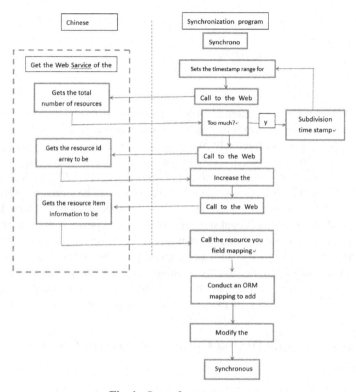

Fig. 1. Struts frame structure

As for cloud platform services, which can be considered as end-user devices, two basic issues need to be considered. One is internal digital Kn, which represents the communication time between the ith robot and the ith service on the platform. The value of drama culture resource cost Cr is shown in Eq. (1).

$$C_r = \sum_{t=1}^{M} \left(\sum_{i=1}^{N} c_i r_{ii} + \sum_{i=1}^{N} e_i k_{ti} \right) \tag{1}$$

where c_i and e_i are the costs of corresponding service invocations for remote and internal communication. Rti is calculated by Eq. (2). Kti is represented by Eq. (3).

$$r_{ti} = \frac{L_i}{RP_t} \tag{2}$$

$$k_{ti} = \frac{L_{data_i} + L_{req-i}}{B_t} \tag{3}$$

where RPt represents different processing capabilities. Li is the service length, which is also considered the primary QoS constraint. Ldata − i and Lreq − i represent the length of service transmitted in the robot. Bt is a robot bandwidth identifier. In addition, rti is the cost of the ith service Si called by the th Rt [14]. The cost matrix for invoking cloud services is shown in Eq. (4).

$$CostMap = \begin{bmatrix} r_{11} & r_{12} & \cdots & r_{1i} \\ r_{21} & r_{22} & \cdots & r_{2i} \\ \vdots & \vdots & \ddots & \vdots \\ r_{t1} & r_{t2} & \cdots & r_{ti} \end{bmatrix} \tag{4}$$

The distribution archive system of GFS contains thousands of computers. Therefore, after this distributed file system is installed, it is not a common hardware tool to manage and control all computers effectively. When these computers are accessed in bulk. For example, after a period of time, a variety of faults will occur, which seriously affect the storage and transmission of data, thus abling the entire network. GFS also has the ability to store large numbers of large documents. Larger files can be stored in several small files, usually isolated from each other, lack of contact with each other, unable to access each other, following the traditional standards of archives system. Moreover, its backup and recovery work will take longer, so it is not suitable for long-term use[15]. When used, the user can divide the files into many small files. The GFS stores a large number of large archives. Conversion is quickly possible from one folder to another so you can share data and resources. At the same time, the stored files are efficiently managed to avoid the transmission of files are modified and lost situations.

3 Storage of Ethnic Drama Cultural Resources Based on Cloud Platform

3.1 Data Replication of the HDFS

HDFS uses a distributed archive architecture in Hadoop. The device has high stability and high storage efficiency. The system has a good expansion ability, can flexibly adjust the size of users according to the needs of the documents, to meet the needs of various applications. Ensure that large-capacity documents can be quickly transmitted and stored between multiple computers. At the same time, it also has a variety of backup modes, with a strong data retrieval ability, and the data replication is conducted by the control nodes.

HDFS clusters generally include computers on multiple scaffolds. Since each cabinet has multiple computers, there is a dedicated system for storing and backup data. Two computers on different racks must communicate with switches. For the problem of high redundancy in the network, the copy storage and backup strategy are proposed to reduce the traffic of the network. Make the whole cluster work more efficient. Effectively improve the security of data storage and the use of clusters. Through the analysis and research of the current three mainstream server architectures, a new server architecture——virtual machine technology is proposed, and according to its characteristics, two different complex algorithms can greatly reduce the number of access memory (Table 1).

Table 1. Query results of system

joggle	definition
Job	Express the specific content that a work needs to implement
JobDetail	Indicates a specific implementable scheduler
Trigger	Represents the configuration of scheduling time parameters, and Quartz provides two types of triggers: Simple triggers and the CronTrigger
Scheduler	Indicates a scheduling container that can register multiple JobDetail s and triggers

HDSF has a strategy that reduces read latency. When a user asks to process a special cluster. HDSF can transfer data to the data node closest to the user when it reads it. At the same time, user requests can also be screened to ensure their real-time performance and accuracy. This can effectively accelerate the user's reading speed. At the same time, the network and storage devices are combined to effectively save and manage the data files. Reduce the bandwidth overhead of the system. At the same time, it can also reduce the cost and cost of the system. In most cases, it is used by the user. At the same time, the promotion of WLAN in the future. The entire system is activated. All equipment in the system works normally without being disturbed by other equipment or terminals. The node will be controlled in secure mode. If you want to download a new file, first copy the file to the corresponding repository. When the system is running, the control node detects the new data block. When this data block fails, the security risk will be determined according to the size and location of the detected data block. When the control node confirms that the data block is safe, wait another 30 s, and the security mode state automatically exits.

3.2 Problems Arising in the Process of Hadoop Processing of Massive Small Files

While Hadoop has a great advantage in processing large files, and it can efficiently compress large amounts of data in itself, it can quickly and accurately access the information needed. Not only is the efficiency and accuracy high, but also more secure storage. It is mainly manifested in three aspects: excessive storage pressure of NameNode nodes, low file reading and writing efficiency, and small file I / 0 problems. Here is a specific analysis of these three points:

(1) The memory pressure of the NameNode node is too large

For file systems, it is a critical problem to fast read and write each node in the network. The memory of the NameNode node determines the number of files that the HDFS can store. All the files are divided into blocks of different sizes, and then their corresponding attributes are marked in their respective locations, with different structure and content, so the types of data used are also different. Various kinds of documents, large or small. Thus, in the file system, redundant data is generated that matches the amount of the corresponding metadata. Therefore, in a distributed database system, to improve the system efficiency and storage capacity, an effective replication technology is used. All need to use a certain amount of memory. Such small files occupy large amounts of memory, resulting in a waste of server resources and network congestion. If there are a lot of small files in the cluster. Such meta-data is usually occupied by other processing programs with a larger memory capacity.

(2) Low document reading and writing

For Hadoop, it can also slowly read and write when processing large numbers of small files. To solve this problem, this paper presents a file system based on the distributed scatter list and the dynamic chain list structure, which uses the dynamic chain technology to speed up the document reading while squeezing the storage space. After storing a lot of small files. Because the archives and the database data cannot be fully shared. Customer opportunities to interact with NameNode frequently, which creates many unnecessary operations and data transfer. The read and the written data are of the same size. Small files are much slower than large computers. Smaller files are more than larger ones, and smaller files are slower. This is because the data in small files are randomly generated, and all exist in file systems, while the data in large files are stored in repositories. If the total number of articles is unchanged. Handling small files is more easily recognized by machines than large files. When handling small files, Hadoop performs much worse than in large files.

3.3   Architecture of Cloud Storage Management System

By designing the architecture model of the cloud storage management system as described in Fig. 2, the architecture of the Guizhou ethnic cultural digital resources cloud storage management system is designed into four layers, namely, the user access layer, the application interface layer, the management layer, and the data storage layer, as shown in Fig. 2:

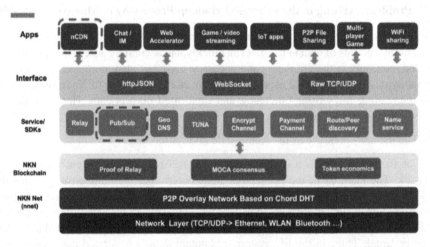

Fig. 2.   System architecture.

The user access layer is designed using a B/S architecture, and cultural cloud users mainly access the background of the cloud storage management system through a browser on the PC side and obtain corresponding services. The user connects to the cultural cloud storage management system through a browser, performs a series of operations on the system, and returns the results to the user after completing the relevant operations.

The application interface layer is designed by load balancing the access system and using REST APIs to reduce the load on related servers and implement operations such as creating, obtaining, modifying, and deleting resources through the HTTP protocol. The application layer provides different service interfaces based on user needs. The service is published through Dubbo, and the corresponding business application system consumes the service, such as the user rights management service interface.

The management layer is responsible for handling specific requests in the system involved in this topic, including user login registration, access control, resource management, tenant management, lease management, system management, and interface servers. Resource management includes directory file management (creating folders, browsing, renaming, and deleting), file access management (uploading, downloading, and deleting files), tenant management mainly manages the basic information of tenants (adding tenants, updating tenants, and so on), and lease management includes four modules: package service management, system lease service, expansion lease service, and order management System management mainly consists of three parts: metadata management (viewing metadata uploaded by FastDFS, etc.), cluster management (viewing memory, CPU, and hard disk information of a device in a FastDFS cluster), and device management (tracker, storage, WEB, database, and other server devices). Cluster management is mainly used to view the memory, CPU, and hard disk information of a device in a FastDFS cluster; Metadata management is mainly used to view metadata uploaded by FastDFS; Device management is mainly used by system administrators to view, start, and lock devices (including storage, WEB, database, and other server devices). The interface server encapsulates the FastDFS' client interface, connecting key functional modules of the management layer with the FastDFS cluster, and meeting a certain amount of concurrency.

The data storage layer is mainly composed of two parts: one is the storage cluster of FastDFS, and the other is to use the MyCAT database to achieve MySQL read/write separation and build a MySQL database cluster.

4   Optimization Design of Storage Process Based on Hadoop Platform

(1) Optimization design of small file storage

Small file storage services. If you need files from other departments, just open the corresponding folder. When files are archived, sub department files can be stored in the file. If you are looking for a small file, simply open the file name and property and discover the file. Group together the names of departments and store them in a database. This method can solve the resource waste caused by information overlap between multiple file systems in advance. This can improve the localization of access to small documents and reduce the pressure on node storage. At the same time, when users request, they can directly read and process small files. It can also improve HDFS I/O performance. Pre extraction and caching mechanisms have been introduced into the system, and replacement strategies have been added. The storage volume consists of a user mounted client, a metadata management node, and a block data storage node. Manage the cStor cloud storage system through the management monitoring center, such as checking whether the service is abnormal. The architecture of the cStor cloud storage system is shown in Fig. 3:

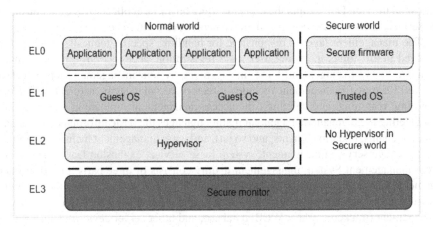

Fig. 3. CStor cloud storage system architecture

(2) Optimization and design of file retrieval

A reading program to obtain the original file. On this basis, the relevant properties of different documents are used to compare them with the existing data, and then compare them to the related data to classify them into the database. At a node, an archive will be accessed. Following this message, the associations of these maps are integrated. The client first esses the name node to obtain the correspondence between the object file and the block. When transferring one or more files to a server, you can use image data retrieval technology to handle this problem. Then connect to the corresponding DataNode and then read the information. We can divide a file into several subfiles, and then store it according to the type of file, according to its corresponding index method. On this basis, the document query is optimized. The method is retrieved according to the custom index construction of the archives to obtain the desired information and locations. While reading the large document, you still use the previous method. Therefore, a new method can be used to obtain the characteristic information of the small profile from the database. And read less in the archives. Then based on this data to determine whether a small file has been correctly written into the memory, and determine its own memory. First of all, according to the shorter file name, to obtain the larger file information and the geographic information of the data node. Then the name of the small file is combined with the size to determine whether the small file can be properly written into the large file. Memory loading was then performed to obtain larger files, and smaller files of movement.

5 Conclusion

Different from the processing of the original HDFS access and delete files. The customer has the opportunity to write this information into the array corresponding to the content of the file, and then query the information in the database, as the current file name. Optimizing the above storage mode can effectively reduce the load of the file system and shorten the working time of the user. Greatly reduce the number of archive elements stored in the node. At the same time, documents can be read and written in different sizes. Processing of file access control processes provides better performance and faster file reading. Strong system expansion ability and strong adaptive ability. So, if there are many more files to read. The advantages of its access performance are also becoming increasingly obvious.

Acknowledgements. Scientific Research Program Funded by Education Department of Shaanxi Provincial Government (Program No. 21JK0166).

References

1. Wang, H., Du, Z.: Research on application of teaching informatization construction based on cloud computing. Inter. J. Innovation Educ. Res. **9**(5), 288–294 (2021)
2. Liu, H.: Research on secure cloud storage of regional economic data network based on blockchain technology. In: International Conference on Machine Learning for Cyber Security. Springer, Cham (2023). https://doi.org/10.1007/978-3-031-20096-0_14
3. Huang J , Li X . Research on traditional costume design and application based on cloud computing. J. Phys. Conf. Ser. **1881**(4), 042064 (6pp) (2021)
4. Su, L., Wen, D., Fu. L.: Research on the boundary delimitation method of national park based on cultural service protection. Polish J. Environ. Stud.(1 Pt.2), 31 (2022)
5. Zuo, L., Cao, X., Zhu, L., et al.: Research on the design method of UHF antenna under the condition of changing tag distribution density. J. Electron. Inf. Technol. **45**(1), 158–167 (2022)
6. Wang, Z., Muthu, B.A., Kadry, S.N.: Research on the design of analytical communication and information model for teaching resources with haring platform. Comput. Appli. Eng. Educ. (1) (2021)
7. Octavian, B., Burluc, R.M., Baston, O.: Research on influence ecological storage of wheat at low temperatures on the flour starch content (2022)
8. Sun., H.: Research on the Application of Artificial Intelligence Technology and Cloud Computing in Smart Elderly Care Information Platform (2021)
9. Fang, J., Xu, Q., Tang, R., et al.: Research on demand management of hybrid energy storage system in industrial park based on variational mode decomposition and Wigner-Ville distribution. J. Energy Storage **42**(1), 103073 (2021)
10. Yang, Y., Du, S.Q., Chen, Y.: Real-time pricing method for smart grid based on social welfare maximization model. J. Indust. Manag. Optimization **19**(3), 2206–2225 (2023)
11. Liu, J, Yang, X., Cheng, H., Jiang, H., Zhang, Y., Wang, Y.: Progress of China's Space Debris Res. **42**(4), 824–829 (2022)

12. Li, Z.Z., Jia, D.L., Wang, H., et al.: To research the effects of storage time on autotransfusion based on erythrocyte oxygen-carrying capacity and oxidative damage characteristics. Cell Trans. **30**, 096368972110056 (2021)
13. Tang, L.F., Wang, Q.: Research on the method of eliminating duplicated encrypted data in cloud storage based on generated countermeasure network. In: International Conference on Multimedia Technology and Enhanced Learning. Springer, Cham (2021). https://doi.org/10.1007/978-3-030-82562-1_57
14. Sun, W.: Research on the integration of preschool language education resources based on metadata storage. J. Math. **2022** (2022)
15. Zhao, B.: Research on National Dance Culture Education and Teaching Based on Data Mining Algorithm (2023)

Development and Application of Intraoral Science Microcourses Based on Cloud Platform

Yurui Jiang [✉] and Jing Li

Yunnan Medical Health College, Kunming 650000, China
kinooo@126.com

Abstract. "Internet plus education" is a good opportunity for information technology curriculum reform. Under the background of vigorously promoting programming education at the basic education stage, and in combination with the development status of programming education in the region, we carried out practical research on the school-based elective course of "creative programming" in junior high schools. In order to solve the layered teaching difficulties encountered in programming teaching, based on the Chifeng Smart Education Cloud Platform and guided by the new constructivist theory, the "teacher guided inquiry" teaching mode is selected for layered teaching design, improving students' autonomous and collaborative learning abilities, and promoting students' comprehensive development. At the same time, the "Smart Education Cloud Platform" is vigorously promoted to provide new ideas and approaches for information based education and teaching reform. The continuous improvement of cloud computing technology has changed people's work, study and living habits. Micro-curriculum is a new form of education in the current education field. Oral medicine science is a required course in colleges and universities. The use of modern computer technology to realize the development of micro-courses can effectively use modern scientific and technological means and the Internet for teaching, so as to change the teaching method, effectively improve the teaching effect and cultivate students' self-study ability.

Keywords: cloud platform · oral cavity science micro-course · development and application

1 Introduction

The progress of computer science and technology in the 20th century has promoted the transformation of the model of prosthodontics. The French dental expert Duret pioneered the introduction of CAD/CAM technology into the design and manufacture of dental prostheses, triggering a major technological revolution in the field of prosthodontics, making digital dental prosthetics a new technology with epoch-making significance in the field of prosthodontics, and fundamentally changing the traditional way of making artificial teeth. Since the emergence of the first ceramic dental crown in 1985, this technology has been greatly developed and gradually commercialized due to its high

Y. Zhang and N. Shah (Eds.): BigIoT-EDU 2023, LNICST 583, pp. 347–359, 2024.
https://doi.org/10.1007/978-3-031-63139-9_37

efficiency and intelligent characteristics [1]. Among them, 3Shape (Denmark), Delcam (UK), Duret (France), Dental System (Denmark), and CERCE3D (Germany) are the most representative and popular among dentists. Compared with foreign countries, domestic scholars are only limited to the exploration stage of basic theories and methods, and the application research of digital design and manufacturing technology for oral prosthesis is in the initial stage [2]. In 2002, Professor Lv Peijun from Peking University reported that the team had initially developed the first set of dental prosthetic CAD/CAM system with independent intellectual property rights in China, and successfully designed and manufactured an artificial crown. Han Jingyun and others from Beijing University of Technology have designed personalized molar inlays using UG and Surfacer software [3]. Dai Ning et al. developed a prototype of DentalCAD software system for oral prosthesis. In addition, some domestic dental schools have successively developed relevant software and hardware system equipment with independent intellectual property rights in China. Among them, Dr. Sun Yuchun, Director of the School of Stomatology at Peking University, has developed a digital complete denture design system with functional ease of use [4].

With the transformation of China's medical system and the deepening of medical teaching reform, the training of oral professional and technical personnel in higher vocational colleges has put forward new needs. Oral medicine is a required course in clinical medicine, with many contents, short class hours and many learning tasks. The theoretical foundation of this course is very strong, the knowledge points are more scattered, and the knowledge structure is more complex. If the traditional teaching methods, the theoretical knowledge is relatively abstract, and the teaching methods and means are relatively backward. At the same time, the practice and experiment time is also relatively short [5]. Due to the learning difficulties of students, leading to the inefficient classroom teaching. In view of the above problems, micro-courses should be applied in clinical medicine students to achieve better teaching results. The development and use of micro-courses, to provide medical students with a broad learning space, students can use the mobile phone Internet for independent learning, to make up for the shortcomings in the classroom, the effect is significant, worthy of great publicity [6].

With the continuous development of "micro class", "micro class" has gradually become an indispensable and new driving force in the reform of higher vocational education in China. As a comprehensive discipline, "Oral Medicine" plays a pivotal role in the whole field of stomatology. It is an important part of the national assessment of oral teaching assistant and stomatology, and also an important course in the future clinical practice. Therefore, how to use information technology for computer-aided teaching is a top priority [7]. We develop and apply "Oral science" micro course, make it a serialized, curriculum, systematic, rich, high-quality micro course resources, and constantly innovate teaching mode, deepen curriculum reform, expand students' independent learning channels and methods. In class, students who make full use of online platforms to carry out extracurricular activities can not only improve the quality of classroom teaching, but also improve teachers' teaching level and professional practice level [8].

2 Related Work

2.1 Characteristics of Micro-courses

The course content is short and concise. The traditional "one class" is relatively rich in content, while the teaching content of "micro class" mainly focuses on "specific knowledge points", "skill operation point" and other related issues. So that students can personally experience the process of the generation and development of knowledge and the internal rules. Microclasses are usually 5–10 min. Therefore, teachers can use the micro-class hours in the class, the abstract, boring knowledge points are concrete; convenient for students to learn and use.(2) Vivid and intuitive [9]. This course integrates video, image, animation, PPT and other forms; all resources are direct. Through observation and learning, people can have a deeper impression, and easier to understand than simple reading.(3) Diversified learning methods. Micro-course resources are not limited by time and space, and have their own unique online teaching characteristics. Students can watch repeatedly, choose mobile phone teaching, independent learning, cooperative learning and other learning methods.

Teaching status quo:

(1) Teaching methods are outdated and backward

In today's society, with the development of information and network, traditional medical education methods have been out of date, most of them are teachers, little discussion and communication in class, only students passively accept, low enthusiasm for learning and low teaching effectiveness.

(2) The theoretical teaching quality is not high

The teaching of oral cavity science major requires students to master more basic theoretical knowledge, and the teaching task is heavy. Therefore, the current teaching methods should be reformed, and a variety of teaching methods should be adopted to improve the teaching quality and achieve the ideal goal. At present, the traditional teaching methods have the contradiction between "short time" and "rich", which increases the difficulty of students' learning and leads to the inefficiency of classroom teaching [10].

(3) The practical teaching foundation is weak

At present, due to the in-depth combination of traditional theory courses and experimental courses, the practical application level of the stomatology department is getting higher and higher. Less internship period, experimental training teaching conditions and medical technology development, backward equipment, low number of students participating in tests, insufficient time, and so on; the performance of students' practical operation skills is mediocre.

In view of the above problems, we should give full play to the computer-aided technology, actively develop and apply the micro-courses, expand the classroom teaching, reform the traditional teaching methods, and make up for the shortcomings of the classroom. With its short, targeted micro-curriculum, it can make students overcome difficulties in the teaching process and improve the quality of teaching [11]. On this basis, teachers should build a "cloud platform" to concentrate the learning resources in the "micro-class" on the "cloud", and realize "sharing" and "creation" and "learning"; let the students in their free time. Make full use of modern electronic tools for self-education, improve the learning effect.

2.2 Performance of Microchannel Plates

There are many technical indicators that describe microchannel boards. This section briefly describes the performance indicators of MCPs that affect the main performance of MCP-PMTs.

(1) Gain

The gain of MCP refers to the ratio of anode output current to input current. Due to the saturation effect, the gain of MCP operating in DC mode and pulse mode is different; Due to ion feedback, MCP gains that have not undergone thorough degassing treatment and that have undergone strict degassing treatment (such as vacuum high-temperature baking, electronic cleaning) are also different.

The multiplication of electrons in MCP is a random process, and its gain needs to be represented by an average value. The gain of MCP is related to its applied bias voltage U, the small aspect ratio of the secondary electron emission coefficient 8 of the first impact, the material secondary electron emission coefficient of the inner wall of the channel, the number of module cascades, and the electrode immersion depth, but not its absolute size [12]. Therefore, within a certain range, as long as the aspect ratio is the same, scaling the size of the MCP will not affect its gain. In unsaturated mode, the gain of MCP increases exponentially with its bias voltage.

(2) Noise characteristics

The noise characteristics of MCP can be described by signal to noise ratio, dark current, and dark count. The noise characteristics of the MCP are influenced by the material and process of the MCP, and are also related to the degassing process, the work function of the channel inner wall material, the surface state, and bias voltage. As the working voltage increases, the dark current also increases [13].

When there is no input signal from the MCP, the current output at the anode is called dark current. The main sources are: 1) hot electron emission current; 2) Ionic current caused by ionization of residual gas; 3) Current generated by field emission from the inner wall of the channel; 4) Leakage current of electrodes and their supporting materials; 5) Environmental background (such as glass radioactivity, cosmic rays, etc.) causes glass luminescence to cause noise currents.

Due to the small anode dark current of MCPs, the dark current of a single MCP is usually less than 0.5pA/cm2 (when the bias voltage is 1kV), so it can be described by a dark count. A component with two or three MCPs superimposed has a hidden count of less than 3/cm2 s. Therefore, extremely weak input signals can be detected [14].

Assuming that the incident electron energy is Ep, the number of internal secondary electrons generated per unit distance from the solid surface is n (x, Ep), and the probability of internal secondary electrons escaping from the surface is f (x), the secondary electron emission coefficient is δ It can be represented by Eq. (1):

$$\delta = \int n(x, E_P) f(x) dx \tag{1}$$

It is generally believed that n (x, Ep) is proportional to the average energy loss in the material

$$n(x, E_P) = -\frac{1}{\varepsilon} \frac{dE}{dx} \tag{2}$$

The probability of secondary electron migration and escape from the solid surface is shown by Eq. (3),

$$f(x) = Be^{-x/\lambda}, B1 \tag{3}$$

among λ Is the average escape depth of the internal secondary electrons, B being equivalent to the surface escape probability, which is related to the material properties.

Young believes that the loss of incident electron energy within a solid is approximately constant:

$$-\frac{dE}{dx} = E_p/R \tag{4}$$

The dark current of MCP cannot be eliminated, and the following measures are usually taken to suppress or reduce it, such as cooling, shielding, selecting non radioactive raw materials, thorough electronic cleaning and aging, plating an anti ion feedback film on its input surface, bending the channel MCP, improving the manufacturing process, and eliminating stray light inside the device [15].

3 Development and Application of Micro-courses Based on Cloud Platform

3.1 Cloud Platform

The concept of "cloud" was proposed in 2007. Current cloud computing services are concentrated in universities, hospitals, government agencies and some companies. Nowadays, with the rapid development of cloud computing technology, and facing practical problems, the establishment of corresponding cloud service platforms is becoming more and more widely used in the enterprise community. It can access to remote databases and servers, for users' teaching, scientific research, business and other fields. Cloud computing is an Internet-based technology that allocates software and information based on user needs to devices such as computers and stores them on a computer. Data is stored in the Internet data center rather than on the computer's hard disk, which can be done on the computer and handled by the cloud Services department. The system uses virtual technology, to reduce the teaching system use cost, to achieve dynamic management; has a good scalability, easy to access and fast advantages.

Currently, the major cloud platforms in the world include Google Cloud Platform, Amazon Cloud Platform, Microsoft Cloud Computing Platform, and IBM Cloud Platform. With the in-depth integration of informatization and education, cloud platforms have been applied to university education, making university education informationization, personalization, specialization, and diversification. In clinical practice, due to its discipline characteristics, clinical characteristics, and students' learning habits, conventional classroom teaching is difficult to achieve ideal results, so it is necessary to introduce cloud computing technology for teaching innovation. With the rapid development of information technology and computer technology, cloud platforms are gradually becoming popular, and micro courses, turnover classes, etc. are widely welcomed by teachers and students. On this basis, we should establish a micro course resource for clinical applications, as shown in Fig. 1. Currently, we choose Baidu Cloud Disk, 360 Cloud Disk, and Tencent Cloud Disk as cloud disks, and conduct research and development of oral science micro classes in cloud disks.

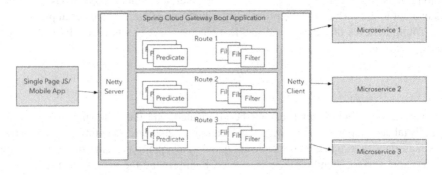

Cloud Platform Microcourse Resource Model

Fig. 1. Cloud Platform Microcourse Resource Model

3.2 Micro Course

Micro-teaching is a short film of more than ten minutes as the medium, and teachers can explain the teaching of a subject in detail. Micro-classroom is a new learning method, which can make the learning content simpler. Usually, in class, the teachers will cut the key points and difficult points, so that each knowledge point becomes a class. Teachers can also cut the knowledge points into a section. Micro-curriculum is highly targeted, small capacity and portable; it has the characteristics of resources, and modern educational needs, suitable for different levels, different types of schools and groups for teaching. The teaching video of the micro-class is simple, the teaching content is clear, and the test results are simple and fast. Therefore, it is very suitable for using mobile phone learning after class, tablet computers and other electronic products, mobile phone learning, network learning, which is a very good auxiliary means. Micro-courses are famous for their large knowledge capacity, strong pertinacity and strong interest. At the same time, students can communicate online with teachers and students anytime and anywhere, to get learning support, and have the characteristics of autonomy and personality. Micro class with its "fine", "short" characteristics, by the majority of teachers and teachers " welcome. Through cloud teaching, 4 G and other technologies, microclassroom serves as an online teaching and online teaching method [3] By the majority, teachers and students' favor.

3.3 The Development Process of Micro-courses

There are three ways to make micro courses, one is shot with a camera, one is shot with a digital device, another is used to record the screen, and with the screen recording software recording is the most convenient, also known as the "electronic whiteboard". In traditional teaching, the use of electronic screens not only takes a lot of time and energy. We used the screen recording software Camtasiastudio and PPT to record the microteaching of intraoral science. In class, first of all, use the electronic courseware to explain the relevant knowledge in the oral cavity, and then the students in the electronic courseware, but also in the corresponding operation. Oral internal science is one of the most common diseases in human beings, mainly including: periodontal tissue disease, periapical disease, oral mucosal disease, dental pulp disease and so on. In the teaching process, it is necessary to first make clear the key points and difficult points of each chapter, and then design video clips according to different teaching methods, and select relevant examples for demonstration. Each knowledge content has three levels of short films, each short film is about the explanation of the knowledge points, and the teacher mainly explains the knowledge points according to the case. Micro-video tape of knowledge expansion is mainly for the expansion of relevant knowledge points, and the purpose is to let students can apply the knowledge they have learned to practice, so as to improve their practical use ability. The specific micro-course production process is as follows (as shown in Table 1):

(1) Material preparation. Select the teaching content, determine the teaching purpose, collect relevant materials (such as text, pictures, medical record and video, etc.), And write the PPT
(2) Record the micro-lessons. The video was shot with a digital camera and can be entered directly into the computer for playback. Turn on, debug, and then turn on Camtasia Studio's videotape and PPT to start recording. Teachers demonstrate, explain, and cooperate with the sign tools or other software and teaching materials, and strive to make the classroom lively
(3) Processing and beautification of micro-courses. After making the good teaching video, the recorded micro video has been specially processed
(4) Upload the videos of the micro-course to the cloud platform
(5) Feedback feedback and application.

Teachers send text messages to students through SMS and software push, and ask them to log on the platform for micro-class account and password. Students can decide whether to download it to their own mobile phone. Before the class, students can log in to the designated online learning platform, watch the micro-video of the teaching, and set up effective classroom teaching objectives and tasks. Software is used to carry out micro-course teaching, with knowledge points as the center, practice practice module design

Table 1. Query results of system

Order number	Learning content, course design	
1	Caries treatment	① caries formation; ② caries diagnosis; ③ hole shape preparation; ④ silver amalgam filling; ⑤ glass ion filling; ⑥ composite resin filling
2	Treatment of abnormal dental development	① enamel hypoplasia: ② fluorosis; ③ tetracycline; ④ central tip
3	Treatment of acute dental injury	① tooth shock treatment; ② tooth dislocation treatment: ③ tooth fracture treatment
4	Treatment of chronic dental injury	① tooth wear treatment; ② tooth fissure treatment: ③ wedge defect treatment
5	dental hypersensitiveness	Dentine hypersensitivity treatment
6	Treatment of pulp disease	① compound pulpitis; ② acute pulpitis; ③ chronic pulpitis; ④ osteotomy; ⑤ pulp plasticizer
7	Treatment of periapical disease	① acute apical inflammation treatment: ② chronic apical inflammation treatment; ③ root canal treatment
8	Treatment of gum disease	① chronic gingivitis; ② adolescent gingivitis; ③ gestational gingivitis; ④ drug gingivitis; ⑤ acute gingival papillitis
9	Treatment of periodontitis	① chronic periodontitis treatment: ② special type of periodontal disease treatment
10	Treatment of oral mucosal infectious diseases	① herpes simplex treatment: ② oral candidiasis treatment: ③ hand, foot and mouth disease treatment
11	Treatment of the ulcerative disease of the oral mucosa	① recurrent averta ulcer treatment; ② Beaset syndrome treatment
12	Treatment of allergic diseases in the oral mucosa	① allergic stomatitis treatment: ② angioneuroedema treatment
13	Treatment of oral mucosal plaque-type diseases	① leukoplakia treatment; ② lichen planus treatment
14	Lip and tongue disease treatment	① chronic non-specific labitis treatment: ② photolabitis treatment; ③ keratitis treatment: ④ treatment

and development. In class, teachers guide students to discuss and communicate, and can timely help them to analyze and answer their questions; so that students can internalize their knowledge, and improve their problem analysis and problem handling. This course adopts the teaching method of "one problem more solution" and "one practice more use". Taking knowledge as the unit, the questions are divided into several small questions and give corresponding answers. The teaching process of the micro-class is as shown in Fig. 2:

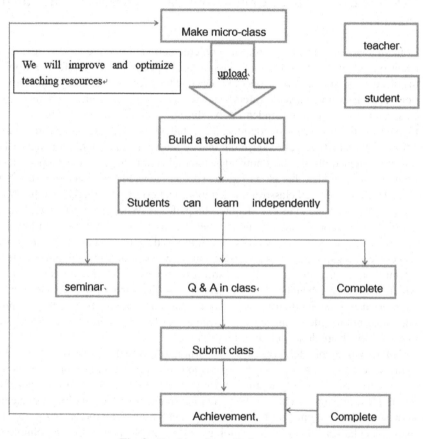

Fig. 2. Teaching steps of micro-courses

The 2021 stomatology class of our hospital implemented micro-class assisted teaching and received good feedback.

(1) Can stimulate students' interest in learning, let them learn in a relaxed and happy environment. The teaching content of micro-class is simple and clear, easy to master, which can improve the teaching effect.

(2) The operability of the course content, and the teaching content of the micro-course is practical and problem-oriented, so that students can immediately use the knowledge

they have learned to solve practical problems, and improve their ability to solve problems.

(3) Flexible learning methods. Classroom teaching is limited by time, place and other factors, and applying it to the research of micro-curriculum not only expands students' learning space, but also enables students to master the degree and time according to their own knowledge. In the flexible choice of teaching content, cultivate students' autonomy.

4 Development of Micro Courses in Oral Science Based on Cloud Platform

(1) Combine with flipped classroom. The implementation of micro courses in universities is often combined with flipped classrooms. Flipped classroom refers to flipping the place where the two processes of knowledge transfer and knowledge internalization occur. In simple terms, it refers to students studying the course content before class, and teachers helping students solve difficult problems during the formal class time. From the perspective of cognitive load, students receiving learning and training before class can effectively reduce internal cognitive load and achieve better learning performance during the knowledge internalization stage of the flipped classroom teaching model, that is, during the second knowledge transfer from teachers to students. The flipped classroom teaching model originated in 2007 and has been rapidly promoted due to its excellent teaching effects. When universities implement the flipped classroom teaching model, they mainly provide students with learning materials based on video resources. Considering that flipped classes place course content learning in the off class time, students may not be able to maintain long-term learning, so teachers create off class learning resources in the form of micro courses, which will be very beneficial for students to use their spare time for learning. In addition, using this method for teaching by teachers can also reduce the teaching burden, as micro videos can be used repeatedly, as long as maintenance and student Q&A feedback are done well at ordinary times.

(2) Combine with mobile learning. Mobile learning refers to the effective combination of mobile computing technology based on cloud platform learning to bring learners a new experience of learning anytime and anywhere. Mobile learning is considered as a future learning mode. The development of current network technology can enable networks to have higher traffic throughput capabilities. The increasingly popular intelligent platform, using Web technology and app application software technology, can provide mobile terminals with powerful resource display, communication and interaction capabilities. Taking the cloud platform as an example, it not only has a huge amount of online disk space to expand the capacity of handheld devices, but also can integrate common text, image, and audio/video formats for online browsing through powerful multimedia online browsing functions. At the same time, the cloud platform also provides an interactive system that can ask questions and evaluate resources. Therefore, combining the implementation of micro courses with mobile learning greatly facilitates learners. The light weight and openness of micro courses can also be reflected in mobile learning, promoting students to gradually develop the habit of using their spare time to learn anytime and anywhere.

Generally, a microlesson can be generated by achieving the three-level goal. A micro course requires core resources to explain the content of the knowledge unit, and supporting resources to support core resources. At the same time, core resources and supporting resources need to be associated with external micro courses and other resources through interfaces. Micro courses are not only organized into a curriculum structure with other micro courses within the course, but also generate knowledge links with other micro course resources, reflecting the openness of micro courses, as shown in Fig. 3.

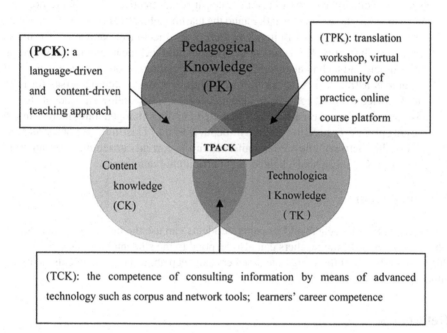

Fig. 3. Microcourse Structure Chart

In summary, the main resources that micro courses should provide should include the following three aspects, as shown in Fig. 3.

(1) Curriculum core resources. The core resource of the course is the central content of the resource package, and the presentation form is micro video. Micro video should undertake the main teaching tasks of current micro courses, carry the knowledge unit content of micro courses, and complete the main micro course teaching process. Micro videos are usually limited to about 10 min, with a maximum of 15 min. The micro video includes a classroom guidance section, a knowledge explanation section, a case analysis section, a task assignment section, and a classroom summary section, among which the task assignment is an optional section. Knowledge explanation can be combined with case analysis, such as explaining cases while summarizing principles.

(2) Course support resources. The course support resources mainly include support resources for the knowledge taught in the micro video, mainly including the chapter knowledge structure diagram of this course, relevant case texts and material source

files mentioned by the teacher during the micro video teaching, literature supporting learning theories, links to network resources, and related tests.

(3) Course information resources. Curriculum information resources mainly describe the construction of micro curriculum resources. The main advantages of establishing curriculum information resources include: describing curriculum construction information to provide reference for the follow-up resource construction of micro courses; Describing the curriculum objectives, key and difficult points, and precautions can facilitate teachers to test the integrity and effectiveness of micro courses, and also facilitate students to understand the learning objectives and key points when using micro courses for learning; The recording of technical parameters for micro video recording provides technical information and technical templates, providing data support and technical specifications for subsequent resource maintenance and resource construction; A description of the construction of micro courses for relevant knowledge points reflects the openness of the course, allowing students to use this "interface" to externally "link" knowledge points that generate interest in the learning process or need to continue in-depth learning. This "link" is not a structural relationship between knowledge units within the current curriculum, but rather an external link that can span chapters and curriculum boundaries.

5 Conclusion

Timely opinions of teachers and students. Students can use the micro-class platform to ask the teachers, and the teachers can also respond to the students' questions in time in different methods. At the same time, teachers can keep abreast of the students' learning situation at any time.

References

1. Wei, W., Ren, X., Du, S., et al.: Development and application of transient electronic based on degradable materials. IOP Conf. Ser. Earth Environ. Sci. **714**(3), 032045 (9pp) (2021)
2. Dunn, A.L., Li, X.: Development of a high-throughput kinetics protocol and application to an aza-michael reaction. Organic Process Res. Developm. **26**(3), 795–803 (2022)
3. Gao, J., Dong, L.I., Dan, S.U., et al.: Research progress on the extraction technology of seabuckthorn fruit oil and the application of nutritional factors. Sci. Technol. Food Industry **43**(13), 400–407 (2022)
4. Chao, Z., Xinglong, W., Shugang, L., et al.: Development and application of a new compound wetting agent for coal seam water infusion. Fuel: J. Fuel Sci., 314 (2022)
5. Zhang, Y.: Characteristics and effective application of online education platform for ideological theory courses in universities based on big data technology (2021)
6. Zhang, L.: Optimization of the marketing management system based on cloud computing and big data. Complexity **2021** (2021)
7. Chen, N., Leiming, X.U., Song, Z., et al.: Development and application of prestack seismic fracture detection software based on P-wave azimuthal anisotropy. Geophys. Prospecting Petrol. **57**(6), 914–926 (2022)
8. Fu, D., Xiao, H., Su, F., et al.: Remote sensing cloud computing platform development and Earth science application (2021)

9. Li, K., Wang, S.: Development and application of VR course resources based on embedded system in open education. Microprocessors Microsyst. **83**, 103989 (2021)
10. Hong, S.Y., Sang, W.L.: Development and Application of Elementary School Environmental Education Program Based on Coding Education (2021)
11. Schwarz, D.: Form, function, development and evolution of intraoral food processing in salamanders (2021)
12. Barone, V., Carnimeo, I., Mancini, G., et al.: Development, validation, and pilot application of a generalized fluctuating charge model for computational spectroscopy in solution. ACS Omega **7**(15), 13382–13394 (2022)
13. Khademi, S., Salemi, A., Jochmann, M., et al.: Development and comparison of direct immersion solid phase micro extraction Arrow-GC-MS for the determination of selected pesticides in water. Microchem. J. Devoted Appli. Microtech. Branches Sci., 164 (2021)
14. Zhang, C., Du, B., Li, K., et al.: Selection of the effective characteristic spectra based on the chemical structure and its application in rapid analysis of ethanol content in gasoline. ACS Omega **7**(23), 20291–20297 (2022)
15. Payero, J.O., Marshall, M.W., Farmaha, B.S., et al.: Development and application of cell-phone-based Internet of Things (IoT) Systems for Soil Moisture Monitoring. Agricult. Sci. (2021)

Implementation of College Educational Administration and Student Management System Based on B/S

Feng Cheng (✉)

Yunnan College of Business Management, Yunnan 650106, China
18187103632@163.com

Abstract. For colleges and universities, educational administration management is a link of their daily school affairs. At the same time, it has the characteristics of strong concept of time, heavy tasks and high accuracy requirements. It is often necessary to consider many aspects, such as education and teaching resources, student information, student examination information, teaching plan and so on. The traditional educational administration work is based on the full manual management mode, which brings a lot of inconvenience to the educational administration work. By analyzing and designing a scientific and reasonable university educational administration management system, it plays an important role in improving the efficiency and level of daily educational administration management and the quality of education and teaching. It can not only improve the management efficiency, but also realize the four modernization levels of educational administration in Colleges and universities, that is, it can achieve a new level of scientificity, standardization and intelligence.

Keywords: Information management · Educational administration system · B/S structure

1 Introduction

Student management of educational administration in Colleges and universities is one of the basic contents of daily management in Colleges and universities. Its fundamental goal is to reasonably integrate and utilize student status management, course selection management, achievement management and attendance management according to the planned talent training scheme, so as to form a high-efficiency process student management mode. Specifically, the daily work of student management in domestic colleges and universities mostly covers important links such as student status management, student course selection management, student achievement management and student attendance management. With the rapid development of computer technology and network information technology, the economy and society has entered the Internet era, Computer information network resources have gradually become an important driving force for the development of education [1]. With the help of network and information technology,

Y. Zhang and N. Shah (Eds.): BigIoT-EDU 2023, LNICST 583, pp. 360–365, 2024.
https://doi.org/10.1007/978-3-031-63139-9_38

we can greatly speed up the pace of information construction in Colleges and universities, which is also the basic strategic goal of rejuvenating the country through science and education. Information construction in Colleges and universities is also the basic content for the country to achieve the goal of information construction. From the perspective of the current era of knowledge economy, it is also the basic environment for the survival and development of colleges and universities in the future, which is a trend. At present, many domestic colleges and universities have gradually realized the campus network, which provides a better learning, working and living environment for students and teachers. At the same time, it can also promote the development of the comprehensive management level of education and teaching in Colleges and universities.

Strengthening the educational administration information management, fully excavating the basic information resources provided by the campus network, so as to realize the sharing of information resources and improve the management level of colleges and universities as a whole has become the basic problem to be solved in Colleges and universities. The management level of education and teaching in Colleges and universities will inevitably affect the management efficiency of education and teaching in Colleges and universities. Among them, educational administration management is the cornerstone of the current daily management of colleges and universities, which will involve the basic work of various teaching departments, teachers, students and so on, With the rapid increase in the number of students brought by the expansion of college enrollment and the continuous in-depth development of the reform of education and teaching system, the educational administration management in Colleges and universities has become increasingly complex and cumbersome. The traditional educational administration management mode and its means obviously can not meet the needs of the development of colleges and Universities under the new situation.

2   Key Technologies of the System

2.1   ado.net Technology

Ado.net technology mainly includes a set of object-oriented class libraries for communication and interaction with data sources to realize database access. In most cases, the data source refers to the database. However, it can also be a text file or the format of office software, such as excel table or XML file. Ado.net technology can realize the communication and interaction of different types of data source sets for database system [2]. It should be noted that there is no series of classes related to this to complete database access. This is mainly because different data sources need different communication protocols, which requires corresponding protocols for different data sources. For some older data sources, most of them use ODBC database access protocol, For many new data sources, OLEDB database access protocol is used. For more data source access protocols that are still developing and launching, they are generally universal and downward compatible. In ASP. Net, ADO. Net class library collection can easily realize database access and processing. Ado.net class library provides public access methods related to communication and interaction with data sources, and a set of different object class libraries are used for different data sources. Generally, these class libraries are called data providers database access providers. For ado.net component objects, they are named according to the communication protocol and the type of data source. Ado.net mainly includes connection object, command object, datareader object, dataset object and DataAdapter object.

2.2 LIS

Information server IIS is a kind of server launched by Microsoft company. It includes a variety of servers (WWW server, FTP server and SMTP server). It realizes the integration with Windows operating system. It is mainly used for web servers that publish information on public Internet or Internet. IIS server transmits network information by using Hypertext Transfer Protocol HTTP protocol, and can also provide file transfer protocol FTP and gopher services by configuring Internet information server. In the visual studio platform, the integration of IIS server is realized, which can provide a powerful system running platform for web applications on the. Net platform, and a secure web system can be built through IIS.

Compared with other types of web servers, IIS has the following advantages:

1. IIS and windows operating system realize seamless integration, so IIS has strong advantages in security, management, operation and so on.
2. IIS provides a rich and complete development platform for the development of web system, and supports the architecture mode of distributed network system.
3. It widely supports a variety of scripting languages, including VBScript and JScript, and supports a variety of ways to access and access databases.
4. IIS can support a variety of system solutions, such as enterprise websites, LAN workstations, etc.
5. IIS supports a variety of server functions, such as FTP, WWW, SMTP, etc.

3 System Requirements Analysis

The workflow of daily affairs management of educational administration in Colleges and universities takes the educational administration department as the competent department to centrally and uniformly manage the relevant data and information generated in the development and management of educational administration and teaching daily work. For other departments, such as the educational administration management personnel of the secondary college, after being respectively authorized by the users of the relevant competent departments of the educational administration department of the general college, they can add, modify, query, count and print the data information of the system according to the established authority [3]. At the same time, with the deepening of the reform of higher education and teaching system and the continuous expansion of the number of colleges and universities, educational affairs have become cumbersome and complex (for example, the addition, modification, query and statistics of basic transaction data such as student basic information management, student status management, student course selection management, teacher information management, course information management, student achievement management and teaching effect evaluation management) According to the principle of departmental division of labor and cooperation, it is distributed to various grass-roots departments and units, so as to promote the division of labor and cooperation of educational administration management and realize the goal of quickly and efficiently analyzing and processing data and information. Among them, the main business model takes talent training as the central goal, combined with students' basic information, students' student status data, students' course selection information, teachers' information Therefore, the fundamental purpose of studying and implementing the university educational administration student management information system is to realize the real-time collection, analysis, processing and release of all student data information in the process of daily teaching activities for the purpose of teaching, including student teaching The main purpose is to lay a foundation for the development and planning of colleges and universities, and also provide decision support for the school management. For our university, the educational administration management system should include the following system user roles: system administrator user and educational administration user Staff users (mainly refer to the staff of the relevant competent departments of the school's educational administration and the educational administration staff of the Department of the College of Education) After analyzing the business processing mode of the daily work management of the educational administration of our university, it can be concluded that the main goal of the college educational administration student management information system is to realize the information management of the educational administration of our university. Then, according to the task division of the role of the system user, the main system functions of the system can be determined.

According to the system demand analysis and system business process analysis, combined with the structured programming idea, we designed the software structure of the new management system. The top module calls its lower module and each module cooperates with each other to realize the complete function of the program, that is, the overall function is divided into several functional modules, and each functional module is subdivided into several sub modules The sub module completes a corresponding sub function. If the function is still complex, it can continue to be divided downward, and the module can be organized into a good hierarchical system in this way. The following gives a detailed analysis respectively, and gives a reasonable function module design in combination with the analysis. According to the demand analysis and business process of the system, the system should include student information management and student course selection management Student attendance management, student achievement management, auxiliary management, system maintenance and other functional modules are shown in Fig. 1.

4   B/S Educational Administration Management System

The college educational administration student management system is a relatively large system project. The system function structure is complex, involving more system users, more functions, cumbersome and complex business. Moreover, the operation process and details of its corresponding users will involve all aspects of the daily teaching management of colleges and universities, and the business level involved is relatively broad, The business process is very complex [4].

The system as a whole adopts the "centralized storage/distributed management" architecture. Users such as teachers or students can access the system through the web.

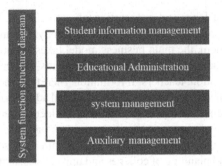

Fig. 1. Overall functional structure diagram of the system

Authorized educational administrators use the client to access the system, and use the client to directly access the database, or the system functions provided by the web site to realize limited management functions. In the B/s browser, the system will process the information submitted by the user, and then allocate the system menu according to the user's authority, which can ensure the security of the system and the rights and interests of the user. The system deployment diagram of the system is given below, as shown in Fig. 2.

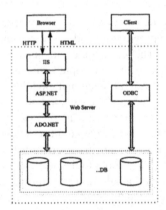

Fig. 2. System deployment structure diagram

To sum up, the users of the university educational administration student management system are mainly the university educational administration administrators, teachers and students. According to the different permissions and functions of the users, the overall application of the system functions is divided into two categories according to the needs: the educational administration managers mainly use the client of B/S structure, and the system administrator assigns corresponding operation permissions according to their work responsibilities, Use client software to directly operate relevant educational administration data through LAN; General users, such as teachers and students, are assigned to the corresponding permissions through the B/S structure and the authentication when logging in through the web page to complete the corresponding operations.

System administrators and general educational administration managers can also operate the data through the web.

5 Conclusion

With the deepening of the reform of education and teaching system, colleges and universities continue to expand the enrollment scale, but also increase the task of daily educational administration and teaching management. How to use modern management facilities and technology to further improve the educational administration of colleges and universities has become a major problem faced by colleges and universities. Today, with the rapid development and application of information technology, especially the popularization, promotion and application of Internet technology, has accelerated the implementation process of educational administration informatization in Colleges and universities. With the help of increasingly mature information technology and Internet technology, the research and design of college educational administration student management system is conducive to improve the scientificity of the implementation of college education, the openness and transparency of teaching management, and the sustainable development of colleges and universities.

In this context, by understanding the mainstream technologies and means of the current electronic educational administration system, this paper makes an in-depth analysis and Research on the student management part of the current educational administration management, absorbs the advantages of the existing excellent system, summarizes the existing problems and deficiencies, and uses the. Net program development platform, Delphi system development language Oracle background database and other technologies design and implement the development of college educational administration student management system based on B/S mode.

References

1. Tang, S.: Application of educational administration management system in College Educational Administration. Fujian Comput. (07) (2011)
2. Xu, S., Lin, Q., Guan, M.: Informatization solutions to meet the individual needs of small and medium-sized enterprises. Comput. Age (07) (2007)
3. Fan, W., Deng, Z., Zhao, Z.: Implementation of college management information system based on web services. Microprocessor (01) (2009)
4. Tao, L., Xu, D.: Network transplantation of CAD system based on Web Service. J. Jiangnan Univ. (Nat. Sci. Edn.) (05) (2005)

The Design and Implementation of the Fine Art Teaching System Based on B/S Structure

Fang Feng[1,2]([envelope]) and Shuyuan Piao[1,2]

[1] School of Design and Art, Lanzhou University of Technology, Gansu 730050, China
ffhfzh@163.com
[2] Yunnan Engineering Vocational College, Yunnan 650304, China

Abstract. Art teaching is an art discipline that focuses on visual communication and emphasizes touch, emotion, and mental perception. It holds a very important position in modern education. For schools, having an art course website that requires hands-on and interactive learning is crucial. In order to better promote the modernization transformation of art education, an art teaching system based on B/S structure has emerged. The art teaching system based on B/S structure can achieve a variety of teaching methods, such as online teaching, video tutorials, task assessment, etc. Based on the B/S architecture, developers can develop online art teaching applications using web technology and distribute the applications to all clients using the HTTP protocol. This article introduces the design and implementation of a primary school art course website. A detailed analysis of the system's requirements was conducted and an implementation plan for the system was provided. It has a good structure, strong interactivity, strong scalability, and is suitable for teaching and learning. It has established a student-centered teaching model to promote students' exploration and innovation, thereby improving the quality of teaching. The art teaching system based on B/S structure permeates modern educational concepts and management ideas, helping education achieve digitization, remoteness, and intelligence, greatly improving the quality and efficiency of art education.

Keywords: Teaching system · Fine arts · B/S architecture

1 Introduction

With the development of modern education, online teaching has become an important mode of teaching in universities. Online teaching refers to the use of network communication technology and multimedia technology to carry out various interactive teaching activities in an open network environment. Online teaching, with its advanced teaching methods and approaches, has advantages in terms of time, space, and content that traditional teaching models cannot match. It not only builds a platform for teaching resources for teachers and students, strengthens communication between teachers and students, enables students to quickly access various teaching resources, but also enhances students' learning interest and initiative, and improves the efficiency and effectiveness of

Y. Zhang and N. Shah (Eds.): BigIoT-EDU 2023, LNICST 583, pp. 366–373, 2024.
https://doi.org/10.1007/978-3-031-63139-9_39

education and teaching [1]. As a discipline closely related to visual spirit, art education has emerged with many new art teaching models under the influence of digital technology, among which the art teaching system based on B/S structure has received much attention.

The art teaching system based on B/S structure refers to a system that connects art course resources, teaching content, teaching tasks, teachers, and students through the network. It is based on internet technology and uses a new distributed client/server computer model for data transmission and application operation, with the advantages of flexibility, security, and easy maintenance.

This system is mainly used for remote and online art education, and can provide corresponding education services and operation platforms for various art education institutions. Students and teachers can complete various teaching and assessment requirements for art teaching through the art teaching system [2]. This not only improves teaching efficiency and quality, but also enables the sharing of educational resources, maximizing the satisfaction of students' personalized learning needs.

The art teaching system based on B/S structure has the following characteristics:

(1) Diversified functions The art teaching system can not only provide basic functions such as course Q&A and online teaching, but also achieve rich functions such as interactive communication between teachers and students, video tutorial playback, and online homework submission.
(2) Intelligent teaching assistants During the teaching and learning process, the system can achieve automated teaching assistant functions such as intelligent evaluation and learning path planning. Students can receive more personalized and precise services, and teachers can better grasp students' learning situations.
(3) Educational security The art teaching system can achieve multi-level and decentralized management, ensuring the security of educational content and student data.
(4) Multi platform applications The system can run on both desktop and mobile devices, and can support multiple operating systems.

Art education is an important discipline for cultivating and refining students' artistic literacy and aesthetic abilities, and the introduction of an art teaching system based on the B/S structure provides a more advanced, efficient, vivid, and practical form of art education.

2 System Architecture

Current software development models can be divided into C/S (Client/Server), B/S (Bowser/Server) and SOA (Service-Oriented Architecture). Service-Oriented Architecture is a popular component model today, but the development of SOA architecture is not yet complete, and many technical guidelines have yet to be improved and validated.

Advantages of the B/S architecture:

(1) The B/S and C/S architectures are fully exploited, making up for the shortcomings of both. Full consideration is given to the interests of the user, ensuring the convenience of the viewer and also making the system easy to update, simple and flexible maintenance, and easy to operate.

(2) Information dissemination using B/S structure, maintaining the advantages of the thin client. The software loaded into the client can use a unified WWW browser. And because the Www browser and the network integrated server are based on industry standards, they can work on all platforms.

(3) The database side uses a C/S structure and is connected via ODBC/JDBC. This part only involves system maintenance, data update, etc. There are no disadvantages such as large maintenance workload on the client side brought about by the complete adoption of C/S structure. And in the client can be constructed very complex applications, friendly and flexible interface, easy to operate, can solve many of the inherent shortcomings of the existence of B / S.

(4) For the original application based on C/S architecture, it is easier to upgrade to this architecture, only need to develop the Www interface for publishing, can retain some subsystems of the original C/S structure, fully utilise the resources of the existing system, so that the existing system or resources can be connected to use without major transformation, protecting the user's previous investment[3].

(5) By embedding ActiveX controls in the browser, functions that cannot be achieved in the browser or are difficult to achieve can be achieved. For example, responding to reports via the browser. In addition, the addition of ActiveX controls on the client side can enrich HTML pages and produce surprising effects.

(6) The server side is divided into two parts: the WEB server and the WEB application, which uses component technology to implement the business logic part of the three-tier architecture, to encapsulate the source code and protect intellectual property rights. COM +, the non-coastal extension set of COM, has powerful features such as memory database and load balancing.

Therefore, the art course website in this paper is designed using a B/S architecture.

3 Requirements Analysis of the System

3.1 Principles of Requirements Analysis

The requirements statute provides the software designer and the client with a basis for quality assessment after the software has been built.

Before requirements analysis, it is important to understand the categories of requirements, so that when acquiring requirements, they are not easily missed if they are dealt with by category. There are many different ways of classifying requirements, one of which tells us that requirements should include:

(1) Functional requirements, which specify the services that the system must provide and which should be classified by the requirements analysis as all the functions that the system must perform;

(2) Reliability and availability requirements, which specify the reliability and availability of the system in quantitative terms;

(3) Interface requirements, interface requirements describe the format of communication between the application system and its environment;

(4) constraints, constraints describe the constraints that the application system should comply with, in the requirements analysis phase of such requirements, is not to replace the design (or implementation) process, which only reflects the constraints imposed on the project by the user or the environment, common constraints are: accuracy constraints, tools and language constraints, design constraints, the standards that should be used, the hardware platform that should be used, etc.;

(5) Reverse requirements, reverse requirements state what the software system should not do. There are theoretically an infinite number of reverse requirements, and we should only select those that clarify the true requirements and eliminate misunderstandings that occur;

(6) Possible future requirements, which should be explicitly listed as requirements that are not part of the current system development, but which are analysed as likely to come up in the future. The purpose of this is to prepare the system for possible future expansions and modifications during the design process, so that such expansions and modifications can be made more easily if they are actually needed.

3.2 Application Requirements

With the continuous development of internet technology, art teaching systems based on B/S structure are also receiving increasing attention. The advantage of this system is that it can achieve remote online teaching for students through the network, providing students with a more convenient and efficient learning experience. Students can use this website to learn art, stay up-to-date with the latest information posted, complete their assignments and work, and log in to forums to communicate with teachers and classmates [4]. As shown in Fig. 1. Below, I will provide a detailed explanation of the requirements for an art teaching system based on the B/S structure.

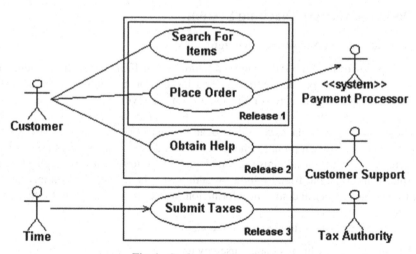

Fig. 1. Student use case diagram

Firstly, the art teaching system needs to have a good user interface that is concise, easy to understand, intuitive, and easy for users to operate. Students can log in to the website or client of the teaching system and enter their own learning interface to start learning. Teachers can have different permissions to manage or modify content such as courses and lesson plans in the system. In addition, the art teaching system should also support multiple users to operate online simultaneously and have good fault-tolerant processing capabilities. Secondly, the art teaching system needs to be designed for different learning stages and content. The teaching system should provide basic courses and advanced courses, and can be evaluated based on academic performance, so that students can better grasp knowledge. In the advanced course module, it is necessary to strengthen the training and assessment of painting skills, and support students to communicate and evaluate each other to improve learning outcomes. In addition, the teaching system should be able to support different types of art works, such as oil paintings, watercolors, sketches, etc., to meet the learning needs of different students. Once again, the teaching system needs to provide good learning resources and interactive functions. The teaching system should build a comprehensive learning resource library and work display library, including teaching courseware, student works, famous works, etc., for students and teachers to learn and communicate. In addition, multimedia interactive functions such as online practice, virtual galleries, social media, etc. should also be provided to facilitate interaction and communication between students and teachers, and improve learning outcomes. Finally, the art teaching system needs to have good scalability and security. The teaching system should have good scalability, support the continuous addition of new learning resources, and be able to seamlessly connect with other systems. At the same time, the teaching system also needs to have a high degree of security, including data confidentiality, backup and recovery, and network security. In addition, the system also needs to provide a comprehensive learning feedback mechanism for teachers and students to provide feedback and continuously improve the system.

4   Design of the Art Teaching System

4.1   Overall System Architecture Design

The web pages of the Fine Art mainly structured using Iframes, which are generally known as inline frames or floating frames. By using an Iframe, an inline frame is inserted section of the site, so that there is no inside a main page with a FrameSet tag, as is the case before using a normal frame. Here, each inline frame can be sized independently.

The mainly using the Java, using JavaBean to connect to the SQL database, so that the implements the registration, teacher and student, downloading student assignments by teachers, etc., while the administrator implements functions such as managing teacher and student information, friendly links, in addition to the above. The administrator is able to manage teacher and student information, friend links in addition to the above, maximising.

The course website is divided into three main sections:

(1) The web service, which is mainly used by users to send requests.
(2) The middle tier server, which is mainly used to execute the business logic.
(3) The course database, which is mainly used to store information about teachers, students and administrators, the latest information posted by administrators, and the assignments posted by teachers.

The system structure is shown in Fig. 2.

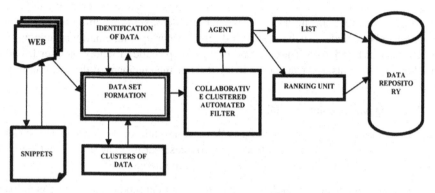

Fig. 2. System architecture diagram

4.2 Overall System Functional Module Structure Design

The overall functional module structure of the system is shown in Fig. 3.

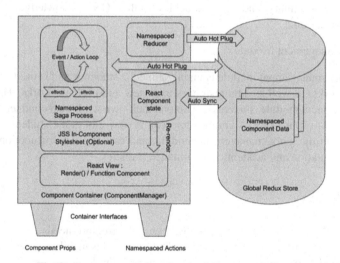

Fig. 3. System overall function module structure diagram

The overall functional module structure design of the art teaching system includes three major modules: user management, learning management, and work management. These modules are interconnected and interact with each other, collectively forming a system that meets teaching needs. Next, I will introduce these three modules in sequence.

(1) User Management Module

The user management module mainly includes two roles: student and teacher. Among them, students can register, log in, modify personal information, and other operations through this module; Teachers can conduct teaching management, curriculum design, and other operations. In the user management module, some common user functions should also be included, such as password reset, avatar upload, email verification, forgotten password, and so on. The user module needs to provide a friendly and user-friendly interface for students and teachers to facilitate user management of their accounts and information.

(2) Learning Management Module

The learning management module is the core module of the art teaching system, which enables the management of teaching resources, learning interaction, and learning feedback. Specifically, the learning management module includes:

- Course management: Through the course management module, teachers can upload, edit, and publish courses and course materials, and set different learning goals and plans for courses.
- Resource management: Through the resource management module, teachers can upload and manage multimedia resources, learning materials, and journals based on different learning objectives.
- Learning and communication: Through the learning and communication module, students and teachers can engage in online communication, interactive learning, discussion and summary, and can also achieve online Q&A, knowledge sharing, and image correction.

(3) Work Management Module

The work management module is mainly aimed at students, and is used for students to submit works, as well as administrators to review and evaluate works. Through the work management module, students can upload their own works and conduct online and teacher-student evaluations. Administrators can review and grade students' uploaded works through the work management module, and can also set up functions such as statistical evaluation and academic performance statistics.

5 Conclusion

The design of an art teaching system based on B/S structure needs to consider three aspects: front-end, back-end, and database. The front-end is mainly responsible for user interaction and display, using popular web technology for development; The backend is mainly responsible for processing business logic, using common backend frameworks for development; The database mainly stores and manages data. Common relational database and NoSQL database can be used. At the same time of design, it is necessary to pay attention to the user interaction experience, data security, and scalability. In terms of functional module design, the art teaching system is mainly divided into user management module, learning management module, and work management module. In short, the art teaching system based on B/S structure is a teaching model that conforms to contemporary educational concepts and student needs, especially in the context of remote online education under the influence of the epidemic, which has received more attention. Major universities, training institutions, and educational institutions can use the B/S structured art teaching system to enhance students' learning experience and teachers' teaching effectiveness.

Acknowledgements. 1. Research on the talent matching degree of art and design education adapting to the labor market, the 12th Five Year Plan Project of Gansu Education Science, Gansu social science planning office;

2. "Promoting the construction of Chinese civilization inheritance and Innovation Zone with the construction of Dunhuang school", scientific research project of colleges and universities in Gansu Province, Department of education of Gansu Province;

3. Research on ceramic art design, national "big innovation " project, Ministry of education of the people's Republic of China;

4. College students' innovative project "color sketch art ", Lanzhou University of technology.

References

1. Qi, X., Zhang, H.: The construction of an interactive online teaching platform for high-quality courses. Sci. Technol. Inform. **29** (2008)
2. Zhaoging: Network teaching in universities. Small Medium-Sized Enterprise Manag. Technol. **8**, 56- 60 (2009)
3. Dai, R.: Analysis of the connotation of online teaching effectiveness. China Dis. Educ. **2**, 45–48 (2009)
4. Xu, Q.: Online teaching and learning: models and development. New Course (Comprehensive Edn.) **7**, 75–79 (2009)

Teaching Mode of "Online and Offline" Human Resource Management Based on Internet

Qian Wen[1($\boxtimes$)], Zhirong Tian[1], and Siyu Zhou[2]

[1] School of Economics and Management, Guangxi University of Science and Technology, LiuZhou 545001, China
gxustbs@163.com
[2] Ministry of Sports, Nanguo Business School, Guangdong University of Foreign Studies and Foreign Trade, Guangdong 510545, China

Abstract. The research on "online and offline" teaching mode based on the Internet is a research focusing on the relationship between online and offline learning. This study was conducted by many researchers from different countries such as South Korea, Japan and China. The main purpose of this study is to understand how students use online and offline modes to learn from teachers. There are two types of research: one is to investigate the effectiveness of online education by comparing online education with traditional education (i.e., classroom based teaching), while the other is to compare offline education with classroom based education. The research of human resource management teaching mode is to find the best teaching mode. This study will be conducted through investigation, interview and observation. The main purpose of this study is to determine the most effective teaching methods related to human resource management. The results of this study will serve as the basis for future research on human resource management.

Keywords: Human resources management · Online and offline · internet · teaching model

1 Introduction

As an important combination of science and technology as the first productive force and talent as the first resource, higher education plays a very important role in national development. With the development of the national economy and the development of science and technology education, mankind has entered the era of knowledge economy. With the economic globalization under the knowledge economy, education plays a direct role in promoting progress, especially higher education. A large amount of spiritual and material wealth originates from high-quality talents. Higher education has become the most fundamental method to cultivate high-quality talents [1].

In 2015, in the government work report, Premier Li Keqiang emphasized the Internet for many times and put forward the strategic plan of "Internet+", saying that we should actively promote the rapid development of Internet information technology, big data and

Y. Zhang and N. Shah (Eds.): BigIoT-EDU 2023, LNICST 583, pp. 374–384, 2024.
https://doi.org/10.1007/978-3-031-63139-9_40

cloud computing, and comprehensively promote the rapid progress of industrial Internet, e-commerce and Internet Finance, so as to lay a solid foundation for Internet enterprises to develop the international market. "@" Since then, "Internet+" as a national strategy has pointed out the direction for all fields of the country in the future and will have a revolutionary impact on all fields of society [2]. The combination of "Internet+" and education will also promote major changes in the education industry. With the help of "Internet+", the place, mode, content, evaluation and organizational form of teaching and learning will undergo major changes. How to achieve the coordination and integration of the Internet and education scientifically is also a hot topic in the current education field [3].

In accordance with the spirit of the credit system reform of the Ministry of Education, in order to cultivate students' independent innovation ability, universities have gradually reduced the proportion of compulsory courses and shortened teaching hours. Currently, human resource management has 48 class hours, which can complete the teaching of all knowledge points in the syllabus, but cannot expand the content in depth and horizontally. If classroom teaching alone, students can only "learn the skin" and cannot seek the essence.

The original intention of reducing class hours is to increase the time and space for students to learn independently. However, many students are accustomed to the traditional "cramming" mode of teaching, and their learning enthusiasm is poor. In addition, erroneous public opinion such as "reading is useless" and "what you learn at school is different from what you actually do" also plays a misleading role, causing many students to "sacrifice their roots for the end" and not attach importance to the accumulation of knowledge during school. Although becoming an excellent human resource manager requires extensive work experience, changes cannot be separated from their roots, and a lack of solid theoretical foundation cannot cope with seemingly complex practical problems. Improper learning attitudes not only waste a lot of valuable time, but also reduce the competitiveness of students in future job hunting.

Learning ability focuses on learning methods and skills, which are not formed overnight and require long-term deliberate practice. Traditional teaching methods of human resource management often use classroom questioning and homework assignments to improve students' learning abilities, but the results have been minimal. On the one hand, due to limited time in class, there are individual differences in students' understanding of knowledge, and teachers cannot take into account everyone; On the other hand, teachers and students lack effective communication channels after class. In addition, the effectiveness of traditional teaching models in collecting and reading human resource management literature, using data analysis software, and improving observation and understanding is not satisfactory. Some students with negative learning attitudes rarely actively seek extracurricular books and materials to improve their professional skills. They are difficult to cope with flexible test questions or practical training, and have weak innovative spirit and practical ability.

Therefore, under the traditional teaching model, it is difficult for universities to provide learning content that meets both social development and student characteristics, and students' doubts about the three questions "What do I want to learn? Where do I learn to use it? How should I learn?" directly affect their learning attitude and ability.

In June 2018, the Ministry of Education proposed "40 new era higher education items", explicitly proposing "promoting the construction of smart classrooms and constructing a teaching model combining online and offline", which provides policy guidance for the construction of an online platform for human resource management teaching.

The major of human resource management is mainly to cultivate specialized talents who have knowledge in economics, law, management, and human resource management, and can carry out human resource management work in units or departments. In essence, human resource management has the characteristics of strong operability and practicality, while the existing teaching platform is only limited to the theoretical teaching direction, unable to meet the current social demand for human resource management talents.

To some extent, the traditional education mode suppresses students' creativity and solidifies their thinking mode. Under the requirements of the development of knowledge economy, how to break through the limitations of the established education mode and establish a work mode that is people-oriented and can fully stimulate the creativity of students is an important task of higher education reform in the new era. The key is to effectively draw on the perspective of human resources development to design, shape students' personality, cultivate students' innovation consciousness and enhance students' innovation ability according to the development needs of people [4].

2 Related Work

2.1 Research Status of Online and Offline Teaching Mode

The concept of "online and offline teaching" was first introduced by domestic scholars from abroad and appeared in China from 2003 to 2004. In December 2003, Professor He Kekang formally advocated "online and offline teaching" in China for the first time at the seventh global Chinese computer education application conference, which opened the prelude of domestic research on "online and offline teaching". With the continuous enrichment of online and offline teaching applications, domestic scholars have conducted in-depth research from different angles. The framework of online and offline teaching mode is shown below (Fig. 1).

Definition of online and offline Teaching: Ma Meng and he Kekang (2008) understand online and offline teaching as a collaborative combination of the advantages of traditional teaching and the advantages of e-learning (digital network learning). On the one hand, it can fully highlight the role of teachers in guidance, inspiration and supervision; on the other hand, it can stimulate students' initiative in learning and highlight students' dominant position in learning [5]. According to Ma Wulin and Zhang Xiaopeng, blended learning is not only a simple mixture of face-to-face learning and online learning, but also an organic integration of multiple elements. It includes the mixture of different learning styles, learning environments, learning participants, learning resources and learning media.

The value and significance of online and offline Teaching: for example, Zhang Qiliang and Wang Aichun (2014) discussed the value of online and offline teaching from five dimensions: teaching form, teaching technology, teaching means, teaching objectives and teaching evaluation. In terms of teaching form, they emphasized the combination of traditional classroom teaching and network teaching, and in terms of teaching

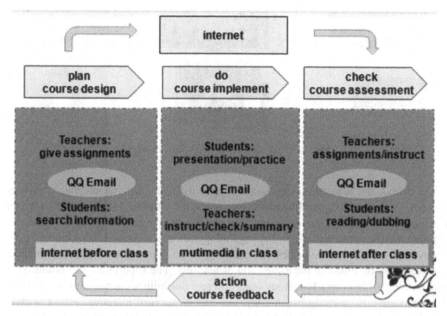

Fig. 1. Framework of online and offline teaching mode

technology, they highlighted the comprehensive use of diversified media technologies, In terms of teaching means, it emphasizes the organic integration of traditional teaching and information technology teaching means [6]. In terms of teaching objectives, it emphasizes the students' dominant position and the teachers' guiding role. In terms of teaching evaluation, it emphasizes the comprehensive application of various evaluation methods such as process evaluation and result evaluation.

2.2 The Internet Promotes the Combination of Offline and Online Teaching Methods of Human Resources Management

The specific name "online and offline" teaching on the Internet actually derives from the English word. In fact, it refers to an Internet "online and offline" teaching mode involved in the specific teaching process, which is an "online + offline" teaching mode. It combines the traditional and current popular teaching modes, and combines offline and online teaching modes, giving play to the advantages of the two teaching modes and guiding students to transition from shallow learning to deep learning. Scholars at home and abroad have various interpretations of "online and offline" teaching on the Internet, interpreting the concept of "online and offline" teaching on the Internet into broad and narrow senses. The broad sense of "online and offline" teaching on the Internet refers to the integration of multiple technologies or media with traditional face-to-face classroom activities. From a narrow sense of concept, it actually refers to a teaching trend that further integrates online teaching and classroom education. Internet online and offline teaching is shown in Fig. 2 below.

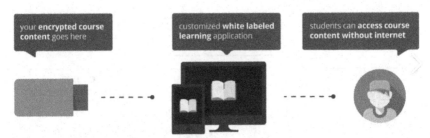

Fig. 2. F Internet online and offline teaching

Enriching and renovating various teaching activities, digitizing teaching resources, and developing and using online platforms are not the ultimate goals pursued by hybrid teaching. Their ultimate goal is to achieve a significant increase in the depth of learners' learning. On the premise that learning psychology can be recognized as a science, we can believe that certain learning rules and more convenient and effective learning methods and paths can be found in the dimension of learning. The superficial phenomena such as "teaching without fixed methods" and different disciplines cannot confuse us. From the perspective of learning psychology, the classification of learning content is clear, and there will be no changes. In terms of various types of learning, scientific laws are relatively fixed. Similarly, there must be laws to follow in the teaching of this type of content. At this time, the "teaching indeterminate method", contrary to our previous view of it, has become a surface formal problem, because various teaching methods have a certain logic to follow. Of course, in the actual teaching process, it is not always possible to carry out teaching according to the best conditions. We should adopt the most appropriate and optimized processing method based on the actual situation. In summary, in order to achieve learners' ability to enhance deep learning, we need to maximize the use of learning and teaching laws.

There are many problems in the traditional teaching of human resources management in Colleges and universities, such as single teaching content, slow updating speed, outdated cases and single teaching methods. Students have few opportunities to practice English, their self-learning ability cannot be effectively trained and improved, and their comprehensive language use ability cannot be trained at all. However, the traditional teaching method also has its advantages. For example, the communication between teachers and students in the traditional classroom is a very effective way of emotional interaction between teachers and students. The face-to-face communication, interaction, correction and reinforcement of teachers and students are more conducive to the timely and effective training of learning strategies and the timely evaluation and feedback of the results. In the "Internet+" environment, the use of Internet tools and methods can effectively solve these problems, obtain them more quickly, and promote the implementation of teaching more convenient and efficient. Teachers can also use various Internet tools to make rich and up-to-date case teaching courseware, and can use Internet communication tools to strengthen interaction with students and enrich the forms of teaching activities [7]. It can be said that "Internet+" has promoted the combination of online and offline teaching methods of human resources management in Colleges and universities. The advantages of the two methods are complementary, enriching the mixed teaching content of human resources management in Colleges and universities, and promoting the improvement of teaching effect. It is mainly reflected in the following aspects: ① the teaching tools provided by "Internet+" accelerate the production of teaching plans and courseware, break the traditional blackboard teaching, and update the teaching methods; ② "Internet+" makes teachers' teaching methods more colorful. With the development of information technology, a variety of teaching methods have emerged, such as mooching and flipping class; ③ "Internet+" breaks the boundaries of time and space, so that teaching is no longer limited to the classroom, so that learners can start learning at any place and at any time, so as to promote teaching communication between teachers and students, and enable teaching feedback to be obtained more quickly to improve teaching effect [8].

2.3 Course Teaching Mode

Guided by job needs, closely adhering to professional ability needs, and promoting the "121" teaching model of "one main line, two realities, and one cooperation". "One main line" refers to taking vocational application ability as the main line and running through the entire teaching process; "Two Realities" refers to the construction of consistency between students' school learning situations and actual work situations based on simulated reality and work task reality; "One Cooperation" That is, schools cooperate with enterprises, establish a school-enterprise cooperation base, and organize students to go deep into the enterprise to conduct practical work. Design and innovate teaching models based on different learning scenarios to effectively implement the action oriented "121" teaching model of work-study alternation, task driven, project oriented, classroom and internship location integration. The teaching of this course, regardless of the selection of course content or the organization of teaching content, always revolves around the main line of cultivating application ability, integrating teaching into the solution of practical work tasks, highlighting the applicability of the knowledge learned, and cultivating students' practical operation ability.

This course system is divided into six modules, with projects under the modules and scenarios subdivided under the projects. Each knowledge module is divided into projects based on actual work tasks and work processes, and on the basis of dividing the projects, teaching is organized into teaching scenarios. The practical training projects submitted to students in the course teaching scenarios are carefully organized and selected based on various key points from human resource management. Each scenario is closely related to actual human resource management, truly reflecting the professional application ability needs of the position.

This course implements the concept of combining work and learning in teaching, and the teaching process is no longer limited to the classroom. Instead, it organizes teaching with real work tasks. Combining theory with practice, combining work with learning, and using flexible learning to build a bridge between schools and enterprises for employment.

One cooperation refers to the cooperation between schools and enterprises, the signing of school-enterprise cooperation agreements, and the establishment of internship and training bases. This cooperation mainly focuses on lectures given by enterprises to schools, and internships offered by students to enterprises. Students conduct research on enterprises under the guidance of teachers, participate in curriculum construction, select curriculum content, and formulate curriculum standards.

3 Internet Based "Online and Offline" Human Resource Management Teaching Mode

3.1 Human Resources Management Mechanism

The so-called human resource management mechanism refers to the "competitive elimination mechanism", "constraint mechanism", "incentive mechanism" and "traction mechanism" of human resources. Human resource management mechanism is an idea. The essence of this idea is to reveal the human resource management system through the mechanism of various elements, so as to integrate the human resources of enterprises. In order to fully express the effect and state of human resource management after enterprise integration from different dimensions, and to improve the core talent competitiveness of enterprises, it is necessary to fully understand and apply the human resource management mechanism [9]. From the perspective of human resource management mode development, it not only includes the intellectual development of human resources, but also covers moral awareness or the ideological and cultural quality of human resources; It is not only to give full play to the existing human resources, but also to fully tap their potential. From the perspective of management, it is not only necessary to build a training system, but also involves the prediction and analysis of human resources development.

The main contents of the human resources management mechanism include the following six aspects:

Fifth, performance management. The purpose of performance management is to evaluate the matching degree and contribution degree of employees in different positions. By evaluating the work achievements of employees in different positions at different stages, the purpose of employees' growth incentive is realized, so as to achieve the comprehensive improvement of the performance of employees, departments and the whole enterprise [10].

Fifth, labor relations. Labor relations mainly refer to the relationship between employees and enterprises in terms of employment and employment. With the continuous development of economy and society, human resource management mechanism is also experiencing continuous development and innovation. Not only that, the practical application of innovative human resource management mechanism is also constantly strengthened and deepened. The innovation and application of enterprise human resource management mechanism should be based on the innovation of employment mechanism, talent incentive and training mechanism. Through the continuous development of information management, technological reform and scientific innovation human resource management mechanisms, the enterprise's human resource management will eventually achieve the improvement of strategic management level.

3.2 Basic Model of Online and Offline Human Resource Management Teaching Mode

The teaching design of human resources management courses in Colleges and universities can make the teaching process or mode more suitable for the development needs of students, stimulate students' interest in learning, make students love learning, and harvest growth.

The basic model of teaching design in this study (as shown in Fig. 3) is mainly designed from three aspects. The first is the design of pre class questions, which mainly involves the analysis of teaching materials and learning conditions by teachers and the design of questions. Then there is the problem-solving in the class, mainly including the problem-solving, problem analysis and problem-solving. Finally, after-school problem development, which is mainly for teachers to assign new learning tasks to students according to the contents of chapters, students to analyze and solve problems and submit reports, and teachers to give ordinary grades.

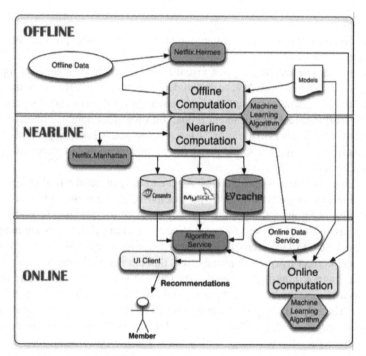

Fig. 3. Internet "online and offline" human resource management teaching mode

The core of the online and offline teaching mode is the design of teaching problems. The whole teaching process will focus on the analysis and solution of problems. First of all, teachers need to systematically analyze the knowledge points of the course before teaching to confirm the applicable teaching methods for each part. Understand the characteristics of students, analyze how to effectively show the course content to students, and how to improve students' interest in learning. Then, according to the learning content, think about the ways and situations to show the problems to the students.

Teachers should clarify teaching objectives and inform students before launching new courses. Teaching objectives include knowledge objectives, skills objectives and emotional objectives. And should be set according to the teaching content. On the basis of clarifying the teaching objectives, teachers should also clarify the key and difficult points of curriculum teaching, so that students can have a plan for learning.

How to design situational display is very important. For example, ask questions through cases and let students think about solutions in the situations specified in the cases; Through role play, let students think about how to solve problems in their own roles; Using game teaching to mobilize students' learning mood, improve students' participation and learning enthusiasm, and reduce the difficulty of students' understanding of abstract and empty concepts and theories in the textbooks; Through the situation simulation, the participating students can truly show how to solve the real problems.

4 Two Kinds of Instructional Design

Online Teaching

The instructional design will arrange the introduction, learning objectives, and the introduction process online.

Introduction: The teacher imports visual resources such as interesting topics and pictures through teaching software, so that students' learning initiative can be maximized, thereby increasing learners' interest in classroom learning. This has great significance in subsequent learning, making sufficient preparation for classroom teaching, and online learning can enable learners to use suitable learning methods Choose appropriate learning time to complete teaching tasks, and gain a deeper understanding of your own problems and shortcomings.

Determination of teaching objectives: After carefully planned introduction, teachers propose achievable objectives from the perspective of learners, through which learners can clarify the key points, difficulties, and key cores of the content. Teachers propose learning goals in the classroom in order to solve learning difficulties encountered in the classroom face to face, classify and apply learning content in an orderly manner, and solve and correct learning thinking errors that learners fall into. This is a learning process of advanced thinking. The goal is the top priority, which is the main body of all subsequent work and the basis for the design of activities at each stage.

Pre test: The effect of the pre test session is to focus on learners' difficulties in certain specific knowledge and skills. On the one hand, teachers can design corresponding test questions to prepare for teaching on this basis. On the other hand, they can enable learners to understand their difficulties in learning and the key points of future learning, and give them a clear positioning. Focused questions refer not only to the key and difficult points in objective conditions (cultural knowledge), but also to some problems in subjective conditions (learners themselves), all of which should be discovered during autonomous online learning. This process allows learners to recall previously mastered or deepen previously blurred knowledge points, thereby learning to consolidate. The main purpose of our online teaching activities is to focus on learners' problems, thereby better improving the efficiency of the classroom teaching process. Online teaching activities related to the introduction, goal, and pretest of BOPPPS greatly facilitate the arrangement of follow-up work.

Offline Teaching

In the specific teaching design process, the participatory learning, post test, and summary links are arranged into the offline learning process. Participatory learning:

Classroom teaching is the key to learners' learning. It is important to effectively use this time to give learners simple and necessary knowledge and skills, and to be able to make reasonable use of the skills "wealth" in their hands. Compared to pre class introductions, goals, and pretests, during these steps in the classroom, teachers and learners can interact face-to-face. Teachers can adjust the content and progress of the next teaching based on learners' understanding of the goals and pretests. In the classroom, learners are divided into groups for discussion, in which they learn about the thinking habits of others, learn from each other based on their own cognition, broaden their thinking, and solve problems in a diverse manner. This premise is based on effective discussions on commonly familiar content, so teachers need to specify learning objectives or content before discussing. When encountering difficult problems beyond the scope of learners' cognition and abilities, teachers need to gradually guide and digest the learners, understand the key issues, and guide them to form rigorous thinking habits. Learning to organize the learning content and find the key to the problem is the focus of learning.

Post test: The post test is also very important in the learning process. After leading the learners to complete the learning of the classroom content, the teacher guides the learners to complete the exercises related to the content of this section. Through the learners' problem-solving status, it can be known how well the learners master the content. This is an acceptance of the learners' learning achievements to see if the learning objectives have been achieved. Based on the learners' mastery, arrangements will be made after class, Either review and consolidate the pre class content to deepen the impression or assign homework after class to continue with the exercises.

Summary: At the end of the class, there is no shortage of summary, which is very necessary. Sorting out the knowledge points, key and difficult points of this content, and mentioning the goals again can better deepen the impression of the learners. It can also allow the learners to discuss first, while the teacher is making supplements, so that the effect of active learning is better.

5 Conclusion

The incomplete teaching materials and teaching equipment required by online and offline mode teaching have an impact on the development of online and offline mode teaching of human resources management in Colleges and universities to a certain extent. Colleges and universities will establish supporting training rooms, improve corresponding teaching equipment, develop new resources and other measures to provide strong support for the development of online and offline teaching. Or the current situation can be improved through the transformation of existing equipment. For example, the training room can be built into a real human resource management work scene, equipped with the equipment required for the post and the resources for simulation work, so that students can practice and learn new knowledge in the actual post. Therefore, enterprise experts, teachers with rich practical experience and teachers with human resources management experience are organized to jointly develop and compile supporting teaching materials to further improve the industry and enterprise databases required for online and offline mode teaching. The compilation of teaching materials should closely follow the needs of the current enterprise development, and integrate the theoretical knowledge and practical operation of human resources management. At the same time, it calls on the state to support the human resources management and teaching resources of colleges and universities.

References

1. Wang, J., Li, Q., Chen, M.: Mixed method research on technological teaching system based on human resource management practices (HRMP): study pertaining to majors in nursing undergraduate programme. Technol. Invest. **13**(2), 13 (2022)
2. Li, L., Zhang, C.: Teaching quality evaluation method of human resource management based on big data. In: Fu, W., Liu, S., Dai, J. (eds.) eLEOT. LNICSSITE, vol. 390, pp. 341–353. Springer, Cham (2021). https://doi.org/10.1007/978-3-030-84386-1_28
3. Long, J., Yuan, H., Zhang, J., et al.: Research and practice of online and offline mixed classroom teaching of pathology based on computer technology. J. Phys. Conf. Ser. **1744**(3), 032127 (2021)
4. Liu, Q., Jiang, Y.: Application of online and offline teaching mode in the course of "embedded system" under the background of internet. J. Phys. Conf. Ser. **1992**(4), 042023 (2021). (6pp)
5. Research on online and offline blended teaching mode of digital signal processing based on smart classroom. Creat. Educ. Stud. **09**(3), 565–569 (2021)
6. Korová, E., Afránková, J.M.: Teaching new trends in human resources management at university. Int. J. Teach. Educ. **10**, 1–65 (2022)
7. Hendy, N.T.: The effectiveness of technology delivered instruction in teaching Human Resource Management. Int. J. Manage. Educ. **19**(2), 100479 (2021)
8. Chung, C.-H., Lin, Y.Y.: Online 3D gamification for teaching a human resource development course. J. Comput. Assist. Learn. **38**(3), 692–706 (2022)
9. Zhou, Y.: Mobile information system for English teaching based on edge computing and VR. Mobile Inf. Syst. **2021**, 1–9 (2021). https://doi.org/10.1155/2021/9741244
10. Wu, C.: Effect of online and offline blended teaching of college English based on data mining algorithm. J. Inf. Knowl. Manage. **21**(Supp02) (2022)

Basic Database and Integrated Management Service Platform of Preschool Education Based on Cloud Computing

Yufei Zhou[✉]

Yunnan University of Business Management, Anning 650300, Yunnan, China
58255353@qq.com

Abstract. The computer is increasingly becoming an important part of children's learning and living environment. On the contrary, the lag of preschool education in informatization level hinders children's development. Cloud computing, as a rapidly developing emerging industry, provides a good platform for preschool education to keep up with the development of the times. Cloud computing separates computing from storage, which enables many users to share and use the same basic resources. As the focus of today's society, cloud computing is playing an increasingly important role in the development of all fields of society, and is regarded as the core of the new generation of information technology reform and business application mode reform. In the 12th Five Year Plan, the management and construction of early childhood education is an important topic. This paper will introduce the implementation of preschool education resource management platform and explore the construction of preschool education resource management platform under cloud computing mode. The platform mainly includes five modules: user management module, view resource module, search resource module, upload resource module and download resource module. Preschool education is related to the national quality education infrastructure. Under the background of the increasing development of information technology, the construction of teaching resource database of preschool education obviously lags behind the needs of social development. The realization of preschool education resource management platform provides a better educational environment for preschool education.

Keywords: Cloud computing · Preschool education · Comprehensive management services

1 Introduction

The development of preschool education in China is in good condition, attracting many scientific research institutes and enterprises to join, studying from different aspects of education and teaching resources and methods, and introducing many advanced technologies, such as Internet, cloud computing, big data and so on. The universal implementation of the comprehensive two-child policy not only promotes the vigorous development of the number of preschool education institutions, but also puts forward higher

Y. Zhang and N. Shah (Eds.): BigIoT-EDU 2023, LNICST 583, pp. 385–392, 2024.
https://doi.org/10.1007/978-3-031-63139-9_41

requirements for their service quality. The increase in the number of preschool children will inevitably lead to an increase in the gap of preschool teachers and the shortage of high-quality preschool education resources [1]. From the current situation of preschool education teachers in China, on the one hand, the number of preschool teachers is growing rapidly, on the other hand, there are a large number of preschool teachers without professional training, low educational level, and serious imbalance between quantity and quality. Children in kindergarten are young, and they have strong curiosity about all new things. In addition, preschool education is the fastest stage for children to receive knowledge and cultivate children's cognition. Therefore, the design of educational activities in kindergartens should be updated in time. Only in this way can we meet the needs of children's development and improve the existence value of kindergartens [2].

The Internet of Things, big data, cloud computing and artificial intelligence are the latest directions of today's science and technology frontier, which are valued and supported by government departments at all levels, and become key projects supported and developed by governments at all levels. Not only that, the acquisition of parenting knowledge of preschool children's parents, the sharing of parenting experience, the improvement of kindergarten education quality and the professional development of teachers are increasingly relying on computer networks [3]. The application of computer technology plays an important role in building a learning society. Because the state and local governments' investment in preschool education is far less than that in quality education and other fields of education, the information technology level of preschool education is far lower than that in various fields of education at all levels, which is not suitable for the development of the times. Cloud computing is a computing model, which has made great progress at home and abroad. The outline of the national medium and long term education reform and development plan for one year emphasizes that information technology has a revolutionary impact on education development and must be highly valued [4]. In the national 12th Five Year Plan, the management and construction of early childhood education is an important topic. After a lot of research and combined with specific practical application, the construction of early childhood education resource management platform has been realized. Cloud computing provides a rapid development opportunity for pre-school education with tight funds because of its advantages such as low cost, high performance, super computing power and super large storage capacity.

2   Cloud Computing

2.1   Definition of Cloud Computing

Before introducing the concept of cloud computing, we must first introduce grid technology, which is the predecessor of cloud computing model. The development of grid computing has a history of more than ten years. The emergence of grid computing was originally to solve the new computing mode of complex scientific computing. It made full use of the sharing advantages of the Internet, organized computers scattered in different geographical locations, and divided large tasks into many small tasks to run in parallel on different computers. Each computer involved in it is a node, and the whole computing is carried out by a grid composed of thousands of nodes. This computing method is called grid computing [5]. The design and development of preschool education resource management platform based on cloud computing, first of all, is to build a preschool education resource management platform, which is designed and developed for preschool teachers in kindergartens and provides them with shared, fast and effective preschool education resources. The platform mainly includes five modules: user management module, view resource module, search resource module, upload resource module and download resource module. The user management module manages users who can log in and use the platform, including kindergarten teachers in various kindergartens. They can search, view, upload and download preschool education resources on the platform, as well as system administrators. In addition to searching, viewing, uploading and downloading preschool education resources on the platform, they can also manage the permissions of other users [6]. Due to the lack of commercial implementation of grid computing, its computing power, equipment overhead, idle resources and other problems make it difficult to apply on a large scale. Figure 1 shows a database service responder based on redirection mode.

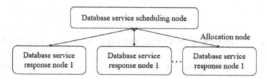

Fig. 1. Database Service Responder

2.2 Design Requirements of Cloud Service Management Platform

The cloud database service management platform is a platform for providing database services to users. Users can customize their own services according to their needs, such as service duration, space size, etc. if users need to use these services, they need to sign corresponding contracts with the service provider, and can use the services in the platform only after paying successfully. According to the actual requirements, this section analyzes the functional and performance requirements of the cloud database service management platform. View resources module: after logging in successfully, users can view the preschool education resources on the platform. Resources include TXT text format, MP3 format, word format, SWF video format, JPG picture format, etc. [7]. The platform provides online viewing function, which enables online viewing of resources in any format. The cloud database service management system is generated according to the user's database service requirements. The cloud service management platform provides database services externally and uses basic services internally. The design process needs to focus on two services: database service and basic service. Cloud service management platform needs to have effective representation and management of database services and basic services. Cloud computing infrastructure cluster is very powerful, so it can provide large-scale storage space for preschool education majors. To build the teaching resource base of preschool education specialty based on cloud computing, it is necessary to set up basic equipment, cloud platform and server-side applications in the cloud. Unified and coordinated management through the school's cloud management platform to provide efficient services for users. Figure 2 is a block diagram of the service dispatching center.

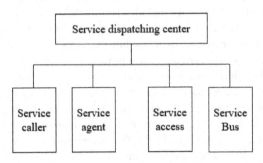

Fig. 2. Service dispatch center

2.3 Management Strategies of Service Management System Without Database

The research of service management strategy in cloud computing mainly focuses on the realization mode of multi-tenant services, effective allocation of virtual services to physical resources, service monitoring, storage of service monitoring data, description of service level agreements, directory management of services, calling services according to service requirements and system load method based on request verification, etc. Cloud computing applications using basic service management strategies generally include the following four main components: service directory; Service monitoring component; Service scheduling component; Manage database components. The application of cloud computing technology in database construction can increase teaching service resources, save the cost of software and hardware for ordinary users, provide conditions for resource pool managers to quickly integrate resources and improve the quality of resource pool construction. In order to dig deep into users' behavior of using teaching resource database, we should pay attention to the contribution, acquisition and exchange of teaching resources on the surface of customers' inquiry, so we should provide experiential services. Virtualization is an important technology of cloud computing, which is widely used in cloud computing data center. This kind of virtual network community construction provides conditions for users to directly build teaching resource database. Put forward performance and security requirements for multi tenant mechanism, service invocation strategy, service life cycle management process and service invocation process [8]. In order to ensure the performance of database service, two performance requirements are put forward: high availability; Simplicity and ease of use. Data security has always been a key issue worthy of attention in database systems. Due to the loose coupling service mode for a large number of users, cloud database puts forward more requirements for data security: multi tenant data isolation; Data failure processing.

3 Construction of Teaching Resource Database for Preschool Education Specialty Based on Cloud Computing

At present, there are many types of preschool education institutions in China, and a diversified pattern of public parks as a model, schools run by social forces as the main body, and multi-ownership kindergartens and preschool training institutions developing together has been initially formed. The development of kindergarten education activities mainly depends on some auxiliary equipment. Without perfect equipment, teachers can only convey some knowledge to children by preaching. However, due to the limited learning ability of young children, they can't understand this knowledge from the teacher's explanation. As a result, the smooth development of preschool education is seriously affected, and it is difficult to guarantee educational activities. In this case, parents will lose confidence in kindergarten, and the number of kindergarten students will be affected. This will form a vicious circle, which is not conducive to the sustainable development of kindergartens. The entry of private capital into preschool education industry helps to solve the problem of "difficulty in entering the park", but it also faces the problem of the conflict between capital profit seeking and educational public welfare. Public parks and public parks will also lead to insufficient or unfair allocation of educational resources due to government failure [9]. Preschool education is a kind of trust. It is difficult for parents to know the quality of service in advance. Only after experience can they know the quality of service; For preschool education consumers and third parties, a unified observation point is needed to observe and measure in order to accurately judge and verify the quality of preschool education; For the preschool institutions themselves, if they want to improve the efficiency of operation and management and improve the service quality, they need a scientific service system to improve the internal governance.

In the cloud database service management system, the database service DBS is a triple $DBS(DEXPR, DLF, DSI)$.

Where DEXPR represents the organization form of database services, which is the representation of database services in cloud database. It can be expressed as:

$$DEXPR = (INTER, CONS, ENTI, SLB, SPACK) \qquad (1)$$

INTER represents the interface of the database, CONS represents the service contract, ENTI represents the service entity, SLB represents the business logic representation of the service, and SPACK represents the representation of the service in the bus service container.

$$INTER = (JDBC, WEB) \qquad (2)$$

JDBC and WEB are two service interfaces of cloud database.

The basic service IBS in the cloud database service management system is a triple:

$$IBS(IEXPR, ILF, ISI) \qquad (3)$$

Among them, IEXPR represents the organizational form of basic services, ILF represents the life cycle of basic services, and ISF represents the use strategy of basic services.

The system service platform is provided by the cloud computing service provider, and the knowledge theme framework is established by the senior education experts of the school. It can save the space of resource library and provide users with efficient and lightweight services. Collaboration refers to the business collaboration between teaching resource databases. It can greatly save investment and time, and facilitate the application and promotion of cloud computing technology in the resource database. Users can accept real-time digital shared courses through wireless digital mobile devices. In the cloud computing environment, to improve the construction effect of preschool education resource database, we should establish personal files for users. Cloud computing can analyze the laws and key preferences of users' interest resource database, establish information records, create users' personalized use logs, and then sort out and analyze users' personalized behavior characteristics, so as to provide services more accurately and efficiently. The development and realization of the preschool education resource management platform adopts MVC design pattern, adopts B/S mode, users access the system through browsers and carry out corresponding operations, and the system development applies java language and SSH three framework technologies. Struts mainly focuses on the management and development of visual layers, and a large number of business operations in the system are placed in the business logic layer, and the business logic layer is designed by Spring framework. Mysql database is used in the background. The operation of business generally needs to operate the database, and the persistence layer based on Hibernate framework is used in the business layer and data layer [10]. The system architecture is shown in Fig. 3. Public cloud is a technical model in which cloud service providers provide resources to various organizations through the Internet. Users only need to pay for computing resources, and do not need to buy and install related operation and maintenance servers and other equipment, so it is cheap and easy to operate.

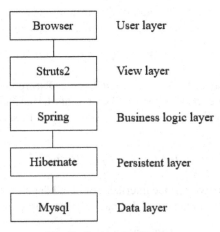

Fig. 3. System Architecture

It is the internal cloud model of a private cloud unit, which refers to the technical construction data center of a unit based on cloud computing, which embodies the comprehensive application of virtual technology, and is also the main form of the school cloud computing model. The construction cost of private cloud is relatively high, because the upfront funds such as equipment and technology have to be invested, and the use and maintenance costs have to be paid. The core data inside the school can transmit network information on campus, and process and store preschool education resources on private cloud, thus ensuring the security of internal confidential resources. The innovation of preschool education mainly comes from teachers' reflection and summary. Only when preschool teachers find problems in educational activities and reflect on them can they realize the innovation of preschool education. However, after investigation, it is found that most kindergarten teachers are graduates of secondary vocational schools and higher vocational colleges. Their professional ability is insufficient, and they lack innovative consciousness and innovative ability in educational activities. This will not only fail to achieve teaching innovation, but also seriously affect the teaching effect of preschool education. The public cloud can provide resources for multiple campuses at the same time, realize the multi school sharing of preschool education professional resources, and improve the utilization of resources. Generally, private cloud and public cloud can be used comprehensively to build a hybrid cloud. Sensitive and confidential information can be processed internally. There is an internal cloud. The rest can be put on the public cloud to share with other colleges and universities, reduce the use cost and optimize the utilization effect of resources, so as to achieve the ideal model of cloud computing to build the teaching resource database of preschool education specialty.

4 Conclusions

After the personal computer revolution and the Internet revolution, cloud computing is regarded as the third IT wave and an important part of China's strategic emerging industries. It will bring about fundamental changes in life, production mode and business model, and cloud computing will become the focus of the whole society at present. In this paper, cloud computing and the construction of teaching resource database for preschool education specialty are studied. As a new computing mode, cloud computing provides virtual resource space and super computing power for data computing and storage management, which enables users to enjoy services cheaply, efficiently and flexibly. With its shared architecture mode, cloud computing connects a large number of preschool education resource information, realizes the cloud platform of preschool education resources, and provides a new way for the co construction, sharing and mutual knowledge of preschool education resources. In short, there are still many areas to be improved in the construction of cloud computing teaching resource database. Our preschool education teachers should scientifically integrate the teaching resources in the database, delete the fully inefficient resources on the premise of overall planning, classify the resources according to the teaching objectives and types, and focus on cloud computing, It provides an efficient and reasonable resource base for the modern teaching process of preschool education.

References

1. Penghua, L.: The application of artificial intelligence in the management of primary and secondary schools and preschool education. Modern Commun. (2), 2 (2018)
2. Xiaomei, S.: Research on the construction plan of preschool education and teaching resource platform in the "Internet +" era. Inf. Technol. Inf. (3), 2 (2020)
3. Li, Z.: Research on the current situation and countermeasures of preschool education development. Sci. Educ. J. Electron. Ed. (4), 2 (2020)
4. Shanshan, X.: Application of cloud computing in archives management. North S. Bridge (18), 1 (2019)
5. Youyin, M., Qiping, M., Yan, M., et al.: Research on mathematical model of preschool education diagnosis in colleges and universities under the background of big data. Electron. World (1), 2 (2021)
6. Xiaomei, S.: Using "Internet +" to promote the information construction of preschool education. Comput. Telecommun. (3), 3 (2019)
7. Zhanxia, T.: Effective application of multimedia technology in early childhood education. Reading Writing: Early Years (3), 1 (2018)
8. Shanshan, W.: On the innovation and practice of kindergarten preschool education. Sci. Consult. (14), 1 (2020)
9. Ting, H.: Analysis of the importance of preschool education to the development of children's personality. Tomorrow (39), 1 (2019)
10. Dongqun, Z.: Analysis of the path of supply-side reform in preschool education. J. Shaanxi Preschool Teachers College **35**(9), 6 (2019)

Establish Efficient Education Management Data Warehouse System

Jin Chen[1(⊠)], Weimin Guo[1,2], and Xizhen Ai[2]

[1] Wuhan University of Technology, Wuhan 430070, China
ccjj123001@163.com
[2] Nanchang Institute of Science and Technology, Nanchang 330000, Jiangxi, China

Abstract. The information construction in the field of higher education continues to advance, and the value of business data such as teaching operation is required to be fully reflected. The study of curriculum evaluation based on education data analysis and the personalized management of undergraduate curriculum learning has theoretical significance and application value. At present, the management information system of many colleges and universities has been improved day by day, and all aspects of information has been recorded more and more comprehensively, such as some student achievement information, student status information, teachers' teaching information, teaching plans and other detailed information. But 80% of the information is simply stored in the database, and the potential information hidden in the data is idle and cannot be fully utilized. If we can reasonably use these data and dig out useful but often overlooked important information, or find out some rules formed with the dynamic changes of various factors, it will undoubtedly be of great help to the management decision-making of colleges and universities. So we put forward the idea of applying data warehouse technology to college teaching management. From this point of view, this paper sets up a university teaching management data warehouse system, analyzes the data with the corresponding data mining algorithm, finds the rules hidden in these data, and thus achieves the purpose of assisting teaching decision analysis.

Keywords: Education management · Data warehouse · data mining

1 Introduction

Since human civilization entered the era of rapid development of information technology, people have paid more and more attention to the important role played by computers in this process. In particular, its effective management of a large number of persistent, shared data that need to be stored in the database for a long time has brought people infinite convenience. Since the late 1960s, computers have been used for management on a larger and larger scale, with more and more applications, and the amount of data has increased dramatically. At the same time, the requirement for multiple applications and languages to share data sets with each other has become increasingly strong [1]. The

© ICST Institute for Computer Sciences, Social Informatics and Telecommunications Engineering 2024
Published by Springer Nature Switzerland AG 2024. All Rights Reserved
Y. Zhang and N. Shah (Eds.): BigIoT-EDU 2023, LNICST 583, pp. 393–403, 2024.
https://doi.org/10.1007/978-3-031-63139-9_42

price of hardware decreases, while the price of software increases. In terms of processing mode, online real-time processing requires more, and began to propose and consider distributed processing. In order to solve the needs of multi-user and multi application sharing data and make data serve as many applications as possible, database technology came into being, developed rapidly and was widely used. Hierarchical database management system and mesh database management system appeared. Especially in the 1970s, relational database became the mainstream of the market with its advanced non process language interface, good data independence and commercialized relationship DBMS [2]. Later, distributed database management system, object-oriented database management system, knowledge base system and so on appeared.

However, with the development and popularization of the Internet, data is growing at an exponential rate. In the face of massive data, the data query and report functions provided by the existing information management system (MIS) can no longer meet people's needs. In order to change the state of inflexibility of the system, new technologies are needed to extract valuable information from massive data to provide support for decision-makers, so as to completely change the situation of "rich data but poor knowledge" [3]. Data storage theory and data analysis technology oriented to decision support have been produced and widely used. This is the data warehouse technology, online analytical processing (OLAP) technology, and data mining (DMi) technology. The decision support system (DSS) based on this technology was born, and went deep into various fields, such as economy, scientific research, and education. Many enterprises and institutions have established their own data warehouse systems. Colleges and universities are important bases for teaching and scientific research, as well as important places for training talents. If you want to handle a large amount of data information reasonably and efficiently, you must establish a complete data warehouse system.

The construction of "golden courses" in colleges and universities deployed by the Ministry of Education, that is, the construction of first-class courses, is related to the construction effect of the basic unit of talent cultivation of first-class majors and the success or failure of first-class undergraduate education. Curriculum evaluation is a powerful grasp of curriculum construction, and the results of curriculum evaluation can better provide curriculum practice for college education. To this end, the Ministry of Education has formulated a curriculum evaluation index system that includes teaching team, teaching content, teaching resources and other dimensions. Understanding the relationship between evaluation indicators can provide effective support for the educational management decision-making of colleges and universities. Data-driven management and decision-making is a useful supplement and extension of the traditional model-driven or process-driven decision-making paradigm.

At present, due to the strong support of the state and relevant departments for the construction of educational informatization, most colleges and universities have introduced teaching management systems to enable college students to learn online and offline. These systems more or less preserve the data left by students in the process of use. With the increase of the number of students and the cumulative number of times of use, these data are growing exponentially, It creates opportunities for analyzing online learning behavior of college students. In addition, educational administrators and educational researchers have become very important in analyzing students' online learning behaviors. The differences in online learning behaviors of college students may indirectly affect their grades. Through studying the online learning behaviors of students in a school of economics and management, such as signing in before class, discussing in class, watching video preview before class, and other behaviors, we can find out the specific behavior patterns of college students, Study the relationship between these behavior patterns and their performance. According to the above results, students with learning difficulties should be found in time, given academic early warning, and help teaching management personnel to intervene in students' learning behavior, so as to help students graduate smoothly.

For different learners and researchers, the significance of educational data mining is very different: learners' attention to data mining can help them understand their learning level, learning efficiency and learning results in a timely manner; Educators are more hopeful that data mining can bring convenience to their work, such as more objective teaching feedback, learners' understanding of the teaching content, which can be used as a reference to adjust their teaching plans and teaching content, and to predict whether their teaching objectives are achieved by predicting learners' achievements. To sum up, the mining of educational data can not only promote efficient learning, but also play a significant role in improving the quality of courses, and is of great significance for the development of education.

2 Related Work

2.1 Research Status at Home and Abroad

In foreign countries, data warehouse has become another technology hotspot after Internet. Large enterprises are almost establishing their own data warehouses, and database manufacturers have also launched their own data warehouse solutions. At present, the data warehouse application systems established and used by foreign enterprises have achieved obvious economic benefits, showing strong vitality in the market competition. In China, some large enterprises have also implemented data warehouse plans, and some successful data warehouse application examples have emerged. There are many mature data warehouse products abroad. All major companies have successively launched their own products, such as Microsoft's Analysis Services, Informix's OLAP product Meta Cube, Oracle's Designer/2000 and Discover/2000, and Sybase IQ, which have been successfully applied to enterprise management and decision support, and are increasingly improving with the continuous use [4].

With the development of data warehouse, OLAP and decision support system technology, decision support is more and more widely used in data intensive industries. The application of decision support technology in banking, finance, telecommunications, insurance and other industries with a high degree of informatization in China has become increasingly mature. Most of them have developed their own decision support systems and obtained good economic benefits. The decision support system based on data warehouse is a specific application of data warehouse technology. Many foreign companies have established such application systems. According to the investigation and research of foreign META groups, data warehouse technology has a very broad application prospect in the financial industry, manufacturing industry, trade industry and social services [5]. The research on DSS in China began in the mid-1980s, especially after 1985. The introduction of DSS research topics, various practical systems and a few successful cases has increasingly appeared in relevant publications and reports. In recent years, China has made great progress in applying data warehouse technology to decision support [6].

Compared with foreign countries, China's colleges and universities started relatively late in the field of educational research and invested relatively little. However, with the attention paid to higher education by the state and relevant education departments, more support has been given to project research in education related fields. In recent years, many fields have introduced machine learning, data mining, artificial intelligence and other technologies. Although machine learning technology and artificial intelligence have been applied in many fields, their development in the field of education is very slow, mainly because of the different requirements for the application of educational data in different universities. Nevertheless, many researchers have analyzed and studied education data according to different needs, and have made great progress. Domestic scholars often use decision tree algorithm, naive Bayes and other machine learning algorithms when analyzing educational data, and have achieved good results. For example, Ren et al. improved the frequent item set generation of Apriori algorithm through the view, analyzed the teaching evaluation data line, and found that education, professional title and teaching age affect the course quality. Li et al. verified the feasibility of outlier detection algorithm in educational data research by using outlier detection algorithm to analyze teaching evaluation data. Guo et al. filtered the strong rules generated by Apriori algorithm by adding interest degree, and analyzed the scores of different courses using the improved Apriori algorithm, and found that there was a certain correlation between the courses. Li Yan 'analyzed the data of more than 1000 people and 20 courses in his college by building a data warehouse, and analyzed the students' grades related to those factors through the decision tree algorithm. The relatively accurate analysis showed that the factors such as course type and major have a great impact on the learning results. By establishing a data warehouse, Liu Chunyang analyzed college students' scores, and concluded that the teaching effect has a certain relationship with the gender of teachers and students. When the gender of teachers and students is the same, most students' scores are better. When Li Xiaolin excavates, analyzes and studies the academic achievements of college students, he carries out a preliminary understanding of the achievement data through the overall distribution characteristics of the achievements, finds out the comprehensive influencing factors, and analyzes the main factors affecting the achievements of college students according to the decision tree.

2.2 Data Warehouse Definition and Characteristics

With the continuous development of the Internet, the data in various fields are growing exponentially, which provides a good data base for data analysis in this paper. However, people's use of data is mostly limited to statistics, query and other aspects, and cannot further find the intrinsic value information. People urgently need a technology that can help them get deeper information, and data mining technology has been applied and promoted.

Data mining is the process of revealing potentially useful information and knowledge hidden in many data by using a specific means from the data generated by practical applications. Data mining has greatly changed the way people used data in the past. It has changed the way people use pre-designed schemes for data analysis in daily life. Through direct search of data, they can find hidden value information, as shown in Fig. 1.

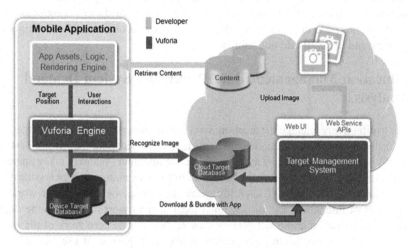

Fig. 1. The process of data mining

Data Warehouse is a subject oriented, integrated, non volatile, time variant data set used to support management decisions. We can understand the concept of data warehouse from two levels. First, data warehouse is used to support decision-making and is oriented to analytical data processing, which is different from the existing operational databases of enterprises; Secondly, the data warehouse is an effective integration of multiple heterogeneous data sources [7]. After integration, it is reorganized according to the theme and contains historical data, and the data stored in the data warehouse is generally not modified. In addition to the sharing, integrity and data independence of the traditional database management system, the data warehouse has the following four characteristics:

(1) Theme oriented. The data organization of operational database is oriented to transaction processing tasks, and each business system is separated from each other, while the data in the data warehouse is subject oriented. The topic is an abstract concept, which integrates, classifies and analyzes the data in the enterprise information system at a higher level, and corresponds to the analysis object involved in a macro analysis field in the enterprise. The data organized based on the theme is divided into independent fields, each of which has its own logical connotation and does not intersect.

(2) Integrated. Transaction oriented operational databases are usually related to some specific applications. Data are independent and often heterogeneous. The data to be managed by the data warehouse is distributed in multiple databases and involves multiple applications. Therefore, the data warehouse should collect and organize

these decentralized, cross platform, heterogeneous operational data, and systematically process, summarize and sort them on the basis of extraction and cleaning. After unification and integration, it can eliminate the inconsistency in the source data and ensure that the information in the data warehouse is consistent global information about the entire enterprise, That is, standardize the source data.

(3) Not updatable. The data in the operational database is usually updated in real time, and the data changes in time as required [8]. The data of the data warehouse is mainly used for enterprise decision analysis. The data operations involved are mainly data queries, and generally do not modify.

3 Education Management Data Warehouse System Demand Analysis

In order to effectively manage the teaching work, most universities have established their own educational information management systems. The teaching data warehouse system in this paper is mainly aimed at the teaching management system of a key university in China. In recent years, the school has made full use of mature and rich educational network resources in teaching, scientific research, management and other work, and used a series of interactive and professional local area networks to realize the digitalization, informatization and intelligence of the school. As the core work of the school, the educational administration management is ahead of the rest. It uses the advanced technical means of information management to achieve the close integration of students, teachers and management personnel and greatly improve the quality of comprehensive education. In the years of accumulation and construction, the school has built a relatively complete educational administration management system, which has realized strict process management of student status management, course scheduling management, course selection management, scientific research management, score management, examination management, teaching evaluation, teacher management, information query, graduate review, etc., greatly relieving the pressure of the management department [9]. At the same time, it also keeps a lot of detailed information about students' achievements, teachers' teaching information and teaching plans. These data truly reflect the teaching situation of the school, which can be used to query various information within the educational administration system (for example, it can give the information about the students who failed or had excellent grades in a certain course in a certain semester, and the student performance of a class taught by a teacher, etc.), and can also generate various statistical reports.

Association rules refer to the discovery of dependencies and correlations between things from a large number of seemingly unrelated data, which is used to discover the internal hidden relationship between things. It is proposed by researchers when studying shopping basket data. Association rules are also the case that multiple events have certain associations. If some specific events occur, other events can be predicted.

In the analysis of association rules, the two most commonly used indicators are support and confidence. Through these two indicators, we can determine which are strong association rules and which are weak association rules. The extraction of association rules also depends on the threshold of these two indicators. The design of the threshold has a great impact on the mining results. Next, we will introduce these two thresholds further.

Support is one of the metrics for association rule extraction. It reflects the proportion of the number of simultaneous transactions of X and Y in all transactions in the transaction database, that is, the frequency of the number of simultaneous transactions of X and Y in the transaction set, which is recorded as Support (X → Y). The calculation method is shown in formula (1):

$$Support(X \Rightarrow Y) = P(XY) = \frac{number(XY)}{number(D)} \tag{1}$$

The Apriori algorithm model can be roughly divided into the following parts: First, we need to extract all frequent itemsets that meet the mining conditions in the dataset by constructing the dataset; Then, mining the association rules that meet the minimum support and minimum confidence from all the frequent items that meet the conditions; Finally, the mining association rules are analyzed, and some guiding suggestions are put forward for the development of this field. The Apriori algorithm flowchart is shown in Fig. 2.

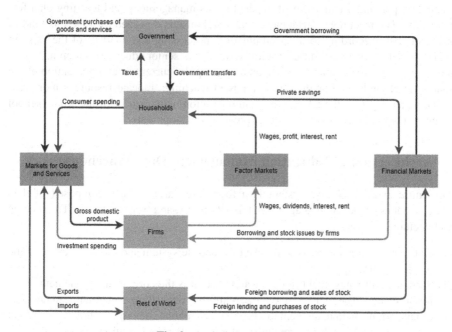

Fig. 2. Apriori algorithm flow

The key to talent cultivation is curriculum. The construction of "golden courses" in colleges and universities deployed by the Ministry of Education, that is, the construction of first-class courses, is related to the construction effect of the basic unit of talent cultivation of first-class majors and the success or failure of first-class undergraduate education. Curriculum evaluation is a powerful grip on curriculum construction, and the evaluation results can be used to guide the direction of curriculum construction and curriculum reform practice. To this end, the Ministry of Education has formulated a curriculum evaluation index system including teaching content, teaching team, teaching resources and other dimensions. Understanding the relationship between evaluation indicators can provide effective support for the educational management decision-making of colleges and universities. Data-driven management and decision-making is a useful supplement and extension of the traditional model-driven or process-driven decision-making paradigm. Data analysis and data mining provide management and decision-making technology for data-driven. By mining the course evaluation data, valuable knowledge can be extracted and the basis for decision-making of course management can be provided. Aiming at the curriculum evaluation in colleges and universities, the data-driven teaching management and decision-making issues are studied.

However, the school has not explored and utilized the value implied by these data (for example, it cannot find out what different characteristics the students who failed in the exam and had excellent grades have in what aspects, and how to reasonably suggest students who failed in the exam to improve their grades. It cannot find out what courses the excellent graduates learned that made them stand out in the employment army). Such saved data information is difficult to provide scientific basis for management decisions (including personnel management, student status management, and teaching plan formulation). The teaching management data warehouse is designed to solve this kind of problem [10]. According to the accumulation, processing and analysis of the existing transactional educational administration system data, senior educational administration management personnel can more accurately grasp the current teaching situation of the school, track and monitor the latest trends in teaching, allocate resources more reasonably and organize the educational administration management of the whole school compared with the history and trend of previous development.

4   Architecture of Education Management Data Warehouse

The entire data warehouse system is a four tiered architecture: composed of data sources, data storage and management, OLAP servers, and front-end tools. The specific architecture is shown in Fig. 3.

(1) Data source: it is the basis of the data warehouse system and the data source of the whole system.
(2) Storage and management of data warehouse: it is the core of the whole data warehouse system. The real key of data warehouse is data storage and management. The organization and management mode of data warehouse determines that it is different from traditional databases, and also determines its representation of external data.
(3) OLAP Server: Effectively integrate the data needed for analysis, and organize it according to multidimensional models for analysis. Its specific implementation can be divided into ROLAP, MOLAP and HOLAPl9'. ROLAP basic data and aggregate data are stored in RDBMS; Both types of MOLAP data are stored in the multidimensional database; The HOIAP basic data is stored in the RDBMS, and the aggregated data is stored in the multi-dimensional database.

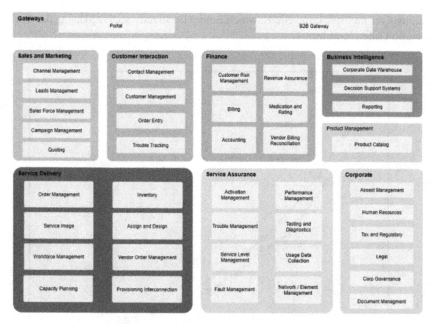

Fig. 3. Data warehouse architecture diagram

(4) Front end tools: mainly include various report tools, query tools, data analysis tools, data mining tools and various application development tools based on data warehouse or data mart. Among them, data analysis tools are mainly for OLAP server, report tools, and data mining tools are mainly for data warehouse.

In the original data collected by the questionnaire system, due to human factors, such as all positive or negative comments, this part of data has been deleted. Due to the influence of system or human factors when the questionnaire system collects data, the collection results of some indicators are missing, and the missing data items should not be deleted due to the limitations of the dataset. After analysis, it is found that some of the options appear more than 50% of the time, so this chapter adopts the mode filling method. After data processing, the number of records is 412, accounting for 98.1% of the sample data.

Apriori algorithm is mainly applicable to single-dimensional attribute value data. In other words, the attribute value of data can be seen as a simple form of whether A exists. However, in reality, data is often multidimensional, which means that Apriori algorithm cannot be directly used to mine association rules. According to the evaluation of national quality courses and the reform requirements of education and teaching, the first-level evaluation indicators, teaching team, teaching content and teaching conditions, etc., are designed. In order to more comprehensively express the first-level indicators, the second-level indicators need to be designed under the first-level indicators, including the course leader and lecturer, the structure and overall quality of teaching team, teaching reform and research, etc. However, the data collected according to the course evaluation index involves multiple dimensions, which cannot be directly analyzed using the Apriori association rule algorithm.

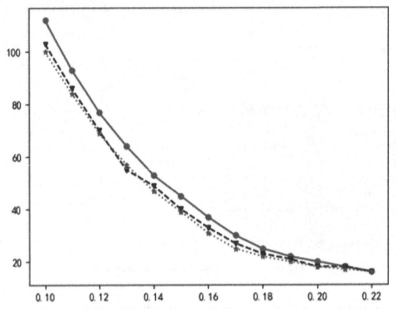

Fig. 4. Comparison of the number of rules extracted by three algorithms under different support levels

Figure 4 under the premise of setting the confidence and interest parameters, with the increase of support, the number of rules extracted by the improved Apriori algorithm initially decreased significantly compared with the traditional algorithm, and finally gradually approached. While the number of rules extracted by the improved Apriori algorithm is more than that of the Apriori algorithm with probability interest, the overall trend is still less than that of the Apriori algorithm with probability interest, It shows that Apriori algorithm with interest degree can reduce the generation of misleading rules, and Apriori algorithm with different interest degree can reduce the generation of misleading rules.

5 Conclusion

At present, data warehouse, OLAP and data mining technology are developing very rapidly, and they are applied in more and more industries. In recent years, with the continuous improvement of the level of teaching informatization in colleges and universities at home and abroad, teaching management has begun to develop towards standardization, informatization and networking. Decision makers and relevant researchers began to pay attention to the application of data warehouse, multidimensional analysis and data mining technology to analyze the historical data of teaching operation, improve teaching quality and guide teaching management. The main research goal of this paper is to use a large amount of data in the existing university management information system to build a teaching data warehouse system, improve the level of university informatization, mine hidden regular information, and support teaching management decisions.

References

1. Subanti, S., Rahmaningrum, A.: Establish efficient portofolio on LQ45 index using stochastic dominance. In: The Third International Conference on Mathematics: Education, Theory and Application (2021)
2. He, Q., Lu, L., Xu, X.: University sports information management system based on big data. J. Phys. Conf. Ser. **1881**(3), 032058 (2021)
3. Yang, Q., Cai, Y., Shen, L., et al.: Research on data management of power grid enterprises based on data middle platform. IOP Conf. Ser. Earth Environ. Sci. **714**(4), 042012 (2021). (5pp)
4. Wilbur, M., Pugliese, P., Laszka, A., et al.: Efficient data management for intelligent urban mobility systems (2021)
5. Tang, J.: Dimensional modeling method discussion for the profits from mineral rights transfer management. Modern Econ. Manag. Forum **3**(2), 81–88 (2022)
6. Hu, T.L.: Customizing pore system in a microporous metal-organic framework for efficient C2H2 separation from CO2 and C2H4. Molecules **27**, 5929 (2022)
7. Fitzsimon, J., Agrawal, S., Khade, K., et al.: A shapley value index for market basket analysis: efficient computation using an Harsanyi dividend representation. Int. Game Theory Rev. **24** (2022)
8. Danilov, M., Buinov, K., Lei, L., et al.: Efficient capacity management for a data storage system, US11093163B2[P] (2021)
9. Tang, M., Liu, T., Zhao, T., et al.: Establish a pharmaceutical emergency management system in China: lessons learned from the COVID-19. Int. J. Clin. Pharm. **6**, 43 (2021)
10. Zhang, X., Lin, D.: University education management system exploration and practice based on big data analysis from the perspective of humanism. J. Phys. Conf. Ser. **1744**(4), 042054 (2021). (4pp)

Design, Research and Practice of Blockchain Based Smart Education Cloud Platform

Lin Zhu[1(✉)], Ying Xu[2], Zheng Mei[3], and li Lu[3]

[1] Sias International University, Zhengzhou 451150, Henan, China
mashayingying@163.com
[2] Ningbo University of Finance and Economics, Ningbo 315100, Zhejiang, China
[3] College of General Education, Xi'an Eurasian University, Xi'an 710065, Shaan-Xi, China

Abstract. With the rapid development of the Internet industry and information technology, big data technology, artificial intelligence, blockchain technology, etc. have received extensive attention and research. The smart education cloud platform is an important part of the smart campus, in which the academic early warning module can conduct intelligent early warning for potential or existing academic problems. How to inform relevant personnel of the correct early warning information safely and efficiently has become an urgent problem to be solved. In the blockchain world, we have many education platforms under development. The main purpose of these platforms is to provide education and training for people who want to know about blockchain. However, there are some problems with these platforms, such as the high cost of using them because they charge for each video or course. They only provide video, but not other types of content, such as audio lectures, books, etc. This means that users must pay more if they want to get any additional information (such as audio lectures). These platforms do not allow users from all over the world.

Keywords: Wisdom education · Blockchain · Cloud platform

1 Introduction

Since the enrollment expansion of colleges and universities at the end of the last century, the number of students in colleges and universities across the country has increased rapidly, and the scale of colleges and universities has continued to expand. With the completion of the reform of the credit system in colleges and universities, students have been able to give full play to their autonomy in learning time and course selection. Even so, the problems caused by the sharp increase in the number of students are endless. Due to the uneven quality of students and the academic pressure after enrollment, a large number of students lack self-control, resulting in the problem students can not successfully complete their studies in this environment. "The relevant person in charge of the Department of Higher Education Students of the Ministry of Education once disclosed at the" Training Seminar on the Management Regulations of Students in General Higher Education "that the dropout rate of college students in China has risen to 2.6%". College

Y. Zhang and N. Shah (Eds.): BigIoT-EDU 2023, LNICST 583, pp. 404–415, 2024.
https://doi.org/10.1007/978-3-031-63139-9_43

students have more and more academic problems in the process of learning at school. This situation not only causes a waste of social resources, but also brings great trauma to the family. The most important thing is that it causes a decline in the quality of talent training. Now, the 5G era has come, and faster and faster technological innovation will continue to promote the sustainable development of the information revolution. The Internet of Things technology, Internet medical technology and VR technology will certainly change people's existing lifestyle. As these cutting-edge technologies enter our lives, massive data will be generated. In this context, the lifestyle and learning style of college students have also undergone tremendous changes. This will inevitably lead to a wider range of educational data sources, and also make qualitative changes in the types of data generated. Looking at the overall situation, the ecological environment based on campus big data has basically formed. In this new situation, how to make good use of these data and excavate the hidden information and value has become a hot research topic.

In order to solve the problem of remote data integrity verification, many experts and scholars have proposed many data integrity verification mechanisms according to different application backgrounds and security models in recent years. The data integrity verification mechanism can be divided into two types according to whether the fault-tolerant preprocessing is adopted: the proof of data possession (PDP) and the proof of data recovery (POR). PDP can quickly identify whether the data in cloud storage is damaged. POR can not only verify the integrity of data, but also recover the data whose integrity has been damaged. The audit work of the early verification mechanism is completed by the user himself, which makes the user bear heavy computing and communication costs. The introduction of the Third Party Auditor (TPA) replaces the user's audit of data, reducing the user's computational burden and communication overhead. Although the above methods have effectively solved the problem of data integrity verification in cloud storage, the following problems still exist. (1) The risk of collusion attack between TPA and cloud providers and data disclosure by third-party auditors. (2) When data is damaged, it is impossible to provide effective evidence to determine whether the cloud provider has damaged the data or whether malicious users have intentionally damaged the data in order to claim from the cloud provider. (3) When data integrity is damaged, effective proof cannot be provided to explain the extent of data damage or the size of data integrity damaged, and effective proof cannot be provided for claim.

With the gradual deepening of the research, it is found that after college students enter the campus, their learning habits and learning methods have changed greatly, and the self-management and autonomous learning mode are prominent. This situation not only makes the cultivation of college students face many problems, but also makes the management of students more complex and difficult. Therefore, the real-time tracking and feedback processing of college students' academic data has become the main issue of university management. In order to further improve the management efficiency and quality of colleges and universities and better serve students, the construction of smart campus is imminent [1].

The academic early warning system adopts a new college management mode of cooperation between students, parents and schools. The main goal is to find students with learning difficulties in time and develop assistance measures. Trying to solve the academic problems in the learning process can ultimately enable students to achieve the established quality objectives of talent training and help students successfully complete their studies [2].

Facing the problems encountered in college education, it is imperative to use information technology to solve these problems, which is also an inevitable way to scientifically improve the comprehensive quality of college students and achieve the established goal of talent training quality.

Smart education cloud platform is an important part of smart campus, and academic early warning module is the help of students combining information technology from the perspective of learning.

2   Related Work

2.1   Research Status

China's research on the integration of cloud computing and education mainly focuses on education science and computer science. The discipline of education science focuses on the concept of education cloud, overview of education cloud research, characteristics of education cloud ontology, classification and application mode of education cloud, etc. For example, Feng Jian described the architecture and basic characteristics of modern distance education based on cloud computing, analyzed the changes of distance education cloud on education and teaching methods, and made prospects for its deployment; Lu Beirong and others summarized the advanced features of the education cloud in terms of efficient infrastructure organization, sharing of educational resources, reducing R&D investment, saving management and operation costs, etc. [3].

Computer science is more concerned with the infrastructure and implementation technology of education cloud services. For example, Huang et al. proposed a cloud architecture model based on the shared content object reference model, which broke through the learning mode of traditional learning system solidification, and realized the unified storage and flexible distribution of educational resources such as courses and learning materials through the construction of content access middleware [4]; Xiao and others described the transformation mode from traditional E-learning to cloud services and cloud service architecture, and discussed the commercialization model of education cloud services and the potential risks of their promotion and operation.

Some scholars have sampled and analyzed the papers on cloud computing education applications in China's educational technology academic journals in recent years: the research on education science accounts for 60% of the total sample, of which the research on education cloud concept and research review accounts for 46% of the total sample, and the research on education cloud body and classification accounts for 14% of the total sample; Research on computer science accounts for 40% of the total number of samples, of which 39% are about education cloud application cases and architecture design, and 1% are about education cloud application mode and operation mechanism [5]. It can be seen that the research of the educational science community mainly stays at the level of macro concept and overview, while the concept definition of the education cloud and the construction of domain knowledge information base need to be further investigated. The research of the computer science community mainly focuses on the design of the education cloud infrastructure model, and there is no mature practice on the large-scale application deployment and industrialized operation of education cloud services.

Li Tanlin uses SQL Server for data mining and online analysis of the data in the educational administration information management system, and takes the evaluation of public elective courses as an example and the evaluation of students' comprehensive quality for experimental verification, indicating that the rules or rules of mining can provide some reference for the educational administration management and operation.

Wang Yongjuan uses Apriori algorithm to calculate and analyze the historical data of college students, and concludes that the key factor affecting students' performance is the stability of students' family status. There is no direct relationship between the college entrance examination results, student origin and other information on students' academic performance.

Wang Jiasheng studied the analysis of students' borrowing data from the library based on the association rule algorithm. Through setting a variety of different rules, he carried out multi-level and multi-dimensional calculations on the relevant data, and obtained the association relationship between student types, grades and books borrowed.

Sen B et al. predicted the grading performance of corresponding students when they entered school by mining the potential information of data in Türkiye's education system.

Wang Kaicheng's research shows that in the process of mining and analyzing students' historical achievements, the neural network algorithm has the highest prediction probability among the four mining algorithms used: decision tree algorithm, clustering analysis algorithm, neural network algorithm and logical regression algorithm.

Salehi M studied the K-means algorithm (KM). After mining and analyzing a variety of learning materials, the research results obtained can, to a certain extent, provide suitable learning materials for different students.

Chen Yijun and others used the Weighted Naive Bayes Classification Algorithm (WNBC) to analyze the correlation between students' CET4 passing and online behavior, and found the correlation between online behavior and passing rate.

2.2 Smart Education

Smart education is an advanced education mode. It applies information technology to education, teaching, education management, scientific research evaluation and other educational activities in depth, providing digital and intelligent support for the smooth development of education and teaching and the distribution and sharing of relevant educational resources, human, material and financial resources.

The basic characteristics of smart education are openness, sharing, interaction and collaboration. Different from the traditional education information system, intelligent education organizes and manages various teaching equipment and educational resources well [6]. At the same time, it can intelligently identify the user's terminal equipment, software environment, access request, service demand and other information according to the situation, and conduct efficient resource scheduling. Smart education has a variety of educational application functions, and can extract, classify, analyze and summarize all kinds of information generated in information-based education activities that students, teachers, education administrators and other users participate in, and constantly optimize and improve themselves through learning strategies to provide better functional services.

In addition, smart education is user centered, which can provide targeted services such as resource retrieval and information push based on the individual characteristics of users, and create an intelligent education ecosystem by simulating human brain thinking [7].

The 12th Five Year Plan of the Ministry of Education has made requirements for accelerating the process of education informatization. Smart education is an important model to promote China's information construction. It greatly impacts the traditional education ideas and teaching methods, significantly improves learners' learning ability and comprehensive quality through information technology, and brings about significant innovation in education models. Vigorously developing smart education is an inevitable choice to keep pace with the times in the field of education [8]. It is of far-reaching significance to deepen the reform of the educational system, improve the quality and benefits of teaching, and cultivate high-quality innovative talents.

At present and in the future, the development of smart education focuses on the integration with cloud computing technology. Based on the big data computing and storage, resource virtualization and other capabilities provided by the cloud environment, we can build stable, reliable and easy to expand education cloud services that meet the characteristics of smart education.

The application of blockchain technology in education by foreign researchers mainly focuses on the research and development of learning certificate platform and the construction of learning record platform. In fact, blockchain technology has other broader application space in the field of education, which domestic researchers have conducted in-depth discussions. Yang Xianmin et al.; Jin Yifu (2017) analyzed the demand for blockchain from the aspects of education resource construction, teaching process evaluation and education input and output, constructed the system framework of "blockchain + education", and proposed a partially decentralized hybrid deployment model; Li Qing et al. (2017) believed that blockchain could provide decentralized learning records and credit banking services, reduce the cost of study, job hunting and talent employment, and establish a more convenient and reliable certificate system; Fang Haiguang et al. (2017) designed intelligent learning robots based on blockchain technology from four aspects: resource sharing, common learning sites, resource construction, and learning achievement recording, aiming to achieve the purpose of in-depth personalized learning in large-scale learning services. It can be seen that blockchain technology has broad development space and application value in the field of education, which is worthy of further research and exploration.

3 Blockchain Technology

3.1 Blockchain Infrastructure

The protocol layering has the advantages of good independence, good flexibility, easy to distinguish and refine business logic, easy to implement, and efficiency improvement. Like the seven layer protocol in the computer network, the typical blockchain basic framework theory includes six layers - application layer, contract layer, incentive layer, consensus layer, network layer and data layer, as shown in Fig. 1.

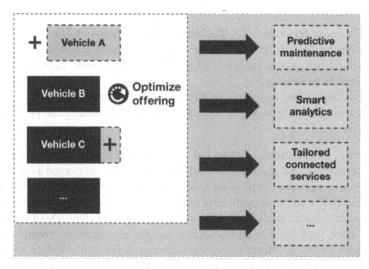

Fig. 1. Blockchain infrastructure

(1) The data layer encapsulates the underlying block data, timestamp, asymmetric encryption based on elliptic curve cryptography algorithm and other information. Its main function is to verify the validity of block data, and store specific transaction data to each data node in the blockchain network in a distributed manner.

(2) The consensus layer mainly includes various consensus algorithms in the blockchain network under different application scenarios, including proof of equity mechanism (PoS), proof of workload mechanism (PoW), and proof of authorized shares mechanism (DPoS). It can adapt to the efficiency requirements of each data node to reach consensus on the generation of new blocks under different application scenarios, which is one of the core technologies of the blockchain.

(3) The network layer includes the formation mechanism, data verification and data transmission mechanism of P2P network. The network layer has built the transaction channel, formulated the node reward rule, and built the network environment of the entire blockchain.

(4) The incentive layer incorporates the economic factors in social life into the blockchain technology system, including the distribution mechanism and the issuance mechanism of incentive economy. The most common reward mechanism is the classic blockchain network represented by Bitcoin, which is often referred to as "mining" reward. The allocation mechanism is a distribution scheme proposed by the joint mining pool based on the participation of each data node after the mining is successful. In the alliance chain and private chain, the incentive mechanism has been diluted. Especially in the private chain, there is no need for a reward mechanism, because the nodes participating in bookkeeping often complete the competitive game of bookkeeping rights outside the chain, and require to participate in bookkeeping through force or voluntary.

(5) The contract layer encapsulates various smart contracts, scripts and algorithms, which is an important basis for blockchain technology to enter the second stage of programmable features. It is the algorithm and business logic built on the blockchain virtual machine, and is the basis of the blockchain system data operation and diversified programming.

(6) The application layer seals various cases and application scenarios of blockchain, mainly including programmable society, programmable finance and programmable currency.

In essence, blockchain is a public ledger jointly maintained by many data nodes, featuring decentralization, data security and reliability. In the distributed database where all transaction records and events in the block can be traced, the data of the uplink block is recognized by the whole network after reaching a consensus on the data nodes of the whole network. All data is distributed and stored in data nodes throughout the network. Each data node fully records all transaction records and executed events shared by all blockchain nodes [9]. Because every transaction in the public ledger is packaged into a new uplink block through the accounting node after the consensus algorithm is completed. Therefore, once the bookkeeping is successful, the data will always be saved on the blockchain and will not be deleted. Blockchain is based on financial concepts such as reward mechanism and public ledger and computer science and technology such as linked list, P2P network and distributed database; At the same time, it combines digital signature, public key and private key encryption primitives, Hash hash and other technologies that are integrated and cross combined.

$$
\begin{cases}
Trust = \{T \mid r = 1, 2, 3, 4, 5\} \\
\quad t_r = 0, False \\
\quad t_r = 1, True
\end{cases}
\tag{1}
$$

3.2 Data Structure of Blockchain

In the currency system based on blockchain technology, the transaction represents the transfer of digital currency of one user address to another user address or addresses of multiple users in the blockchain network, which is a one-to-one or one-to-many interaction process. A legal transaction includes at least the output of the transaction, the input of the transaction, the digital fingerprint of the transaction, and the specific amount of the transaction.

Transaction output: contains the specific amount of digital assets to be received and the user address of the receiver. Each output must specify the number of digital assets transferred by the exporter to the receiver, and the receiver must have the private key of the address to control the digital assets.

Digital fingerprint of transaction: each transaction has a unique identifier.

Transaction input: usually includes two aspects: address list for transferring digital assets and specific amount input. For example, in the Bitcoin system, the address balance is obtained by calling the past transaction records of the address, so the digital assets will not change. In the entire monetary system, users will not increase or decrease existing digital assets without transactions. However, users can reorganize assets, combine multiple digital assets or re-segment a single digital asset. According to the rules, all users need to use digital signatures to ensure the legitimacy of the transaction initiated by the input address.

$$\mathbf{e}_{TN}^i = \frac{\sum_{n=1}^{N_K} S_K^n}{N_K} \tag{2}$$

Transaction Amount: corresponding to the specific amount of the input address and output address.

In all blockchain systems, block data is connected in series to form a chain. As shown in Fig. 2:

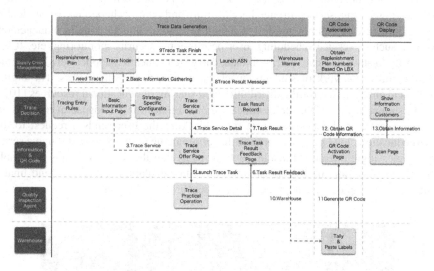

Fig. 2. Block chain structure diagram

Merkle tree was named after mathematician Ralph Merkle, who first discovered that a single hash value can be used to represent a large amount of information. It is generally divided into three steps: first, hash the metadata; Second, combine the obtained hash values in pairs from left to right, and do the hash calculation. Repeat this step; Third, the final Merkle tree becomes a hash value, which is also called the root of the Merkle tree. It represents all information on the whole Merkel tree in a relatively short string.

The root hash is an effective mechanism to summarize the transactions in the block and verify the existence of a transaction in the data block. This structure can ensure that the data sent in the distributed network is valid, because any change to the data will cause the change of the root hash value to be detected.

$$Hash(N_K^m, TN_i^m, TN_i^s,) <= \text{TARGET} = 2^{256 \cdot targelB} \tag{3}$$

Due to the emergence of Merkle tree, blockchain has been greatly optimized. Users can choose to create a "lightweight wallet" or "lightweight node", without downloading and storing the entire blockchain, just to verify when the transaction enters the block. For a user's wallet, you only need to download and store the block header and Merkle root (and the Merkle evidence they receive from the full node) to verify whether a transaction is legal.

4 Design of Blockchain Based Smart Education Cloud Platform

The traditional education information system has the disadvantages of oneness and heterogeneity. Generally, a set of education information system only provides one or several limited services, and different systems cannot effectively allocate and share education resources flexibly due to the differences in architecture.

The smart education cloud platform has solved the above problems. Based on cloud service engineering, service-oriented architecture and other technologies, it can deploy advanced hardware equipment, design a well layered architecture, build management systems such as service scheduling, user permissions, security monitoring, etc. It has the ability to store massive education data, carry rich education applications, and build a collaborative network of students, teachers, managers and other users, The digital ecological environment for the distribution and sharing of educational resources [10].

As shown in Fig. 3, the smart education cloud platform is transparent to users, as long as users can obtain services on demand. After the user sends a request to the smart education cloud platform through the terminal, the platform goes through a series of complex logic operations inside, such as: analyzing the request, finding a suitable service interface, and packaging the relevant data calculation and format, and finally returning the adapted education services and resources to the user.

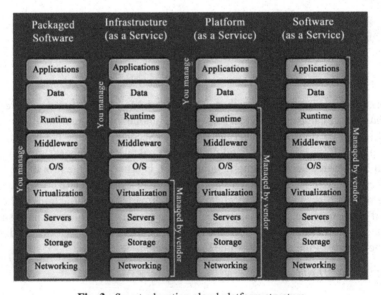

Fig. 3. Smart education cloud platform structure

The smart education cloud platform consists of two parts: the smart education client and the smart education server. The smart education client is the unified entrance for education cloud users to access the platform. It can build targeted service scenarios based on users' roles and push them to different service contents. The smart education service end is responsible for providing specific educational application service resources, and at the same time, organizing and managing various educational services organically.

In order to verify the impact of credit evaluation on the speed of block-out in the academic early warning blockchain, the scenario of academic early warning blockchain is simulated on the basis of the experimental environment in Sect. 3. Set five credit values with different grades, randomly simulate 80 data nodes MN with randomly distributed credit values between 1 and 100, to evaluate the relationship between the average credit of data nodes and the consensus reached in the new area. First, two sets of experiments are set up to test the relationship between the credit values of book-entry data nodes and verification data nodes in the whole consensus process in the academic warning blockchain. Then, the experimental environment was rearranged, and three groups of comparative experiments were set up to realize the PoW consensus algorithm, DPoS consensus algorithm, and PoS consensus algorithm. The impact of the data nodes introduced into the credit evaluation on the outbound speed of the academic early warning blockchain network was compared and analyzed, so as to judge the containment degree of the strategy on malicious nodes.

In the current environment of simulating the academic warning blockchain, the following three groups of comparative experiments are set up to implement the consensus algorithm as PoW consensus algorithm, PoS consensus algorithm, and DPoS consensus algorithm. The experimental comparison is made with the CDPoS consensus algorithm proposed in this paper, as shown in Fig. 4.

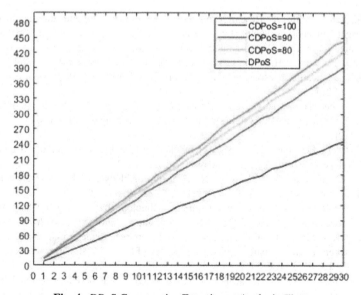

Fig. 4. DPoS Comparative Experiment Analysis Chart

As shown in Fig. 4, the experimental test is carried out with blocks with a generation height of 30. The experimental results show that under the current experimental environment, the DPoS consensus algorithm takes nearly 450s to complete the experimental goal. From the figure, it can also be seen intuitively that when the credit value of CDPoS is reduced to 80, the block generation speed is very close to the DPoS consensus algorithm.

5 Conclusion

Based on the relevant concepts in the field of education and cloud service engineering technology, and based on the SOA design pattern, this research has realized a large-scale, flexible configuration and expansion of smart education platform based on cloud computing. The cloud based smart education platform has built a multi-party collaborative smart education digital ecological environment for learners, educators, education managers, service resources, etc. The platform supports the rapid deployment of education service applications, provides rich education service content, carries massive education resource data, and education cloud users can transparently obtain the required service resources.

Acknowledgements. The Natural Science Foundation of Zhejiang Province (LY20G030025); The MOE Layout Program of Humanities and Social Sciences(20YJC630241); National Social Science Foundation of China (18BGL184).

References

1. Liu, S., Yang, Y., Shi, X.: Research and design of E-portfolio for education practice growth of normal university students. In: CIPAE 2021: 2021 2nd International Conference on Computers, Information Processing and Advanced Education (2021)
2. Zhou, Q., Lu, J., Yin, H., et al.: Layout guide for journal of physics: design and research of distributed educational resource sharing platform based on IPFS. J. Phys. Conf. Ser. **1971**(1), 012026 (2021)
3. Sun, X., Chen, H., Wang, Q., et al.: Research and design of online training platform based on spring cloud distributed system structure and computer big data. J. Phys. Conf. Ser. **1952**, 042087 (2021). (7pp)
4. Kassanuk, T., Phasinam, K.: Design of blockchain based smart agriculture framework to ensure safety and security. Mater. Today Proc. **51**, 2313–2316 (2022)
5. Kiyeng, D., Karume, S.M., Masese, N.: A design of blockchain based smart contract for tendering. Int. J. Coms. Apps. Tech. Res. **10**(10), 222–225 (2022)
6. Zhang, Y.: Research on multiparty payment technology based on blockchain and smart contract mechanism. J. Math. **2022**, 1–14 (2022). https://doi.org/10.1155/2022/3434954
7. Wang, S.T., Li, M.H., Lien, C.C.: Analysis of the optimal application of blockchain-based smart lockers in the logistics industry based on FFD-SAGA and grey decision-making. Symmetry **13**(2), 329 (2021)
8. Liu, Z., Zhao, H., Liu, J., et al.: Research and design of VR-based mechanical simulation interaction and network experiment platform. IOP Conf. Ser. Mater. Sci. Eng. **1126**, 012024 (2021)

9. Møller, H., Skov, S.S.: Education as Framed Sense-Making A Design Based Research contribution to the theory and practice of play in higher education. J. Play Adulthood **3**(1), 31–51 (2021)

10. Wu, D., Guo, P., Zhang, C., Hou, C., Wang, Q., Yang, Z.: Research and practice of data structure curriculum reform based on outcome-based education and chaoxing platform. Int. J. Inf. Educ. Technol. **11**(8), 375–380 (2021). https://doi.org/10.18178/ijiet.2021.11.8.1537

Design of Ideological and Political Network Education Platform Based on Genetic Algorithm

Qiutao Qin, Yuting Chen(✉), and Meijin Luo

Hechi University, Yizhou 546300, Guangxi, China
790567088@qq.com, 18020@hcnu.edu.cn

Abstract. How to realize the effective combination of politica party construction course and network platform is the key to the full implementation of "whole process education" under the political education mode in the new era. It is not only related to the formation of students' own values and correct ideas, but also related to the overall comprehensive quality and patriotic feelings of our people. Especially for students studying public courses, strengthening their political education will help to improve the comprehensive quality level of students studying public courses. College Party building, ideological and political network integrity education and platform development can design the content of ideological and political education in colleges and universities and the problems existing in ideological and political education in colleges and universities, and encourage the general public to participate in the network symbolic building. Therefore, it is necessary to build a service framework, which can optimize the core ideological and political content and combine the ideological and political content of other personnel to realize the integration of information and thought.

Keyword: Service architecture · Party building and political thinking · Network education · Platform development

1 Introduction

At present, there are certain deficiencies in the overall research on ideological and political education in colleges and universities, which are mainly reflected in some problems in the optimization of information [1, 2], information combination and information collation and analysis, and there are also some problems in a number of contents and key indicators in another game, so it is necessary to judge according to the various contents and indicators in colleges and universities, and some people's graduate education is the 2006 college education development and efficient optimization of colleges and universities, which happened the day before yesterday, that is, it is believed that part of the content of ideological education in colleges and universities needs to be carried out, which will be a problem of education, which will not be conducive to the overall development of education, education is the core of education, and the intellectual development of colleges and universities also has one Qualitative physique should be

Y. Zhang and N. Shah (Eds.): BigIoT-EDU 2023, LNICST 583, pp. 416–423, 2024.
https://doi.org/10.1007/978-3-031-63139-9_44

coped with [3, 4], so it is the main research direction to carry out ideological research and ideological analysis in college education, and the formation and construction of ideological analysis is the main research direction at present, but the lack of data in the process of research direction is not conducive to the collation and integration of the entire data and gold medals, so it is necessary to conduct comprehensive judgment and analysis of students' ideological and political education in colleges and universities, and better conduct research, so it is necessary to optimize the content of colleges and universities, identify the problems existing in the ideological and political education of Chinese universities [5–7], and better develop and judge, especially for the construction of platforms in colleges and universities, which can optimize their main contents, and inevitably judge the key content and key indicators in colleges and universities. The instructor will provide you with relevant work and analysis [8–10].

2   Service Architecture System Overall Model

2.1   Basic Framework of the System

In the style of service architecture, Efficient fitness is a process, so it is necessary to judge the data resources and analysis process [11]. In addition to this neutral feature that does not depend on specific technologies, the ability of dynamic query, location, routing and mediation is supported through the service registry and the service engine driven bus, Good realization of comprehensive optimization and legal analysis of data [12]. The basic framework of service architecture implementation is shown in Fig. 1.

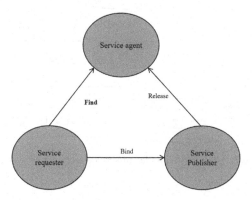

Fig. 1. Basic structure framework of service architecture implementation

There are big problems in the whole process of ideological and political education, but it needs to [13]. The interoperability of the education system and the sharing of resources are the primary issues. Service system architecture is currently the hottest topic in the IT industry. With the continuous maturity of service system architecture technology, people have a deeper understanding of service system architecture, and there is a good demand environment for service system architecture models and application promotion. Based on the principles and ideas of the service system architecture. Combine actual business situation requirements. An integrated platform structure framework for educational informationization is proposed [14]. The knowledge base of the education industry is constructed through service registration, intelligent service aggregation is carried out through the registration knowledge base of each business module service, and a component library of user services is formed, and the business process is defined by the user through the workflow engine system of the service bus. Form a user-specific business integration system [15] Through the unified integration of user business systems and data integration, the basic knowledge information base of regional education industry can be formed, which provides information data support services for knowledge mining, data analysis, early warning and other business intelligence development of education industry The overall design idea of the service architecture system is shown in Fig. 2.

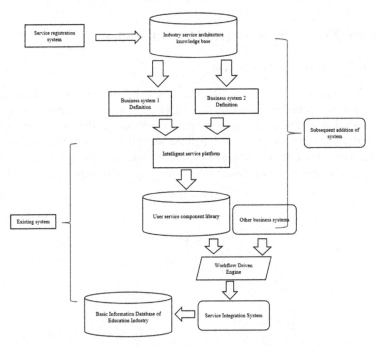

Fig. 2. Overall design idea of service architecture system

2.2 Application Mode of the System

Due to the complex types of users in the education field, the actual situation of user informatization development in various regions is very uneven, so the system has designed different architecture management application modes for different types of users. Among them, the centralized and distributed management mode is mainly for the basic campus network environment and hardware facilities of various universities in the region, and the information maintenance technical staff is relatively complete. For universities and colleges with more business requirements, it is more suitable for the distributed information management mode. Colleges and universities in remote areas generally do not have the ability of distributed information management. First, they do not have the supporting hardware facilities of the information center. Second, they are not equipped with high-end technicians to maintain the network ability of the University Information Center. Such an environment is more suitable for host server hosting or service, that is, software centralized information management mode. We can adopt the regional centralized management mode for educational institutions in more developed cities with complete regional infrastructure and hardware construction facilities and relatively concentrated technical force.

It is also impossible to realize the complete sharing and intercommunication of data among various systems in a short time. In order to facilitate users' work and use and ensure the consistency of data, we will gradually integrate and transform each system. At present, we can adopt different unified authentication strategies according to the system applications of different colleges and universities, and finally achieve the usage of all office systems integration and unified single sign-on for users. WeChat has a huge user base, and among the many services of WeChat, WeChat official account platform is one of the good choices for building an online education platform. WeChat official account WeChat generally provides functions such as downloading courseware and viewing the content of ideological and political courses. If students want to communicate with teachers, they only need to send corresponding messages. Teachers can view the real-time message content in the back end, and one-to-one communication with students can be realized through the reply function. The use process of WeChat service platform in WeChat official account is shown in Fig. 3.

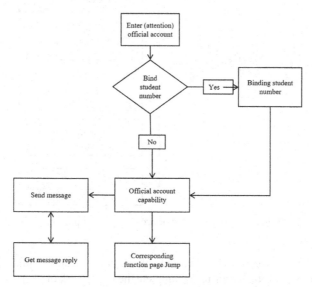

Fig. 3. WeChat official account service platform usage flow

3   Construction of Network Education Platform for Ideological and Political Courses in Colleges and Universities

3.1   Necessity of Platform Construction and Development

Data in the whole analysis process, mainly plays a key basic role, and the platform construction can promote the optimization of data, the sum of data and the overall analysis of data can promote the optimization of data structure to achieve the overall level of the platform. The emergence of a high platform can more in-depth analysis of data resources, the construction of reasonable logical thinking, promote the development of ideological and political education, and form a more comprehensive and complete ideological and political education system. In the process of multi-heating and multi-angle analysis of the ideological and political education system, the construction of teaching system can also have strong relevance, can better promote the development of data, and form useful data models and data regulations to guide data related work. Diversified analysis of data and multi-dimensional analysis of data can also better mine data in depth, so as to realize comprehensive judgment of data and make it clear that this is the status of education (Fig. 4).

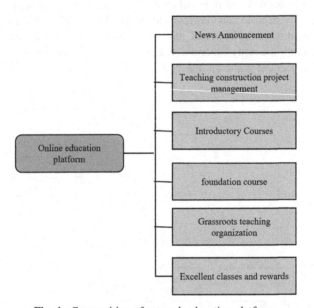

Fig. 4. Composition of network education platform.

It is necessary to construct new data and online platform, and establish the saturation relationship between data platforms to complete the basic work of data. In addition, it is necessary to judge the overall analysis content of basic courses and teachers, and then realize the comprehensive index and category of data. For different teaching contents and teaching methods, it is necessary to adopt diversified analysis content and structure to better judge the data. In addition, the data should reflect the problems existing in ideological and political education, the actual data and the content of ideological and political education, the later analysis and the overall theoretical research.

3.2 Application Path of Platform Construction

In the course ideological and political network education platform construction, we should focus on the basic framework, and do a good job of comprehensive construction with ideological elements as the leading factor, theoretical elements as the framework, institutional elements as the premise, resource elements as the foundation and technical elements as the support. At present, there are still some problems such as poor practicability and interactivity in the process of constructing the network teaching platform of ideological and political courses in colleges and universities in China. Educational resource management platform is an ideological framework system based on service framework system. At the beginning of the design, the flexibility and scalability of the system were fully considered. It can fully realize the loose coupling of various functional modules and the reuse of modules, making the development faster, avoiding repeated development, and having good scalability and maintainability. The functional modules of the educational resource service platform are shown in Fig. 5.

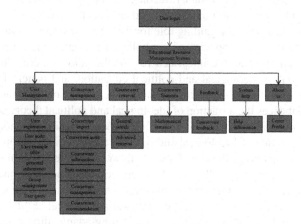

Fig. 5. Functional modules of education resource service platform

In order to enhance the functionality and professionalism of the ideological and political network education platform, professionals from various fields should be gathered, so that front-line political education can communicate effectively with curriculum teachers, launch corresponding hot courses, help students studying public courses to make progress, and guide students studying public courses to learn more effective political education knowledge, and jointly create a big pattern and platform for collaborative education. In the planning of network platform construction of teaching reform, We should pay more attention to the data analysis process and the overall structure of the data. In addition, we should judge the key points and key contents in the data and the comprehensiveness of the index data. We should pay attention to the mining problems in the data, analyze the data continuously, and compare the types of different data to better analyze and identify the data.It is also necessary to judge the key points in the data and the coupling between the data, and give corresponding prepositions, improve the network courseware, and clarify the corresponding guarantee and incentive system. Network credit mutual recognition mechanism for students' resumes, and gradually cultivate students' good ideological and political learning habits [7]. Guide teachers to update the teaching system, encourage teachers to develop ideological and political courseware by establishing topics, and reflect it on the ideological and political network education platform.

4   Conclusions

Under the background of the new era, the party's construction has a broader development space and a better management mode. This requires us to actively keep up with the trend of the times and put Party building in the first place. Actively combine the most advanced tools to form the "Internet plus party building" mode, do well in Party member management and party work study, strengthen ideological and political work in party affairs, and the relationship between data, in order to enhance the comprehensiveness of data and promote its better development.the times, professional academic learning is on the one hand, and more importantly, ideological and moral education and training. The contents and key points of some data should be specially identified and screened, so as to find out the data with key guiding role for the whole research results, and provide support for the formal development of symbolic education at one time. At the same time, it is necessary to play the integrated role of the platform, complete the overall education and goal of ideological and political education, and better play the role of war education.enriches teaching methods, enriches teaching contents, integrates teaching resources, enhances the attraction of Ideological and political theory courses, and is conducive to stimulating students' learning interest and learning autonomy. Initiative. In the teaching practice of Ideological and political theory course, through reasonable teaching settings, encourage the use of shared network service platform of Ideological and political theory course in Colleges and universities. The students trained by colleges and universities have been widely praised by employers because of their strong political quality, solid foundation, excellent technology, strong practical ability, good comprehensive quality, high loyalty to enterprises and strong adaptability to work, and their social reputation and comprehensive school running strength have been continuously improved.

Acknowledgements. Research Topics on Theory and Practice of political education for College Students in Guangxi in 2021"Exploration and Research on the Social Practice Education Mode of the Communist Youth League in Colleges and Universities Based on the New Development Concept"(2021SZ075); 2020 National Social Science Fund Project "Research on the History of Peasant Movement in Guangxi (1921–1927)", (20XDJ015); Key construction projects of demonstration teaching and research team of Ministry of Education in 2019: Research on the Construction of Teaching Resources of Outline of Modern Chinese History (19JDSZK014) ; Guangxi Higher Education Undergraduate Teaching Reform Project (2021JGZ152): Research and Practice on Improving the Course Construction Ability of Science and Engineering Teachers on Politics and Ideology in Local Application-oriented Universities.

References

1. Xiaobei, G.: Development of ideological and political online teaching platform based on VEM framework. Microcomput. Appl. **36**(8), 3 (2020)
2. Yongan, L.: Development and design of an ideological and political network teaching system based on .NET. Autom. Instrum. (11), 3 (2016)
3. Xiaoping, W.: Development and design of ideological and political network teaching system based on VOD. Electron. Design Eng. (3), 4 (2017)
4. Xiaoping, W.: Development and design of ideological and political network teaching system based on VOD. Electron. Design Eng. **25**(3), 49–52 (2017)
5. Xiaoxia. D.: Development and design of ideological and political network teaching system based on B/S mode. Autom. Instrum. (5), 3 (2017)
6. Fei, Z.: The adjustment of industrial structure facing the world. Shanghai Party History and Party Build. (3), 1 (2018)
7. Hongwei, L.: Exploring new ideas for the development of party building in secondary vocational schools in the new era. J. Tianjin Vocat. Coll. **20**(6), 4 (2018)
8. Yu, X.: Development of online political education works based on the needs of university students. Ideol. Educ. Res. **8**(5) (2020)
9. Minmin, Z., Yuerong, T.: Development and design of a network education management platform for student party members. Gansu Sci. Technol. **34**(24), 4 (2018)
10. Siyan, H., Xiqian, X.: Discussion on the optimization and integration of network teaching resources of ideological and political courses in colleges and universities in the era of big data. Contemp. Tourism (7), 220 (2018)
11. Yan, W., Yan, C.: Research on the practice of the development mode of "wei thoughts and politics" for college counselors based on WeChat public platform. Inner Mongolia Educ. (2), 2 (2020)
12. Jing, W.: The construction of a new model of political education management in colleges and universities oriented to the WeChat platform. New Gener. Inf. Technol. **3**(15), 5 (2020)
13. Jun, Z., Xiaoyan, R., Jianwei, W.: Design and implementation of smart village management system. Guizhou Agric. Sci. **48**(12), 5 (2020)
14. Qin, W., Cheng, F.: Exploration of the construction of university teaching and administrative party branch from the perspective of discipline. Contemp. Educ. Pract. Teach. Res. Electron. Ed. (5), 2 (2018)
15. Pingjuan, Z., Shuangxi, L., Tingting, W.: Design and implementation of community education platform based on the concept of microservices. J. Hebei Univ. Eng. Soc. Sci. Ed. **37**(3), 5 (2020)

Application Research
of Computer-Aided Online Intelligent
Teaching

Realization of Computer Course Scheduling Algorithm in Higher Vocational Colleges Based on ML

Ping Wu[1,2](✉)

[1] Heilongjiang Polytechnic, Harbin 150025, Heilongjiang, China
837602581@qq.com
[2] Chongqing University of Arts and Sciences, Chongqing 402160, China

Abstract. Today, with the rapid development of message technique, all higher vocational colleges have established perfect message management systems, among which educational administration management system is the core of the whole message system. In the educational administration, course arrangement is the first step to ensure the teaching quality. It arranges the time and place for the courses set by the school, so that the whole teaching can be carried out in a planned and orderly way. With the continuous deepening of education reform, the reform of course scheduling is also underway, arranging more scientific and humanized school courses, and the individual needs and individual development of students and teachers are also the focus of current curriculum arrangements. Implementing the comprehensive management of school teaching through computer teaching management system is an effective means to improve the level of school teaching management and promote the progress of school management. This paper uses ML algorithm to establish computer course scheduling algorithm. ML (machine learning) uses computer simulation technique to study the learning process of human knowledge acquisition, and from it, it innovates existing knowledge, promotes analysis and solves problems. Through the research of this paper, it is concluded that the algorithm in this paper has remarkable effect and is suitable for being widely used.

Keyword: ML · Higher vocational colleges · Computer courses · Course scheduling algorithm

1 Introduction

Anyone who is very familiar with the educational administration in colleges and universities knows that the curriculum arrangement is the one that occupies a large percentage of the workload of educational administration. Today, with the rapid development of message technique, colleges and universities standing at the forefront of technique have used modern educational administration systems to liberate a large number of manpower from the complicated educational administration [1]. If the traditional manual scheduling method is adopted, the courses of each semester will take more than two months to

Y. Zhang and N. Shah (Eds.): BigIoT-EDU 2023, LNICST 583, pp. 427–435, 2024.
https://doi.org/10.1007/978-3-031-63139-9_45

complete. Even if so much time and human resources are invested, the conflict between the time occupation, teacher occupation and classroom occupation of the starting unit cannot be avoided [2]. In the current educational administration work, the problem of course scheduling presents an increasingly complex situation in both space and time. If individuals are transformed into students themselves, the more difficult course scheduling work will follow. Manual course scheduling needs to be carried out according to various factors, which will lead to a large error rate and easy to conflict. At least, there may be individual conflicts between students, teachers and the classroom, and the change of course readjustment will be very large, which will affect the normal teaching of the school, as well as the problem of teaching accidents [3]. In serious cases, the curriculum can't be reasonably arranged, let alone the reform of teaching and education system. In all the educational administration work, course arrangement is the most basic, the most complex, and at the same time the core work. The essence of course scheduling is to arrange the right teachers to take the right courses at the right time and place, which is the basic guarantee for the whole teaching to be carried out in an orderly and planned way. Because the course arrangement is characterized by large scale, complex requirements and constantly changing nature, the course arrangement problem has always been one of the interesting topics [4]. This paper studies the course scheduling algorithm based on ML algorithm, so as to meet the new teaching system. Make the school's teaching and educational administration work go smoothly, make better use of the school's resources, and then promote the reform process of the education system.

2   Computer General Education and ML Course Scheduling Algorithm

2.1   Computer General Education

Man's all-round development theory is Marx's basic theory about man's development, which mainly refers to the full development of man's ability and potential, physical strength and intelligence, body and heart, and the continuous satisfaction of various needs of man [5]. In order to cultivate high-quality talents to adapt to the 21st century and implement computer general education in vocational education, we must change our educational concept and establish the concept of general education. It is necessary to understand the significance of implementing general education ideologically and realize its position and importance in vocational education [6]. Although higher vocational colleges aim at cultivating skilled talents, the premise of skilled talents is a high-quality citizen, otherwise they will become deformed talents with skills but no morality. By strengthening general education, students' moral quality and comprehensive quality can be improved, and their moral, intellectual, physical, aesthetic and labor development can be promoted in an all-round way, so that students can become a useful talent with sound body and mind, strong moral and excellent skills [7]. The talent training mode is shown in Fig. 1.

Colleges and universities can divide computer general education courses into two types according to their own situation: small-scale teaching and popular teaching. The courses are composed of teachers' lectures, organizing discussions, and autonomous

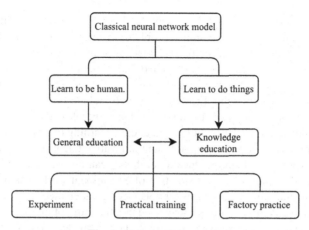

Fig. 1. Talent training mode

learning. At present, the mode of "lecture in lobby and discussion in small classroom" is widely adopted. However, the practical experience of general education has proved that tutorial system will be more effective in a small area. Implementing general education and improving educational ideas are the forerunner, and whether the educational ideas are correct or not is directly related to the direction of educational reform. Relatively speaking, the higher vocational education has little resistance to the implementation of computer general education [8]. Higher vocational education does not have the burden of exam-oriented education, nor the pressure of entering a higher school. As a new type of education, it does not have many inherent models. However, higher vocational education is largely developed by inheriting the traditional educational model, and the traditional educational concept is very stable and lacks the motivation of self-innovation.

General education teaches not only knowledge, but also wisdom, so it appeals not only to reason, but also to emotion and belief [9]. Its carrier is not only words, or even images and sounds. General education is inseparable from harmonious teacher-student relationship, beautiful campus environment and lively cultural life. In terms of curriculum content, it is necessary to unify computer general education with professional education and with social needs [10]. Many people think that higher vocational education is mainly to impart knowledge and cultivate skills, and it is a kind of "technical education". In fact, this view is one-sided and ignores the essence of education. Admittedly, training technical talents is the educational goal of higher vocational colleges, but we can't just train a person who only knows computers or can do accounts. If so, the school can only be a workshop for training "instrumental" talents at best [11].

2.2 ML in Course Scheduling Algorithm

After the development of computer technique to a certain stage, one of the branches of computer science, artificial intelligence, emerged. The main research of artificial intelligence is to simulate the human brain with computer, operate various artificial intelligence activities, explain them with popular language, and realize a series of reasoning, planning and thinking activities carried out by the human brain with computer, that is, artificial intelligence, which solves some complex problems that need human beings to complete.

In order to ensure the scientificity, systematicness and feasibility of the curriculum schedule, a set of scientific curriculum scheduling principles is needed to realize the planned and realizable systematic project. The main factor considered in the algorithm is how to make full use of school resources, which include time resources, classroom resources and teacher resources. Students play a dominant role in the whole school education and teaching activities. By stimulating students' learning motivation and improving students' learning efficiency, high-quality and innovative talents can be cultivated, and the educational goals in modern educational theory can be realized. According to the educational reform and the present situation of educational work arrangement in general schools, the daily management of schools faces great challenges. It is necessary to pay attention to the flexibility, convenience and practicability of the course arrangement system in the design. It is necessary to fully fit the various teaching resources used by schools and maximize the teaching quality. Especially in higher vocational colleges, because it is to train skilled professionals, the teaching plan aimed at cultivating students' innovative spirit and practical ability involves many courses of different natures according to the laws of students' physical and psychological development at different stages.

The system should be able to directly restrict the course arrangement and the course itself. When arranging the course, it is also necessary to analyze the actual situation of the course itself and the actual psychological characteristics of students, so as to arrange the course scientifically and reasonably. Since the student-oriented management concept is embodied, the course arrangement should highlight the student-centered position, fully consider the students' psychological and physiological laws, and enable students to learn the appropriate courses at the right time, thus improving their learning efficiency. For example, the theory course should not be arranged in the morning and it is best not to be too dense. It is best to arrange different classes in the same course every other day. It is also necessary to analyze the actual situation of the class, and then arrange the course, for example, at a certain characteristic time of the week, a class needs to carry out practical activities, etc. When you meet the above situation, you can't arrange courses for them. In addition, we should give full play to the leading role of teachers. Teachers play a very important role in the whole teaching work, so the quality of teachers' teaching directly determines whether the training goal of the college can be achieved. Therefore, when arranging classes, we should try our best to meet the reasonable requirements of teachers and improve their enthusiasm.

3 Discussion on ML Algorithms and Results

3.1 ML Algorithm

In the past, the classical data mining algorithm was to optimize the ML algorithm based on the data set. However, from the current aspects of collection, retrieval, storage, sharing, analysis and processing, this traditional ML method has been difficult to meet the demand of mining data in the current large amount of heterogeneous data. ML refers to the behavior of computers and other machines to improve their system performance through their own experience. People have strong learning and imitation ability, and their learning is a very complicated process. This so-called process is ML theory. ML is the behavior of using computer simulation technique to study the learning process of human beings to acquire knowledge, and to innovate the existing knowledge and improve the means of analyzing and solving problems. At present, there are many interpretations of the word "calculation". The classical neural network model is shown in Fig. 2.

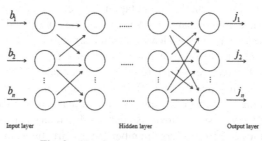

Fig. 2. Classical neural network model

There are different meanings and expressions in different scientific fields and practical situations. One of the abstract expressions is the execution of an algorithm or a series of rules: it is carried out by a set of successive rules or instructions. As far as computers are concerned, "computing" is not an ontological meaning with realistic characteristics, but a formal and logical method. This requires a certain theoretical and logical basis of calculation. From this point of view, the research of "algorithm" undoubtedly has the most direct promoting significance for the further analysis of the concept of "calculation". It is of great practical significance to study the ML algorithm in the big data environment, that is, to use ML to mine the valuable knowledge points existing in the current dynamic complex database.

If, in the whole, there is a relationship between y and x with a univariate normal error model, for the given x_i, there are:

$$y_i = \beta_0 + \beta_1 x_i + \xi_i \tag{1}$$

So the question is: What are the overall parameters β_0, β_1? Because all the data can't be studied, β_0 and β_1 can only be estimated by sampling. Record the estimated parameter as $\hat{\beta}_0 = b_0$, $\hat{\beta}_1 = b_1$. Assuming that the estimated values b_0, β_1 of β_0 and β_1 are found by a certain method, the estimation equation can be obtained:

$$\hat{y}_i = b_0 + b_1 x_i, \quad i = 1, 2, \ldots, n \tag{2}$$

For each x_i, this estimation equation has a definite $\hat{y}_i$ corresponding to it. Obviously, $\hat{y}_i$ is often equal to the actual observed value y_i, but there is a deviation of e_i, namely:

$$e_i = (y_i - \hat{y}_i) \tag{3}$$

e_i Sometimes referred to as residual error. In order to express the deviation of all the observed values y_i from the regression estimated value $\hat{y}_i$, the sum of squares of residuals is generally considered:

$$\sum_{i=1}^{n} e_i^2 = \sum_{i=1}^{n} (y_i - \hat{y}_i)^2 = \sum_{i=1}^{n} (y_i - b_0 - b_1 x_i)^2 \qquad (4)$$

As we know, a general-purpose computer runs the described system according to the input, which is called a virtual machine. The process of human brain's cognition of the outside world is very similar to the operation method of this computer. If our brain has already started to implement the computational structure that represents the external system, it more or less shows that we have realized the understanding of the external world. The most essential purpose of learning is to learn knowledge from a large amount of data analysis. In recent years, more and more experts have begun to pay attention to big data technique. Big data technique refers to the technical ability to quickly obtain useful message from all kinds of data. Traditional data analysis pays more attention to the advance setting of statistical methods in data analysis to realize valuable data message. Compared with past data analysis methods, Big data technique extracts hidden and valuable data message from a large number of data structures, thus maximizing the value of data. In the current big data environment, how to adopt effective learning means is the significance of ML at present, and ML will also become a widely respected and popular learning and service technique. Data analysis based on ML, how to deal with a large amount of data message quickly and effectively, is the key research direction of ML at present.

3.2 Results and Discussion

Before designing the system, the system needs analysis should be carried out first. The system needs analysis is one of the most important links in the system development work, and the comprehensive investigation of seeking truth from facts is the basis of the analysis and design. The conceptual design of database is the process of abstracting the user's needs obtained by the system analysis into the message structure reflecting the user's point of view, that is, describing real things in a way that does not depend on any data model, with the aim of correctly reflecting real things and the relationship between things in the form of symbols. The main factor considered in the algorithm is how to make full use of school resources, which include time resources, classroom resources and teacher resources. Although we have developed a course scheduling system from class schedule to class schedule and individual course scheduling system, in practical application, most of the teaching progress is regular. We can classify the progress of the same class to reduce the scale of problems and avoid problems such as difficulty in printing the schedule due to scattered results of similar schedule scheduling. It can be seen from Tables 1 and 2, Figs. 3 and 4 that different control parameters can get different control results. The results of system verification are consistent with the results of theoretical analysis and the changing trend, which proves the correctness of the algorithm in this paper to realize virtual simulation object control.

Usually, the courses taught by each teacher are determined by the educational administration department according to the teachers' characteristics and through consultation with teachers, so the corresponding relationship between courses and teachers is relatively certain. In the design of the algorithm, it can be considered that there is no

Table 1. Distance error of table parameters

	0	20	40	60	80	100
Parameter 1	0.92	0.28	0.83	0.68	0.52	0.21
Parameter 2	0.96	0.66	0.58	0.53	0.8	0.15

Table 2. Angle error of table parameters

	0	20	40	60	80	100
Parameter 1	0.22	0.23	0.81	0.33	0.41	0.21
Parameter 2	0.66	0.97	0.35	0.7	0.88	0.28

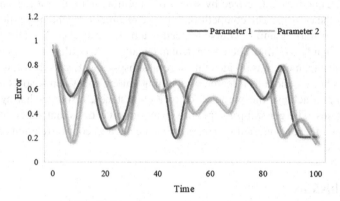

Fig. 3. Distance error of table parameters

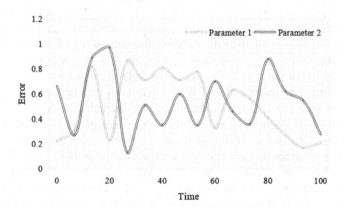

Fig. 4. Angle error of parameters

competition of teachers' resources, which not only takes care of the strong subjectivity of teachers' resource allocation, but also makes the course scheduling algorithm not need to consider teachers' automatic allocation, which simplifies the complexity of algorithm design and reduces the amount of data storage and calculation. In the whole process of software development, programming is only a relatively small part. The real decisive factor of software development comes from the early conceptual problems, rather than the later implementation problems. Only by recognizing, understanding and correctly expressing the memory essence of application problems can a good design be made, and then, it is the concrete programming realization.

As a special course scheduling system, security is also an important issue to be considered, so this system designs a login interface that requires password input and authentication. Before entering the system, the user must enter the user name, password and identity through the login interface. These message will be automatically checked with the data in the system database, and only when they are correct can they log in to the system. Time is characterized by strong competition, not only for the starting units but also for the courses. The competition for time resources is generally reflected in the desire of each starting unit or course to occupy a better time slice. Usually, we can get the general standard of time slice from demand analysis. According to the requirements of system management, it is divided into several subsystems. Each subsystem has a high degree of cohesion and a low degree of coupling among subsystems, so as to facilitate application and achieve the purposes of data consistency, resource sharing and clear responsibilities. The general principle of subsystem division is that subsystems should be relatively independent, and unnecessary data calls and control relationships should be minimized.

4 Conclusions

Course arrangement is a very important work in educational administration, which relates to the quality and efficiency of the whole teaching activities. The application of artificial intelligence theory in the design of course arrangement system can promote the daily management of schools and make the daily management of schools more scientific and efficient, so the design of course arrangement system plays a very important role in the daily management of schools. A reasonable schedule can make full use of all kinds of teaching resources, stimulate students' interest in learning, and improve teachers' enthusiasm and teaching effect. However, the unreasonable curriculum will have a negative impact on the whole teaching activities, even the management of the whole school. The problem of computer course scheduling is a classic problem, and the idea of solving this kind of problem also has important reference value in other problem fields. It is believed that with the improvement of computer theory level such as artificial intelligence and the in-depth development of scientific workers' research on this problem, more scientific methods will be explored and become a classic problem, providing important scientific reference for people to solve similar problems.

References

1. Dougherty, J.P.: Math CountsMathematics for a human-computer interaction course. ACM Inroads **10**(1), 26–27 (2019)
2. Urquiza-Fuentes, J., Paredes-Velasco, M.: Investigating the effect of realistic projects on students' motivation, the case of Human-Computer interaction course. Comput. Hum. Behav. **72**, 692–700 (2017). https://doi.org/10.1016/j.chb.2016.07.020
3. Srimadhaven, T., Junni, A.C., Harshith, N., et al.: Learning analytics: virtual reality for programming course in higher education. Procedia Comput. Sci. **172**, 433–437 (2020)
4. Kaushik, M.: Evaluating a first-year engineering course for project based learning (PBL) essentials. Procedia Comput. Sci. **172**, 364–369 (2020)
5. DeBenedictis, E.P.: Plotting a socially responsible course for computers using cybersecurity as an example. Computer **50**(12), 86–90 (2017). https://doi.org/10.1109/MC.2017.4451217
6. Catanese, H., Hauser, C., Gebremedhin, A.H.: Evaluation of native and transfer students' success in a computer science course. ACM Inroads **9**(2), 53–57 (2018)
7. Hammami, J., Khemaja, M.: Towards agile and gamified flipped learning design models: application to the system and data integration course - ScienceDirect. Procedia Comput. Sci. **164**, 239–244 (2019)
8. Olson, J.S., Wang, D., Olson, G.M., et al.: How people write together now: beginning the investigation with advanced undergraduates in a project course. ACM Trans. Comput.-Hum. Interact. **24**(1), 1–40 (2017)
9. Souza, A., Filho, M.R., Soares, C.: Production and evaluation of an educational process for human-computer interaction (HCI) courses. IEEE Trans. Educ. **99**, 1–8 (2020)
10. Willison, R., Lowry, P.B.: Disentangling the motivations for organizational insider computer abuse through the rational choice and life course perspectives. Data Base Adv. Message Syst. **49**(4), 81–102 (2018)
11. Amato, F., Coppolino, L., D'Antonio, S., et al.: An abstract reasoning architecture for privacy policies monitoring. Futur. Gener. Comput. Syst.Comput. Syst. **106**(5), 393–400 (2020)

The Teaching Reform of Animal Pathology Course in Application Oriented Universities Based on Computer Technology

Chunhua Li[✉], Cuiqing Zhao, Huayong Wei, and Qianhong Liu

Jilin Agricultural Science and Technology University, Jilin, China
chunhuali2009@sina.com

Abstract. Animal pathology is an important discipline in the field of veterinary medicine. It involves the study of diseases affecting animals and their causes, symptoms, diagnosis, and treatment. The reform of animal pathology teaching in applied universities is an important aspect that needs to be explored and studied to improve the quality of student education. The current teaching methods used in animal pathology may not be sufficient to meet the needs of students. Therefore, it is necessary to carry out reforms to ensure that students gain comprehensive knowledge about animal diseases. The exploration and research of teaching reform can help identify areas for improvement, such as curriculum development, teaching strategies, and evaluation methods. Using technology in the teaching of animal pathology can provide students with an interactive learning experience, thereby improving learning outcomes. There are practical problems and current situations in applied universities, such as unclear teaching objectives, unclear teaching paths, and lack of teaching practice. Based on this, this article first analyzes the current teaching situation of animal pathology courses in applied universities, then studies the teaching mode of animal pathology in applied universities from the perspective of computer technology, and finally proposes teaching reform strategies for applied animal pathology. In addition, combining practical courses such as laboratory experiments can help students apply theoretical knowledge to practice. In short, exploring and researching the teaching reform of animal pathology is crucial to improving the quality of education for veterinary students. This will ensure that they gain comprehensive knowledge of animal diseases and effectively address them in their future veterinary careers.

Keywords: Teaching Reform · Animal Pathology Course · Computer Tech

1 Introduction

With the iterative progress and maturity of computer tech, it has been widely and deeply studied and popularized in many fields, especially the utilization of computer tech represented by multimedia and database in the teaching reform of animal pathology course in utilization-oriented undergraduate colleges, which greatly accelerates the teaching

Y. Zhang and N. Shah (Eds.): BigIoT-EDU 2023, LNICST 583, pp. 436–446, 2024.
https://doi.org/10.1007/978-3-031-63139-9_46

innovation and reform of animal pathology professional course [1]. At present, with the progress of society and the continuous amelioration of people's living standards, both the demand for animal meat consumption and the demand for pet market are constantly expanding. In this context, the rapid growth of the demand for animal pathological treatment in society has brought new opportunities and challenges to the development of veterinary industry [2]. On the one hand, the growing market makes the animal husbandry and veterinary industry have a broad demand for professional animal medicine talents; on the other hand, the practical literacy of students in animal husbandry and veterinary colleges needs to be further ameliorated, and the matching and adaptability between them need to be further ameliorated.

In order to further strengthen the practical utilization and operation ability of students majoring in animal pathology in utilization-oriented universities, so that they can better serve and protect the practical needs of animal husbandry and veterinary industry, we need to strengthen the utilization and integration of computer, network and info tech in animal pathology course. Secondly, in view of the current practical problems and status quo of animal pathology course in utilization-oriented universities, such as unclear teaching objectives, unclear teaching paths and insufficient teaching practicality, it is helpful to establish a practical teaching platform by using computer tech and actively carry out the teaching reform of the course, so as to clarify the training objectives and programs of the course, and accelerate the teaching reform and optimization of the course [3].

In addition, in view of the practical characteristics of animal pathology course, it is necessary to use computer tech to establish the organic connection between the theory and practice of the subject, so as to open up all links of the course teaching [4]. The use of computer info platform enables students to further verify and strengthen their theoretical understanding in practical operation, accelerates the cultivation of students' ability to observe, analyze and solve problems, and releases students' learning initiative and innovative thinking. By using computer tech to build a virtual experimental operation platform, students' practice process can get rid of the shortage of resources and the limitation of practice scene, space and time, so that students' practice can be more fully guaranteed [5].

In short, the organic integration of computer tech and animal pathology course in utilization-oriented universities can accelerate the teaching reform of the course; significantly ameliorate the professionalism of teaching objectives, the practicability of teaching content and the practicality of teaching methods. The in-depth utilization of computer tech is also helpful to cultivate more professional and practical talents for the animal husbandry and veterinary industry, and ameliorate the students' professional quality of animal pathology diagnosis from several aspects as shown in Fig. 1 below. Therefore, it is of great practical value to study the teaching reform of animal pathology in utilization-oriented universities on account of computer tech.

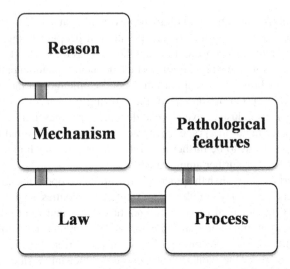

Fig. 1. Specialized elements of animal pathological diagnosis

2 Current Situation of Animal Pathology Teaching in Utilization Oriented Universities

2.1 Challenges Faced by Animal Pathology Teaching in Utilization Oriented Universities

Under the current network info conditions, the teaching of animal pathology course in utilization-oriented universities is facing the challenges of info overload and fragmentation of learning time and content. The hyperlink structure leads to the fragmentation of knowledge, learning and time, and the connection between knowledge is cut off because of multi task and fast pace. Secondly, due to the interruption of the connection between knowledge in the network era, it is unable to form a complete system, which aggravates the phenomenon of info overload in the process of students' learning knowledge, leading to passive acceptance, lack of deep thinking, distraction, and even cognitive bias in most cases [6]. In addition, a large number of false, inferior, incomplete and inaccurate components in the fragmented info occupy a large number of students' extracurricular time, causing serious interference to students' systematic learning.

2.2 Opportunities for Animal Pathology Teaching in Utilization Oriented Universities

Under the condition of Internet, using computer tech to carry out the teaching reform of animal pathology helps students to allocate their learning time more flexibly and freely, and makes the content of the subject easier for students to master and obtain [7]. Secondly, the use of Internet tech to establish animal pathology teaching platform helps to maintain students' interest in learning, so as to facilitate the efficient use of fragmented time. In addition, the utilization of Internet tech makes teaching resources and materials more abundant, so as to better accelerate students' absorption of knowledge, so that they can obtain the most cutting-edge knowledge in the field of the subject, so as to restructure the knowledge structure.

2.3 Current Situation of Animal Pathology Teaching in Utilization Oriented Universities

At present, most of the applied undergraduate courses of animal pathology teaching mainly focus on the diagnosis and quality of animal diseases, through the traditional clinical observation means, the disease symptoms, disease consultation and pathological examination of animals are analyzed, thus generating diagnosis opinions. It can be seen that the current teaching methods and teaching objectives are mainly focused on the training of the theoretical knowledge, concept and animal pathogenesis of animal pathology, so that students can understand and master the changes of functional activities in the course of animal disease [8]. The current teaching mode cannot effectively classify the students' levels. Therefore, it is necessary to optimize the course system of animal pathology to meet the students' individual characteristics and needs, so that students have more solid theoretical and practical operation skills.

3 Teaching Mode of Animal Pathology on Account of Computer Tech

3.1 The Premise of Teaching Animal Pathology Course on Account of Computer Tech

First of all, advanced info tech should be widely used to accelerate the teaching of animal pathology on account of computer and network, so as to provide a good info learning environment and conditions for students [9]. Secondly, the relevant utilization-oriented universities should make full use of multimedia and network tech, adopt new teaching mode to ameliorate the single teaching mode of animal pathology course, give full play to students' learning initiative and dominant position, and make the learning process of the course more interactive and experiential. In addition, the teaching mode of animal pathology course on account of computer tech should be fully supported by modern info tech, especially network tech, so that the teaching process, especially the practical teaching link, is not limited by time and place, and can assist students to carry out autonomous learning according to their individual characteristics [10].

3.2 Curriculum System of Animal Pathology on Account of Computer

The cultivation of applied talents in animal medicine mainly refers to the cultivation of professional and technical personnel who can effectively diagnose and treat various clinical animal diseases, and the prerequisite for effective treatment of animal diseases is accurate diagnosis. Currently, for diseases of economic animals (such as chickens, pigs, etc.) and companion animals (such as dogs, cats, etc.), the main diagnostic methods are traditional observation of animal clinical symptoms, consultation with livestock owners, pathological autopsy of animal carcasses, and laboratory testing (such as routine paraffin sectioning, etc.). Animal pathology is an authoritative first level clinical diagnostic discipline [11]. Therefore, the basic teaching objectives of the course "Animal Pathology" are determined as follows: to enable students to master the basic concepts of diseases, the main pathological changes of diseases, and the occurrence and development process of diseases; To cultivate students' ability to diagnose clinical diseases, in particular, they should understand the interrelationship between the morphological structure, material metabolism, and functional activities of animals at different stages during the occurrence and development of diseases [12]. Specifically, a ladder type talent structure is adopted for training, and different curriculum objectives are set according to different employment directions and career requirements of students majoring in animal medicine, and different types of jobs. Students majoring in animal medicine are divided into practical classes and innovative classes based on their future employment orientation [13]. The practical class students will mainly engage in clinical work in the future, with the curriculum function focusing on the cultivation of pathological diagnostic skills. The innovative class students will mainly engage in scientific research in the future, with the curriculum function focusing on the cultivation of design experimental skills. In order to adjust the curriculum structure, it is possible to hire corresponding enterprise leaders, industry experts, and teachers with rich teaching experience to assist in formulating the curriculum outline and curriculum plan, making the curriculum structure more close to actual work needs [14]. According to students at different levels and different employment needs, optimize the curriculum system, and through comprehensive basic training, enable students to firmly grasp the theoretical knowledge and application skills of basic animal pathology.

The computer-based animal pathology curriculum system mainly includes several aspects as shown in Fig. 2 below. The Internet tech is used to divide the curriculum system, and then the Internet is used as the center to build a new system and structure. Secondly, we use computer tech to build collaborative and exploratory teaching mechanism of animal pathology course, hybrid mechanism represented by micro class and MOOC, and mobile classroom teaching mode of self-organization and maker's zero deposit and lump sum [15]. With the help of computer multimedia courseware, an autonomous learning mode is established, in which students can freely control their learning time, choose learning contents and participate in teachers' teaching guidance under the guidance of teachers.

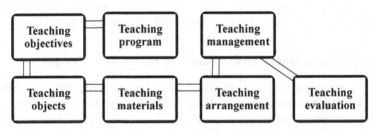

Fig. 2. The computer-based animal pathology curriculum system

3.3 Teaching Mode of Animal Pathology on Account of Computer Tech

Taking the course of active pathology as the center, the discussion of the subject was completed through different tasks, and the training of students' various skills was completed at the same time. Secondly, in addition to cultivating students' professional knowledge, students' comprehensive practical utilization ability of animal pathology knowledge was also ameliorated through a series of practical tasks. In addition, by highlighting the teaching concept of teacher-centered and student-centered, each unit gives students a certain amount of time, and takes the group as the unit to show students' understanding and expanding thinking of animal pathology course. Through the reform and innovation of computer-based animal pathology course, the teaching effect and students' learning satisfaction can be significantly ameliorated, and the results are shown in Fig. 3 below.

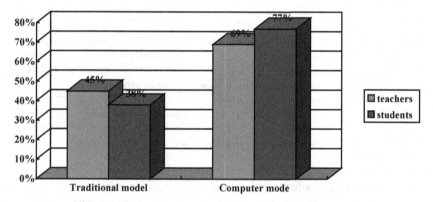

Fig. 3. The effect of animal pathology curriculum reform on account of computer

4 Teaching Reform Strategy of Animal Pathology on Account of Computer Tech

4.1 Optimizing Teaching Mode on Account of Computer Tech

According to the content of the textbook and under the guidance of the teacher, students independently preview and learn the course content of animal pathology, answer teachers' or students' questions about the content of animal pathology, rewrite the text, complete the textbook exercises, and discuss based on the textbook exercises. Secondly, the teaching mode of "two teachers in the same class" should be adopted, and the teaching method of "integration of production, education, and research" should be constructed. The construction and utilization of computer teaching resources should be strengthened, and teaching methods and means should be enriched, as shown in Fig. 4. In addition, computer technology should be used to strengthen the practical teaching of animal pathology, reform the examination methods of animal pathology, and strengthen the cultivation of students' practical and scientific research abilities.

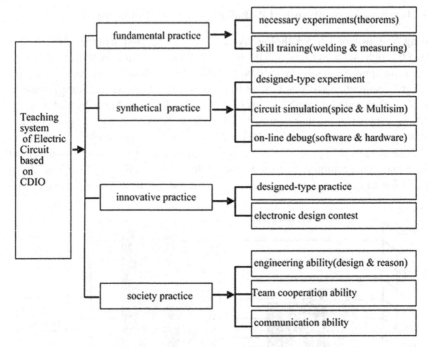

Fig. 4. Optimizing Teaching Mode of Computer Technology

Absorbing advanced educational and teaching concepts, achievements, and information technology means, we have developed a variety of curriculum activities with multi-dimensional classroom interaction, and established new teaching methods suitable for improving students' practical abilities. To this end, use teaching methods such as lecturing, heuristic, participatory, exploratory, and discussion to fully mobilize students' learning enthusiasm.

(1) Case Teaching Method

Case teaching method is an open and interactive new teaching method with clear purpose, objectivity, authenticity, and comprehensiveness. It can inspire students and increase their subjective role in classroom teaching. During the teaching process of Animal Pathology, the description of pathological changes by teachers using language alone is too abstract for students to understand. To address the above issues, clinical animal cases are used as teaching materials to allow students to observe pathological changes and correctly describe and analyze them. In addition, during the teaching process, students are required to simultaneously conduct clinical pathological dissection changes and laboratory histopathological observations to understand the consistency between microscopic and macroscopic changes, thereby better understanding the pathological changes of animal tissues and organs. For example, when introducing the pathology of the respiratory system, with reference to porcine reproductive and respiratory dysfunction syndrome and avian influenza, we will introduce lobar pneumonia. We will select one case of infectious pleuropneumonia, perform visual and microscopic examinations of the stages of hyperemia and edema, red liver transformation, gray liver transformation, and dissipation, analyze the pathological changes, and guide students through differential diagnosis on how to analyze such cases. Combining theoretical knowledge with clinical cases to analyze the occurrence and development process of diseases can enable students to firmly grasp basic theoretical knowledge, while also cultivating students' clinical practical skills.

(2) "Micro class", "Mu class", and "offline" teaching methods.

According to the course plan, we will organically integrate classroom teaching through online tutorials, experimental teaching multimedia teaching software, and micro class videos, while sharing learning resources on animal pathology with students through microblogging, WeChat, and QQ platforms. Before the experiment class, release the experiment operation video for students to preview in advance, and solve and discuss difficult issues through the network platform. For example, when learning Gram dyeing technology, first place a video of the Gram dyeing process on Weibo and WeChat platforms for students to preview before class. On the platform, students can ask questions of interest, and the teacher can provide timely answers. The videos of microenterprise courses played during the teaching process are vivid and vivid, making the classroom teaching atmosphere more active, and achieving good classroom teaching results.

(3) PBL teaching method

PBL teaching method "Problem Based Learning" is a problem-based teaching method that solves practical problems through teacher guidance and group collaboration. For example, in teaching, students are provided with gross pathological anatomy images and histopathological sections based on specific case analysis, and the teacher provides appropriate explanations. Then, students are divided into groups of 4–6 people. After class, they independently query information and discuss in groups to complete pathological speculation and preliminary diagnosis. In class Each group will make a summary statement, and the teacher will provide answers to difficult questions encountered by students. Finally, a summary of the case will be provided. The above teaching process can greatly enhance students' learning enthusiasm and cultivate their awareness of autonomous learning and unity and cooperation.

4.2 Teaching Reform Strategy of Animal Pathology on Account of Computer Tech

First of all, it should carry out diversified teaching with the help of computer carrier and platform, reasonably adjust the experimental teaching projects, and reform the experimental teaching assessment mode. Among them, in the reform of experimental teaching assessment mode, a unified experimental teaching and assessment mode of animal pathology was established with the help of computer tech. Secondly, in the reasonable adjustment of experimental teaching project level, with the help of computer tech to establish a concrete understanding of knowledge model, so as to help students better grasp abstract knowledge, and better integrate with practice. In addition, it should actively ameliorate the teaching methods and means under the blessing of computer tech, constantly ameliorate the classroom teaching effect, increase the construction of experimental training room and practice training base, optimize the hardware conditions of practice teaching, and create a multi-link practice assessment system.

Currently, many colleges and universities have fewer experimental hours for animal pathology. Generally, 4 to 6 experiments are arranged in the second half of the second semester of grade, with each experimental class lasting about 3 h, totaling 18 to 20 class hours. The content of experimental courses is mostly observation of pathological sections of specimens, and the teaching method is relatively simple, which often puts students in a passive state of accepting knowledge. The classroom teaching effect is poor. In order to strengthen the practical teaching process and increase the corresponding class hours, the practical teaching is divided into three stages: In the first stage, the pathology course is offered in the second semester of the second grade, while the pathology experimental course is offered, and the pathological anatomy practice is added, so that students can deepen their understanding of the pathological characteristics of diseases and changes, and enhance basic operation and skill training; Stage 2: In the second semester of Grade 3, an experimental course on veterinary skills will be offered, including the dissection and film reading of animal pathology. In Stage 3, during the senior year internship, written descriptions of cases encountered in the clinical pathological diagnosis of animal diseases will be provided, typical clinical cases will be collected, and students will be allowed to observe a large number of visual and microscopic specimens, multimedia courseware, slides, and wall charts to carry out pathological practical teaching at multiple levels and angles. During the above three stages of teaching, the TBL (Team Based Learning) teaching model can be introduced into the traditional experimental teaching of animal pathology. For example, the School of Life Sciences of Longyan University has established more than ten comprehensive and designed experimental projects using favorable experimental platform conditions such as the Institute of Animal Medicine and the Fujian Swine Epidemic Prevention and Control Engineering Center, such as clinical symptom observation and pathological dissection of Newcastle disease in chickens, establishment of a mouse tetrachloride liver injury model, observation of acute heat stress damage to mouse tissues and organs, and pathological dissection and observation of Pasteurella infected rabbits, Divide students into free groups, with 5 to 6 people in each group. Each group randomly selects an experimental project, and completes related learning tasks such as collecting and sorting relevant data, observing, analyzing, and drawing pathological specimens, producing and presenting PowerPoint presentations, and interactive Q&A. In class, each group will present the learning situation to the entire class in turn, leading them to learn the content of the experimental project together. After the speech, interactive questions and answers will be conducted, and student representatives and teachers from each group will grade the entire group. Finally, the teacher will provide comments and necessary analysis.

During the Pathological Anatomy Internship Week, based on some pathological cases submitted for clinical examination, students are required to diagnose the diseases suffered by animals from the pathological changes (including visual and microscopic examinations) found during clinical manifestations and physical signs, discuss the evolution and development of the diseases, and analyze the causes of death. For example, yellow diarrhea in piglets and white diarrhea in piglets are both acute and fatal intestinal infectious diseases caused by pathogenic Escherichia coli in newborn piglets. The differences are in the age of onset, stool color, and mortality rate. Both infectious gastroenteritis and epidemic diarrhea in pigs can cause diarrhea in piglets, but the mortality rate of piglets is different. According to pathological sections, the ratio of villus length to intestinal gland recess is different. In this way, students can draw inferences from one example by analyzing diseases with similar symptoms.

In addition, a comprehensive experimental performance evaluation system based on four indicators, namely, experimental class performance, experimental reports, film reading assessment, and group learning demonstration, has been established. Through microscopic examination of specimens, case analysis, defense, and other means of investigation, it can be more in-depth and specific to understand the degree to which students master practical operating skills.

5 Conclusion

In summary, by using computer tech to build a virtual experimental operation platform, students' practice process can get rid of the shortage of resources and the limitation of practice scene, space and time, so that students' practice can be more fully guaranteed. On account of the analysis of the current situation of animal pathology teaching in utilization-oriented universities, this paper studies the opportunities of animal pathology teaching in utilization-oriented universities. Through the research on the teaching mode of animal pathology on account of computer tech, the teaching mode of animal pathology on account of computer tech was analyzed, and the teaching reform strategy of animal pathology on account of computer tech was given.

Acknowledgments. Research and practice on the reform of animal pathology course combine application-oriented colleges with directional culture mode.

References

1. Han, T.: Research on the teaching reform path of operational research course of engineering management major based on computer technology. J. Phys. Conf. Ser. **1744**(3), 032238 (2021). (4pp)
2. Feng, W., Zhang, C., Liu, Q.: Research on computer teaching in universities based on computational thinking. J. Phys. Conf. Ser. **1915**(2), 022041 (2021)
3. Maher, R.A., Osman, A.G.E., Fahmy, K., et al.: Out come of wide local excision with and without corticosteroid therapy in management of idiopathic granulomatous mastitis. Tumori J. **107**(1_suppl), 13–13 (2021)
4. Cheng, Q., Li, B., Zhou, Y.: Research on evaluation system of classroom teaching quality in colleges and universities based on 5G environment (2021)
5. Wu, X.: Research on the reform of ideological and political teaching evaluation method of college English course based on "online and offline" teaching. J. High. Educ. Res. **3**(1), 87–90 (2022)

6. Xu, J., Feng, L.: Research on the Application of "Production-Oriented Approach" Based on Blended Teaching in College English Writing Teaching in Private Undergraduate Colleges. Destech Publications, Inc (2021)
7. Hode, A.K., Dedjan, H., Sondjo, F.M.: Peripheral neuropathy and associated factors in diabetics at the CNHU-HKM of Cotonou in 2021. J. Diabetes Mellitus **13**(1), 11 (2023)
8. Xiong, Y.: Research on practical courses and scientific teaching of accounting major in colleges and universities based on computer technology. J. Phys. Conf. Ser. **1744**(4), 042082012 (2021)
9. Li, L., Sun, M.: Research on the teaching mode of the interior design studio system in universities based on computer. J. Phys. Conf. Ser. **1744**(3), 032173 (2021). (4pp)
10. Yuan, Z., Fang, L., Yi, S.: Research on the teaching innovation of environmental art design specialty based on computer VR technology. J. Phys. Conf. Ser. **1992**(3), 032001 (2021)
11. Wang, L.: The reform of college music education mode based on computer delay factor algorithm music technology. In: Hung, J.C., Chang, JW., Pei, Y., Wu, WC. (eds.) Innovative Computing. LNEE, vol. 791, pp. 1699–1704. Springer, Singapore (2022). https://doi.org/10.1007/978-981-16-4258-6_218
12. Jia, S., Zhang, X.: Teaching mode of psychology and pedagogy in colleges and universities based on artificial intelligence technology. J. Phys. Conf. Ser. **1852**(3), 032033 (2021)
13. Guan, Y.: Research on the reform of ideological and political theory courses in colleges and universities in the big data era. J. Phys. Conf. Ser. **1852**(2), 022061 (2021)
14. Liu, J.: Research on English teaching reform based on information technology. J. Phys. Conf. Ser. **1744**(4), 042234 (2021). (5pp)
15. Zhan, S., Wu, J.: Research on physical experiment teaching reform based on internet environment. J. Phys. Conf. Ser. **1802**(2), 022055 (2021)

Intelligent Optimization of Computer Image Processing Technology Analysis

Huayong Wei[✉]

Anhui Communications Vocational and Technical College, Hefei, China
hyweisky@126.com

Abstract. Intelligent optimization algorithm is an advanced computing technology, which simulates the biological evolution process in nature or the logical thinking of human beings to find a solution to the problem. In computer image processing, intelligent optimization algorithms are widely used, mainly in image enhancement, image restoration, image segmentation, feature extraction, image recognition and so on. Intelligent optimization algorithms have developed rapidly, and many excellent algorithms with different characteristics have emerged, which have achieved good results in practical applications. Image analysis is the basis for realizing machine vision, including image enhancement, image fusion, image recognition, image tracking, image retrieval and many other technologies. It has a great demand in medicine, transportation, military, aerospace and other fields. In particular, the development of many industries and fields such as intelligent robots, smart medicine, and smart cities has brought many optimization challenges to image analysis, At present, image analysis based on swarm intelligence optimization algorithm has become an important research hotspot.

Keywords: computer · Intelligent optimization algorithm · image processing

1 Introduction

Intelligent optimization algorithm plays an important role in computer image processing technology, and is widely used in image enhancement, restoration, segmentation, feature extraction and recognition. With the continuous development of technology, the application of intelligent optimization algorithm in computer image processing will be more extensive and in-depth, which is helpful to improve the effect and efficiency of image processing. At the same time, for researchers and technology developers, a deep understanding of the principles and characteristics of these algorithms, as well as their limitations and advantages in specific applications, is the key to achieve efficient and practical computer image processing [1].

DImage enhancement is the use of intelligent optimization algorithm to improve the visual effect of the image in order to better extract useful information. For example, intelligent optimization algorithms such as genetic algorithm and particle swarm optimization can be used to adjust the contrast, brightness and color of the image, so as to

Y. Zhang and N. Shah (Eds.): BigIoT-EDU 2023, LNICST 583, pp. 447–456, 2024.
https://doi.org/10.1007/978-3-031-63139-9_47

achieve the enhancement effect [2]. Image restoration is to restore the real image from the degraded image as much as possible. By using intelligent optimization algorithms, such as simulated annealing, genetic algorithm, etc., we can effectively solve the problems of image blurring and distortion.Image segmentation is to divide an image into several meaningful regions or objects. Image segmentation techniques based on intelligent optimization algorithms, such as ant colony algorithm and simulated annealing algorithm, can identify and segment complex images more accurately.Computer image processing technology has a wide range of applications in many fields, and with the continuous progress and development of technology, its application prospects are becoming more and more extensive. However, computer image processing technology still faces many challenges, such as large amount of data, real-time and intelligence. In order to overcome these challenges, it is necessary to continuously carry out technological innovation and research to improve the efficiency and accuracy of computer image processing. At the same time, it is necessary to combine other related technologies, such as artificial intelligence, machine learning, etc., in order to further improve the application value and practicability of computer image processing.

Cloud computing models have certain limitations in production applications. With the development of the Internet of Things technology, the number of monitoring devices, networked industrial devices, and a series of smart home terminal devices such as sweeping robots and smart refrigerators has increased rapidly. The amount of data generated by these terminal devices is growing rapidly, and the growth rate has exceeded the speed of network bandwidth development. At the same time, some application scenarios have higher requirements for real-time data processing and security and privacy. Traditional cloud computing models require data to be transmitted to the cloud for centralized processing. However, the limitations of such computing models have become increasingly prominent, mainly manifested in: a) In unmanned driving and other application scenarios, high real-time and stability are required. Cloud computing processing methods can generate high delays, and data transmission through the network cannot ensure its stability. Therefore, these scenarios cannot process data through cloud computing. b) Data processing is limited by cloud server computing bottlenecks. Although cloud servers have powerful computing capabilities, they are still unable to meet the explosive growth of intelligent optimized data processing requirements. At the same time, there are peaks and troughs in computing requirements at different time periods. When the demand peaks, the data provided by intelligent optimization devices must be queued for processing, seriously affecting the normal operation of intelligent optimization devices;

Intelligent optimized computing models can effectively solve the problems existing in the cloud computing models mentioned above. The core of intelligent optimization computing is to perform data calculation and processing locally on the collected data information, and only report the data processing results to the cloud. The advantages of intelligent optimization computing mainly include: a) reducing data transmission and dependence on the network. In the intelligent optimization calculation model, data processing is performed on local devices, greatly reducing the amount of data transmission, reducing dependence on the network, and reducing the cost of network transmission. b) Ensure real-time and stability of data processing. In intelligent optimization computing, data is processed in local devices, and only the data processing results are transmitted to the cloud. This can not only alleviate the computing pressure of the cloud computing center, but also avoid the uncertainty caused by network fluctuations, effectively improving the stability and real-time performance of data processing operations. c) Ensure data security and de privacy. Intelligent optimized computing only transmits the processed data results to the cloud, without the risk of disclosing private data, ensuring the security of user information.

The purpose of this paper is how to use the best swarm intelligence optimization algorithm to solve various problems in image analysis more effectively [3]. First of all, in the basic research of swarm intelligence optimization algorithm, the algorithm performance is improved to avoid its defects in high-dimensional, multimodal, discontinuous and complex optimization problems. Secondly, aiming at the five problems of image enhancement, image fusion, image recognition, image tracking and image retrieval, through in-depth study of the mechanism and characteristics of various swarm intelligent optimization algorithms, the most effective optimization algorithms are determined to obtain the best results for solving practical engineering problems.

2 Related Work

2.1 Overview of Intelligent Algorithm Research and Development

Since the intelligent algorithm was proposed, it has attracted extensive attention of many scholars at home and abroad. After years of development and creation, intelligent optimization algorithm has been successfully applied in various fields of the national economy, providing an efficient and feasible solution to many complex problems in production and life, and has become an important research direction in the academic field [4].

At present, the research on intelligent algorithm is generally divided into three aspects: first, directly improve on the basis of the original algorithm; Second, according to the advantages and disadvantages of different algorithms, different algorithms are combined in a certain way to create a hybrid intelligent optimization algorithm with better performance. The third is to obtain inspiration by observing the collective behavior of people and animals in the nature, and then establish mathematical models to describe various swarm intelligent behaviors, creating new intelligent optimization algorithms [5].An image is a two-dimensional matrix of pixels, and each pixel has a color value. Common color models are RGB model and HSV model. In computers, images are usually stored in binary form, that is, the color value of each pixel is represented by several binary bits are shown in Fig. 1.

$$J_m(U, V) = \sum_{j=1}^{C} \sum_{i=1}^{N} u_{ij}^m d_{ij}^2 \tag{1}$$

tor V is calculated by the following formula:

$$v_j^{(t)} = \frac{\sum_{i=1}^{N} (\mu_{ij}^{(t-1)})^m x_i}{\sum_{i=1}^{N} (\mu_{ij}^{(t-1)})^m} j = 1, \ldots C \tag{2}$$

Step 2. Given the new cluster center V (t), the member value μ (t) ij can be updated to:

$$\mu_{ij} = \frac{1}{\sum_{k=1}^{C} (\frac{d_j}{d_k})^{\frac{2}{(m-1)}}} i = 1, \ldots, Nj = 1, \ldots C \qquad (3)$$

$$F(U, V) = \frac{1}{J_m + \varepsilon} \varepsilon > 0 \qquad (4)$$

The ReLU function is hard saturated in the $(-\infty, 0)$ interval, and the derivative value is constant in the $(0, +\infty)$ interval. It can maintain the gradient without attenuation in the $(0, +\infty)$ interval. The ReLU function not only solves the problem of gradient disappearance, but also significantly increases the speed of model convergence during training and reduces computational complexity. Therefore, functions such as ReLU are now widely used as activation functions for convolutional neural networks.

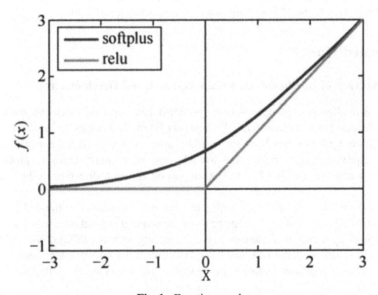

Fig. 1. Function graph

Genetic algorithm, ant colony algorithm and particle swarm algorithm are commonly used intelligent algorithms at present. The development and application of these algorithms have been relatively mature. Cuckoo algorithm, Tianniushu algorithm, etc. are emerging intelligent algorithms proposed in recent years. The theoretical innovation and engineering application of these algorithms have become a research hotspot in the field of intelligent algorithms.

2.2 Application and Feasibility Analysis of Intelligent Algorithm in Image Processing

Image processing refers to the processing and transformation of images to achieve specific purposes. The methods of image processing include image enhancement, image restoration, image segmentation, feature extraction, image recognition and so on. Common image processing methods include filter, histogram equalization, threshold segmentation, edge detection and so on [6]. Algorithm is the core part of image processing. The design and implementation of the algorithm need to be optimized and adjusted according to the specific application requirements. Common image processing algorithms include linear algebra method, Fourier transform, wavelet transform and so on.the sensor technology, the amount of digital image data is getting larger and larger, and the requirement of data processing speed is getting higher and higher. Therefore, how to deal with a large amount of data quickly has become an important challenge. At the same time, real-time has become an important issue, especially in some application scenarios, such as automatic driving, it is necessary to process sensor data in real time.The data obtained is becoming more and more diversified, so how to effectively integrate these data and extract more abundant information has become an important challenge. Multi-source data fusion can be realized in many ways, such as feature fusion based on deep learning and multi-modal information fusion. In the future, multi-source data fusion will become an important trend of computer image processing, which will further improve the effect and application range of computer image processing.The requirements for data processing speed are getting higher and higher. Therefore, how to deal with a large amount of data quickly has become an important challenge. At the same time, real-time has become an important issue, especially in some application scenarios, such as automatic driving, it is necessary to process sensor data in real time [7]. Therefore, this algorithm has important guiding significance for image processing and analysis, which can improve and optimize the overall effect of the image, and effectively identify and analyze the key points in the image.In the field of image processing, color space refers to a mathematical model that can provide appropriate color descriptions for image processing. Its familiar RGB (red, green, and blue) is a common color space. This article uses an HSV color space, which can be obtained by non-linear transformation based on RGB:

$$Q = \frac{1}{m} \int_0^t F(C_{\text{in}} - C_{\text{eff}})dt \tag{5}$$

$$sim_{u,v} = \frac{|N(u)N(v)|}{|N(u)N(v)|} \tag{6}$$

Or:

$$sim_{u,v} = \frac{|N(u)N(v)|}{\sqrt{|N(u)| \times |N(v)|}} \tag{7}$$

$$sim_{u,v} = \frac{\frac{\sum_{i \in N(u) \cap N(v)} 1}{\log(1+N)(i)1}}{\sqrt{1N(u)| \times |N(v)|}} \tag{8}$$

When optimizing visual communication effects, first use the RGB to HSV color space transformation formula described in Eqs. (5) to (6) to obtain the representation of the image in HSV space, and then optimize it. The algorithm flow in this article is shown in Fig. 2.

In the image acquisition module and processing module, PiCamera is used as the image acquisition module and the raspberry pie processor is used as the edge processor.

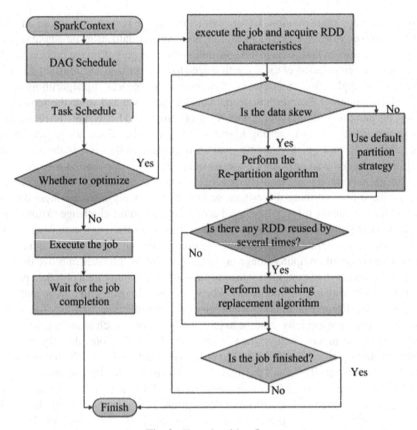

Fig. 2. Text algorithm flow

The camera transmits 640 * 480 image data to the raspberry pie, and the number of people in the node is obtained through neural network operations on the raspberry pie.

3   Overview of Intelligent Algorithms

Different intelligent algorithms will find that in the process of intelligent algorithm analysis, the commonly used algorithms are stealth algorithm, keyword algorithm and joint equation algorithm, but in the process of algorithm, there will be the overall structure of complex data collection, difficult effective examples and experiments of key points and key indicators, so it is necessary to set the initial value of data in the process of data analysis, and realize orderly and effective iteration to improve the overall situation of data. The joint use of analytical intelligent algorithms is one of the commonly used methods at present, which can make up for the shortcomings between different algorithms, optimize the algorithm as a whole, and highlight and complete the key points and key problems in the algorithm.There are also some shortcomings in the process of optimization recognition, and the key points and key comparisons of the algorithm are also the main purpose of optimization.

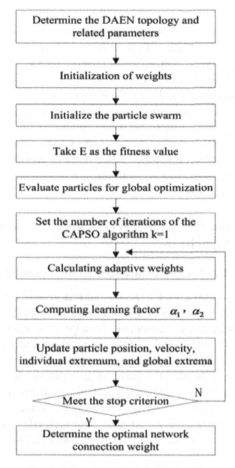

Fig. 3. Flowchart of BAS-CS algorithm

With the development of image processing technology, the problems to be optimized in image processing become more and more complex. Therefore, higher requirements have been made for the performance of intelligent optimization algorithms, which require both high optimization accuracy and high optimization efficiency. Therefore, in order to meet the requirements for accuracy and efficiency in image processing, scholars at home and abroad have made many improvements to intelligent optimization algorithms, In addition to improving the algorithm itself, many scholars also integrate several different optimization algorithms to create intelligent optimization algorithms with better performance. In order to better solve the increasingly complex optimization problems in the image field, this paper combines two new intelligent optimization algorithms BAS algorithm and CS algorithm to create a new hybrid intelligent algorithm (BAS-CS) with better optimization performance [9].

On the one hand, BAS algorithm has high global search performance and convergence speed, but it also has the defects of low convergence accuracy and easy to fall into local optimum. Considering that the random bird nest elimination mechanism in CS algorithm is conducive to eliminating the suboptimal solution, introducing the random bird nest elimination idea in CS algorithm into BAS algorithm is conducive to enhancing the ability of BAS algorithm to jump out of local optimum. On the other hand, using the location update mechanism in BAS algorithm to replace the location update mechanism in CS algorithm is conducive to reducing the blindness caused by Levy's flight search mechanism in CS, improving the convergence speed while ensuring the global search performance of CS algorithm, which shows that combining the two algorithms is conducive to improving the defects of the two algorithms and combining the advantages of the two algorithms. Therefore, this paper, based on BAS algorithm and CS algorithm, Combining the advantages of the two algorithms, a new hybrid intelligent algorithm BAS-CS is proposed, as shown in Fig. 3.

4 Computer Image Processing Technology Based on Intelligent Optimization Algorithm

4.1 Basic Framework of Image Feature Extraction Algorithm

Using BAS-CS algorithm for model selection and feature selection, the optimal model and feature combination can be found quickly. For example, in neural network training, using BAS-CS algorithm can automatically adjust the learning rate and network structure, thus improving the model performance and generalization ability [10–13]. Bayesian optimization is a global optimization algorithm, which searches by establishing a probability model of the objective function. Its basic idea is to model the objective function as a stochastic process, and then use Bayesian theorem to model and reason the stochastic process, so as to find the position of the minimum value of the function. Bayesian optimization method has the advantages of high efficiency and accuracy, and has been widely used in optimization problems in various fields (Fig. 4).

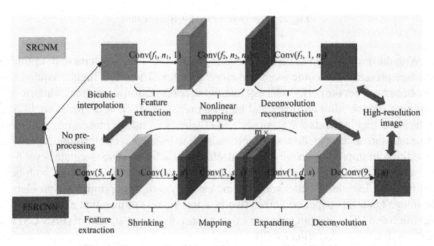

Fig. 4. Framework of image feature extraction algorithm

4.2 Image Processing

In this study, support vector machine is used to extract image features. This model can be used to solve regression analysis, classification and recognition problems On the basis of acquiring the characteristics of the labeled image data, input the image labels and image feature data to the support vector machine classifier, and finally complete the image classification processing [14].

Adaptive sampling is an improved technique of Bayesian optimization method. Its main idea is to dynamically adjust the sampling strategy by analyzing the historical sampling data, so as to reduce the number of samples and computational complexity while ensuring the search accuracy. Specifically, adaptive sampling technology can select the appropriate sampling points according to the changing trend of the objective function, and avoid sampling some useless or redundant points. This can greatly improve the search efficiency and accuracy [15]. Samples are collected according to the prior distribution p (f), and a set of observation data $D = \{(xi, fi)\}$, $i = 1, 2, ..., n$ is obtained. Where xi represents the coordinates of the i-th sampling point and fi represents the function value of the i-th sampling point. At the same time, the predicted mean μ and standard deviation σ of these sample points are calculated as parameters of posterior distribution [16]. Based on the above design scheme, the image feature extraction algorithm designed in this research adopts the following operation process:

(1) Input image; (2) Extracting image blocks based on the original image; (3) Regularization processing based on image blocks; (4) Whitening is performed based on the regularized image; (5) The dictionary is extracted by distributed BAS-CS algorithm; (6) The feature extraction function is established according to the obtained dictionary; (7) Input image features into the support vector machine classifier and classify the images [17–20]; (8) Output classified images.

5 Conclusion

Because the combination of computer science and image processing technology can greatly improve the performance and efficiency of image processing, image processing technology has been widely used in military, remote sensing, medicine, industry and other fields, providing great convenience for people's production and life, greatly promoting the development of social productivity, but also promoting their own continuous innovation and development. Therefore, as a field closely related to people's production and life, digital image processing technology has a lot of problems waiting for us to study and solve in both theoretical research and engineering application.

Acknowledgements. 2020jxtd065 (Project category: Anhui quality engineering, project name: teaching team of computer specialty, Project No: 2020jxtd065).

References

1. Li, Y., Chu, L., Zhang, Y., et al.: Intelligent transportation video tracking technology based on computer and image processing technology. J. Intell. Fuzzy Syst. Appl. Eng. Technol. **37**(3Pt.1), 3347–3356 (2019)

2. Sun, J., Zhai, Y., Li, L.: Research on image texture noise processing based on intelligent blind restoration algorithm. In: 2020 2nd International Conference on Information Technology and Computer Application (ITCA) (2020)

3. Yu, G., Sang, J., Sun, Y.: Thermal energy diagnosis of boiler plant by computer image processing and neural network technology. Therm. Sci. **24**, 128 (2020)

4. Huang, M., Yan, X., Bai, Z., Zhang, H., Zeen, X.: Key technologies of intelligent transportation based on image recognition and optimization control. Int. J. Pattern Recognit. Artif. Intell. **34**(10), 2054024 (2020). https://doi.org/10.1142/S0218001420540245

5. Nag, S.: A type–II fuzzy entropy based multi-level image thresholding using adaptive plant prop-agation algorithm (2017). https://doi.org/10.17605/OSF.IO/5KQZD

6. Zhang, R., Chen, Q., Niu, Q.S., et al.: An image segmentation method based on bean optimization algorithm. Comput. Knowl. Technol. (2019)

7. Chen, Q., Li, W., Chen, Z.: Analysis of microstructure characteristics of high sulfur steel based on computer image processing technology. Results Phys. **12**, 392–397 (2019). https://doi.org/10.1016/j.rinp.2018.10.037

8. Xu, C., Wang, Y., Sheng, R., Lu, W.: Intelligent express delivery system based on video processing. In: Zeng, J., Qin, P., Jing, W., Song, X., Lu, Z. (eds.) ICPCSEE 2021. CCIS, vol. 1451, pp. 370–379. Springer, Singapore (2021). https://doi.org/10.1007/978-981-16-5940-9_28

9. Hiener, D.C., Hutchison, G.R.: Pareto optimization of oligomer polarizability and dipole moment using a genetic algorithm. J. Phys. Chem. A **126**(17), 2750–2760 (2022)

10. Optimization of coal seam permeability improvement technology by radial multi-branch borehole high pressure combined water jet **52**(2), 88–92, 97 (2021)

11. Sulistyo, S., Woo, W.L., Dlay, S., et al.: Building a globally optimized computational intelligent image processing algorithm for on-site nitrogen status analysis in plants. IEEE Intell. Syst. **33**, 15–26 (2018)

12. Li, W., Du, W., Tang, W., et al.: Parallel algorithm of multiobjective optimization harmony search based on cloud computing. J. Algorithms Comput. Technol. **11**(3), 174830181771318 (2017)

13. Liu, K.: Research on computer image processing technology in web design based on visual communication. Revista de la Facultad de Ingenieria **32**(11), 90–95 (2017)

14. Wang, C.: Research on panoramic image processing technology based on virtual reality technolo-gy. In: 2019 International Conference on Virtual Reality and Intelligent Systems (ICVRIS). IEEE (2019)

15. Guo, L.I., Zhou, Y.S.: Research and implementation of automatic printing quality inspection method based on high robustness genetic algorithm. J. Xichang Univ. (Nat. Sci. Edn.) (2017)

16. Wang, T.: Research on image coding based on rate distortion optimization. Intell. Comput. Appl. (2017)

17. Feng, Z.: An image detection method based on parameter optimization of support vector machine. Int. J. Circuits **15**, 306–314 (2021)

18. Kung, W.: Research on signal processing technology optimization of contact image sensor based on BP neural network algorithm. J. Intell. Fuzzy Syst. Appl. Eng. Technol. **38**(4Pta1), 3911–3919 (2020)

19. Wang, K., Yu, Q.: Simulation analysis of 3D medical image reconstruction based on ant colony optimization algorithm. J. Intell. Fuzzy Syst. Appl. Eng. Technol. **38**(4 Pt.1), 3893–3902 (2020)

20. Lu, Y., Wang, Y., Liu, J., et al.: Improved biogeography-based optimization algorithm. Comput. Eng. Appl. (2016)

The Commercialized Operation Mode of Training Applied Talents of Business Administration Major in Colleges and Universities Based on Computer Technology

Jilin Xu[1], Haoyue Liu[2], Xiaobing Zhang[1(✉)], and Jia Zhao[3]

[1] Huaiyin Institute of Technology University Business College, Huaian, Jiangsu, China
zhende18909249907@163.com
[2] Jiangsu College of Nursing College of Marxism, Huaian, Jiangsu, China
[3] Department of Economics and Management, Hebei University of Environmental Engineering, Hebei, China

Abstract. Colleges and universities are the main positions for training business management professionals. Excellent business management professionals can solve various management problems faced by enterprise development and promote sustainable and stable social and economic development. With the development of enterprises, the competition and cooperation requirements are getting higher and higher, and the requirements of enterprises for business management professionals are also getting higher and higher. The purpose of this study is to explore the commercial operation mode of the training of Applied Talents in Business Administration Major in Colleges and universities. The main purpose of this study is to understand the commercial operation mode of the training of Applied Talents in Business Administration Major in universities and its impact on students. The second goal is to understand the impact, problems and challenges faced by business administration students in the process of university learning.

Keywords: Talent training · Computer technology · Business administration · Commercialization

1 Introduction

Business administration is an applied discipline closely related to social and economic development. In recent years, the contradiction between the demand and supply of business management talents has become more and more obvious. With the acceleration of the process of global integration and the strengthening of economic ties among countries, China's economy will develop at a high speed driven by the international economy, which will lay a solid foundation for the employment of business administration graduates in the future. China is in the critical period of macro system reform and the establishment of modern enterprise system, which urgently needs a large number of high-quality business

Y. Zhang and N. Shah (Eds.): BigIoT-EDU 2023, LNICST 583, pp. 457–467, 2024.
https://doi.org/10.1007/978-3-031-63139-9_48

management talents to join. China's economic transformation also needs professional business management talents [1]. Generally speaking, the demand for business management talents is on the rise. At the same time, most enterprises find it difficult to find qualified talents who can be competent for their corresponding management positions, and their needs can not be met. Colleges and universities have set up business administration majors and trained a large number of business administration talents, but some of them can not find satisfactory posts, and some of them can not meet the requirements of posts [2]. According to the 2011 employment report, among the majors with the highest unemployment rate of undergraduate graduates in 2010, business administration ranked sixth. Many universities also included business administration in the list of reducing enrollment due to the high unemployment rate. On the one hand, the society's demand for high-quality business management talents is increasing; on the other hand, there is a relative surplus of business management talents. The important reason for this is that the training of business management talents in Colleges and universities is misplaced with the needs of the market, that is, business management talents can not adapt well to the needs of the market and society, and the training of business management talents in higher education can not serve the social economy well. The decline of talent quality is another important factor that causes the contradiction between the demand and supply of business management talents. Since the enrollment expansion in 1998, China's higher education has changed from elite to popular [3]. The number of students on campus has increased, the number of hardware facilities is small, the number of college teachers is short, and the quality of talent training has not been guaranteed. As a result, higher education can not train high-quality talents for the society [4].

However, nowadays, there are still many limitations and shortcomings in the process of cultivating big data business management talents in universities. From the perspective of the real demand of the market, the demand for talents in the market is no longer limited to traditional professional and technical fields such as data analysis and algorithm engineers. More and more non-technical positions are also eager for the emergence of talents capable of processing data, reading data, and mining data value. This requires big data business management talents to possess relevant knowledge of big data business management, They also need to possess the abilities and skills of other professions required for these positions. The cultivation of big data business management technical talents is characterized by multi-disciplinary and multi technology integration, which covers an increasingly wide range of disciplines and technologies, and the market demand is becoming increasingly comprehensive. However, due to limitations such as class hours, teachers, and training models, universities cannot cover all aspects, and a single college education cannot meet the personalized learning needs of big data business management talents.

Many online education platforms have emerged in response to the lack of training in universities. There are specialized platforms for providing vocational examination training courses, there are Muke platforms that provide university curriculum resources, there are vocational skills training platforms that provide practical courses oriented towards employment, and various online education platforms emerge in an endless stream. More and more school students are refining their professional knowledge and learning other professional knowledge through online education platforms; The incumbents who have already been employed learn new skills through online education platforms to enhance their competitiveness in the workplace; Graduates facing employment are trained in practice and application skills in advance through online education platforms, which have gradually taken a place in the big data business management talent training system.

The online education industry is developing in full swing, with a strong momentum, and there are also many problems. When developing online education platforms, many enterprises face problems such as a lack of operational experience and high-quality educational content, resulting in a lack of representative leading enterprises despite the emergence of online education platforms. Most online education platforms also face a series of issues such as low user stickiness and low satisfaction. How should online education platforms position themselves to make up for the shortcomings of university training? What is the current development status of these platforms, and have they played their due role under their own positioning? Can each platform be recognized by users and meet the needs of the market? These issues need to be studied.

In this context, the talent training of undergraduate business administration must be adjusted and innovated according to the needs of society and market, improve the quality of talent training, and adapt to the needs of enterprises.

2 Related Work

2.1 Talent Training Mode

Chinese scholars' research on talent training mode began in the 1990s, and scholars have different expressions on talent training mode. Wang Qianxin believes that "talent training mode refers to the structural style and operational mode of the training process adopted by colleges and universities to achieve the training objectives, including professional setting, curriculum system, teaching design, education methods, training channels and characteristics, composition of teachers, practical teaching and other elements." Zeng Lingqi and Zhang Xisheng believe that the talent training mode refers to the implementation of talent training under the guidance of certain ideas, according to certain training objectives, with certain teaching contents, curriculum systems, management systems and evaluation methods. It consists of four aspects: training objectives, training systems and training evaluation [5]. Li Zhiguo proposed the talent training model, which refers to the implementation paradigm for teachers to achieve a certain standard of knowledge, ability and quality structure for students within a certain time limit under the guidance of certain educational concepts, guided by social needs and training objectives, and relying on their own school running conditions, as well as to achieve the stability of this structure. From the synthesis of the above statements, it can be seen that scholars generally believe that talent training mode is an educational idea and teaching operation method based on it, including educational objectives, training specifications and training methods, and its extension is professional setting, teaching arrangements, curriculum system, etc. [6]. In the process of talent training, the talent training mode is in a guiding position, and the talent training mode determines the whole process of education and teaching activities. The talent cultivation research model is shown in Fig. 1 below.

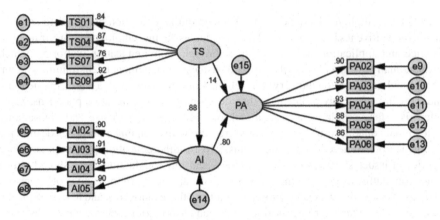

Fig. 1. Research model of talent cultivation

Talent training goal is a kind of prediction of the results of talent training activities before people carry out talent training activities. "Training objectives are the requirements and standards of talent training, the core of building a talent training model, and play a guiding, normative and regulatory role in talent training activities." Talent training specifications mainly include quality, ability, knowledge and other elements. The curriculum system organizes the teaching contents according to a certain structure in order to achieve the school's training objectives, and is the sum of the teaching process and teaching contents. Through analysis and synthesis, each part of the curriculum system is arranged in a certain order and connected. Training measures refer to the methods and approaches adopted to achieve certain goals according to the talent training plan, including classroom teaching, practical teaching and other links, teaching management systems and operational requirements [7]. Teaching measures are the essential elements of talent training mode. Good teaching measures can improve teaching efficiency and realize the rational, scientific and orderly talent training. Training evaluation is "an evaluation standard and method that is compatible with the training program, training goal and training process to ensure the implementation of the training goal." Training evaluation is the last link in the talent training activities. In the talent training mode, on the one hand, training evaluation is to see whether the talent training activities have reached the expected talent training objectives; On the other hand, training evaluation can effectively monitor the process of talent training activities, find and correct deviant behaviors in time, and people can also find out the shortcomings in talent training activities through talent training evaluation so as to improve and optimize talent training programs.

2.2 Analysis on the Necessity of Commercializing the Training of Applied Talents in Business Administration Major in Universities

Nowadays, with the development of cloud computing, the Internet of Things, and other technologies, various industries are accumulating massive amounts of data. These "new oil" require talents skilled in big data business management technology to explore and process, so as to achieve data value-added. The so-called big data business management talents are the talents who can professionally process these precious data resources.

Big data is widely used in business management in China, and has broad application prospects in intelligent manufacturing, agriculture, news production, and other fields, whether in industry, finance, research, office work, media, or daily life, Both cannot be separated from the support of big data business management [? 2. The State Council's Action Plan for Promoting the Development of Big Data Business Management] China also proposed to develop the application of big data business management in industries such as industry, emerging industries, agriculture and rural areas, and apply big data business management technology to the entire industrial chain. It can be seen that the wide application of big data business management requires big data business management talents to play a role in various industries.

Generally speaking, as big data business management talents need to handle massive, unstructured, or semi structured data, the most important thing is to master corresponding distributed processing and other big data business management technologies. Big data business management talents are also equated with distributed and cloud computing practitioners. Since the development of the big data business management industry, its connotation has become increasingly rich. In positions where the amount of data to be processed may be small, such as human resources, accounting, and operations, there is also a need for big data business management talents. Behind big data business management talents is not only simple technologies such as distributed and cloud computing, but also a kind of data science thinking. Big data business management talents can not only explore the value of data in complex and massive data, but also apply scientific and innovative thinking in structured and limited data to explore new value of data, without regarding the volume and structure of data. In reality, the second application scenario is often more common in the industry and more efficient in achieving data value-added.

To sum up, big data business management talents are not limited to a certain industry, let alone a certain type of position. Where there is data, there is a need for big data business management talents. These people who can explore the value of data can be broadly referred to as big data business management talents.

As more and more universities have established majors related to big data business management at the undergraduate level, a number of outstanding big data business management talents have emerged, and the abilities of undergraduate graduates have also been trusted by employers. Job seekers with undergraduate degrees have received a more systematic higher education, have basic professional abilities, and are highly malleable. Employers rank second in terms of talent demand for college degrees, due to the existence of many positions with low educational requirements, such as data annotation. As mentioned earlier, where there is data, there is a need for big data business management talents. These positions seem to have no technical content, but to achieve results, they still need data science thinking and professional and technical skills. For these job seekers, The variety of courses offered in online education platforms is a good tool. The cultivation of business management talents is shown in Fig. 2 below.

(1) It is beneficial to improve the competitiveness of colleges and universities

Due to the limitation of funds, colleges and universities have insufficient investment in teaching facilities and equipment. If they cooperate with professional training

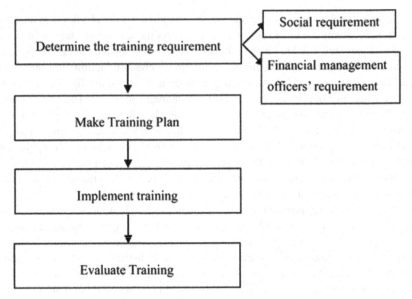

Fig. 2. Training of Business Administration Talents

institutions in society, they can make full use of their existing resources, reduce the capital investment of colleges and universities, save the cost of running schools, and use the limited funds to improve the teaching environment, so as to improve the competitiveness of colleges and universities.

(2) It is beneficial to improve the employment rate of college students

After the cooperation between colleges and professional training institutions, on the one hand, professional training institutions have a lot of enterprise resources. As a medium between enterprises and colleges, they can provide phased internship opportunities according to students' professional characteristics and personal wishes, improve students' practical ability, and lay a good foundation for future employment. On the other hand, professional training institutions will conduct phased training according to the professional characteristics of students before they formally take up their jobs, so that students can master the basic skills required by future jobs, which is conducive to students' employment and improves the employment rate of college students [8].

3   Thoughts on the Construction of the Commercialized Operation Mode for the Training of Applied Talents in Business Administration Major of Colleges and Universities

3.1   Framework of Talent Cultivation Mode

The business administration major aims to strengthen the students' practical ability in enterprises, conducts in-depth enterprise research, closely combines the school's positioning and the realistic needs of modern economic and social development for enterprise management talents, studies the curriculum plan with enterprises, formulates practical and innovative talent training plans closely integrated with the needs of enterprise development, actively explores and constantly improves and innovates talent training models, That is, the new talent training mode of "actively innovating, expanding and developing new methods, and expanding and improving the diversified practice platform of practice, experiment, training and practice based on the enterprise experimental base" through the guidance of talent training objectives, focusing on the two levels of "teaching" and "learning", and on the basis of ERP Experimental simulation, management case competition, marketing planning competition and other training paths[9], It has formed a "1 + 2 + n" innovative, developmental and open talent training mode for business administration majors with the connotation of "school training - Enterprise Training - students' self-cultivation", as shown in Fig. 3.

Teachers play an important role in teaching activities, and their ability directly affects the quality of students' learning. The survey results of the overall level of teachers indicate that there is still a large proportion of teachers whose teaching level needs to be improved. The survey on the proportion of professional course teachers with management experience shows that a large proportion of teachers have no experience in enterprise management, so they cannot understand management theory well, combine management practice with theory, and impart knowledge to students well. The above problems are caused by the following reasons: first, the teachers' educational background is not high, and second, the school does not have a relevant system to ensure that teachers practice in enterprises and have management experience.

In the survey of the abilities of business management talents that need to be strengthened, most students believe that innovation ability, teamwork and communication ability, and management and decision-making ability need to be strengthened, while some students believe that organizational and coordination ability needs to be strengthened. The survey results, on the one hand, reveal the requirements of enterprises for the ability of business management talents from the perspective of students, and on the other hand, indicate the lack of training for students' abilities above. Innovation ability, team cooperation and communication ability, and management and decision-making ability can all be strengthened in practice, indicating that the school has insufficient training for students' practical ability and should be strengthened.

A survey of the employment prospects of business administration majors shows that more than half of the people have a very optimistic and optimistic attitude towards employment, while nearly half of the people have a moderate and pessimistic attitude towards the employment prospects. There are several reasons for the lack of confidence in the employment prospects. First, they do not understand the market demand and do not know what their major can do in the future. Second, they are skeptical about their professional abilities and whether they are competent for the job. Third, their professional direction is not clear.

For colleges and universities, making full use of the resources of professional training institutions can improve their teaching quality and the employment rate of students, which will improve the reputation and status of colleges and universities in society and promote their sustainable development; For professional training institutions, students are the "products" they process. The successful employment of the college students

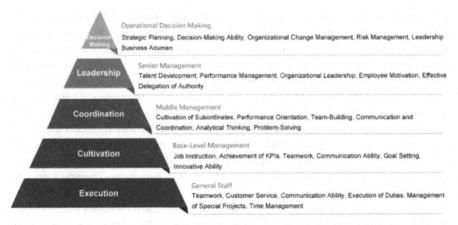

Operational Decision Making
Strategic Planning, Decision-Making Ability, Organizational Change Management, Risk Management, Leadership
Business Acumen

Senior Management
Talent Development, Performance Management, Organizational Leadership, Employee Motivation, Effective
Delegation of Authority

Middle Management
Cultivation of Subordinates, Performance Orientation, Team-Building, Communication and
Coordination, Analytical Thinking, Problem-Solving

Base-Level Management
Job Instruction, Achievement of KPIs, Teamwork, Communication Ability, Goal Setting,
Innovative Ability

General Staff
Teamwork, Customer Service, Communication Ability, Execution of Duties, Management
of Special Projects, Time Management

Fig. 3. "1 + 2 + n" talent training model framework

they train and the improvement of their employment success rate also mean that their "products" are marketable, which will also improve the social reputation, peer competitiveness and economic benefits of professional training institutions, which is also the basis of their foothold in the market.

3.2 The Realistic Demand for Enterprise Management Talents

The main capabilities that companies believe need to be strengthened include teamwork, innovation, and computer and English skills. In future work, more and more tasks require teamwork to complete [10]. Therefore, it is very important for business management professionals to cooperate with others and how to cooperate better. The quality of teamwork is also related to the achievement of enterprise goals. Team work skills can be strengthened in practice and in some experimental courses. The ability of divergent thinking, the ability to handle unexpected events, and the ability to solve problems together constitute a very important innovation ability for students. For the cultivation of students' innovative thinking and ability, first of all, it should focus on the continuous improvement of theoretical knowledge and basic qualities; Secondly, relevant training in creative courses should also be conducted; The most important thing is to continuously strengthen social practice and internship to continuously broaden students' horizons. After experiencing some practical problems, students will have more and more good ideas. Enterprises believe that the ability to use foreign language computers should be strengthened. In the context of economic globalization, more and more domestic enterprises are cooperating with foreign enterprises [11]. Foreign language proficiency can affect the exchange of talents in cooperation with foreign enterprises, as well as the internationalization perspective of talents, thereby affecting the development of enterprises. With the rapid development of the Internet and information technology, computers have not only become an important means of information exchange within enterprises, between enterprises and the outside, but also an important tool for enterprises to obtain, release, and process information. Therefore, enterprises believe that graduates should have good computer skills, including data processing capabilities, software application capabilities, and so on.

The knowledge that enterprises believe needs to be strengthened includes marketing knowledge, financial knowledge, and statistical knowledge. Knowledge of marketing and finance is very important for enterprises. Marketing concepts have a significant impact on product design, production, and revenue generation; Finance is a very important part of an enterprise, which can reflect the operation of the enterprise. Therefore, enterprises must pay more attention to financial marketing knowledge. If an enterprise wants to develop for a longer time, it should pay attention to the continuous updating and improvement of financial marketing knowledge. Data statistics are becoming increasingly important in the management of enterprises, and schools should attach importance to and strengthen statistical courses.

The knowledge that the enterprise believes does not need to be strengthened includes information management knowledge, humanistic knowledge, and management theoretical knowledge, which indicates that the enterprise believes that the training of students in the three knowledge areas in universities is sufficient and may not be strengthened. On the other hand, this reflects the lack of understanding of management theory and humanistic knowledge in enterprises. Both management theory and humanistic knowledge belong to basic knowledge, and the value of learning basic knowledge can only be seen in the future. Information management knowledge belongs to the preliminary application of computers, which proves that undergraduate colleges and universities are sufficient in cultivating preliminary computer skills [12]. What companies believe is not needed to strengthen is interpersonal relationships and professionalism, which proves that schools cultivate the ability to get along with students and good professional qualities in their usual theoretical and practical teaching.

4 Ways to Cultivate Applied Talents in Business Administration

Although the talents created by the business administration specialty meet the needs of society to a certain extent, there are shortcomings and contradictions. Each university should combine its own characteristics, take its essence and discard its dross, and put forward new solutions.

(1) Reform the teaching mode. Students are the future of the motherland and should occupy a dominant position in teaching. Schools should break the traditional teacher centered education model and guide students to actively study and explore in teaching. In classroom teaching, we should increase students' discussion time. After teaching, teachers organize students to discuss, encourage students to ask questions, and solve problems with students, so that students can understand the learning content more deeply and improve their interest in learning. Internet resources keep pace with the times and contain the latest and most comprehensive content. In addition to obtaining knowledge from textbooks, teachers should actively guide students to learn by using Internet resources.

(2) Reform the teaching content. The traditional teaching content of compulsory courses accounts for a large proportion, leaving few places for elective courses. These conditions tend to cause students to rely too much on textbook knowledge and lack innovation and practical ability [13]. Under the new educational background, we should increase the proportion of elective courses, let students understand the connotation of business administration in all aspects, and cultivate them into comprehensive talents. In the context of globalization, the requirements for students' English quality are getting higher and higher [14]. Bilingual teaching should be advocated, and foreign professionals can be hired at high salaries to teach students. Cases should also be embedded in the teaching, and it is forbidden to talk on paper. The content of business administration textbooks is too theoretical, which is easy to cause students' incomprehensible understanding and incomplete mastery. Classic cases should be introduced during teaching, and students should be led or guided to discuss. In the teaching process, supervision should be strengthened, and the attendance system can be implemented. School teachers and school leaders can be organized to listen to classes, so as to find problems and solve them.

(3) Pay attention to practical links. Practice is the only criterion for testing truth, and practice produces true knowledge. Schools and teachers should actively provide students with efficient practical ways. Under their own conditions, students can practice through the computer Internet. Use computers to create a practical case of the operation and management of an enterprise over the years for students, and let students simulate various activities of enterprise production and management through computer software [15]. The school should also establish cooperative relations with major enterprises, regularly organize students to visit, and organize students to practice during holidays.

5 Conclusion

In short, in view of the specific situation of limited funds, insufficient resources and weak practical experience and ability of teachers in Colleges and universities, we should explore cooperation with professional vocational training institutions and other social organizations, make full use of social education resources, and realize the profit goal of social organizations while realizing the training goal of applied talents in Business Administration Major in Colleges and universities through commercialization and market-oriented operation. This kind of commercialized operation mode has its theoretical basis and practical significance, and provides a practical and feasible operation mode for improving the training quality of application-oriented talents and the employment competitiveness of students in Business Administration Major in Colleges and universities at this stage.

Acknowledgements. Research on Under the background of "Internet+" the green agricultural products marketing and agricultural economy in Jiangsu Province (JSSCL2020B022); Research on urban-rural Integration development under the background of rural revitalization (2021SJA1820); Research on the rural settlement transformation under the Background of New Urbanization (2021SJA1805).

References

1. He, C., Miao, H., Chu, Y., Li, X.: Study on the practical teaching reform of business administration major in colleges and universities under the economic transformation of resourcebased cities(2018)
2. Liu, T.: Research on personnel training mode of business administration major based on OBE. Modern Manag. Forum **5**(1), 238 (2021)
3. Zhu, F.: Research and practice on the construction of first-class business English major in local colleges and universities — taking Taizhou University as an example. J. High. Educ. Res. **3**(2), 120–127 (2022)
4. Huimin, M.A., Shao, X.: Research on the training mode of "three-quality talents" in application-oriented universities based on OBE. Asian Agric. Res. **14**(12), 3 (2022)
5. Shen, D.: Exploration of smart classroom teaching mode of basic courses of visual communication design major in colleges and universities based on MOOC + flipped classroom. In: ICIMTECH 2021: The Sixth International Conference on Information Management and Technology (2021)
6. Zhang, Y., Xiang, L., Yan, H.U.: The path selection in training applied innovative-minded talents for business administration major: based on analysis of the newly-built local undergraduate colleges and universities from the perspective of the national norm for teaching quality. J. Neijiang Normal University (2019)
7. Liu, N., Liu, J.: The construction of practical teaching system of physical education specialty in local colleges and universities. J. Anshun University (2019)
8. Zhang, J.W.: Research on the training of applied talents of electronic information major in local colleges and universities——taking Baoji University of Arts and Sciences as an example. Educ. Modernization (2018)
9. Pan, X.: Reform practice of talents training mode of economics specialty in applied undergraduate colleges and universities. Educ. Teach. Forum (2019)
10. Cai, C.H., Cai-Lian, G.U.: Research on the training mode of agricultural electrification major applied talents in the transformation and development situation for colleges and universities. J. Shenyang Inst. Eng. (Soc. Sci.) (2018)
11. Huang, Y., Business, S.O.: Modular teaching reform of financial management major in applied colleges and universities——based on the experience of universities of applied sciences in Germany. J. Putian Univ. (2017)
12. Chen, S.A., Gao, J., Xing, J.M., et al.: Thinking on the undergraduates training mode of aquaculture major in local colleges and universities in northwest region. Animal Husbandry Feed Sci. (2018)
13. Ou, F.-R., Li, X.: Practical research on the training mode of school-enterprise cooperative talents of leisure sports major in private colleges and universities. J. Guangzhou Sport Univ. (2019)
14. Fan, X.: Innovation of marketing talent training mode of colleges and universities in transformation. Bus. Econ. (2019)
15. Zhang, Y.L.: Training stands and strategies of applied music talents in local universities. J. Hub Univ. Educ. (2018)

Online Teaching System of National Music Theory Course Based on Mobile Terminal

XinZhu Li[✉]

MuDanJiang Normal University, Mudanjiang 157011, Heilongjiang, China
Xinzhu_li@outlook.com

Abstract. With the continuous progress of science and technology, people are getting used to doing more things on the Internet anytime, anywhere. The foundation of the network teaching platform is mobile devices. Using this platform can make the teaching method break through the limitation of time and place, make the digital learning more extensive, meet the individual needs of learners as much as possible, and at the same time, make the teachers' teaching method fundamentally change. The online teaching system of national music theory course based on mobile terminal is an extension of mobile learning, which adds mathematics-assisted learning to mobile learning and provides a platform for students, teachers and students to interact with each other. Ethnic music is the music of all ethnic groups, which is a music ensemble shared by ethnic groups or certain cultural and social groups and continued to be passed down. However, the teaching concept of national music under the cultural concept has always been the focus of its attention, and it is the general trend to introduce it into traditional music teaching in China. According to the characteristics of online teaching, the teaching is carried out in the form of project the online teaching of folk music can effectively improve the teaching effect Based on the mobile terminal, as long as it is installed on the student's smartphone, it can help the student ask the teacher online at any time. After the teacher finds the problem, he can directly answer it online and explain the knowledge points for the students until the students understand it. Whether after class or on weekends, with this app, students don't have to worry about finding a teacher when they have problems. The design of this paper is the online teaching system of national music theory course based on mobile terminal, which is used to assist daily teaching. It is hoped to make full use of the existing network resources and mobile computing technology to improve the teaching quality and efficiency.

Keywords: National music theory · Mobile terminal · Online teaching

1 Introduction

With the rapid development of the Internet, the application of the Internet has gradually entered every corner of people's lives [1]. Online education is a hot field recently [2]. As a new type of education method, mobile network teaching plays an increasingly important role in the development of education, which can not be ignored [3]. It can

Y. Zhang and N. Shah (Eds.): BigIoT-EDU 2023, LNICST 583, pp. 468–475, 2024.
https://doi.org/10.1007/978-3-031-63139-9_49

assist teachers in teaching, avoid many disadvantages of traditional teaching, and make great contributions to the modernization and technology of education [4]. Based on this consideration, the online teaching model of online national music theory course "paying equal attention to learning and teaching" is put forward: it is necessary to fully reflect the role of students as the main body of study, and not neglect the guiding role of teachers; Give full play to teachers' leading role and fully reflect students' cognitive subject role [5]. In the traditional school education mode, students spend a lot of time in the process of teaching by teachers. Although this traditional model has its advantages, its disadvantages are also obvious.

Therefore, in recent years, with the rapid popularization of computers and networks, a new education model, online education, has emerged [6]. In the course of national music, the online teaching method can completely change the state that teachers completely instill the key points and results of the course in the traditional teaching mode, so that students can explore the teaching objectives in the form of completing projects and independently find appropriate solutions [7]. After the problem is solved, teachers should organize students to conduct self-evaluation and mutual evaluation, help students find problems and solutions in the process of project completion, and improve the learning ability of the whole class in communication [8]. For the traditional teaching theory, the teaching method it adopts is to teach. However, in the case of constructivism teaching theory, teaching methods different from lecturing are adopted, in which collaboration and discussion are both very important methods and also very important organizational forms. When designing the network teaching platform, we should make reasonable grouping and discussion according to the specific situation [9]. We must make a clear concept. Online education is not the same as distance education. It can also be short-range and combined with traditional education methods [10]. Compared with the traditional school education model, online education makes students more free, and they can make their own personalized learning plans that match their abilities and living habits.

For the teaching quality, it is not only closely related to the teaching content, but also very key to the teaching methods. In addition, the strategies and forms of expression used in the implementation of teaching are also very important. For example, the previous computer-aided teaching can teach students through projectors, and online education can also teach in the classroom through the network. Each student and teacher has a terminal. All terminals are connected to the same LAN. The teacher's teaching content is synchronously sent to the student's terminal through the LAN. Students can see the teaching content more clearly and quickly, and then students can mark their questions and send them to the teacher's terminal. This will certainly become another key symbol of modernization and scientization in the field of education.

2 Theoretical Thinking Based on Curriculum Teaching

2.1 Clarify the Importance and Objectives of the Course

At present, the music departments of many colleges and universities in China have successively set up national music theory courses based on mobile terminals. The purpose is to enable students to learn and understand the diversity and diversity of world national music culture, cultivate their "dual musical ability" and form their music cultural relativism values. The Internet has narrowed the distance between students and teachers, allowing them to communicate more and have more one-to-one communication time. The English teaching structure realized according to this idea and goal is called "both learning and teaching" mode. Here are two main network teaching modes, as shown in Fig. 1.

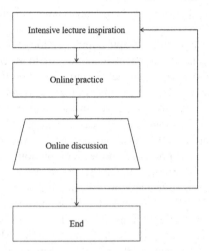

Fig. 1. Online classroom network teaching mode

Students can put forward their own questions online at any time after class or on weekends, waiting for the answers of countless famous teachers online. The so-called "teaching students in accordance with their aptitude" has got the best continuous explanation in the concept of online education. China's ethnomusicology, as a discipline, can be said to be completely based on the third stage in the sense of Europe and America from its formal introduction to China, and this academic idea was introduced into China's higher education institutions. However, at present, there are some obvious shortcomings and problems in the course of offering the theory of national music in the music department of colleges and universities, which have seriously affected the smooth development of this course in colleges and universities. For teachers, the process of changing from the dominant position to the guiding position is essentially changing themselves from the transmitter of folk music knowledge to the promoter of students' learning. Online teaching is praised by users in terms of learner autonomy and knowledge richness. For "mobile education", it mainly constructs the information network of "mobile education". In order to provide teachers and students with life information, teaching management, education and scientific research, it makes full use of GPRS platform and SMS platform in the research process, which can also provide them with enough preferential telephone services. Mobile learning can enable students to learn at any time and in various ways, but there are still unsolved problems in many aspects, such as feedback speed, network bandwidth, memory of mobile terminal, quality of video and audio, weight of mobile terminal, power life time and price of equipment. Therefore, in order to fully understand

and absorb the essence of the outstanding music culture of other countries or nations, we should set up a national music theory course based on mobile terminals, clarify the diversity and diversity of music culture of all ethnic groups in the world, and cultivate our aesthetic values and attitudes of "beauty, beauty, beauty and communion".

2.2 Teaching with Diversified Methods and Means

According to the curriculum characteristics and purpose of national music theory course, what teaching methods and means should we use as teachers to present holographic knowledge? For the school, using the project curriculum model can achieve the school running goal, which is equivalent to a better publicity for the school. The project curriculum model can also use the optimization of assessment and teaching to improve the school running level, which has a significant effect on the improvement of the curriculum system. The network teaching mode of diversified learning is shown in Fig. 2 below.

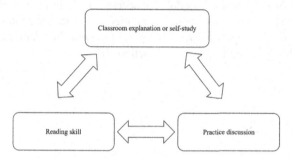

Fig. 2. Diversified online education model

By summarizing the current trend through the survey results, we find that the learning method using mobile devices is beginning to become the trend of people's learning methods, especially among students and employees, the proportion of learning knowledge on the mobile side is over 70%. Secondly, it is necessary to establish a special service station system, the main scope of which is some major university campuses, and provide telecom cards, wireless networks, even notebooks, handheld computers and other related products for users participating in this project. Thanks to unremitting efforts and research and development, China has also made many achievements in mobile learning, mainly the SMS group sending system based on smart phones, as well as the experimental project established in Peking University and the mobile campus established in Shanghai Radio and TV University. These projects all illustrate the development status of China in this field to a certain extent, and the main feature is the low level. Therefore, continuous exploration and research are needed. From the perspective of ethnomusicology, musicology is actually the organic integration of Ethnology and musicology. In theory, ethnology is indisputable and involves cultural expression. Therefore, teachers need to present ethnic music teaching contents through web server, explain them through microphone, and make students synchronize when browsing these contents.

As far as its characteristics are concerned, the knowledge content contained in the course of national music theory belongs to the culture of others, which is quite different from our culture. For most students, they are rarely exposed to it. Therefore, applying the project-based curriculum model to the teaching of ethnic music can be correctly mastered by the teachers in a short time. The advantage of this type of application lies in the convenience of obtaining high-quality online resources, including knowledge points and teachers, and it saves time. In addition, it has the advantages of multi-orientation, multi-level and multi-function. It is based on these advantages that the campus has no walls, providing more scholars with opportunities for continuous learning and education.

3 Design and Analysis of Network Teaching System

3.1 Server Design Analysis

The server should meet the processing of a large number of events. In order to meet the needs of data security and speed, it needs to be designed. In order to achieve the system design scheme of the server, it needs to analyze the functions of students, teachers and access server. When dividing the modules of access server, they are mainly divided into configuration module and access module, and their functions are configuration module and access module. This application is divided into student client and teacher client. The student client should have the following functions (Fig. 3):

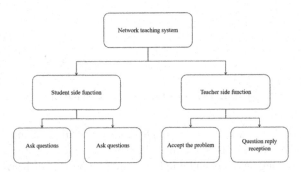

Fig. 3. Student client functions

Students can post questions in this interface. The main purpose is to promote the terminal and networking of learning, so that people can study independently or communicate with others at any time in any place with network. The server presents the feedback information to the teacher, and the teacher makes further explanation and response according to the students' feedback information. If teachers only instill music knowledge into students rationally from the theoretical aspect, but do not give them the training of audio-visual perceptual experience, students can not obtain an in-depth understanding of other music culture and achieve the goal of cultivating students' multiple music aesthetic ability. In order to ensure that every student must participate in teaching evaluation, the system adopts mandatory processing. Therefore, information entropy is used to quantify the information content contained in a system, so as to optimize the system or judge the system. It is defined as follows:

$$H(X) = -\sum_{x \in X} p_i \log p_i \qquad (1)$$

Therefore, in the teaching of ethnic music, the project curriculum model can enable teachers and students to participate in the construction, implementation and evaluation of the project together, and teachers can grasp the progress of students' projects in the whole process, so as to ensure the correct direction of students' project research. In designing the server system, it is necessary to design the basic framework, and when designing the related framework of the server, it involves the following issues: first, divide the functions of the system; when developing the system, the principle used is object-oriented. The user interface design of the system is also very consistent with the user's thinking and habits, which is simple and easy to use. The system also designs simple and easy to understand icons and text descriptions for each function, which can be understood by the user at a glance. For the system, abstracting requirements into functions requires better division of functions, which can greatly reduce the difficulty of developing the system and make the system more scalable. The real-time design of the system needs to make enough efforts. The real-time communication protocol and polling transmission mode should be adopted to make the audio and video data sent to the server in real time and reduce the delay of video transmission. In this mode, the role of the Internet is similar to that of the database. The main technology to realize this role is FTP service (i.e. upload service). For example, online lecture notes, homework and course information can be uploaded to students' web pages through FTP, and self-study can be carried out according to the downloaded content.

3.2 Client Design Analysis

For the Android system, the main components of applications on mobile phones are user interface classes and activity classes, as well as program object classes and resource management. Among them, the user interface class is the thread class in the application program. It circularly detects various messages received and calculates the specific state of the program. It is also necessary to calculate the corresponding screen redrawing for the drawing events. The basic idea is to calculate the frequency of each attribute value of each sample data in the attribute value, and then calculate the frequency AVF of the sample data according to the frequency of each attribute of each sample. The more the frequency of the sample data is, the more abnormal it is. The calculation formula of sample data frequency is as follows:

$$\text{AVF}(x_i) = \frac{1}{m} \sum\nolimits_{j+1}^{m} f(x_{ij}) \tag{2}$$

For shareSDK, it integrates some sharing excuses of social networks and is applied by developers in mobile phones. Through this, program developers can add the function of social circle sharing to mobile phone applications more quickly. In the system of this paper, the technical feature is that there are many network interactions between the server and the client, and all kinds of operations should be abstracted as simple modules and then processed. If it is a network perspective, then the interaction between the client and the server is shown in Fig. 4:

The network module mainly sends the content of the screen or the video stream data recorded by the camera to the server in real time, and the server processes these data

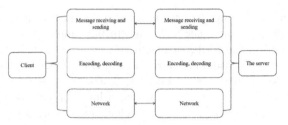

Fig. 4. Interaction between client and server

and transmits them to other clients, and then receives the audio and video data of other clients needed by this client to play. At the same time, you can also run CIA software written in Java language directly on the Internet. As the basic execution unit of the program, the lease of the activity class is to control the application life cycle, mainly to control the start and pause of the program, as well as the operation of running and exiting. Abstracting the elements in the program is the application object, which controls the behavior and switching between these components through messages. Therefore, the two distance similarity measurement methods have their own advantages and are suitable for different models. For any sample data, the calculation model of other chord distances is as follows:

$$\text{Sim}(X, Y) = \cos(X, Y) = \frac{XY}{\|X\| \cdot \|Y\|} \tag{3}$$

The main task of the Model layer is to formulate data flow, state of processing objects and rules of processing. The model layer is the core of this model, which receives and processes the data transmitted by the interface view and returns the final result to the interface. JavaCAI software in Whe page greatly enhances the interactivity and real-time of ethnic music teaching materials, which is very vivid and can leave a deep impression (such as drills, explanations, simulations, demonstrations, games, etc.), thus truly creating an individualized learning system based on Internet network. In the program, as long as it is visible, it can belong to the program object and is an actual moving entity. The main function of the program object is to perform the definition operation on the object. If it is determined that an event occurs, the program object will perform logical action on it. It divides the model in more detail from a technical point of view, so that all components contained in it can play a full role, but it can not be used as a framework. For the client, its main functions include helping users register, modifying user information, logging in and obtaining server list.

4   Conclusions

Ethnomusicology is obviously a new discipline, an interdisciplinary discipline, and the fusion of ethnology and musicology. Ethnomusicology is the study of music from the perspective of ethnology. It is undoubtedly one of the most convenient ways to learn about the world and master the music culture of different nationalities in the world by offering online teaching of national music theory courses for college students of music department in colleges and universities. The online teaching system of national music theory course based on mobile terminal makes use of the advantages of mobile terminal anytime and anywhere and the convenience of network, which shortens the distance between teachers and students, and makes it easier for students to ask questions and answers from teachers. It can not only carry out distance learning and communication through the camera, but also realize the network teaching function, that is, transmit the content of the terminal screen to the server. This paper makes a theoretical thinking on the course based teaching, and expounds the architecture design of the server and the function design of the client. Both questions and answers can be combined randomly by text, voice and pictures to help users ask and answer more comprehensively. The online teaching system of ethnic music theory course based on mobile terminal is of great significance to the teaching system. The system framework and design mode proposed in this paper have great reference value for the realization of mobile network teaching in the future.

Acknowledgements. 2021 youth cultivation project of basic scientific research business expenses of Heilongjiang Provincial Colleges and universities: research and Practice on innovative mode of vocal music talent cultivation in Local Normal Universities in the new era, Project No: 1451MSYQN003.

References

1. Zhang, H.: Analysis on the reform measures of national music theory teaching in Colleges and Universities. Digit. User (7), 200–201 (2014)
2. Xu, S.: Discussion on the application of project curriculum model in national music theory teaching. J. Chifeng Univ.: Nat. Sci. Edn. **30**(4), 2 (2014)
3. Ma, J., Han, X., Zhou, Q., et al.: An empirical study on online teaching group behavior of college teachers and students based on learning analysis. Audio Visual Educ. Res. **35**(2), 7 (2014)
4. Liang, H., Yin, Z.Q.: Analysis on the development status of online national music education platform. New Gen.: Theor. Edn. (10), 2 (2019)
5. Wu, Y.: National music theory teaching in music education in Chinese colleges and universities. Northern Music (10), 1 (2016)
6. Zhao, Y.: Application of project curriculum model in national music theory teaching. Innov. Pract. Teach. Methods **2**(2), 3 (2019)
7. Wei, S.: Learning analysis from the perspective of online education managers—construction and application of online teaching performance evaluation model. Mod. Educ. Technol. **24**(9), 8 (2014)
8. Li, W.: On the shortcomings and optimization path of national music theory teaching in Colleges and universities. Northern Music **37**(17), 1 (2017)
9. Lu, P.: On the implementation and exploration of national music in music teaching in senior high school. Tomorrow (39), 1 (2019)
10. Yang, M.: Some views on the current situation of ethnomusicology theory teaching in music colleges and universities. People's Music (11), 4 (2016)

A Study of Phonetic Conversion in German Online Learning System

Xiaofen Li[1][(✉)], Danyang Gong[2], and Lei Ji[2]

[1] Wuhan Business University, Hubei 430056, China
20180138@wbu.edu.cn
[2] Sports Department, Shenyang Jianzhu University, Shenyang 110168, Liaoning, China

Abstract. In the mobile internet environment, various terminal applications emerge in endlessly, the popularity of mobile terminal equipment and the rapid development of wireless network communication technology provide good material conditions and technical basis for the implementation of mobile online education. Compared with the traditional learning methods, mobile online education has played its own strong advantages, making its learning have the characteristics of mobility, interactivity, situational and personalized learning. It is an extension of traditional education in the mobile internet environment, which can meet the needs of modern learners' online learning, and can bring greater convenience and good experience to learners. Speech conversion is usually a difficult problem that some German online learning systems must solve. Speech conversion research in German online learning system is a free online course for students who want to learn how to pronounce words and phrases correctly. This course will teach you the basic knowledge of German pronunciation, including pronunciation rules and exceptions. The goal of this course is to help you improve your pronunciation so that it sounds more natural when talking or listening to native speakers of English. This online course teaches how to pronounce German words using the International Phonetic Alphabet (IPA). You can use this IPA chart as a reference when learning new words and phrases. After completing each course, you can check your progress by clicking.

Keywords: Online learning system · German · grapheme-to-phoneme conversion

1 Introduction

The rapid development of information technology has promoted the process of world informatization, accelerated the integration of information technology and traditional industries, and also promoted the pace of education modernization. Educational technology has gone through from traditional educational technology to multimedia technology education to network education. Driven by the development of information technology, education has moved to any place where information and communication technology

Y. Zhang and N. Shah (Eds.): BigIoT-EDU 2023, LNICST 583, pp. 476–486, 2024.
https://doi.org/10.1007/978-3-031-63139-9_50

can reach. However, with the rapid development of the mobile internet and the popularity of intelligent terminal devices, the development of online education on the PC has entered a saturation state, and more and more network users choose to use intelligent terminal devices for fragmented learning. According to the statistics of China Internet Network Information Center (CNNIC), in recent years, the growth of the number of Internet users at the PC end has been basically fixed, and its growth trend has tended to be flat, and under the influence of the mobile Internet, many PC end users will turn to mobile terminals. Therefore, the mode and structure of PC-based online education under the traditional network has been fixed; In addition, due to the limitation of network interconnection, the place and time of use of PC are fixed and limited. Therefore, these inherent defects eventually lead to a smaller and smaller market for all kinds of education and learning under PC.

An important function of some German online learning systems (such as German learning websites or German Chinese online dictionaries) is to provide phonetic symbols and pronunciations for searching words. So how are these phonetic symbols and pronunciations obtained? The most direct idea is that these phonetic symbols and pronunciations (recorded by real people in advance) are stored in the database of the server in advance. Once the user retrieves a word in the browser on the client side, he can obtain its phonetic symbols and pronunciations by looking up the database. However, have we ever thought of such a problem that with the continuous development of linguistics, a large number of new words will be generated every year, In addition, German allows people to create compound words at will according to certain rules, which determines that German has almost unlimited vocabulary [1]. Therefore, no matter how large a thesaurus is built, there are always some words that cannot be found in the thesaurus. How to solve the pronunciation of these words? Obviously, it must be solved by the technology of character to sound conversion in German speech synthesis [2].

With the rapid development of science and technology, the knowledge economy has also emerged. The two major characteristics of the knowledge economy are the innovation of knowledge and technology. The arrival of the new era also requires high standards for knowledge education. For contemporary education, it is necessary to seek a new way, which will be of great benefit to the future education and training of talents, as well as the development of innovative knowledge economy. Students are the main body of learning, and also the sender of learning. Therefore, how to give full play to students' autonomy, how to guide students' learning enthusiasm, how to cultivate good learning methods, and how to shape the concept of lifelong learning are all issues that contemporary educators should consider. Therefore, research in this area becomes more meaningful [3].

In the current Internet era, with the development of wireless communication technology and the rise of smart phone applications, the popularity of mobile Internet technology has led to the rise of mobile learning. Online education based on mobile platforms has once again enriched the networked education methods. Respect for personalized learning methods has become a unique new learning method in the field of independent learning. Mobile learning is based on digital learning. Online education based on mobile platform has huge market and potential. In this case, the innovative model of online education based on mobile platform has become the focus of attention and the trend of future development. With the deepening of mobile learning, the number of user learning groups is also increasing, and the functions of mobile learning education applications are constantly enriched, which meet the diverse learning needs of people in modern society. Through mobile online learning system, learners can learn independently anywhere, anytime and at will, no longer subject to the constraints of time, place and space, and achieve self-centered self-learning based on learning tasks, It brings new feelings and experiences to learners, enhances learners' learning enthusiasm through situational interaction, and makes learning more convenient, more extensive and more universal. In the wireless network environment, learners can view the learning resources they are interested in through the fragmented time. Of course, some of these resources can be downloaded for free. In the learning platform, users with common learning interests and learning objectives can also communicate online at any time, initiate collective discussions on a professional issue, and carry out the collision of ideas and inspiration, so as to deepen the understanding of the problem through in-depth interactive communication. It is a model of autonomous learning and interactive learning, a new learning method, and also triggered the reform and innovation of traditional education.

The previous learning methods were all book learning, so the learning method of Internet learning can make learning more convenient, unrestricted, and break the previous learning habits. Systematic learning can be carried out at any time, anywhere, and online learning can be carried out for any chapter and any course. The world's excellent educational resources can be learned by online learning scholars, and the autonomy of learning is also higher. Internet education and learning has the advantages of information interaction, freedom from time and place restrictions, wide resources and other advantages [4]. It is growing up in the education cause. It has more than one form of learning for scholars who can learn flexibly. At the same time, it has opened up a way of learning for those who can not carry out higher education, which is impossible in the past education.

2   Related Work

2.1   Research Status at Home and Abroad

With the development of network technology in modern society, network learning will be the global learning trend. Through the analysis of relevant research works at home and abroad in recent years. It can be found that some large training institutions have gradually introduced online learning and training models, developed various targeted network databases to reasonably manage teaching content, and used a variety of tools to assist learning and teaching activities.

Gu Yanfen and Huang Liping explored the web-based learning system with complex functions, and established an education system integrating resources and management according to the needs of students and the actual situation. Wu Hongyan proposed the network teaching management system on the basis of the existing network teaching research in China, which should be based on the actual needs of students, and on the basis of providing students with learning resources, should strengthen the supervision of the system, adjust students' learning attitude in time, and accurately master each learner's learning progress and learning situation [5]. Wu Xiangen et al. (2017) pointed out in the article that the biggest difference between online teaching and actual teaching is not the sharing of resources, It is about the management of learners. Through the analysis of the existing online learning platform, it can be found that at present, entity teaching is still the most important teaching form to supervise students' learning attitude and adjust students' learning methods. Fu Jia (2019) took Chinese language teaching as the specific research object in the research. This paper analyzes the educational achievements of Chinese language teaching in network platform education, and explores the significance of visual education for the operation of the entire education and learning system [6].

For now, both at home and abroad have paid close attention to networked education, and have also conducted in-depth research on all factors affecting online courses, learning tools, environment and so on. The theory of autonomous learning is the central idea of network teaching design, and learners design learning mode uniquely [7]. Autonomous learning is the biggest feature of network teaching, so the basic structure and function of the network are designed reasonably around the learners' own needs.

Voice conversion technology is an important branch of speech synthesis. Since 1950, computer-based speech synthesis technology has been attracting researchers' attention, and people have been trying to find an effective way to manually control speech properties. The attributes of speech mainly include three parts: 1) semantic features. The whole structure of pronunciation is closely related, which constitutes the basic features of pronunciation content, including grammar, lexical choice, language expression habits, etc.; 2) Global characteristics. It reflects the rhythm of the whole sentence, the gender characteristics of the speaker, and the overall pitch; 3) Local attributes. It shows the characteristics in a short time, such as resonance peak and spectrum change. Although people have made great progress in controlling these attributes, speech conversion still has a long way to go. With the increasing popularity of human-computer interaction and the continuous improvement of the computing ability of devices, more and more researchers are engaged in the research wave of improving the effect of voice conversion.

A typical speech conversion technology is usually divided into three basic steps: feature extraction, transformation mapping, and speech reconstruction. Figure 1 depicts the general framework of general speech conversion technology. First, feature extraction extracts the serialized semantic information and global speaker information of speech into different features, and then the mapping module transforms and merges the extracted features to generate the target speaker's voice features. Finally, the vocoder reconstructs the target speaker's voice features into a time-domain signal. The mapping module is the core of the whole voice conversion, and the mapping methods vary greatly. From the data form, it can be divided into parallel data and non-parallel data, and from the statistical model, it can be divided into parametric and non-parametric models.

2.2 Research Significance

The German online learning system will take the improvement of the remote education teaching level of the majority of secondary vocational schools as the starting point, and design a remote education mechanism for the leaders, teachers and students of secondary vocational schools to achieve communication based on the current scale, network technology, practice base and other actual conditions of the majority of secondary vocational schools. This can play a crucial role in the enhancement of its teaching service quality.

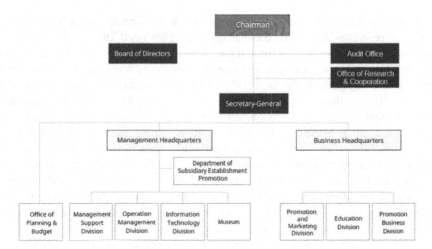

Fig. 1. General framework of voice conversion technology

In this paper, the corresponding research and development of the system is carried out according to the actual situation of the distance education work in relevant colleges and universities and the actual needs of development. The system has diversified functions. Among them, five key functions are more important. They are data, practice enterprises, remote education bases and processes, and performance management [8]. Its research runs through the whole process of distance education, covering the corresponding processes such as pre preparation, in-process management and control, and post evaluation. It plays an important role in dealing with the corresponding problems in the internal and external distance education of secondary vocational schools.

By providing multimedia education module, online student question and answer module and business module of learning website, it provides students with numerous learning resources, improves students' participation and problem analysis ability, trains students to solve problems, learn theoretical knowledge and solve educational priorities. Improve the difficulty and students' comprehensive ability. Multimedia course modules usually provide students with knowledge about structure display through static web pages [9]. This page allows students to answer, discuss homework and interact with other interactive modules through this page.

At present, with the gradual reduction of price and the continuous improvement of performance, smart phones have become more and more popular, which provides the necessary material basis for mobile learning. At the same time, the development of wireless network technology provides efficient technical support for mobile online learning, enabling the wide development and application of various applications based on Android system, such as entertainment, office, shopping and other fields are being penetrated. In the field of education and training, the learning mode has changed from the previous PC platform to the mobile platform, and the various mobile online learning systems generated based on the mobile intelligent terminal platform are changing people's learning mode, making learning can be carried out anytime and anywhere, no matter students in school or employees in the unit can walk on the road, subway_ You can use fragmented time for learning. Learners can arrange their own learning according to their actual situation, so as to achieve autonomous learning, accelerate the speed of knowledge updating, and make learning more efficient, more intelligent and more humanized.

In the mobile internet environment, the mobile online learning system based on Android is beneficial for learners to use fragmented time for learning. Through the interactive design of the system, the friendliness and stickiness of learners' experience is enhanced, which will greatly facilitate the promotion and popularization of mobile learning software. At the same time, it has promoted a learning mode of "anytime, anywhere and everywhere" to the whole society. This learning mode has brought users a good user experience and opened up a new way to realize "lifelong learning" and "independent learning". Therefore, the mobile online learning system based on mobile internet conforms to the modern life and learning habits, has broad market prospects, and can bring huge economic value and social benefits.

3 Outline Design of Online Learning System

A complete learning system is composed of various molecular modules. When designing the system, we need not only the overall design scheme, but also the design scheme of each functional module. The overall architecture of this design and the implementation method of each sub module will be described in detail below.

3.1 Function Module Design Summary

The online learning system in the network mainly includes the following parts: first, account registration, second, course information, online testing and management. If users do not register, they can only access the online learning page and the course information interface. If the registered student users want to take the test, they need to log in the user name first and then enter the online test interface. Moreover, the implementation user can only access the management center. The previous interface cannot access the management center. This part is mainly used for teacher management, maintenance and addition of question bank, etc. It can also directly query the examination materials of student users, find the materials of a student, and modify them. The student users who have not logged in cannot reply and comment on the platform, but can only view.

The system design of online learning mainly adopts modularization. The modularization method subdivides the system into several units according to functions, and adopts different implementation methods for different functional units. When all the functions of each unit are realized, It is integrated. In the website, different functional units are also modularized, and each module is a separate file, which can achieve the optimal function after merging. The designated file is placed in the webpage to add more content to the webpage. The design of the network system is divided into front-end management and back-end management systems.

In general online learning systems, the domain ontology built by domain experts is mainly used to build the knowledge system in the learning system. Such knowledge system only has the universality of the learning system, and can not build the knowledge that meets the cognitive needs of learners according to specific learning resources. At the same time, a single learning resource cannot be applied to learners with different learning backgrounds, and learning resources at different levels cannot enjoy the same knowledge structure. In view of the above problems, this paper designs an online learning system resource construction model. The public knowledge provided in the system is mainly divided into two parts: the static knowledge corresponding to the domain ontology and the dynamic knowledge built for the resources provided by the system. Their existence makes the learning system not only meet the setting of learning resource structure by domain experts, but also meet the learning needs of different learners.

The basic model of online learning system resource construction is shown in Fig. 2. First, select the learning resource text required by learners, extract the conceptual entities with cognitive value and predefined semantic relationships with the help of auxiliary prediction base and rule set, and finally integrate the scattered semantic links into a complete semantic chain network with the help of inference rules. In the part of public knowledge construction, for the construction of static knowledge, we build the relationship between the knowledge points defined by the domain experts by establishing the construction rules to form a fixed static knowledge structure in the system. For the construction of dynamic knowledge, we first need to extract dynamic conceptual entities based on the content of resources provided in the learning system, combined with the auxiliary corpus, and then establish appropriate semantic associations between them through pre-defined semantic relationships and rule sets used to extract entities and build semantic associations, so as to transform unstructured knowledge text into scattered semantic links with semantic associations. Then, by setting the semantic inference rule set, the semantic subgraphs containing semantic links are integrated into a complete dynamic knowledge semantic chain network diagram.

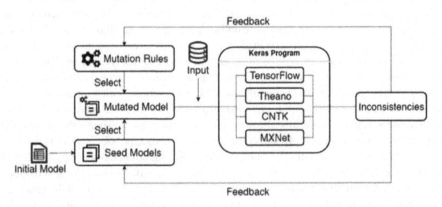

Fig. 2. Basic model of resource construction of online learning system.

3.2 System Architecture

In this design, the 3-tier architecture of Browser/Web/DataBase is adopted, as shown in Fig. 3. Users in Browser/Server can send query requests to the server through the browser, process and forward from the server, and finally return to the browser to achieve the purpose of query. The advantage of this architecture is that users can directly read and edit information through the browser. In the process of installation and operation, more work will be added to the server's operation. For example, when accessing the database or executing a program, it will be directly reflected in the server, which makes the server's work more arduous. When the browser sends a request, it is usually processed by the server, which will process the request in depth, and finally draw a conclusion to return the result to web.rver for completion [10].

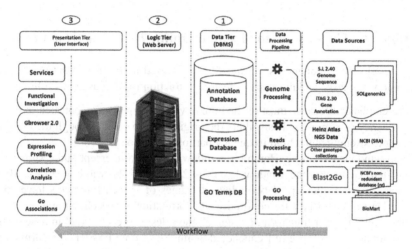

Fig. 3. Browser/Web/DataBase architecture

In software engineering and project management, before any project is launched, it is necessary to conduct a feasibility analysis to determine whether the project has the necessary conditions for development and whether the existing resources can be reasonably utilized to achieve the expected social and economic benefits. In order to conduct a comprehensive feasibility analysis, the feasibility analysis of the online learning system based on Android will be carried out from three aspects: operational feasibility, technical feasibility and economic feasibility. Among them, the operational feasibility analysis focuses on the user's skill level and practical operation basis; Technical feasibility considers whether the mobile learning system can be completed within the specified time with the existing technical conditions, whether there are technical risks, and the cost of developers learning new technologies; The economic feasibility considers whether the mobile learning system can bring actual economic benefits, mainly from the comparison and analysis of input and output.

Android mobile terminal devices have been widely used, and learners have the basic hardware conditions. In terms of system coverage of smart phone market, Android has achieved 73 The proportion of 1% ranks first. Therefore, using Android smart phones as terminal devices for mobile learning provides material conditions for mobile learning. In terms of operation, users who can use smart phones can basically operate general apps. In addition, the openness of the Android platform, freedom from operator constraints, and rich hardware choices provide good conditions for the popularity of Android phones. These factors are very conducive to developers to develop mobile learning client software with rich main interface content and good user experience. Therefore, from the perspective of users, Mobile learning system has no operational obstacles and difficulties. In terms of technology, mobile learning system involves mobile terminal, wireless communication technology and mobile internet technology, but these technologies are relatively mature at present, so there are no technical difficulties and risks for developers. To sum up, the development of online learning system based on Android meets the feasibility at all levels.

4 Phonetic Conversion in German Online Learning System

In this work, Mel frequency spectrum feature is used as the final feature of speech conversion synthesis, and the steps of feature extraction for corpus are as follows:

(1) Pre-emphasis. Because most of the human voice energy is concentrated in the low frequency part, pre-emphasis filters the original audio signal through the high-pass filter to strengthen the high frequency part of the audio.
(2) Add window and frame. Hamming window is used to intercept audio signals step by step. Generally, the window length is 25 ms, and the window shift is 10 ms. Therefore, the intercepted two adjacent frames of speech fragments have 15 ms overlap, which ensures the continuity and correlation of speech features.
(3) Short time Fourier transform. In general, the rules of speech signal in time domain are not as rich as those in frequency domain. Short time Fourier transform can be used to map the time domain information to the frequency domain for the subsequent calculation of Mel filter bank filtering. Let x (n) be the voice signal in time domain, n is the sampling point in time, and N is the number of short-time Fourier transform points, then the calculation of Fourier transform is:

$$X(k) = [\sum_{n=0}^{N-1} x(n)e^{-j\frac{2\pi}{N}kn}], k = 0,1, 2, \ldots, N - 1 \tag{1}$$

(4) Mel filter bank. Due to the characteristics of human ears, people's sensitivity to sound signals presents nonlinear characteristics, and Mel filter banks can simulate audio nonlinearly, as shown in Fig. 4. Mel transform of spectrum is

$$Mel(f) = 2595\lg(1 + f/700) \tag{2}$$

where, Mel (.) represents Mel frequency transformation, f represents the value of speech frequency, and Mel filter is expressed as:

$$H_m(k) \begin{cases} 0 & k < f(m-1) \\ \frac{k-f(m-1)}{f(m)-f(m-1)} & f(m-1) \leq k < f(m) \\ \frac{f(m+1)-k}{f(m+1)-f(m)} & f(m) \leq k < f(m+1) \\ 0 & k \geq f(m+1) \end{cases} \tag{3}$$

By running the above algorithm on the whole thesaurus, it is found that there are errors in 2602 words conversion, that is, the correct string of words conversion is 92.3%. After analyzing the sample of conversion errors, it is found that some words are only converted from long to short sounds. For example, the second a in Kalabrien [ala: bri2n] should be a long sound/a/, but it has been converted into a short sound/a/. There are 711 such words. Because this kind of error is not serious, it is barely acceptable. If this part of error is ignored, the overall conversion accuracy can reach 94.4%. Then analyze the remaining words with conversion errors, most of which are foreign words, mainly from English words, such as Jeans [d3i: nz]. For these foreign words, Because their pronunciation is much more complicated than that of German words and their proportion is small, it is unnecessary to study their pronunciation rules in German speech synthesis. They and their pronunciations can be added to a special case library as special cases, so that if such words are encountered during speech synthesis, their pronunciations can be directly extracted from the special case library.

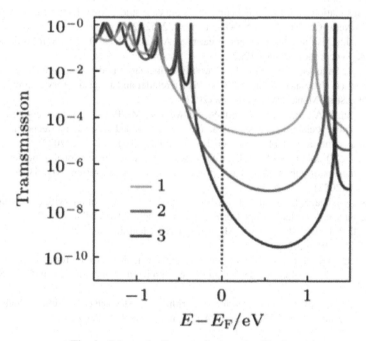

Fig. 4. Schematic diagram of triangular filtering

5 Conclusion

It is often an important function of German online learning system to provide phonetic symbols and pronunciations for searching words. Because German has almost unlimited vocabulary, no matter how large a thesaurus is built, there are always some words that cannot be found in the thesaurus. Obviously, to solve the pronunciation of these words, we must use the word to sound conversion technology. In this paper, we propose a rule driven algorithm for morpheme to phoneme conversion of finite state transcribers. In this algorithm, some rules for word to sound conversion are first formulated on the basis of a thesaurus, and then all the phonemes in German words are converted into phonemes through an iterative finite state transcriber on the basis of this rule. Through the algorithm test of the whole thesaurus, the correct rate of word to sound conversion can reach 923%, and if the error of long short sound conversion is ignored, the correct string can reach 94.4%. Obviously, this algorithm provides some reference value for other western languages, such as English, French and so on.

References

1. Pritzen, J., Gref, M., Zühlke, D., et al.: Multitask Learning for Grapheme-to-Phoneme Conversion of Anglicisms in German Speech Recognition (2021)
2. Ghanadbashi, S., Golpayegani, F.: Using ontology to guide reinforcement learning agents in unseen situations a traffic signal control system case study. Appl. Intell.: Int. J. Artif. Intell. Neural Netw. Complex Prob. Solving Technol. 2, 52 (2022)
3. Zhang, J.: Designed for Equitable Learning: A Study of UCD and Liquid Syllabus in an Online Synchronous Course (2021)
4. Haag, L., Sandberg, E., Sallns, U.: Towards an increased understanding of learning: a case study of a collaborative relationship between a retailer and a logistics service provider. Int. J. Retail Distrib. Manag. 50(13), 44–58 (2021)
5. Hellmann, K.A., Mikelskis-Seifert, S., Schwichow, M.: Pre-service teachers perception of competence, social relatedness, and autonomy in a flipped classroom: effects on learning to notice student preconceptions. J. Sci. Teacher Educ. 33(3), 282–302 (2022)
6. Fashiku, C.O., Olujoke, J.E., Baba, A.O.: Computer-assisted instructional strategies and learning outcomes of pupils in pre-basic private schools in Southwestern Nigeria. Am. J. Educ. Learn. 7 (2022)
7. Fu, X., Krishna, K.L., Sabitha, R.: Artificial intelligence applications with e-learning system for china's higher education platform. J. Interconnect. Netw. 22(Supp02) (2022)
8. Perry, D.P., Knight, B.L., Jeck, E.M., et al.: Machine learning in an online agricultural system. US11138677B2 (2021)
9. Hemmer, P., Kühl, N., Schffer, J.: Utilizing active machine learning for quality assurance: a case study of virtual car renderings in the automotive industry. Hawaii Int. Conf. Syst. Sci. (2021)
10. Li, N.: An improved machine learning algorithm for text-voice conversion of English letters into phonemes. J. Intell. Fuzzy Syst.: Appl. Eng. Technol. 2, 40 (2021)

Design and Implementation of Online Dance Teaching System

Pengying Sui[1]($\boxtimes$), Zhe Jiang[1], and Cuiying Wang[2]

[1] Dalian Art College, Liaoning 116000, China
sophiespy@163.com
[2] Xianyang Normal University, Xianyang 712000, Shaanxi, China

Abstract. The design and implementation of online dance teaching system is a process involving the design, development, testing and deployment of an interactive electronic platform for dance education. The goal is to create an effective tool for teachers to teach students through digital media. This enables them to improve their teaching skills and enable them to acquire new ways of interacting with students. How does the design and implementation of online dance teaching system work? The design phase involves creating a user interface that teachers will use to teach. It also includes the content that the design will display on the screen, such as images. It is designed for teachers and students who want to learn different dance steps. The system is developed to help people know more about their bodies, improve their coordination ability, and build confidence in themselves as dancers.

Keywords: Dance teaching · System design · Online learning

1 Introduction

This project is an online dance teaching system. It is developed to provide a simple and effective way to learn dance steps, choreography and other related topics. Based on the concept of "virtual dance studio", this project provides students with all the necessary tools to learn dance steps, choreography and other related topics. This tool will help develop the skills required for professional and home dancing. The main goal behind the project is to provide a platform for people to easily access information about all aspects, such as dance steps, choreography, music theory, other dance related topics.

For the teaching of dance majors in colleges and universities, this online teaching practice for emergency purposes has broken the dependence of dance practical teaching on the traditional teaching mode of "face to face" and "hand to hand". At the same time, the connection between the Internet and dance teaching in colleges and universities has also reached an unprecedented degree of closeness, bringing many possibilities for future dance teaching in colleges and universities. For a long time, due to the particularity of dance teaching, few dance educators in colleges and universities carried out online dance teaching practice before the outbreak of the epidemic, especially today, when the country continues to promote the modernization and informatization of higher education,

Y. Zhang and N. Shah (Eds.): BigIoT-EDU 2023, LNICST 583, pp. 487–497, 2024.
https://doi.org/10.1007/978-3-031-63139-9_51

and the concept of "Internet plus education" in other disciplines and online teaching achievements such as MOOC, micro class, flipped classroom are "everywhere". Under the epidemic, in order to ensure the teaching order of dance majors in universities, online teaching has become an inevitable choice. On the one hand, it promotes the development and exploration of online teaching of dance practice in universities, and on the other hand, we have a clearer understanding of the respective advantages and disadvantages of online and traditional dance teaching modes in universities. In the post epidemic era, we should fully consider the significance of online dance teaching in the future for the teaching of dance majors in colleges and universities based on the basic purpose of summarizing the existing online teaching experience to provide guarantee for the order of dance teaching in colleges and universities. Therefore, the purpose and significance of this study are mainly summarized in the following three points:

Based on this, this paper studies the design and application of dance teaching system based on Moodle platform. The evaluation standard of college teaching level has changed to the direction of informatization [1]. The informatization degree of college teaching management directly determines the level of teaching quality. Through scientific management methods and using network technology, information technology and other cutting-edge technologies as the core, the information construction of teaching management in Colleges and universities has played a key role in improving the level of teaching management in Colleges and universities [1]. The informatization of teaching management in Colleges and universities can scientifically, efficiently and quickly complete the purpose of teaching and learning, effectively organize teaching activities and reasonably allocate teaching resources.

The dance is rich in content, with its pleasing dancing posture and moving music, which has great attraction to college students and makes college students have a strong desire and enthusiasm for learning. Dance is divided into two categories: modern dance and Latin dance. Modern dance is divided into five types: Waltz, Vienna waltz, tango, trot and Foxtrot. Latin dance is divided into five types: Rumba, Cha Cha, samba, cowboy and bullfight. There are ten kinds of dances in total. How to organically combine these ten kinds of dances to build a dance teaching program system and improve the quality of dance teaching, This puts forward a new topic for dance teachers in Colleges and universities. The design phase includes creating a learning management system (LMS) to manage student records, a content delivery system to provide course materials and web-based tools for teachers to interact with students. The development phase includes the use of various technologies (such as video lectures, recordings or textbooks) to create course content. Finally, it involves deploying LMS and all necessary software components on the server to provide users with access to their courses through the Internet.

2 Related Work

2.1 Online Learning Digital Media Applications

The design and implementation of Luo dance teaching system is a complex process. This process involves analysis, planning, design and implementation. In the first stage of this process, we need to analyze the problems that our system needs to solve. We need to study the current situation to understand what problems students face when learning dance or teaching dance? What are their difficulties? How can we improve these difficulties? Once we understand all these things, it will be easier for us to design our online dance teaching system. Digital media is a highly comprehensive interdisciplinary of science and art, which is dominated by information science and digital technology, based on mass communication theory and guided by modern art, and applies information communication technology to the fields of culture, art, commerce, education and management. Digital media technology integrates computer graphics, network technology, communication technology, digital art, digital audio, media interaction, two-dimensional animation, three-dimensional animation, digital video and audio processing and other technologies and creative links. Digital media involves a wide range of industries, including film and television, publishing, news, entertainment, games, advertising and other industries, as well as television stations, network companies and other units [2]. The framework of the online learning environment is shown in Fig. 1 below.

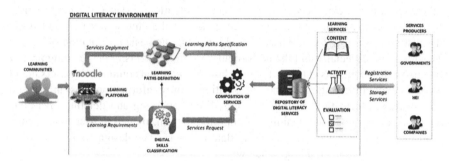

Fig. 1. Framework for an online learning environment

Its products include animation, online games, mobile games, digital movies, digital TV, mobile TV, digital publications, digital education and other scientific research institutions. According to a recent research report released by strategy analytics, the global digital media revenue will exceed the film entertainment revenue for the first time in 2008. In the media industry, the revenue growth of traditional distribution channels will slow down, and the digital media business model will provide key growth opportunities for the entire industry. It can be said that the digital media industry is full of opportunities.

As the leader of online dance teaching in universities, the online teaching ability of dance professional teachers is crucial to the quality of online dance teaching. First of all, online dance teaching has its own particularity and involves more links than traditional dance teaching, such as the use and selection of different online teaching platforms, the use of online dance teaching resources, how to conduct classroom interaction, tracking after class learning and other links. As a dance professional teacher, only by ensuring that they have a clear understanding of all aspects of online dance teaching can they grasp the quality of online dance teaching. Accordingly, the online teaching ability of dance teachers naturally includes more aspects. The most important abilities can be summarized in the following three aspects: First, teachers should have the ability to design teaching for online particularities, which is a concentrated manifestation of teachers' online teaching ability and directly affects the learning effect of students. 2、 Teachers should have the ability to understand and operate software and hardware functions, which is the most fundamental part of online teaching. 3、 Teachers need to have a certain ability to organize online classes, and it is crucial for teachers to effectively organize classes and fully mobilize students' enthusiasm. During the epidemic prevention and control period, college dance teachers were constrained by the lack of online teaching experience and experience, and their online teaching ability was significantly insufficient.

2.2 Design and Application of Teaching System

The design and implementation of online dance teaching system is one of the most important things in this field. We have many design options, but we must follow some rules to make it better. In the authority control of the dance teaching management information system, except for the system administrator, other roles of the system are controlled through the role of the system administrator. The system administrator has the highest authority in the system. According to the actual situation of dance teaching management, three user roles are set: teacher user, educational administrator user and system administrator user [3]. Teacher users mainly manage the basic information of students in each period, especially add the performance of any students in the learning process, so as to evaluate students at the end of the class; Educational administrator users mainly manage student information, teacher information, course information, class information and schedule information, mainly adding, editing, querying and deleting operations; System administrator users mainly maintain the system, including user management, authority management, data backup and data recovery. The design framework of the teaching system is shown in Fig. 2 below.

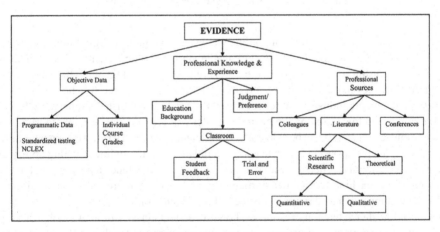

Fig. 2. Design framework of teaching system

The main task of curriculum managers is to manage and maintain the system, including whether the target system can operate normally and whether the school-based curriculum teaching activities can be carried out normally. Curriculum administrator is the unity of the two roles of curriculum system administrator and curriculum teaching administrator.

2.3 Utilize Platform Features to Enhance Interaction

In the traditional dance teaching process, teachers usually can intuitively capture the learning situation of students based on their eyes, expressions, and gestures, and carry out teaching activities based on the received teaching feedback information. However, due to the limitations of software functions and hardware devices in online live dance teaching, it is difficult to receive real-time teaching feedback. Firstly, there is currently no online teaching software that can accommodate an entire class of students without switching screens, so teachers cannot simultaneously observe the learning of each student's dance movements in real-time. Secondly, electronic screens separate and compress the body dynamics of all students into individual blocks. Due to the size and resolution of the screen, the dance learning screen presented by each student to the teacher is only a few centimeters in diameter, making it difficult to capture the students' expressions and movement details. Teachers are often required to check the learning effect one-on-one, resulting in reduced classroom efficiency and slowing classroom progress. Finally, as a very important means in traditional dance teaching, during the "follow dance" process, students rely on real-time imitation and verbal guidance from teachers to complete the learning of dance movements. However, due to equipment constraints in online live teaching, when performing dance movements or combinations that contain spatial scheduling, teachers cannot teach dance movements while watching students' dance learning, and cannot verbally correct students' errors in a timely manner. In summary, how to better receive real-time teaching feedback from students in online dance teaching is a key issue that needs to be addressed in online live teaching.

During the online live dance teaching process, teachers can use the "picture in picture" method to better collect students' real-time teaching and learning effects. Firstly, dance teachers can divide the pre recorded teaching content into several sections and share it with students through teaching software, giving them time to learn independently. At this time, dance teachers can observe students' learning situation in real time through a small window, answer students' questions and record them, and focus on solving them in the next stage of demonstration teaching. After the students have basically mastered the dance movements, the teacher can start organizing the overall teaching of the class. On the one hand, it avoids the situation of inaccurate synchronization of sound and picture in live dance courses. On the other hand, like traditional dance classes, the teacher can also call for a stop at any time to point out the problems existing in the students, so as to correct the wrong dance movements of the students in real time. Secondly, in the final stage of the live class, dance teachers need to focus on organizing students to answer questions, focus on solving difficult problems commonly raised by students, and conduct real-time action demonstration teaching; Focusing on solving individual student problems, online live teaching not only captures the real-time learning situation of students, but also improves teaching efficiency and reduces the pressure of online teaching.

In the online dance teaching process, image resources can be used to achieve intuitive teaching effects. Access to Internet image resources is convenient, and online dance teaching can be applied to the teaching of hand shapes, foot positions, and static large dance poses. During online live teaching, dance teachers can free themselves from live teaching by allowing students to imitate personally demonstrated images to facilitate their own guidance for students. In addition, teachers can also create some mind map type pictures to enhance the logic of dance teaching, so as to facilitate students to remember the context relationships in some dance movements. For example, the five main teaching materials in the classical dance body rhyme teaching include Cloud Shoulder Turning Waist, Swallow Crossing the Forest, Green Dragon Probe Claw, Cloud Hand, and Wind Fire Wheel. "Cloud Shoulder and Waist Rotation is a typical flat circular motion that connects the seven basic elements of classical dance: lifting, sinking, rushing, leaning, containing, thrusting, and moving.". However, it is difficult to form logic by relying solely on verbal cues from teachers without certain memory points. Therefore, the form of mind mapping can be used to make students remember more deeply and systematically.

In online dance teaching in universities, short dance videos can be used to inspire and guide students to learn independently. Due to the short video resources, which mostly take a few minutes or so, the content is brief and highlights the key points, making it useful as an auxiliary material for online dance teaching. For example, relatively short videos can be used to inspire students in live or recorded classes, such as the movement routes of limbs in dance, and the scheduling of formation. Long short videos are more suitable for sharing to students in the form of web links, for use in micro appreciation, key teaching, and so on. It is not suitable to use it in live teaching or courseware production of recorded courses to save online dance teaching time.

3   Design and Implementation of Online Dance Teaching System

Designing and implementing an online dance teaching system is a software that helps teachers provide students with the best learning experience. It allows teachers to create personalized curriculum plans, which will be provided in an interactive format. This means that teachers can make changes at any time without affecting others. Students' progress will be displayed on the dashboard, which allows parents to easily monitor their children's progress, as well as allow them to access other resources, such as videos or other materials [4]. The user interface of Laban Editor is shown in Fig. 3 below: (a) the main editing window of Laban Editor, and (b) the dance animation display window.

The design of the system is based on the analysis of the existing dance teaching system. The main purpose of this study is to find out the problems in these systems and how we can improve them. Therefore, a questionnaire is compiled, which consists of four parts: (1) dance teaching system; (2) Dance teacher education; (3) Online service delivery; (4) Evaluation method. Since 2006, this questionnaire has been sent to all teachers who teach at least one class using the online dance teaching system. The response rate of respondents was 31%.

(1) Expand demonstration methods. The traditional dance teaching process is embodied as: demonstration - imitation - display. That is, the teacher first makes demonstration actions, and then the students imitate learning according to the demonstration. Finally, the learning results are displayed under the guidance of the teacher. The first two links, namely "demonstration" and "imitation", are inseparable from the demonstration guidance of teachers. Therefore, the level of teachers' demonstration will directly affect

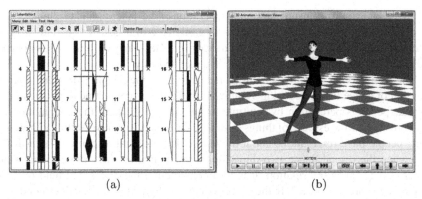

(a)   (b)

Fig. 3. User interface of Laban Editor: (a) Laban Editor main editing window, (b) dance animation display window

the learning effect of students [5]. The demonstration level of dance teachers is often restricted and affected by age, health, mentality and other factors. The influence of any factor may lead to the inaccuracy of demonstration and bring learning errors. If we use the dance digital teaching system, in the teaching process, the teachers play relevant dance video materials according to the teaching needs, which is like inviting the best dancers to the classroom for demonstration, so that students can see the standard demonstration and accurate action specifications, and then accept the demonstration and explanation of the teachers, Realizing the synchronous influence of multi-point visual perception and action form analysis will greatly improve the effect of dance teaching. Figure 4 below shows the design process of the teaching system.

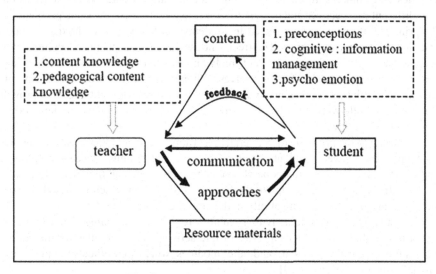

Fig. 4. Teaching system design process

At the same time, to ensure the smooth operation of the dance digital teaching system, we need to train professional technicians to participate in it, and we need to carry out special training for teachers who use the dance digital teaching system. This is not easy, and we need to implement it step by step in a planned way.

The confusion of using dance digital technology. Some people worry that after the adoption of dance digital teaching system, although dance communication extends and expands people's perception by multiple means, it also weakens the imagination and ability to analyze the essence of things of students who lack a positive attitude. Therefore, many people have reservations about the use of dance digital teaching system. But in fact, when the digital dance two-dimensional and imitation three-dimensional world planarizes all dance information, it is also constructing the diversified field of dance education in another way [6]. In the process of dance digital teaching, it does not deviate from the core proposition of body technology. Only through physical skill training can all information be digested and absorbed, so that dance teaching can move from closed art learning to open life exploration.

4 Simulation Analysis

The design and implementation of online dance teaching system is a project involving the design, development and implementation of educational software, with the purpose of providing dance education for students. The main objective of the project is to develop an effective tool to learn dance skills in a practical way through the use of modern technology. The software will also help teachers teach students effectively without any obstacles or constraints. Android's school-based dance curriculum design and teaching should go out of the self closed mode to provide students with a broader space for activities and thinking. In course teaching, students are encouraged to ask questions from different perspectives and design different answers to solve the same problem [7]. The principle of openness is reflected in: students can freely choose the dance course content they like and are interested in, freely choose the course concept and learning tools designed according to themselves, and freely choose the course learning methods and course assignments suitable for themselves. When developing and designing Android network school-based courses, we must plan from all directions and angles to provide learners with a relatively open learning environment. The system development code is shown in Fig. 5 below.

According to the principle of cooperative learning, we should vigorously strengthen the cooperation between students when developing and teaching dance school-based Android courses. The form of cooperation can be team, so that all members of the team can learn from each other, complete the learning tasks of dance school-based courses, and cultivate students' learning ability in the course of learning [8].

Generally speaking, interactivity is mainly reflected in teaching. Android dance school-based platform provides a series of interactive activity modules for the course, such as forum, email, blog, Wiki and other modules, which well reflects the interactive principles in course learning [9].

Just as people in modern society pay more and more attention to the purification and optimization of living environment, dance teaching must first pay attention to the

```
return set([word[0:i]+word[i+1:] for i in range(n)] +

[word[0:i]+word[i+1]+word[i]+word[i+2:] for i in range(n-1)] +

[word[0:i]+c+word[i+1:] for i in range(n) for c in alphabet] +

[word[0:i]+c+word[i:] for i in range(n+1) for c in alphabet])

def known_edits2(word):

return set(e2 for e1 in edits1(word) for e2 in edits1(e1) if e2 in NWORDS)

def known(words):

return set(w for w in words if w in NWORDS)

def correct(word):

candidates = known([word]) or known(edits1(word)) or known_edits2(word) or [word]

return max(candidates, key = lambda w:NWORDS[w])
```

Fig. 5. System development code

basic teaching system and take it as a necessary condition for the whole dance teaching. Specifically, the basic teaching system, a subsystem of dance teaching, mainly includes the following subsystems:

(1) Character system. Including cultivating students' thought, character, morality, character and so on. That is, to achieve both morality and art, to avoid the occurrence of phenomena such as emphasizing specialty over morality and having art without morality, and to get out of the misunderstanding of the lack of Ideological and moral education.

(2) Psychological system. It includes cultivating students' psychological qualities such as learning interest, desire, will, inspiration, emotion and understanding, and improving students' psychological endurance and psychological regulation.

(3) Cultural system. Standing at the height of "big culture" and observing dance teaching, we will fully realize that dance art is bound to be restricted and affected by dance culture, and cultural atmosphere and cultural conditions directly determine the professional level and artistic creativity of dance artists, so we will pay full attention to the creation of cultural heritage and cultural taste in dance teaching, And the construction of dance culture [10]. The online chart of the number of teachers and students is shown in Fig. 6 below.

Teaching content system. The teaching content system is not only the carrier and support of the whole dance teaching system, but also an important means and reliable guarantee. The author believes that the reform of the teaching content system of dance teaching is imperative. It is necessary to change the old puppet state of traditional content and replace it with new and dynamic teaching content with large amount of information and strong update of information, such as women's solo dance The spirit of sparrow,

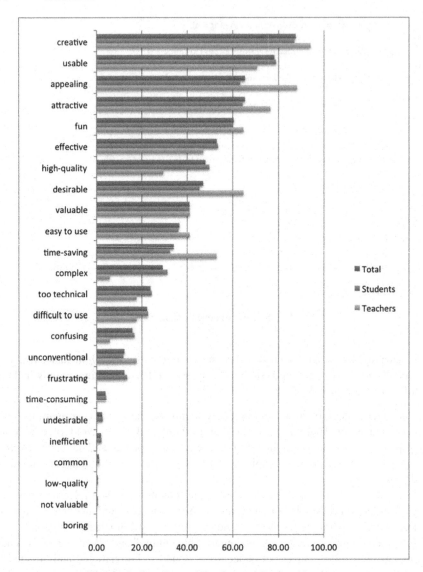

Fig. 6. Online Chart of Teacher and Student Numbers

the group dance thousand hands Guanyin, modern dance and street dance should be incorporated into the formal teaching content system as soon as possible, so as to make the dance teaching full of vitality and strong vitality.

5 Conclusion

The design and implementation of online dance teaching system is the process of designing and developing a system to provide students with an effective and efficient learning experience. The design includes user interface, content management, data storage, search engine and so on. Implementation involves designing a database structure that will store information about all students enrolled in this course. It also involves integration with other systems, such as email servers and web servers, so that anyone can access it anytime, anywhere on any device.

Acknowledgements. 2021 Dalian University of Art "Faith Youth" bidding project "Faith Youth Original Musical Dance Creation and Practice" YP202118.

References

1. Tian, F., Zhu, Y., Li, Y.: Design and implementation of dance teaching system based on unity3D. In: 2021 6th International Conference on Intelligent Computing and Signal Processing (ICSP) (2021)
2. Liu, G.: The design and implementation of sports dance teaching system based on digital media technology. In: The 1st EAI International Conference on Multimedia Technology and Enhanced Learning (2017)
3. Mao, Y.: Design and Implementation of Virtual Dance Training System under the Background of Artificial Intelligence Technology (2021)
4. Fox, V.: Improving Development in Youth: My Implementation of an After-School Dance Program (2016)
5. Chatterjee, A.: Implementation of Dance Movement Therapy Among Hearing Impaired Children – A Case Study (2016)
6. Zhao, X., Chen, C., Li, Y.: Implementation of online teaching behavior analysis system. 11 (2021)
7. Widodo, A., Nursaptini, N., Erfan, M.: Implementation of multicultural education through Sasambo Dance at the University of Mataram (2021)
8. Rosala, D.A.: Local Wisdom-Based Dance Learning: Teaching Characters to Children through Movements. Mimbar Sekolah Dasar (2020)
9. Zhu, L., Sun, J., Zhou, M.: Design and implementation of dance video teaching system based on Spring MVC architecture. Mod. Electron. Techniq. (2019)
10. Zhang, C.: University B: Design and implementation on dance teaching live system for iOS platform. Comput. Technol. Develop. (2016)

Design and Implementation of Online College English Teaching Based on OBE

Jing Guo and Jijie Liu[✉]

East University of Heilongjiang, Heilongjiang 150000, China
huaw545@aliyun.com

Abstract. English is the second foreign language taught in most schools and one of the most important languages in technical and professional work. In this regard, EFL learners not only need to learn English as a means of communication, but also because they are interested in studying abroad. For these reasons, there is a growing demand for English education, especially among college students. Although many universities offer foreign language general education courses, few universities offer courses designed specifically for our society's EFL learning needs. However, there is no similar study on the effect of EFL teaching. A large number of studies have been conducted to test the effectiveness of teacher centered EFL teaching. But to what extent can this teaching be applied to other environments? To solve this problem, we introduce online college English teaching based on OBE (OCT).

Keywords: College English · OBE · Online teaching

1 Introduction

Online teaching and learning has become an irresistible trend, but Chinese students generally have weak language practice ability and low participation in online learning, which makes online learning or online assisted physical classroom unable to achieve ideal results. In online learning, learners' learning engagement is generally average, which is obviously lower than the performance level of learning engagement in offline traditional classroom, which needs to be further improved.

However, learning input has an important impact on learning gains and learning performance. Learning input has a direct positive impact on learning performance. That is to say, learning input is an important guarantee for achieving good learning results. Without a high degree of learning input, any learning will be difficult to gain. Therefore, learning input has also been included in the key indicators of the quality evaluation of university education [1]. The degree of learning engagement is so important to the learning effect, but the current college students' learning effect is generally poor, and the learning engagement is at a general level. Therefore, how to effectively improve the online learning engagement level of learners has attracted more and more scholars' attention.

Y. Zhang and N. Shah (Eds.): BigIoT-EDU 2023, LNICST 583, pp. 498–504, 2024.
https://doi.org/10.1007/978-3-031-63139-9_52

OBE (Output Based Education) means an education model based on learning output, It is also called "results oriented education". In "Internet plus" In the era, classroom teaching has been effectively supplemented through online resources, and students have also achieved a better learning effect. Through the content based screening and refining of knowledge points, the teaching unit with content as a module can be constructed. Through various forms such as micro classes and mu classes, appropriate and reasonable interaction between teachers and students can be designed to improve students' enthusiasm for learning and enable students to participate in teaching activities. Students participate in online learning and generally choose the learning content for the purpose of solving problems in learning [2]. Therefore, students have a high interest in learning, a clear purpose and a good learning effect. This research will design an online teaching model from the perspective of OBE, and pay more attention to the quality of students' training through continuous attention to students' learning effects.

2 Related Work

2.1 Research Status of OBE Concept

The concept of OBE first originated abroad. In 1981, the American scholar Spady W.D. first proposed the concept of OBE in his article. Later, he made a systematic exposition of the concept of OBE, defining OBE as "a clear focus on and architecture of the education system, to ensure that students master the experience of substantive success and control the future life". In addition, other foreign scholars have also conducted a series of studies on OBE. For example, the Western Australian Education Department defines OBE as "an education and teaching process that helps students achieve specific output through learning" [3]. In 2002, Harden R.M. summarized twelve advantages of OBE compared with traditional education, and introduced the detailed development of OBE from 1981 to 2002. In general, the research results of OBE education concept abroad provide a rich theoretical basis for our research.

The domestic research on OBE concept is relatively late, but domestic scholars attach great importance to the research on OBE and have made some beneficial explorations. Advanced search was carried out on CNKI with the theme of "OBE" or "achievement oriented" [4]. By February 2020, 4820 articles had been retrieved. According to the quantitative visual analysis of CNKI, the trend of the number of articles published was shown in Fig. 1. When OBE was first proposed, there was less research. Only in 2008, the number of articles published reached a small peak, a total of 90 articles. The real research started after China became a signatory to the Washington Agreement in 2013, It broke out in the year of becoming a full member. Since 2014, the number of papers published has gradually increased, especially in recent years. It can be seen that the research on OBE education concept is becoming more and more popular [5].

2.2 Online Open Courses

Online open courses are literally translated from "MOOC", that is, "large-scale open online courses". On September 16, 2012, Wikipedia defined MOOC as "a course with

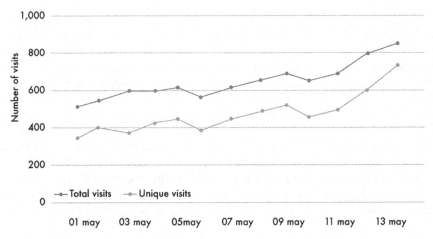

Fig. 1. OBE/result oriented document quantity trend chart

participation distributed in various places and course materials distributed in the network". On September 20, 2012, the definition evolved into: "MOOC is - MOOC is a new development in the field of distance education, as well as a new development of the open education concept advocated by open education resources."

Each excellent course is a "technology platform + content resources", so the online open course is a course that relies on the network platform, realizes the sharing of educational resources, and can be learned anytime and anywhere. With the rapid development of information technology, various MOOC platforms have also emerged, such as "Love Curriculum", "Superstar Fanya", "Wisdom Tree", "School Online", etc. Building online open courses based on these platforms can have a huge impact on today's educational reform, which is worth our serious research [6].

OBE is an education model based on results or output orientation, which was initially applied in the basic education reform in the United States, Australia and other countries. Since the 1990s, the member countries of the Washington Agreement, such as the United States, Britain and Canada, have taken the OBE model as the mainstream idea of their educational reform. The OBE education concept emphasizes the students' learning achievements, pays attention to the output of the teaching process rather than its input, and needs to reverse design teaching activities based on the students' learning output. Under the background of education informatization, this research has carried out teaching reform practice on information technology curriculum in junior high school based on OBE education concept, combined with the current teaching situation of information technology curriculum in junior high school, and explored how to build an OBE teaching mode suitable for information technology curriculum in junior high school with the help of digital superstar platform [7].

3   Design of Online College English Teaching Based on OBE

The implementation of OBE concept to the curriculum level needs to integrate English online courses from the three dimensions of cognition, ability and emotion, determine the teaching content and teaching strategies from top to bottom, and build an online course teaching design framework that focuses on emotional experience and learning results. It can be implemented in four steps, namely, defining project results, simulating language environment, realizing project results, and applying project results.

(1) Define project outcomes

The online classroom adopts the teaching mode of "outcome oriented", with the design of "simulation projects" related to each unit as the foothold, taking listening and speaking training, text analysis, reading training, and cultural development as the knowledge and ability reserves for project realization, and finally realizing the ladder like improvement of English comprehensive application ability through the display of project results [8].

(2) Simulation Language Environment

Foreign language learning has high requirements for language environment. Integrated English online course expands single textbook knowledge to rich English online audio-visual resources to create a simulated language learning environment; With the help of strong sensory stimulation and project experience, it can arouse learners' emotional resonance; Relying on a series of common English learning software such as mobile terminals, course official account, and online apps, we will build a digital language learning environment that everyone can learn, everywhere, and from time to time.

(3) Achieve project results

Realizing project achievements is the practice link of OBE concept implementation. The online comprehensive English course provides learning maps for online classes and guidance on learning methods to enhance independent learning ability; Stimulate the desire for knowledge through task guidance; Train logical thinking through mind mapping; Improve learners' English pragmatic competence through situational activities; Relying on the "cloud classroom" to achieve learner autonomy in learning, testing, and real-time feedback, so as to meet the personalized learning needs of learners, and achieve "a space for life, with characteristics for life".

(4) Application project achievements

Through the research on online learning behavior big data and multi-level learning achievements, the online comprehensive English course can form a semi open teaching closed loop and provide application feedback for the following three levels of groups. The first is the learner. According to the mastery of knowledge points reflected in the online test, the system provides learners with personalized assessment of cognitive level and learning suggestions in combination with error frequency, and recommends corresponding expansion courses [9]. The second is the teacher. With reference to the big data related to the online learning process, such as homework submission, attendance, etc., teachers can quickly understand the basic situation of learners and classify them, adjust teaching strategies and priorities for learners of different types and foundations, fully respect learners' differences in goal setting, homework design and evaluation content, and put forward grading requirements. The third is the third party of the project. Through the screening and integration of student simulation project results, excellent projects have the opportunity to share with a third party through the "cloud platform" display, and actually apply to foreign language exchanges and other teaching and research activities in real situations.

4   Comprehensive English Online Course Practice Based on OBE Concept

(1) Course introduction and learning analysis

Comprehensive English is a professional basic course in the curriculum system of English majors in higher vocational colleges. It is a main compulsory course that presents English language knowledge, comprehensively trains language skills such as listening, speaking, reading and writing, increases students' knowledge and life experience, and cultivates students' comprehensive English ability. The textbook is "Practical English (Comprehensive Course)" (second edition) published by Foreign Language Teaching and Research Press. The textbook adopts the idea of task oriented activity design, but the language materials are not new enough and the visual online resources are insufficient. The teaching objects are sophomores majoring in English education. The main characteristics of the students are: 100% of them have the hardware conditions for remote online classes, and they are skilled in using the hybrid teaching network platform[10]. Their English foundation and language expression ability are uneven, and they are eager to express freely in English, but their vocabulary is limited and their expression is not smooth; I like interesting and intuitive online learning, and I am curious about the online teaching mode of this course during the epidemic.

(2) Online teaching platform and unit learning map configuration

The integrated English online interactive learning platform mainly includes Brainstorm WeChat group, campus official account, Superstar Learning Link and Pigai intelligent assessment system for exercises.

Before class, learners log in to the app official account (iChat Comprehensive English Microschool) via mobile phones or computers to receive the unit simulation project and online learning index designed by this course group, as shown in Fig. 2. First of all, learners memorize words through root and affix memory methods and complete online independent tests. The system automatically marks and gives statistical feedback. Secondly, after obtaining the online reading guide of the background information required by the unit simulation project, the learners use English to carry out the relevant topic "cloud discussion", and strengthen the memory and application of the important and difficult English words of the text in a relaxed and pleasant brainstorming.

In the class, learners completed the knowledge and skills reserve of simulation project reporting through video listening and speaking training, reading comprehension, key

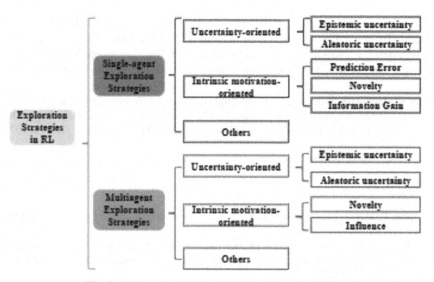

Fig. 2. Comprehensive English Online Learning Index

points refining, reading training, question answering exercises, etc., and met the needs of personalized learning with the help of "cloud classroom" intelligent knowledge point recognition technology to carry out independent reading and vocabulary expansion. Teachers online focus on helping learners to overcome the obstacles of long and difficult sentences and text understanding, and expand the depth and breadth of thinking.

After class, learners can follow the text independently with the help of intelligent voice evaluation software, and constantly break through the pronunciation difficulties according to the system prompts. The project script is submitted online through pigai's intelligent assessment system for exercises, and is modified repeatedly. The oral practice and unit simulation project are completed and uploaded to the "Cloud Classroom". Teachers and students select the best works from various assignments and display them on the campus official account. At the same time, teachers selected high-quality Mooc resources of Love Course in combination with unit learning content, and distributed relevant learning tasks in real time through the online interactive platform.

5   Conclusion

The online teaching design based on the OBE perspective monitors the quality of the whole teaching process and evaluates the teaching, which is convenient to understand the learners' learning status and online learning effects, and depends on how to choose and apply the learning objectives and teaching strategies. The establishment of learning objectives should be based on graduation requirements. The selection and achievement of learning objectives determine the differentiation of teaching strategies. The evaluation of learning output belongs to the whole process evaluation, which focuses on the process evaluation. At the same time, it combines with the summative evaluation and pays attention to the effect of the summative evaluation, forming a multi-level, multi angle, multi subject online learning evaluation method, which is reflected in the evaluation process. By evaluating the degree of achievement of teaching objectives of learning achievements, we will adjust the training objectives, teaching methods, content design and other aspects in the next round of teaching, so as to achieve better learning outcomes.

Acknowledgements. General Project of Higher Education Teaching Reform of Education Department of Heilongjiang Province in 2021 "A Study on the Practice of College English Ideological and Political Teaching Based on the Concept of OBE" (Project Number: SJGY20210736).

References

1. Ling, Y.: Design and implementation of the platform for multimedia resource sharing based on cloud technology. (7) (2022)
2. Mo, L., Shao, X.: Design and implementation of an interactive english translation system based on the information-assisted processing function of the internet of things. Math. Probl. Eng. **2022**, 1–13 (2022)
3. Hc, A., Envelope, X.: Design and implementation of human resource management system based on B/S mode. Procedia Comput. Sci. **208**, 442–449 (2022)
4. Zhai, H., Wang, Y.: Design and implementation of earthquake information publishing system based on mobile computing and machine learning technology in GIS. J. Interconnect. Netw. (2022)
5. Li, Y., Luo, H., Zhou, Y.: Design and implementation of virtual campus roaming system based on Unity3d. J. Phys.: Conf. Ser. **2173**(1), 012038 (2022)
6. Liu, Z., Mei, E., Fan, J., Zhang, Y.: Design and implementation of single-phase power quality monitor based on IM1281B. J. Phys.: Conf. Ser. **2290**(1), 012046 (2022). https://doi.org/10.1088/1742-6596/2290/1/012046
7. Palaoag, T.D.: Design and implementation of intelligent pig house environment monitor system based on Internet plus (2022)
8. Kunitz, S., Berggren, J., Haglind, M., Löfquist, A.: Getting students to talk: a practice-based study on the design and implementation of problem-solving tasks in the EFL classroom. Languages **7**(2), 75 (2022). https://doi.org/10.3390/languages7020075
9. Han, Y., Liu, L.: Design and practice of "Student-Centered" teaching method based on OBE concept: the case of theory and practice of cross-border E-commerce course. Open J. Soc. Sci. (2022)
10. Nafise, S., Ranjbar, A.A., Gorji, T.B.: Design and implementation of a new portable hybrid solar atmospheric water-generation system. Clean Energy **6**, 6 (2022)

Construction of Practical Teaching Platform of College Physics Education Under the Background of Information Technology

Bingtao Wei[✉] and Tang Kun

School of Artificial Intelligence, Wenshan University, Wenshan 663000, China
bingtaowei@sina.com

Abstract. With the development of science and technology and the arrival of information society, information technology has increasingly become a creative tool to expand human capabilities. The two platforms of traditional education and information technology are presented to educators. How to integrate information technology and subject teaching has become a new hot spot in the reform of basic education in the 21st century. It is very important to establish a teaching platform that can be used as the basis of physical education practice and learning. The construction of this platform will provide students with a wide range of knowledge and skills, which are necessary for their future career in the field of physics education. In order to achieve this goal, it is necessary to develop an appropriate model. On this basis, we can put forward our own ideas on how to organize all aspects of the teaching process: from content and methods, through teaching tools and materials (Textbooks), to the final evaluation.

Keyword: Information technology · College physics education · Practical teaching platform

1 Introduction

With the continuous development of information technology, university education has gradually developed from the initial manual education and teaching methods to practical teaching systems and computer-assisted learning (CAL), and then to the stage of information technology and curriculum integration (IITC). The construction of a web-based practical teaching platform in vocational colleges has become the key to achieving IITC. At present, such educational and teaching methods and platforms are extremely rare, especially for a certain university, building an information based university has become an inevitable way for the development of the school. Therefore, from the perspective of the actual situation of the school, it has become an urgent issue to build a teaching platform that applies IITC fields, has wide teaching coverage, extensive teaching content, supports diversified teaching, and is suitable for practical teaching models [1].

As an experimental science, physics is the theoretical foundation of all science and engineering majors. With the continuous deepening of teaching reform, the role of experiments in teaching has been increasingly valued by people. Experiments play a very

Y. Zhang and N. Shah (Eds.): BigIoT-EDU 2023, LNICST 583, pp. 505–516, 2024.
https://doi.org/10.1007/978-3-031-63139-9_53

important role in scientific research and social production activities. The basic teaching content of physical experiment course is greatly different from that of physical theory course, and cannot be replaced, such as the use of instruments, physical testing methods, and the processing and analysis of experimental data. Physical experiments are also the foundation of other professional experiments, which can deepen students' understanding of physics theory, strengthen the connection between theory and practice, and cultivate students' good scientific literacy, practical ability, and innovative thinking.

The Outline of the National Medium and Long Term Education Reform and Development Plan (2010–2020) sets forth requirements for teachers to fully recognize and respect the individual differences of students, establish a teaching concept of cultivating personalized and diverse talents, and then pay attention to the individual characteristics of students, so as to help each student develop their strengths and potentials as much as possible, and teach students in accordance with their aptitude. Some educational researchers believe that college physics experimental courses are different from scientific research. Their main purpose is to achieve knowledge transfer and cultivate students' scientific quality through various links in the experimental process, rather than exploring new physical laws and phenomena. This view precisely illustrates the actual teaching objectives of current college physics experimental courses. However, to some extent, such teaching objectives not only limit the teaching content and resources of college physics experimental courses to a certain set range, but also constrain the innovative thinking of learners, which is not conducive to personalized cultivation of students. Moreover, due to problems such as a single teaching model, outdated teaching methods, imperfect assessment systems, and inconsistent assessment standards, the evaluation perspective of learners' learning effects is single and incomplete, learners ignore experimental preparation, the experimental process is operated mechanically and does not explore the thinking principles, and later, they do not pay attention to experimental error correction. This ultimately leads to the "virtual reality" of college physics experiments.

With the advent of the information age and the widespread promotion and application of Internet and network technology, human learning activities have begun to exhibit distinct characteristics from traditional learning, with personalized learning models, virtual learning environments, and collaborative learning processes. Especially in the online context, the learning behavior of online course learners is characterized by multiple structures and levels [2]. In the era of big data, online learning conducted through the network utilizes data mining technology, learning analysis technology, and other methods to fully record, track, and visualize learners' learning behaviors, learning needs, and learning styles, while establishing different learning models to adapt to different types of students. Personalized learning paths and personalized learning trajectory dynamics are tailored for different individual learners. By pushing flexible and personalized learning resources, each person's learning content has a personal specificity, and is no longer the same. Therefore, the purpose of the research has shifted from improving the overall level to focusing on individual personalized development, seemingly from "overall" to "individual". In fact, it can be more targeted and effective in optimizing students' learning outcomes and optimizing the learning environment for the second time.

Currently, this practical teaching platform suitable for teaching is extremely rare. Due to financial, human, technical, and awareness reasons, many colleges and universities have no intention of developing this system at all. However, as education becomes increasingly widespread, establishing such an education system has gradually become a trend and a contradiction that must be resolved. Especially for Xinjiang Changji Vocational and Technical College, whose teaching coverage is large, teaching content is wide, and teaching methods are diverse, there is an urgent need to build a teaching platform suitable for practical teaching classroom teaching mode. Therefore, we should optimize the rational allocation of resources, make full use of scarce teaching resources, and effectively handle the increasing amount of management information. The construction of campus LAN provides a new management mode for experimental teaching in vocational colleges. According to scientific experimental teaching management, advanced computer network technology, database technology, build a powerful experimental teaching network management platform.

The platform is based on practical teaching, continuously improving students' learning initiative and interest, fully mobilizing their potential to acquire new knowledge and technology, and vigorously cultivating their innovative awareness [3]; At the same time, establish learning modules, continuously improve the quality of teachers, constantly seek professional development, and improve the level of education and teaching. So as to achieve the effect of teacher-student interaction.

2 Related Work

2.1 Current Situation of the Integration of Information Technology and High School Physics Teaching

In today's society, information technology based on computer multimedia and network is constantly penetrating into various fields of subject teaching. In the "Outline of Basic Education Curriculum Reform (Trial)", The Ministry of Education emphasizes that "vigorously promoting the universal application of information technology in the teaching process, promoting the integration of information technology and subject teaching, gradually realizing the transformation of teaching content presentation methods, student learning methods, teacher teaching methods, and teacher-student interaction methods, and providing a rich and colorful educational environment," curriculum integration, "has become a new perspective for China's basic education reform in the 21st century." [4]. In some remote and backward local middle schools in China, due to a lack of funds, even the most basic computer projectors cannot achieve the integration of information technology and college physics teaching. In some demonstration universities in cities, despite the complete hardware facilities, people are still accustomed to the era of one piece of chalk and one mouth. The vast majority of college physics teachers believe that the integration of information technology and college physics teaching is not only time-consuming and laborious, but also not necessarily effective [5]. Only when they are in public classes do they make some slides to deal with errands. In addition, many college physics teachers are more intimidated by the limitations of computer skills. As a student, I urgently need to learn college physics from both visual and auditory aspects. In order to solve this contradiction, we must mobilize the enthusiasm of college physics educators, let the idea of combining information technology with college physics teaching take root in the hearts of the people, and let them truly think and act. In various public classes and lecture competitions held at the national, provincial, and municipal levels, the integration of information technology and college physics teaching is becoming increasingly demanding [6]. In recent years, the Ministry of Education has regularly urged provincial and municipal education commissions to organize computer level training and examinations for college teachers to improve their computer skills and meet the requirements of combining information technology with college physics teaching. At the same time, the Ministry of Education has increased educational funding for local universities to improve their computer projectors and other hardware facilities. The construction of experimental teaching platform is shown in Fig. 1 below.

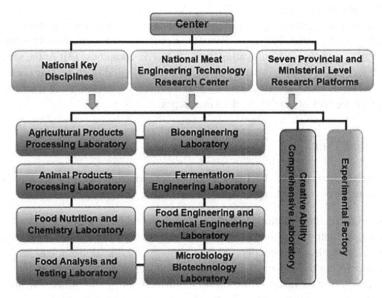

Fig. 1. Construction of experimental teaching platform

From a theoretical perspective, currently, in the relevant research that has been conducted, research combining learning behavior data in teaching platforms is very limited. This study aims to explore new ways to evaluate the performance of college physics experimental courses. Based on this, we will develop teaching resources that can stimulate students' innovative thinking and scientifically evaluate teaching effectiveness, enrich theoretical achievements related to innovative education in college physics experiments for undergraduate students, and provide effective reference for domestic research in this field. It is also of great academic significance to achieve the training objectives of universities and promote the development of undergraduate students' personality and innovation ability.

At the same time, in order to solve the practical problems in the current college physics experiment teaching, it is of important practical significance to combine the traditional college physics experiment evaluation considerations with the new connotation of learning behavior data (classifying and organizing the data, establishing a data model, and a new grade weight table), and constructing a teaching platform that can achieve flexible and multi-dimensional evaluation of the learning effectiveness of college physics experiment students.

2.2 Main Problems in Existing Practical Teaching

Analyze the existing practical teaching system and draw the following conclusions:

(1) Hardware is divorced from modern good education.

After the 1990s, China's higher vocational colleges have been newly established and rebuilt, but most of them were upgraded or merged from junior colleges, staff universities, colleges of education and secondary professional schools. The teaching resources of these schools are old and can't keep up with the requirements of higher vocational education. Moreover, under the condition of insufficient and scarce teaching resources, China's colleges and universities have expanded their enrollment, Under such circumstances, the construction of teaching facilities is difficult. In addition, these vocational colleges with weak foundation have limited hematopoietic function and do not have the funds to update teaching equipment, which can not meet the training and experiment class rate, and can not improve the construction standard of training base [7].

(2) The level of practical teaching management is low.

At present, many higher vocational colleges still design courses according to the traditional segmented method, resulting in many problems. First, the goal of practical teaching is not clear, which causes many problems in practical teaching. The teaching process does not reflect the teaching guiding ideology of "taking comprehensive quality as the basis, application as the main line, and ability as the center". Second, the design of practical teaching is not organically integrated with theoretical teaching, and theoretical teaching is disconnected from practical courses. In practical teaching, the application of the learned theory is not highlighted, especially the comprehensive application of the learned professional knowledge, and the ability to solve technical problems is poor, which affects the function and role of practical teaching [8]. The practice teaching management in higher vocational colleges is loose, and a complete set of management system and corresponding quality management and evaluation system on practice teaching have not been established. The quality of practice teaching management completely depends on the responsibility of instructors. There are differences in the abilities of instructors of different practical courses, which will inevitably affect the effect of practical training. Some know that teachers, limited by their own practical ability, social experience, educational background and other conditions, cannot correctly guide students to complete experimental training tasks, and cannot let students complete professional skill training comprehensively, systematically and with high quality. Some even mislead students, and the practical training effect is greatly reduced.

(3) The assessment method of practical teaching is unscientific

At present, most higher vocational colleges arrange skill training (practice link) to the final stage according to the requirements of curriculum and training plan, so that students can choose one of several designed practical projects to complete. The progress and content of students' curriculum design should be carried out completely according to the teacher's plan. Professional teachers are responsible for students' internship assessment. According to students' completion of the project, peacetime performance and discipline, grades are given respectively, and weighted synthesis [9]. This assessment method can not reflect students' learning ability and practical ability. Take the completion of students' projects as the basis for assessment, and do not pay attention to the assessment of project completion process. This assessment method belongs to target assessment, which only pays attention to the results, and does not pay attention to the quality of practical teaching process, which can not stimulate students' learning enthusiasm and initiative. During the completion of the project, students can "clone and copy" and so on.

3 Construction of Practical Teaching Platform for College Physics Education

3.1 Analysis of Overall System Structure

The integration of information technology and high school physics teaching has four elements: teachers, students, content, and teaching media. These four elements are not isolated, but interconnected and interactive as a whole. Students are the core element of this system, reflecting the status of students as the main body, reflecting the physical and mental development of students, and reflecting the main task of cultivating students' thinking quality. The three elements of teacher content and teaching media serve as the central elements of students. In a sense, teaching media directly serves teaching content. Teaching media can make teaching content more orderly, form more beautiful, and scene more abundant. Teachers are the creators and executors of these two elements. Only through teachers can teaching content and information technology be organically combined. These four elements are inseparable [10]. If any one of them goes wrong, it will affect the function of other elements, the function of the entire system, and the learning effect of students.

According to user demand analysis, the practical teaching platform needs to have the following functions:

(1) Practical teaching management includes many contents. As the core of practical teaching management system, it includes teaching document management, teaching process management, personnel management, asset and fund management, etc.
(2) The design of the system should conform to the process of practical teaching, combining advanced technology with the needs of the unit, and designing and standardizing the system from multiple perspectives and directions to improve work efficiency and workflow.
(3) The system can meet the needs of open practical teaching management, and has been widely recognized. The dynamic use of the training room greatly improves the

utilization rate and is also conducive to the cultivation of students' practical abilities, thereby meeting the needs.

(4) The system can publish exercise information, faithfully follow the schedule of the training room, automatically update based on the latest exercise information, and issue notifications.

3.2 Platform Structure and Functional Design

According to the actual teaching situation, user demand analysis, and the relationship between platform components, the overall architecture of the college physics experimental teaching platform that supports learning behavior data analysis includes the following parts: extracurricular learning information platform, course teaching resource platform, online teacher-student interaction platform, learning behavior statistics platform, and teacher evaluation management platform.

(1) Extracurricular learning information platform. The home page of the platform provides teachers and students with jump pages for educational administration information related to schools and colleges, facilitating users to learn relevant information in a timely manner. At the same time, it regularly updates anecdotes related to college physics and college physics experiments, stimulating learners' interest in college physics learning and guiding students' innovative thinking.

(2) Course teaching resource platform. The platform follows the actual and complete learning process of learners, and divides college physics experiment course resources into pre class preview resources, in class experiment data records, after class reflection, and expansion questions.

(3) Network teacher-student interaction platform. In order to improve the traditional teaching environment in which teachers and students, even students, do not have a backtrack after the completion of physics experiment classes, and there is often no communication between students' after-class thoughts or questions, an interactive platform has been specially designed for teachers and students to post and comment for communication.

(4) Learning behavior statistics platform. The platform records online behaviors of learners during online learning through the background to help teachers better understand students. For example, in the preview section, the monitoring of learners' viewing time of preview videos is added, and the traces of learners doing questions are recorded during exercise tests. At the same time, the platform realizes the correct and incorrect judgment of multiple choice questions and automatic scoring, and calculates and merges the scores of each part according to the established score weight table.

(5) Teacher evaluation management platform. Teachers provide standard answers to some objective questions to the platform, which enables automatic scoring. In addition, teachers can view relevant data of students during online learning and provide personalized evaluations based on the situation. The structural diagram of the college physics experiment teaching platform is shown in Fig. 2 below.

Based on the actual needs of college physics experiments, the platform should have the following functions: information release and management function, online learning

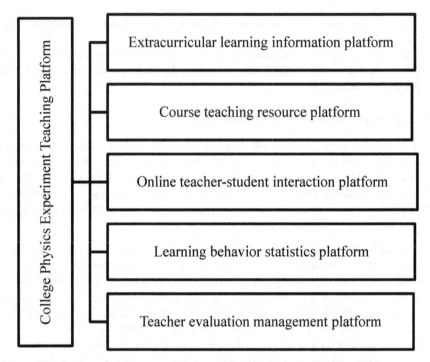

Fig. 2. Structural Diagram of College Physics Experiment Teaching Platform

function, interactive function, teaching resource service and management function, and data analysis and statistics function.

(1) Information release and management functions. Release timely educational and teaching information, as well as anecdotes related to college physics and experiments, and conduct management and maintenance.
(2) Online learning function. Provide students with video and graphic resources related to the course, enabling online learning anytime and anywhere.
(3) Interactive functionality. Provide an interactive platform between teachers and students, students and students, as well as human-computer interaction, enabling users to conduct synchronous and asynchronous interaction, and conduct online discussion and question answering or problem solving.
(4) Teaching resource service and management functions. This includes uploading and managing course videos, course documents, and graphic resources, as well as timely updating extracurricular development resources.
(5) Data analysis and statistics function. The platform automatically judges and calculates objective question scores, while recording and analyzing online behavioral data of learners, helping teachers understand the effectiveness of students' online learning and assisted learning, and timely adjusting teaching methods.

3.3 Platform Process Design

The users of the practical teaching platform of higher vocational colleges are required to be educational administrators, school leaders, practical course teachers and students. The process of the system is: first, the user logs in to the system and enters the corresponding user name and password. The system will check whether the user is legal. If it is legal, the system will ask whether it is an administrator. If it is an administrator, the system allows the administrator to allocate user rights, manage teaching documents, manage teaching processes, manage personnel information, and manage assets and funds. If you are not an administrator, you can operate part of the work within the permission according to the permission assigned by the administrator. The specific implementation is shown in Fig. 3:

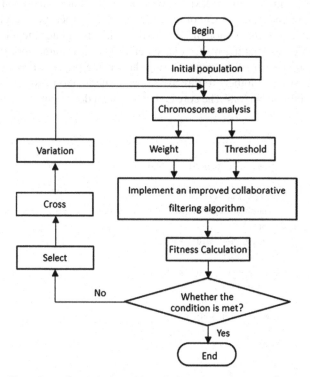

Fig. 3. Flow chart of practical teaching platform in Higher Vocational Colleges

4 System Development

As a carrier tool for teaching, the university physics experiment platform needs to develop a set of supporting teaching resources suitable for the platform in order to truly play a role in the teaching process. Therefore, the teaching process based on the university physics experiment teaching platform has been designed to guide teachers to better use the platform to carry out teaching activities, while combining high-quality teaching resources, giving full play to the characteristics of the platform, Provide students with personalized learning space to help them better conduct collaborative learning and inquiry learning.

HbuilderX, or HX for short, is a mainstream front-end development tool that is currently widely used in the cross platform client field and supports HTML5 hypertext technology. The tool was fully developed by Digital Paradise (Beijing) Network Technology Co., Ltd. (hereinafter referred to as Digital Paradise), and is a Web integrated development environment developed for the majority of Uni-App developers. As the next generation version of HBuilder, it has a very powerful syntax prompt function, and is extremely responsive to startup speed, large document opening speed, and coding prompts. During the production process of HBuilder, Digital Paradise used four languages for development, namely Java, C, Web, and Ruby, but its main body was written in Java. The front-end development of the college physics experiment teaching platform uses the app development version of HBuilderX, which integrates the relevant plug-ins needed in most cases, making it very convenient. There is a framework syntax prompt in the lower right corner of the page. During the writing process, there will be a code assistant. Press Alt + numbers to directly select an item, and press Ctrl + left mouse button to add multiple cursors. The core code for system development is shown in Fig. 4 below.

```
@Override
public boolean registered(UserInfoDomain userInfo) {
    try {
        long userId = CommonUtils.getRandomLong();
        int count = loginDao.setUserInfo(userInfo.getUserName(), userId, userInfo.getPassword());
        log.info("registered count: " + count);
        if (1 > count) {
            log.info("registerd failed");
            return false;
        }
    } catch (Exception e) {
        log.error("registerd failed: " + e.getMessage());
        return false;
    }
    return true;
}
```

Fig. 4. Core code

After entering the university physics experiment teaching platform, users can directly see the extracurricular resources displayed on the home page. The extracurricular resources are presented in a card format. Mobile phone users can scroll up and down the screen to select, while PC users can use the mouse to scroll up and down to select, click on the extracurricular resources they are interested in to view, and when clicking on the educational administration information, they will automatically jump to the official website of the school or college for viewing, When clicking on extracurricular resources that interest you, they are displayed directly in the form of a web page. The learning resource interface is shown in Fig. 5 below.

Fig. 5. Learning Resource Interface

Developed using Uni-App, it can achieve multiple forms of publishing such as clients, applets, and web pages. Considering the simplicity and ease of operation, as well as mobile phone users of different Android and IOS systems, the preferred form of publishing is web pages, which are suitable for cross browser applications and have the advantages of good compatibility, fast startup speed, short reaction time, and low traffic consumption. Other forms of publishing and compatibility testing can be conducted as required in the future, The WeText Tencent quality open platform can be used for compatibility testing of clients and applets. The platform provides complete compatibility testing, performance testing, security testing, and cloud based real machine testing. It provides a dual end scanning, penetration, and reinforcement of internal overall risk monitoring tools for applets.

5 Conclusion

Starting from the analysis of system requirements, this paper establishes the system framework according to the idea of software engineering, and puts forward the design objectives of the server and client software of the practical teaching platform in higher vocational colleges. According to the requirements of practical teaching in higher vocational colleges, this paper designs a set of practical teaching platform with simple and practical operation interface. The practical teaching platform of higher vocational colleges has realized the information management of practical teaching in our school, greatly reducing the heavy workload of equipment management and teaching management in practical teaching in our school, facilitating users, administrators and decision makers to dynamically grasp the practical teaching information of our school, improving work efficiency and saving personnel costs. After being tested, the practical teaching platform in Higher Vocational Colleges runs stably, operates conveniently and quickly, meets the needs of practical teaching in schools, reduces costs, improves efficiency, makes practical teaching more scientific and reasonable, and meets the teaching needs of schools.

References

1. Hu, C., Liu, Y.: Construction and application of micro technology platform in applied technology universities under the background of internet plus. J. Phys.: Conf. Ser. **1533**(2), 022112 (2020) (6pp)
2. Chen, L., Li, Y.: The significance and practical path of outward bound training in college. Phys. Educ. Teach. **8**(1), 5 (2019)
3. Huang, C.: Exploration and research of information technology in college english teaching. J. Phys.: Conf. Ser. **1648**(2), 022021 2020 (5pp)
4. Wei, C., Yuan, L.: Reflection on college informationized teaching model under the background of educational informationization. In: 2019 IEEE International Conference on Computer Science and Educational Informatization (CSEI). IEEE (2019)
5. Wei, W., Wei, J., Peng, J.: Practical application of sports basketball teaching APP under the background of the new media. J. Phys.: Conf. Ser. **1744**(4), 042230 (2021) (7pp)
6. Zhao, F., Chen, L.: Empirical study on the teaching quality evaluation system of college physics informatization based on fuzzy comprehensive evaluation method. Rev. Facult. Ingen. **32**(14), 58–66 (2017)
7. Wei, W., Wei, J., Fang, W.: Application analysis of flipped classroom based on wechat public platform in basketball physical education teaching. J. Phys: Conf. Ser. **1744**(4), 042228 (2021)
8. Zhang, J.Q., Zhang, Z.L.: Research on the reform strategy of college physical education under the background of internet. J. Heb Univ. Eng. (Soc. Edn.) (2019)
9. Qiang, L.I., Department, F.L.: Paths for ecological classroom construction of college English under the background of education informatization. J. Hubei Corresp. Univ. (2018)
10. Wang, H., Zou, Y., Li, J., et al.: Exploration and practice of college physics experiment innovation teaching under the background of emerging engineering education. China Mod. Educ. Equip. (2019)

Application Study of Virtual Reality Technology Assisted Training in College Physical Education

Xun Sun[1(✉)] and Xue Qian[2]

[1] Physical Education Institute, Tongling University, Tongling 244061, Anhui, China
xunsun66@163.com
[2] Zaozhuang Vocational College of Science and Technology, Zaozhuang 277599, Shandong, China

Abstract. With the sustainable development and progress of social economy, the level of science and information technology is also constantly improved. VR technology arises at the historic moment in this era environment. As the talent cultivation base, colleges and universities should also adapt to the social development, innovate the mode of running schools, introduce science and technology into the teaching classroom, make reasonable use of accurate and efficient VR technology, innovate the physical education teaching mode, and provide objective data support for the development of physical education teaching activities. However, considering the actual situation, it is not difficult to find that the application of VR technology in college sports is still in the initial stage, and some schools and teachers have not yet realized the value of VR technology. Based on this, the following will be an analysis of the importance and application of VR technology in physical education teaching in colleges and universities, hoping to provide suggestions for educators.

Keyword: virtual reality technology · colleges and universities · physical education teaching

1 Introduction

Under the background of the sustainable development and progress of science and technology, computer technology has been popularized in all fields. The field of education should also follow the pace of The Times, realize the importance of science and technology, and effectively combine teaching activities with science and technology. Physical education teaching in institutions of higher learning, has always been difficult and key, physical education for the role of students' physical quality, but part of the sports risk coefficient, higher demand for venues and equipment, under the limited cost, colleges and universities cannot create conform to the requirements of the practice environment, this caused a bad effect for sports teaching. With the use of VR technology, colleges and universities can create a one-to-one virtual scene, provide students with a practice platform for students, improve students 'physical education learning effect, exercise students' physical quality, and let students make continuous progress under the assistance of VR.

Y. Zhang and N. Shah (Eds.): BigIoT-EDU 2023, LNICST 583, pp. 517–527, 2024.
https://doi.org/10.1007/978-3-031-63139-9_54

in recent years, The Ministry of Education has proposed a number of guidance plans related to virtual reality technology for the reform of teaching methods: in the "13th Five Year Plan" for Education Informatization, it included accelerating the construction of demonstration virtual simulation experiment teaching projects in the "Deepening the Integration of Information Technology and Higher Education Teaching"; it proposed in the "Education Informatization 2.0 Action Plan" in 2018 "In order to integrate the development of 5G technology, we will strengthen the construction of large capacity intelligent teaching resources through the construction of national high-quality online open courses, demonstration virtual simulation experiment teaching projects, and other carriers"; "Key Points for Education Informatization and Network Security in 2019" proposes to "promote the in-depth application of new technologies such as big data, virtual reality, and artificial intelligence in education and teaching." In sports teaching, virtual reality technology can generate various virtual sports equipment models and different climate environments through computers, enabling students to obtain near real experiences through virtual environments, thereby solving the problems of lack of teaching resources, single teaching methods, and unsatisfactory teaching content, and achieving intelligent, modern, and efficient sports teaching.

In the post epidemic era, the COVID-19 is still lurking and breaking out all over the country, and online sports teaching has gradually become normalized. However, the sense of distance between teachers and students, and the sense of separation between teaching and learning still make online teaching unable to better complete the interaction between teachers and students, and ensure the quality of teaching. As a new technological means, virtual reality technology has advanced modern teaching concepts and features such as immersion, interactivity, and multi perception. It provides the possibility to break time and space constraints, improve the home class experience, and create real teaching scenarios. In terms of educational theory, virtual reality technology connects users with the virtual environment, creating an "autonomous learning" environment and realizing the presence of people. The traditional "teaching for learning" learning method has also been updated, transforming it into an "interactive" learning method in which students gain knowledge and skills through the interaction of themselves, information, and the environment, making up for the limitations caused by objective conditions such as weather effects, insufficient training venues, equipment, and funding in teaching, and achieving the advantage of being able to exercise without leaving home. The popularization and promotion of virtual reality teaching method during the epidemic situation is not only conducive to turning the COVID-19 epidemic situation into an opportunity, but also conducive to promoting the quality and upgrading of online sports teaching. The scoring criteria for physical training using virtual reality technology are shown in Fig. 1 below.

With the accelerated pace of education and teaching reform in universities and the development of modern education informatization, VR technology has gradually been applied to education and teaching in universities. The impact of VR technology on college education and teaching reform is comprehensive and profound, and its impact on college physical education cannot be ignored. As is well known, students' low interest in physical education can be described as a common phenomenon and difficulty in physical education teaching in ordinary colleges and universities. The reason for this is

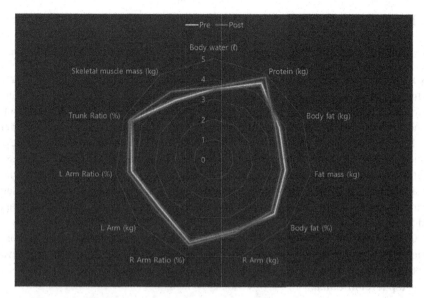

Fig. 1. The Scoring Standard of Virtual Reality Technology for Sports Training

undeniable, to some extent, due to the outdated existing teaching content, teaching methods, and means. Traditional physical education textbooks and teaching methods cannot enable teachers to teach sports technical movements well, nor are they conducive to students' refined perception and understanding of sports technical movements. However, the application of VR technology to physical education teaching can enable teachers and students to interact and analyze data through actions, language, and other aspects in the sports world created by virtual reality technology, providing a new direction and idea for the learning of sports technology, and can design and display sports technology actions in a targeted manner, making physical education more intuitive and detailed, both innovating traditional physical education methods, It can also stimulate students' interest in sports learning. In particular, the construction of a VR sharing platform for college physical education can promote resource sharing in college physical education at a certain level, and will also promote the return of college physical education to the essence of education, which will have a profound impact on cultivating innovative practical talents and establishing a lifelong view of physical education. However, literature searches have found that research on the application of VR technology to physical education is quite rare in the academic community, while research on the construction of a VR sharing platform for physical education is almost non-existent, which is indeed not conducive to the current requirements of educational informatization reform for the reform and development of physical education in colleges and universities. In view of this, this article intends to explore the construction of a VR training platform for physical education teaching in ordinary colleges and universities, in order to attract valuable insights.

2 Related Work

2.1 Definition of "VR Technology"

VR is an abbreviation for Virtual Reality, which is translated into virtual reality. Virtual reality technology is a computer simulation technology that can create and experience a virtual world. It uses computers to generate an interactive three-dimensional dynamic scene, and its physical behavior simulation system can immerse users in the environment.

The concept of VR originated in the United States, which leads the world in the development and application of VR technology. In the 1980s, the United States established multiple laboratories for the development of VR technology, and conducted research on the application of VR technology in aerospace, optics, and other fields during the same period. In the short term, it has quickly been widely studied in European countries, Japan and South Korea.

China introduced VR technology relatively late, and conducted research on it through national projects, using university laboratories as research bases. Currently, the relevant VR technology achievements of Beijing University of Aeronautics and Astronautics are at the top level in China.

2.2 Overseas Research on the Application of VR Technology

The level of VR technology application in the United States represents the development level of VR applications in the world, including basic research, aerospace, and telescopic observation, and the establishment of a VR education system. Among them, computer laboratories in universities use VR technology to explore and apply areas such as molecular modeling, surgical simulation, and architectural simulation. At the same time, VR design has been introduced into the fields of design, entertainment, and manufacturing. The UK is a leader in Europe in the design of VR auxiliary equipment and product applications, and has established multiple research centers that apply VR technology, including the use of VR technology to design the cockpit of advanced fighter jets. Japan is adept at producing VR games and has established a large-scale VR knowledge base, which has been effectively analyzed and applied in motion recognition and expression capture in image processing technology. In addition, experiments have also been conducted on the interaction between virtual organisms and virtual environments, and more research and exploration have been conducted on human actions (faces, limbs) in virtual reality.

Osmo et al. conducted experiments on subjects in an immersive virtual reality (VR) forest environment. Before and after using virtual reality applications, they measured the degree of recovery effects on participants through perceived recovery results, vitality, and emotions. Before and after using virtual reality applications, the degree of recovery effect on participants is measured by perceived recovery results, vitality, and emotions. Although virtual reality technology has effective recovery capabilities in schools or workdays that cannot access highly restorative natural environments, it has also proven to be able to meet some basic recovery needs.

Bisso et al. used VR technology to alleviate schizophrenia. Researchers conducted a systematic review to explore the therapeutic application of immersive virtual reality technology in the spectrum of schizophrenia. The results showed that VR treatment had significant effects compared to conventional treatment, without significant side effects, and had significant therapeutic effects for patients with drug resistance. Such research will provide a reference for immersive virtual reality technology in the treatment of mental diseases, and effectively replace drug treatment, thereby providing protection for the safety and stability of patients with mental diseases.

In summary, the application of VR technology in foreign countries has been specifically carried out for a long time, and involves various industry fields. Various practical studies are also quite comprehensive. There are many valuable experiences that can be summarized to continuously fill the gaps in the field of VR technology application.

2.3 VR Technology is Important in Physical Education Teaching

(1) Avoid accidental injury

The intensity of practice in physical education in colleges and universities is usually relatively large. Some of the sports programs will inevitably lead to students 'injuries in the actual teaching and practice, which has a bad impact on the teaching quality and students' physical condition. However, if VR technology can be introduced and used in physical education teaching to simulate and demonstrate the possible highly dangerous links in physical education practice in advance, then the generation of accidents and dangers can be effectively avoided to avoid the adverse effects on students' bodies. With the help of VR technology, students can train various sports events in simulation situations without worrying about accidental physical injuries and accidents. (As shown in Table 1) Not only that, the computer VR scenario can also monitor every movement made by students in the training in real time, record the students 'non-standard movements, correct the shortcomings of students' shortcomings in time, and improve the quality of physical education teaching [1].

Table 1. Application of VR technique in avoiding teaching injuries

Application of computer virtual reality technology							
Bodybuilding teaching	Basketball teaching	Volleyball teaching	Football teaching	Taekwondo teaching	Beven and even bar teaching	Swimming teaching	Boxing teaching
Action normative guidance	Exercise normative guidance to avoid physical contact injury	Exercise normative guidance to avoid physical contact injury	Exercise normative guidance to avoid physical contact injury	Exercise normative guidance to avoid physical contact injury	Exercise normative guidance to avoid physical contact injury	Action normative guidance	Exercise normative guidance to avoid physical contact injury

(2) The lack of optimized material conditions

In the physical education teaching in colleges and universities, because there are many types of sports, the venues and equipment required for each kind of sports are also completely different, which puts forward strict requirements for colleges and universities. Some schools have limited conditions to fully meet the needs of sports exercise, so colleges and universities have to allocate most of the limited funds to purchase sports equipment. In this situation, many physical education teaching projects can not be carried out effectively because of the limitation of financial conditions, and have to give up. However, through the application of VR technology, this problem is effectively solved. Virtual reality technology can create virtual practice scenarios for students, so that students can conduct sports exercises in the computer scene, enrich the practice experience in the senses, and improve the quality of physical education teaching. The test design for current sports training research is shown in Fig. 2 below.

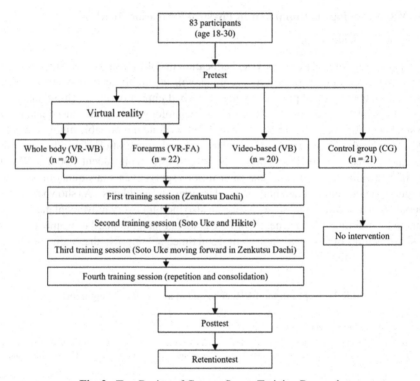

Fig. 2. Test Design of Current Sports Training Research

3   Application of Virtual Reality Technology in Physical Education Teaching

(1) Application of VR technology and equipment

In recent years, the visual technology development rate rapidly, in the process of VR technology, the requirement for equipment is small, don't need teachers to install some sensor kind of equipment, only need teachers control and set some simple camera and processor, at the same time can through the camera receive real-time image information, to obtain the students in sports in every posture, again through the computer processing to VR scenario in real and virtual interaction, greatly improve the quality of sports training, reduce human causes[2]. In the computer VR technology use system, there are many plates and systems, such as image pretreatment plate, three-dimensional reconstruction plate, etc. In order to accurately obtain the parts of the students, and in the sports movement form information, so it should be in the students playground around set up some cameras, in order to real-time to capture the students movement information, all-round no dead Angle to input and shooting, for VR to provide more accurate information transmission system. After the corresponding image information is successfully obtained, the three-dimensional reconstruction technology in the computer vision plate can automatically form the three-dimensional model persistence information in the students' movement, which can provide intuitive image data for teachers and help teachers to better analyze the movement state of students.

(2) Training scene creation

Application of virtual reality technology in the process of colleges and universities sports teaching, usually can play the function of two aspects, one is by capture the continuity of the students in the movement of 3 d action information, analyze the students' sports movement integrity, and detailed research and contrast, to correct action for the follow-up practice authentic guidance. The second is that through the three-dimensional 3 d modeling plate, to conduct the virtual creation of the actual practice environment, so as to provide students with a more real virtual training environment.

For the first function, when the students finish the creation of the three-dimensional model of the training movements, they can directly see their own action completion and action display results on the display screen. Through manual analysis, we can find out the mistakes and deficiencies in the training movements. On this basis, the teachers can directly guide the students to correct them[3]. In addition, we can also create a more automatic objective evaluation method, to carry out a fully automatic evaluation of students' sports training movements, and assist artificial analysis. To achieve this goal, you can use the simulation technology in virtual reality technology. First of all, teachers can first collect the correct three-dimensional images of the movements in the sports exercise, create a three-dimensional movement structure framework, and then collect the training images of the students 'training posture, and expand the data analysis, and compare the students' movement posture through the three-dimensional reconstruction technology. Next, the teacher can compare the students' motion and posture images according to the previously collected 3 D images of the correct behavior, and give the manual assessment results. In this way, it can be effectively realized under the application of fully automatic auxiliary technology, to determine whether the students' sports movements are standard, whether correct, this way is more accurate, but also to reduce the manual error.

For the second function, the focus is on the interaction design of the virtual situation and the actual environment. In general, the improvement of students' actual experience in the exercise process in the virtual situation should be taken as the core design point.

Therefore, when creating the situation, we should also focus on considering the simulation construction process of three-dimensional reconstruction. Real environment and virtual environment interaction, is the center of this function, through a detailed and comprehensive analysis of movement, create a more accurate simulation model, when the students complete the sports action, with the help of stereo reconstruction technology, will all the collected action information input into the model, the computer can be based on the design of the automatic output situation feedback.

(3) Image preprocessing

In VR technology created a virtual scene, visual input information has important influence for the use of the whole system, the computer with the aid of cameras, recording the students in the process of movement of every action, and obtain the scene material through VR scene, in the VR technology, the camera itself jitter situation or the students in the movement will lead to the clarity of the final imaging is affected. However, such a fuzzy image usually makes the subsequent three-dimensional reconstruction function unable to operate reasonably, and more importantly, it fails to create accurate and comprehensive three-dimensional information, resulting in serious errors in VR calculation and reducing the application experience of VR technology. Therefore, in order to avoid this situation, image pretreatment technology arises at the historic moment, teachers in the creation of VR frame, must be image preprocessing technology, if the image is fuzzy, and the initial clear image convolution, so simple processing fuzzy image become the necessary function of this technology. If an image only has a fixed blur point, a clearer image can be processed in advance. However, in the actual use of this technology, in addition to the point blur cases, there will also be more complex coupling blur cases. For example, the jitter of the camera itself and the high-speed movement of students in the training process will lead to the blur points in different parts of the image. For this kind of image blur, some technical workers put forward a processing way, is fuzzy extraction technology [4]. For the case of poor image clarity, BAYES is reasonably applied to intercept the fuzzy points in each frame, and then the fuzzy image is reconstructed through the form of reverse volume, so as to achieve a more effective blur elimination effect. Such a way does not require manual adjustment of parameters at all, and is well adapted, so it is widely used in the VR system creation.

(4) Three-dimensional Reconstruction Technology

The three-dimensional reconstruction technology is the technology of recording the students' movement in a virtual scene and creating a simulation situation. On the basis of the stereo reconstruction technology, the camera can directly capture all aspects of students' motion parameters, and then analyze the parameter information, such as shadow, focus, etc., to expand the stereo reconstruction to reconstruct the position of the simulated situation [5]. The process corresponding to this technology is shown in Table 2:

This technology needs according to the camera image information to run, after the camera to the students movement and motion finished, transmission to stereo reconstruction in the VR system, stereo reconstruction technology can be combined with image elements, such as information, action, light, point, three-dimensional reconstruction, through surface, three-dimensional reconstruction way, uphold the principle of

Table 2. Technical process of stereo reconstruction

Stereo reconstruction technology process
Input multi-perspective image —— feature point check —— feature point matching —— stereo model estimate —— point cloud registration —— point cloud grid

luminosity consistency, based on the sparse point cloud for dense point group [6]. In general, it is necessary to comprehensively collect the perfect three-dimensional information of various objects and elements in the scene. At the same time, the camera must be designed as different angles of the object, so as to realize the unification of the information of the three-dimensional reconstruction point cloud in a coordinate, so that the three-dimensional structure information can be displayed more perfect. Under the use of three-dimensional reconstruction technology, it can help teachers to analyze students 'physical training more comprehensively, and let teachers observe whether students' movements are standard from multiple angles and multiple aspects. In the past, two-dimensional plane images can only let teachers watch from one Angle, but three-dimensional reconstruction can allow teachers to 360° to watch whether students' sports movements meet the standard, which is more conducive to the improvement of teaching quality.

4   VR Sports Training Teaching

The existing immersive, interactive, and imaginative advantages of virtual reality technology can quickly drive the visual, auditory, and proprioceptive sensations of the experimenter to maintain high intensity real-time feedback, enhance strong sensory input, and enhance the effect of motion output. The human sensory system can automatically generate relevant perceptual memories by receiving and processing information about past events [7]. That is to say, after a long period of VR sports training, sports athletes generate relevant memories by processing the scenes, stimuli, operations, etc. they strongly perceive in the created virtual environment through the brain, and then transfer their cognitive and sports experiences in the virtual scene to the real environment through the memory regeneration process, Complete the mastery of the ability to improve exercise density.

The key technologies included in virtual reality technology, such as dynamic environment modeling, real-time three-dimensional animation, three-dimensional display sensing, accurate and fast tracking, and system transformation integration, all determine the depth of integration of the experience in the virtual environment. Network signal is one of the important factors affecting accurate and fast tracking [8]. The VR sports training system in this study uses a variety of means to compensate for network delay and other factors that interfere with training. For example, it will predict the amount of advance or delay injury calculation according to the current form direction and speed of the limbs, and adjust the results after the system integrates the actions of both parties at the same supervisor time point. A series of software support ensures that sports athletes deepen their sports imprint and stabilize the output state of athletes' perceived induced stimuli in a virtual environment to real-world training scenarios [9].

From a psychological perspective, VR sports training reflects a trend to enhance the sense of reality by overlaying stimulating information in the virtual training environment with psychological activities in the inner world, strengthening the psychological activities of sports athletes in cognitive aspects such as spatial cognition and behavioral cognition. In the human spatial cognitive system, there is an information processing module that maintains strong contact with the body. When athletes generate similar scene cognition, their physical actions and behaviors will significantly bias towards maintaining the movement state under the cognitive impression [10]. In VR sports training, there will be continuous and random bright spots that stimulate athletes to exercise, increasing the number of sports without arousing the athletes' awareness. When athletes conduct tests after the experiment, their brains will project visual cognitive scenes in the virtual scene, and their sports actions, frequencies, and other states will also be similar to them, resulting in a significant increase in sports density.

5 Tag

To sum up, VR technology system design is very simple, the cost is low, but the high degree of science and technology, in the college physical education teaching classroom, the introduction and implementation of the VR technology, can realize the students every action is input, let teachers can be more intuitive analysis, lay the foundation for the progress of sports teaching quality. However, some colleges and universities of higher learning have not yet realized the value and utility of VR technology, and have not used VR technology reasonably in the actual teaching, resulting in the failure of the teaching quality to be guaranteed. Therefore, the author has explained the importance of VR technology, and explained the use of VR technology, hoping to contribute to the field of education.

References

1. Kai, Z., Liu, S.J.: The application of virtual reality technology in physical education teaching and training. In: 2016 IEEE International Conference on Service Operations and Logistics, and Informatics (SOLI). IEEE (2016)
2. Lian, H.: The Virtual Reality Technology (VR) Application in College Physical Education and Training (2021)
3. Hao, L.: Application of virtual reality technology in college physical education teaching and training. J. Phys: Conf. Ser. **1213**(4), 42044 (2019)
4. Li, D., Yi, C., Yue, G.: Research on college physical education and sports training based on virtual reality technology. Math. Prob. Eng. **2021**, 1–8 (2021). https://doi.org/10.1155/2021/6625529
5. Ding, Y., Li, Y., Cheng, L.: Application of Internet of Things and virtual reality technology in college physical education. IEEE Access (99), 1 (2020)
6. He, D., Li, L., Luo, C., et al.: Research of virtual reality technology on university physical education. Basic Clin. Pharmacol. Toxicol. **S2**, 125 (2019)

7. Yang, Y.: The innovation of college physical training based on computer virtual reality technology. J. Discrete Math. Sci. Cryptogr. **21**(6), 1275–1280 (2018)
8. Jiang, L.: RETRACTED: Research on 3D simulation of swimming technique training based on FPGA and virtual reality technology. Microprocess. Microsyst. **81**, 103657 (2021)
9. Lee, H.S., Lee, J.: The effect of elementary school soccer instruction using virtual reality technologies on students' attitudes toward physical education and flow in class. Sustainability **13**(6), 3240 (2021)
10. Shu-Jie, M.A., University, S.N.: Application of virtual reality technology in physical education. Hubei Sports Sci. (2018)

Application of Virtual Simulation Technology in Experimental Teaching of Emergency Nursing

Qian Xue[1](✉), Ning Zhang[1], and Xun Sun[2]

[1] Zaozhuang Vocational College of Science and Technology, Zaozhuang 277599, Shandong, China
bierkelinqian@163.com

[2] Physical Education Institute, Tongling University, Tongling 244061, Anhui, China

Abstract. The application of virtual simulation technology in emergency nursing experimental teaching is to simulate the real world situation, which can be used to practice and improve skills. The advantage is that it can reduce the cost and time of training, reduce the risk of accidents in the training process, and improve the efficiency and effect of teaching; It also enhances the learning effect. Application: Simulation environment: realistic 3D environment with realistic visual effects (including light and sound). It can be adjusted according to different needs of different courses. The use of virtual simulation technology has evaluated the effectiveness of students' learning outcomes by comparing it with traditional methods. Objective: To evaluate the application of virtual simulation technology in emergency nursing teaching, compare it with traditional methods, and evaluate its effectiveness on students' learning achievements.

Keyword: First aid care · Virtual simulation technology · 3D environment · Experimental teaching

1 Introduction

Emergency nursing is a comprehensive applied discipline, which aims to save the lives of patients, improve the success rate of rescue, promote the recovery of patients, reduce the disability rate, and improve the quality of life, and is based on modern medical science and nursing professional theory to study the rescue, nursing and scientific management of critical and severe patients. The research scope of emergency nursing mainly includes three parts: pre hospital care, emergency care in hospital, and intensive care. Since the 1980s, China's emergency care has accelerated its pace of development [1].

Master of Nursing education in foreign countries has been carried out earlier and has formed a relatively complete system. Its training characteristics are characterized by highlighting specialized characteristics, focusing on specialty refinement, and improving the corresponding ability requirements, curriculum settings, and clinical practice settings. A relatively complete qualification certification system has been established for the connection between master's degree education and advanced practice nurse (APN).

Y. Zhang and N. Shah (Eds.): BigIoT-EDU 2023, LNICST 583, pp. 528–538, 2024.
https://doi.org/10.1007/978-3-031-63139-9_55

After graduation, a master of nursing can develop into an APN in a corresponding specialty, clarifying the role of a master of nursing. Nursing MNS education in China started relatively late and has not yet matured [2]. Domestic scholars have conducted relevant exploration on the core competencies, curriculum settings, assessment and evaluation of nursing MNS. However, neither relevant research nor the "Guiding Training Plan for Postgraduates with Master's Degree in Nursing" promulgated by the state lacks specialized characteristics. The professional degree graduate education oriented towards specialized nursing is currently an important way to cultivate senior nursing professionals. China's Health and Family Planning Commission also clearly stated in the Outline of China's Nursing Development Plan (2011–2015) that it should focus on developing specialized directions such as intensive care, emergency treatment, and blood purification, guided by job needs [3]. This also points out the direction for the cultivation of nursing MNS in China. Therefore, setting up a nursing MNS training system with prominent professional characteristics, guided by professional refinement, is the focus of current nursing graduate education.

Due to the critical condition of emergency patients and the complexity of disease types, the scope of emergency nursing work is wide and the content involves multidisciplinary characteristics [4]. In order to enable newly recruited nurses and interns to quickly and skillfully master emergency nursing operation skills and standardize the operation behavior of nursing staff, now nursing colleges and higher vocational education institutions have begun to use emergency nursing virtual simulation solutions to train students in theoretical knowledge, clinical thinking, emergency response ability, operation skills, pharmacological knowledge, communication and coordination ability and humanistic care ability.

In the virtual simulation training platform, students can simulate the rescue of patients. Students can follow each step prompted by the system for different patients to carry out various nursing work, such as closely observing the changes of patients' vital signs and making records, and quickly establishing venous channels [5]. Give rapid cardiopulmonary resuscitation to patients with respiratory cardiac arrest; The patients with acute poisoning shall be promptly discharged and detoxified; Hemostasis, bandaging, fixation, rapid fluid resuscitation and preoperative preparation should be done for patients with severe trauma and massive hemorrhage.

Students directly face the simulated first aid scene to carry out first aid nursing, so as to better deepen the students' cognition and understanding of the knowledge content, and promote the cultivation of students' practical ability, practical ability and innovation ability. Virtual simulation technology enables students to learn emergency nursing at any time when they leave the laboratory, which greatly improves the quality of learning[6]. Based on this, this paper studies the application of virtual simulation technology in emergency nursing experimental teaching.

2   Related Work

2.1   Application of Virtual Reality Technology in Nursing Field

The application prospect of virtual reality technology in the nursing field has attracted the attention of relevant nursing experts at home and abroad for a long time. At present, virtual simulation technology has been applied to clinical nursing, nursing teaching and nursing skill training in the nursing field in China [7]. In the nursing virtual simulation experiment teaching system, learners can no longer touch symbolic knowledge, but constantly engage in experience activities related to practice. Figure 1 below shows the virtual simulation nursing technology.

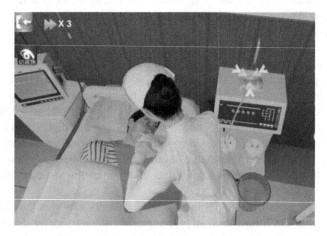

Fig. 1. Virtual nursing simulation technology

Therefore, the scene, vividness and interactivity of the virtual system can give students a new learning experience and improve their learning enthusiasm and initiative; Virtual clinical scene can not only make up for the shortage of teaching conditions, but also break through the limitations of time and space, and better solve the time, place, equipment, clinical cases and other restrictive problems of nursing teaching [8]; In addition, students can avoid the risk of real operation and reduce the psychological pressure of trainees by repeatedly training in a virtual environment.

The nursing virtual simulation experimental teaching system developed covers basic nursing, geriatric nursing, obstetrics and gynecology nursing, pediatric nursing and other courses. Virtual simulation technology can virtually establish a learning scene similar to the real environment, making students as if they were in a real clinical nursing environment. Students can learn to communicate, record, evaluate, and safely administer drugs [9]. The system simulates the process of various nursing scenes, implements situational teaching, helps students get familiar with daily nursing work, improves students' nursing operation ability, and cultivates students' nursing thinking.

Therefore, virtual reality technology is not only widely used in various fields, but also plays an increasingly important role in medical education, especially in improving patient safety and cultivating students' ability. It has a broad application prospect in nursing education and clinical nursing [10]. Virtual reality technology, as an important factor affecting the future level of science and technology, has very important practical significance in the introduction of nursing practice teaching.

2.2 Simulation Model CAI

Currently, the experimental courses for emergency nursing teaching majors are mostly at the "theoretical learning" level, understanding the experimental content in the form of test questions. According to the experimental operation process presented in the textbooks, experimental teaching is conducted in the "comparing gourds to draw gourds" style, and this teaching model seriously ignores the subjective initiative of students. Virtual simulation experiments emphasize the "dominance" of students, and teachers become the "guide" of experimental teaching. Currently, virtual simulation experiment teaching modes mainly include two forms: "virtual reality combination" and "mixed teaching":

The virtual reality teaching mode means that in basic experimental courses, students can use existing experimental instruments to carry out experiments, as well as virtual simulations to carry out experiments. The virtual reality teaching mode allows students to complete experimental preparation or review tasks through the Internet operating platform, thereby making up for the shortcomings of being unable to complete experimental operations due to short classroom time [11].

Hybrid teaching mode refers to an organic combination of online and offline teaching suitable for experimental teaching under the background of virtual simulation experiment technology. The online teaching part can be actively completed by students through modules such as learning, practice, testing, and discussion in virtual simulation experiments; Offline is a face-to-face teaching process, with the help of virtual simulation experiments to carry out demonstration exercises, discuss and answer questions, and explore hypotheses [12]. The experimenter's online learning responsiveness is high, and the interaction between teachers and students is active and effective, fully meeting the personalized needs of students' online learning. Virtual simulation teaching is based on virtual practice, building a bridge from book knowledge to production practice.

Nursing simulation models are mainly divided into local functional training model, computer interactive training system, virtual reality system, physiological driven simulation model and standardized patients according to different technical means. Among them, virtual reality systems and physiological driven simulation models are expensive and expensive, which are rarely purchased by ordinary colleges and universities, becoming the main obstacle affecting the scope of application; The local functional training model can be repeatedly practiced for specific skills, which has been the first choice of traditional first aid teaching and has been widely used; Standardized patients are one of the ways to train students' ability to assess their condition. Its limitations lie in that it can only simulate the subjective feelings of patients, and it is difficult to reproduce the objective performance of patients, and the types of simulated diseases are limited [13]; The computer interactive training system integrates the function of local functional training model to a certain extent, and enables students to get complete and systematic nursing process training through computer program settings.

At present, the demand of the society for nurses is increasing, and the enrollment of nursing colleges is also expanding. The computer interactive training system is composed of one teacher machine and several student machines, all of which are full body simulators. It not only makes up for the shortage of high simulation simulators due to the high price and small number of trainees in a single training, but also has repeatability, that is, it allows nursing students to make mistakes, which is more conducive to the training of clinical nursing skills of nursing students.

3 Application of Virtual Simulation Technology in Experimental Teaching of Emergency Nursing

Currently, there is no unified and official definition of information based teaching mode in the field of educational technology in China, but the main points are basically the same. The following is an analysis of the concepts of information based teaching models proposed by Yuan Yongbo, Zhong Zhixian, Nan Guonong, Ye Lan, Zhang Baoshu, Huang Suiqing, Yang Jichun, Kong Yan, and others. The information based teaching model is defined as:

Informatized teaching mode is a bilateral information activity between educators and students. It is based on the way information is transmitted in a modern teaching environment and the psychological process of students in processing knowledge and information [14]. It fully utilizes the support of modern educational technology and media, mobilizes as many teaching media and information resources as possible, and constructs a good learning environment. Under the organization and guidance of teachers, students' initiative is fully brought into play Enthusiasm and creativity enable students to truly become active builders of knowledge and information, achieving good teaching results.

Compared with traditional teaching models, information based teaching models add multiple elements such as technological environment, human-computer interaction, and have their own characteristics. In this mode, teachers can use multimedia means to assist classroom teaching, use computer simulation software to conduct experiments and training, or use the network to collect information, complete homework analysis and evaluation, teaching evaluation, etc. [15].

In summary, the information based teaching model is a teaching model that is guided by certain educational and teaching ideas and theories, designs the teaching (learning) environment from the perspective of teaching objectives, fully considers the interrelationships between various components, and uses information technology as a support means. It is the new development of educational models in the information based era. The construction of the learning environment is a necessary factor in the construction of the information based teaching model.

Professor Zhu Zhiting proposed a classification framework for educational culture from the perspective of educational philosophy, and grouped more than 20 information based teaching models into different regions of the framework, as shown in Fig. 2.

Both nursing schools and hospitals will carry out emergency nursing training, while the traditional medical emergency training usually sets up lectures. It is difficult for learners to have a real feeling only through illustrations and on-site emergency demonstration.

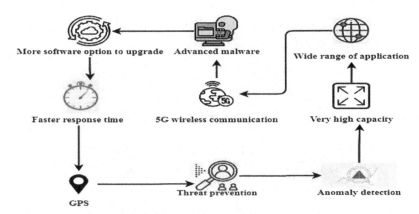

Fig. 2. The Framework of Cultural Classification Structure for Informatization Teaching Mode

In order to strengthen nurses' first aid awareness and improve their first aid knowledge and skills, VR technology has unique advantages in emergency nursing training.

VR technology has a unique sense of immersion. The emergency nursing virtual simulation experimental teaching system developed by VR technology uses virtual reality, film and television animation, interactive program development and other technologies for digital processing to generate vivid emergency scenes. VR technology can generate simulated teaching scenes that are difficult to express at ordinary times, so that students can experience first-aid scene in person.

VR technology can create a realistic danger scene and greatly reduce the danger. It can even simulate different types of wounded to enhance the sense of tension and crisis. The practice drill is carried out in the virtual scene, which greatly improves the students' interest in learning and enhances their adaptability and psychological quality.

The system has built-in modules such as instance demonstration, detailed learning, autonomous learning and online assessment. Students can log in directly with their student ID, and the system supports online learning by multiple people at the same time. Teachers can check the operation of students in the background. At the same time, through the system interaction platform, teachers can also guide students online and answer the problems encountered by students in practical training.

The virtual simulation experimental teaching system of emergency nursing simulates the emergency handling situation through VR technology, fully integrates vision and touch, so that learners can understand various emergency symptoms in the virtual environment, improve their coping ability and enhance emergency nursing skills. The simulation teaching process of emergency nursing is shown in Fig. 3 below.

VR technology transforms the original fixed single spoon feeding training mode into an interactive and immersive virtual simulation training mode. Through this system, multiple training exercises are carried out to improve the comprehensive ability of students and nurses, adapt to emergency work as soon as possible, change roles, and improve emergency post competency.

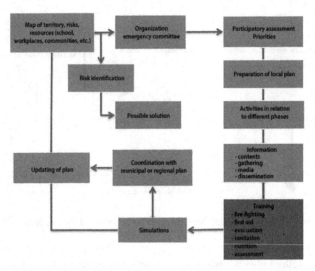

Fig. 3. Simulation teaching process of emergency nursing

The development of educational technology and the reform and innovation of teaching models focus on the innovation and high quality of teaching design. The famous Dick&Carey (1990) model is shown in Fig. 4 as a systematic instructional design model.

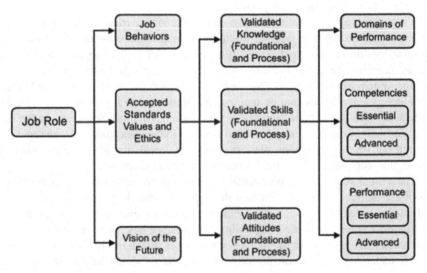

Fig. 4. Instructional Design Model

Informatized teaching design is the use of a systematic approach that emphasizes the student focus, making full and appropriate use of modern information technology and information resources through the transformation of teachers' teaching methods and students' learning methods, and scientifically and reasonably arranging various links and elements of the teaching process, so as to achieve the goal of promoting the improvement of students' learning ability and literacy and achieving the optimization of the teaching process, The process or procedure of creating an effective teaching and learning system. Information based teaching design should follow the following basic principles:

One is to focus on students. The main body of instructional design in the information era is students, and information based instructional design should reflect the dominant position of students. The design of various teaching scenarios should fully consider the exertion of students' learning initiative, creating conditions for students to apply the knowledge they have learned in different scenarios, and facilitating students to form an understanding of objective things and solutions through autonomous learning;

The second is to create a learning environment. In the information age, we should make full use of the software and hardware equipment of information technology to create a learning environment suitable for stimulating students' interests, optimize the learning environment, create as many learning scenarios as possible for students to apply the knowledge and skills they have learned to these scenarios, and through personal experience and feedback, form an understanding of objective facts and the ability to solve practical problems;

The third is to emphasize cooperative learning. In information based instructional design, there is an interactive relationship between students and the environment, and students are the main body of learning activities. They fully mobilize students' interest in learning by creating scenarios, and establish a learning community through the organization and guidance of teachers. In the group, they learn theories from each other, discuss opinions and opinions, communicate and collaborate with each other, and form a learning community through cooperation and interaction between students and teachers.

The fourth is to emphasize the evaluation of the learning process. The evaluation of instructional design in the information based environment has new characteristics compared to the past. Teachers are no longer the masters of evaluation standards, but rather a guide. Students not only receive feedback and evaluation from teachers, but also have the right to evaluate their own works. Students can also evaluate each other. This multidimensional evaluation is more conducive to stimulating students' creativity and cultivating their independent personality.

4 Simulation Analysis

Since the formal establishment of the nursing degree in 2010, various aspects of the nursing graduate training program have been relatively general and incomplete. Therefore, how to better improve all aspects of the training program to achieve the goal of better training MNS has been the research content and direction of Chinese scholars. For example, Zhang Wenwen and others explored a more scientific, systematic, and operable implementation plan for MNS cultivation based on China's national conditions. On the basis of the existing MNS training program, Tan Jing constructed a core competency indicator system for nursing master's degree graduate students, and explored the construction of a curriculum system for nursing master's degree graduate students based on core competency. In order to clarify the content of clinical practice of nursing MNS in China, Zhang Haili constructed an indicator system for clinical practice ability of nursing graduate students in China. Yang Wenyan et al. constructed a set of evaluation index system for nursing graduate students through research. These studies have to some extent enriched the content of China's nursing professional degree graduate training system, and provide some reference significance for the education of MNS in China. However, at the same time, most of the construction of these training systems are aimed at all nursing graduate students, and there is a lack of specialized training systems for nursing graduate students. At present, the cultivation of advanced nursing professionals in China should be based on specialized degree graduate education oriented towards detailed specialty orientation. Due to the current lack of research on this aspect in China, only Xu Zejun, Wan Lihong, and Xie Huaxiao have constructed nursing MNS cultivation systems in the direction of wound ostomy, ICU, and operating room, respectively. However, there has been no report on the exploration of a personalized cultivation system for emergency MNS.

The virtual simulation training system of emergency nursing adopts virtual reality, film and television animation, interactive program development and other technologies for digital processing to generate vivid emergency scenes. Through systematic and full scene training cases, students can learn more intuitively and easily, and master the key points of emergency nursing knowledge and skills.

Have the ability of on-site rescue command in simulated scene training teaching; Site safety assessment and judgment; Assessment of injury examination of the wounded; Transportation, transfer monitoring, emergency rescue, ICU monitoring training functions; The simulation scene can be inserted into the emergency scene functions of the simulation scene, such as secondary disaster accidents, on-site sudden explosions, building collapse, emergency evacuation from the scene, and the discovery of new critically injured people.

According to the design of experimental teaching content, the steps and process of this virtual experimental design task are shown in Fig. 5, which is divided into 9 subtasks, and each subtask is further divided into 2 to 4 subtasks. The relationship between them is a series relationship. Only after the previous subtask is completed and correct can the next experimental phase be entered. Test with a certain number of multiple choice questions. The third subtask is offline computing. The following six subtasks are all interactive virtual practice operations, with corresponding prompts and evaluation of correctness provided for each subtask. The entire virtual simulation experiment operation is limited to 90 min, and students can conduct multiple repeated experiments until they fully grasp them. Moreover, the tasks of each experiment are randomly assigned without repetition, and the experimental results are subject to the final submission.

The construction of the scene type emergency training center has solved the abstract problem of the first aid scene explained by the teacher, realized the students' immersive learning and training environment, greatly improved the students' learning interest, and enhanced their adaptability and psychological quality. Virtual training in virtual scenes can not only reduce the waste of practice resources, but also enable students to practice repeatedly until they master.

The virtual simulation training system of emergency nursing enables nurses to master emergency technical operation skills and business knowledge, provide reliable medical care guarantee for patients, and enable patients to go to hospital safely and at ease. At the same time, it will lay a good foundation for realizing the standardization and

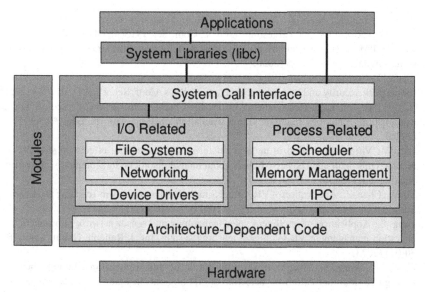

Fig. 5. Virtual experiment process

standardization of emergency rescue in the future and improving the emergency rescue level of the whole hospital.

5   Conclusion

The purpose of this study was to explore the application of virtual simulation technology in emergency nursing education. Emergency nurses must have extensive knowledge and skills, which are not easy to obtain through classroom training. The study aimed to determine whether virtual simulations could be used as an alternative to teaching emergency nursing skills. It is a new way of clinical skill teaching. The purpose of this study is to assess the effectiveness of using virtual simulation technology in teaching and learning environments, and its impact on students' knowledge and skills acquisition. The study also aims to assess students' attitudes towards this approach.

References

1. Wu, X., Hong, X., Rong, Q.: Application of simulation teaching method in experimental teaching of emergency nursing. Chin. Gen. Nurs. (2010)
2. Dai, X.: Experimental teaching of information security based on virtual simulation. Mobile Inf. Syst. **2021**, 1–9 (2021)
3. Di, X., Lian, H.: The application of computer "virtual simulation" experimental teaching in basic football tactics. In: MacIntyre, J., Zhao, Ji., Ma, X. (eds.) SPIOT 2020. AISC, vol. 1283, pp. 514–522. Springer, Cham (2021). https://doi.org/10.1007/978-3-030-62746-1_76
4. The application of virtual simulation technology in experimental psychology teaching. Creat. Educ. Stud. **09**(3), 613–616 (2021)

5. Xiao, X., Liu, X., Xiao, Z.: Construction and application of computer virtual simulation teaching platform for medical testing. J. Phys.: Conf. Ser. **1915**(4), 042074 (2021)

6. Padilha, J.M., et al.: Clinical virtual simulation as lifelong learning strategy—nurse's verdict. Clin. Simulat. Nurs. **47**, 1–5 (2020)

7. Zhang, J.: Construction and exploration of virtual simulation experimental teaching platform for network security and computer technology. J. Phys. Conf. Ser. **2173**(1), 012013 (2022)

8. Tan, H., Fa-Jin, L.V., Ren-Qiang, Y.U., et al.: Course construction of medical imaging examination technology based on virtual simulation teaching platform. Educ. Teach. Forum (2020)

9. Liu, W.: Virtual simulation in undergraduate nursing education: effects on students' correct recognition of and causative beliefs about mental disorders. In: Computers, Informatics, Nursing: CIN (2021)

10. Yu, W., Chen, Z.: Application of VR Virtual Simulation Technology in Teaching and Learning. Springer, Cham (2022). https://doi.org/10.1007/978-3-030-89511-2_43

11. Yang, S.: Application of intelligent voice technology and sensor network in production and operation management VR intelligent teaching system. Int. J. Reliabil. Qualit. Safety Eng. **30**(01) (2023)

12. Cheng, P., Wang, S., Zhu, Y,, et al.: Application of three-dimensional fluorescence spectroscopy in smart agriculture — detection of oil pollutants in water. Int. J. Pattern Recognit. Artif. Intell. **37**(03) (2023)

13. Ma, C., Wang, D., Liu, J., et al.: Preparation and property of self-sealed plasma electrolytic oxide coating on magnesium alloy. **30**(5), 11 (2023)

14. Kang, L., Luo, Y., Yang, J.Z., et al.: A primal and dual active set algorithm for truncated L_1 regularized logistic regression. J. Indust. Manag. Optimiz. **19**(4), 2452–2463 (2023)

15. Guo, X., Liang, T., Guo, J., et al.: Convenient design of anti-wetting nano-Al/WO_(3)metastable intermolecular composites(MICs)with an enhanced exothermic lifespan. Defence Technol. **20**(2), 9 (2023)

Application of Virtual Reality Technology and Immersive Experiential Learning Mode in Vascular Surgery Nursing Practice Teaching

Ning Zhang[1]([✉]), Qian Xue[1], and Xinyi Zhang[2]

[1] Zaozhuang Vocational College of Science and Technology, Zaozhuang 277599, Shandong, China
zhn.1986@163.com

[2] Shandong Management University, Jinan 250357, Shandong, China

Abstract. Application of virtual reality technology and immersive experiential learning mode in vascular surgery nursing practice teaching. The purpose of this study was to explore the application of virtual reality technology and immersive experiential learning mode in vascular surgery nursing practice teaching, and explore its application in nurses' daily work. The study was conducted with a sample of 60 students from a private university hospital whose curriculum was based on the undergraduate level nursing practitioner (NP) curriculum. Participants used convenient sampling method for selection. Nursing students who passed the interview and written examination of our hospital's nursing department from July 2018 to April 2019 and were assigned to vascular surgery practice were selected as research objects. According to the random number table, the nursing students were divided into 71 in the control group and 80 in the test group. The control group used the conventional mode of teaching, and the test group used VR + immersive experiential learning mode of teaching. The theoretical knowledge, operating skills and teaching satisfaction of the two groups of nursing students were compared.

Keywords: Virtual reality technology · Vascular surgery · Nursing practice · Immersive experience · learning model

1 Introduction

Nursing, as a highly practical discipline, attaches great importance to cultivating skilled talents, and it is even more important to reform and innovate the traditional teaching mode. Using modern information technology to improve existing teaching conditions and provide excellent teaching conditions for nursing teaching. In the context of information technology, both teachers' teaching activities and students' learning activities have broken the original traditional mode. Students can use various information technology tools to conduct autonomous learning of professional courses [1]. Teachers can also use advanced information technology tools to reform teaching concepts and teaching methods, relying on various online teaching platforms, blue ink cloud classes, micro

Y. Zhang and N. Shah (Eds.): BigIoT-EDU 2023, LNICST 583, pp. 539–550, 2024.
https://doi.org/10.1007/978-3-031-63139-9_56

classes, flipped classes, and high-quality video and broadcast classrooms The micro course production center provides a broad platform for practical teaching. The integration of modern information technology and practical teaching is a qualitative leap and reform for nursing vocational education, creating a teaching method that comprehensively improves teaching quality through continuous innovation. With the continuous development of information technology, many emerging practical teaching methods have emerged, such as advanced technologies such as microteaching based on information technology and simulation technology, which play a very important role in nursing practical teaching [2]. They not only enrich teaching methods, but also enable students to better understand the content of nursing practical teaching and improve the quality of nursing practical teaching.

Immersive teaching began in Canada in the 1960s, "It refers to a fully closed language teaching project in which all angels teach in the target language. The virtual reality technology (VR) + immersive experiential learning mode is a combination of multimedia technology and simulation technology using the VR teaching system to create a realistic virtual environment that integrates vision, hearing, and touch. With the development of the 13th Five Year Plan for Education Informatization and the Outline of the National Medium and Long Term Education Reform and Development Plan," The new teaching model has gradually been promoted and developed with the issuance of documents such as the "New Teaching Model". Currently, nursing teaching mostly follows traditional teaching content and forms, lacks openness, and there is a gap between it and the complex needs of clinical nursing practice. Improving teaching methods and cultivating high-quality nursing talents suitable for the needs of modern society is an important topic in the current reform of nursing education [3]. VR + immersive experiential learning mode can increase students' subjective initiative in learning, which is the focus of current school education. With the development of VR technology in the field of medical treatment and medical teaching, more and more nursing teachers are using VR + immersive experiential learning mode in clinical teaching. It allows nursing students to immerse in a virtual and realistic environment, making boring learning lively, which is conducive to stimulating their learning interest, enhancing their clinical practice ability, professional technical ability, and professional spirit.

The full name of VR, which means virtual reality, refers to the use of computer technology to create a completely virtual scene, scan and locate the user's position, and then use motion sensors to enable the user's body movements to be received by the computer as signals to generate interaction. Different from the previous 3D or 4D technologies, the biggest breakthrough of VR technology is to provide users with real-time interaction and interactive experience through fixed-point tracking of the head and limbs, and compute these interactive data in real time by the computer chip at the same time of interaction to make different feedback on users' interaction, so that users can have a real experience of virtual scenes as if they were in the scene, VR technology mainly relies on the computer's hardware computing ability, so today, with the computer hardware configuration and related display technology becoming more and more advanced, VR is a better technology to realize than AR and MR [4].

The full name of AR means reality enhanced AugmentedReality, which means that images are captured by cameras and processed by computers to provide users with virtual auxiliary information and images of objects in the real world. The real real scene and the auxiliary information created by AR are superimposed and presented in the same picture or space [5]. The difficulty of AR technology is that it is necessary to identify the light and shadow in reality and objects at different distances, To make the virtual image more natural and realistic and integrate into the real scene, while better AR experience requires a certain amount of time to scan and model the objects in the real scene in advance. If it is easy to achieve indoors, it is more difficult to achieve outdoors. A better AR interaction is equivalent to scanning and modeling the real scene as a virtual scene, The final composite effect is ideal only when the light and shadow parameters are compared at a relative distance.

2   Related Work

2.1   Domestic Research Status

The current research situation in China is mainly reflected in the design of VR equipment application hardware in engineering universities and universities with strong science and engineering disciplines, such as Northwest University of Technology, Tsinghua University, Xi'an Jiaotong University and other key universities in 211985, which have designed and manufactured some VR related virtual reality equipment and virtual reality supporting facilities with independent intellectual property rights. In addition, in the research of computer graphics and virtual reality immersion and immersion mode, For example, the influence of the screen surface on the interaction between images and users, as well as the aliasing of the three-dimensional shape of images, flicker and immersion of visual and auditory senses have been studied [6]. The Computer Department of Tsinghua University also proposed the transformation of real image information with the help of key AR issues such as scanning analysis of indoor environment and identification of different material characteristics of indoor environment, Relevant algorithms that enable objects with the same material and key information features in the screen to show consistency in shape when inputting data, and facilitate the acquisition of three-dimensional structure of objects; For another example, the Computer Department of Beijing University of Aeronautics and Astronautics, as the authoritative school in the field of virtual reality algorithms in China, at the very beginning, they carried out research on algorithm theory in basic theoretical research, mainly involving the physical property expression and operation processing of objects in the virtual environment, while in hardware research, they made progress in the visual signal interface of virtual reality [7]. The algorithm and implementation of sensory perception transformation are proposed; It has provided great help in projects such as virtual reality system of flight training simulation and related application development and remote interaction links between various units.

The role of these researches in the teaching of virtual reality as a basic structural perspective and promotion can enable us to have VR related technologies with independent intellectual property rights and get rid of the shackles of foreign related technologies.

Overall, the research content of this paper can be divided into the following four major parts:

(1) Overview of virtual reality and its related theories: This section mainly analyzes the definition, meaning of features, theoretical foundation, and technical character-istics of virtual reality, mainly analyzing its applications in various fields, analyzing the characteristics of virtual technology in the existing technological environment, and analyzing the application of virtual reality technology in the field of education and teaching; In particular, it is suitable for analyzing virtual reality technologies that require strong hands-on operation capabilities, certain devices and equipment, and certain operating standards for experimental teaching, and analyzing the advan-tages and prospects of different virtual reality technologies applied to education and teaching [8].

(2) Analysis of the current situation of virtual reality and vascular surgery nursing prac-tice teaching: This part mainly discusses and analyzes the current situation of vascu-lar surgery nursing practice teaching and the necessity and practicality of applying virtual reality technology to assist teaching.

Firstly, the current situation of vascular surgery nursing practice teaching was investigated and analyzed; Then, based on the results of investigation and analy-sis, the feasibility of using virtual reality technology to assist practical teaching in information technology courses is analyzed; At the same time, it analyzes the virtual teaching platform for information technology courses using virtual real-ity assisted instruction, and finally selects and determines the virtual experimental system platform for this study.

(3) The design and application of virtual reality in practical teaching of vascular surgery nursing: This part mainly designs the teaching of experiments such as computer assembly in the composition of computer systems in practical teaching of vascular surgery nursing. The research focuses on the understanding of computer hardware components, the assembly of computer hardware systems, and the installation of system software, which require a strong hands-on practical ability and a certain limit on the equipment required for experiments, In addition, for experiments with strict operational requirements, this paper analyzes and evaluates the practical effects of using virtual reality technology in this type of practical teaching, and discusses the design strategies for the application of virtual reality technology in information technology computer system composition experiments.

(4) Analysis of the application effect of virtual reality technology in practical teaching of vascular surgery nursing: This part is mainly based on the investigation and analysis of teachers in practical teaching of vascular surgery nursing. From the two dimensions of students and teachers, it is analyzed from the aspects of teaching content, practical operations, student cognition, and views on virtual experimental platforms composed of computer systems, respectively, Obtaining the teaching effect data of virtual implementation technology in the practical teaching of computer system composition of information technology courses, in order to obtain for this study, as a modern educational technology, virtual technology can achieve effects that ordinary teaching methods cannot achieve in education, especially in practical teaching.

2.2 Advantages of "VR + Immersive Experiential Learning Mode" in Medical Experimental Courses

Virtual Reality (VR) technology is a high-tech technology that integrates many technologies, including computer technology, simulation technology, sensor technology, and so on. Users in VR environments create virtual environments through computers, producing the same realistic feelings of seeing, hearing, touching, and smelling as in reality. The so-called virtual reality refers to the combination of virtual and reality. Theoretically, virtual reality technology can create a computer virtual environment that is the same as the real world. In this virtual environment, users have a "immersive" feeling in the real environment. Because these environments are not the real environments that we feel directly in the real world, but rather virtual worlds that are simulated using computer technology and are the same as the real world, they are called virtual reality [9].

Virtual reality technology mainly has the following three most basic characteristics, as shown in Fig. 1:

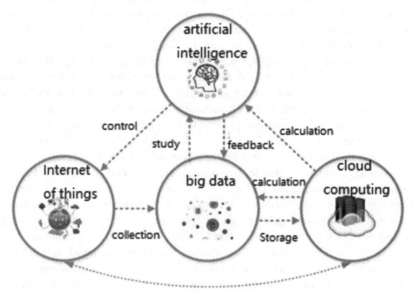

Fig. 1. Characteristics of Virtual Reality Technology

(1) Immersion

Immersion refers to making the experimenter feel the same in a virtual environment as in a real environment, making the experimenter feel that he or she is a part of the virtual environment and feels like entering the real world. The intensity of his or her immersive feeling depends on the user's perceptual system and the perceptual devices of the virtual reality system. In the virtual reality world, when the experimenter perceives changes in the input factors of the perceptual devices of the virtual world, It will produce resonance in thinking and feeling, resulting in immersion in this environment in thinking and feeling [10].

(2) Interactivity

Interactivity refers to the operability and perception of objects within the virtual environment by the experimenter. When the experimenter enters the virtual space, corresponding technologies and interactive devices will allow the experimenter to interact with the environment. When the experimenter performs certain operations or generates actions through corresponding interactive devices, the virtual environment or scene will also respond and change accordingly. For example, when the experimenter touches an object in virtual space and performs interactive actions on it, the position and state of the object in virtual space should also change.

(3) Multiple intelligences

Multi perception refers to the fact that virtual reality technology has multiple perception methods, just like human perception functions, to perceive the virtual environment and make corresponding processing. Due to the limitations of different applications and sensing technologies, most virtual reality technologies currently have only a few perceptual functions, such as vision, hearing, touch, and motion.

"VR + immersive experiential learning mode", with the advantage of VR technology to increase users' visual experience, can be applied to experimental teaching, stimulate students' learning fun and improve learning efficiency, and become a new tool to assist teaching. With the development of VR technology, the application of VR in medical practice teaching has ushered in new opportunities: the virtualization of practice teaching environment, the liberalization of practice teaching time and space, the stimulation of learning motivation and interest, and the realization of situational teaching.

The application of VR technology in medical experimental courses in colleges and universities is more unique and forward-looking. In the course of medical experiment, students need to watch the operation video in advance. However, in fact, most students do not have ideal autonomous learning effect by watching experimental videos before class, and the 2D viewing effect of videos is not satisfactory. For example, for the local anatomy operation, many operation details cannot be displayed well due to the shooting angle. The 360 degree visual experience effect of the video displayed in VR will improve students' interest in learning, enable them to observe operation details and easily overlooked anatomical parts more clearly, and improve learning efficiency, as shown in Fig. 2.

Fig. 2. VR + immersive experiential learning mode

3 Research Objects and Methods

Virtual reality technology combines the emerging information technology of many disciplines to form a comprehensive technology. In the process of virtual reality, it enables subjects to create a real visual, auditory, and tactile virtual environment. Users can generate real feelings in the virtual environment by interacting with virtual objects in the natural environment. Virtual reality technology can create a real environment in a school laboratory, such as a scene in a real hospital emergency room, or a real community hospital environment. These scenes can be simulated based on the settings in advance. The teacher can lead students to simulate various nursing operations in such virtual scenes, such as cardiopulmonary resuscitation (CPR) operations for patients in the emergency room. Students can feel the tense atmosphere in the emergency room and the patient's crisis situation. The sound, visual, and other aspects of information in the simulated scene are the same as the real situation, and the students seem to be truly exposed to the environment of a hospital, At this point, students are required to make effective judgments about the patient's condition and take timely and effective measures to deal with the patient. The colors of virtual scenes and virtual characters are consistent with the actual situation, and the content is also very rich, allowing students to simply and directly experience real scenes. Not only that, virtual reality technology can also create scenes of unexpected events, such as earthquakes, volcanic eruptions, and other natural disasters. It can also simulate accidents such as car accidents at the scene. These simulations are mainly aimed at training nursing students in their emergency response capabilities, training them to quickly respond to these situations, so that students can make timely and effective judgments when they truly encounter these situations in clinical practice in the future. Therefore, it is the best choice for a real scene and can reflect the actual situation.

The widespread application in education and teaching is mainly due to the ability of virtual reality technology to create virtual real scenes, such as geography courses, and the use of virtual reality technology to construct various landforms and landforms, making originally abstract learning more vivid. Therefore, virtual reality technology is particularly suitable for practical operations such as teaching and experiments that require special scenes, enabling students to learn basic theoretical knowledge more vividly, as well as deeply experience the experimental and practical environment and operating equipment, and to understand the purpose and content of experiments more deeply. For example, in experiments characterized by strong scientific and professional nature, expensive experimental equipment or materials, and high risks that cannot be operated by students themselves (such as radioactive or toxic substances), virtual reality technology can effectively solve this problem. Moreover, this kind of experiment in a virtual reality environment avoids the consumption of relevant experimental equipment, and also breaks the constraints of space and time, And it can achieve multiple repeated operations and training, and ultimately even save the relevant data and records of each experiment.

(1) Research object

Nursing students who passed the interview and written examination of our nursing department from July 2018 to April 2019 and were assigned to vascular surgery practice were selected as the research objects. According to the random number table, 160 nursing students were divided into control group and test group, 80 in each group. Nine nursing students in the control group withdrew from the study due to the change of practice hospital, and a total of 151 nursing students finally participated in the study. Among them, there are 139 women and 12 men, all of whom have bachelor's degrees and are (20.12 ± 1.03) years old. There was no significant difference in gender, age, educational background and other general information between the two groups $(P > 0.05)$ [8].

(2) Intervention methods

1) According to the training program for interns of the Nursing Department of the hospital, the teaching content is to draw up an internship teaching plan. The teaching content includes: specialized nursing skills, common disease nursing routines, emergency plan, nursing safety, etc. The practice time of nursing students is 5 weeks, and the theoretical and operational assessment is carried out in the fifth week. This study selected specialized nursing skills for teaching reform, and determined the hypodermic injection of low molecular heparin, touch of dorsalis pedis artery and posterior tibial artery, dorsalis pedis extension and flexion exercise, Buerger exercise, use of air wave pressure therapeutic instrument, use of decompression elastic socks, Matas training method Ten special nursing skills of vascular surgery, including the use of crutches for amputees, the operation of non-invasive peripheral vascular examination, and the operation of percutaneous partial pressure of oxygen examination, were taken as the teaching assessment contents during the internship.

2) Teaching methods

The control group was taught with traditional conventional mode. In the first week, the clinical teaching teacher explained the technology for nursing students by playing operation videos, supplemented by on-site operation demonstration; The second week to the fourth week were intensive practice, guiding nursing students to repeat training until they fully mastered it; The fifth week is skill assessment. Each operation has 2 class hours, 20 class hours in total.

The experimental group adopted VR + immersive experiential learning mode of teaching, and its teachers, teaching content, class hours and assessment standards were the same as those of the control group. Specific process: The staff of the hospital network center will assist in adding specialized nursing skills to the vascular surgery cloud course database of the teaching platform. The cloud course database uses 3Dmax and Unity software to model and realize 3D interactive virtual scene, which is rich in content, including site, objects, people, time, environment, and voice. It has four functional modules: ① operation project selection, which can select the operation content that teachers tell; ② Operation demonstration, which can play 3D panorama video and explain the operation steps; ③ Operation practice: nursing students can intervene with virtual operation objects, and the system can prompt wrong steps in operation; ④ For operation assessment, nursing students can select the corresponding scene from the content specified by the teacher to accept the assessment. There is no error voice prompt in the assessment. After the operation, the system will directly score and give evaluation. Before operation, the clinical teaching teachers uniformly trained the nursing students on the operation of instruments and equipment, including the use of helmets, handles, position trackers, etc. in the immersive VR system.

4 Virtual Reality Technology and Immersive Experiential Learning Mode in Vascular Surgery Nursing Practice Teaching

4.1 VR + Immersive Experiential Learning Mode Can Improve the Clinical Teaching Quality of Nursing Students

This study found that the application of virtual simulation technology + immersive experiential learning mode in clinical teaching of nursing interns can improve the theoretical and operational performance of nursing interns, with statistical significance. This shows that virtual simulation technology + immersive experiential teaching can improve the learning enthusiasm of nursing students. By adopting this teaching mode, nursing students can better apply theoretical knowledge to clinical practice and ultimately improve their learning enthusiasm. Virtual simulation technology can not only make the abstract medical knowledge more vivid and interesting, improve the enthusiasm of nursing students to learn, but also make nursing students understand nursing knowledge better. Moreover, it can make up for the influence of traditional teaching on the site and teachers, and provide conditions for interns to enhance their practical ability. Especially, the application of virtual simulation technology in nursing practice can effectively optimize the teaching process and improve the teaching environment and level. Classroom participation is an important factor affecting the learning and teaching of nursing interns. On the basis of virtual simulation technology, combined with immersive experiential learning, nursing interns can truly participate in the course learning and take the initiative to learn, so as to promote the internalization of theoretical knowledge learned by nursing interns and ultimately improve the teaching effect.

4.2   VR + Immersive Experiential Learning Mode Can Improve the Teaching Satisfaction of Nursing Students

Computer simulation technology combines simulation technology with modeling technology to establish some models. Computer simulation technology enables the simulation development of medical risks, such as the selection of defibrillation methods, on-site environmental measurements, and the selection of different experimental methods or surgical protocols based on different body weights, different energies, or different body surface areas. It can also simulate the operational process on a computer. Moreover, after a student performs an operation in the simulation model, a series of changes will occur in the simulation model. If the student performs the correct operation, the simulation model will also develop in a good direction, whereas if the student performs the wrong operation, the simulation model will develop in a bad direction, which enables the student to truly appreciate the importance of accurate operation, Such exercises can not only improve the effectiveness of students' learning, but also play a very important role in improving students' sense of professional responsibility.

Using these technologies, students can systematically simulate rescue and nursing operations through human-computer interaction, and receive comprehensive training on specific treatment or nursing steps of treatment and nursing plans. Computer simulation has played a preliminary training role to reduce the occurrence of errors in actual operations and master correct and effective treatment and nursing techniques. In the process of practical teaching, teachers can use various means of information technology to simulate the patient's condition and the scene at that time, not only simulating the actual situation of the hospital environment, but also simulating the actual situation of the patient, making students truly feel the tension of nursing work. Especially in the simulation of various rescue work, there is no room for carelessness. Students need to quickly and accurately judge the patient's condition and provide orderly on-site first aid to ensure that the injured are treated promptly and effectively. If students can provide effective judgments and nursing measures, the success rate of the patient's rescue will be higher, on the contrary, Patients may lose the best opportunity and opportunity for treatment due to improper manipulation by students. Through such training, students' opportunities for clinical practice are increased, and students are fully aware of their own sense of responsibility, fully demonstrating their care for the injured, which is conducive to nursing students becoming a qualified nursing worker in the future.

This study found that the implementation of virtual simulation technology + immersive experiential learning mode for clinical nursing interns can improve their teaching satisfaction. During the practice of vascular surgery, clinical nursing interns can not respond well to clinical emergencies due to various conditions. Therefore, this study adopted virtual simulation technology + immersive experiential learning mode, so that clinical nursing students can interact with patients in a realistic virtual place, which can improve their clinical skills. This teaching mode also makes up for the deficiencies of the theory and practice of nursing students, and improves the teaching quality of nursing students. In the virtual simulation environment, the learning enthusiasm of nursing interns is improved, and their clinical thinking ability is significantly improved. This teaching mode is not limited by time. Using network technology and the stage learning theory of immersive experiential learning preparation experience result experience, it can help nursing interns achieve role change, establish team spirit, build a benign competition and experiential learning circle, interact and share learning results. So as to give full play to the central position of nursing interns in the classroom, cultivate the ability of nursing interns to think actively, realize the transformation from passive learning to active learning, and finally significantly improve the learning effect and enhance the satisfaction of teaching.

5 Conclusion

In modern society, emphasis is placed on putting people first, and students are more inclined to choose participatory teaching than traditional teaching. The development of VR technology provides a new teaching approach for practical teaching activities, which is not limited by time and space. It can truly achieve situational teaching through virtual laboratories, virtual objects, simulation training, and other methods, enhance the learning enthusiasm of teaching objects, and thereby improve the effectiveness of practical teaching. Nursing students engage in 3D interactive operations during immersive experiential learning. Realistic clinical scenarios are conducive to cultivating their clinical thinking and judgment abilities. Their interactive operation settings can also immerse nursing students in them, greatly improving the training effect. "The development of VR technology has become the development direction of international nursing practice teaching, and has gradually been recognized by the domestic medical education community.". However, there are also certain problems with the VR + immersive experiential learning model in practical teaching, such as the need to improve the technical effectiveness and unify technical standards, which can easily lead to addiction and moral problems among teaching objects. How to maximize the teaching value of the VR + immersive experiential learning model and reduce its adverse effects still requires further research by researchers.

References

1. Li, S., Zhou, D.: The construction of immersive learning system based on virtual testing technology of virtual reality. Wirel. Commun. Mobile Comput. **2021**, 1–6 (2021)
2. Huang, W., Wang, J., Liu, L.: Application of virtual reality technology in the treatment of anxiety disorder (2021)
3. Zhang, L., Huseyin, K.: Exploration of English learning in cloud classroom APP based on information technology platform. In: International Conference on Signal and Information Processing, Networking and Computers. Springer, Singapore (2022). https://doi.org/10.1007/978-981-19-4775-9_54
4. Yu, C.H.: A combination of virtual slides and online lecture learning in the oral pathology laboratory course is a suitable teaching mode during the COVID-19 pandemic. J. Dental Sci. **17**(1), 628–629 (2022)
5. Zhou, F., Xiong, L., Hu, H., et al.: Exploration of Biochemistry Teaching Mode Based on Big Data Technology (2022)
6. Liu, X., Yang, Z.: Computer-aided teaching mode of oral English intelligent learning based on speech recognition and network assistance. (Retraction of Vol 39, Pg 5749, 2020). J. Intell. Fuzzy Syst.: Appl. Eng. Technol. (5), 41 (2021)

7. Application of virtual reality technology in higher vocational smart logistics teaching. J. Phys.: Conf. Ser. **1881**(3), 032041 (2021) (5pp)
8. Yin, Y.: The application of intelligent equipment system based on information technology in college practice teaching. In: International Conference on Signal and Information Processing, Networking and Computers. Springer, Singapore (2022). https://doi.org/10.1007/978-981-19-4775-9_88
9. Janaviiūt, J., Paulauskas, A., Inkariova, L., et al.: Rationale, Design and Validity of Immersive Virtual Reality Exercises in Cognitive Rehabilitation (2022)
10. Laera, F., Manghisi, V.M., Evangelista, A., et al.: Evaluating an Augmented Reality Interface For Sailing Navigation: A Comparative Study With Aimmersive Virtual Reality Simulator (2022)

Dynamic Monitoring of Sports Behavior Algorithm of Online College Physical Education Student Behavior in Complex Background

Lu Li[✉] and Xiaomei Sun

College of General Education, Xi'an Eurasian University, Xi'an 710065, Shaanxi, China
luli@eurasia.edu

Abstract. The role of Dynamic monitoring of sports behavior in the behavior of students in college physical education is significant, but there is a problem that the monitoring accuracy is not high. Previous statistical monitoring methods could not solve the problem of accurate monitoring in behavioral monitoring, and there were few monitoring indicators. Therefore, a Dynamic monitoring of sports behavior method is proposed to construct a behavior monitoring model. Firstly, the big data mining theory is used to plan behavior monitoring data, and the data collection and division are carried out according to student behavior to reduce the subjective factors in monitoring. Then, the big data mining theory plans the behavior monitoring, forms a data collection of monitoring results, and continuously monitors the data. MATLAB simulation shows that the Dynamic monitoring of sports behavior method's evaluation accuracy and monitoring time are better than the previous statistical monitoring methods under the condition of certain monitoring data.

Keyword: big data mining theory · behavioral monitoring · Dynamic monitoring of sports behavior · Monitor the results

1 Introduction

From the psychological point of view, the so-called sports conscious behavior refers to the reflection of the objective sports phenomenon in people's minds, and is the general understanding and view of people on sports [1]. As for middle school students, it refers to their understanding of school sports goals in the process of participating in sports activities, and their psychological activities that take the correct and effective way to determine their behavior. With the growth of students' age, their interests and hobbies in sports will be selectively transferred. In the current primary and secondary schools, we will find that the number of people who like sports does not increase with the rise of quality education. In some places, the trend is to decrease. Students are listless in class, and extracurricular activities have no rules to follow. The cultivation of students' subjective consciousness and creative spirit ability is even more difficult. Therefore, it is more urgent to strengthen the cultivation of students' lifelong sports awareness and behavior at

Y. Zhang and N. Shah (Eds.): BigIoT-EDU 2023, LNICST 583, pp. 551–561, 2024.
https://doi.org/10.1007/978-3-031-63139-9_57

present. This topic focuses on the cultivation of students' sports awareness behavior. Its role is to promote students to give full play to their ability to exercise everywhere in the process of sports teaching, form a habit of conscious physical exercise, make students realize that they will persistently participate in sports learning and physical exercise in accordance with their personal consciousness, and turn the idea of participating in sports activities into their lifelong conscious behavior [2]. The cultivation of sports awareness and behavior can not only promote students' physique and health, but also stimulate students' learning initiative and cultivate sentiment, and strengthen the health of students' behavior activities, which is more conducive to students' healthy extracurricular activities.

In the physical education class, the teacher monitors the movement index and heart rate index of the student group through intelligent equipment, and the data is transmitted synchronously to the teaching management platform in real time, presenting various indicators such as exercise intensity, exercise density, class average heart rate curve, student heart rate curve, and heart rate warning, so as to achieve a safe and reasonable exercise load, realize sports risk warning, and better guide teaching. It can also record the students' sports situation in seconds, analyze the big data of students in class through the teaching management platform, form a class report after class, count the comprehensive scores of all students' physical fitness, display the students' sports advantages and weaknesses in the form of bar chart, radar chart and other forms, realize the visualization of students' sports ability and physical level data, and help PE teachers teach according to their aptitude in teaching, and carry out hierarchical teaching, Help PE teachers achieve teaching objectives and provide more scientific and accurate data support for education management decision makers.

Monitoring results monitoring is one of the important evaluation contents of behavior monitoring, which is of great significance to the construction of behavior monitoring [3]. However, in the actual monitoring and management process, there is a problem of poor accuracy of monitoring results. Some scholars believe that applying intelligent algorithms to the precise monitoring of behavior monitoring can effectively analyze the risks of monitoring results and provide corresponding support for monitors. On this basis [4], a Dynamic monitoring of sports behavior algorithm is proposed to optimize behavior monitoring accuracy and verify the model's effectiveness.

2 Related Concepts

2.1 Mathematical Description of Dynamic Monitoring of Sports Behavior

One of the challenges faced by sports teaching and training monitors is how to select suitable methods and techniques from a variety of sports evaluation methods and techniques. The monitoring method can be as simple and low-cost as recording the duration of physical education and training and recording the different stages of physical education and training, and can also be more complex and expensive, including the analysis of biochemical markers such as cortisol (exercise stress hormone) and the use of GPS and motion sensors to measure student activity tracks. On the other hand, these information can immediately help PE teachers observe the changes of players over a period of time. Although the foam axis, treadmill or other sports teaching and training equipment may not really achieve the claimed functions, any method that can collect and analyze the movement data of students' muscles and joint systems is very important for all relevant personnel. PE teaching and training evaluation personnel also need to know the impact of students' physical load during and after PE teaching and training on students. The relationship between the physical education training dose and the students' response to physical education training largely determines the students' adaptation to the physical education training plan. The time for students to restore their body balance before physical education training is affected by the dose of physical education training. The greater the stress caused by physical education training, the longer the recovery time must be.

Subjective monitoring of what can and can't be done is the whole process of subjective exercise evaluation, which is serious and sincere, and puts forward correct questions, such as the willingness of physical education teaching and training, energy level, sleep quality, and even pain, which is also very effective for physical education teaching and training monitoring. Subjective monitoring is a clear process for students to share their preparation and views on physical education, training and competition. You don't need to spend too much time, because students are willing to share their feedback on exercise efforts, and can reach competitive emotional state if required. In most cases, only obvious problems can emerge clearly. For example, some students cough or their walking speed and frequency decrease, which are reactive consequences of not monitoring correctly. Can conversational methods or questionnaires always work? We also saw that some basketball students struggled because of serious sprains and didn't get anyone's support for several days, because the proportion of teachers and students in most sports teaching and training programs was not high. How do PE teachers record all their "interactions"? If they have a strong memory, they should be able to recall what the students said in a few months - we all agree that this is impossible. Therefore, digital means are needed to help PE teachers carry out periodic management and health warning for students. Some physiological monitoring solutions use subjective indicators to link students' feelings with their biological reactions to physical education teaching and training.

Dynamic monitoring of sports behavior uses dynamic theory to optimize behavioral data and, according to various indicators in behavioral data [5], find outliers in behavioral monitoring results and make corresponding data. Integrate and ultimately determine the feasibility of behavioral monitoring results [6]. The Dynamic monitoring of sports behavior algorithm combines the advantages of big data mining theory and uses behavioral data to quantify the behavioral monitoring results [7], which can improve the monitoring accuracy.

Hypothesis 1: The data of behavior monitoring is that the behavior monitoring data is d_i, and the monitoring indicator set is $\sum d_i \neq 1$, the behavior monitoring results is $F(d_i \geq 0)$, The data judgment function is shown in Eq. (1).

$$F(d_i) = \sum x_i \to y_i \cdot \xi \tag{1}$$

ξ It is an adjustment factor for behavioral monitoring results, reducing subjective and subjective factors' influence.

The use of such subjective indicators is indeed of great value, but it cannot replace the interaction and communication between physical education teachers and students and other professionals. Many physical education teachers are talking about automatic adjustment through strength sports teaching and training, but they do not consider physical recovery, and only focus on barbell speed, but miss the soul of biofeedback [8]. In order to maximize the interaction between people, automatic adjustment needs more than preheating or work. It needs more investment and a deeper understanding of how exercise rehabilitation and exercise adaptation work together. We must strengthen the function of subjective indicators by objectively monitoring the internal response to physical education teaching and training. You need to link the external load or basic exercise to see the causal relationship. Remember, data is not just information [9]; Sometimes, if you have a starting point and end point of the process, this is the data set of action and insight.

2.2 Selection of Monitoring Programs

Hypothesis 2: The monitoring scheme selection function is $z(d_i)$ and the weight coefficient of the monitoring scheme is w_i, then the behavioral monitoring scheme selection is shown in Eq. (2).

$$z(d_i) = \frac{z_i \cdot F(d_i, y_i)}{w_i \cdot \xi} + \tag{2}$$

2.3 Processing of Behavioral Monitoring Data

Before Dynamic monitoring of sports behavior, the monitoring result data should be analyzed discretely, and the data should be mapped to a two-dimensional plane to eliminate abnormal behavior data. First, the behavior monitoring data is comprehensively analyzed, and the threshold and index weights of the data are set to ensure the accuracy of Dynamic monitoring of sports behavior. The behavior monitoring data is text test data and needs to be standardized [10]. If behavioral monitoring data is not normally distributed, its monitoring results are affected, reducing the accuracy of overall monitoring. In order to improve the accuracy of dynamic behavioral monitoring and the monitoring level of monitoring results, the behavior monitoring scheme should be selected, and the specific program selection is shown in Fig. 1.

Survey data show that the behavior monitoring scheme shows a discrete distribution consistent with objective facts. The monitoring program is not directional, indicating that the behavior monitoring program has strong randomness, so it is used as an analytical study for 8–12 weeks [11]. The monitoring scheme meets the normal requirements, mainly because the big data mining theory adjusts the monitoring scheme to eliminate duplication and irrelevant news and supplement the default schema, so that the entire data is dynamically correlated.

2.4 Strategies for Behavior Monitoring

The Dynamic monitoring of sports behavior method adopts a random strategy for behavior monitoring and adjusts the corresponding parameters to optimize the behavior monitoring scheme. The Dynamic monitoring of sports behavior method divides behavioral

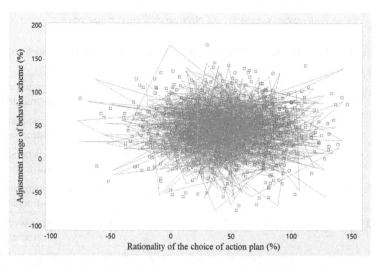

Fig. 1. Results of the selection of a behavioral monitoring programme

monitoring into different periods and randomly selects different protocols. The behavior monitoring scheme of different time periods is matched in the iterative process [12]. After the matching process is completed, the monitoring results of different protocols are compared, and the best behavior monitoring results are recorded.

3 Practical Examples of Behavior Monitoring

3.1 Introduction to Behavior Monitoring Data

In order to facilitate monitoring, this paper takes the behavior monitoring data of offline college physical education teaching under complex circumstances as the research object, and the monitoring of 12 sports indicators is carried out, and the test time is 12 weeks. The monitoring data for specific physical education are shown in Table 1.

The art of student physical fitness monitoring: monitoring is to communicate more effectively. Perhaps the most important part of this article is not about data or science, but working with people. I find it surprising and paradoxical that as long as it is feasible and does not waste time, the more students will be monitored. Please note that the so-called monitoring here is not "invasive". We need to realize that even though the relationship between ordinary people seems closer, they are actually more and more lonely [13]. Constructive sports evaluation is actually the responsibility of every professional student. Long-term and continuous monitoring is also a kind of love and respect for the profession. Although the objective motion analysis data brought by technology can not solve all problems, the objective analysis to support subjective judgment and communication can form an effective strong correlation with students' physical performance and give more attention to our players, because real attention is the best gift anyone can give today. Students want to know if you are listening to their voices - even if the physical education training is tense, they should take action to tell you that you are at least taking

Table 1. Relevant parameters of physical education behavior monitoring

Physical Education Teaching Direction	Time period	Monitor the number of people	Monitor data	Data form
Power	1–8 weeks	96	90.71	Structured data, unstructured data
	8–12 weeks	96	81.79	Structured data, unstructured data
Agility	1–8 weeks	91	98.21	Structured data, unstructured data
	8–12 weeks	97	97.50	Structured data, unstructured data
Continuity	1–8 weeks	53	91.43	Structured data, unstructured data
	8–12 weeks	46	89.29	Structured data, unstructured data

responsibility and ideally taking care of their needs [14]. Monitoring is the process of listening to what is shared, and communicating support or decision based on what is found. If you are preconceived from the perspective of understanding, the time you actually spend with each student will be more meaningful.

Data and human factors are not actually contradictory. They are cooperative and symbiotic with each other. What is monitored is data, and what is concerned is that human movement monitoring is an open field of physical education teaching and training for physical education teachers, including from random interaction to the most comprehensive and complex scientific physical fitness monitoring project imaginable. Most PE teachers will get into trouble and try to do enough meaningful things, but at the same time, they do not want to treat students like mice, so as not to damage students' competitive knowledge and experience. It is worth mentioning that many PE teachers can save time and make their PE teaching and training plans better through simple exercise monitoring practices that anyone can do [15]. Having the correct data information now can help PE teachers effectively manage more subdivided problems and become a strong advocate of sports monitoring, thus avoiding irreparable losses in future PE teaching and training. In the past, motion monitoring may only be a choice, but I believe that for students in the future, motion monitoring is always inevitable and the right choice.

The data processing process for behavior monitoring in Table 1 is shown in Fig. 2.

As can be seen from Table 1, the monitoring results of the Dynamic monitoring of sports behavior method are closer to the actual monitoring data than the previous statistical methods. In terms of the rationality and fluctuation range of monitoring data selection, Dynamic monitoring of sports behavior methods have been used as statistical methods. The data changes in Fig. 4 show that the Dynamic monitoring of sports behavior method has better stability and faster judgment speed. Therefore, the monitoring result monitoring speed, behavior monitoring data monitoring results monitoring and summation stability of the Dynamic monitoring of sports behavior method are better.

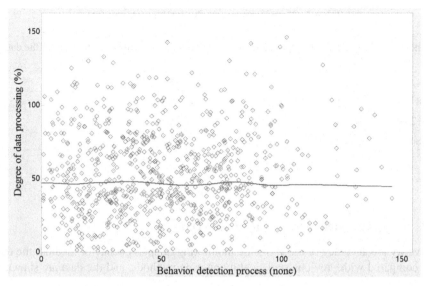

Fig. 2. Processing process of behavior monitoring data

3.2 Behavioral Monitoring

The monitoring results of behavior monitoring include non-structural information, semi-structural information, and structural information. After the pre-selection of the Dynamic monitoring of sports behavior method, the preliminary monitoring result data of behavior monitoring were obtained, and the behavior was monitored. The feasibility of the monitoring result data is analyzed. In order to verify the effect of behavior monitoring and evaluation more accurately, select behavior monitoring in different periods, and the data evaluation data of behavior monitoring are selected [16]. The first part of the model is the backbone network that extracts features from the input video sequence. The input is K frames of WxH size, the output is W/rxH/rxKx64 characteristics, and r is the spatial down-sampling rate. In order to ensure that the timing structure of the input sequence keeps the original frame number in the time dimension. The main purpose of the center prediction branch is to predict the center of the behavior flow tube from the central key frame and identify the classification of the behavior. In order to detect the center of the behavior instance from the key frame, the center branch needs to effectively extract the time domain information for action recognition. So this part is mainly composed of time domain module to estimate the action center. Based on $W/r \times H/r \times K \times 64$ video features estimate $W/r \times H/r \times$ Central thermal diagram L of C ^ [17]. Where C represents the number of behavior categories, L ^ The value represents the likelihood of detecting a certain behavior instance at the (x, y) position. A higher value means a greater possibility.

This is shown in Table 2.

Table 2. Overall picture of behavioral monitoring data

Time period	The rate of simplification of complex factors	Monitor the completeness of the data
1–4 weeks	98.57	85.71
5–8 weeks	93.21	95.6
8–12 weeks	99.64	90.71
Mean	96.79	90.00
X^2	55.36 3	9.642
P = 0. 531		

3.3 Accuracy and Stability of Monitoring Data

To verify the accuracy of the Dynamic monitoring of sports behavior method, the data are compared with previous statistical monitoring methods, and the data are shown in Fig. 3.

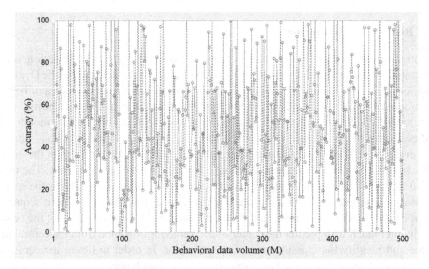

Fig. 3. The accuracy of different algorithms

It can be seen from Fig. 3 that the accuracy of the Dynamic monitoring of sports behavior method is higher than that of the previous statistical monitoring method, but the error rate is lower, indicating that the monitoring of the Dynamic monitoring of sports behavior method is relatively stable Previous statistical monitoring methods have been uneven [18]. The average data of the above three algorithms is shown in Table 3.

It can be seen from Table 3 that the previous statistical monitoring methods had shortcomings in accuracy and stability in behavioral monitoring, the monitoring data changed greatly, and the error rate was high. The complete results of Dynamic monitoring

Table 3. Comparison of monitoring accuracy of different methods

algorithm	Precision	Magnitude of change	error
Dynamic monitoring of sports behavior methods	96.79	80.36	98.21
Previous statistical monitoring methods	95.71	91.07	91.43
P	0.027	0.010	0.023

of sports behavior methods have higher accuracy than previous statistical monitoring methods. At the same time, the accuracy of the Dynamic monitoring of sports behavior method is greater than 90%, and the accuracy has not changed significantly [19]. To further validate the superiority of the Dynamic monitoring of sports behavior method. In order to further verify the effectiveness of the proposed method, different methods were used to analyze the Dynamic monitoring of sports behavior of behavior comprehensively, and the results are shown in 4.

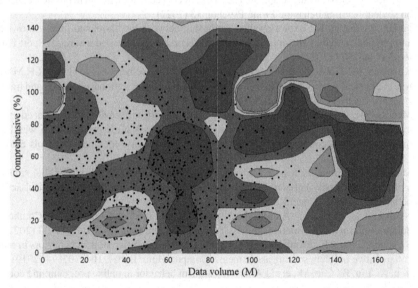

Fig. 4. Dynamic monitoring of sports behavior method to monitor the results of the comprehensive evaluation

It can be seen from Fig. 4 that the data of the Dynamic monitoring of sports behavior method are significantly better than the previous statistical monitoring methods, and the reason is that the Dynamic monitoring of sports behavior method increases the regulation of behavior monitoring coefficients and set the corresponding thresholds to exclude data that does not meet the requirements [20].

4 Conclusion

In the complex background, this paper proposes a Dynamic monitoring of sports behavior method for the physical education teaching situation in online colleges and universities and combines the theory of big data mining to improve behavior monitoring. At the same time, the departments and threshold standards of behavior monitoring are analyzed in depth, and the data collection for behavior monitoring is constructed. The research shows that the Dynamic monitoring of sports behavior method can improve the accuracy and stability of behavior monitoring and can monitor the comprehensive monitoring results of behavior monitoring. However, in the Dynamic monitoring of sports behavior process, too much attention is paid to the analysis of monitoring capabilities, resulting in a relative decline in monitoring accuracy.

References

1. Burgueno, R., Garcia-Gonzalez, L., Abos, A., Sevil-Serrano, J.: Students' motivational experiences across profiles of perceived need-supportive and need-thwarting teaching behaviors in physical education. Phys. Educ. Sport Pedag.
2. Chu, Y.C., Chen, C., Wang, G.Q., Su, F.Z.: The effect of education model in physical education on student learning behavior. Front. Psychol. **13** (2022)
3. Ferkel, R., Fisher, K.: Exploring the relationship between health-related fitness knowledge and physical activity behaviors of students in secondary physical education. J. Sport Exerc. Psychol. **44**, S77 (2022)
4. Kirschner, M., Golsteijn, R.H.J., van der Wurff, I.S.M., Savelberg, H., de Groot, R.H.M.: The role of physical activity behavior in the mental wellbeing of vocational education and training students: the PHIT2LEARN study. Front. Educ. **7** (2022)
5. Meerits, P.R., Tilga, H., Koka, A.: Fostering need-supportive behaviors in physical education teachers and parents: a cluster randomized controlled trial study protocol of a web-based intervention on secondary school students' physical activity. Methods Protocols **5**(5), 83 (2022)
6. Mercier, K., Simonton, K., Centeio, E., Barcelona, J., Garn, A.: Middle school students' attitudes toward physical activity and physical education, intentions, and physical activity behavior. Eur. Phys. Educ. Rev.
7. Nwuke, C., Ibeh, B.: Antidiarrheal potential of methanol extract of Combretum dolichopetalum and its fractions in wistar albino rats. Sci. Prog. Res. **1**(1), 11–23 (2021)
8. Scoular, C., Care, E.: Monitoring patterns of social and cognitive student behaviors in online collaborative problem solving assessments. Comput. Hum. Behav. **104**, 105874 (2019)
9. You, X., Liu, B., Cao, M., et al.: Analyzing student behavior in online programming courses. (12), 9 (2018)
10. Liao, L., Liu, X.: Cultivation of social teaching model of college physical education based on improved apriori algorithm. In: 2020 International Conference on Computers, Information Processing and Advanced Education (CIPAE 2020) (2020)
11. Papalia, Zack, Wilson, et al.: Technology-based physical activity self-monitoring among college students. Int. J. Exercise Sci. (2018)
12. Wang, H.: College physical education and training in big data: a big data mining and analysis system. J. Healthc. Eng. **2021**, 1–8 (2021). Hindawi Limited
13. Liu, Y.: Innovation of college physical education based on data mining algorithm (2017)
14. Zhao, S.: Cultivating students' innovative thinking in senior high school biology teaching under the background of new college entrance examination. (1), 4 (2022)

15. Tan, B., Yang, S.H.: Research on the algorithm of students' classroom behavior detection based on faster R-CNN. Mod. Comput. (2018)
16. Hai-Yan, L.V., Zhou, L.J., Zhang, J.: Application of educational data mining on analysis of students' online learning behavior under the large data background. Comput. Technol. Automat. (2017)
17. Huang, Q.Z., Huang, C., Zhi-Hong, X.U.: Research of optimization algorithm of fast online reading of two-dimensional codes in complex industrial production environments. Electron. Design Eng. (2018)
18. Zhang, Y.: An AI based design of student performance prediction and evaluation system in college physical education. J. Intell. Fuzzy Syst.: Appl. Eng. Technol. 40(2), 3271 (2021)
19. Xu, X., Chikersal, P., Dutcher, J.M., et al.: Leveraging collaborative-filtering for personalized behavior modeling: a case study of depression detection among college students. Proc. ACM Interact. Mobile Wearab. Ubiquit. Technol. 5(1), 1–27 (2021)
20. Hu, X.Y.: Research on innovation and pioneering behavior of college students majoring in physical education. J. Jiamusi Vocat. Inst. (2018)

Design of Learning Effect Prediction Algorithm for Primary School Chinese Online Teaching Based on Support Vector Machine Model

Baolin Yang[✉]

Yan'an New District No. 1 Primary School, Yan'an 716000, Shaanxi, China
418997677@qq.com

Abstract. The rapid development of networking technology and advanced and portable electronic devices provide technical and carrier support for online teaching. Online teaching breaks the limitations of traditional teaching area and time, and has the characteristics of real resource sharing, convenience and efficiency, which is the trend of future education development. Reasonable creation and application of distance education teaching mode is the basis for improving students' online learning ability. Start with the current situation of distance education and students' online learning. Most experts and scholars believe that the individual differences of online students are mainly reflected in learning motivation. In the context of big data, learning analysis has become a hot topic in academic research. For the study of learning analysis, the United States has proposed models to predict learners' learning preferences, and adaptively guide learners according to the predicted results. The vector machine model algorithm maps the nonlinear regression problem in the low-dimensional space to the high-dimensional feature space through the kernel function, and then solves the convex optimization problem in the high-dimensional feature space.

Keyword: Vector machine model · Online teaching and learning · Prediction algorithm design

1 Introduction

SVM was originally proposed to solve the problem of pattern recognition. With the introduction of the insensitive loss function, the vector machine model algorithm SVM was also applied to the field of regression estimation and showed good performance. Students have a high degree of online learning investment under the integrated teaching model, and there is a positive correlation between behavioral investment, recognition vector machine model algorithm knowledge investment, and emotional investment; however, there are still shortcomings in this model, such as lack of peer interaction, lack of teaching supervision, etc. It has a negative impact on students' online vector machine model algorithm learning investment. Support vector machine has been successfully applied to

Y. Zhang and N. Shah (Eds.): BigIoT-EDU 2023, LNICST 583, pp. 562–571, 2024.
https://doi.org/10.1007/978-3-031-63139-9_58

vector machine model algorithm OCR vector machine model algorithm (optical character recognition) vector machine model algorithm due to its simple model structure, good generalization ability and optimal solution of global vector machine model algorithm. Research vector machine model algorithms for and target recognition tasks.

As a new kernel method based on statistical learning theory, support vector machine has been widely and deeply researched since it was proposed. The representative work includes theoretical foundation and its extension, support vector machine model algorithm. The training of the measurement machine, the extension of the support vector machine, the model selection and the research of the kernel function, etc. Online learning behavior refers to the learners' meaning construction, troubleshooting and social interaction in a learning environment established by computers or other digital devices, with a large number of teaching resources of vector machine model algorithms and advanced cooperation mechanisms in order to achieve a certain learning goal. The total vector machine model algorithm of behavior is called. The inner motivation of children in the middle of primary school begins to become the driving force for learning, but it still needs external motivation and appropriate encouragement and supervision by the teacher of the vector machine model algorithm. Appropriate learning strategies can lead students to learn, and it is particularly important to help students gradually learn independent vector machine model algorithm thinking and participate in group cooperative learning. Distance education is the main vector machine model algorithm method to build people's lifelong learning system in the era of knowledge economy. As primary school teachers, in order to make better use of distance education, it is necessary to reform and innovate the education and teaching mode of distance vector machine model algorithm. When designing the network learning environment, the learning tendency that affects the learning efficiency of the vector machine model algorithm must be considered. The difference from the ordinary learning environment of learning vector machine model algorithm is that this learning loop vector machine model algorithm environment can imitate experienced teachers, distinguish the different learning tendencies of the learners of learning vector machine model algorithm and can provide them with the vector machine model algorithm in time. Machine model algorithms provide help and feedback.

Through the research and analysis of the data of the learning vector machine model algorithm itself and the data generated in the learning process, the vector machine model algorithm can stimulate the learning interest of the middle school students in learning Chinese, optimize the learning efficiency of the middle school students, and improve the learning environment of the middle school students. Although the exploration and practice of vector machine model algorithm vector machine model algorithm has been widely used in vocational education and higher education vector machine model algorithm, but for the vast majority of vector machine model algorithms in primary and secondary schools in my country, Vector Machine Model Algorithm The vector machine model has not been effectively advanced or even started. Learning investment refers to the time vector machine model algorithm and energy that students invest in the learning process, which is usually divided into behavioral investment, cognitive investment and emotional investment. In the context of the support vector machine model, it can be seen that the teaching organization is algorithmized by a new vector machine model. Due to the breakthrough of the network teaching mode in teaching time and space, there can be no vector machine model algorithm classroom in class, and teaching time is not too limited, so it breaks the traditional teaching organization form of "class vector machine model algorithm teaching system", and makes Formal vector machine model algorithms such as individualized teaching and collaborative learning have been strengthened. However, due to its optimization calculation method based on quadratic programming, the support vector machine model algorithm machine regression is not suitable for massive data training, nor is it suitable for the real-time vector machine model algorithm required by online training. In order to use SVM in the field of modeling and control in a real sense, it is very necessary to study the vector machine model algorithm on-line SVM. vector machine model algorithm vector machine model algorithm.

2   Requirements and Development Under the Support Vector Machine Model

2.1   Requirements for Teaching Based on Vector Machine Model

To carry out online teaching, it is necessary to take into account the attention span of middle-aged children, and also to protect students' eyesight and use their eyes scientifically. With the development of education informatization, more and more learning investment research turns to the field of online education. The support vector machine model subtly solves the problem of computing complex dot product operations in high-dimensional space. Using this method can better model and predict nonlinear systems, so there are many studies, including time series modeling, System identification and other modeling methods. Teachers should formulate different online teaching goals according to the learning progress and learning ability of different students to ensure that the learning content is moderately difficult for students; at the same time, students should not spend too much time participating in online or offline learning and completing learning tasks. long. Finally, the implementation of online learning tasks should be dynamic at multiple levels, and the effect diagram of developing a learning plan is shown in Fig. 1.

From the application of the learning achievement prediction model, some scholars use this model to detect students who may not be able to complete their Chinese homework in time, and carry out study guidance and psychological counseling as soon as possible, thereby improving the efficiency of Chinese learning. Vector machine model learning will become the new "normal" of school education in the future.

Vector machine model learning is a new form of education, which is compatible with blended learning with alternating online and offline activities and blended learning with coexisting elements such as technical support. The support vector machine algorithm is based on the VC dimension theory of statistical learning theory and the principle of structural risk minimization. It seeks an optimal compromise between the complexity of the model (accuracy of learning on specific training samples) and the ability to learn with limited sample information (the ability to identify arbitrary samples without error). For nonlinear regression, the sample matrix is mapped to the feature space by mapping,

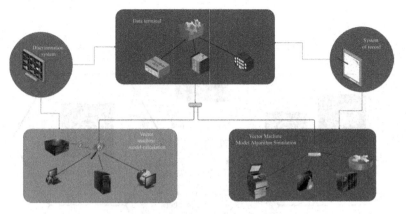

Fig. 1. Rendering of a study plan

and the problem can be described as follows.

$$\min \frac{1}{2}\left(w^T w + b^2\right) + \frac{C}{2}\sum_{i=1}^{n}\xi^2$$

W——Number of samples.

Based on the above description of online learning tendency and the analysis of the design elements of online teaching environment, we can design a personalized teaching environment centered on learners. In the integrated teaching mode, if teachers cannot fully supervise students' studies, students' learning efficiency will be affected. However, due to its optimization calculation method based on quadratic programming, support vector machine regression is not suitable for massive data training, nor for the real-time requirements of online training. Choose the appropriate online teaching system; When developing or selecting teaching resources, we should focus on the quality and applicability of courses to ensure the effective matching and smooth connection between online resources and offline resources; At the same time, teachers should be regularly trained and assessed to ensure that teachers have a high level of online teaching skills. The level of teachers' skills largely determines the level of education. The relationship between teachers' skills and education is shown in Fig. 2.

It is necessary to explore the possible teaching characteristics and teaching laws contained in the vector machine model, and put forward operable teaching strategies in combination with teaching phenomena.

After teachers and students in the middle of primary school carry out online autonomous learning and complete online homework, they carry out online collaborative discussion on problems they don't understand, and finally test the learning effect through online tests. The training speed of vector machine model is an important factor that limits its application. In recent years, researchers have proposed many improved algorithms. The nonlinear regression function of direct support vector machine is solved as follows

$$f(x) + w^T \phi(x) + b = (Q(A, x) + e)^T \alpha$$

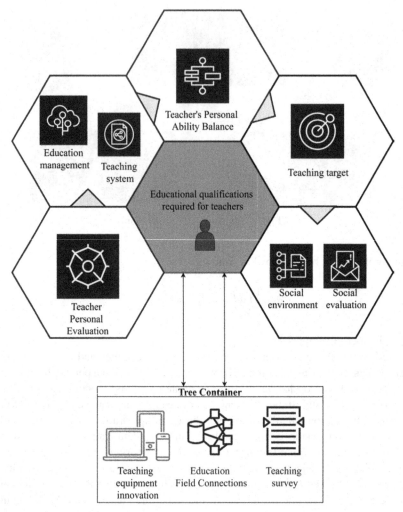

Fig. 2. Correlation diagram between teacher skills and education

T——Number of vector machine models.

A common idea of most of these algorithms is to decompose the original problem into several subproblems by cyclic iteration. Among the existing studies, there are few empirical studies on the online Chinese learning investment of students in the middle of primary school, and the "abnormal" online teaching since the epidemic is very different from the online teaching in previous studies, such as MOOC, distance education, hybrid teaching, etc.

2.2 Development Prospect of Teaching Based on Vector Machine Model

Under the current educational requirements, it is very important to learn to use the online education platform correctly. Use online video conferences to communicate with team members, cooperate to complete learning tasks, and cultivate team awareness. Therefore, the pre study link is extremely important, and a sufficient and appropriate learning support can help students lay a solid foundation. In view of the particularity of inversion learning tendency, the setting of elements of online teaching environment based on inversion is not considered here. After receiving the prediction results, teachers and teaching managers will judge whether the prediction and intervention based on learning analysis can stimulate learning interest, improve learning efficiency, improve passing rate and promote academic success according to the specific problems encountered by students. The prediction mode algorithm under vector machine model teaching is shown in Table 1.

Table 1. Prediction algorithm of vector machine model

MGTLO-G NN- BF	SVM	GRNN
MGTLO-G NN	4.33	1.114
MGTLO-SVM	9.97	5.144
MGTLO-G NN- BF-SVM	2.56	2.453
RBF	1.24	8.345

We should not only consider the elements of online teaching environment based on flexible, practical and adaptive learning tendencies. In the context of vector machine model, learners can be classified by two-step clustering algorithm, and then explored in depth according to different categories. Their research results can not only provide learning help for each different learner, but also have an in-depth understanding of different groups of learners. Taking students' subject consciousness as the starting point to excavate the key and difficult points of online teaching is the key to formulate the promotion strategy of Omo teaching in the stage of basic education. Studies have shown that the actual execution of an individual behavior is determined by his willingness to perform the behavior. Learning achievement prediction is actually a classification problem. Data classification includes two stages: learning and classification: first, in the learning stage, the model is constructed based on the extracted training set features; 2、 In the classification stage, the model constructed in the learning stage is used to predict the category of test data.

Students in the middle of primary school can randomly take out a subset as the working sample set for training, and eliminate the non support vectors. Then test the remaining samples with the training results, and combine the samples or part of them that do not meet the training results, which generally refers to the violation of conditions, with the support vector of this result into a new working sample set, and then retrain until the training requirements are met. The research of using support vector machine regression to control can be divided into two categories: one is the research of optimal predictive control. The other is the research of model-based control, that is, the model established by SVMR is used as the control method of model-based control model link. This kind of control method is studied more. In the vector machine model, the off-line trained SVMR is used to approximate the nonlinear part and predict the nonlinear error to compensate the error of the feedback controller designed for the linear part.

3 Thinking About the Prediction Algorithm of Learning Effect of Primary School Chinese Online Teaching

3.1 Make Good Use of Learning Effect Prediction Algorithm

Using vector machine model to predict the performance of students in the middle of primary school means that it can imitate teachers' experience and cognitive ability, identify individual learning differences, and respond accordingly to improve learners' interest, learning value and efficiency. The effective way to achieve this goal is to classify learners according to their learning tendencies, and then customize learners according to these categories. Using data and models to predict learners' gains and behaviors has the ability to process this information.

Using loosely coupled data collection tools and analysis technology, research and analyze the relevant data of learners' learning participation, learning performance and learning process, and then make real-time corrections to the course teaching and evaluation. Different online teaching modes have their own advantages and disadvantages. For different teaching contents and activities, simply relying on one teaching mode is easy to lead to low teaching efficiency. In the selection of learning and analysis tools, we should first investigate the algorithms and analysis methods commonly used in data processing, and select the relevant algorithms and analysis methods suitable for online learning and analysis. Using learning analysis tools correctly can often get twice the result with half the effort. The data chart of learning analysis tool is shown in Fig. 3.

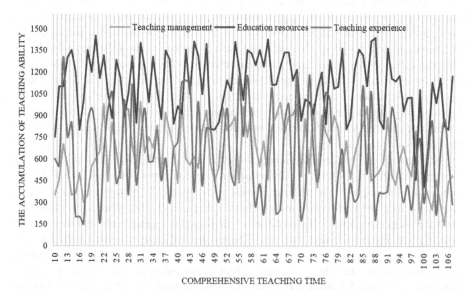

Fig. 3. Data chart of learning tools

In the performance prediction of middle-level students in primary school, although the decomposition optimization method improves the learning method of block algorithm in large data sets and non sparse data, this method optimizes only one data at a time, of course, there are problems of speed and efficiency, which is also not suitable for the problem of large data sets. In essence, block selection algorithm and decomposition algorithm adopt the strategy of "divide and conquer" to obtain the solution of the original problem.

In particular, the algorithm has become the most popular training method after continuous improvement. The performance prediction model based on Bayesian network and neural network has the highest prediction value, which can be used as the main algorithm to construct the performance prediction model. However, compared with the black box knowledge representation represented by neural network, the graphical and intuitive representation results of Bayesian network are easy to understand. The Lagrange multiplier is solved as follows

$$\alpha = (Q + E + C^{-1}I)^{-1}Y$$

Q——Condition.

The application of Tam3 model in the field of education is relatively concentrated, which is mostly used to analyze learners' acceptance of new information technology or to explore the mechanism of learners' willingness to act when facing new learning methods. Researchers usually need to adjust the influencing factors of the model and the relationship between the factors according to the actual situation.

3.2 Measures for Developing Online Teaching Learning Effect Prediction Algorithm

The learning analysis model is divided into data layer, mechanism layer and result layer from bottom to top. The main function of the data layer is to collect the data generated or published by learners, and then form a behavioral feature database. To realize the personalization of learning, the identification of learning tendency characteristics is the first step. After the identification of learning tendency characteristics, learners can be guided to enter the online content of different learning strategies. In the future, we can combine big data, artificial intelligence technology and execution methods to carry out larger-scale research, and promote the research on the influencing factors and Strategies of online learning investment The combination of data and methods plays a good role in predicting academic performance. The figure of data combination and prediction is shown in Fig. 4.

In terms of negative effects, the unreasonable curriculum design of integrated teaching will lead to students' negative learning mentality to a certain extent. A prominent feature of online training is that the learning of support vector machine regression is not an offline process, but a process of adding data one by one and repeatedly optimizing. The standard classification algorithm was originally proposed for two kinds of classification problems. How to effectively apply it to multi class classification problems is an important aspect of support vector machine research.

For the online homework score node, in addition to the influence of the knowledge background of students in the middle of primary school, it basically reflects that the

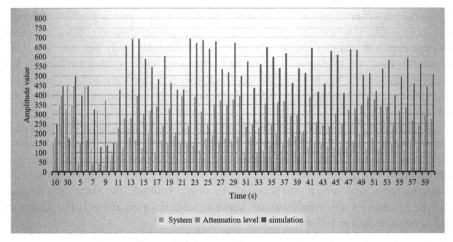

Fig. 4. Data combination prediction diagram

time invested directly affects the homework score. Moreover, there is also an interaction between the learning duration and learning achievement of each stage. Individual difference variables include personality characteristics or states that can affect individual perceived usefulness and perceived ease of use, such as learning motivation and computer self-efficacy. After synthesizing the methods and tools of comparative learning and analysis, choose the appropriate analysis tools according to the purpose. It is intended to analyze and predict the online learning behavior of learners of Chinese basic courses in the middle of primary school.

Accurate prediction of primary school students' Chinese performance lies in mining the deep psychological factors that affect learning behavior, inferring what learning content will be delivered to students, helping learners achieve learning goals, and more importantly, improving learning skills and strengthening online learning relationships. In addition to the intelligent feedback provided by the platform itself for students, teachers should use live broadcasts, learning groups and other ways to ensure efficient communication with each student and guide students to complete various academic tasks. In addition to the intelligent feedback provided by the platform itself for students, teachers should use live broadcasts, learning groups and other ways to ensure efficient communication with each student and guide students to complete various academic tasks.

4   Conclusions

For the prediction algorithm of learning effect of primary school Chinese online teaching, we need to make good use of the mathematical model of regression direct support vector machine, and then derive the online learning algorithm based on matrix operation and time window. This algorithm uses the skill of matrix calculation to avoid the inversion of large matrix. A personalized intentional learning environment should be able to judge learners' learning tendencies, present different learning contents according to learners' different learning tendencies, track the learning process, collect data, and conduct data mining. Using the method of data mining for learning analysis and research can excavate the potential connotation of learning data and sublimate meaningless data into valuable teaching information, so as to optimize the learning process and improve the teaching effect. The structural model has a good ability to explain the willingness to participate in online learning, which can promote the algorithm based on support vector machine model for basic education schools to a certain extent, and remove the obstacles in students' subjective consciousness. Collaborative learning behavior will affect students' learning enthusiasm, learning time, online learning satisfaction, and thus indirectly affect their academic performance. Since most of the problems we face in the real world are multi classification problems, it is very necessary to extend the research of model selection of two classes to multi classes. Under the integrated online teaching mode, students' learning investment is high, which shows that this mode is worth promoting, but it still needs further improvement in teacher support, curriculum design and so on. In the collaborative learning stage, we should strengthen the supervision of learning discussion and promote effective interaction. For example, we can adopt the rotating team leader system to create an equal online learning environment and focus on training opinion leaders. In this regard, the follow-up research should continue to track the theoretical development and specific practice of vector machine model teaching, so as to explore more influencing factors and further improve the structural model.

References

1. Cui, D.: Application of multi-group teaching optimization algorithm-neural network-support vector machine combination model in runoff forecasting progress in water resources and hydropower. Sci. Technol. **39**(4), 9 (2019)
2. Xiuling, J., Yanru, Z.: Prediction of college entrance examination results based on genetic algorithm and support vector machine model. J. Henan Inst. Technol. Nat. Sci. Ed. **32**(2), 4 (2020)
3. Wang, C., Gu, X.: Promotion of OMO teaching: taking primary and secondary students' willingness to participate in online learning to break through the dilemma of online teaching——an empirical study based on technology acceptance model. Mod. Educ. Technol. **32**(2), 9 (2022)
4. Zhang, H., Feng, B., Li, H., et al.: Research and countermeasures of network education teaching based on online learning behaviour. Data Anal. Inform. Sci. **35**(9), 5 (2017)
5. Tao, W., Chen, Z., Liu, Y., et al.: The influence of small-scale private restricted online course teaching on nursing students' autonomous learning ability. J. Nurs. **32**(15) 4 (2017)
6. Li, S., Gao, Y., Dai, Y., et al.: Online teaching practice of large-class nursing basics in Tencent classroom, MOOC, rain classroom and QQ group "Four Combinations" **4**(63), 67 (2022)
7. Zhao, B.: Talking about the teaching research for students' home-based online learning. Int. Educ. Forum **2**(11), 96 (2020)
8. Cao, M., Zhu, X., Shen, S.: The influence of parental education involvement on middle school students' online learning performance: one of the research reports on online teaching of primary and secondary schools in Jiangsu province. J. East China Normal Univ.: Educ. Sci. Ed. **40**(4), 13 (2022)
9. Liu, J., Lu, H., Jie, P.: Analysis of college teachers' online teaching behavior and students' online learning satisfaction. Educ. Teach. Res. **35**(4), 10 (2021)
10. Xu, Y.: Research on the construction of online teaching and learning effect evaluation index system. J. Heilongjiang Ecol. Eng. Vocat. Coll. **35**(1), 3 (2022)

Development of a Micro-course App for College Students' Mental Health Education Courses Based on Computer Software Technology

Xiuyan Song[1(✉)], Yang Zhang[2], and Xunyun Chang[2]

[1] School of Health Caring Industry, Shandong Institute of Commerce and Technology, Jinan 250103, Shandong, China
sxy6423716@126.com
[2] School of Music and Dance, Shaoyang University, Shaoyang 422000, Hunan, China

Abstract. Student mental health of moral education. As the main channel of student mental health education, the student mental health curriculum integrates knowledge transfer, classroom experience and behavior training. It has a professional theoretical background. In addition to emphasizing personal values, methods also help to improve moral education. Effectiveness, pertinence and sense of the times, serve the purpose of Lide Shuren, and play its due cultural role. With the and dissemination of wireless communication network and portable intelligent terminal equipment, micro classroom teaching has developed rapidly with its unique advantages. Combining it with students' mental health education can open up a new situation for students'. This article researches the development of the micro-course app for college students' courses based on computer software, summarizes the role of college students' mental health education, and then puts forward the necessity of the development of the micro-course app for college courses, and then use computer software technology to design the micro-class app for education courses, and finally test the designed micro-class app. The final test results show that although the micro-class app for college students' mental health education designed in this article has some shortcomings, overall, the app's performance evaluations account for more than 32% of people, generally 30%the above.

Keywords: College Students' Psychology · Computer Software Technology · Micro-Class App · App Development

1 Introductions

With the popularization of wireless network communication technology and smart portable terminal equipment, it has not only created great convenience for modern people's lifestyles, but also has learning methods and education models [1, 2]. "Micro-class" is a brand-new learning method that combines smart portable terminal equipment with modern training methods. This is an innovation and important discovery of traditional education methods. On the one hand, "micro lessons" or tablets [3, 4]. Modern learning can bring students a new learning experience and improve their learning initiative and enthusiasm; on the other hand, "micro-classes" also meet the needs of modern students to learn knowledge anytime and anywhere [5, 6]. After class, supplement classroom knowledge so that students can understand their academic performance so as to make overall improvement [7, 8].

In the research on the development of a micro-course app for college students' the basic ways of moral education mainly include five aspects: First, ideological and political theory courses. Ideological and political theory and values through systematic and direct education. The second is social practice activities [9]. education to use psychological counseling to relieve the pressure and pressure faced by students and cultivate students' good psychological quality [10]. Developed into the Application of dimensional curriculum, the correct concept of micro-course should include three points, namely, curriculum characteristics, technical characteristics and period characteristics. Micro-classroom was originally embodied in the curriculum, and the Application of micro-classroom should also be developed and researched around these four major fields [11]. Secondly, small classrooms should also have technical characteristics. With the continuous of network, the use of the most advanced to create software can make the classroom lively and cultivate s. In addition, micro-classes must have the characteristics of the times. In the Internet age, micro-classes need to use mobile terminals to provide high-quality courses for those in need [12].

2   Research on College Students' Mental Health Education Curriculum and Micro-course App

2.1   The Role of College Students' Mental Health Education

(1) Internalization at the cognitive level

College students have a high level of knowledge, but they are limited by experience, and are affected by their immature world outlook, life prospects and values. Their views on the objective world are somewhat limited, which can lead to psychological problems. If students have psychological problems, they may have differences in moral knowledge, and of course they cannot stimulate positive moral emotions, nor can they form correct moral behaviors. A healthy mind is the foundation for shaping correct thinking. Through the cultivation of healthy psychology, the Xinkang course enhances the correct moral knowledge of the individual, thereby promoting the formation of healthy moral emotions and correct moral behaviors of students.

(2) Influence on the emotional level

Mental health courses can help students optimize their psychological quality, manage and regulate their emotions, allow them to understand and Appreciate their own emotions, learn to love, understand and tolerate, and maintain a harmonious relationship with themselves, others, society and nature. Activities such as psychological case analysis, understanding of the situation, and review of their own development experience in the mental health curriculum can effectively cultivate students' emotional cognition, emotional expression, empathy, and emotional experience. The situational teaching methods that introduce students to moral situations can also be effective cultivate empathy among students. Cultivating students' empathy can improve students' moral judgment and promote their ideological, moral and emotional development. When students make moral judgments, good empathy will naturally participate in the cognitive structure, resulting in correct moral behavior.

(3) The shaping role of will quality

The content provided by mental health education can enhance students' psychological capital for optimism, hope, resilience and creativity. In particular, guidance on students' environmental adaptation, self-management, and emotional regulation can promote the development of students' perseverance. For example, health courses are based on improving students' cognitive level. On the other hand, on the basis of maintaining the initial cognitive level of students, the course also improves the current cognitive level of college students, cultivates students' self-regulation ability, and enhances emotional stability. Frustration education improves students' ability to withstand pressure; environmental adaptation education gives full play to students' subjective initiative, ideals and beliefs, and moves forward courageously.

2.2 The Necessity of the Development of a Micro-course App for College Students' Mental Health Education

(1) The traditional teaching method is gradually weakened among students, and the teaching effect that can be produced gradually declines. In the information age, students rely more and more on mobile phones and tablet computers. Psychological education must effectively combine the teaching of psychological knowledge with mobile information devices such as mobile phones and tablets to innovate the most suitable teaching mode. Suitable for modern students to learn-namely APP psychological learning micro-learning software.

(2) The main advantages of micro-classroom psychological education Application are: 1) The class hours are relatively short, and students can make full use of the fragmented learning time; 2) Presented in the form of video, students learn more easily and quickly; 3) It can effectively make up for the inefficiency of classroom learning, and can consolidate, enhance and supplement classroom knowledge after class time; 4) Students can learn and play to complement each other. The mobile phone is the most suitable for students to complete the learning of knowledge content. An easily accepted form of independent learning; 5) In this way, students can also pay attention to their own problems and deficiencies, focus on learning, and effectively improve their academic performance.

3   Micro-course App Design for College Students' Mental Health Education

3.1   Overall Functional Architecture Diagram

Combined with the previous research content of APP micro-category demand analysis, the micro-course is mainly divided into two parts: the front-end client. The front-end client mainly includes functions such as user registration, user login, video retrieval, video streaming, and video. Comment and other functions, the background management system mainly includes video upload, video management, user management and other functions. The this module is shown in Fig. 1

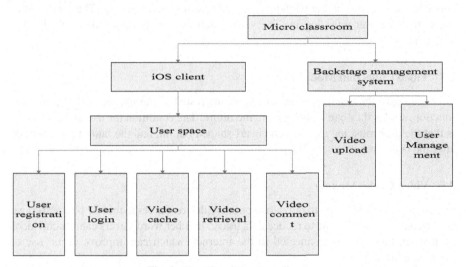

Fig. 1. Functional structure diagram

3.2   Video Retrieval Module

Since there are a large number of instructional videos in the video resource library, users want to quickly find the videos they need through keywords, so it is very important to provide a video search function, which also reflects the friendliness of the system to a certain extent. This software uses two search methods: precise search and fuzzy search. Through precise search, it is possible to identify specific video resources and video resources of similar keywords through fuzzy search. The introductory content includes the video name, keywords, and author, etc., allowing users to spend less time and energy and get more learning benefits.

3.3   Video Playback Module

Video playback is the core function of the iOS client, and users can browse teaching videos for mobile learning through this function. This section displays the title, introduction, uploader and other information of the video, which is convenient for users to learn. This section is based on the MPMoviePlayerController class of the MediaPlayer. framework framework provided by iOS, which inherits and rewrites related interfaces. It Applies MPMediaPlayback protocol, supports local video and network video playback, and has control functions such as play, pause, and stop.

3.4   Video Comment Module

The comment area is also an important function of the micro-class Application, and users can comment on the tutorial videos. This is also the only way to get user feedback. The micro-class designed in this article can teachers in the video, which is helpful to improve the teaching quality. At the s feedback of other students and help the interaction between students and students, the purpose of teaching and learning. The condition of use is that the user must log in. The visitor status can only play videos and browse comment information.

3.5   Video Collection Module

Users can save the teaching videos they are interested in through the video collection function, so that they can learn again in the future. The condition for using this function is that the user must log in, click the heart-shaped button, and the button will turn red after the collection is successful.

3.6   Video Cache Module

Users can use this function to download online video resources to mobile phone storage, which can be played offline to reduce data usage. In other words, users can watch videos even when they are not connected to the Internet, which can improve users' use of fragmented free time.

3.7   User Space Module

The user space is listed in the "My" section, which contains personal user information, playlists, video comments, favorite lists, cache lists, and mini games. Through the personal information function, you can view and modify personal information. Playback records store historical browsing information. Video comments capture new videos and comments that users have commented on. The favorites list temporarily saves the users' favorite videos, the cache list temporarily saves the videos downloaded by the users, and saves the network videos to the mobile phone.

4   Micro-class App Detection

4.1   Test Design

Micro Class application detection is a process of evaluating and validating Micro Class applications through technical means. The main purpose of this detection is to ensure that the functionality, performance, and security of Micro Class applications meet expectations and provide a satisfactory user experience.

4.2 Data Processing

In Micro Class application detection, a series of testing methods and tools can be used to evaluate whether the application's functionality is functioning properly. For example, functional testing can be conducted to verify whether the various functions of the application work according to the design requirements and meet the needs of users. In addition, performance testing can also be conducted to test the response speed and resource consumption of the application under different loads and conditions. Security testing can also be conducted to check for potential security vulnerabilities in the application and take corresponding measures to fix them.

Micro Class application detection also needs to focus on user experience, including user-friendly interface design, smooth operation, and other aspects. Through user experience testing, feedback and opinions from users can be obtained to further improve and optimize the application. Among them, the commonly used calculation formula is expressed as:

$$r = \frac{S^\wedge 2xy}{Sx\,Sy} = \frac{\sum (x - \bar{x})(y - \bar{y})/n}{\sqrt{\sum (x - \bar{x})^\wedge 2/n}\sqrt{\sum (y - \bar{y})^\wedge 2/n}} \tag{1}$$

$$r = \frac{n\sum xy - \sum x \sum y}{\sqrt{n\sum x^\wedge 2 - (\sum \bar{x})^\wedge}\sqrt{2(n\sum y^\wedge 2 - (\sum \bar{y})^\wedge 2)}} \tag{2}$$

4.3 Result Analysis

Micro Class application testing is a comprehensive evaluation and validation process aimed at ensuring that the functionality, performance, security, and user experience of the application meet the expected requirements, providing users with a high-quality Micro Class learning experience. The survey results are shown in Table 1:

Table 1. Test results of the micro-course APP for college students' mental health education

	Experimental interface effects	System response time	Facilitate project management	Content design
Good	46%	34%	48%	32%
General	32%	45%	30%	47%
Not good	10%	9%	13%	12%
Do not know	12%	12%	9%	9%

It can be seen from Fig. 2 that although the micro-class APP for college students' has some shortcomings, in general, more than 32% of the APP's performance evaluations are relatively good more than 30%.

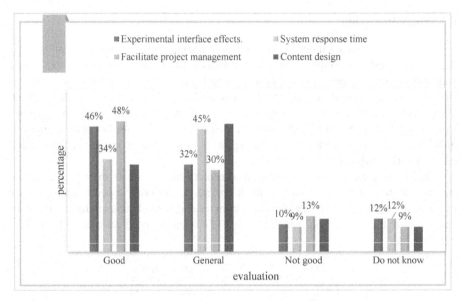

Fig. 2. Test results of the micro-course APP for college students' mental health education

4.4 Psychological Management

Psychological management data includes unstructured information. After the pre-selection of AHP algorithm, the preliminary psychological teaching management is obtained, and the feasibility of the psychological management data of the accounting results is analyzed. In the effect of the analysis, different time periods of education are selected, as shown in Table 2.

Table 2. Overall situation of psychological teaching management

Time period	Psycho-teaching data	Psychological management data
1~4 weeks	88.66	90.72
5~8 weeks	84.54	83.51
8~12 weeks	89.69	88.66
mean	83.72	85.75
X^2	1.75	8.66
P = 0.032		

4.5 Accuracy and Stability of Psychological Teaching Management

In the accuracy of the AHP algorithm, the psychological data with the statistical method, and the psychological data is shown in Fig. 3.

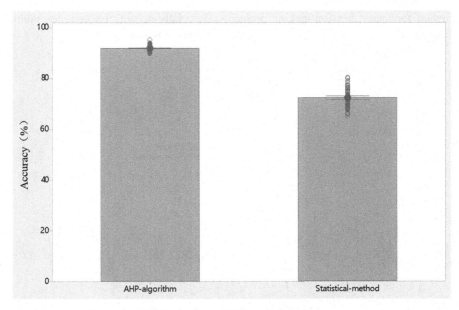

Fig. 3. Accuracy of different algorithms

It from Fig. 4 that the accuracy of the AHP algorithm that of the statistical method, but the indicating that the analysis of the AHP algorithm, while the analysis of the statistical method is uneven. The average psychological data of the are shown in Table 3.

Table 3. Comparison of analysis accuracy of different methods

algorithm	accuracy	Magnitude of change	error
AHP algorithm	90.72	8.66	1.57
Statistical methods	85.57	8.60	2.78
P	9.69	3.51	9.69

As can be seen from Table 3, there are deficiencies in the accuracy and stability of statistical methods in analysis, large changes in educational programs, and high error rates. The accuracy of the comprehensive results of the AHP algorithm is higher than that of statistical methods. The AHP algorithm decomposes and organizes complex decision problems through the construction of a hierarchical structure and comparison matrix, making the relationships between decision factors clearer. Compared to statistical methods, the AHP algorithm can more meticulously consider the relative importance of various factors, reducing information loss. Compared to statistical methods, the higher accuracy of AHP algorithm's comprehensive results is mainly attributed to its more detailed factor decomposition and organization, full consideration of subjective factors, and logical consistency testing mechanism. This makes the AHP algorithm the preferred method for many decision-making problems, especially suitable for complex multi-dimensional decision-making situations, and the result 4 is shown.

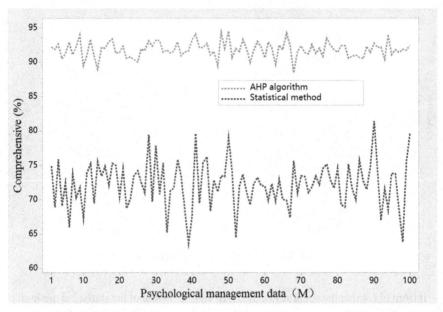

Fig. 4. Comprehensive results of AHP algorithm on psychological management

It Fig. 4 that the psychological management data of the AHP better than the statistical method, and the AHP the management of psychological teaching and sets the corresponding standard. Exclude substandard psychological management data.

5   Conclusions

This article takes the role of the heart health curriculum from the perspective of moral education as the core, and conducts research from the theoretical and empirical levels. At the theoretical level, the external and internal effects of the Xinkang course on moral education are discussed, and then the psychological education micro-course APP design is carried out. Through user evaluation, it is concluded that the overall effect of the micro-course APP designed in this article is better.

Acknowledgements. Research and Practice of Higher Vocational General Education Reform based on Higher level Target Cultivation under the digitalization context. (NO:23A3011).

References

1. Mitchell, J.J., Reason, R.D., Hemer, K.M., et al.: Perceptions of campus climates for civic learning as predictors of college students' mental health. J. College Character **17**(1), 40–52 (2016)
2. An, B.D., Cho, K.D.: Moderating effect of mental health of college students. Asia Life Sci. **2**, 977–987 (2018)
3. Chan, C.W.: Moral education in Hong Kong kindergartens: an analysis of the preschool curriculum guides. Global Studies of Childhood, **10**(2), 156–169 (2019)
4. Kichuk, A.: The emotional component of the present-day students' psychically health: the question analysis. Bull. Taras Shevchenko Nat. Univ. Kyiv Ser. "Psychol." **1**(10), 48–50 (2019)
5. Rolé, S.: The identification of key online learning dispositions of college students learning in a blended learning course. Eur. J. Teach. Educ. **2**(3), 1–11 (2020)
6. Wang, Q., Du, T.: Implementation of the college student mental health education course (CSMHEC) in undergraduate medical curriculum: effects and insights. BMC Med. Educ. **20**(1), 1–12 (2020)
7. Robert, M., et al.: Impact of a mental health curriculum on knowledge and stigma among high school students: a randomized controlled trial - sciencedirect. J. Am. Acad. Child Adolesc. Psychiatry **55**(5), 383–391 (2016)
8. Meireles, M., Fernandes, C., Silva, L.: Curricular guidelines and medical education: expectations of first year medical students at a higher education institution. Revista Brasileira de Educação Médica **43**(2), 67–78 (2019)
9. Ahmet, A.: The analysis on sport attitudes of students at high school education in Turkey. Educ. Res. Rev. **11**(5), 194–203 (2016)
10. Burbach, F.R., Sherbersky, H., Whitlock, R., et al.: A unique regional family interventions training programme. J. Mental Health Training Educ. Pract. **13**(5), 273–282 (2018)
11. Scholz, M., Neumann, C., Wild, K., et al.: Teaching to relax: development of a program to potentiate stress-results of a feasibility study with medical undergraduate students. Appl. Psychophysiol. Biofeedbackl. Psychophysiol. Biofeedback **41**(3), 275–281 (2016)
12. Ross, S.J., Owens, K., Roberts, A., et al.: Mindfulness training: success in reducing first year health professional students' study and exam related stress. Health Prof. Educ. **6**(2), 162–169 (2020)

Research on the Investigation Model of the Implementation of Mooc/spoc Mixed Teaching Mode in Colleges and Universities Based on Computer

Liu Lu[1][(✉)], Xianli Zen[2], and Liu Min[3]

[1] Harbin Normal University, Harbin 150000, China
13796099081@163.com
[2] Guilin University of Electronic Technology, Guilin 541004, Guangxi, China
[3] Shangqiu Normal University, Shangqiu 476000, Henan, China

Abstract. The hybrid teaching mode combining information-based teaching with traditional teaching is not new, but whether it has become a mature, systematic and effective classroom teaching mode needs empirical research. This study aims to explore the investigation mode of mooc/spoc mixed teaching mode in Colleges and universities. The purpose of this study is to test the effectiveness of online course delivery system in Colleges and universities. We use content analysis (CAT), one of the qualitative data collection methods, to analyze the investigation model of mooc/spoc mixed teaching mode. The results show that MOOC has three elements: (1) content, (2) learning process, (3) teaching practice; These elements can be divided into two parts: content and learning process. Based on the results of cat, we identified four categories for each element: knowledge structure, teaching method structure, and knowledge. In view of the problems and deficiencies in the teaching of "college computer", in combination with the latest basic requirements of college computer teaching revised by the College Computer Course Teaching Steering Committee of the Ministry of Education, and in combination with the characteristics of professional disciplines, the curriculum content reform of "college computer basic" course is carried out with the teaching goal of cultivating computational thinking, and the content system of college computer course is constructed based on the integration of disciplines; Cooperate with famous schools to build MOOC and SPOC for every teacher in our school, and provide high-quality teaching resources and online learning environment for the realization of curriculum teaching objectives; Create a new flipped classroom teaching mode of "College Computer Foundation" based on "MOOC + SPOC", which includes four steps: pre-class preparation and learning, classroom presentation and discussion, after-class improvement and submission, and student mutual evaluation and evaluation, providing an efficient and feasible implementation plan.

Keyword: MOOC · SPOC · Computer · Mixed teaching

X. Zeng—Student Affairs Office

© ICST Institute for Computer Sciences, Social Informatics and Telecommunications Engineering 2024
Published by Springer Nature Switzerland AG 2024. All Rights Reserved
Y. Zhang and N. Shah (Eds.): BigIoT-EDU 2023, LNICST 583, pp. 582–592, 2024.
https://doi.org/10.1007/978-3-031-63139-9_60

1 Introduction

With the continuous maturity of Internet technology, using the network to learn has gradually become a trend. The existence of wechat, wechat official account, Moke and other resources has changed the way human beings learn and receive education. With the development of network education platform, network teaching software, network teaching video and other technical means, learners have more channels to obtain learning resources. These new learning methods are also respected and loved by more and more people. The continuous development of "Internet + education" has led to revolutionary changes in the traditional way of education. Students begin to acquire more knowledge through online learning, which constantly strengthens the ability of autonomous learning [1]. However, although abundant learning resources can be obtained through online network learning, the efficiency of learning is difficult to evaluate and ensure. Although the traditional classroom teaching mode is not conducive to the cultivation of students' innovative ability and autonomy, it can make the teaching content complete efficiently and orderly. Both have their own advantages. The mixed teaching mode can organically combine the advantages of the two [2].

In recent years, MOOC has risen quietly, and the construction of various platforms at home and abroad has surged. The number of online courses and users has increased by leaps and bounds. In 2014, the MOOC of Chinese universities was launched. At present, more than 400 courses have been opened, and nearly 10 courses of "College Computer Foundation" have been opened online. However, the huge increase in the number of MOOC platforms, online courses and student registrations has triggered a quality crisis. The research shows that "no prerequisite" and "no scale limit" are both advantages and limitations for students and universities. MOOC has little impact on university physical courses, and there are also doubts about the improvement of teaching quality of the university. SPOC just solved these problems. SPOC is the organic integration of MOOC and traditional campus teaching. It is a solution to change the current situation of traditional higher education through MOOC resources. Its basic form is to use MOOC lecture video or online evaluation and other functions to assist classroom teaching in traditional campus classroom. SPOC not only promotes the external brand of the university, but also promotes the teaching reform in the university and improves the teaching quality in the university. Many colleges and universities have built SPOCs that meet their teaching needs.

In 2017, the state revised the general curriculum standard, in which the core quality of physics has higher requirements for teachers and students. Teachers should be based on students' core quality education, scientific development education and discipline thinking education, and pay attention not only to imparting knowledge, but also to the development of students' ability, especially students' innovation ability. The progress and development of the country need innovative talents. The new curriculum reform requires teachers to have the ability to cultivate students' innovative consciousness, mobilize students' enthusiasm, create a harmonious learning environment, and enhance students' ability of autonomous learning.

Traditional teaching mode has its advantages, but with the development of society, the disadvantages of traditional teaching mode are gradually exposed. For a long time, it has been widely believed that school education is the center of knowledge learning, classroom learning is the focus of students' learning, and teachers are the key to the whole classroom, so students can not effectively participate in the classroom [3]. In a word, the teaching methods and activities used by the traditional teaching mode are carried out around teachers, and most colleges and universities also use this teaching mode.

2   Related Work

2.1   Concept of Mooc+spoc Hybrid Teaching Mode

(1) MooC。MOOC (massive open online course) has the characteristics of large-scale (massive, the number of students studying each course at the same time is often thousands to tens of thousands, or even hundreds of thousands), open (open, the learning content is free), online (online, all learning resources are stored and broadcast through the Internet). At the same time, its content is relatively complete, and it can be called a course, as shown in Fig. 1. Therefore, MOOC is an online open course involving large-scale learners, focusing on free and open learning content and aiming at learning effect feedback obtained after online learning [4].

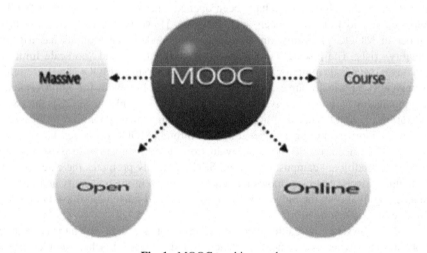

Fig. 1. MOOC teaching mode

(2) SPOC。SPOC (small private online course), literally translated as a small-scale limited online course. Small refers to massive in MOOC, which refers to the implementation of flipped classroom. The number of objects is school students, and the number is small; Private refers to open in MOOC, which means that only recognized learners on campus have access to these resources. "Minority" refers to the number of students, generally between dozens and hundreds. Therefore, it has also become a "private broadcast class" [5].

(3) Mooc+spoc new hybrid teaching mode. Teaching mode refers to the relatively stable structure and procedure of teaching activities established under the guidance of certain teaching ideas or teaching theories. The mooc+spoc new hybrid teaching mode in this paper is a new teaching activity framework and activity procedure formed by effectively matching and deeply integrating various high-quality teaching resources such as MOOC online video resources, simulation exercises, discussion areas and other high-quality teaching resources with the characteristic teaching resources of SPOC links (customized and private online courses and offline flipped classes) [6].

The new model not only combines the respective advantages of MOOC and SPOC, but also makes up for the quality crisis caused by MOOC's large-scale learning. In the MOOC link, the teaching content, teaching form, educational concept and technical platform of MOOC are improved. SPOC classroom activities adopt team learning, collaborative training, inquiry learning and other learning methods, which to a certain extent realizes the comprehensive and deep integration of online learning and traditional classroom teaching.

Cockrum believes that hybrid teaching uses technical means to impart knowledge asynchronously, liberate classroom time, and carry out learner-centered personalized learning activities. It increases the interaction and personalized contact time between learners and teachers, improves the teaching effect, and is a personalized teaching environment; Driscoll believes that blended teaching improves the teaching effect by combining the advantages of traditional learning and digital learning through face-to-face, real-time e-learning and self-paced learning; Zhang et al. confirmed through relevant research that the effect of independent and interpretive online teaching is obviously inferior to that of collaborative and teacher-led independent online teaching; Professor Cross believes that the guidance of curriculum learning from teachers is the most important part of curriculum teaching. His view is based on the survey of learners of a MOOC course; Fox believes that blended teaching can improve teachers' adjustment ability, learners' passing rate and learners' mastery and participation. It can be used as a supplement but not a substitute for classroom teaching; Shen Xinyi designed a series of strategies to improve the teaching effect, which are based on the theory of knowledge contextualization and peer evaluation; Zhang Xiaojuan and others, with the help of the technology, resources, interaction and other multi-dimensional support of the SPOC platform, integrate the network virtual field with the classroom physical field, online teaching and offline teaching, and build a deep teaching model; Zheng Yuanyuan and others took the information retrieval course of Shihezi University as an example to evaluate the teaching effect evaluation indicators of the information retrieval course under the mixed teaching mode;

2.2 Mooc+spoc Hybrid Teaching Mode Knowledge Interaction

To define the learning effect of blended teaching mode, some scholars once thought that blended learning was a combination of cognitivism, behaviorism and constructivism; Arlen believes that learners' learning effects describe our expectations for learners' learning - what learners know, understand and can do after completing the course, professional study or degree acquisition, which is commonly referred to as knowledge and understanding (cognition), practical skills (skills), attitudes and values (emotion) and individual behavior; Sandeen believes that the quality of peer evaluation will affect the learning effect; Russell believes that peer evaluation can well achieve the evaluation of learners' learning effect and performance evaluation in the course with thousands or even tens of thousands of learners participating; Jiang Feng proposed an online learning effect evaluation model based on fuzzy mathematics, which uses fuzzy mathematics theory to comprehensively evaluate the learning effect and teaching effect; Ding Hui and others built a learning evaluation mechanism based on MOOC's mixed teaching model, including learning interactive evaluation, process evaluation and summative evaluation; Xie Maosen et al. carried out reliability analysis and factor analysis on the self-test items of learners' learning process evaluation under the space teaching mode, and then determined the evaluation gauge of learners' learning process under the space teaching mode, so as to improve the learning effect; Chen Chunjin et al. adopted the multiple analysis method and concluded that blended learning is more conducive to improving and improving learners' learning effect than pure online learning and face-to-face learning.

Yan Yali and others pointed out that the so-called network group interaction is that learners can critically learn new ideas and facts in the interaction, integrate into the original cognitive structure, and transfer existing knowledge to new situations to make decisions and solve problems; Wasko proposed that in the network environment, both sides must have the willingness to communicate, and knowledge interaction can only be carried out if they have mutual needs for knowledge; Senge pointed out that the essence of knowledge interaction is that there is a positive desire for interaction between the interactive subjects, both knowledge transferors and knowledge receivers are indispensable, and these knowledge providers are not only willing to share their knowledge for free, but also more willing to help others acquire knowledge, and the last knowledge demanders can digest and absorb this knowledge [7].

This study focuses on the knowledge interaction of the new model, and defines its concept as: in the context of mooc+spoc, teachers and learners, learners follow the law of teaching and learning, and discuss, communicate and collide difficult knowledge through online video learning, stage tests, topic discussions, after-school assignments, assessment and evaluation, and offline flipped classes, so as to stimulate learners to analyze, question and think deeply about problems, Finally, we can achieve the internalization and transfer of knowledge and the dynamic behavior process of knowledge innovation.

The traditional teaching mode mainly completes a series of teaching activities offline, including teachers' classroom teaching, arranging after-school homework, organizing final exams and after-school practice. The traditional teaching mode pays more attention to how teachers teach and ignores how students learn, so the teaching effect is not ideal. The new model pays more attention to the integration of online and offline: the MOOC part adopts the form of online teaching, that is, teachers and learners communicate through the virtual environment and platform of the Internet, such as course videos, discussion areas, virtual communities, etc. MOOC has the advantages of large-scale, free and online, but it can't effectively preach, teach and solve doubts in the process of teaching and learning. In order to make up for the shortcomings of MOOC, SPOC came into being. As the complementarity of MOOC, it realizes the face-to-face knowledge exchange in offline physical classes [8]. Therefore, the new model realizes the integration of online and offline teaching, and emphasizes the cultivation of learners' enthusiasm, initiative and creativity through collaborative and exploratory learning methods, with the goal of realizing deep knowledge interaction.

3 Research on the Current Situation of the Implementation of Computer-Based Mooc/spoc Hybrid Teaching Model in Colleges and Universities

3.1 Current Situation of Hybrid Teaching Mode

In 2002, American scholars Smith J. and ellette marcier put forward the concept of hybrid teaching, which essentially combines traditional classroom teaching with online education to achieve complementary advantages. At present, the domestic academic circles have not formed a unified concept of hybrid teaching. The core meaning of hybrid teaching is to form a teaching mode of offline and online collaboration. Unlike the previous one-way classroom structure from online to offline, hybrid teaching has formed a two-way closed-loop structure from online to offline and then online. Based on the two dimensions of physical characteristics and teaching characteristics, Feng Xiaoying and others divided the development of Hybrid Teaching in China into technology application stage, technology integration stage and "Internet +" stage. The focus of hybrid teaching research and attention has also risen from the level of technical support and application to the level of students' knowledge and ability acquisition [9]. The implementation path of hybrid teaching mainly includes three aspects, namely, the construction and quality assurance of online curriculum resources, the organization and implementation of offline teaching, the similarity and improvement of online teaching, and the feedback and evaluation of students' learning. After more than 20 years of development, hybrid teaching at home and abroad has been widely used in all kinds of education in China, especially in the field of higher education. It has become the focus of educational research and reform carried out by educational administrative departments (educational policy makers), educational and teaching researchers, teachers (Teaching implementers) and teaching managers. Domestic scholars prefer the research on resource mixing, and most of them are in the field of higher education and vocational education. Its form is mainly combined with other teaching methods or modern information technology, such as the combination of Hybrid Teaching and learning, hybrid teaching and cloud classroom, hybrid teaching and flipped classroom, etc. On the whole, the current hybrid teaching mode is still in the exploratory stage, and there are some problems, such as the theory and practice of reform need to be deepened, the incentive system has not been established or improved, the general lack of overall planning and construction standards, the urgent need to improve teachers' education and teaching ability, and the lack of pertinence of teaching quality evaluation indicators [10].

SPOc is to customize courses for students and provide targeted and differentiated learning activities by limiting the access conditions and scale of courses. The new MOOC+SPOC model advocates the hybrid learning of online and offline integration in knowledge interaction, in which online activities adopt the integrated MOOC model of micro-video, test, exercise, feedback evaluation, interactive discussion, etc.; In the physical class, the limited, small-scale, in-class organization and interactive SPOC teaching mode is adopted. Teachers organize learners to carry out interactive discussion of knowledge based on situational problems, and summarize, feedback and answer questions about the discussion content. Therefore, the technological transformation of MOOC and SPOC integration under the new model is promoting an educational revolution. Learners change from knowledge receivers of traditional knowledge interaction to active learners of knowledge. They can not only acquire knowledge, but also use technical means to help themselves overcome the obstacles in the process of knowledge interaction and obtain support services; In the process of traditional knowledge interaction, teachers monitor students' progress, evaluate learning results, provide learning feedback, etc., while the new model provides data that monitors learners' homework submission and topic discussion anytime and anywhere. Therefore, the new model changes learners' knowledge interaction mode, and is the innovation and development of traditional knowledge interaction mode.

3.2   Investigation Model of the Implementation Status of Mixed Teaching Mode

(1) Online part of the course

A major feature of Moke is to highlight the value of students' learning and respect students' learning subject status. Therefore, under the mixed teaching mode based on Mu class, students need to log in to Mu class platform to complete autonomous learning task list and related learning tasks. For example, "dividing subnets and constructing hypernets" are divided into three knowledge points. In the process of learning, students must first watch the teaching videos recorded by teachers, and then solve the problems of dissent and incomprehension through group cooperation, online discussion and other learning methods. In this process, students' autonomous learning ability and teamwork ability have been cultivated. In addition, in the process of students discussing and solving problems, teachers should guide students to read relevant expansion materials to better assist students in learning.

Teachers also log on to the Moke teaching platform to understand the students' learning progress, the scores of each knowledge point and each learning link. Through the summary and analysis, the teacher found that most students master the two knowledge points of "the method of dividing subnets" and "the forwarding process of packets when using subnets", while they do not understand the knowledge point of "the method of constructing network reading" deeply enough, and students have some difficulties in completing it. Based on the understanding of these aspects, teachers can determine the focus and targeted points of online teaching.

(2) Offline part of the course

First, mixed teaching methods. For students who attend the meeting class on site, the teacher shall record their attendance and give corresponding credits; Students participating in the live meeting class can interact by sending bullets, voting, liking and asking questions, obtain automatic attendance and scoring, and realize online and offline real-time interaction and Q & A.

Second, focus on the content. Taking "molecular networks and building hypernets" as an example, teachers should focus on "the method of dividing subnets and the packet forwarding process when using subnets" according to the students' online learning and the students' questions fed back by the Mu class platform. At the same time, in the specific explanation process, students should be encouraged to raise their own problems, and teachers and students should discuss, analyze and solve problems together, as shown in Fig. 2.

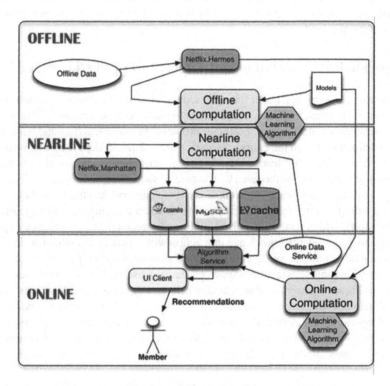

Fig. 2. Mixed teaching mode

Third, group cooperative learning. Combined with the teaching content of this lesson, the teacher organized students to discuss the "calculation method of unclassified address" in groups. Each group consists of 3–5 members. Teachers can ask questions at any time in class, and students in online class can ask questions and discuss online through the Mu class platform. In the process of students' autonomous learning and discussion, the teacher gives supervision and troubleshooting, which takes about 30 min. After that, each group will send representatives to show, speak and explain.

Fourth, summarize comments and sublimation. After the representatives of the group finished the presentation and explanation of the results, the teacher commented on the key points and difficulties of the students' works. Aiming at the students' hand-in-hand teaching of design program cases, it reveals the difficulties of technology application and expands the teaching depth; For students in online classes, teachers can explain face-to-face, so as to solve students' learning problems.

Fifth, submit your homework online. The purpose of arranging after-school test questions is to consolidate students' mastery of knowledge points. Teachers upload the questions to MOOC teaching platform and push them to students. On the Mu class platform, students can submit homework online and add attachments, which teachers can view at any time; For students who have not submitted homework, teachers can make online key statistics. Teachers can issue activities such as signing in and answering questions in response to the submission of homework, so as to ensure and expand the effectiveness of mixed teaching.

4   Specific Implementation and Effect of Flipped Classroom

The knowledge interaction under the new model includes: ① learners' attention and discussion on the learning content when participating in the course learning; ② The in-depth communication and discussion of difficult problems between teachers and learners and between learners through the course discussion area; ③ the in-depth knowledge interaction between teachers and learners and between learners through virtual communities, including QQ, WeChat, Weibo, etc.; ④ The face-to-face in-depth knowledge interaction between teachers and learners, as well as between learners, through flipped classroom. Learners will encounter many difficult problems when carrying out online learning in the new mode, which cannot be solved in a timely manner. Therefore, they expect to have face-to-face in-depth knowledge interaction with teachers and other learners, solve doubts, and obtain interactive sense of value, so as to improve their performance expectations and learning satisfaction. Perceived ease of use and interactive value have a significant impact on users' online learning behavior intention; The higher the interactivity of network resources, the stronger the users' perceived performance expectations and willingness to participate; The interaction of the discussion area can promote learners' perceived performance expectations and willingness to participate; Teachers guide and help learners' discussion, which has a good role in helping learners improve their learning effect.

In the whole teaching process, the knowledge content of computer software and hardware system is selected to implement the teaching mode of classroom flipping. The implementation process is divided into pre-class preparation and learning, classroom presentation and discussion, after-class improvement and submission, and student mutual evaluation and evaluation.

(1) Preparation and study before class.

① Grouping: Each class is divided into three groups, with one group leader and one deputy group leader. The list of each group is sent to the mailbox designated by the teacher in advance.

② Topic selection: The teacher will release the discussion questions according to the flipped content, and each group will choose.

③ Learning: log in to the "MOOC+SPOC" platform to learn the video content specified by the teacher, and check the materials for further learning.

④ Production: group discussion and production of learning results into PPT.

(2) Class presentation and discussion.

Classroom is divided into three parts:

① Display: According to the divided groups, the teacher will randomly assign one student to display the group's work. The operation demonstration should be carried out in combination with the actual problems, and others can supplement.

② Discussion: After the presentation of each group, students and teachers from other groups will ask questions. Each student in the group can answer questions.

③ Summary: The teacher summarizes the discussion of the whole course and summarizes the key points and difficulties of this part.

(3) After-class improvement and submission.

① Improvement: Each group modifies their display works according to the questions raised by teachers and students. ② Submit: submit the work to the FTP server as required by the teacher.

(4) Students' mutual evaluation and evaluation.

The work submitted by students will be published on our WeChat public platform. Students and teachers will evaluate and score each work independently, calculate the scoring results, and the teacher will give the final evaluation results according to the students' classroom performance. Figure 3 shows the results of students' mutual evaluation.

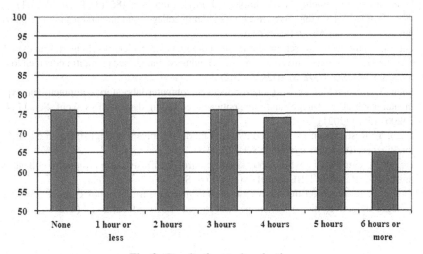

Fig. 3. Result of mutual evaluation

5 Conclusion

This paper reviews and combs the relevant research on the new model and the new model knowledge interaction, analyzes the concept and characteristics of the new model, and defines the new model knowledge interaction. On this basis, it analyzes and demonstrates the influencing factors of the willingness to participate in the knowledge interaction of the new model, reveals the key influencing factors of the knowledge interaction behavior of the new model, designs the supporting system model of the knowledge interaction of the new model, constructs the evaluation index of the effect of the new model based on the knowledge interaction, and tests it through an example. Finally, it puts forward the improvement strategy of the knowledge interaction of the new model.

Acknowledgements. Educational Reform Project of Colleges and Universities in Heilongjiang Province (Project No.SJGY20200371).

References

1. Yuan, C., Men, S.: Thoughts on the mixed teaching mode of ideological and political courses in colleges and universities based on the MOOC platform. In: IPEC 2021: 2021 2nd Asia-Pacific Conference on Image Processing, Electronics and Computers (2021)
2. Lu, J.L.: Research on the ideological and political teaching mode of dual system curriculum in colleges and universities based on MOOC (2021)
3. Wu, H., Ma, R.: Research on the teaching mode of software engineering in colleges and universities based on big data analysis (2021)
4. Jia, S., Zhang, X.: Teaching mode of psychology and pedagogy in colleges and universities based on artificial intelligence technology. J. Phys. Conf. Ser. **1852**(3), 032033 (2021)
5. Wei, B.: Research on the mixed teaching model in colleges and universities in the context of "Internet+". Asian Agric. Res. **12** (2021)
6. Qiu, S., Yang, L.: Research on the mode of short video project teaching and media talent training in colleges and universities under 5G industry chain based on multimedia technology. J. Phys. Conf. Ser. **1992**(2), 022057 (2021)
7. Shen, Y.: Research on network management of computer laboratory equipment and experimental teaching in colleges and universities based on big data. J. Phys. Conf. Ser. **1744**(4), 042067 (5pp) (2021)
8. Zhao, Y.: Research on the blended teaching model of university English Based on artificial intelligence. Tobacco Regulatory Sci. (2021)
9. Lu, Y.: Research on the whole process cost control of infrastructure projects in colleges and universities Based on DBB model. Archit. Eng. Sci. **3**(1), 24–28 (2022)
10. Zhang, J.: Research on the innovation driving mechanism of campus cultural activities in colleges and universities based on the background of network culture. **2** (2021)

Construction of Computer-Based Collaborative Evaluation Model for Labor Education in Local Colleges and Universities

Lin Lin[✉]

Harbin Normal University, Harbin 150000, China
linlin3273@163.com

Abstract. Constructing a computer-based collaborative evaluation model of labor education in local colleges and universities is a tool for teachers to evaluate students' performance. The model consists of two parts: the first part is the evaluation part, which evaluates students' performance according to their academic performance, work experience, attitude and other related factors; The second part is the feedback part, which provides information that needs to be improved to improve students' performance. The main purpose of this project is to build a computer-based collaborative evaluation model of labor education in local colleges and universities. This paper comprehensively scores students' labor education according to their labor education course examinations, personal labor practice activities, and collective labor practice activities. The evaluation method is efficient and accurate.

Keyword: Labor education · computer · Local universities · Collaborative evaluation

1 Introduction

On the issue of "the true meaning of education", Tang Jiangpeng, a member of the National Committee of the Chinese People's Political Consultative Conference and the principal of Xishan High School in Jiangsu Province, said that at the 2021 National People's Congress, it was succinctly pointed out that "students cannot win the future only by their achievements. Achievements are not the whole content of education, let alone the fundamental goal of education. Education only focuses on the enrollment rate, and the country will have no core competitiveness." At present, China is moving towards the direction of strengthening the country with talents. Science and technology in the new era are the primary productive forces. We should not only train scientific and technological innovation talents, but also train high-quality innovative talents with the fundamental task of "building morality and cultivating people" to achieve the goal of strengthening the country with talents [1]. Looking at the historical development logic of labor education, we can see that labor plays an indispensable role in the process of talent training. Under the educational background of different periods, the purpose and form of labor education are different, the practice methods and evaluation methods are different.

© ICST Institute for Computer Sciences, Social Informatics and Telecommunications Engineering 2024
Published by Springer Nature Switzerland AG 2024. All Rights Reserved
Y. Zhang and N. Shah (Eds.): BigIoT-EDU 2023, LNICST 583, pp. 593–603, 2024.
https://doi.org/10.1007/978-3-031-63139-9_61

Cultivate virtue through labor, increase wisdom through labor, cultivate beauty through labor, and innovate through labor. After a preliminary understanding of the current situation of labor education in Rizhao City through interviews with teachers from the Rizhao Education Bureau, the practice team once again went to primary and secondary schools in Rizhao City, hoping to carry out in-depth practice through individual cases of labor education courses in local schools. The practice team members first introduced the background and purpose of this social practice in detail to the interviewees, including school teachers, students and some parents, and said that they would excavate local characteristics in this practice process, ignite the creative torch of the labor education curriculum for middle school students in the new era, seek to learn from experience, and develop reasonable and feasible wisdom programs for implementation and promotion. "At the beginning of the implementation of labor education, due to the lack of experience for reference, the labor education model adopted by the school was relatively simple, and the evaluation criteria were relatively one-sided. The students seemed to be walking through the motions, and our teacher's evaluation was not easy. "When talking about the early labor education, the teacher said frankly. At the same time, she regretted that the school had considered the way of combining education with pleasure and teaching with work to carry out diversified labor education courses, but it lacked the corresponding funds and resources, so it has not been promoted. It can only simply open the class labor corner and the school labor park, so that students can start from the small work around them, so as to return to the true joy of labor education. After talking with the teacher After point-to-point and face-to-face interviews, the members of the practice team also distributed questionnaires to the majority of teachers and students. Many students took the initiative to fill in the questionnaires and actively answered the questions of the members of the practice team, showing a strong interest in labor education. " In the labor education carried out by the school, I have not only gained simple labor results, but also realized the joy and difficulty of labor. I hope that the school can carry out more different labor education, take us to walk in the sun and look in the fields. "A student said to the members of the practice team with great expectation.

As an important position for the development of labor education, schools must establish a strong security mechanism, and evaluation, as the internal power to promote the construction and development of labor education curriculum, must be sound and perfect. The evaluation contents shall include the number of labor participants, labor attitude, actual operation, labor results, etc. The specific labor conditions and relevant factual materials should be recorded in the comprehensive quality file of students and serve as an important reference for students' enrollment and evaluation. School labor education is developing in continuous exploration, but the evaluation of labor education is still in a vacancy. In October 2020, the CPC Central Committee and the State Council issued the Overall Plan for Deepening the Reform of Educational Evaluation in the New Era, which proposed to improve the evaluation of results, strengthen process evaluation, explore value-added evaluation, improve comprehensive evaluation, give full play to the role of evaluation baton, problem-oriented, closely link with reality, promote the reform of key areas of educational evaluation, carry out substantive and effective evaluation reform, and make full use of modern information technology, Improve the scientificity, objectivity and professionalism of evaluation ". Quality education aims to improve the quality of the people. In the evaluation reform, attention should be paid to the innovative ability and practical ability of students [3] Through the interpretation of the relevant documents and policies of labor education in recent years, the implementation of labor education in schools is more reasonable and well documented, which builds a bridge for the construction of labor education system, points out the direction for the implementation of school labor education, and provides new guidance for the evaluation of labor education. With the increasing emphasis on labor education, the evaluation of labor education has changed from the establishment of student evaluation system to the whole process of labor education and the implementation of quality inspection. Thus, establishing and improving the labor education evaluation system is an important link in promoting the development of labor education curriculum in the new era.

2 Related Work

2.1 Research on Labor Education Evaluation

Dai Jiafang et al. (2017) believed that the most prominent problem of current school labor education is the lack of corresponding labor education effect evaluation dimensions and standards, and proposed to establish relevant evaluation standards from the four evaluation dimensions of labor common sense based on the realization of labor education goals, including labor emotion, labor will and labor behavior [3].

In the paper "Research on the Evaluation of Labor Education in Colleges and Universities Based on Practice Guidance" (2020), Liu Maoxiang believed that the establishment of labor education evaluation system in colleges and universities is an important subject to promote the development of labor education in colleges and universities, and an important way to solve the practical difficulties of labor education. The purpose of labor education evaluation is to improve students' labor literacy [4]. He has established corresponding evaluation points from the perspective of labor quality of college students and labor education practice of college students. On the basis of comprehensively promoting labor education, he has guided all kinds of education at all levels to build a characteristic labor education system according to the actual situation of the region. In addition, based on the above point of view, scholar Liu Maoxiang put forward the important strategies of implementing the combination of labor education and local characteristics, the combination of professional labor education curriculum development and subject curriculum, and accelerating the implementation of vocational labor education teacher training [5].

In the article "Historical Logic and System Construction of Labor Quality Evaluation in Colleges and Universities in the New Era" (2020), Gong Chunyan and others took "education monitoring and evaluation" based on cognitive diagnosis theory and project response theory as the evaluation model of labor education, recorded and analyzed relevant data and information in the process of labor education activities, to assess whether students and groups have conscious labor behavior, love labor Ability to work efficiently and other labor qualities. Based on this evaluation theory, scholars have incorporated the evaluation of students' labor literacy into the labor situation and established a framework model, as shown in Fig. 1:

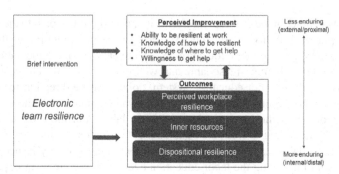

Fig. 1. Labor quality evaluation model

2.2 Regional Collaborative Innovation System

The regional collaborative innovation system is a comprehensive innovation system composed of the regional internal collaborative innovation system and the regional external collaborative innovation system. The essence of the regional external collaborative innovation system is the innovation network system that forms the benefit distribution pattern through the collaborative interaction between regions. In the process of regional external collaborative innovation, the division of benefit distribution is particularly complex. For the purpose of research, this paper uses the idea of capacity structure for reference, and plans to use the capacity structure relationship model to divide the regional benefit distribution. According to the definition of capacity structure, when two regions carry out collaborative innovation, the level of collaborative innovation within the region directly affects the possibility and stability of collaborative innovation between regions, It also determines the distribution of benefits in the process of inter-regional collaborative innovation. Therefore, theoretically, the development level of the regional external collaborative innovation system depends on the development level of the regional internal collaborative innovation, and changes with the change of the internal system. Therefore, when constructing the evaluation index system of the regional collaborative innovation system, it should mainly be based on the internal system of the regional collaborative innovation system. The regional collaborative innovation system is shown in Fig. 2.

From the perspective of capability structure and the concept of regional collaborative innovation system, the regional collaborative innovation system can be divided into four parts: knowledge innovation capability subsystem, knowledge allocation capability subsystem, knowledge application capability subsystem and innovation environment support capability subsystem. In view of the actual connotation of the four capability subsystems, referring to the relevant research results, on the basis of following the principles of comprehensive, scientific, systematic and operational indicator selection, and taking the use frequency of indicators as the preliminary screening principle, the evaluation indicator system of the regional collaborative innovation system is initially constructed, and then the under-represented variables are removed by direct clustering and correlation analysis, Further screening shall be conducted for the primary selected indicators to achieve the comprehensiveness and accuracy of the indicator system.

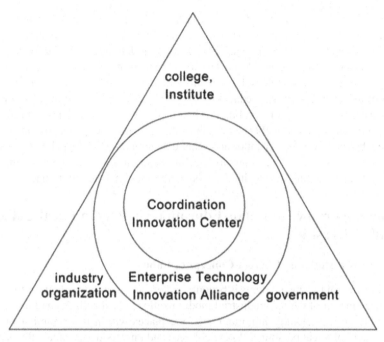

Fig. 2. Regional collaborative innovation system

2.3 Labor Education

Human beings have labor. The Chinese encyclopedia dictionary defines "labor" as: "labor is a process in which human beings cause, adjust and control any material transformation between nature with their own activities. It is a unique attribute of human beings and the basis for the existence and development of human society." The concise knowledge dictionary interprets "labor" as: "labor is a purposeful activity that people use labor tools to change natural things and make them suitable for their own needs, the use or consumption of labor, a unique social practice of human beings, and the first basic condition for the existence and development of human society." "Ci Hai" expounds labor as follows: "Labor plays a decisive role in the formation of human beings. It is a purposeful activity that people change the object of labor to make it more suitable for their own needs. It is the most basic condition for the existence and development of human society. Labor has different social attributes under different social systems. In the selection of slavery, feudal system and capitalist system, the labor of workers is manifested as slave labor, serf labor and wage labor, which are different The nature of exploited labor. Under socialist public ownership, workers have become the masters of the state and enterprises, and are no longer exploited [6]. After entering communism, labor is not only a means of making a living, but also will become the first need of people's life. "

Labor and education are two different concepts. When the two are combined, labor is endowed with education, and education cannot ignore labor. The Encyclopedia of China (Education volume) defines labor education as: "labor education is an education that enables students to establish correct labor views and attitudes, love labor and working people, and develop labor habits. It is one of the contents of moral education". In the dictionary of teachers' encyclopedia, labor education is defined as: "Labor education is to spread the basic knowledge and skills of modern production to the educated, and cultivate them to have correct labor views, labor habits and feelings of loving the working people and labor achievements. Labor education attaches great importance to the intellectual factors in the process of labor, combines ordinary labor with creative labor, and combines simple labor with knowledgeable labor. Labor education includes productive labor, social welfare labor and Self service labor and other educational activities [7]. " The scope of labor education is much larger than labor technology. Labor technology is an important part of it. Understanding new technology is an important part of labor education.

3 The Importance of Labor Education Courses in Local Colleges and Universities

3.1 Cultivate Students' Correct Concept of Labor

The cultivation of technical talents is becoming more and more important for the continuous development of China's industrial modernization. Local colleges and universities, which play an increasingly important role, are places with a large number of scientific and technological personnel. Local colleges and universities graduate thousands of undergraduates every year, which effectively promotes the development of China's social economy. Most college students in local colleges and universities are only children, and they participate in labor education courses [8, 9]. There are no good labor habits, weak labor consciousness, weak labor concept, lack of labor education and other problems. Therefore, in order to explore labor education courses suitable for local college students, local colleges and universities should combine the characteristics of educational objects and the actual situation of their students, and comply with the requirements of the development of the new era. The labor education courses in local colleges and universities are to cultivate students' labor consciousness, labor skills and correct labor concept; For the improvement of students' practical ability and the mastery of technical skills, it is beneficial to set up labor education courses; For students to realize the glory of labor, from the role of students to the role of technicians, it is necessary to set up labor education courses [10]. The cultivation of students' hard-working spirit can be achieved through labor education classes, which will make full psychological preparations for their future to be a dignified, high-quality and happy person in society.

3.2 Improve Students' Physical Quality

Family work is strange to many students, because most of them are only children, who live a carefree life from childhood to childhood. They never need to work at home, and their daily life is also arranged by parents, which makes students lack teamwork ability, poor labor skills, low labor quality, and their ability to communicate with others in society needs to be improved. In this way, it is difficult to improve students' comprehensive quality, and the process of developing labor education will be very slow [11], The comprehensive quality of students cannot be improved. When you graduate from university and go to work in a unit, the labor intensity will be much greater than that of the school. You can't do without good physical fitness, and many students don't pay attention to their physical exercise. In the learning process of the new era, it is necessary to increase students' physical training. The labor content in the labor education curriculum is not large, which is much less than that in physical education [12]. There are many kinds of labor, which can be arranged according to students' personal hobbies to improve students' labor ability. Labor education curriculum can be achieved.

3.3 Indicator Screening

After obtaining the primary indicator system, in order to ensure the comprehensiveness and accuracy of the indicator system, this paper will use the method of correlation analysis and direct clustering for further screening. The basic steps are:

Step 1: Index correlation analysis. Calculate the correlation coefficient between the secondary indicators under each primary indicator, that is, compare the indicators in pairs to obtain the correlation coefficient matrix R [13].

Step 2: Determine whether to filter indicators. If the correlation coefficient in the correlation coefficient matrix exceeds the threshold value (generally 0.8), it means that there are similar attributes between the information, and further screening of indicators is required. Otherwise, indicator screening is not required.

Step 3: index cluster analysis. If it is necessary to screen indicators, cluster the indicators first. This paper mainly uses the direct clustering method in cluster analysis to cluster. The specific idea is to first sort all the different elements Y in the correlation coefficient matrix R, except diagonal elements, in the order of the largest to the smallest, that is, $1 = \gamma_1 > \gamma_2 > \gamma_3... > \gamma_n$; then take the threshold value $\gamma = \gamma_k \in [0,1]$, when $r_{j*} \geq \gamma_k (j \neq j^*)$, the index X and index X are considered; Have the same characteristics and classify them into one category. At the same time, let A and 4 indicate that the clustering threshold is γ. The two classes of are said to be similar when $A_1 \cap A_2 \neq \phi$; Finally, all similar classes are combined into one class, and the clustering threshold is? Equivalent classification of. Because of the clustering threshold γ The classification results are different with different values [14]. The closer the value is to 1, the finer the classification will be. Therefore, in order to determine the value more accurately, this paper adopts the method of γ C to determine the clustering threshold? Optimal value of:

$$C_k = \frac{\gamma_{k-1} - \gamma_k}{n_{k-1} - n_k} \qquad (1)$$

where: n_k and n_{k-1} Is the number of objects in the $k - 1$ and k clustering, γ_k and γ_{k-1} are the threshold values of the $k - 1$ and k clustering, respectively. If $C_e = \max_k(C_k)$, the threshold value of the e-th clustering is considered to be the optimal value. This is because the change rate C of the clustering threshold γ_k. The larger the number of adjacent clusters, the greater the difference between classes, and the more obvious the difference between classes [15].

There are n decision-making units, x_j and y_j represent the input vector and output vector of the decision-making unit, and the specific expression is:

$$\sum_{j=1}^{n} \lambda_j x_j + s^- = \theta x_{j0} \qquad (2)$$

$$\sum_{j=1}^{n} \lambda_j y_j - s^+ = y_{j0} \tag{3}$$

$$\lambda_j \geq 0, j = 1, 2, \cdots, n \tag{4}$$

where: s^- is the relaxation variable, s^+ is the residual variable, and if $\theta^* = 1, s^{-*} = s^{+*} = 0$, then unit j is DEA effective; if there is non-zero value in $0 = 1$, s and s″ *, then unit y_{j0} is DEA weak effective.

$$d_{ik} = \frac{a_{ik}}{\frac{1}{n} \sum_{i=1}^{n} a_{ik}} \tag{5}$$

Normalization of indicator matrix. Because the unit and index properties of the original data are different, the accuracy and rationality of the evaluation results will be affected if the calculation is carried out directly, so the original index matrix cannot be directly calculated, and it needs to be processed, that is, the normalization of the index, and the commonly used transformation methods of canonical variables include mean value transformation and extreme value transformation [16].

4 Computer Based Collaborative Evaluation of Labor Education in Local Colleges and Universities

Labor education can enable students to establish correct labor views and attitudes, love labor and working people, and develop labor habits. It is one of the main contents of the all-round development of morality, intelligence, physique, art and labor. The "opinions on Comprehensively Strengthening labor education in large, medium and primary schools in the new era" clearly points out that it is necessary to improve the position of labor education and place labor education in a prominent position as the key work of comprehensively implementing the party's education policy at present. Guided by the Marxist concept of labor, adhere to the overall, all-round and whole process design, clarify the general objectives of labor education and the curriculum, content requirements and assessment methods of different stages and different types of schools, and form a labor education system. However, at present, the major domestic colleges and universities lack an effective labor education evaluation system [17]. As long as the time or number of labor practice activities that students participate in meet certain requirements, the implementation example of this paper aims to solve the above problems.

In this embodiment, whenever a student completes a labor education course examination, the first type of evaluation points obtained by the student through the labor education course are obtained, and the first type of evaluation points are obtained according to the credits of the education course and the examination results; Whenever students complete a personal labor practice activity, they get the second type of evaluation points obtained by the students through the personal labor practice activity [18]. The second type of evaluation points are obtained according to the working hours of labor practice activities and the completion score. Every time students complete a labor practice activity, there will be a teacher to score; Whenever students participate in and complete a collective labor practice activity, they will get the third type of evaluation points obtained by the students through the collective labor practice activity. The third type of evaluation points are obtained according to the working hours of the collective labor practice activity, the completion score of the collective labor practice activity, and the comprehensive score of the students. Every time students complete a collective labor practice activity, teachers will score the local tasks and collective tasks; At the end of each semester, when it is necessary to obtain the student's labor education evaluation score, input the student's labor education evaluation instruction. The student's labor education evaluation instruction includes the student's name, student number and other information, and retrieve all the first class evaluation points, second class evaluation points and third class evaluation points of the student in this semester [19]. In the embodiment of the invention, the retrieved first class evaluation points The second type of evaluation score and the third type of evaluation score are input into the evaluation model, and the labor education evaluation score of the student is automatically output. The algorithm of the evaluation model is: labor education evaluation score $=k1*$ study the first type of evaluation score $+k2*$ (third type of evaluation score $+e$ third type of evaluation score), where K1 represents the proportion coefficient of theoretical education, K2 represents the proportion coefficient of practical education, and the specific values of K1 and K2 are set by high efficiency according to needs [20], The embodiment of the invention can comprehensively score the labor education of students according to the labor education course examination, personal labor practice activities and collective labor practice activities that students participate in, and the evaluation method is efficient and accurate, as shown in Fig. 3.

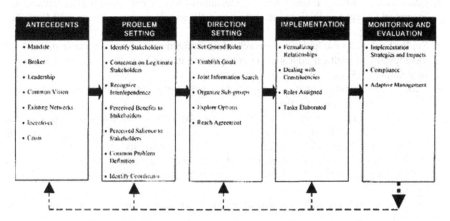

Fig. 3. Collaborative evaluation process of labor education

5 Conclusion

The reform and implementation of labor education curriculum have new requirements in the new era. Local colleges and universities should see the shortcomings in their own school labor education courses, and need to improve according to the transformation of people's teaching ideas and the needs of society for talents, so that the labor education courses of local colleges and universities can keep pace with the pace of the times, so that students will consciously improve their labor ability through labor, professional skills will also be improved, and their life values will be clear, and they will not think that labor education courses are not open, This is a leap from quantitative change to qualitative change. Students will prefer to take labor classes. Labor education courses can not be replaced by general scientific research training, let alone dispensable. The characteristics of labor education courses should have the unity of knowledge and practice, and apply what they have learned. Only in this way can they have a unique comprehensive educational function. The healthy growth of young students in labor education courses should be seriously treated and valued by local colleges and universities.

Acknowledgements. Research on the collaborative evaluation mechanism of labor education in Colleges and universities in Heilongjiang Province under the background of artificial intelligence (21EDC193) ;Construction and test of labor education evaluation index system of local colleges and universities driven by the data of excellent youth project of central support fund for local colleges and Universities.

References

1. Yong, L.I., Education, D.O., University, S.: Research on school-locality collaborative development of entrepreneurship education in local colleges and universities based on big data. J. Tibet Univ. (2019)
2. Chu, Z., Liu, P., Liu, C.: Evaluation of the education quality of innovation and entrepreneurship in applied colleges and universities based on AHP and BP neural network. IOP Conf. Ser. Mater. Sci. Eng. **392**(6), 062184 (2018)
3. Su, R.: Evaluation-model-based research on the combination of internet platforms with the ideological and political education in colleges and universities. Revista de la Facultad de Ingenieria **32**(13), 681–686 (2017)
4. Gao, N.: To give full scope to labor quality evaluation of youth of the new era as the baton. Rev. Educ. Theor. **3**(3), 67 (2020)
5. Liang, Yi., Wang, H., Hong, W.-C.: Sustainable development evaluation of innovation and entrepreneurship education of clean energy major in colleges and universities based on SPA-VFS and GRNN optimized by chaos bat algorithm. Sustainability **13**(11), 5960 (2021)
6. Quan, L., Zhou, H.: Evaluation of innovation and entrepreneurship education capability in colleges and universities based on entropy TOPSIS-a case study. Kuram ve Uygulamada Egitim Bilimleri **18** (2018)
7. Franklin, S.: A computer-based model of crick and koch's framework for consciousness (2022)
8. Zheng, L.: The model of task design in computer-supported collaborative learning (2021)
9. Ren, X.: Research on development-based financial aid model for needy students in local colleges and universities. China Educ. Technol. Equipment (2017)
10. Yang, G.Y.: Exploration on the electronic and information major in local colleges and universities based on CDIO education concept. Mod. Comput. (2019)
11. Zhang, Y.: Study on the training evaluation model for first line young teachers in colleges and universities based on data mining. Boletin Tecnico/Tech. Bull. **55**(16), 650–656 (2017)
12. Hou, K.K., Tan, J.Y.: Exploration on teaching reform of ACCESS database for non-computer majors in colleges and universities. Comput. Knowl. Technol. (2018)

13. Yuan, M.A., Jiang, T., Zhong, W.: The path analysis of collaborative-innovation talent training of universities in China——based on pervasive computing and information chain theory. Sci. Technol. Manag. Res. (2016)
14. Jiansheng, W.U., Tang, X., Xie, Y.: An analysis of the construction of computer specialty groups in applied undergraduate colleges under the model of integration of labor and education and collaborative education (2019)
15. Chen, B., Wang, X.Y., Wang, Q.: Multidimensional thoughts on strengthening marxism theory education of leading cadres of colleges and universities. J. East China Univ. Technol. (Soc. Sci.) (2019)
16. Luo, Y., Zhang, G.: Research on the reform of computer public course in local undergraduate colleges and universities based on transformation and development. Wirel. Internet Technol. (2016)
17. Liu, J.F., Hou, X.C., Zhi-Jun, M.A., et al.: Research on the evaluation system of public PE teachers' teaching ability in local colleges and universities in Heilongjiang province. J. Mudanjiang Normal Univ. (Nat. Sci. Edn.) (2019)
18. Jin-Mei, L.V., Gao, S.T.: Research on the quality evaluation of innovation and entrepreneurship education in colleges and universities——based on group G1 method. J. Anhui Univ. Sci. Technol. (Soc. Sci.) (2018)
19. Hui, W.H.: Study on practice of collaborative teaching model in local colleges and universities. J. Weinan Normal Univ. (2017)
20. Liang, H.T., Fang, Z.H., Yang X.Y., et al.: Research on data service model of teaching evaluation in colleges and universities based on SOA. Comput. Eng. Softw. (2016)

Research on the Construction of E-commerce Course System Based on Computer Internet

Jun Zhang$^{(\boxtimes)}$, Libo Zhu, and Dongping Chen

Department of Economics and Management, Weifang Engineering Vocational College,
Qingzhou 262500, Shandong, China
Zhangjun.1220@163.com

Abstract. With the popularity of the Internet, E-commerce has become a part of people's life. Therefore, E-commerce has affected people's traditional way of life and work, which also requires Colleges to constantly adapt to the needs of society. Based on the current situation of computer Internet, Colleges must cultivate new E-commerce talents, which will better promote the development of E-commerce. However, there are still many problems in the current E-commerce curriculum system (hereinafter referred to as ECCS) in Colleges, such as single teaching method, weak teachers, old curriculum content, etc., which will seriously affect the cultivation of E-commerce comprehensive talents in Colleges. In order to meet the social needs, Colleges need to build ECCS, which will cultivate comprehensive quality E-commerce talents. First of all, this paper analyzes the necessity of E-commerce curriculum reform in Colleges. Then, this paper constructs the ECCS. Finally, this paper puts forward some suggestions, which can better cultivate comprehensive talents.

Keywords: Computer Internet · E-commerce Curriculum System · Construction

1 Introduction

At present, E-commerce has become the most popular industry, which requires a large number of professional talents. Therefore, Colleges must cultivate more professional talents, which will adapt to the impact of the society on various E-commerce majors [1]. Therefore, practical E-commerce talents are an important foundation for the development of E-commerce, which can be engaged in various specialties of E-commerce, such as software technical support, page beautification, negotiation and so on [2]. Therefore, Colleges must reform the curriculum, which will better meet the needs of E-commerce for all aspects of talent. At present, many Colleges have begun to highlight their traditional advantages, which will better set the integrity of E-commerce discipline. By emphasizing the practicality of the course, we can build a practice and training base [3–6]. However, some Colleges have different emphasis on curriculum and skills training, which will be difficult to form ECCS. Therefore, Colleges must build ECCS, which will better complete the E-commerce professional training [7].

Y. Zhang and N. Shah (Eds.): BigIoT-EDU 2023, LNICST 583, pp. 604–609, 2024.
https://doi.org/10.1007/978-3-031-63139-9_62

2   The Necessity of E-commerce Curriculum Reform

With the social demand for comprehensive E-commerce talents, we must constantly reform the E-commerce curriculum, which is very necessary, as shown in Fig. 1.

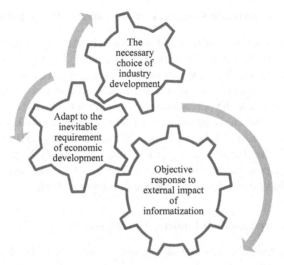

Fig. 1. The necessity of E-commerce curriculum reform.

2.1   Objective Response to External Impact of Informatization

With the capital market entering the new normal, we need to constantly improve the operation mechanism of E-commerce market. E-commerce comprehensive management has become the main trend of E-commerce development. At present, E-commerce professional education is still in the exploratory stage, and the teaching content is mainly theoretical research. With the development of E-commerce information and globalization, Colleges must reform the ECCS. By adjusting the curriculum objectives and specific content, we can reasonably position E-commerce problems and development opportunities, which need to update the teaching philosophy [8]. At present, the E-commerce market has basically realized fast payment, which can help the supply and demand sides to achieve transactions without intermediary. Colleges need to cater to the overall trend and characteristics of the development of E-commerce industry, which can guide students to pay attention to the speed of E-commerce innovation. By focusing on the development of E-commerce industry, we can enhance the research on new models such as third-party payment, P2P E-commerce and Internet E-commerce, which will break through the traditional curriculum. By increasing social practice activities, we must meet the needs of E-commerce market. Based on the development of information technology, E-commerce professional education in Colleges should develop in the direction of mobile payment, search engine, cloud computing, etc., which needs to enhance students' network information technology and data analysis ability [9].

2.2 Adapt to the Inevitable Requirement of Economic Development

E-commerce major includes macro and micro levels. At present, the ECCS major in Colleges mainly focuses on the theoretical development. The main courses still stay in the field of E-commerce policy, which is far from meeting the actual needs of market economy [10]. At present, the micro talent training mode and goal setting of some universities still continue the planned economy mode, which will be lack of perceptual knowledge and innovation. Teachers are used to learning by the book, which will restrict the enthusiasm of students. At the same time, the implementation of E-commerce courses in Colleges lacks the characteristics of the times, which needs the specific curriculum content and lacks practicality. Therefore, Colleges must reform the ECCS, which will better adapt to the requirements of economic development [11].

2.3 The Necessary Choice of Industry Development

From the perspective of macroeconomic development, affected by the downward economic growth rate, the non-performing assets of E-commerce institutions continue to increase, which will cause the business performance of E-commerce institutions to show a downward trend [12]. At present, E-commerce and third-party payment of E-commerce institutions will be gradually replaced. With the rapid development of E-commerce, Colleges must put forward higher requirements, which will meet the development of the industry, which will better meet the requirements of the job market. At present, Colleges must change the teaching concept, which will better adjust the personnel training mode. According to the changes of the industry, Colleges must adjust the internal ECCS, which will better meet the needs of the development of big data E-commerce [13]. Through various forms of development, students can create a more open E-commerce teaching environment, which will better adapt to the dynamic needs of market changes. By improving the old teaching mode, we can enrich the content of curriculum design, which will better improve the enthusiasm of students to participate in curriculum teaching [14].

3   Construction of ECCS

3.1   Scientific Establishment of Trinity ECCS

According to the different positioning of Colleges, Colleges should treat the ECCS specialty differently according to their own actual situation. According to the internal students' learning situation, students must fully understand the concerns and interests, which will build a unique and personalized development direction. Therefore, what Colleges need to emphasize is the goal of information teaching, which is the basic ability to cultivate students' all-round development. Therefore, we must have a complete

ECCS Specialty in Colleges, which will better meet the comprehensive requirements of students' knowledge, ability, technology and quality. This paper develops a trinity ECCS, as shown in Fig. 2.

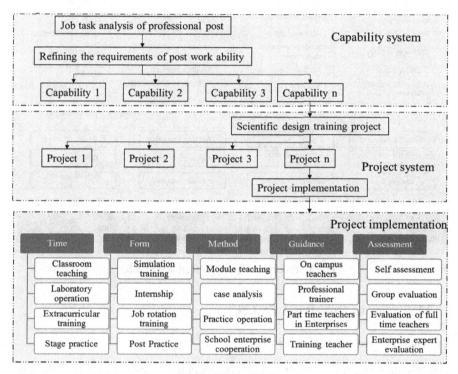

Fig. 2. Trinity ECCS.

3.2 Process Design of Professional ECCS

Systematic oriented curriculum breaks the order of subject knowledge, which solves the problem of knowledge reconstruction. According to the actual working process of the enterprise, we can sort the knowledge, which will maximize the experience. Therefore, the name of E-commerce course based on work process systematization does not point to work process, which will form a complete work process, which will better cultivate students' ability to complete the specific work process. The design process of professional ECCS is shown in Fig. 3.

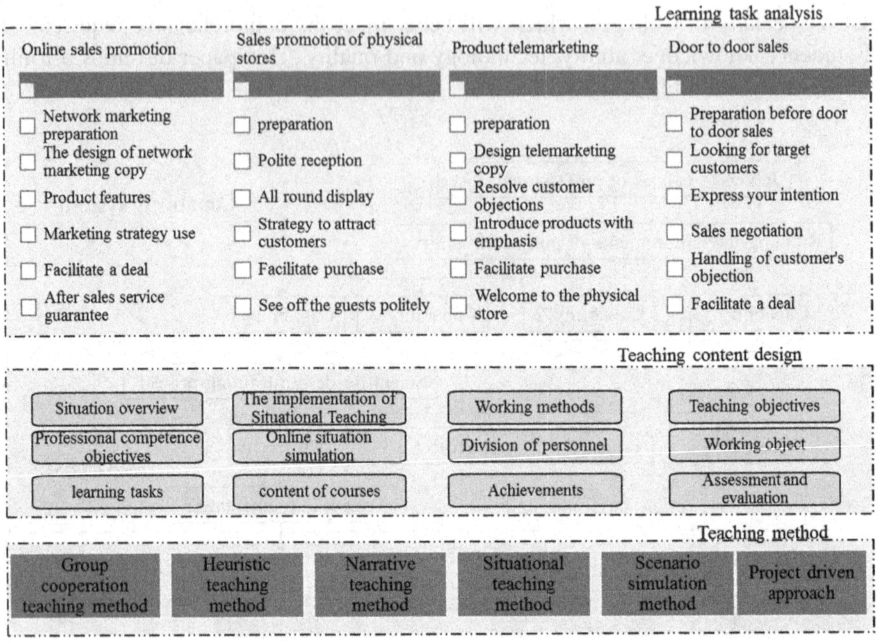

Learning task analysis

Online sales promotion	Sales promotion of physical stores	Product telemarketing	Door to door sales
☐ Network marketing preparation	☐ preparation	☐ preparation	☐ Preparation before door to door sales
☐ The design of network marketing copy	☐ Polite reception	☐ Design telemarketing copy	☐ Looking for target customers
☐ Product features	☐ All round display	☐ Resolve customer objections	☐ Express your intention
☐ Marketing strategy use	☐ Strategy to attract customers	☐ Introduce products with emphasis	☐ Sales negotiation
☐ Facilitate a deal	☐ Facilitate purchase	☐ Facilitate purchase	☐ Handling of customer's objection
☐ After sales service guarantee	☐ See off the guests politely	☐ Welcome to the physical store	☐ Facilitate a deal

Teaching content design

Situation overview	The implementation of Situational Teaching	Working methods	Teaching objectives
Professional competence objectives	Online situation simulation	Division of personnel	Working object
learning tasks	content of courses	Achievements	Assessment and evaluation

Teaching method

Group cooperation teaching method	Heuristic teaching method	Narrative teaching method	Situational teaching method	Scenario simulation method	Project driven approach

Fig. 3. Process design of professional ECCS.

4   Measures to Construct ECCS

4.1   Increase Teaching Practice

Colleges should bring E-commerce skills competition into practice teaching, which will improve students' professional skills. At the same time, Colleges should encourage students to actively participate in large-scale national professional skills competitions such as "three innovations", so that students can get the guidance of relevant teachers before leaving the school. Through teaching practice, Colleges can build a bridge between classroom knowledge and off campus practice. Through the teaching practice platform, Colleges can test the reserve of knowledge, which will improve the practical ability. By stimulating students' entrepreneurial enthusiasm, Colleges can enhance the comprehensive quality of E-commerce teachers.

4.2   Reforming Teaching Resources

Colleges must build a teaching material development team, which needs to compile characteristic teaching materials. Through the cooperation with school enterprise cooperation units, Colleges can establish the training system according to the post needs of enterprises to cultivate applied talents. Based on the social needs, we can develop the training guide book with the characteristics of E-commerce teaching materials as the leading. Through the establishment of network portal quality courses, we can share the "E-commerce" quality resources, which can be shared to the school's portal website, including syllabus, electronic courseware, knowledge question bank, computer instruction, competition notice, etc.

5 Conclusion

With the rapid development of E-commerce, Colleges must build and improve the ECCS, which will better input professionals suitable for social development. According to the actual needs of the post, Colleges can identify the talent gap in the market, which will establish a more suitable ECCS.

References

1. Cao, B., Xiang, G.: Constructing the ECCS of "theory practice integration" of cross border E-commerce in application-oriented Universities. J. Chizhou Univ. **33**(01), 148–150 (2019)
2. Xueqin, C.: Research on the construction of ECCS based on application. J. Shandong Agric. Eng. Univ. **32**(08), 37–38 (2015)
3. Peng, D., Yuyan, Z.: Research on the teaching reform of E-commerce course based on the concept of innovation and entrepreneurship plus "CDIO." J. Xingtai Univ. **35**(01), 184–187 (2020)
4. Gao, L., Tang, P., Diao, P.: Research on evaluation of ECCS construction in higher vocational colleges based on market demand. E-commerce (09), 93–94 (2020)
5. Cong, J., Chunxiao, Y., Chunying, W.: ECCS of pharmaceutical E-commerce based on modern talent training. Mod. Enterprise (04), 94–95 (2019)
6. Yang, L., Xiaoke, S.: Teaching reform of E-commerce course. J. Zhengzhou Inst. Aeronaut. Indus. Manag. (SOCIAL SCIENCE EDITION) **29**(05), 151–153 (2010)
7. Huishu, L.: E-commerce curriculum reform and practice based on "entrepreneurship and innovation" in Application-oriented Universities. J. Jilin Normal Univ. Eng. Technol. **34**(12), 43–45 (2018)
8. Ming, L., Huan, C., Xi, Y.: Research on the ECCS of cross border E-commerce Specialty under the guidance of CBE. J. Higher Educ. **14**, 10–14 (2020)
9. Wang, M.Y.: Reform of the ECCS specialty from the perspective of Internet plus. Ind. Innovation Res. (04), 69+103 (2019)
10. Ke, W.: Analysis on the reform of Higher Vocational ECCS guided by post demand. Fireworks Technol. Market **03**, 172 (2020)
11. Xingkai, Y.: Optimization and practice of ECCS. E-commerce **06**, 78–80 (2014)
12. Zhihong, Y.: Research on the construction of ECCS under the guidance of innovation and entrepreneurship. J. Wuhan Bus. Univ. **31**(02), 94–96 (2017)
13. Zhang Guangxia, X., Dong, W.Z.: Research on ECCS specialty based on working process. Bus. Econ. **04**, 118–119 (2010)
14. Zhang, J., Su, Y.: Research on the teaching reform of E-commerce course based on the cultivation of entrepreneurship and innovation ability. J. Huanggang Normal Univ. **39**(03), 124–128 (2019)

The Design and Implementation of Teaching Assistant System for Excellent Courses Based on WEB

Jie Zhang[1(✉)], Zijiang Li[1], Chengyi Niu[1], and Yang Zhang[2]

[1] Shandong Institute of Commerce and Technology, Jinan 250103, Shandong, China
191810649@163.com
[2] Lanzhou Resources and Environment Voc-Tech University, Lanzhou 730020, Gansu, China

Abstract. The construction of quality courses is the key to the reform of college education and the comprehensive embodiment of college education level, which is related to the sustainable development of colleges and universities. The online auxiliary teaching system of quality courses is an important part of the information construction of quality courses. Design and Implementation of Teaching Assistant System for Excellent Courses Based on WEB is a book that allows readers to deeply understand the design and implementation of teaching assistant system for excellent courses based on WEB. This book aims to give students a comprehensive understanding of how to design, implement and evaluate teaching assistant systems in their respective academic institutions. It also includes some practical examples to help readers understand the concepts presented in this book. The author uses real scenarios to illustrate the design, implementation and evaluation of the web-based high-quality course teaching assistance system.

Keywords: Excellent courses · WEB · Teaching assistant system

1 Introduction

The current online courses are relatively rigid. At present, in foreign countries, people are more aware of the importance of the learning environment. It is very important to create an interactive learning environment. To make the network play a role, we should not copy some things on the network, but create a virtual interactive course environment. In the current traditional learning mode, when people are learning, they can consult teachers and students, as well as go to libraries and laboratories to view various materials. If these things are put on the virtual network, the course will be boring [1]. In classroom teaching, teachers always play a vital role and face many challenges. The first is how to get students' immediate and accurate teaching feedback. Teachers can rely on a variety of information, including classroom questions, tests, student responses, and students' facial expressions, gestures, and body movements to evaluate students' learning performance. However, these information are often rough and cannot cover or track the real-time learning situation of each student. Another challenge is how to

Y. Zhang and N. Shah (Eds.): BigIoT-EDU 2023, LNICST 583, pp. 610–621, 2024.
https://doi.org/10.1007/978-3-031-63139-9_63

accurately record and model students' learning, which is crucial for assessing students' status and personalized teaching. To establish an accurate personal learning time series model, it is necessary to ensure that the whole teaching process is recorded on a purely quantitative and computable basis.

Therefore, in order to achieve the goal of personalized teaching, it is necessary to accurately and effectively track the learning situation of students' various knowledge points through student models. As the most commonly used student model, the knowledge point tracking model models the various learning behaviors of students through their historical learning tracks, so as to continuously track the students' mastery of knowledge points at various time points. However, most of the existing student models are based on flashcard learning mode. In most common teaching processes, there is a direct or indirect relationship between a series of knowledge points, which is not consistent with the situation of flashcards.

In addition, teachers often need to make teaching plans according to the given teaching objectives, including some specific objectives, such as 95% of students can pass the final exam. This means that teachers must reasonably arrange the teaching details of each class and each student group in the teaching plan. For example, teaching more basic knowledge points can help ordinary students better pass the exam, while spending more time on more difficult knowledge points is more beneficial to some excellent students. The core question is which choice is better for the improvement of the whole class, and how to reasonably arrange a large number of teaching content to achieve the predetermined teaching objectives. However, this teaching planning ability is usually difficult to master, and most teachers are used to arranging their work according to experience. Especially in the face of multiple complex teaching objectives, it is difficult to find the best teaching plan for all students.To make our interaction process manifest, we should create a teaching environment that can interact and communicate, so that everyone can not only learn individually, but also cooperate in groups to learn and communicate together, This learning environment is not only the learning of content, but also the actual operation and application. At present, in foreign countries, high-quality courses have been in the practical operation link, and the course interaction system of many websites has been implemented, and many people are using this. In many cases, the quality of the curriculum is directly related to the quality of learning [2]. The current knowledge is changing rapidly, and the number is also very large. We should not only hear the teacher's explanation in the actual learning, but also learn more application knowledge in the process of interactive fields, to mine more data information, and then sort out the data information for analysis and application, so as to create a high-tech era, It is imperative that a set of online learning courses include an interactive environment.

Some requirements have been put forward by the education department for the construction and improvement of quality courses. At the first stage, it is necessary to develop an auxiliary teaching system for teachers, students and learners. The current computer high-tech technology and network tools can be used to design a reasonable module application. This module application allows learners to conduct interactive learning anytime and anywhere, and communicate well with teachers. This system can also let teachers publish some good courses on it to meet people's learning needs [3]. Such good resources can be shared by everyone, and can form a good platform for interconnection and communication. At the same time, the auxiliary teaching system of high-quality courses also plays a key role. It can sort out these courses and subjects, manage and maintain the application of the system, which can improve the efficiency of the teaching system.

2   Related Work

2.1   Current Situation of Teaching and Research on Quality Courses

At present, the construction of high-quality courses jointly initiated by the competent education departments and colleges and universities in China has begun to take shape, gradually forming a three-level high-quality course system of "national, provincial and municipal, and school". The development level and scale of quality courses have also made some achievements, and their social influence is also increasing. With the attention and efforts of all parties, the number of high-quality courses in China is increasing (Joseph J Pearl, Darlene E Crone Todd. 2002). By the end of 2009, 3146 national excellent courses had been approved, including 2084 ordinary undergraduate courses, involving professional courses, elective courses and public courses of first, second and third level disciplines. 814 vocational and technical courses, 149 online courses, covering 13 first level disciplines, 400 national excellent undergraduate courses and 200 national excellent vocational and technical courses were reviewed in 2009, There are 50 national excellent courses of online education and 29 national excellent courses of military colleges and universities. Through the construction of national quality courses, more than 15000 provincial quality courses and more school level quality courses have been driven [4].

With the rapid development of information technology, the construction of high-quality courses has become an effective measure of educational innovation in colleges and universities, creating and providing more and more high-quality educational resources. However, as colleges and universities continue to strengthen the construction of the quality curriculum system, the number of quality curriculum systems and the number of users are also increasing. Some schools' quality curriculum systems can no longer meet the teaching needs, which has a certain impact on the construction of the quality curriculum system and its positive role, limiting the driving and demonstration of the quality curriculum. First of all, the system structure of quality courses is not perfect, systematic learning cannot be realized, and the innovation and practicality of related construction work still need to be improved; Secondly, the functional modules of the quality course system are single and unreasonable, and the system navigation design is not clear enough; Thirdly, the system mostly displays the content with static web pages, with poor interactivity; Finally, system developers only upload courses roughly, and the content logic is poor. It is difficult for students to learn systematically, teachers cannot update and manage the website in time, and managers cannot scientifically evaluate diversified high-quality course systems [5].

At present, the construction of the teaching assistant system of quality courses is still in the early stage of development and cannot completely replace the traditional classroom teaching. However, the outstanding problems exposed in the traditional course teaching, such as the backward teaching methods and technologies, have greatly affected the students' learning effect and the quality of education and teaching, and have also hit the students' enthusiasm for learning. How to integrate traditional classroom teaching and emerging network teaching on the basis of existing hardware, software and teaching resources, and innovate in teaching forms and teaching resources has become a very necessary research topic.

2.2 B/S Architecture

The software architecture depends on different databases and deployment environments. Therefore, it is necessary to define the system architecture to provide better application services. The system architecture can be roughly divided into the following stages: First, in the 1960s and 1980s, the software system in this period was mainly a centralized architecture -- mainly due to the constraints of the technology at that time. By the early 1990s, the architecture of the computer management system had also changed with the development of computer application technology. At the beginning of the 21st century, The paging architecture of C/S structure based on the application of C/S mode is gradually formed, which is mainly due to the application development of stand-alone system and local area network. Figure 1 shows the structure of software development process [6].

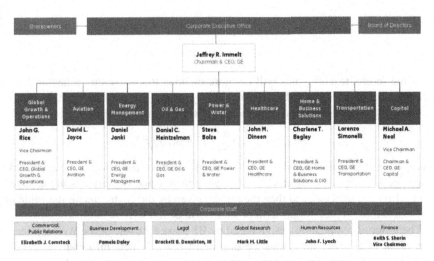

Fig. 1. B/S Software System Development Structure Chart

B/S is an expansion and development of C/S (Client/Server) application mode. It is also a product of the rapid development of Internet technology, and is the best support and guarantee for browser applications that are more popular in current applications.

The system design is based on B/S mode, which reduces the system coupling. The front end page only displays the data from the background, and the specific business logic is realized by the background processing, and is displayed to different front end pages through the same controller, so the low coupling is realized. In the front end page display, the technologies commonly used include HTML, CSS and some controls. The same is true in the implementation of this system. The front end page is implemented using JSP technology, JS technology, CSS technology and the use of some controls. After the background business logic processing, it is displayed to the front end page and presented to users [7].

The students who study well and the students who get excellent results in the exam are not completely equivalent. Because the test results will be affected by many factors, the most important of which is the test skills. The test skill set is composed of two parameters (s, g). s represents the probability that students choose the wrong answer in the test after fully mastering a knowledge point, and g represents the probability that students choose the correct answer in the test without mastering a knowledge point.

State transfer formula: The model can calculate the probability of knowledge point mastery at the next moment through the students' learning ability and the probability of knowledge point mastery at the last moment. The formula is shown in formula (1):

$$k^{t+1} = k^t + l(1 - k^t) \tag{1}$$

where, k^t represents the probability of knowledge point mastery at time t.

The probability formula of correct answer in the test: Formula (2) represents the probability that students can correctly answer the question of this knowledge point in the test:

$$C = k(1 - s) + g(1 - k) \tag{2}$$

$$W = 1 - C \tag{3}$$

In the future, teaching aids will be more inclined to choose this behavior. On the contrary, teaching aids will reduce the probability of such behavior. In MDP, the ultimate goal is to get an optimal action strategy, as shown in formula (4):

$$\pi^* = \text{argmax} \sum \gamma'' R(s_i, a_i, \pi) \tag{4}$$

where, s_i represents the state of the environment at time t; a_i Indicates the action taken by the agent when it is in state s; $R(s_i, a_i, \pi)$ indicates that strategy z is in the state s_i, when action a is selected, and then the reward given by the environment: the value of y indicates that users prefer long-term or short-term benefits.

The program application design based on BS makes the role of the Web application page of the client only limited to the display of business data information, and does not need to participate in the processing of business logic as traditional. Because the application based on B/S makes the page not directly interact with the database, it avoids the modification of page logic caused by the change of business logic, but only needs to be adjusted uniformly on the server side, Furthermore, the design goal of high cohesion and low coupling in program development is realized [8].

3   Demand Analysis of Quality Course Teaching Assistance System

In the existing research, there is no mature system to help support the offline teaching activities of the whole class. Considering the good performance of intelligent assistants in online learning websites, it is very meaningful to integrate such intelligent assistants into offline teaching [9]. By implementing a system with intelligent teaching auxiliary function, teachers' teaching and students' learning can be observed and recorded in a fine-grained manner. Personalized teaching is supported by accurate student models, students can easily understand their learning status, and teachers can get teaching plans optimized by multiple objectives and factors.

Based on the above objectives, the system functional requirements are shown in Fig. 2, including the system management function module, the course data management function module, the classroom service function module, the examination service function module, the student model function module and the recommendation function module, in order to achieve the management of the access users and the relevant data involved in the course, the collection and provision of classroom interaction information and examination information [10]. The construction and updating of student models and the recommendation of student learning and teacher teaching.

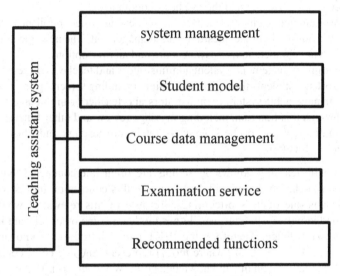

Fig. 2. System function module diagram

Functional requirements refer to the functions or services to be realized by users using the system. The main functions of the system are:

(1) Account management: the administrator configures the basic information of system users, including exam settings, teacher account settings, etc. Teachers log in to the system teacher management background through the account and password assigned by the administrator to view personal information and update and modify personal information [11]. At the same time, teachers can add and delete student accounts and passwords in batches through the system or import student accounts and passwords in batches through the database; Students log in to the student management background through the teacher's pre assigned account to view their personal information, and can update and modify their personal information;

(2) System settings: administrators can initialize system parameters through system parameter settings, including initial system password, total exam score, exam time and other initial system information.

(3) Data management: teachers add, modify and delete learning materials; Students can use this function to learn online the learning materials uploaded by teachers.

(4) Homework management: Teachers can assign homework to students through the system's homework management module, or use the system to grade and write comments on the homework submitted by students. After students submit their homework, teachers can make corrections in the background of the system. If students' homework scores exceed 80, they will be rated as excellent homework. Students can use the system to obtain the homework assigned by the teacher, or they can query the specified homework by the homework name; At the same time, you can also use the system background to submit jobs [12]. If the jobs have been received or expired, they cannot be submitted. Students check the grades of the homework that the teacher has corrected and the teacher's comments.

(5) Question bank management: teachers can set new, modified, published, deleted and invalidated questions in the question bank management. The new questions include question type, number, stem, answer, score and answer options.

(6) Work sharing management: system administrators and teachers can review the published works of students through this function, including screening and cancellation.

(7) Forum management: system administrators and teachers can manage forum messages through this function, including message review and other functions.

(8) Test parameter setting: teachers can set the total score, test time and other information through this function.

In systematic learning, knowledge points are often interconnected, but the BKT model ignores such correlation and does not take this connection into account in the model, which is one of its shortcomings. Because of this relevance, when learning some knowledge points, students usually need to learn some other relevant knowledge points as pre-knowledge. Therefore, the IBKT model introduces a knowledge point association matrix $m(i, j) \in M$, where $m(i, j)$ represents the degree of dependence of the i-th knowledge point on the jth knowledge point. When $m(i, j)$ is 0, it means that the two knowledge points are completely unrelated. When $m(i, j)$ is 1, it means that learning the jth knowledge point is the necessary prerequisite for learning the i-th knowledge point and has the strongest dependence.

The model sets an initial learning ability l, which represents the efficiency of learning the ith knowledge point without being affected by any pre-knowledge point, that is, $m(i, j)$ is O Or the knowledge point j has fully mastered [13]. This initial learning ability only depends on one's intellectual conditions and learning habits. After considering the relevance of knowledge points, the model uses i to express the real learning efficiency of the ith knowledge point. The formula is shown in formula (5):

$$\tilde{l}_i = l_i \Pi_{j=1}^{j-1}[1 - m(i, j) \cdot (1 - k_j)] \tag{5}$$

In the formula, the model only calculates the impact of the first knowledge point to the i-1 knowledge point on the knowledge point i. This is because the order of the knowledge points in the system corresponds to the learning order of the knowledge points in the curriculum plan, so the subsequent knowledge points will not be used as the pre-knowledge points of the i-th knowledge point.

$$k_i^{t+1} = k_i^t + \left(1 - k_i^t\right)\tilde{l}_i \cdot h \tag{6}$$

In the formula, t represents the current time at k_i^t represents the student's mastery of the ith knowledge point at time t; H refers to the class hours occupied by the learning duration of this knowledge point from the last learning to the present. Usually, a class hour is set as 15 min [14].

After modeling the students, the system can predict the progress he/she can make after a certain teaching activity and the results he/she can achieve in the exam based on the model according to the knowledge points and learning ability of all students. Based on this, the system can formulate more reasonable learning or teaching plans for students or teachers according to teaching objectives, so as to better improve the overall teaching performance of each student and class.

4 Design of Teaching Assistant System for High-Quality Courses Based on WEB

4.1 System Architecture Design

At present, there are various technologies for developing websites, such as use Net, asp, php, java, CH, etc. Conceptually, Design pattern is to systematically write, classify and summarize according to the most reasonable pattern. The purpose of its use includes providing code, designing modules, upgrading system functions, etc. From this point of view, designers should base code preparation on the most basic use functions. To realize engineering design, it is necessary to establish an effective structure of software projects.

The system implements the J2EE based business relationship according to the three-tier B/S system. When the current platform, the middle platform and the background need to be discussed separately, the data is analyzed according to the logical relationship in the program. When the system is revised or upgraded, the protection layer is vulnerable, and many software and structures are vulnerable to attacks [15]. The existence of a three-tier protection structure can not only improve stability and security, but also reduce maintenance and upgrade costs. The overall structure of the system is shown in Fig. 3.

4.2 System Development Environment

Before the implementation, installation and debugging of the system, first prepare the platform environment of the system, mainly for the configuration of the server side and the client side:

(1) Server configuration:
   Hardware configuration: CPU: Core i5 5200U; Memory: 16G; Hard disk: 500G
   Software configuration: Windows 7 Professional; MYSQL2008;

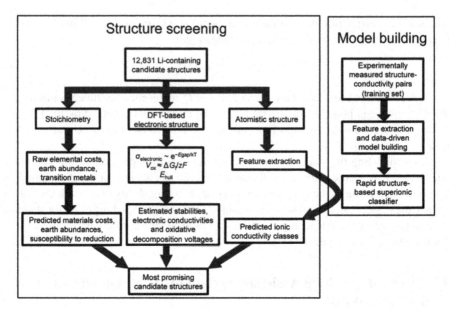

Fig. 3. Overall Structure Diagram of the Teaching System of Excellent Courses

(2) Client configuration:

Hardware configuration: CPU: Core i55200U; Memory: 4G; Hard disk: 500G Software configuration: Windows 7 Professional; IE9.0; Word, Excel, etc. Then, detailed arrangements are made for the preparation of the participants, mainly for the staffing of the system commissioning and official launch.

Finally, in order to ensure the trial operation and online work of the system, the training of relevant personnel was also carried out. For the end users of the system, the training shall be carried out in stages and [16]. From the pilot stage to the trial operation stage, and then to the final official launch stage, comprehensive training will be conducted in batches for users who use the system at each stage. In order to make the training work achieve the best effect, the project team has made the training plan in advance, and has modified and improved the training courseware for many times. Through on-site explanation and computer operation, users can master the use and operation of the system more quickly and easily.

The system is implemented under the Web environment and based on the BS structure. The client can be accessed as long as I browser is installed. The system interface design is friendly [17]. The web page is implemented by JSP. The database is MYSQL. The system selects Tomcat 6.0 server.

4.3 System Database Simulation Analysis

When implementing data storage and management through database technology, data is directly stored in the database. If the operator wants to obtain relevant data information, he must extract data from the database through relevant operation methods. If the amount of data is large, the query speed of data will be very slow. In order to improve the speed of data extraction, it is a good solution to establish a cache mechanism. Extract the frequently used data into the cache [18]. If the user extracts the same data again, it will be directly extracted from the cache and no database operation will be performed. Since the query of the cache is much faster than the query of the database, the establishment of the cache mechanism will improve the response time of the data operation and greatly improve the user's experience. If the amount of data in the database is large and the amount of data that users need to operate the database is large, it is inconvenient to archive [19]. To solve this problem, creating indexes is a good solution. Create indexes in key fields to improve the speed of data operation and enhance the user's experience. Data simulation is shown in Fig. 4 below.

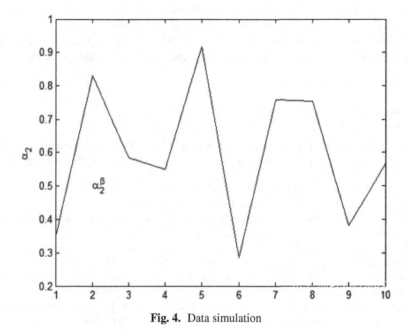

Fig. 4. Data simulation

The algorithm also binds the sum value of students' feedback with the length of time without learning to strengthen the association, and sets a vector of length m to replace the original length of time without learning. In this vector, only the index bit data corresponding to the sum value of student feedback is set to log (delay + 1), and the rest positions are 0. After processing the data, the complete input of the neural network is the processed knowledge points, the processed non-learning time, the current time and student feedback [20].

Through such processing, the neural network can deal with the high complexity problems caused by the observation space of the whole class, and achieve a good training effect in the recommendation of teachers' teaching knowledge points.

5   Conclusion

The online assistant teaching system of quality courses is related to the process of information construction in colleges and universities. Only through the network can quality courses be rapidly disseminated. Based on the actual needs of quality courses, this paper designs and implements the online auxiliary teaching system of quality courses, and develops the system using the object-oriented thinking, which builds a platform for the teaching management and communication between teachers and students. With the development of the Internet, there are more and more data in the web-based quality courses aided teaching management system, which brings difficulties to the teaching of quality courses. How to manage the online aided teaching of quality courses is the focus of attention. This paper designs and implements a web-based quality course aided teaching system. First, it investigates the requirements of the system. On the basis of the requirements, it designs and implements the system, including system outline design, detailed design, and database design. Finally, it tests the system. The test results show that each functional module of the system operates stably and achieves the established goal.

References

1. Wang, M., Li, J., Jia, Q., et al.: Design and implementation of an assistant teaching system for english creative writing based on dynamic reference recommendation. Comput. Appl. Softw. (2019)
2. Li, W.: Design and implementation of music teaching assistant platform based on Internet of Things. Trans. Emerg. Telecommun. T echnol. **30**(9), e3606 (2019)
3. Yang, L.: Design and implementation of the teaching assistant system in the digital music classroom. Agro Food Indus. Hi Tech **28**(1), 2705–2708 (2017)
4. Design and Implementation of Solfeggio and Ear Training Learning Assistant System Based on Computer Cat Technology. J. Phys. Conf. Ser. **1881**(2), 022034 (2021)
5. Muhammad, E.A.: The implementation of the Fulbright English teaching assistant program in Malaysia: An evaluation on students' language proficiency (2017)
6. Flaherty, A., O'Dwyer, A., Mannix-McNamara, P., Leahy, J.J.: Evaluating the impact of the "teaching as a chemistry laboratory graduate teaching assistant" program on cognitive and psychomotor verbal interactions in the laboratory. J. Chem. Educ. **94**(12), 1831–1843 (2017)
7. Liu, Z.: Research and Implementation of Digital Art Media System Based on Big Data Aesthetics (2022)
8. Ferrante, C.A.: An insight into a whole school experience: the implementation of teaching teams to support learning and teaching. Athens J. Educ. **4**(4), 339–350 (2017)
9. Patel, S.J., Cafferty, P., Klein, M., et al.: Nutrition and preventative medicine across the lifespan: implementation of a physician assistant team-based learning curriculum on pediatric preventative medicine. J. Phys. Assistant Educ. **31**(4), 198–203 (2020)
10. Jia, T.-J., Yang, et al.: Design and Implementation of Cloud Crypto Secure Server System for Power System Based on Sharing Encryption Resource (2018)
11. Ali, S.: Design and Implementation of Web-Based Distance Learning System for Computer Architecture Subject (2021)
12. Wei, D., Yu, W., et al.: Design and implementation of gasifier flame detection system based on SCNN. **28**(4), 10 (2022)

13. Lv, Z., Zhang, C., et al.: Design and implementation of an eye gesture perception system based on electrooculography. Expert Syst. Appl. **91**, 310–321 (2018)
14. Cao, Y.H.: Design and implementation of LP model standardization teaching assistant software. Comput. Knowl. Technol. (2018)
15. Xie, X.J., Xiang-Ju, L.I., Cao, F.P., et al.: Research and Implementation of E-learning Teaching Assistant System Based on Improving C4.5. J. Jiamusi Univ. (Natural Science Edition) (2018)
16. Yueming, L.I., Zheng, G., Che, Y., et al.: Design and implementation of emergency traffic management system based on WebGIS. J. Mil. Transp. Univ. (2016)
17. Rong, M.: Design and implementation of top-quality course website system based on SaaS. Electron. Des. Eng. (2018)
18. Qi, S., Li, S., Zhang, J.: Designing a teaching assistant system for physical education using web technology. Mob. Inf. Syst. **2021**(6), 1–11 (2021)
19. Gang, C.: Design and implementation of network teaching system based on android platform. China Comput. Commun. (2017)
20. Liu, X., Zhang, W., Polytechnic, C.: Design and implementation of data visualization teaching system based on Web technology. Electron. Des. Eng. (2019)

Research on the Construction
of Computer-Aided Dynamic Simulation Model
# of Labor Education Evaluation in Local
Colleges and Universities

Lin Lin[1]([✉]), Jia Lu[2], and Minjia Liu[3]

[1] Harbin Normal University, Harbin 150000, China
linlin3273@163.com
[2] Wuhan University of Engineering Science, Wuhan 430060, China
[3] Shanghai University of Electric Power, Shanghai 201306, China

Abstract. Labor education in local universities is one of the important activities for students on campus, and evaluating the quality and level of labor education in local universities is of great significance. However, traditional evaluation methods have problems such as incomplete evaluation items and non real-time evaluation results, which cannot comprehensively and accurately reflect the actual situation. Therefore, this article proposes a computer-aided dynamic simulation model construction method that utilizes the dynamic simulation technology of the model to evaluate labor education in local universities.

In this article, we first reviewed and analyzed existing evaluation methods, and proposed improvement ideas for their existing problems. Secondly, we utilized the ideas of system dynamics to construct an evaluation model for labor education in local universities, and trained the model using multi-layer neural network algorithms. Finally, we used dynamic simulation technology to simulate and implement the model, and obtained dynamic results of labor education evaluation.

The research results of this article indicate that the evaluation method for labor education in local universities based on computer-aided dynamic simulation models can effectively evaluate the quality and level of labor education. This method has the advantages of comprehensive evaluation items, real-time evaluation results, and visualization, which can help school managers better understand the operation of labor education and adjust and improve labor education plans in a timely manner. This is of great significance for improving the level of labor education in schools and creating an excellent learning environment.

Keywords: Labor education · computer-aided · Simulation model · Local universities · Educational evaluation

1 Introduction

The moral and quality education of local university students is one of the hot topics in current education reform. Especially in recent years, "labor education" has become an indispensable part of local universities. By giving students the opportunity to participate

Y. Zhang and N. Shah (Eds.): BigIoT-EDU 2023, LNICST 583, pp. 622–632, 2024.
https://doi.org/10.1007/978-3-031-63139-9_64

in various labor and practical activities, they can improve their practical abilities, exercise their willpower, and better adapt to social changes. However, how to scientifically and accurately evaluate the use of labor education to promote students' quality improvement in local universities is a challenge that local universities face. The traditional evaluation of labor education in local universities is mainly conducted through questionnaires, surveys, organizational research, inspections, and other methods. Although this method can grasp a certain situation, problems such as incomplete evaluation content, long evaluation cycle, and non real-time evaluation results have hindered the development of labor education in local universities. Therefore, it is particularly important and necessary to use computer-aided dynamic simulation models to construct evaluation methods for labor education in local universities.

The design and implementation of labor education evaluation methods for local universities need to consider the following aspects: on the one hand, the evaluation method needs to take into account the characteristics of local universities themselves, combined with the educational goals, student characteristics, educational resources and other factors of local universities [1]. On the other hand, the evaluation method should also take into account the current trend of rapid technological development and use advanced computer technology to assist in evaluation and simulation. To address the above issues, this article explores the use of computer-aided dynamic simulation models to construct a method for evaluating labor education in local universities. Specifically, the research content of this article mainly includes the following steps:

Firstly, we analyze the current problems in the evaluation of labor education in local universities from the perspectives of evaluation and methodology, in order to clarify the theoretical basis for constructing an evaluation model. Secondly, we apply the concept of system dynamics to construct a dynamic model for the evaluation of labor education in local universities. This model not only considers the impact of labor education on students, but also models the entire educational environment. It also includes multiple aspects such as the goals of labor education, curriculum design, and teacher-student interaction, more comprehensively reflecting the situation of labor education in local universities [2]. Then, we train the model using techniques such as artificial neural networks to optimize the model parameters and improve the simulation accuracy of the model. Next, we used computer simulation technology to dynamically simulate the evaluation of labor education in local universities based on the constructed model, and analyzed the simulation results. Finally, we improved and optimized the evaluation method of labor education in local universities by combining model parameters and simulation analysis results.

In summary, this study aims to explore how to construct a local university labor education evaluation model through computer-aided dynamic simulation models. By constructing appropriate models, conducting comprehensive data analysis and design, supplemented by technical means, the evaluation results can be more accurate and persuasive. In addition, this method can also help universities to, Lack of labor teachers, sites and funds; Take labor as a means of punishing students; Only physical labor without ideological education is common [3]. From the perspective of family, the number of only children is huge, and parents often only care about and require their children's academic performance, not only do not require their children to engage in domestic work, but also do all the major and minor things. From a social perspective, the idea of getting something for nothing and "looking at money" has spread, and it is common to despise labor and workers. The mismatch between the specific requirements of enterprises for talents and the training objectives of colleges and universities for college students has become increasingly prominent [4]. Therefore, it is urgent to carry out labor education for college students and improve their labor quality. This paper studies the construction of computer-aided dynamic simulation model of labor education evaluation in local colleges and universities.

2 Related Work

2.1 Labor Education

The dictionary of Encyclopedia of literature, history and philosophy and the dictionary of education define labor as "the use and consumption of labor", including mental labor in addition to physical labor. Marx, Deng Xianhong, Fu Junsheng and Mao Liyan believed that labor is the medium of material exchange and transformation between human beings and nature, the process of interaction between human beings and nature, and also a unique activity of human beings. In this practice process, people use labor tools and natural resources to purposefully transform the objective world according to their own needs, which not only creates material and spiritual wealth, promotes social progress, but also promotes the all-round development of human beings [5].

The content of labor education, and clearly point out the need to cultivate educatees to love labor and working people. Cihai and Encyclopedia of teachers also specifically point out the need to cherish and love the fruits of labor. In addition to the Encyclopedia of China education, other dictionaries which can promote students to continuously exercise their hands and brains creatively, which will cultivate many new people of the times and provide talent reserves for the realization of an innovative country. Feng Gang and Liu Wenbo (2019) stressed that carrying out labor education in the new era can train workers to have innovative ways of thinking, professional technology and rich scientific knowledge, not only inject fresh blood into social and economic development.

2.2 The Important Position and Significance of Labor Education in Talent Training in Colleges and Universities

Human beings are created by labor, and the history of human evolution is a history of labor development. It can be said that since the emergence of human beings on the earth, the first historical activity is labor, because labor has gradually multiplied and created human civilization [6]. The so-called labor here is labor in a broad sense, that is, the general designation of human practical activities to understand and transform the world.

The fundamental purpose of running schools is to cultivate comprehensively developed socialist builders and successors. Marxist labor view points out that in the period of rapid development of socialized industry, if we want to make the talents trained by education meet the requirements of social production progress, we can only achieve it by combining education and productive labor, that is, carrying out labor view education.

This labor concept education method can make students familiar with every link of the production mode and production system quickly, which not only meets the needs of talents for the development of socialized industry, but also provides practical skilled talents to the society;

With the rapid development of society, the demand and requirements for talent in enterprises have become increasingly high. As a place for cultivating talents, universities have a very important component in talent cultivation - labor education. Labor education is an educational method used to popularize the awareness of labor education among students and promote their comprehensive development [7]. The importance of labor education in talent cultivation in universities cannot be ignored.

Firstly, labor education is an important way to cultivate students' innovative awareness. In labor education, students need to participate in various practices or labor, which can promote students to establish correct labor and values, further enhance their innovation awareness, cultivate innovative talents, and make contributions to social and economic development.

Secondly, labor education can improve students' vocational skills. Nowadays, professional skills in various industries are upgrading towards the demand side, and the occupational requirements for talents are also constantly increasing. In labor education, students have the opportunity to learn various vocational skills and accumulate relevant experience, which can directly improve their employment competitiveness.

Once again, labor education can promote students' self-development and cultivate their vitality and courage. In labor education, students tap into their own potential and strengths, explore and innovate through continuous practice, continuously improve their vitality and courage, and face broader life challenges.

Finally, labor education helps to enhance students' sense of social responsibility. In labor education, students need to take the initiative to take on work, learn to collaborate effectively with teams, manage time, identify risks, etc., which can make students think about the direction of talent growth, improve their sense of social responsibility, and promote social development [8].

In short, the position and significance of labor education in talent cultivation in universities are extremely important. The importance of labor education is reflected in helping students establish correct labor concepts and values, improving their vocational skills, promoting their self-development, and enhancing their sense of social responsibility [9, 10]. Therefore, universities should pay attention to the teaching and management of labor education, provide students with a better labor education environment and opportunities, and fully play the important role of labor education in talent cultivation in universities.

3 Current Situation of Labor Education Evaluation in Local Colleges and Universities

3.1 Investigation on the Current Situation of Labor Education in Colleges and Universities

In order to understand the current situation of labor education in universities, we conducted a questionnaire survey and collected a total of 200 valid questionnaires. The questionnaire includes multiple aspects such as the implementation of labor education, student participation, teacher management methods, and students' perception of the significance of labor education. The survey results are as follows:

1. Implementation of labor education

94.5% of universities have established labor education courses or related practical activities, including social practice, technological innovation, volunteer services, and campus gardening projects. In addition, 5.5% of universities have not set up related activities.

2. Student engagement level

Among the students participating in practical activities, 42.5% of them believe that they have fully participated in the activities, while 18% of students believe that they have not fully participated in the activities, especially in social practice projects such as volunteer services. In addition, 39.5% of students have not expressed their level of participation.

3. Teacher management methods

When students participate in practical activities, 46.5% of the activities are led or managed by teachers, 22% of the activities are independently organized and managed by students, 21.5% of the activities are led by professional teachers, and 10% of the activities are handled by professional institutions outside of school.

4. The significance of labor education perceived by students

In the eyes of students, the significance of labor education is mainly reflected in the following aspects: cultivating students' abilities and qualities (47.5%), helping students understand society (19%), promoting students' communication (15.5%), and increasing students' practical experience (11%).

The survey results show that most universities offer labor education courses or practical activities, but there are still some students who believe they have not fully participated. There are various ways of managing teachers, but they are mainly led or assisted by teachers, and there is a relative lack of student autonomy in management. Therefore, it is necessary to strengthen student participation. In addition, students have a relatively clear understanding of the significance of labor education, but their expressions are slightly singular. According to the survey results, further improvement and enhancement of the quality and level of labor education in universities should focus on increasing students' participation, emphasizing their subjectivity, and strengthening their independent management and practical abilities.

3.2 Research Results

About 78.67% of the students think that there are some problems in the current social concept of labor (the data result has two decimal places, and the method of rounding is adopted), 18% of the students hold a negative attitude to this view, and another 3.33% of the students say that they have "never cared" about this problem, which indicates that many college students and have begun to think about it. At the same time, 98.7% believed that labor education was "helpful" to their own growth and development; The proportion of labor education organized by "very willing to participate", "willing to participate", "can participate or not participate", "unwilling to participate" and "very unwilling to

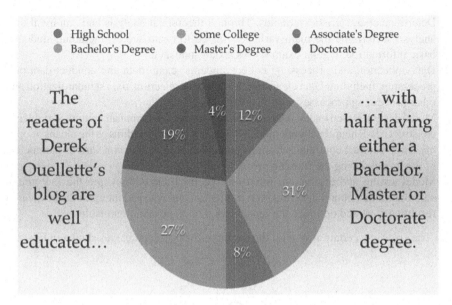

Fig. 1. Survey results

participate" schools is 82.67%, 14%, 2.67%, 0.67% and 0 respectively, which indicates that the majority of students are still very supportive, as shown in Fig. 1.

In response to the question "whether your school has opened labor education related courses or explicitly included labor education in the training plan", the results of the teacher questionnaire and the student questionnaire are that 10.37% and 11.33% or have no clear labor education implementation plan, respectively. "Yes, but imperfect" accounts for 51.89% and 54% respectively, and the results of the two groups of data are relatively consistent, It has high reference value. Carry out relevant activities in one of the four years of University. In the question of "how to arrange the class hours during the period when your school offers labor education courses", the proportion of "1–2 times a week" is only 13.68%, and the proportion of "1–2 times a month" is 22.11%, "1–2 times per semester" is 21.05%, and "1–2 times per academic year" is 7.37%, and the rest is "carried out irregularly" It shows that more than half of the schools have a perfunctory attitude towards labor education, and the frequency of activities is not high, which cannot guarantee a certain amount of class hours.

3.3 Dynamic Simulation Model of Labor Education Evaluation Status

B-P neural network is a commonly used neural network model that can generate effective models for prediction and decision-making through learning and training existing data.

When designing a comprehensive evaluation model for exam scores, B-P neural network technology can be used to select input and output settings based on the selected feature variables, and then use existing exam score data for training and optimization.

Specifically, a comprehensive evaluation model for exam scores can be established through the following steps:

1. Determine characteristic variables: Through theoretical analysis and empirical data analysis, determine the main variables related to exam scores, including students' basic information, regular exam scores, exam status, etc.
2. Data collection and processing: collect students' exam data and conduct data pre-processing, including Data cleansing, feature data selection, data standardization and other processing processes.
3. Model design: Based on the selected feature variables, set input and output variables to construct a B-P neural network model. Select learning algorithms as the means of optimization, conduct continuous training and debugging, and obtain various parameters of the model during the training process.
4. Model testing and evaluation: Input the specified test dataset into the B-P neural network model, obtain the evaluation results, and analyze and interpret the evaluation results. Adjust and optimize the model based on the evaluation results.

The error in a certain way until the system error is acceptable, as shown in Fig. 2.

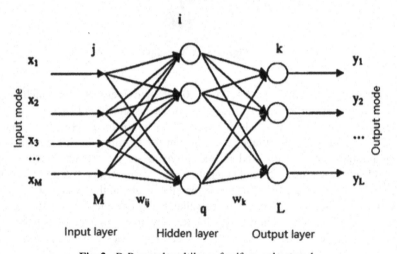

Fig. 2. B-P neural multilayer feedforward network

The ultimate goal of our comprehensive evaluation of students' grades is to get a quantitative value that can accurately and objectively reflect students' learning level, that is, evaluation value.

$$E(w, b) = \sum_{j=0}^{n-1} (d_j - y_j)^2 \tag{1}$$

Secondly, carry out simulation experiments. Open the course evaluation simulation model kc that has been successfully established in Chapter 5_ Pinjia.mdl, input the data of sample 1 through input1, conduct the simulation experiment, and get the simulation output value oUT of sample 1 in the Workspace interface_ Data. Use the same method to calculate other sample data through simulation.

Finally, the simulation results are analyzed. This course has 10 valid samples, each of which has an output value, and the grade is marked according to the actual application of the evaluation example of the higher vocational college in which the graduate student belongs. Through the comparative analysis of the two programs, the final evaluation grade of this course is obtained.

Each time a student completes an examination of a labor education course, he/she will receive the first class of evaluation points obtained by the student through the labor education course. The first class of evaluation points will be obtained according to the credits of the education course and the examination results; Each time a student completes a personal labor practice activity, he/she will get the second type of evaluation points obtained by the student through the personal labor practice activity. The second type of evaluation points will be obtained according to the working hours of the labor practice activity and the completion score. Each time the student completes a labor practice activity, the teacher will give a score; Each time a student participates in and completes a collective labor practice activity, he/she will receive the third type of evaluation points obtained by the said student through the said collective labor practice activity. The third type of evaluation points will be obtained according to the working hours of the collective labor practice activity, the completion score of the collective labor practice activity, and the comprehensive score of the said student. Each time a student completes a collective labor practice activity, a teacher will score the local task and the collective task; At the end of each semester, when it is necessary to obtain the student's labor education evaluation score, enter the student's labor education evaluation instruction, which contains the student's name, student number and other information, and retrieve all the first class evaluation score, second class evaluation score and third class evaluation score of the student in this semester. In the implementation of the invention, the first class evaluation score The type of evaluation score are input into the evaluation model, and the student's labor education evaluation score is automatically output. The algorithm of the evaluation model is: labor education evaluation score = K1 * and the first type of evaluation score + K2 * (and the second type of evaluation score + the second and third type of evaluation score), where K1 represents the proportion coefficient of theoretical education, K2 represents the proportion coefficient of practical education, and the specific values of K1 and K2 are set by the efficient according to the needs, so, The implementation example of the invention can comprehensively score students' labor education according to the labor education course examination, individual labor practice activities and collective labor practice activities that students participate in, and the evaluation method is efficient and accurate.

4 Simulation Results and Analysis

This article uses a computer-aided dynamic simulation model to construct an evaluation model for labor education in local universities. Through optimization of model parameters and dynamic simulation analysis, it aims to evaluate and improve the quality and level of labor education in local universities. Below will be a detailed introduction to the specific process and result analysis of the research experiment.

Experimental process:

1. Data collection

Firstly, before conducting the experiment, we collected data on the implementation of labor education in local universities, mainly including data on curriculum design, number of participants, teacher resources, and practical activities. Through data collection and induction, we have obtained a dataset that can be used to construct the model.

2. Build an evaluation model

Based on the dataset, we adopt the idea of system dynamics to construct a dynamic model for the evaluation of labor education in local universities. This model includes various influencing factors of labor education, such as educational objectives, curriculum design, and teacher-student interaction, fully reflecting the actual situation of labor education.

3. Training model parameters

Next, we use techniques such as artificial neural networks to train the evaluation model, in order to optimize the model parameters and improve the simulation accuracy of the model. During the training process, we used a large number of datasets to optimize and train the model parameters.

4. Conduct dynamic simulation experiments

After optimizing and training the model parameters, we used computer simulation technology to evaluate labor education in local universities based on the constructed evaluation model. In the simulation experiment, we simulated labor education activities in different scenarios, evaluated their quality and level through experiments, and analyzed the simulation results. The simulation results are shown in Fig. 3.

Experimental results and analysis:

Through experimental simulation, we obtained real-time dynamic results of various variables, such as student participation and students' understanding of labor education. The experimental results indicate that through dynamic simulation technology, the quality and level of labor education in local universities can be comprehensively evaluated, and improved and optimized in the simulation.

Specifically, through dynamic simulation, we can dynamically analyze each variable, identify problems, and improve them to improve the actual effectiveness of labor education. For example, in situations where students' participation is low, we can adjust teaching methods appropriately or strengthen on-site labor education to increase students' participation. For students with a relatively limited understanding of the significance of labor education, it is possible to strengthen their awareness and promotion of labor education, and participate in more targeted and extensive educational activities. In summary, through the results of simulation experiments, we can discover the importance of labor education in talent cultivation in universities and explore a scientific and accurate evaluation method.

In addition, we also used system dynamics thinking to simulate and analyze the impact of labor education on students' self-development, vocational skill enhancement, and other aspects. The experimental results indicate that labor education can promote students' self-development and enhance vocational skills, which are all very important parts of talent cultivation in universities. At the same time, if the educational environment

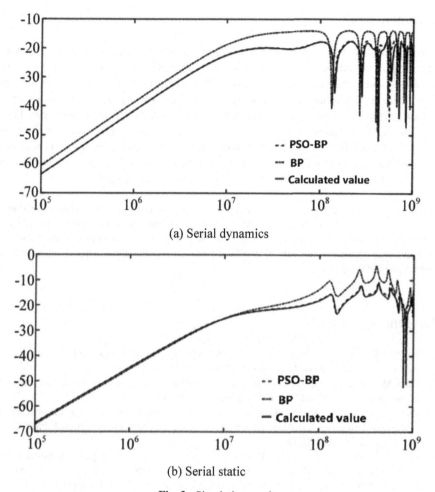

(a) Serial dynamics

(b) Serial static

Fig. 3. Simulation result

and teacher-student interaction are not effectively implemented and improved, it will also have a negative impact on the actual effectiveness of labor education.

In summary, through the construction and experimental analysis of computer-aided dynamic simulation models, we can comprehensively and scientifically evaluate the quality and level of labor education in local universities, and improve and optimize them in the simulation. At the same time, we can also have a deeper understanding of the importance of labor education in talent cultivation in universities, providing valuable reference opinions for educational reform.

5 Conclusion

Labor education involves all aspects of College Students' growth and success. It is not a "monologue" of colleges and universities, but requires the joint commitment and efforts of colleges and universities, families and society, and strive to build a "Trinity" collaborative education mechanism of colleges, families and society, and establish a correct outlook on job selection, labor and social responsibility by allowing, voluntary labor and professional experience in communities, enterprises and rural areas. For example, during the COVID-19, the deeds of Wuhan community volunteers are vivid teaching materials for social labor education. Through these measures, colleges and universities can realize the "one body and two wings" labor education linkage.

Acknowledgements. Research on the collaborative evaluation mechanism of labor education in Colleges and universities in Heilongjiang Province under the background of artificial intelligence (21EDC193); Construction and test of labor education evaluation index system of local colleges and universities driven by the data of excellent youth project of central support fund for local colleges and Universities.

References

1. Ye, M.: Research on computer BIM technology in whole process dynamic control of construction cost. J. Phys. Conf. Ser. **1915**(3), 032079 (2021)
2. Feng, M.: Research on the construction of student ability evaluation system based on computer application. J. Phys. Conf. Ser. **1915**(2), 022037 (2021)
3. Zhao, J., Ying, F.: Research on the construction of virtual simulation experiment teaching center based on computer-aided civil engineering in colleges and universities. J. Phys. Conf. Ser. **1744**(3), 032115 (2021)
4. Lei, S., Gu, Z., Cui, Y., Tang, H.: Research on the construction of the quality maturity evaluation in the product R&D phase. In: Salvendy, G., Wei, J. (eds.) Design, Operation and Evaluation of Mobile Communications. HCII 2022. LNCS, vol. 13337. Springer, Cham (2022). https://doi.org/10.1007/978-3-031-05014-5_12
5. Lanchun, L., Wei, C., Kaimo, G., et al.: Research on the evaluation system construction of county innovation driven development-based on evaluation and measurement model (2022)
6. Pan, L., Sun, J., Zhou, R.: Research on the Construction of Age-Friendly Community Based on Fuzzy Comprehensive Evaluation Model: Evidence from Community in Hefei of China. Dove Press (2021)
7. Yin, H., Wu, H., Tsai, S.B.: Innovative research on the construction of learner's emotional cognitive model in e-learning by big data analysis. Math. Probl. Eng. **2021** (2021)
8. Gao, K.: Research on the Construction of Internet + Educational Simulation English Education Platform under Modern Education Technology (2021)
9. Zheng, C.: Complex network propagation effect based on SIRS model and research on the necessity of smart city credit system construction. AEJ - Alexandria Eng. J. **61**(1), 403–418 (2021)
10. Tang, M., Gui, Y., Liu, H.: Research on the construction of nurses' core competence knowledge network based on computer mind mapping. J. Phys. Conf. Ser. **1992**(3), 032027 (2021)

Research on the Innovation of College Education Model Based on the Perspective of Scientific Research in the Era of Financial Media

Minjia Liu[✉]

Shanghai University of Electric Power, Shanghai 201306, China
mingal@shiep.edu.cn

Abstract. The innovation of higher education model based on scientific research in the era of media integration is a new form of higher education development and operation. From this point of view, it can be said that this model has been applied to many universities around the world. The transformation from traditional university system to innovative university system is an important goal of many countries. For the first time, I think we should pay attention to the following aspects: 1. The education system should meet people's needs; 2. The education system must be able to provide comprehensive and reliable information; 3. The education system should have a good level of scientific research; 4. For students' initiative, the education system should have enough freedom and flexibility in managing resources and personnel; 5. This is an important aspect of higher education innovation.

Keywords: Innovative education · higher education · higher education model

1 Introduction

It is one of the important innovative measures of higher education and teaching in China to promote teaching through scientific research and cultivate high-quality compound talents. The core task of teaching and research universities is to organize teaching activities, and on this basis, strive to improve their own teaching and research innovation capabilities. Based on the students' comprehensive quality evaluation of teaching activities, we can effectively improve the quality of education and teaching by doing a good job in teaching research reform, summarizing experiences and lessons, and making up for weaknesses. Teaching and research universities must establish scientific research awareness, remove barriers between teaching and scientific research, promote the integrated development of teaching and scientific research, implement the whole process and all-round three-dimensional all staff education model, and cultivate high-quality compound innovative talents. For teaching and research universities, only by organically combining teaching and scientific research can they have their own characteristics and level and constantly improve the quality of talent training [1]. Accelerating the construction of the policy system of promoting the efficient operation of teaching through scientific research and making scientific research achievements teaching and teaching activities scientific

Y. Zhang and N. Shah (Eds.): BigIoT-EDU 2023, LNICST 583, pp. 633–637, 2024.
https://doi.org/10.1007/978-3-031-63139-9_65

research is an active exploration and beneficial attempt for colleges and universities to highlight the characteristics of the discipline, improve the discipline system, grasp the direction of the discipline, and build a new teaching system and school running mode with modern education concepts. This paper is based on the research perspective of the financial media era of the university education model innovation.

2 Related Work

2.1 Transformation and Innovation of School Education Mode

The transformation and innovation of the school's education mode won the special prize of the national achievement award of basic education. At that time, the achievements were mainly based on the curriculum reform, which was more reflected in the transformation of various courses, course selection and class selection, tutorial system and other training modes. In fact, in this process, teaching methods have changed imperceptibly in the minds of teachers. Take the curriculum as an example. When the curriculum is diversified, each discipline has its own classroom, and different classes go to different classrooms. Subject resources are all in the classroom, including subject books, instruments, specimens, models and experimental equipment. Resources are in front of us. They are teachers, and the classroom will be enriched [2]. The experiment does not need to wait until the experimental class. Open the drawer, open the cabinet, and all the equipment is in front of you. Students can experiment at any time according to their needs. It does not need a certain class. According to the learning content, the experiment is carried out at the time of the experiment. If you need to read, you can read. If you need to speak, you can speak. When the teacher is teaching, students can also consult other materials. When audio-visual resources enter the classroom, students have their own equipment to check [3]. "Teacher, what you said is wrong" "Teacher, there is another way of saying this problem on the Internet"... Students can always challenge you and question you. Some students began to learn by themselves in their own ways, not necessarily according to the ideas designed by teachers. That is to say, students' learning methods began to change. The construction of this kind of subject classroom, the abundant resources around, and the change of students' learning methods have brought great touch and reflection to teachers.

Both teachers and students are undergoing subtle changes. Although we were talking about curriculum reform at that time, the classroom has actually changed. In addition, the organizational structure of the school is a flat management that directly points to the front line of teaching. Some emergency needs of teachers and students can be responded in a timely manner. These also affect the change of teachers' views on students. In the classroom, teachers are more respectful of students, and more respectful of students' learning needs and learning differences.

2.2 Financial Media and Its Basic Characteristics

The concept of "financial media" is a product of the development of the Internet. Financial media combines the characteristics of traditional media and new media, and has its own uniqueness. The financial media not only realizes the integration of various social media in terms of manpower, content and publicity, but also achieves resource sharing and publicity. Different scholars have different views on financial media. Zhou Kunpeng has more accurately defined financial media. He believes that "financial media is a new type of media that is organically integrated with traditional media and new media based on Internet thinking. It is not the result of the evolution of a single media form, but the latest form of media development in the new era [4]."

With the development of Internet technology, various elements of media are rearranged and combined to maximize the interests of organizations in terms of communication technology, communication platform and communication impact. The meaning of financial media includes five aspects of integration: first, concept integration, which affects the operation of organizational media with new concepts such as systematic thinking and Internet thinking. Financial media is not only the development of a single media form, but also the joint development of media organizations. We can understand the concept of financial media integration from a comprehensive perspective. The second is platform integration. Through cross platform and cross media, the operation mode of multiple media has been transformed into that of an integrated media, and the operation mode has changed. The third is technology integration, the integration of Internet technology, financial media analysis technology and new media technology. Fourth, content integration, which breaks through the limitation of content presentation of different media, is compatible with pictures, words, sounds and images, and uses diversified media communication forms to enhance media communication content and promote the value of media. Fifth, organizational integration [5]. Media organizations should cooperate according to the changes of time and situation, coordinate the interests of all parties, cooperate with institutions in other relevant fields, enhance the joint benefits of media, and reduce artificial resistance.

In short, financial media is based on the promotion of Internet technology. It integrates different media and their elements with an integrated thinking, so as to achieve the mutual integration of educational objectives, educational content, educational means, educational carriers and other resources, and realize the talent training goal of colleges and universities based on students.

3   Research on the Innovation of College Education Model Based on the Scientific Research Perspective of the Financial Media Era

Scientific research education refers to that from the perspective of pedagogy or higher education, teachers cultivate students' moral character and sound personality in the process of scientific research or through scientific research activities, cooperate with teaching education and other aspects, promote the comprehensive development of students' moral, intellectual, physical and aesthetic, and aim to implement the goal of talent training in colleges and universities.

The idea of borderless education is applied to the education of people in colleges and universities, which is mainly reflected in three aspects: first, to break the physical boundary and achieve the integration inside and outside the school. It believes that colleges and universities should push down the "wall", integrate with their communities, break the boundaries of schools, expand the boundaries of colleges and universities through cooperation with the government and industry, education and research, and combine practical knowledge and theoretical knowledge outside the classroom to influence and promote each other. Second, universities should also break the barriers between departments, and combine personnel, teaching, scientific research, student education and other functional departments to form an effective linkage [6]. Third, the integration and development of university Internet platforms. With the rapid development of information technology, Internet technology has been used in the education of college students to share the information resources of the school. College students can obtain the information resources they need with the help of the network platform. They can learn the professional knowledge they are interested in through online courses or virtual universities, such as learning the courses of other college teachers on the university MOOC. The development of online education breaks through the boundaries of colleges and universities, uses other resources of colleges and universities for our own use, and regards the university education of the whole society as a community of interests, forming a good interaction effect through complementary advantages.

Teachers and students can really participate in scientific research practice. In scientific research projects with common goals and interests, students can assist each other in scientific research. The observation and research on teachers and students show that UR is an intellectual experience process: it provides students with a learning opportunity to practice science, and improves the cognitive skills of higher education to a certain extent. Stimulating students' enthusiasm and independence in learning, understanding the practical significance of scientific research and accumulating practical experience are of guiding significance for future work and education development direction and career planning. In a broad sense, undergraduate research itself is the purest teaching method [7]. Teachers believe that students' participation in scientific research will help to build students' cognitive level, cultivate their technical level, communication and expression ability, and promote their personal development. Students believe that participating in scientific research is conducive to deepening the theme of academic field, solving problems and learning moral standards.

From the perspective of media, scientific research education can be regarded as a way of moral education in colleges and universities, not only because of the educational nature of scientific research itself, but also because of its particularity. Scientific research is a double-edged sword. The combination of scientific research and education can achieve the same effect as teaching and education, or even achieve half the result with twice the effort [8]. On the contrary, if scientific research is separated from people, it will have many adverse effects, ranging from no benefit to students' training, affecting teachers' values, to harming the society and harming the country, which is contrary to the original educational goal of the school. Colleges and universities shoulder the important task of cultivating builders and successors for the socialist modernization drive, and they also cultivate talents with high scientific and cultural quality and ideological and moral quality. Scientific research and education in the perspective of media integration is an organic combination of the two, which is the call of the times for higher education reform in the new situation [9]. Teachers bring scientific research into the classroom, so that students can understand the latest scientific research achievements, which will help students enrich and update their knowledge system; The process of students' participation in scientific research activities is conducive to the training of thinking ability, the cultivation of scientific research spirit and the enhancement of team consciousness. Participants in scientific research, not only teachers, but also undergraduates and postgraduates should participate. Through various forms of scientific research activities, students can understand scientific research, understand scientific research and enter into scientific research, which is not only conducive to the cultivation of scientific research spirit and moral quality, but also can learn to apply in future study and work, and be independent, which can stimulate patriotism and promote national spirit [10]. Scientific research and education in the perspective of media is a process of "educating students in virtue", which is in line with the fundamental education of virtue first in colleges and universities.

4 Conclusion

In the era of financial media, college education model is not only facing the crisis of teaching and learning, but also facing many problems in research. Based on scientific research, we should look for new ways to innovate in higher education. This paper aims to explore the innovation of college education model from the perspective of scientific and technological development, combined with financial media.

References

1. Tang, X., Wei, X., Wang, W.: Innovation of college students' ideological and political education in the new media era. Guide Sci. Educ. (2017)
2. Tao, E.J., Jia, Y.M., Wang, X., et al.: On the all media innovation of ideological and political education for college students in the era of internet plus. J. Jiangsu Inst. Commer. (2018)
3. Luo, W.: The innovation of college ideological and political education based on double micro-platforms in the perspective of new media. J. Longdong Univ. (2019)
4. Lei, J., Management, S.O.: Research on the structural model of college students' wechat business entrepreneurship ability from the perspective of psychological capital. J. Sichuan Vocat. Tech. Coll. (2019)
5. Jiang, H.: Innovation of ideological and political education in colleges and universities from the perspective of network public opinion. J. Contemp. Educ. Res. (2021)
6. Tang, X., Marxism, S.O.: Analysis on the education innovation mechanism of university network ideology and politics from the perspective of new media. Theor. Pract. Innovation Entrepreneurship (2018)
7. Guan, H.: Research on the innovation of the training mode of financial professionals in undergraduate universities in the era of "Internet+". Sci. Educ. Art. Collects (2019)
8. Wang, T., Fan, Y., Wang, Y., et al.: Research on the innovation of the ideological and political education in colleges and universities based on entrepreneurship education. J. Huainan Vocat. Tech. Coll. (2017)
9. Cui, X.H.: On college English education innovation in the era of mass media information. J. Qiqihar Junior Teachers' Coll. (2016)
10. Liu, J.Y., University, S.: Research on ideological and political education innovation in the era of big data. J. Liaoning High. Vocat. (2018)

Author Index

Printed in the United States
by Baker & Taylor Publisher Services